Introduction to Outdoor Recreation

Providing and Managing Natural Resource Based Opportunities

Introduction to Outdoor Recreation

Providing and Managing Natural Resource Based Opportunities

Roger L. Moore and B. L. Driver

Venture Publishing, Inc.
State College, Pennsylvania

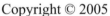
Production Manager: Richard Yocum
Manuscript Editing: Michele L. Barbin, Valerie Fowler, Richard Yocum

Library of Congress Catalogue Card Number: 2005921951
ISBN-10: 1-892132-50-8
ISBN-13: 978-1-892132-50-5

We dedicate this text to outdoor recreation professionals everywhere—in classrooms, research settings, and most of all in the field providing the outdoor recreation opportunities on which this text focuses. The work you are doing and will do is vitally important. We know you do it from a passion to serve the environment and the people who, like you, love it. Thank you from all of us!

Table of Contents

List of Tables and Figures

Acknowledgments

We would like to acknowledge and thank the many special people who helped make this text possible. We would first like to thank our families for their generous support and the sacrifices they made while we focused on writing. Their constant encouragement made a sometimes grueling task much more pleasant. Of course, we would like to thank everyone at Venture Publishing: Geoff Godbey for doggedly encouraging us to write the book in the first place and then prodding us until it was completed, and Valerie Fowler, Richard Yocum, and Michele L. Barbin for their expert and tireless editing and production efforts. Thanks, too, to Dennis Perry for assistance with a number of graphics and figures and Catherine Dorwart for her work in preparing much of Appendix B. Special thanks to Joyce Hart for interpreting and typing Bev's scribble!

We owe a special debt to our colleagues past and present. Their work has built and sustained the outdoor recreation profession, and their encouragement has helped us to introduce the fundamentals of that profession in this book. It is particularly appropriate here to thank our international colleagues. Their perspectives and expertise have strongly influenced our interpretations of the concepts and principles presented here. For example, our interpretations of the concept of leisure (Chapter 1), our understanding of the appropriate social and economic roles of leisure in a society (Chapters 1 and 2), the information on outdoor recreation around the world (Chapter 10), and our stance regarding recreation entrance and user fees (Chapter 19) were strongly influenced by our professional associates in many other countries. In particular, the discussions of the beneficial outcomes approach to leisure (BOAL) and benefits-based management (BBM) in Chapter 13 were strongly influenced by our association with several superb outdoor recreation professionals with the New Zealand Department of Conservation. We thank them and a host other recreation professionals for what they have done for the field and for what they have taught us. In no way do we believe that we "Yank" authors have any unique handles on the topics we have presented in this book.

The authors and publisher wish to thank the following people and organizations for their assistance in obtaining various illustrations and graphics used in this book:

Bureau of Land Management, National Science and Technology Center
  Barbara Campbell
  Ethel Coontz
  Brian Diethorn
  Randy Hayes
  William L. Jackson
  Janine Koselak

Bureau of Reclamation
  Jerry Leggate

USDA Forest Service
  Shela Mou

US Geological Survey
  Harry Allan
  Cheryl O'Brien
  Loreen Utz

Although too numerous to mention here, many people and organizations provided photographs to enhance this text. Photos without an acknowledgement were provided by Roger Moore.

And finally we would like to acknowledge the role that many authors of previous publications played in the preparation of this text, especially Scott Shafer, who coauthored a 2001 article with one of us that enriched parts of the trails and greenways section of Chapter 18. The coauthor of this text has authored or coauthored over 200 published and unpublished (but widely distributed) papers. The contents of many of those papers were integrated into several chapters of this text, especially Chapters 2, 12, and 13. Naturally, a concerted effort has been made to cite and acknowledge all the published work that was drawn on for this text. However, it is possible that some material included here will be very similar to our previously published work and not fully cited. This was not intentional, but results from having written about those subjects so often in the past. Similar thoughts can only be expressed in so many different ways without repetition.

Once again, thank you to all those who contributed in any way to making this text a reality. We hope that it serves a valuable purpose and does justice to your help and support.

Preface

Scope of This Text

- Sharing tall tales beside a fading campfire deep in a national forest
- Jogging on a carriage road in New York's Central Park
- Riding the last descent on a rugged mountain bike trail in Utah
- Photographing the "cloud forest" in a Costa Rican national park
- Rock climbing the face of El Capitan
- Enjoying the company of good friends
- Testing skills
- Learning about nature
- Feeling success after meeting a challenge
- Wondering about one's place in the universe
- Making memories
- Realizing the benefits of close families, healthy people, strong economies, and communities committed to sustaining their natural environments

These are all parts of *outdoor recreation*. So are hundreds of other activities, satisfying experiences, and beneficial outcomes. This text is about outdoor recreation: what it is, providing opportunities for it, and professionally managing the places where it takes place.

Despite its diversity, all outdoor recreation has one thing in common. By definition, outdoor recreation depends in some way on natural environments. The natural setting might be a pristine wilderness area virtually untouched by humans, or it could be a carefully designed and highly modified urban park or greenway. Outdoor recreation can occur days from the nearest road or in a tiny park in the heart of downtown. This text attempts to introduce the concepts and skills needed to be effective outdoor recreation professionals and providers in the myriad settings where it occurs. The information that follows focuses on areas allowing public access, regardless of whether the lands are public or private and regardless of whether fees are charged for their use.

This text is intended primarily for people interested in pursuing careers as outdoor recreation professionals. By *outdoor recreation professional*, we refer to any person who has responsibilities for providing outdoor recreation opportunities and managing outdoor recreation resources and who has acquired and applies the professional body of knowledge necessary to do so effectively. The primary purpose of this text is to introduce the essentials of this professional body of knowledge.

This text introduces many aspects of outdoor recreation and recreation resource management. Because of the scope and importance of outdoor recreation and related amenities throughout the world, this book is somewhat deficient by concentrating mostly on the United States. Although we have used many examples from other countries, our focus on the United States was necessary to keep the text's size reasonable. While the types and amounts of outdoor recreation resources and opportunities provided do differ from country to country, we believe the essential principles and recommendations described here have applications in all countries, whether more economically advanced ones that have exhibited a long tradition of recreation professionalism or ones that are currently developing and applying expertise. This belief is based on our professional experiences beyond the United States and extensive interactions with professional associates from around the world.

Why Does This Field and Education in It Matter?

We have chosen outdoor recreation as our profession and have written this book because we are convinced that outdoor recreation management is an extremely important field and an honorable profession. At its most basic level, outdoor recreation involves interactions between two elements: people and natural environments. Humans cannot live without the natural resources provided by the natural environment and cannot *live well* without contact with the natural world. Likewise, the natural environment cannot be sustained on a planet with over six billion people unless we carefully manage our finite land and resources and control our appetites for the goods and services available from them. Outdoor recreation is one of these uses, and one of humanity's rapidly growing appetites.

Many of the settings where outdoor recreation takes place are fragile; some are unique and irreplaceable. The ecological relationships within these natural areas are extremely complex as well. Changes in one part cause changes—often unexpected and irreversible changes—in other parts. Add to this the intentional and unintentional effects of human activities, including outdoor recreation, and the stewardship of this already complex system becomes immensely challenging.

One of the central themes of this text is that outdoor recreation can be extremely beneficial—more beneficial than most people recognize. We even make the perhaps startling suggestion that the total benefits of recreation equal or exceed the benefits of any other social service and that recreation contributes as much to the total economy as any other type of endeavor. Outdoor recreation, in particular, contributes greatly to these totals. Tangible dollars and cents arguments alone should convince even the most pragmatic decision maker that it is crucial to understand and to carefully manage outdoor recreation opportunities and to be responsible stewards of the environment on which they depend. But there is more than economic benefits: pleasure, joy, beauty, connectedness, and the renewal of human spirits. These are but a few of the less tangible rewards resulting from outdoor recreation that may be hard to quantify, but are no less important.

Careful and skilled planning and management are needed to preserve and conserve outdoor recreation areas while optimizing the many benefits they provide. Perhaps the mission statement of the USDA Forest Service best captures why we feel this field and this text are important. They are both about, "Caring for the land and serving people." In short, planning and managing outdoor recreation is an extremely rewarding and beneficial profession and one that requires both breadth and depth of professional preparation and experience. We hope this text proves to be a step in that direction for each reader.

How This Text Fits In

Not everyone who uses this book will become an outdoor recreation professional, and many who do choose this profession will not continue in that role for their entire careers. We feel strongly, though, that the material included here is important for everyone regardless of educational objectives and career aspirations. Some will apply this material to better provide outdoor recreation opportunities and to better manage recreation areas, most will use it to become more responsible outdoor recreationists, and everyone will use it to be better informed and more responsible voters and citizens.

This text was written to make readers think, to broaden their perspectives, and to introduce them to the concepts and skills needed by outdoor recreation professionals. We believe it is relevant to all students and professionals in any field related to recreation or natural resources. This includes those concentrating in natural resource management, forestry, ecology, and other resource-based fields, because outdoor recreation is a growing use of and impact on natural areas. Its relevance extends to people focused on tourism and commercial recreation because well-managed natural areas are often the primary attraction for tourists. It is important for those directing their efforts toward adventure recreation, because natural areas are typically the destinations that sustain the enterprises that provide these forms of recreation. This text is also relevant to those concentrating on community recreation, because local parks and recreation departments are responsible for many of the natural areas, open spaces, passive recreation areas, and greenways where outdoor recreation occurs. The concepts and practices described apply to students focused on park management, because understanding and managing park resources and visitors is what park managers do. They are even important for those concentrating in sports management, because many recreational sports occur in public natural areas.

Philosophy and Approach

Throughout our careers, each of us is going to make a difference in the world. For some that difference will be great, for some small. Most of the differences we make will be positive, but some, unfortunately, will be negative. The difference we make is based primarily on what we know and what we do with what we know. In the pages that follow, we attempt to present, in a straightforward, practical way, the tools necessary to be an effective outdoor recreation professional. What happens from there is, of course, up to you.

Remember that the world is extremely complex and no single discipline or approach offers the only way to understand it. Recreation and natural resource management are interdisciplinary fields. We attempt to present what we believe is the best perspective and combination of approaches available. We encourage you to be critical thinkers and to disagree with us when you feel that is appropriate. Be dedicated to excellence, and the contributions you make during your careers will bring us all better understanding and management in the future. This is the essence of being a professional, and being a professional is essential to success.

In short, this field is important and therefore educating people well in this field is critical. We take this seriously and sincerely hope you will too. We challenge you to make an important, positive contribution and to have some fun along the way.

Roger L. Moore
B. L. Driver

Part I

Foundations and Background

Chapter 1
Key Concepts

Education concerns the whole [person]; an educated [person] is a [person] with a point of view from which he [or she] takes in the whole world. (Pieper, 1963, p. 36)

Learning Objectives

1. Explain the basic concepts of natural resource management, leisure, recreation, and outdoor recreation.
2. Explain how the definitions of these terms can affect the management of outdoor recreation resources.
3. Describe the types and dynamics of outdoor recreation experiences.

A building is only as sound as the foundation that supports it. In the same way, being an effective outdoor recreation professional depends on having a thorough grounding in some basic concepts. We use the term *outdoor recreation professional* to refer to any person who has responsibilities for providing outdoor recreation opportunities and managing outdoor recreation resources and who has acquired and applies the professional body of knowledge necessary to do so effectively. Developing such an understanding is far more than an academic exercise. Our conceptual underpinnings have real implications for what we do and do not do professionally. They directly affect the kinds of settings planners and managers choose to provide and the types of experiences outdoor recreationists have when they use these settings. By establishing a conceptual foundation on which to hang your thoughts, you begin to develop and to refine a professional philosophy—the point of view from which we each take in the world professionally. In outdoor recreation resource management, the conceptual point of view from which we take in the world guides and influences how we manage resources and how we relate to the people who use and make decisions about resources. Just as every building requires a solid foundation to support it, our profession will not reach its potential or be able to adapt in a changing world if not solidly grounded.

The field of outdoor recreation is built most directly on the concepts of natural resource management, leisure, recreation, and outdoor recreation. Developing a solid professional philosophy grounded in these concepts is crucial for all outdoor recreation professionals. But understanding the distinctions among these concepts is not as simple as it might first appear. This is because few people take the time to examine them carefully, and therefore use the terms less precisely than they should. This confusion and lack of precision is compounded by the fact that the words *leisure* and *recreation* are used as nouns, adjectives, and adverbs, as well as in combination with related words, such as leisure time, leisure activities, leisure experiences, recreation activities, recreation experiences, leisure lifestyle, being at leisure, and leisurely. The objective of this chapter is to examine some of this murky water and to provide a clearer understanding of the concepts of natural resource management, leisure, recreation, and especially outdoor recreation. By the end of this chapter the reader should more clearly understand the distinctions among these concepts and the implications they have for providing outdoor recreation opportunities.

The field of outdoor recreation is inherently multidisciplinary. At the most basic level, however, outdoor recreation and outdoor recreation resource management involve interactions between two distinct elements: people and natural environments (Figure 1.1).

Both human and natural resource elements are essential, whether we are considering recreationists using natural

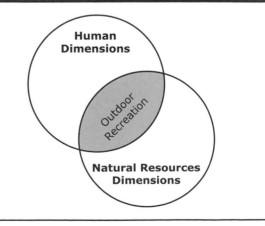

Figure 1.1 Outdoor recreation focuses on the intersection between human dimensions and natural resource dimensions.

settings; professionals understanding, conserving, planning for, and managing natural resources; or policy makers and voters making decisions that affect natural areas. The human aspects of our profession are rooted in psychology, sociology, social psychology, geography, economics, political science, public administration, history, archeology, landscape architecture, and other fields. The natural resource aspects build on the environmental sciences, including biology, ecology, forestry, geology, botany, hydrology, range science, wildlife biology, soil science, and many others. Most public outdoor recreation agencies recognize that all of these disciplines are important to providing outdoor recreation opportunities. Some agencies refer to the natural resource aspects as resource management or resource protection and the human aspects as visitor services. We refer to these two broad areas of outdoor recreation policy making and management as the *natural resource dimensions* and the *human dimensions* of outdoor recreation. Although the level of emphasis on each of these dimensions varies from site to site and agency to agency, the field of outdoor recreation always involves both. We introduce the basic concepts of each of these areas in the remainder of this chapter.

Natural Resource Dimensions of Outdoor Recreation

In the broadest sense, the natural resource dimensions of outdoor recreation involve assuring that high quality, sustainable natural resources and ecosystems are available, now and in the future, for a host of purposes, including outdoor recreation. The programs and management activities needed to accommodate these uses are rarely carried out by outdoor recreation professionals acting on their own. Outdoor recreation professionals typically work in partnership with teams of other professional natural resource managers that can include foresters, biologists, ecologists, geologists, botanists, hydrologists, range scientists, wildlife and fisheries biologists, soil scientists, and other experts. Therefore, it is important that outdoor recreation professionals have a basic knowledge of these other disciplines to understand and to mitigate the effects of their programs and outdoor recreation use on the environment. Even a cursory treatment of these disciplines, however, is beyond the scope of this text. Chapter 5 provides information on the natural resources available for outdoor recreation as well as who owns and manages these recreation lands and waters. Chapter 14 deals directly with assessing and managing the negative impacts recreation use can have on natural resources. We limit our broader discussion of the natural resource dimensions of outdoor recreation here to presenting the following outdoor rec-

reation related natural resource principles. Managers should keep these principles clearly in mind as they carry out their duties.

Outdoor Recreation Depends on the Availability of High-Quality Natural Areas

There are two fundamental ways of viewing life and natural resources: the anthropocentric (i.e., human-centered) perspective and the ecocentric (i.e., life-centered) perspective. The former views humans as the most important species on the planet and sees resources as existing for human benefits. The other perspective sees all life as equally important. Regardless of which view an outdoor recreation professional holds, some natural resources must obviously be preserved and the remainder conserved and used wisely if they are to continue to be available for future generations. This applies to outdoor recreation resources as much as it applies to the land, clean water, forests, wildlife, and minerals necessary for other essential purposes.

Diverse Environments Exist on the Planet, and Outdoor Recreation Takes Place in All of Them

Outdoor recreation occurs in virtually every natural and seminatural setting, in every part of the earth's biosphere, in all major climate zones and regions, and in all environments.

Outdoor Recreation Is an Important Part of Any Ecosystem

An ecosystem is much more than a landscape. An ecosystem is formed by the interaction of all living organisms (including people) with their environment (USDA Forest Service, 1995, p. xi) and can be small or vast. As such, an ecosystem includes flora, fauna, water, air, and humans.

High-quality, sustainable natural settings of many kinds are essential for outdoor recreation.

Outdoor recreation involves people interacting with natural environments. The presence, and especially the behavior, of these recreationists must be taken into account when considering the ecosystem.

Integrity of All Elements of the Ecosystem Is Vital to High-Quality Outdoor Recreation

All elements of an ecosystem (including humans) are interconnected and interact with one another. Therefore, changes in one component affect the other components, including the people who recreate there. For example, forest succession affects food supplies and which animals will thrive, and therefore what hunting opportunities will be available. Similarly, acid precipitation changes species health and composition, which affects the desirability of various sites to recreationists. This can cause changes in visitation patterns and associated economic impacts on local communities. Careless behavior by users can start wildfires which destroy forests and cause siltation of streams, which kills fish, thereby reducing the food available to other species, and so on. In this sense, everything (including outdoor recreation) is connected to everything else ecologically.

Whenever Possible, Outdoor Recreation Areas Should Be Managed From an Ecosystems Management Approach

Sustainable ecosystem management is "the skillful, integrated use of ecological knowledge at various scales to produce desired resource values, products, services and conditions in ways that also sustain the diversity and productivity of ecosystems" (USDA Forest Service, 1995, p. xii). Generally, ecosystems should be managed at the size of a watershed or larger.

Wildlife, an important natural resource, is central to many outdoor recreation experiences. (Photo by Bob Walker)

Each Generation Has the Responsibility to Pass on a Healthy and Sustainable Natural World to the Next

All life has value and biodiversity should be preserved whenever possible. Renewable resources should be conserved and used in a sustainable manner with no waste. Resources should be managed to assure that they continue to remain available in a healthy ecosystem long term. Resources should be viewed and managed under a philosophy of "intergenerational equity" where each person takes responsibility for his or her own actions and leaves the earth at least as good as he or she found it (Miller, 2002).

Not All Outdoor Recreation Requires Large, Wild, or Completely Natural Environments

Outdoor recreation can occur in small, urban "vest-pocket" parks as well as vast wilderness areas and any natural setting between these extremes.

"Outdoor Recreation Resources" Must Be Defined Broadly

Outdoor recreation resources are any natural resources and related facilities that make outdoor recreation possible. This certainly includes the natural resources of land, water, vegetation, wildlife, air, and minerals, but from the perspective of outdoor recreation professionals the term also includes the facilities and other developments used in outdoor recreation engagements. The job description for Outdoor Recreation Planners in federal agencies describes outdoor recreation resources as the land, water, mountains, forests, wildlife, and other outdoor elements useful for recreational purposes (U.S. Office of Personnel Management, 2002a). The Park Ranger job series description uses the word *resource* to include natural, historical, cultural, archeological, or other similar kinds of resources (U.S. Office of Personnel Management, 2002b). To be most accurate and of most use to managers and planners, outdoor recreation resources must be conceived broadly enough to also include trails, marinas, picnic facilities, campgrounds, forest roads, and so forth.

Human Dimensions of Outdoor Recreation

The many definitions of leisure and recreation have caused considerable confusion and created a lack of agreement on what these words mean. Because of that widespread confusion, and the intellectual baggage that goes with it, this section will begin with a brief review of how the words *leisure* and *recreation* are used in this text. We will then elaborate on each concept. The purpose of this review is to assure that the reader will understand clearly how we use these foundational terms in this text.

Herein, the word *leisure* is used in two ways. One is to refer to a state of being (i.e., the state of leisure) in which a person is relatively free to engage in activity (including recreational activity) of his or her own choosing. So, being in the state of leisure is a precondition for such engagement. The other way leisure is used is as an umbrella term that covers all areas of specialization within the broad field of leisure as an area of inquiry and practice. Outdoor recreation is, therefore, a subarea of leisure. In this text *recreation* is defined in experiential terms, with a recreation experience being an intrinsically rewarding experience that results from engagements freely chosen and not accompanied by strong external time pressures. Any human activity that provides this type of experience is a recreational activity, regardless of whether the opportunities to engage in the activity are provided by public or quasi-public agencies, private enterprises, or the individual. With this basic distinction between leisure and recreation in mind, we will now explore each more closely, paying particular attention to how they affect outdoor recreation management.

Leisure

The way individuals think about leisure is extremely important. In conscious and unconscious ways, how we view leisure affects what we choose to do and who we become. The ways individuals think and choose become the rudders that steer societies and cultures. Philosopher Josef Pieper (1963) made a compelling case that leisure is actually the basis of culture. As outdoor recreation professionals, the ways we view leisure, therefore, are crucial. We are the ones who provide the places where people spend much of their free time and the opportunities for them to participate in rewarding activities of their choosing. These are the opportunities for people to achieve a state of mind they find rewarding, and whether or not they can clearly articulate it, these are the places and the opportunities where each person hopes to live out a life he or she believes is worthwhile. In this sense, outdoor recreation professionals have a very important responsibility. What we provide and how we do it affects individuals, and through them can influence many aspects of the larger world. Suddenly, the implications of understanding and providing for leisure become extremely important.

The concept of leisure has been interpreted and defined in many ways. Our word leisure comes from the Latin word *licere* meaning "to be free" (Kelly, 1996, p. 7) and the ancient Greek word *schole* meaning "serious activity without the pressure of necessity" (Godbey, 1994, p. 4). From these roots, however, our current notions of leisure have grown in many directions through the work of psy-

chologists, sociologists, social psychologists, historians, philosophers, economists, anthropologists, and others. Godbey classifies the many existing definitions of leisure into four basic types: time, activities, state of mind, and state of existence. Similarly, Kelly considers three approaches to viewing leisure: time, activity, or condition. They and other experts offer the following observations about these different ways of viewing leisure.

Leisure as Free Time

When most people think of leisure, their ideas relate in one way or another to free time. Many people use the terms leisure and free time synonymously and imply as much by commonly referring to "leisure time." Formal definitions of leisure as free time typically describe it as time unobligated and opposed to work. These definitions present leisure as that time remaining after subsistence (work) and existence (e.g., sleeping, eating, bathing) needs are met. MacLean, Peterson, and Martin (1985, p. 7) defined leisure as "that portion of time not obligated by subsistence or existence demands. It represents discretionary or free time, time in which one may make voluntary choices of experience."

The obvious advantages to thinking about leisure as free or discretionary time is that it seems clear-cut and practical. Leisure viewed this way can be easily quantified, making it possible to identify trends and to compare amounts of leisure among different groups. The emphasis on freedom of choice is also appealing. At first glance, equating leisure with free time seems to make it a concept that nearly everyone can relate to and support. However, *freedom* is a relative term, and the degree of freedom a person experiences varies for different aspects of life and for different situations. Is anyone ever completely free politically, economically, physically, or socially? Is a person's free time actually the goal or simply a necessary precondition that makes something else possible? Doesn't

Outdoor recreation always involves people interacting with natural settings in some way.

leisure have something to do with a certain *quality* rather than just a *quantity*? The ancient Greeks certainly believed it did and most scholars and practitioners today do as well.

Leisure as Particular Activities

Many people think about leisure as engaging in certain activities. This is consistent with the ancient notion of *schole*. When people refer to leisure activities they typically mean pursuits freely chosen, pleasurable, and not participated in for pay. Outdoor recreation planners today routinely estimate participation in activities such as downhill skiing, hiking, birdwatching, and mountain biking, but not pursuits such as studying, working, or singing, even though these and many other activities can occur in outdoor recreation areas. Once again, viewing leisure in terms of certain activities has the advantages of being simple and emphasizing freedom of choice. But again, many feel leisure is more. No activity is leisure to all people in all situations. A ski instructor, for example, may hit the slopes out of financial need and loath every minute spent with students. Likewise, few (if any) activities cannot be leisure to certain people under certain circumstances. While splitting firewood may be an unwanted drudgery to most, it may be a pleasurable, freely chosen challenge to a harried urbanite on vacation in the country. Limiting our idea of leisure to lists of activities is simple, but it ignores peoples' motives and experiences.

Leisure as a State of Mind

Definitions of leisure from psychologists and social psychologists tend to present leisure as a state of mind involving *perceived freedom* and *intrinsic motivation* (Iso-Ahola, 1980; Neulinger, 1994, p. 18). In other words, leisure is something that must be freely chosen and engaged in for reasons intrinsically satisfying rather than for extrinsic reasons, such as money or increased status. Seeing leisure in this way explains why it often seems so situational. Why, for example, one boy scout who is told by his leader to build a campfire on a rainy morning can see it as work, while it is leisure to another if he volunteers to challenge himself. Defining leisure as a state of mind reminds us that it is just as much or more about what something *means* to a person than when it occurs or what the particular activity might be. A shortcoming of leisure defined solely as a state of mind, however, is that it seems to ignore the external world. Should a daydream, hallucination, or drug-induced state of mind be considered leisure? Can having the willpower to think positively about a truly bad situation make it leisure?

Leisure as a State of Being or Existence

Aristotle described leisure as the "absence of the necessity of being occupied" (De Grazia, 1961, p. 19). He and other classical philosophers saw leisure as an ideal condition necessary for individuals to achieve virtue and to perfect themselves. Their belief was that virtuous individuals would contribute to the creation of a more virtuous society and leisure was a crucial ingredient to make this happen. Similarly today, leisure is often thought of as a state of tranquillity, contemplation, spiritual celebration, or even prayerfulness in mind and soul (Pieper, 1963). The appeal of such a definition is that it presents an ideal we can strive for—an ideal with potentially important implications for individuals and society. A possible shortcoming of considering leisure as an ideal condition is that it can be easy to dismiss as unrealistic. Critics point out that such an ideal applies fully to no one. They rightfully note that even if some ancient Greeks got close to this ideal, they did it at the expense of slaves and by creating a society where only free males could be citizens and realistically pursue leisure. Some find a concept of leisure based on an ideal condition to be esoteric and difficult to put into practice today.

How Can the Way We Define Leisure Affect Outdoor Recreation Management?

If outdoor recreation professionals hold the perspective that leisure is simply free time, it is natural to regard leisure as not particularly important. After all, wouldn't leisure, by definition, be essentially "left over time" after attending to other more important priorities? Managers with such a perspective might then simply concentrate on providing visitors with opportunities for entertainment and diversion to fill their leftover time. Such a perspective might even communicate that leisure and things related to it (e.g., parks and recreation areas) are luxuries. Luxuries have low funding priorities for taxpayers and government agencies. Viewing leisure as simply free time does not communicate that leisure provides significant, meaningful, and important outcomes.

Defining leisure only as particular activities inaccurately limits the scope of the outdoor recreation profession and its important contributions. Such an approach could narrow planning and programming to pursuits that happen to appear on particular lists of "leisure activities," when no such list will ever be complete or accurate. Viewing leisure as participation in certain activities makes it easy to count participants and to quantify "production," but ignores the *qualities* crucial to what leisure really is. Providing outdoor recreation should not be about limiting visitors to a menu of approved activities. It also needs to consider what goes on inside visitors—the intangibles they bring with them and take away.

A state of mind characterized by intrinsic motivation and perceived freedom is certainly an important part of leisure. Although outdoor recreation professionals need to consider the psychology of leisure, it is certainly more than just what goes on in a visitor's head. The kinds of leisure considered in this book depend on actual natural settings. There is certainly a role for virtual outdoor recreation, but leisure and outdoor recreation are grounded in the real world, not just in a particular state of mind. Again, viewing leisure solely as a state of mind begs the question of whether leisure has meaningful and important outcomes. Aren't leisure and outdoor recreation more than a feeling? If not, why are natural resources needed for leisure and recreation at all?

The perspective that leisure is a state of being or existence does have important implications for outdoor recreation professionals. By viewing leisure as an *ideal condition* with the potential for great good, leisure could have great value, as the ancient Greeks believed. Such a definition (and professional philosophy) could provide the outdoor recreation professional with important guidance. It implies there is more to leisure and outdoor recreation management than simply providing places and activities to entertain visitors during their leftover time. The focus becomes providing settings, conditions, and opportunities that can be crucial for the enrichment of individuals, communities, and society. Few may ever completely achieve the long-term "absence of the necessity of being occupied" described by Aristotle. But the term *ideal* implies a desired good worthy of effort. Providing opportunities for people that can enrich their existence and improve their world (and encouraging them to do so) are certainly ideals worthy of our effort.

The Definition of Leisure Used in This Text

It should be clear from the foregoing discussion no universally accepted definition of leisure exists, nor is there likely to be one any time soon. The term and the concept itself have a tremendously rich heritage, which continues to provide direction for us as professionals today. Reducing leisure to activities that occur in free time would fall far short of its true meaning and potential. Leisure is more than free time or certain activities. A particular state of mind or state of being are closer to the mark, but neither captures the richness nor the potential of leisure. While each of these perspectives offers some guidance to outdoor recreation professionals, leisure is more.

In this text, leisure is the umbrella concept from which all recreation, including outdoor recreation, flows. However, it differs qualitatively from recreation. We adopt the view that leisure is a state of being (i.e., the state of leisure) in which a person is relatively free to engage in activities of their choosing (including recreational activity). Therefore, *leisure is a precondition for all recreational engagements* and is the state or condition where recreation becomes possible. This state may exist for a few

minutes, a few hours, or much longer for some people. The leisure condition is characterized by relative freedom from obligations and other constraints. But most importantly, this state of leisure is one of opportunity and potential. It allows each of us to choose activities and experiences and ways of living that we find rewarding, satisfying, and worthwhile (Godbey, 1994, p. 11). Leisure begins with the ideal condition Aristotle described as the "absence of the necessity of being occupied." It is the condition of *licere* ("to be free") where the *schole* ("serious activity without the pressure of necessity") can happen. It is an ideal that should be reflected in our planning for and management of recreation opportunities.

Viewing leisure from this perspective should remind outdoor recreation professionals that our efforts are directed toward a part of people's lives where they have the freedom to make important choices. These choices are instrumental in defining who they are and in determining the quality of their individual lives. In turn, their lives can affect our world in meaningful ways. What leisure and outdoor recreation professionals provide in terms of places, activity opportunities, and images of what is possible and desirable shape these important choices for better or worse. The question all outdoor recreation and natural resource professionals should ask themselves and their agencies is: Do we simply help people to fill their free time or do we create desirable, even *ideal* conditions where people have the opportunity to enhance their lives and, perhaps, our world?

Before we leave our discussion of leisure, we want to clarify a point sometimes contentious among recreation professionals and sometimes a misconception about leisure in particular. It relates to a concept we refer to as *visitor sovereignty*. In economics *consumer sovereignty* literally means the consumer is king. In other words, there is the expectation that business will provide the goods and services they believe the consumer demands, and consumers will decide to buy, or not buy, those goods and services based on the utility they expect to derive from them. We approach outdoor recreation resource management in a similar way. That is, managers will generally provide a wide array of outdoor recreation opportunities for people to choose from during their leisure. We know and expect that visitors will choose and use those opportunities that best meet their preferences. The alternative view would be that park and recreation managers should provide only those opportunities that they believe are the "best" ones and the only ones that visitors or customers "should" choose. This alternative approach can rapidly become one that resembles attempts at social engineering and has very little place in the realms of recreation or leisure. This does not mean leisure programming should not be used to reach socially agreed on outcomes, such as promoting environmental responsibility through ecotourism or designing recreation-based interventions for youth at risk. Nor does approaching our field from a perspective of visitor sovereignty mean that we need to provide every opportunity in every setting. Clearly, doing so would not be appropriate and would often conflict with land management objectives. What it does mean is we realize customers will make their own choices of recreation opportunities and experiences and we need to plan accordingly.

Recreation

The word *recreation* comes from the Latin root *recreare* meaning to create anew or to be refreshed. *Re-creation* of mind, body, and spirit captures the essence of recreation. The word *creation* in recreation denotes that recreation includes such things as growth and development, learning, creative expression, and nurturing. The concept of recreation, therefore, includes two important elements. First, pressures and demands (often our work) wear us down, and these are things from which we regularly need to be refreshed or restored. Second, positive, refreshing *outcomes*, such as challenge and growth, result from engaging in recreation.

The concepts of leisure and recreation are obviously related. Definitions of the two sometimes overlap as they relate to free time, activities, and state of mind. Recreation, however, is not the same thing as leisure, even though some people use the two terms interchangeably. In the simplest terms, recreation can be thought of as the activities a person engages in during their leisure and the experiences that result from those activities. Remember, though, that leisure is more than free time. Refreshing "recreation activities," therefore, are not strictly limited to a block of free time in the traditional sense.

While leisure emphasizes the condition characterized by freedom, recreation emphasizes both the activities undertaken during this leisure and the experiences that result from engaging in those activities. Although both leisure and recreation have something to do with a particular state of mind, it is our recreation that most directly produces the refreshing, satisfying experiences. It is incomplete and inaccurate to consider recreation to be just an activity, because the activity is simply the means of achieving certain desired experiences. In sum, recreation always involves activities voluntarily chosen and the resulting experiences.

It is impossible to overemphasize the importance of the experience itself (in contrast to the activity that produces it) in understanding recreation. The idea that people engage in particular recreation activities to realize desired psychological and physiological experiences is the most fundamental aspect of all recreation, including outdoor recreation. A large body of research documents the impor-

tance of experiences to all aspects of leisure and recreation. The concept of recreation experiences, therefore, has become the underpinning of most of the important approaches for planning and managing outdoor recreation opportunities described throughout this text. The management systems discussed in Chapters 12 and 13 are based on the concept of managing recreation resources not only to provide opportunities to engage in particular outdoor activities in particular settings but also ultimately to realize specific types of satisfying experiences. Because the concept of recreation experiences is so fundamental to understanding leisure and recreation, it will be briefly explained here. The types of recreational experiences will be elaborated in Chapter 2.

All human experience is a psychological or physiological response to encountering something, and recreation experience is no exception. Recreation experience is a response to a recreational engagement. All recreation experiences occur at the individual level, albeit strongly influenced by social and cultural influences. The experience can be psychological, physiological, or psychophysiological in nature. Examples include experiencing physical and mental relaxation, enjoyment of natural settings, learning, being with one's family or friends, testing and applying particular skills, introspecting about one's personal values, or nurturing nature-based spirituality.

A widely accepted definition of recreation experience considers it an *intrinsically rewarding* experience that finds its source in *voluntary engagements* during *nonobligated time* (Driver & Tocher, 1970, p. 10). These three essential dimensions—type of reward, freedom to choose, and degree of external time pressure—are at the heart of the recreation experience. An intrinsic reward is a reward inherently satisfying to the individual—something that produces pleasure inherent to the recreational engagement for its own sake rather than rewarding for any external reasons such as financial gain or increased status. Put simply, intrinsic rewards are "internal" to the recreation activity while extrinsic rewards are from some "external" source. For example, a person who hates to play golf may play with his boss in the extrinsic hope of gaining his or her favor, and perhaps eventually a pay increase. The second, often related, defining characteristic of a recreation experience is that the engagement is freely or voluntarily chosen by the participant, rather than an obligation of any kind. Someone who chooses to go deer hunting because he or she really wants to is more likely to have a satisfying recreation experience than someone who goes "because my friends expect me to" (see also Iso-Ahola, 1999) The final characteristic of a recreation experience relates to time considerations, some not immediately apparent in the previous definition. The most basic is that a pure recreation experience is only possible during unobligated time—time not obligated by existence or subsistence demands as mentioned in the earlier discussion of leisure. Once this basic condition has been met, however, the way the individual perceives time continues to be important to his or her recreation experience. For example, the recreation experience is diminished by feelings of external time pressure. A person who feels external pressure to get back to the office by a certain time will have a very different recreation experience than someone who feels little or no time pressure. In contrast, "internal" intrinsically rewarding and voluntarily chosen time pressures do not diminish the recreation experience. Internal time pressure can enhance the recreation experience for some people, and in some cases is essential. This is often the case with competitive experiences, regardless of whether the competition is with others or oneself. Examples would include a person trying to set a personal speed record kayaking a whitewater slalom course or a person who is competing with others to see which team can spot and identify the most species of birds in a 24-hour "big day" birding event. While external time pressures can diminish the recreation experience by bounding it and constraining it, internal time pressures can enhance it for some people in some situations.

The *flow* experience described by Csikszentmihalyi (1990) is a special case regarding the perception of time during a recreation experience. When in flow a person is so engrossed in a particular activity and experience that they lose consciousness of time. This could be the case with a person so perfectly challenged by a particular rock climb that he or she completely loses track of time while absorbed in climbing it. Someone completely in the groove playing in a basketball game or swinging at a fastball might similarly be focused on the moment so intensely that he or she may lose track of time altogether. While the flow experience often occurs during recreation, it is certainly not necessary for a satisfying recreation experience nor is it some sort of "ultimate recreation experience" that should be strived for over all others.

Considering these three dimensions—type of reward, freedom to choose, and degree of external time pressure—the "ideal" recreation experience is one that is voluntarily chosen, intrinsically rewarding, and unaffected by external

time pressures. These three dimensions can be visualized as three continua illustrated in Figure 1.2, which shows the recreation experiences of four hypothetical individuals. The left pole of each continua represents the condition consistent with a purely recreational experience, while the right hand pole does not. Any individual's particular recreation experience could be plotted anywhere along each continuum. To illustrate, assume that four people each take a day-long snowboarding trip as illustrated in Figure 1.2. Person A has a purely recreational experience characterized by a totally intrinsically rewarding experience in which she engaged as a totally voluntary choice and felt no external time pressure while participating. Person B finds much intrinsic reward, does not feel much external time pressure while recreating, but is recreating mostly because his girlfriend wanted him to accompany her. While willing to go with his girlfriend, his decision to recreate was not as voluntary as it would have been if entirely his choice. Person C could be someone who loves to snowboard and chose to take part of the day off to make the trip, but needs to get back to the office for an afternoon meeting and so is experiencing some external time pressure. And Person D could be a college student employed as a part-time ski patroller primarily to earn money. Assume that although she has to hold down a part-time job, her choice of that particular job is made voluntarily because she likes to snowboard. Also assume her work is done within a relatively flexible schedule that requires some consciousness of time but does not create oppressive external time pressure. As such, the work of Person D is also recreational to some extent. Although each of these four people is having a somewhat different experience and some of their experiences are more constrained (and perhaps less "ideal") than others, each is having a recreational experience.

The purpose of comparing Persons A, B, C, and D in Figure 1.2 is not to suggest that any one of those people is getting more recreational enjoyment than another. Instead, it is included to show visually the three most essential characteristics of recreation experiences to help differentiate recreational from other types of human experiences. It is also, and more importantly, included to lay

Points A, B, C, and D represent four different people having different recreation experiences.

Figure 1.2   Three essential dimensions of a recreation experience

the groundwork for a fuller understanding that an experiential definition of outdoor recreation is professionally important from a managerial perspective, elaborated in later chapters (especially Chapters 2, 12, and 13).

From this discussion, one should recognize that perceived freedom is a particularly important dimension of recreation when defined experientially (as we do in this text). The essential role of perceived freedom has important implications for the planners and managers of recreation resources. We emphasize that park and recreation planners and managers must be ever attentive to helping recreationists preserve this sense of perceived freedom. This means among other things not being overly restrictive in rules and regulations imposed in recreation setting. Leisure scientists, as well, must be mindful to not impose too greatly on recreationists when studying their use of the recreation facilities, areas, and sites where they choose to exercise this freedom.

Outdoor Recreation and Related Concepts

The term *outdoor recreation* obviously refers to a particular type of recreation. However, the term has been used in many ways over the past half century and is still defined differently by various groups and providers. Some examples of various perspectives on outdoor recreation include the following:

> Outdoor recreation…is the wholesome recreation that is done without the confines of a building. (Douglas, 2000, p. 4)

> Outdoor recreation includes any sort of fun or enjoyment found in the outdoors that involves resource use for any activity or series of activities of choice. (Cottrell & Cottrell, 1998, p. 65)

…we use the term *outdoor recreation* to encompass the organized free-time activities that are participated in for their own sake and where there is an interaction between the participant and an element of nature. (Ibrahim & Cordes, 1993, p. 4)

> Realizing satisfactory experiences…by participating in preferred recreation activities in preferred surroundings or settings. (USDA Forest Service, 1982)

At some point trying to define exactly what is and what is not outdoor recreation becomes an exercise in semantics. It is, however, very important to clarify what we as outdoor recreation professionals mean by the term. Although the term "outdoor recreation" could imply (and has sometimes been defined as) any recreation that happens to take place outdoors, historically (and for purposes of this text) it is much more specific than that. We will use the following definition:

> **Outdoor recreation:** recreation experiences that result from recreation activities that occur in and depend on the natural environment

This definition emphasizes that like all other types of recreation, outdoor recreation is more than an activity. The activity is the means to achieve some desired experience. It also distinguishes outdoor recreation from the many other forms of recreation in that outdoor recreation occurs in and depends on a natural environment. Figure 1.3 presents this graphically.

A specific example of outdoor recreation might be the solitude and self-reliance that result from wilderness hiking in the high peaks of the Colorado Rockies (Figure 1.4). The actual outdoor recreation trip or outing is referred to as an *outdoor recreation engagement*.

Similarly, think about the excitement of mountain biking in a county park or enjoying the sights and sounds of nature while horseback riding on a greenway trail near

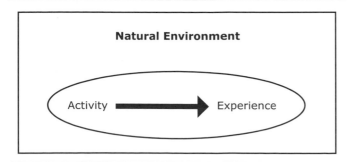

Figure 1.3   Outdoor recreation as activities and experiences occurring in and depending on natural environments

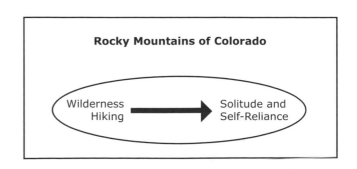

Figure 1.4   Example of an outdoor recreation engagement

an urban area. It is essential for professionals to conceptualize outdoor recreation as the combination of the activity, the outcome (e.g., experience) that results from the action, and the environment where they take place. Although simple lists of "outdoor recreation activities" are commonly generated as can be seen in any State Comprehensive Outdoor Recreation Plan (SCORP), to adequately define outdoor recreation for effective planning and management we must consider what the user is doing, why the user is doing it (i.e., what experience is desired) and the role of the natural environment in the experience. Our definition explicitly directs attention to all three aspects of outdoor recreation.

Notice also this definition addresses two things that distinguish outdoor recreation from other forms of recreation. The first is the extent to which the setting is natural. The second is the extent to which the activity and experience depends on the natural environment. The most extreme degrees of these two dimensions are not necessary for an engagement to be considered outdoor recreation, of course. In fact, each dimension is best viewed as a continuum. Some outdoor recreation settings are completely natural and undeveloped while others are highly modified and include sophisticated constructed facilities. Sometimes the experience is completely dependent on a natural setting (e.g., the solitude often sought in wilderness areas). Other times the natural setting is less crucial (e.g., for people gardening in their backyard or who choose a greenway trail for a walk with a friend rather than a neighborhood sidewalk). Both dimensions can be somewhat subjective as well. A setting that may seem quite "natural" to one person may not be to another. It is also important to remember that the degree of naturalness or how much the experience depends on the natural environment do not

imply a hierarchy where some types of outdoor recreation are necessarily better than others. To clarify what is and what is not outdoor recreation, consider how the field of outdoor recreation fits and often overlaps with other related ones.

Natural Resource Recreation and Resource-Based Recreation

These terms are synonymous with outdoor recreation as defined here and in some ways are more descriptive titles than "outdoor recreation" because they more explicitly indicate the importance of the natural setting.

Wildland Recreation and Forest Recreation

These terms typically refer to subsets of outdoor recreation that take place in particular settings.

Wildland recreation has been viewed as

> …recreational activities conducted outdoors in wildland areas that are dependent on the natural resources of these areas. (Hammitt & Cole, 1998, p. 3)

> …that segment of outdoor recreation activity that takes place in and depends on relatively undeveloped natural environments. (Graefe, 1987, p. 169)

> The term wildland, as used here, refers not only to wilderness, but to any lands where the works of nature, rather than those of people, are the main attractions. (Wellman, 1987, p. 2)

Forest recreation has been defined as

> …any outdoor recreation that takes place in forested areas, whether or not the forest provides the primary purpose for the activity. (Douglas, 2000, p. 10)

Outdoor recreation is, by definition, natural resource-based and occurs in a huge variety of settings.

A large proportion of tourism and commercial recreation focuses on outdoor recreation experiences.

Tourism and Commercial Recreation

The natural resources and environment are "the very basis of much of tourism" (Goeldner & Richie, 2003, p. 14). Tourism has been defined as "the entire world industry of travel, hotels, transportation, and all other components, including promotion, that serves the needs and wants of travelers" (Goeldner & Richie, 2003, p. 592). The World Tourism Organization defines tourism as "the activities of persons traveling to and staying in places outside their usual environment for not more than one consecutive year for leisure, business and other purposes" (Goeldner & Richie, 2003, p. 7). Some, but by no means all, outdoor recreation is consistent with these definitions of tourism. Likewise, many outdoor recreation opportunities are provided by commercial providers, such as guides and outfitters, private ski area corporations, and private campground operators. As such there is considerable overlap between outdoor recreation and tourism and commercial recreation.

Nature Tourism

This particular form of tourism (often referred to as nature-based tourism) has been defined as

> an aspect of adventure tourism where the focus is upon the study and/or observation of flora, fauna and/or landscape. It tends toward the small-scale, but it can become mass or incipient mass tourism in many national parks (e.g., Yosemite). It is sometimes perceived as synonymous with ecotourism since one of its aims is to protect natural areas. (France, 1997, p. 16)

Ecotourism

Much of ecotourism is outdoor recreation as defined in this text. Ecotourism is generally considered to be a form of alternative tourism (as opposed to mass tourism) and a product as well as a principle. "The attributes of ecological and socioeconomic integrity, responsibility and sustainability are qualities that may, or unfortunately may not, pertain to ecotourism as a product." (Cater & Lowman, 1994, p. 3). Ecotourism has been defined as "responsible travel to natural areas which conserves the environment and improves the welfare of local people" (The Ecotourism Society, as cited in Western, 1993, p. 8). It has also been defined as

> a sustainable form of natural resource based tourism that focuses primarily on experiencing and learning about nature, and which is ethically managed to be low-impact, nonconsumptive, and locally oriented (control, benefits, and scale). It typically occurs in natural areas, and should contribute to the conservation or preservation of such areas. (Fennell, 1999, p. 43)

Adventure Recreation, Outdoor Adventure, and Risk Recreation

Most adventure recreation (sometimes referred to as outdoor adventure or risk recreation) is actually a type of outdoor recreation as we define it here. Adventure recreation typically includes activities such as mountaineering, whitewater kayaking and rafting, spelunking, ropes courses, skydiving, and scuba diving. Of course, adventure recreation, such as rock climbing in climbing gyms or bungee jumping off bridges, does not need to occur in or depend on outdoor or natural settings. Outdoor adventure pursuits have been defined as "a variety of self-initiated activities utilizing an interaction with the natural environment that contain elements of real or apparent danger, in which the outcome, while uncertain, can be influenced by the participant and circumstances" (Ewert, 1989, p. 6).

Many experiences can be both outdoor recreation and nature tourism.

Much of ecotourism is outdoor recreation as defined in this text.

Most adventure recreation is built around outdoor recreation experiences. (Photo by Aram Attarian)

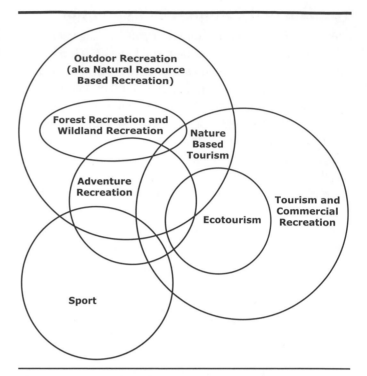

Figure 1.5 Overlap of outdoor recreation with other related fields

Outdoor Sports and Athletics

Because outdoor recreation occurs in and depends on the natural environment, most outdoor athletics and sports are not considered outdoor recreation. However, there are types of outdoor recreation that are clearly sports and visa versa. Eco-Challenge, competitive trail running, and organized mountain bike racing are examples where outdoor sports and outdoor recreation do overlap. Competition can certainly be a part of outdoor recreation for some people at certain times. Note that hunting and fishing are called "sports" although they do not usually involve competition nor are they participated in "in the game form," which are generally defining aspects of a sport.

The previous examples should make it clear that what we are referring to as outdoor recreation is a very broad topic and should emphasize that outdoor recreation as a profession is equally broad. It should also be clear that outdoor recreation, even if called something different, is an important topic in fields as diverse as natural resource management, forest and wildland management, tourism, adventure programming, and even sport. Figure 1.5 presents an illustration of how these and other areas overlap and relate to our concept of outdoor recreation.

Outdoor Recreation Experiences

The experiences that result from outdoor recreation engagements are an important key to managing outdoor recreation resources. Public and private outdoor recreation providers increasingly realize they cannot be responsive and effective unless they have an understanding of the experiences their customers desire. Examples of common

outdoor recreation experiences include solitude, challenge, enjoying the sights and sounds of nature, and testing skills. Chapter 2 will present a more comprehensive list and discuss outdoor recreation experiences. However, several basic concepts need to be introduced here to provide an adequate foundation.

Most outdoor recreation experiences can also be achieved in ways other than engaging in traditional outdoor recreation in natural settings. For example, visiting indoor climbing gyms, using virtual reality units, watching certain movies, or walking with friends in a climate-controlled shopping mall could produce experiences very similar to ones that occur in and depend on a natural environment.

Outdoor recreation is an *experience* that results from an activity that occurs in and depends on a natural environment.

Also, be aware that because achieving these desired experiences is often the motivating force for people to choose to participate in outdoor recreation, these same experiences are sometimes called motives, desired outcomes, experience preferences, or recreation experience preferences.

Where do human motives come from? Some, like hunger, are biological and instinctive. Most of the motives for engaging in outdoor recreation, however, we learn based on past experience and relate to what we and our reference groups enjoy. Some experts organize outdoor recreation motives along a continuum with escape or "push" motives at one end and engagement or "pull" motives at the other. Push motives are often caused by external factors, like stresses from work, and frequently lead to passive recreation behaviors, like sunbathing on a beach. Pull motives are best thought of as an internal draw to some desired experience and more frequently lead to active behaviors, like hiking or birding.

Two final things are important to realize about motivations for outdoor recreation. First, not all motives are conscious to the person engaging in the recreation. Second, most people have multiple motives for engaging in any particular outdoor recreation engagement.

An Outdoor Recreation Experience Model

Outdoor recreation behavior is best viewed from a social psychological perspective, which assumes people participate in outdoor recreation because they hope to gain certain rewards or outcomes, particularly outdoor recreation experiences. This way of thinking about outdoor recreation is based on *expectancy theory*, which proposes people engage in particular behaviors with the expectation the activity will meet their particular needs and help them to achieve what they desire. Outdoor recreation professionals using this perspective commonly refer to it as the *behavioral approach*, because it focuses on why people engage in outdoor recreation and acknowledges the importance of the experiences and other benefits that result (Manning, 1999, p. 3). The essence of the behavioral approach to outdoor recreation management is understanding why

people do what they do and what they hope to gain. This information is essential to effective recreation resource management.

Note that this behavioral perspective implies that managers must consider certain key aspects of any outdoor recreation engagement, including the user's motivations or needs, the recreation activity engaged in, the recreation settings where the activity and experience take place, the companions (if any) for the recreation engagement, and the experience or other desired outcomes that result from the recreation engagement. None of the aspects are complete or adequate when considered alone.

A simple outdoor recreation experience model as provided in Figure 1.6 can help to visualize how these aspects interrelate. Consider this the "who, what, where, and why" of outdoor recreation behavior from the user (or customer) perspective.

Figure 1.6 emphasizes that users engage in outdoor recreation because they have certain recreation-related motivations, preferences, or desires. They bring these preferences with them to recreation settings as the input to this model. Driven by these motives or preferences, users must make certain choices to engage in outdoor recreation. They must choose a setting, an activity, and with whom (if anyone) they will participate. By engaging in the recreation outing based on their choices, users hope to achieve their desired outcome, generally some combination of outdoor recreation experiences.

Viewed in terms of this model, an example of an outdoor recreation experience might be understood as in Figure 1.7 (p. 16). An office worker who had a particularly difficult and stressful week of indoor work spent mostly in meetings and in front of a computer might simply want to escape to find some peace and quiet and fresh air. Based on these desires, she might choose to walk alone on a quiet trail around a lake in a park near her home. As a result of this engagement she hopes to experience a state of solitude and relaxation.

Notice that Figure 1.7 is presented from the user's perspective. Outdoor recreation managers can view this from

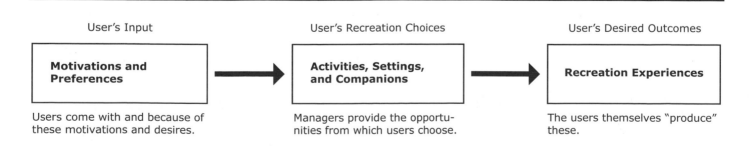

Figure 1.6 A simple outdoor recreation experience model illustrating the "who, what, where, and why" of outdoor recreation behavior

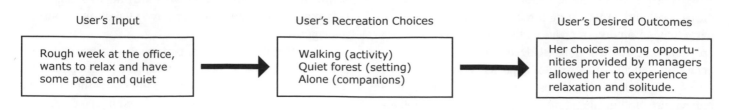

User's Input	User's Recreation Choices	User's Desired Outcomes
Rough week at the office, wants to relax and have some peace and quiet	Walking (activity) Quiet forest (setting) Alone (companions)	Her choices among opportunities provided by managers allowed her to experience relaxation and solitude.

Figure 1.7   An application of the outdoor recreation experience model

their perspective as well to focus on why their visitors or customers do what they do and to begin to anticipate what outcomes their customers desire (Figure 1.8).

Several important things to note about outdoor recreation behavior might not be immediately obvious from these examples. First, because outdoor recreation involves people interacting with natural environments, the setting element of the model is essential and the one over which recreation resource managers and planners typically have the most control. Second, users make their outdoor recreation choices from the settings, activities, and companions available to them. Taken together, these are called *outdoor recreation opportunities*. The USDA Forest Service (1982, p. 4) defines a recreation opportunity as "the availability of a real choice for a user to participate in a preferred activity within a preferred setting, in order to realize those satisfying experiences which are desired." This terminology emphasizes the third important fact: outdoor recreation experiences are produced by the visitor, not the manager. Managers can only provide the outdoor recreation opportunities that make the visitors' engagements and associated experiences possible.

Visitors desire a tremendous variety of experiences from their outdoor recreation engagements. These experiences will be described in Chapter 2. The outdoor recreation experience model (Figure 1.6) illustrates that each experience can be produced by many different combinations of activities, settings, and companions. Similarly, the same combination of opportunities (i.e., setting, activity, and companions) could be used by different people to produce different experiences. The same person

can even use the same recreation opportunities to produce completely different experiences during different engagements. In other words, outdoor recreation experiences can be situational, individually specific, and highly variable, and their meaning to the individual can depend on the context of the engagement..

Finally, notice that we have used both users and customers to refer to the people actually engaging in the outdoor recreation. The term visitors is also commonly used in some circles, such as in the National Park Service, to refer to outdoor recreationists. Each of these terms has advantages. The concept of *user* emphasizes that the person uses a particular opportunity to produce some outcome they desire. The term *visitor* can convey a certain host-guest relationship between managers of an area and those who recreate there. Such a guest, hopefully, finds it easier to remember that they have some responsibility to treat the area and other visitors with respect. Using the term *customers* to refer to outdoor recreationists is growing in popularity among recreation resource managers. The customer concept explicitly requires that managers of outdoor recreation and related amenity resources adapt and apply a customer-oriented style of management. That style is now being used by most effective and successful organizations that provide goods and services and is increasingly important for outdoor recreation resource managers as well. The word customer was first used by the private sector to mean someone who pays a price for a good or service. Despite the fact that some people still hold that definition of customer, that narrow use of the word is now archaic. The word customer now does not necessarily have anything to

Customer's Needs/Desires	Outdoor Recreation Opportunities Provided	Desired Outcomes
Motivations and Preferences	**Activities Settings Companions**	**Recreation Experiences**

Figure 1.8   The outdoor recreation experience model from the outdoor recreation managers' point of view rather than that of the user

do with marketing for profit or requiring that a price be paid. It has everything to do with attempting to meet the preferences of the people who use the goods and services provide, whether provided by a public agency or a private enterprise. We will use the words customers, users, and visitors interchangeably in this text.

The basic ideas illustrated in the outdoor recreation experience model are at the heart of what outdoor recreation management is all about. At its core are the concepts of providing opportunities for desired experiences and doing so in ways that sustain the health and integrity of the natural settings that make the opportunities possible. Therefore, we define outdoor recreation management as follows:

> **Outdoor recreation management:** providing opportunities for satisfying outdoor recreation experiences while sustaining the health of the natural environments on which these opportunities depend

Outdoor recreation management, so defined, intends to direct attention to both the human dimensions and the natural resources dimensions of outdoor recreation. The term *outdoor recreation resources management* refers more specifically to the natural resources dimensions of outdoor recreation. We will use both of these terms in this text, as appropriate.

Timing and Phases of the Outdoor Recreation Experience

The model of outdoor recreation behavior presented here does not explicitly address the important issue of the timing. Obviously, many factors affect the time when a person engages in outdoor recreation, such as when he or she has unobligated time, how far away his or her preferred setting is, when his or her companions are available, weather con-

Traveling to and from the outdoor recreation setting are also phases of the total outdoor recreation experience. (Photo by Reuben Rajala)

ditions, and factors related to the nature of the experience itself. The best birdwatching times are in the early morning, flyfishing is best in the early morning and late evening, and the light conditions and long shadows of afternoon are preferred by many photographers and artists.

A more basic time-related aspect of outdoor recreation participation has to do with what is referred to as the phases of the outdoor recreation experience. It has been recognized for decades that outdoor recreation participation involves much more than simply the time actually spent in the natural setting itself. Five major phases comprise the total outdoor recreation experience (Clausen & Knetsch, 1966, pp. 33–36).

Anticipation

Anticipation includes planning and preparing for the engagement as well as looking forward to it. It may be very short and spontaneous or long and involved. In fact, if the actual recreation outing never occurs, the anticipation could end up being the entire experience.

Travel To

Getting from home or work to the outdoor recreation setting is certainly a part of the total recreation experience. This phase could take minutes, as in walking from home to a nearby suburban park. Or it could last weeks, as in international travel from the United States to Nepal followed by a long trek on foot to a mountaineering base camp in the Himalayas. Travel to recreation settings can be a large or small proportion of the entire experience, inexpensive or costly, enjoyable or a dreaded burden. Likewise, it could involve any or all modes of travel.

On-Site Experience

This phase is the actual participation in the outdoor recreation activities and the experiences that result in the recreation setting. The on-site recreation engagement itself is generally the primary focus of recreation managers, although it should not be their only focus.

Travel Back

Much like travel to the recreation setting, travel back can take many forms. It can be long or brief and involve any or all modes of transit. It could be an enjoyable part of the total experience, but may not. Travel back may be very different from travel to in terms of pace, attitude, energy level, and emotion.

Recollection

The complete outdoor recreation experience generally does not end abruptly when the participant arrives home. Recollection of the experience continues through memories, pictures, and souvenirs. The recollection phase might be the longest and most enjoyable aspect of the total experience (particularly if the participant forgets or minimizes any unpleasant things that occurred during the other four phases). It is also possible that the recollection phase is the most important for some, particularly if the primary motive was obtaining some sort of "trophy," even if the trophy is an accomplishment of some sort.

Note that the five phases of the outdoor recreation experience vary in length and importance depending on the individual and the particular trip. Also notice that outdoor recreation professionals (or any of their partners that help them to provide the recreation opportunities) can influence and enhance the experience during any of these phases. For example, managers provide information and planning assistance in advance. Public land managing agencies place environmental education staff on commercial passenger trains and ferry boats. Providing mass transit and other transportation alternatives within natural areas themselves is also becoming more common. Information and souvenirs can be provided for visitors to take home with them, and newsletters or e-mail updates can be offered for people who want to learn more or to recall pleasant memories long after their trip has ended.

Summary

In this chapter we introduced the foundational concepts needed to be effective and thoughtful outdoor recreation professionals. We demonstrated that outdoor recreation and outdoor recreation management always involve both natural resource dimensions and human dimensions. We emphasized the essential role of high-quality natural resources for outdoor recreation and presented a number of key principles regarding natural resource management. Most of the chapter addressed the human dimensions of our field by clarifying the differences and importance of leisure, recreation, and outdoor recreation. We concluded that how we define these important concepts, especially leisure, can and should affect how we manage outdoor recreation resources. In particular, we advocated that outdoor recreation professionals who define leisure properly will not focus on helping people to fill their free time, but work to create desirable, even *ideal* conditions where people are most likely to enhance their lives. A considerable part of the chapter addressed defining and discussing outdoor recreation and differentiating it from other related fields. The central role of the experience (as opposed to the activity that produces it) was presented and reinforced using a model of outdoor recreation that attempted to focus attention on the who, what, where, and why of outdoor recreation behavior from the users' and the managers'

perspectives. With these basic concepts in mind, we are now ready to more fully address the many benefits of leisure, including outdoor recreation, as well as the increasingly important role of outdoor recreation and outdoor recreation professionals in modern society. These topics are the focus of Chapter 2.

Literature Cited

Cater, E. and Lowman, G. (Eds.). (1994). *Ecotourism: A sustainable option?* Chichester, England: John Wiley & Sons.

Clausen, M. and Knetsch, J. L. (1966). *Economics of outdoor recreation*. Baltimore, MD: Johns Hopkins Press.

Cottrell, S. P. and Cottrell, R. L. (1998, August). What's gone amok in outdoor recreation? *Parks and Recreation*, 65–69.

Csikszentmihalyi, M. (1990). *Flow: The psychology of optimal experience*. New York, NY: Harper and Row.

De Grazia, S. (1961). *Of time, work, and leisure*. New York, NY: The Twentieth Century Fund.

Douglas, R. W. (2000). *Forest recreation* (5th ed.). Prospect Heights, IL: Waveland Press.

Driver, B. L. and Tocher, S. (1970). Toward a behavioral interpretation of recreational engagements, with implications for planning. In B. L. Driver (Ed.), *Elements of outdoor recreation planning* (pp. 9–31). Ann Arbor, MI: The University of Michigan Press.

Ewert, A. W. (1989). *Outdoor adventure pursuits: Foundations, models and theories*. Columbus, OH: Publishing Horizons.

Fennell, D. A. (1999). *Ecotourism: An introduction*. New York, NY: Routledge.

France, L. (Ed.). (1997). *The Earthscan reader in sustainable tourism*. London, England: Earthscan Publications, Ltd.

Godbey, G. (1994). *Leisure in your life: An exploration* (4th ed.). State College, PA: Venture Publishing, Inc.

Goeldner, C. R. and Richie, J. R. B. (2003). *Tourism: Principles, practices and philosophies* (9th ed.). Hoboken, NJ: John Wiley & Sons.

Graefe, A. R. (1987). Wildland recreation. In A. R. Graefe and S. Parker (Eds.), *Recreation and leisure: An introductory handbook* (pp. 169–173). State College, PA: Venture Publishing, Inc.

Hammitt, W. E. and Cole, D. N. (1998). *Wildland recreation: Ecology and management* (2nd ed.). New York, NY: John Wiley & Sons.

Ibrahim, H. and Cordes, K.A. (1993). *Outdoor recreation*. Madison, WI: WCB Brown and Benchmark.

Iso-Ahola, S. (1980). *The social psychology of leisure and recreation*. Dubuque, IA: William C. Brown Company Publishers.

Iso-Ahola, S. (1999). Motivational foundations of leisure. In E. Jackson and T. Burton (Eds.), *Leisure studies: Prospects for the twenty-first century* (pp. 35–51). State College, PA: Venture Publishing, Inc.

Kelly, J. (1996). *Leisure* (3rd ed.). Boston, MA: Allyn & Bacon.

MacLean, J., Peterson, J., and Martin, D. (1985). *Recreation and leisure: The changing scene* (4th ed.). New York, NY: Macmillan Publishing Company.

Manning, R. (1999). *Studies in outdoor recreation: Search and research for satisfaction* (2nd ed.). Corvallis, OR: University of Oregon Press.

Miller, G. T., Jr. (2002). *Living in the environment: Principles, connections, and solutions* (12th ed.). Belmont, CA: Brooks & Cole.

Neulinger, J. (1994). *The psychology of leisure: Research approaches to the study of leisure*. Springfield, IL: Charles Thomas Publishers.

Pieper, J. (1963). *Leisure: The basis of culture*. New York, NY: Random House.

USDA Forest Service (1982). *ROS users guide*. Washington, DC: Author.

USDA Forest Service (1995). *Sustaining ecosystems: A conceptual framework* (R5-EM-TP-001, Version 1.0). Washington, DC: Author.

U.S. Office of Personnel Management (2002a, August). *Position classification standard for outdoor recreation planning series* (GS–0023). Retrieved from http://www.opm.gov/fedclass/html/gsseries.asp

U.S. Office of Personnel Management (2002b, August). *Position classification standard for park ranger series* (GS-0025) Retrieved from http://www.opm.gov/fedclass/html/gsseries.asp

Wellman, J. D. (1987). *Wildland recreation policy: An introduction*. New York, NY: John Wiley & Sons.

Western, D. (1993). Defining ecotourism. In K. Lindberg and D. E. Hawkins (Eds.), *Ecotourism: A guide for planners and managers* (pp. 7–11). North Bennington, VT: The Ecotourism Society.

Chapter 2
Benefits of Leisure and Its Roles in Society

You can lay to rest, once and for all time, the idea that parks and recreation is nothing more than fun and games. (Jordan, 1991, p. 368)

Learning Objectives

1. Explain the concept of "professional" and define leisure and recreation professionals.
2. Understand the three types of leisure benefits and how they encompass all the benefits of leisure, including benefits to individuals, to groups of individuals (e.g., society at large), and to the biophysical environment, whether the benefits are psychological, physiological, social, economic, or environmental.
3. Describe the nature, scope, and magnitude of the benefits of leisure in general and of outdoor recreation in particular.
4. Explain why leisure and recreational professionals must understand the benefits of leisure and the roles of leisure in a society.

This chapter considers the professional aspects of careers in leisure and recreation and explains why understanding the benefits of leisure is fundamental for people pursuing such careers. It then reviews what is known about the benefits of leisure in general and outdoor recreation in particular.

Review of Definitions of Leisure and Recreation

Chapter 1 established that the many definitions of leisure and recreation have caused considerable confusion. Because of this lack of widely accepted definitions, especially of leisure, this chapter begins with a brief review of how the words leisure and recreation are used in this text. The purpose is to assure that the reader understands our use of those terms as we present and discuss the benefits of leisure and recreation.

Herein, the word *leisure* is used in two ways:

1. as a state of being (the state of leisure as defined in Chapter 1) in which a person is relatively free to choose to engage in a recreational activity, so being in that state is a precondition for such engagement

2. as a broad, umbrella term that covers all areas of specialization, such as outdoor recreation, within the broad field of leisure as an area of inquiry and practice

As explained in Chapter 1, this text defines *recreation* experientially, with a recreation experience being one that

is intrinsically rewarding and that occurs from freely chosen engagements and is not accompanied by strong compulsions to temporal demands other than the "time/clock" demands inherent within the engagement (e.g., going as fast as you can). Thus, any human activity that provides this type of experience is a recreational activity, regardless of whether the opportunities to engage in that activity are situated indoors or outdoors or whether they are provided by public or quasi-public agencies, private enterprises, or personally by the individual recreating.

The benefits considered in this chapter are those derived from any type of recreation, including mental engagement, and the benefits of outdoor recreation refer to those that accrue from the management and use of outdoor recreation resources. The term *leisure professional* applies to any professional who specializes in any field of leisure, such as outdoor recreation, and who meets the requirements of a professional defined in the following section. The terms leisure professionals and recreation professionals are used frequently in this text and are equivalent, with the only difference being that the term *recreational professional* denotes a specialization within a specific area of leisure, such as outdoor recreation. Put simply, all recreational professionals are also leisure professionals, just as all medical professionals are also "health" professionals whether they specialize in nursing, family medicine, heart surgery, or pediatrics. The exception to the equivalency between a leisure and recreation professional would be people whose professional efforts are devoted to the broad concept of leisure and not to a particular recreational specialty. Examples include leisure counselors, scholars, or someone who works to create opportunities for more people to experience leisure more often or for longer periods of time.

What Is a Leisure Profession or a Recreation Profession?

People generally understand the characteristics and contributions to society of most professions. In contrast, those of us who study or work in some area of leisure or recreation have frequently been asked by our parents, friends, or other associates, "How can anyone study or work in leisure?" Sometimes, this question teasingly plays on the semantics of *"work in leisure"* or *"work in recreation."* In other instances, the question reflects some understanding of the philosophy of leisure that promotes the concept of leisure as a state of being, and the person asking the question wonders either why anyone would not study philosophy instead of leisure, or how anyone could have a career in leisure so defined. But most often the question reflects widespread lack of understanding about the nature, scope, and benefits of leisure. Shortly, we will explain why this widespread misunderstanding exists more for leisure than for other professions. But first we must establish how we define profession.

A *profession* is commonly defined as an area of expertise founded on an empirically supported body of knowledge. Some writers also like to add that most professions have one or more professional organizations (e.g., the America Medical Association, the Society of American Foresters), which exist

1. to advance professional knowledge, and promote and publicize professional activities.

2. to determine subject areas (normally defined as courses and curricula of formal education) in which a person must demonstrate satisfactory training before admittance to the professional organization is granted.

3. to set up licensing procedures, including tests of professional knowledge.

4. to establish codes of ethics for the profession, such as the Hippocratic oath in the medical professions.

Despite these purposes of professional associations and societies, the most important characteristic of professions distinguishes them from trades and crafts—they are based on a body of scientific knowledge. Members of professions are expected to know, and in many cases, pass periodic tests of that knowledge.

Empirically supported knowledge denotes professional knowledge derived from scientific studies that follow established and accepted methods of scientific research. While personal intuitions and subjective premises may add important and needed dimensions to the art of a profession, they are excluded from the science-based knowledge that must be understood to merit professional standing. Thus, to be considered a professional, one must learn that body of knowledge and continually stay abreast of new additions to that knowledge. Members of a profession cannot perform effectively if they do not keep up with the states of knowledge within their respective professions. This is true for academics, teachers, scientists, doctors, lawyers, engineers, architects, or members of other professions. People would not have confidence in anyone who claimed to be professional if they left the impression they did not possess the professional knowledge expected of them. For example, few of us would seek the services of a medical doctor if we thought he or she could not apply the most recent medical knowledge available and feasible. Nor would we opt to take any elective courses from professors who left the impression they did not know the concepts and principles they wanted us to learn.

The question then arises: Does a sufficient empirically supported body of knowledge now exist so that a person can gain knowledge to entitle him or her to be called a leisure professional? The answer is a definitive yes. Several such bodies of knowledge comprise the different areas of specialization within leisure, such as outdoor recreation. The problem is too few of us pursuing careers in leisure/recreation view ourselves as professionals and behave accordingly by keeping abreast of new knowledge. The major reason other people do not understand what those of us who pursue careers in leisure or recreation do is that we ourselves do not, and cannot, articulate clearly to others what a leisure or recreation professional does and why and what our contributions are. Therefore, other people remain confused about what we do and why, and will ask, "How can you study or work in leisure?" Put simply, the two biggest challenges facing the leisure professions are for each of us (a) to understand the science-based knowledge about the benefits of leisure and its important contributions to a society and (b) to communicate those contributions to others outside our profession.

Crompton (1993) and Crompton and Witt (1998) addressed this challenge by stating that we must "reposition the image" of leisure. We must change people's inaccurate perceptions of leisure away from the idea that leisure is frivolous to the image that leisure services provide benefits to society that equal or exceed those of other social services. This change in image cannot occur until all leisure professionals acquire a thorough understanding of the now readily available results of scientific studies about the diverse benefits of leisure and the relative magnitudes of those benefits. Put simply, we cannot communicate to others the contributions of leisure to society unless we ourselves clearly understand what those benefits are.

The benefits of leisure have been extolled since the days of Aristotle. The roots of the parks and recreation movements in England, Canada, the United States, and other countries were grounded in the concept of the social worth of recreation. Nevertheless, most past and ongoing pronouncements about the benefits of leisure remain largely subjective although they no longer need to. While these subjective opinions about the nature and scope of some of the benefits of leisure might well be correct, an empirically supported (i.e., professional) body of knowledge cannot be based on subjective impressions and opinions, and neither can efforts to "reposition the image" of leisure within the leisure professions. As said, there must be art in any profession, but there must also be science.

While we must reposition the image of leisure within our leisure professions, we have another pressing responsibility. The current pervasive image of leisure being mostly fun and games must also be changed in the minds of people in other professions with whom leisure professionals work. The image of leisure must also be repositioned in the minds of elected officials who decide what public resources will be allocated to the acquisition and management of park and recreation resources, and in the minds of members of the general public who now widely support other social services, such as public education, because they know of their benefits to society (Jordan, 1991). All of these people must come to understand and to appreciate the values added by leisure to the lives of individuals—extending from families through local communities to society at large. Only we can be their teachers.

Benefits of Leisure

Definitions

One reason why the benefits of leisure are not more widely understood is that scientific knowledge about many of those benefits only emerged recently. Another important reason is that no clear and comprehensive definition of what is meant by a benefit of leisure has been widely accepted in the leisure professions. For example, when applications of the beneficial outcomes approach to leisure (BOAL; described in detail in Chapter 13) were first being pilot tested and evaluated systematically in several public park and recreation agencies, it immediately became obvious there was considerable confusion about the meaning of the phrase *benefits of leisure*. The definition of a benefit found in most dictionaries was too restrictive and prevented effective application of the BOAL. Therefore, three types of benefits of leisure were identified and defined that would comprehensively consider all the ben-

efits of leisure and could be applied meaningfully. Those three types of benefits will now be described, because they establish how the words "benefits of leisure" are used this text.

Change in a Condition or State Viewed as More Desirable Than a Previous One

That beneficial change can be to individuals, groups of individuals (e.g., a family, a community, society at large), or biophysical and cultural/heritage resources. Examples include improved mental or physical health, increased learning, closer bonding among members of a family unit, a more economically viable local community, or a refurbished archeological structure. Note this category of benefit requires a change or movement from an existing state or condition to what is viewed as an improved condition or state. This is the definition of a benefit found in most dictionaries.

Maintenance of a Desired Condition and Thereby Prevention of an Unwanted Condition

This prevents an undesired condition from becoming worse, or reduces the unwanted impact of an existing undesired condition. While people commonly recognize that park and recreation agencies facilitate many improved conditions, they often fail to realize that those agencies also maintain many existing desired conditions and prevent worse conditions. In fact, much of the effort of parks and recreation agencies is directed toward these objectives. Examples include maintaining and protecting existing natural and cultural/historic resources, providing opportunities for users to maintain their physical and mental health, stimulating tourism to maintain the economic stability of local communities, helping to prevent some youth from becoming at risk or more at risk, or preventing greater incidences of vandalism. Unlike the previous "improved condition" category of benefits, this second type of benefit does not require a change to occur if an existing desired state is prevented from becoming an undesired state or if an existing undesired state is prevented from becoming worse. However, a change is required if this second type of benefit results from reducing the impacts of an existing undesired condition.

Realization of a Satisfying Recreation Experience

Many, if not most, actions of parks and recreation professionals are directed toward providing opportunities for the realization of satisfying recreation experiences. We include this as a distinct category of benefit because it is not always clear how provision of those opportunities contributes to the realization of either of the previous types of more tangible benefits. For example, the improved conditions that result from experiencing psychophysi-ological relaxation and increased physical fitness are more readily measured and managed scientifically than are any improved conditions that might be realized from recreation-prompted spiritual renewal or enjoyment of a scenic vista. Yet parks and recreation managers cannot ignore these more esoteric types of possibly beneficial experiences just because any associated improved or maintained desired conditions cannot be specified clearly or measured accurately. At first reading, you might think it is perhaps arbitrary to say that a third type of benefit results from the realization of a satisfying psychological experience from a recreational engagement. But, is it not logical to assume that if people feel good about some-thing, they have benefited psychologically for at least some period of time?

Characteristics

To thoroughly understand and appreciate the usefulness of these three types of benefits of leisure, one must be aware of three characteristics.

First, the definitions of the three types of leisure ben-efits do not say anything about whether a particular changed condition, maintained condition, or satisfying recreation experience are socially acceptable because not all people agree on what is acceptable. For example, some cultures and subcultures have no problem with nude bathing at public beaches; others do. Or, a person might gain a sat-isfying experience from painting graffiti of the walls of buildings, but unless that graffiti is socially endorsed, re-alization of that type benefit would be unacceptable social-ly (and often punishable by law). Therefore, there must be reasonable social consensus, especially among mana-gerially relevant stakeholders, before any condition can be considered as beneficial from a public policy or mana-gerial perspective. Fortunately, there is considerable so-cial consensus about many of the benefits of leisure.

Outdoor recreation can lead to a wide range of health-related benefits. (Photo by National Park Service)

Examples include promotion of family bonding, learning about nature and cultural/historic resources, temporarily escaping and recovering from the everyday strains and stress of life, and enhanced pride in one's community.

Second, together the three types cover all the benefits associated with the delivery and use of leisure services, because the benefits can accrue not only to individuals, but also to groups of individuals, as well as to the biophysi-cal and cultural/heritage resources being managed. While most of the benefits result from use of leisure services, some benefits are created just from managerial activities, even when there is no use of the leisure services provided. For example, benefits of increased income are created directly by park and recreation agencies when they pay employees and contractors.

Third, to avoid a common confusion, it should also be understood that the way the three types of benefits are defined is not directly related to the way the word "ben-efit" is used in economic benefit-cost analyses. In those analyses, benefits are defined and measured in terms of some index (e.g., monetary price) of the economic worth of the goods and services that will be provided or pro-tected by the investment being evaluated. In economic terms, the three types of benefits constitute the utility of a leisure service to which economic measures of worth are assigned by market prices or by other means employed by economists to estimate market prices of "unpriced" amenity services. Although this chapter uses a broader definition of benefits than economists do, we also recog-nize the tremendous contributions made by economists in determining and measuring the economic values of recre-ational services and of the economic impacts of recreation and tourism expenditures on local communities, regions, and nations at large. Chapter 19 addresses the economics of outdoor recreation in detail.

The heart of this discussion is that all park and recre-ation policy makers and managers must appreciate that scientific knowledge about all types of benefits is neces-sary for professionalism in our field. This knowledge helps ensure that park and recreation policy makers and man-agers make effective, responsive, cost-effective, efficient, fair, and equitable policy and managerial decisions and do so in an accountable manner.

Evolution of Scientific Knowledge About Benefits of Leisure

As elaborated in Driver (1999a), very little scientific research was done in any of the subareas of leisure before 1960. There were several sociological studies within the context of the broader community, a few investigations of the impacts of outdoor recreationists on the biophysical environment, several efforts to estimate the economic impacts of tourists, and some studies directed at estimating recreational use of dispersed recreation areas. This poverty of empirical research was pointed out in Volume 27 (Bibliography and Literature Review) of the Outdoor Recreation Resources Review Commission (1962). Over 90% of the literature citations were to administrative studies that discussed increasing use rates and other factors that indicated needs to provide more opportunities to meet growing demands. Also indicative of this very recent history of science-based knowledge is the fact that the first research journal in leisure, *Journal of Leisure Research*, was not published until the mid-1960s. Put simply, the knowledge about leisure in 1960 was primarily based on philosophical writings and administrative studies measuring trends in recreational use.

Research on the benefits of leisure began even later. Few results regarding benefits were reported before the early 1980s, and they were limited mostly to the mental and physical health benefits of getting exercise during one's leisure, psychological benefits of participating in sports, and beneficial secondary economic impacts of tourists' expenditures. The notable exceptions were the considerable amount of research on people's economic willingness to pay for leisure services and on different types of beneficial satisfying experiences realized from leisure engagements. Even given these studies, there was little widespread scientific interest in the benefits of leisure before the middle to late 1980s.

Since about 1985, scientific interest in leisure benefits has increased rapidly. That interest was stimulated in part by a growing number of publications on benefits, notably *Benefits of Leisure* (Driver, Brown & Peterson, 1991), *The Benefits of Recreation Research Update* (Sefton & Mummery, 1995), *The Benefits Catalogue* (Canadian Parks/Recreation Association (1997), and *Setting a Course for*

Family bonding and better family relations are common benefits of outdoor recreation participation.

Change: The Benefits Movement (O'Sullivan, 1999). Research now in progress and results of future research will continue to advance our knowledge about the benefits. A good example is the research on at-risk youth (cf. Hurtes, Allen, Stevens & Lee, 2000; Witt & Crompton, 1996).

Perhaps the most important thing to recognize about the evolution of our scientific knowledge base is how far we have come. It is difficult to think of but a few other professions for which the science-based body of knowledge advanced as much as for leisure during the past four decades. Communication sciences, space engineering, and some fields of medicine have done so. But 40 years is an extremely short period of time for any profession to advance from practically no science-based knowledge to where the leisure professions are today. All leisure professionals should be proud of these remarkable achievements.

Nature, Scope, and Magnitude of the Benefits of Leisure

The rest of this chapter gives a general overview of the scientific knowledge about the benefits of leisure. Entire books and other documents have been written on this topic (e.g., Canadian Parks/Recreation Association, 1997; Driver, Brown & Peterson, 1991; O'Sullivan 1999). This review is done in two subsections. The first summarizes science-based knowledge about the benefits of leisure when leisure is defined very broadly. The second subsection summarizes knowledge about the benefits of outdoor recreation, which comprise an important subpart of the total benefits of leisure.

It might seem desirable to focus only on the benefits of outdoor recreation in a text targeted to that area of leisure. But that is impossible and even undesirable. Such an attempt would be subjective, speculative, and overly qualitative, because few benefits of leisure, when taken individually or singly, can be attributed solely to a particular recreational setting, such as outdoor settings. Put differently, most identified benefits of leisure, when considered singly, can be realized in indoor as well as outdoor settings, in one's home, in a city, and in other settings, as elaborated in the next section. For that reason, we first review the benefits of all types of leisure engagements and then relate those benefits to outdoor recreation. Such an approach will better facilitate a professional understanding of the scope, nature, and magnitude of the benefits of leisure and of the sizable contribution of outdoor recreation to those total benefits.

Benefits of Leisure in General

When leisure is broadly defined, we must consider the time, effort, money, and other resources allocated by public agencies, private enterprises, quasi-public or nonprofit organizations, interest groups, and private individuals to provide and to use recreational opportunities. Such a broad concept of leisure includes what is conventionally thought of as recreational activities, but also includes use of public libraries, art galleries, and museums, as well as enrollment in continuing education courses, watching television programs, entertaining in one's home, attending and viewing professional sports, the Olympic games, and much more. Leisure-related proportions of the time and income that people spend on acquiring and using personal computers and vehicles should also be included in this broad definition of leisure, as should all the time, effort, and personal income that go into boats, yachts, airplanes, second and third homes, and other facilitators of recreational pursuits. As such, leisure is a much larger part of the fabric (including the economic fabric) of many societies than commonly realized.

We begin the following discourse on the benefits of leisure, defined broadly, by giving some general descriptions of those benefits. Then we become very specific about the nature, scope, and magnitude of particular types of benefits that have been systematically researched. We will first consider the noneconomic benefits (those measured in other than monetary units) and then the economic ones.

Noneconomic Benefits

Chapter 4 describes some of the many trends and forces in society leading to increasing use of recreational opportunities. Here we briefly discuss some of the more esoteric factors that contribute to increased recreation participation. These selected factors are quite relevant to this chapter,

because they have contributed to people's greater concerns about the quality of their lives, which in turn have lead to greater awareness by people of the contributions of recreation to that perceived quality.

An increasing number of people are now aware that the following factors contribute to the quality of their lives:

- good nutrition
- physical exercise
- avoiding substance abuse (including alcohol and tobacco)
- managing stress
- social networking that provides support and cohesion (including trying to regain a perceived loss of sense of community)
- seeking and using "alternative" medical practices (e.g., acupuncture, use of proven herbal remedies, massage)
- exploring means of facilitating and expanding the spiritual meanings of their lives (including the growing use of natural areas for spiritual renewal)
- presence of local amenities and use of those amenities (e.g., museums, performing arts, green/open spaces, recreation programs and facilities)

Put simply, large numbers of people are becoming more introspective and knowledgeable about how they allocate their unobligated time and other personal resources.

The growing introspection about the positive and negative consequences of alternative personal behaviors to the quality of one's life has pervaded leisure in a way that has become increasingly important to our profession. One result of this introspection is that people now evaluate the consequences of their leisure behaviors more seriously and carefully. They now have a better understanding of the

Social bonding and nurturing others occur during many outdoor recreation experiences.

Historic awareness and contemplation can be important aspects of outdoor recreation.

consequences of alternative leisure choices, meaning that they better understand the benefits they will likely receive from their recreational engagements. This increased awareness of benefits has contributed to growing levels of recreational use. It also is consistent with the tenet of consumer economics that people are generally reasonable about how they expend their scarce resources and do so rather deliberately to gain utility (e.g., satisfaction and other benefits) from a particular good or service purchased or used. This is not to argue that people are completely rational in their decisions, that the pull of habit is not strong, or that people are utility maximizers. Instead, the argument here is that people generally behave reasonably, and as sovereign consumers generally act to optimize their personal utility or welfare over time.

Reliable evidence from several quality of life studies (Allen, 1991; Campbell, 1981; Marans & Mohai, 1991) and other research indicates that people have a fairly good understanding and awareness of the types of satisfying experiences and other benefits they desire from their recreational engagements. Therefore, people who recreate are prudent in expenditures of their scarce personal resources and generally do so to realize those benefits of which they are aware. This means that the documented large percentages of the population of the United States and other countries who participate in many different recreational activities gain a tremendous amount of benefit.

To document the benefits and people's awareness of them, we start with results of a study by Godbey, Graefe, and James (1992). That study, *The Benefits of Local Recreation*, was done for the National Recreation and Park Association, our field's umbrella professional organization, which has several specialized professional branches (e.g., the Society of Park and Recreation Educators). In January and February of 1992, telephone interviews were conducted with a nationally representative sample of 1,305 individuals age 15 and over. Those telephone interviews were followed by a mailed questionnaire to obtain additional information. The questionnaire was sent to 882 of those telephoned. Some key findings were that 75% of the respondents reported that they used local recreation and park services (51% reported they used them occasionally, and 24% said they used them frequently). Respondents to that household survey, and to a very similar one

in Canada by Harper, Neider, Godbey, and Lamont (1997), were asked to report benefits they perceived to themselves individually, to their household, and to their local community. The percentage breakdown of the total benefits that respondents perceived to result from the presence and use of local recreation opportunities are presented in Table 2.1. Percentage results from the Godbey and colleagues (1992) study are listed along with those from the Harper and associates (1997) study.

Notice that the sums of the percentages across each of the second two rows are each greater than 100%. This indicates that the respondents attributed some of the benefits in one category to other categories too. For example, benefits such as improved mental and physical health or closer bonding of families can accrue to households and the local community as well as to individuals.

If one sums the percentages for "some benefit" and "great benefit," it can be seen that 83.7%, 79.2%, and 94.4% of the respondents to the study in the United States (and 86%, 97%, and 94% for the Canadian study) perceived either some or great benefit to them individually, for their household, or for their local community, respectively. Notice how close these summed percentages are for those two nations. Not surprisingly, people perceive that benefits of leisure accrue to them individually and to their households. But these two studies are particularly revealing by showing that 61.3 % (and 58%) of the respondents also perceived great benefit to their local communities. Lastly, both users and nonusers were asked about the benefits they perceived, and 71% of the nonusers reported perceived benefits to themselves, their household, or their local community. This supports the notion that many of the users of recreation resources are off-site users who appreciate the presence of those resources, but might never use them (see Chapter 13). Bear these last two findings in mind when you read the section of this chapter on the roles of leisure in society.

Respondents to both the Godbey and colleagues (1992) and Harper and associates (1997) studies who perceived benefits were asked to name the most important benefit they received and then to list the additional benefits they perceived for themselves, for their household, and for their local community. Space limitations prevent a listing of these specific types of benefits mentioned. Suffice it to say

Table 2.1   Summary of study results from Godbey, Graefe, and James (1992) and Harper, Neider, Godbey, and Lamont (1997)

Amount of Benefit	To Whom Do the Benefits Accrue?					
	Individuals		Households		Community at Large	
	Godbey et al.	Harper et al.	Godbey et al.	Harper et al.	Godbey et al.	Harper et al.
No Benefit	16.3%	14%	20.8%	2%	5.6%	4%
Some Benefit	47.0%	46%	47.9%	52%	33.1%	36%
Great Benefit	36.7%	40%	31.3%	45%	61.3%	58%

that results from both studies support the underlying contention of this chapter that the benefits of leisure are very extensive and of a magnitude not commonly recognized or appreciated. A number of specific types of benefits have been attributed to leisure by systematic research. They are listed in an abbreviated fashion in Table 2.2.

While Table 2.2 lists specific types of benefits, it also includes some general categories of benefits, which subsume some of those specific types, leading to some redundancy. Notice that the 145 benefits of leisure listed in Table 2.2 are organized into several categories, some of which show subclasses of benefits. Those groupings show the general nature of the benefits and what type of impact they have. For example, the personal benefits category is divided into psychological (with three separate types of these benefits shown) and psychophysiological, the category of benefit that focuses most directly on the health-related benefits of recreational activities. Thus, personal benefits accrue to individuals, and the social/cultural benefits impact groups of people, ranging from small groups, such as families, through local communities, to society at large. The economic benefits are really social benefits but of a particular and important type. The environmental benefits designate beneficial outcomes from the protection, management, and use of natural and cultural/heritage resources, and they depict clearly and specifically the very wide scope of the benefits of leisure.

The benefits as presented in Table 2.2 are of central importance to this chapter because they clearly show that benefits of leisure are of a broader scope, more varied, and most probably of greater magnitude than most people would first envision. A close inspection shows the listed benefits pervade all aspects of human behavior and performance, including

- mental and physical health
- family and community relations
- self-concept
- personal value clarification
- perceived personal freedom
- sense of fitting in
- understanding local community and national historical events and cultural characteristics
- pride in one's community and nation
- learning of many types
- performance in school and at work
- sharing
- ethnic identity
- identities formed with sports and sports teams

- formation of close friendships and systems of social support
- spiritual definition, renewal, and facilitation
- involvement in community affairs
- local community cohesion and stability
- environmental understanding and stewardship
- economic development, growth, and stability

It should also be noted that many of the benefits listed in Table 2.2 are experiential in nature and are based on psychological studies of perceived benefits. The results of those psychological studies provide very useful information, but they are sometimes viewed as less reliable than studies using "hard" measures, such as the physiological studies measuring the cardiovascular benefits of activity during leisure. That view is antiquated, because advances in psychological research during the past several decades now give the results of that research much validity and reliability.

Leisure scientists have used different research methods to identify and to measure the psychological and social psychological benefits of leisure. Driver (2003) reviews these different approaches, and why they are used, and gives some results from each. Perhaps the most widely adopted approach has been use of the recreation experience preference (REP) scales developed by Driver and associates (Driver, Tinsley & Manfredo, 1991; Manfredo, Driver & Tarrant, 1996). The REP scales were developed to identify and measure the magnitude of the types of satisfying and dissatisfying psychological experiences salient/dominant in the minds of the some 30,000 recreationists studied after they participated in a wide variety

Outdoor recreation can lead to important stewardship and preservation benefits for the environment and enhanced environmental ethics for visitors.

Table 2.2 Specific types and general categories of benefits attributed to leisure by one or more scientific studies

PERSONAL BENEFITS: PSYCHOLOGICAL

Personal Development and Growth
- Self-esteem
- Self-confidence
- Self-reliance
- Self-competence
- Self-assurance
- Self-affirmation
- Values clarification
- Learn new skills and develop and apply other skills
- Academic/cognitive performance
- Independence/autonomy
- Sense of control over one's life
- Humility
- Leadership ability
- Aesthetic enhancement/greater appreciation of beauty
- Creativity enhancement
- Spiritual growth and greater appreciation/tolerance of different ethnic interpretations of spirituality
- Adaptability

- Cognitive efficiency
- Teamwork/cooperation
- Problem solving
- Nature learning
- Cultural/historic awareness/learning/appreciation
- Environmental awareness/understanding
- Tolerance
- Balanced competitiveness
- Balanced living
- Willingness to take risks
- Acceptance of one's responsibility
- Academic and other mental performance

Mental Health and Maintenance
- Holistic sense of wellness
- Stress management (i.e., prevention, mediation, and restoration)
- Prevention of and reduced depression/anxiety/anger
- Positive changes in mood and emotion
- Catharsis

Personal Appreciation/Satisfaction
- Sense of freedom
- Self-actualization
- Flow/absorption
- Exhilaration
- Stimulation
- Sense of adventure
- Challenge
- Nostalgia
- Perceived quality of life/life satisfaction
- Creative expression
- Aesthetic appreciation
- Nature appreciation
- Spirituality
- Positive change in mood/emotion
- Environmental stewardship
- Identification with special places/feeling of geographical belonging or physical grounding
- Transcendent experiences

PERSONAL BENEFITS: PSYCHOPHYSIOLOGICAL

- Improved perceived quality of life
- Cardiovascular benefits, including prevention of strokes
- Reduced or prevented hypertension
- Reduced serum cholesterol and triglycerides
- Rehabilitation of patients with heart problems
- Improved control and prevention of diabetes
- Reduced risk of lung and colon cancer
- Better muscle strength and joint functioning
- Reduced spinal problems
- Decreased body fat/obesity/weight control

- Improved neuropsychological functioning
- Increased bone mass and strength in children
- Promotion of better balance
- Increased muscle strength and better connective tissue
- Respiratory benefits (e.g., increased lung capacity, benefits to people with asthma)
- Improved response time
- Reduced incidence of disease
- Improved bladder control in the elderly
- Increased life expectancy

- Reduced anxiety and somatic complaints
- Management of menstrual cycles
- Management of arthritis
- Improved functioning of the immune system (i.e., resistance to illness)
- Reduced depression and improved mood
- Reduced consumption of alcohol, tobacco, and other drugs
- Reduced need for some medications

SOCIAL/CULTURAL BENEFITS

- Community satisfaction and morale
- Community identity
- Pride in community/nation (i.e., pride in place/patriotism)
- Cultural/historical awareness and appreciation
- Reduced social alienation
- Reduced illness and social impacts of such
- Community/political involvement
- Increased productivity and job satisfaction
- Ethnic social integration
- Social bonding/cohesion/cooperation
- Conflict resolution/harmony
- Reduced crime
- Greater community involvement in environmental decision making

- Social support
- Support for democratic ideal of freedom
- Family bonding/better family life
- Keeping children engaged/away from less desirable activities
- Higher class attendance
- Lower dropout rates
- Increased trust in others
- Increased compassion for others
- Reduced loneliness
- Reciprocity/sharing
- Social mobility
- Improved image of public agencies
- Community integration
- Promotion of voluntary community efforts

- Nurturing of others
- Understanding and tolerance of others
- Environmental awareness, sensitivity
- Enhanced worldview
- Nurture new community leaders
- Socialization/acculturation
- Cultural identity
- Cultural continuity
- Prevention of social problems by at-risk youth
- Developmental benefits in children
- Increased independence of older people
- Networking by seniors
- Increased longevity and perceived quality of life

ENVIRONMENTAL BENEFITS

- Maintenance of physical facilities
- Stewardship/preservation of options
- Improved air quality through urban forestry
- Husbandry/improved relationships with natural world
- Increases in "leave no trace" use

- Understanding of human dependency on the natural world
- Environmental ethic
- Public involvement in environmental issues
- Environmental protection
- Ecosystem sustainability
- Species biodiversity

- Maintenance of natural scientific laboratories
- Preservation of particular natural sites and areas
- Preservation of cultural/heritage/historic sites and areas
- Promotion of ecotourism

ECONOMIC BENEFITS

- Reduced health costs
- Increased productivity
- Less work absenteeism
- Reduced on-the-job accidents
- Amenity use of hazard areas
- Decreased job turnover

- International balance of payments (from tourism)
- Local and regional economic growth
- Local amenities help attract industry
- Employment opportunities

- Contributions to net national economic development
- Promotion of places to retire and associated economic growth
- Increased property values

Note: Some of the specific types of benefits are subsumed within more general types, so there is some redundancy in this list. Sources: First published in Driver (1990), revised for Driver and Bruns (1999), and revised considerably for this text. Many benefits are supported by more scientific research than are others. The best reference for the scientific bases of these benefits is *The Benefits Catalogue* by the Canadian Parks/Recreation Association (1997).

of recreational engagements. Although the complete REP scales have never been published before, they have been used widely and in several countries, with results published in refereed journals and other outlets. Because many of the psychological benefits listed in Table 2.2 were derived from research that used the REP scales, they are included (with explanatory notes) in Appendix A (p. 315).

The experiential nature of many of the benefits of leisure helps to explain why Chapter 1 discussed in detail the importance of understanding recreation in experiential terms, and why the third type of benefit of leisure defined earlier in this chapter was "the realization of a satisfying recreation experience." While many of the other types of benefits identified in Table 2.2 (e.g., improved or maintained physical growth, protection of natural and cultural heritage resources) are not manifested in experiential terms, most of the benefits listed are realized psychologically or psychophysiologically. If one wanted to, they could even interpret the physical health-related benefits as being experienced physiologically, but normally an experiential definition of recreation refers to psychological and psychophysiological responses. The point is, if one wants to truly appreciate the nature, scope, and magnitude of the benefits of leisure, recreation must be understood in experiential terms. The reader will gain a better understanding of the breadth and scope of these experiential benefits if he or she reflects on a few favorite recreation activities and answers the following questions:

• Do I personally ever receive any of the listed benefits from my recreation?

• Do I believe other individuals probably do so?

• Do groups of people (from family members to local communities to society as a whole) receive the types of social benefits listed?

• Do natural and cultural/historical resources benefit in the ways listed?

Through this simple exercise, one can become more aware of the great number of benefits of leisure that research has identified. Therefore, one will be better prepared to help "reposition the images" held by others of our leisure and recreation professions.

Several characteristics of recreation experiences should also be made clear here. First, people who never visit the facilities, sites, or larger recreation areas being managed realize many of the beneficial experiences listed in Table 2.2. These people are called *off-site users,* and benefit just from knowing the amenities are available and are being protected. Examples of such benefits are improved stewardship and environmental ethic, listed in Table 2.2 under environmental benefits. Many people who receive these types of benefits live long distances from

national and state parks, fish and wildlife refuges, national forests, nature conservancy areas, art centers, and other recreation resources, but know, learn about, and appreciate the existence of these resources from information they obtain from many sources (e.g., TV, lectures, coffee table books, magazine articles). Many of these remote off-site users support the management and protection of these amenities through their tax dollars and voluntary contributions of money, which indicates they value the resources in which they invest. In addition, off-site users who live near the amenities receive other types of experiential benefits. Those benefits relate to the fact that several research studies in the United States and other countries (Allen, 1991; Campbell, 1981; Marans & Mohai, 1991) documented existence of nearby amenities as one of the top-five most important contributors to people's perceived quality of life or satisfaction with their lives. This is the reason residents of the guest/host community and other local communities near recreational opportunities typically value those amenities so highly.

Lastly on Table 2.2, and because of past confusion, it must be emphasized that some of the benefits listed have been defined much more clearly and have been the subject of much more scientific research than have others. Driver (1990) emphasized and documented that point in an earlier paper, which listed a slightly shorter number of benefits than Table 2.2. He presented a chart that showed the degree to which each of the benefits had been clearly defined or specified, as well as the degree to which each benefit had been supported by scientific research. Even today, some of the benefits listed in Table 2.2 remain not well-specified and still receive little scientific research, while most of them are specified (or defined) much better and have been the subject of more research. For example, the cardiovascular benefits of physical exercise have been defined very well and have been the subject of hundreds of studies, but the spiritual benefits remain not well-defined and have received little study as a benefit of leisure. The point emphasized here is that not all of the benefits of leisure listed in Table 2.2 have been defined or specified adequately or have had enough scientific documentation.

Please ponder the broad nature and scope of the benefits listed in Table 2.2, and reflect on the large number of people who receive these benefits. Think about their pervasiveness and total magnitude, and reflect further on the associated benefits they nurture, create, and promote. For example, leisure activities can reduce health care costs, crime, and the high costs of incarceration; increase the economic value of work performance; and promote pride in community and nation. Then ask yourself this rather startling question: Does leisure contribute as many total benefits to society as any other social service, including health and education? Given the wide variety of benefits and how they pervade all aspects of our lives, the authors of this text answer a very definite "yes" to this question. Supporting this contention are the high rates of participation in recreational activities by members of the public, which means that a strong majority of citizens receive many of the benefits listed in Table 2.2.

As we report in detail in Chapter 4, many representative household surveys documented high rates of recreation participation. Godbey and colleagues (1992) reported that 75% of the respondents to their national household survey said they used local recreation and park services either occasionally or frequently. In addition, data from the 1994–1995 National Survey on Recreation and the Environment (Cordell et al., 1999, p. 221) showed that 95% of the population of the United States 16 years of age and older participated at least once in the following selected recreation activity groups between January 1994 and April 1995: fitness activities, outdoor team sport activities, walking, outdoor spectator activities, camping, swimming, and picnicking. A similar household survey was repeated in 2000–2001 and found in general that rates of participation by people ages 16 and older increased in most activities (Cordell, Betz, Green & Mou, 2004). During the 12-month period covered by that survey, percentage participation in frequently engaged in activities were as follows:

- walking for pleasure (83%)
- family gatherings (74%)
- visiting a beach (61%)
- visiting museums and nature centers (57%)
- picnicking (55%)
- sightseeing (52%)
- attending outdoor sporting events (50%)
- visiting historic sites (46%)
- viewing wildlife (45%)

We iterate that these hundreds of millions of people engaging in these and other recreation activities denote a strong multiplier effect on the benefits listed singly or individually in Table 2.2. The total magnitude of the benefits is staggering, and warrants a significant "repositioning of the image" of leisure in the minds of most people.

Economic Benefits

We contended above that when leisure is considered broadly, leisure services probably provide as much total benefit (i.e., add as much value) to an economically developed country (i.e., where needs for food, nutrition, sanitation, housing have been met fairly well) as do any other social service. Another perhaps equally startling contention by the authors of this text is that the leisure services

sector is one of the largest economic sectors in the United States. To explore this proposition, we first need to consider the size of this leisure economic sector.

The economic benefits of leisure are represented by the large amounts of expenditures and investments of money in leisure infrastructures and money spent directly on recreational engagements. The economic benefits that accrue include the following:

- increased employment opportunities
- increased economic security of people receiving income generated from that employment and from sales of recreation equipment and services
- increased local, regional, and national economic growth and stability
- improved international trade balances
- government revenues from sales and recreation property taxes
- other economic benefits related to these flows of money related to leisure

It has been established, but not widely recognized, that the leisure services sector is very big business in the United States and other countries (Stynes, 1993). For example, in many countries recreation and tourism rank in the top three economic sectors as generators of income and employment. It has also been established that expenditures on tourism-related international travel generates greater flows of funds among nations than any other economic transaction, including sales of grain, automobiles, or electronic parts and equipment. In addition, tourism is the primary generator of foreign exchange in many less economically developed countries.

The following statistics on the economic impacts of domestic and international travel document the size of the "leisure industry." They were taken directly from Driver (1999b, pp. 8–9).

In 1995, international travelers spent $79.7 billion in the United States, and American travelers spent $60.2 billion outside the United States, creating a trade balance surplus of $19.5 billion. The size of the surplus rose 4% over 1994. The surplus trade balance from travel grew for the 7th straight year. Travel is one of the few economic sectors that generates a positive trade balance. During 1995, domestic and international travelers together spent $421.5 billion in the United States, which is a 5.8% increase over 1994. When induced and indirect expenditures are added to those expenditures, the estimated total expenditures for 1995 were about $1,017 billion. That total translates into about 16.5 million jobs, travel-related payrolls of about $116 billion and $64 billion in federal, state and local tax revenues for that year. Pleasure-related travel accounted for 69% of all U.S. domestic/residential travel in 1995. Seventeen percent of domestic business trips in 1995 combined business with pleasure, which represents a 4% increase over 1994. I could find no statistic for the percentage of international travel that is estimated to be pleasure-related, but it is logical to assume it is as high or higher than that for resident travelers. In 1995, travel and the related tourism it stimulated was the third largest retail industry in the United States, after automotive dealers and food stores. The projections for the foreseeable future are for expenditures in that sector to continue to increase as a percent of total expenditures of the retail sale industries of the United States. (The Tourism Works for America Council, 1996; U.S. Travel Data Center, 1994)

Statistics such as these document that recreation and tourism are "big business" of great magnitude. But those statistics only touch the surface—they pale in size when compared to other components of the leisure industry that must be considered if one really desires to obtain an accurate picture of the total economic benefits of leisure when defined broadly. The problem is current systems for classifying economic sectors of most countries do not provide for the definitive and accurate identification and inclusion of most leisure industries. For example the *Standard Industrial Classification Manual* of the U.S. government breaks private economic sectors in that country into five-digit categories ranging from very general one-digit designations (such as manufacturing) to very specific delineations of a particular type of manufacturing industry. Unfortunately, leisure industries are poorly represented, with important components of that industry,

Outdoor recreation-related industries create employment opportunities and enhance local and regional economic growth.

such as television, radio, hotels, and restaurants, classified as other industrial/economic sectors.

A full accounting and accurate representation of the great size of the leisure economic sector and its economic significance would require including the cost of planning, constructing, and maintaining all the physical facilities that facilitate many types of leisure pursuits (e.g., janitorial and sanitation services, water repairs and improvements, heating, lighting, security, communication services). Examples of such leisure-related facilities and costs include the following:

- TV and radio stations
- facilities needed to produce DVDs, CDs, videotapes, and audiotapes used during leisure
- publishing houses that publish books used at least in part during leisure
- theme parks
- firms that produce computers used for leisure and the cost of such, including the operating costs
- costs of production, marketing, and producing personal vehicles used totally or in part for leisure, including recreation vehicles (RVs)
- infrastructure for museums, art galleries, libraries, and facilities for providing continuing education courses
- costs associated with the Olympic and other games, including travel costs
- costs of all professional sports, including that of constructing and maintaining stadiums and arenas, the salary and other costs of the professional players (e.g., travel, equipment, health insurance)
- costs of acquiring and operating cruise ships, ferries and other modes of transportation (e.g., scenic railroads and highways) that facilitate leisure engagements
- expenditures and costs related to acquiring, maintaining, and using summer homes, condominiums, boats/yachts, and airplanes used for leisure
- sporting guns, ammunition, fishing rods, and bait
- cameras used for leisure
- clothes for leisure
- use of hotels, restaurants, and tour guides for leisure
- leisure-related payment of taxes and salaries, work benefit packages, and travel-related costs of the people who manage and run these facilities

High proportions of these types of economic costs rightfully belong in the leisure-related accounts for many industries, firms, and publicly provided facilities. They do, if the goods or services provided are used totally or in part for leisure. Put differently, they do if leisure use prompts the investments and expenditures.

The previous list might seem a bit excessive, but hopefully that view of the leisure services economic sector emphasizes how broad the leisure industry account is when one considers leisure broadly as we do in this section. One can reasonably speculate that when it is considered broadly the leisure services economic sector could well be one of the biggest, if not the biggest economic sector of the U.S. economy. If reasonably sovereign consumers and private industries willingly allocate so much of their resources to support and promote the leisure services sector, the benefits they receive must be reasonably commensurate with the expenditures. If so, the, economic benefits of leisure services are extremely great.

In fairness, it should be mentioned that many expenditures on leisure services also lead to disbenefits, such as recreation-related injuries, damage to resources, and other costs, such as those related to abuse of alcohol, but negative impacts accompany all consumer purchases. The purpose here, however, is to develop an appreciation for the scope and magnitude of the contributions of the leisure services sector to a national economy, not to try to interpret the net economic benefits.

We end this section on the noneconomic and economic benefits of leisure by repeating the two propositions we tendered. When leisure is considered broadly (a) it provides as many total benefits (i.e., adds as much value to a society) as any other social service including educational or medical services, and (b) the leisure industry is one of the largest sectors of the economy of many countries, including the United States. Each leisure professional must ponder these propositions. Whatever the outcome of that reflection, one must agree that the total benefits of leisure are very significant indeed. So we return to the

question raised at the beginning of this chapter: Why do so few people both inside and outside the leisure and recreation profession recognize, understand, and appreciate these benefits to a greater degree? And lastly, what will you, as a leisure professional, do to help "reposition the image" of leisure?

Benefits of Outdoor Recreation

In the following section we explore the benefits of outdoor recreation in particular. Remember that most of the benefits listed in Table 2.2 can be realized in outdoor settings. But the first question that must be addressed is: Are any of those benefits uniquely dependent on outdoor environments or settings?

Natural Resource Dependency of Outdoor Recreation Benefits

At the beginning of the discussion of the benefits of leisure in general we stated it is difficult to separate the benefits of outdoor recreation from other forms of recreation. That is because most of the benefits listed in Table 2.2 can also be realized in other than outdoor environments and through nonrecreational activities. Put differently, few benefits of leisure are uniquely dependent on a particular setting, outdoor or otherwise. Thus, most, if not all, benefits of leisure can be realized from alternative human behaviors. At first this statement might seem counterintuitive, because we have come to believe that most specific benefits of leisure can only be realized in particular settings. However, careful reflection about each of the benefits listed in Table 2.2 reveals that each of those benefits individually can be realized in many different environments or settings. One person might prefer to enjoy nature in Central Park in New York City, another person

Challenge and self-reliance are important benefits for many outdoor recreationists. (Photo courtesy of NC Division of Tourism, Film and Sports Development)

Improved self-confidence and problem-solving skills are common outdoor recreation benefits from mountaineering experiences. (Photo by Aram Attarian)

might prefer the vast Boundary Waters Canoe Area, still another while gardening in their backyard, and yet another while watching a television program related to nature on the Discovery Channel. Enjoyment of nature can also occur during a course on environmental education or from reading a book. So, we must be extremely cautious about believing that a particular benefit we realize when engaging in a particular outdoor recreation activity can only be realized that way. Thus, while each of the benefits listed in Table 2.2 can be realized from outdoor recreation, few if any are uniquely dependent on a particular recreation setting or facility when any particular benefit listed in Table 2.2 is considered singly. But setting dependency does occur when more than one of the listed benefits are desired and sought from a particular setting. This is a critical point to understand about outdoor recreation.

Much research has shown that recreationists prefer specific recreation settings for many reasons, including personal tastes, effects of past experience, social and cultural conditioning, cost, time available, skill level, and information available on alternative options. A particularly important factor that determines and guides these preferences for particular recreation settings is the *recreation experience/benefit gestalt*, which relates to the qualitative dimensions of leisure preferences. The experience/benefit gestalt refers to the fact that many dozens of research studies disclosed that a group (i.e., package) of generally four to seven very specific psychological experiences comprise those experiences most highly valued by participants in a particular recreation activity within a particular setting. In combination, this group of most satisfying/gratifying/beneficial experiences represents the "recreation experience/benefit preference gestalt." The word *gestalt* is used purposefully to denote a synergistic/holistic total experience greater than the sum of its parts, with each part

representing a very specific dimension of that total experience. For example, a person hiking in a remote nature area might seek and value most highly the experience/benefit gestalt formed from realizing the specific psychological experiences of getting physical exercise, enjoying nature, enjoying solitude, and releasing some everyday tensions. Alternatively, another person visiting the Anasazi cliff dwellings in Mesa Verde National Park with a spouse and their young children might value most highly the experience/benefit gestalt created synergistically from the interplay between learning about the Anasazi culture, experiencing family bonding, and getting some physical exercise. So just as the separate instruments of a symphony orchestra combine with sound waves from one instrument affecting the sounds produced by other instruments to produce a gestalt melody, so do the limited number of most highly valued specific psychological experiences, just mentioned for the hiker and visitor to the cliff dwelling, synergistically produce a holistic recreation experience/benefit gestalt.

A very critical point now needs to be made about the natural resource dependency of the benefits of outdoor recreation. Although *each* of the small set of specific recreation experiences that create a recreation experience gestalt can be realized independently from many different types of recreational and nonrecreational behaviors, the gestalt created by synergism among those individual experiences generally depends on a specific type of recreational engagement in a particular setting. Put simply, the gestalts, and not the individual recreation experiences, are recreation-setting dependent. Thus, because a satisfying recreation experience was defined earlier as the third type of benefit of leisure, the recreation experience/benefit gestalts are setting dependent, although each experiential benefit taken separately is not setting dependent.

This issue of the setting dependency of the benefits of outdoor and other types of recreation is important for two reasons. First, parks and recreation policy makers and managers always operate with limited funds and other resources, and they cannot allocate resources to meet all the completing demands for different types of recreation opportunities. Managers must mesh their professional skills in managing recreation settings with appraisals of customer needs and preferences to determine which packages of benefit opportunities to provide in which settings. They must use much discretion in determining which recreation opportunities to provide. They frequently must ask whether demands for some recreation activities and experiences/benefits can be met in different types of settings, especially when supply of certain types of outdoor recreation resources is very limited. Second, many leisure scientists and philosophers and others outside the leisure professions argue that if a particular type of benefit can be

Outdoor recreation benefits, like contemplation and stress management for this angler perhaps, can sometimes be dependent on particular types of natural resources. (Photo courtesy of NC Division of Tourism, Film and Sports Development)

realized in several different settings, then scarce public funds and other resources should not be allocated to managing particular types of recreation settings. This argument, for example, has been made against designating large areas to become part of the Wilderness Preservation System, which exists in part to provide "primitive" types of recreation opportunities. This view is uninformed, because as just described, it is not single benefits but the experience/benefit gestalts (e.g., including those available in Wilderness areas) that are resource dependent.

Despite these important reasons for understanding the presence or absence of resource dependency of the benefits of outdoor recreation, that really is not the most important outdoor recreation policy or managerial issue. The important consideration is one of customer preference. Most people who enjoy a particular recreation activity prefer to engage in that activity in a particular type of recreational setting, just as they prefer specific types of wine, beer, soda pop, cars, homes, music, and most other goods and services. Therefore, resource dependency is frequently not the major issue; it is one of customer preference. In a democratic republic, both voter and consumer sovereignty is what "governs." They do in leisure, so long as (a) resources exist to meet preferences for particular recreation settings, (b) provision of opportunities to exercise these preferences are considered by public consensus to be socially acceptable, and (c) consumers are willing and able to bear what is established (in the way of prices, fees, or taxes) as their fair share of the public or private costs of providing those opportunities.

Results of Research That Document the Benefits of Outdoor Recreation

As mentioned here and in Chapter 1, the economic concept of consumer sovereignty contends that people allocate their scarce time, money, and personal resources to optimize the utility or benefit they believe they will receive from the expenditures of these scarce resources. If so, the large amount of money and time spent on outdoor recreational engagements should logically mean that large amounts of benefits are received when aggregations are made across all people making the expenditures. Many surveys of participation in outdoor recreation document very high rates of participation and substantial evidence of the varied and sizable benefits received.

The 1994–1995 National Survey on Recreation and the Environment documented that 95% of the U.S. population ages 16 and over participated at least once during the 12-month period studied in some type of outdoor recreation activity (Cordell et al., 1999, p. 221). More recently, Cordell and colleagues (2004) reported on a very similar survey conducted in 2000–2001, with results shown for the population of the United States ages 16 and over. While

walking for pleasure in all environments showed the highest rates of participation overall (83%), more definitively outdoor recreation activities also showed very high rates of participation, such as visiting a beach (60.9%), visiting a nature center (57%), viewing wildlife (44.7%), and swimming in lakes and streams (41.8%). Remember that these are percentages of the U.S population ages 16 and over, which represents around 200 million people.

In another national household survey, the U.S. Fish and Wildlife Service (2001) found that 66.1 million people in the United States (ages 16 and over) participated in observing, feeding, or photographing wildlife. The magnitude of personal benefits they received and the other types of benefits they helped to create by their expenditures on bird feeders, bird food, cameras, books, binoculars and viewing scopes, travel, and other facilitating expenditures are unquestionably large.

Another periodic national household survey of outdoor recreation in America is done by Roper Starch Worldwide, Inc. for the Recreation Roundtable. The Recreation Roundtable is a group of influential individuals, including CEOs of recreational equipment manufacturing companies, who work with the American Recreation Coalition to promote political and other interests in outdoor recreation. The report of the latest Roper Starch survey, *Outdoor Recreation in America 2000: Addressing Key Societal Concerns*, interviewed 1,986 Americans. Findings from that survey also documented the great benefits of outdoor recreation, as reflected by the following statements taken directly from the "Study Highlights" section of the report (pp. 3–5):

- Americans continue to ascribe many benefits to participation in recreation. This new research confirms motivations of fun, fitness, and family togetherness, but also shows Americans believe outdoor recreation plays a role in addressing various key social concerns, especially those related to young people. For instance, close to 8 in 10 Americans (79%) believe outdoor recreation can improve education.

- Americans also see outdoor recreation playing a role in reducing childhood obesity—a full three quarters of Americans see it as having a role in helping with this problem.

- According to most Americans, participation in outdoor recreation also can significantly aid parent-child communication, with three quarters crediting it as playing a role.

- Even in the case of tough social problems such as juvenile crime (71%), underage drinking (66%), and illegal drug use (64%), outdoor recreation is viewed by a strong majority as playing positive role.

- When it comes to policy-related issues, it is interesting to examine the views of the Influential Americans, a bellwether segment of the public who are politically active in their community. Influentials are significantly more likely than others to endorse the idea that kids who take part in outdoor recreation are less apt to engage in vandalism and other criminal activities (57% of the Influentials strongly agree versus 47% of the general sample). Moreover, Influentials even more than others believe that outdoor recreation is an ingredient in addressing some of the societal issues asked about.

- Overwhelmingly Americans believe that if people participated more in outdoor physical activities, the health effects would be beneficial (93%). Outdoor recreation is seen almost unanimously as the best way to be physically active (90%).

- Another positive benefit seen in outdoor recreation relates to environmental awareness. Virtually all Americans agree that outdoor recreation is a good way to increase people's appreciation for nature and the environment (95%). Similarly, more than 9 in 10 agree that if people spent more time outdoors, they would better understand the importance of environmental protection.

- The study finds continued growth in Americans' participation in outdoor recreation. These data show that two thirds of the American public (66%) are engaging in some type of outdoor recreation at least several times a month. And more than three quarters of Americans (78%) are participating in outdoor recreation at least once a month, an increase of 11 points [sic; 11%] in the last year alone. What's more, outdoor recreation participation has undeniably increased across all age and income categories. This increased participation is likely to have broad societal benefits, because those who participate in outdoor recreation regularly report higher satisfaction with their lives.

- About 40% of all Americans reported a visit to a federally operated recreation site during the past year, with sites associated with large bodies of water attracting the most visitors. Overwhelmingly, visitors reported satisfaction with their experiences at these sites (95%).

- The outdoor recreation industry once again was credited by the public with a high level of environmental responsibility, scoring higher than any other industry.

To further document the benefits of outdoor recreation, the results of two economic studies will be summarized, and other documentation of the economic benefits of outdoor recreation will be discussed in Chapter 19. The first study to be considered, conducted by the U.S. Fish and Wildlife Service (2001), reported that wildlife recreationists spent a total of $108 billion in 2001 which represented 1.1% of the Gross Domestic Product (GDP) of the United States that year. Of that amount, $28 billion was spent on travel costs, $64.5 billion on equipment, and $15.8 billion on other items. These expenditures do not include the money spent by public fish and game agencies, private firms, communities, wildlife-related conservation organizations, and individuals for facilities and services provided for use by wildlife recreationists. Included also should be the costs of books on wildlife, salaries, information brochures, visitor centers, interpretive talks, guided trips, and excursions.

Another report also documents the sizable contribution of outdoor recreation to the value of domestically produced goods and services, or GDP in the United States. The Draft 1995 RPA Program for the USDA Forest Service states

> Forest Service programs in 1993 are estimated to have generated about $123.8 billion toward the GDP; a little less that 2% of the national total. By the year 2000, Forest Service programs, as outlined in this strategic plan, would contribute $130.7 billion to GDP, of which $97.8 billion (75%) would be generated by recreation, $12.9 billion by wildlife and fish, $10.1 billion by minerals, and $3.5 billion by timber.

These high estimates for recreation and the economic impact analyses made for this draft RPA program statement, scheduled for release in 1995, were contested (mostly for political reasons) and were revised downward. Nevertheless, the magnitude of the benefits remain high, and most of the economic activity associated with Forest Service programs continue to be stimulated through use of the recreation, fish, and wildlife resources managed by that agency (USDA Forest Service RPA staff analysts, personal communication). Remember that these estimates of economic benefits of outdoor recreation are for only one federal agency, the USDA Forest Service. When the outdoor recreation-related benefits of all other public agencies that provide outdoor recreation opportunities at all levels of government, plus all other organizations that do so are considered, the economic effects are far greater still.

In summary, wildlife and other outdoor recreation and related amenity resources make large contributions to GDP; the pursuit of outdoor recreation is a major economic engine.

The Role of Leisure in Society

So far we have made the case that leisure plays many important roles in the effective functioning of society by reviewing results of scientific investigations that document how pervasive the many and large benefits of leisure are. We showed that those benefits contribute to all realms of human endeavor and enhance all dimensions of social and economic welfare of a nation, including the extremely important dimension of people's perceived quality of, and satisfaction with, their lives. Specifically, the results of research we summarized demonstrate that opportunities for leisure pursuits contribute positively to

- mental and physical health, a growing concern in all countries as the cost of health care continues to increase rapidly

- important learning experiences, ranging from learning about the history, traditions, and culture of a locality, region, or nation to increased understanding and appreciation of natural ecosystems and human dependency of them

- promotion and maintenance of systems of social support that range from families and other small social groups to improved social cohesion and networking in local communities

- enhanced self-concept/image/esteem of individuals along many dimensions, such as self-confidence and competence

- value clarification of individuals and enhanced perceptions of their sense of fit in the grand scheme of things

- nurturing and maintaining desired ethnic identities

- enhanced performance at work and in school

- economic growth and stability

It is difficult to think of any other social service that impacts a society so positively and in as many ways as leisure does.

Despite these important specific roles, there is another essential, more overriding, synergistic, and philosophical role of leisure in society. This philosophy is quite difficult to describe despite the fact that Aristotle extolled it over 2,000 years ago and many books have been written about it since (cf. Bammel & Burrus-Bammel, 1996; Kelly & Godbey, 1992). People who write about the desirability of a socially healthy philosophy of leisure in a society can sometimes come across as unrealistic utopians regarding what leisure can and *should* be in a society. They sometimes leave the impression they know what is best and want to impose their views and desires on others. We reject that approach, but certainly recognize and appreciate

the importance to a society of having and reflecting a healthy/appropriate philosophy of leisure. So, with considerable trepidation, we attempt to describe this extremely complex concept of a "proper" social philosophy of leisure as being simply one of a civil and balanced perspective reflected by how people live their lives, as appraised by people not a part of that society (i.e., live in another society). That civility and balance is reflected in the attitudes, values, and behaviors of the people who comprise a society and by the policies, pursuits, and behaviors of its public and private sectors.

To expand on what we mean by a civil and balanced society, we offer the following characteristics of a society that we do *not* believe is adequately civil and balanced:

- people oriented primarily toward competitive striving for more money, material possessions, and power

- an obvious overly fast pace of life

- too little apparent concern about aesthetics and human sensitivities in the design of buildings, transportation facilities, and at a broader scale, in its cities

- does not offer adequate protection of amenities afforded by the countryside or urban areas

- governments do not have a ministry, department, or division with names such as cultural affairs

- does not overtly and explicitly recognize and promote the values of leisure by policies, such as providing partial compensation of the costs to people of their annual vacation/holiday (as many countries do)

- when people retire, too many of them are bored, remain driven to stay busy, or in other ways do not know how to enjoy their leisure during their later years

While admittedly speculative, these characteristics combine synergistically to portray the philosophy of leisure of some societies. Alternative philosophies of leisure are readily apparent to someone who has visited different societies, which have more reflective—and we believe more appropriate—philosophies of leisure. Such societies leave the impression that their people have a very balanced perspective of what life is about. Each reader must decide in which type of society he or she wishes to live and nurture professionally.

Summary

At the beginning of this chapter, we emphasized three reasons why knowledge about the benefits of leisure is of critical importance to people who have professional interests in outdoor recreation. First, leisure professionals must have a good understanding of the benefits that accrue from leisure services in general and from outdoor recreation in particular. Second, we cannot change (i.e., reposition) inaccurate perceptions about the purposes, nature, and scope of leisure until we, as leisure professionals ourselves, understand more fully, and then articulate more clearly and convincingly, the tremendous benefits of leisure. Third, a new approach to parks and recreation policy development and management called the beneficial outcomes approach to leisure (BOAL) is rapidly gaining favor. This new approach (described in Chapter 13) requires clear definition and specification of the types of benefits that will be pursued overtly by parks and recreation policy makers and managers. We then introduced the three types of benefits of leisure: (a) a change in a condition or state viewed as more desirable than a previous one; (b) maintenance of a desired condition and thereby prevention of an unwanted condition from occurring, prevention of an undesired condition from becoming worse, or reduction of the unwanted impacts of an existing undesired condition; and (c) the realization of a satisfying recreation experience. We then presented examples of the benefits of leisure and outdoor recreation that are supported by scientific research. Finally, we discussed the essential role of leisure in a society.

Hopefully, this chapter has been thought provoking and enlightening about the nature, scope, and magnitude of the benefits of leisure in general, and outdoor recreation in particular. We hope you now have a better understanding of the vital roles of leisure in a society. Obviously, we are convinced that leisure is a crucial social service, and we are dedicated to advancing leisure and outdoor recreation professionally. We hope you are, or will be, too.

Literature Cited

Allen, L. (1991) Benefits of leisure services to community satisfaction. In. B. L. Driver, P. Brown, and G. Peterson (Eds.), *Benefits of leisure* (pp. 331–350). State College, PA: Venture Publishing, Inc.

Bammel, G. and Burrus-Bammel, L. (1996). *Leisure and human behavior* (3rd ed.). Madison, IA: Brown & Benchmark.

Campbell, A. (1981). *The sense of well-being in America: Recent patterns and trends*. New York, NY: McGraw-Hill.

Canadian Parks/Recreation Association. (1997). *The benefits catalogue*. Gloucester, Ontario, Canada: Author.

Cordell, H. K., Betz, C. J., Bowker, J. M., English, D. B. K., Mou, S. H., Bergstrom, J. C., et al. (1999). *Outdoor recreation in American life: A national assessment of demand and supply trends*. Champaign, IL: Sagamore.

Cordell, H. K., Betz, C., Green, G., and Mou, S. (2004) *Outdoor recreation for 21st century America*. State College, PA: Venture Publishing, Inc.

Crompton, J. (1993). Repositioning recreation and park services: An overview. *Trends, 30*(4) 2–5.

Crompton, J. and Witt, P. (1998, October). Repositioning: The key to building community support. *Parks and Recreation*, 80–90.

Driver, B. L. (1990). The North American experience in measuring the benefits of leisure. In E. Hamilton-Smith (Comp.), *Proceedings: National workshop on the measurement of recreation benefits*. Bandoora, Victoria, Australia: Phillips Institute of Technology.

Driver, B. L. (1999a). Recognizing and celebrating progress in leisure studies. In E. Jackson and T. Burton (Eds.), *Leisure studies: Prospects for the twenty-first century* (pp. 523–544). State College, PA: Venture Publishing, Inc.

Driver, B. L. (1999b). Management of public outdoor recreation and related public amenity resources for the benefits they provide. In H. K. Cordell (Ed.), *A renewable assessment for the Resources Planning Act: Outdoor recreation and wilderness demand and supply trends in the United States* (pp. 2–5, 27–29). Champaign, IL: Sagamore.

Driver, B. L. (2003). Leisure experiences. In J. Jenkins and J. Pigrim (Eds.), *Encyclopedia of leisure and outdoor recreation*. London: Routledge Press.

Driver, B. L., Brown, P., and Peterson, G. (Eds.). (1991). *Benefits of leisure*. State College, PA: Venture Publishing, Inc.

Driver, B. L. and Bruns, D. (1999). Concepts and uses of the benefits approach to leisure. In E. Jackson and T. Burton (Eds.), *Leisure studies: Prospects for the twenty-first century* (pp. 349–368). State College, PA: Venture Publishing, Inc.

Driver, B., Tinsley, H., and Manfredo, M. (1991). The paragraphs about leisure and recreation experience preference scales: Results from two inventories designed to assess the breadth of the perceived psychological benefits of leisure. In. B. L. Driver, P. Brown, and G. Peterson (Eds.), *Benefits of leisure* (pp. 263–286). State College, PA: Venture Publishing, Inc.

Godbey, G., Graefe, A., and James, S. (1992). *The benefits of local recreation and park services: A nationwide study of the perceptions of the American public*. University Park, PA: Pennsylvania State University, School of Hotel, Restaurant and Recreation Management.

Harper, J., Neider, D., Godbey, G., and Lamont, D. (1997). *The use and benefits of local government parks and recreation services: A Canadian perspective*. Winnipeg, Manitoba, Canada: Health, Leisure, and Human Dimensions Research Institute, University of Manitoba.

Hurtes, K., Allen, L., Stevens, B., and Lee, C. (2000). Benefits-based programming: Making an impact on youth. *Journal of Parks and Recreation Administration, 18*(1), 34–49.

Jordan, C. (1991). Parks and recreation: More than fun and games. In. B. L. Driver, P. Brown, and G. Peterson (Eds.), *Benefits of leisure* (pp. 365–368) State College, PA: Venture Publishing, Inc.

Kelly, J. and Godbey, G. (1992). *Sociology of leisure.* State College, PA: Venture Publishing, Inc.

Manfredo, M., Driver, B., and Tarrant, M. (1996). Measuring leisure motivation: A meta-analysis of the recreation experience preference scales. *Journal of Leisure Research, 28*(3), 188–213.

Marans, R. and Mohai, P. (1991). Leisure resources, recreation activity, and the quality of life. In B. L. Driver, P. Brown, and G. Peterson (Eds.), *Benefits of leisure* (pp. 351–363). State College, PA: Venture Publishing, Inc.

O'Sullivan, E. (1999). *Setting a course for change: The benefits movement.* Ashburn, VA. National Recreation and Parks Association.

Outdoor Recreation Resources Review Commission. (1962). *Outdoor recreation for America.* Washington, DC: U.S. Government Printing Office.

Sefton, J. and Mummery, W. (1995). *Benefits of recreation research update.* State College, PA: Venture Publishing, Inc.

Stynes, D. (1993). *Leisure: The new center of the economy.* In Issue Papers prepared and distributed by the Academy of Leisure Sciences.

The Tourism Works for America Council (1996). *Tourism Works for America: 1996 Report.* Washington, DC: Author.

Roper Starch Worldwide, Inc. (2000) *Outdoor recreation in America 2000: Addressing key societal concerns.* Prepared for the Recreation Round Table. Washington, DC: Author.

USDA Forest Service. (1995). *Draft 1995 Resources Planning Act program for the USDA Forest Service.* Washington, DC: Author.

U.S. Fish and Wildlife Service (2001). *2001 national survey of fishing, hunting, and wildlife-related recreation.* Washington, DC: U.S. Department of the Interior.

U.S. Travel Data Center. (1994). *Impact of travel on state economies 1994.* Washington, DC: Travel Industry Association of America.

Witt, P. A. and Crompton, J. (1996). *Recreation programs that work for at-risk youth: The challenge of shaping the future.* State College, PA: Venture Publishing, Inc.

Chapter 3
Historical Context

Anybody who visits the popular outing centers near the large American cities on public holidays cannot fail to be impressed by the immense number of people in search of forest recreation. Almost every possible open spot along the highways will be filled with picnickers and campers cooking their meals, pitching tents, playing games, swinging from trees, and noisily giving vent to pent-up child-like impulses which are rigidly curbed under city regimentation. (Marshall, 1933)

Learning Objectives

1. Know why it is important for outdoor recreation managers to understand their historical context.
2. Explain the characteristics of the major periods of outdoor recreation history.
3. Give examples of key events from each historical period.
4. Understand the historical trends in outdoor recreation participation.

Outdoor Recreation History as Our Context

Why is it important to study the history of outdoor recreation and outdoor recreation resources? The most important reason is that past conditions and events always affect our circumstances and options in the present. One historian has called this "the trajectory set by prior social conditions" (Cranz, 1982, p. x) Social, economic, political, public opinion, and many other forces throughout history have interacted to affect the direction of this trajectory of conditions that influence us today (see Figure 3.1). Some events have major effects, like the terrorist attacks on the United States in 2001, and some have more limited influences, like where Congress decides to set the boundaries of a particular national park. Some historical influences generate macrolevel effects over long periods, like the wilderness preservation movement, and some have microlevel effects over much shorter time frames, like everyday decisions made by a local parks and recreation director. But all these events and forces influence our options as we make decisions in the present. When we think about historical events and forces as affecting the trajectory of current conditions, it is easier to visualize why it is important to understand our outdoor recreation history.

Outdoor recreation professionals who understand and consider the relevant historical trajectories can be more effective, because they can better anticipate what will likely happen and why. For example, all of the public natural areas available for outdoor recreation today were set aside for particular purposes. Although these original purposes might have evolved over time, understanding them and the forces that led up to them can help us to plan and to manage better. In the case of Great Smoky Mountains National Park in North Carolina and Tennessee, for instance, the land for the park was purchased from private landowners beginning in the 1920s rather than set aside from existing federal land, as was the case with most previous national parks in the United States. The land for the Great Smokies was actually purchased by the two states and then donated to the National Park Service. Because a large amount of the money to buy the land was donated by private individuals, including over $1,300 in

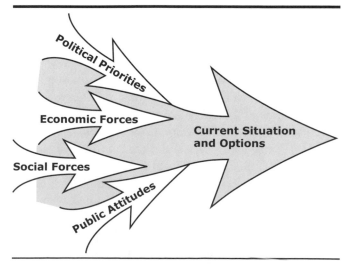

Figure 3.1 How the trajectory of past conditions and events affects the situation and options for outdoor recreation managers

small change from school children (Campbell, 1960, p. 38), the state legislatures in North Carolina and Tennessee added deed restrictions before donating the land, assuring that entrance would always be free. Because of the social, political, economic, and public opinion conditions in the 1920s and 1930s, managers of the Great Smokies today cannot charge an entrance fee like those that generate considerable income for many other large national parks. As a result they have been forced to manage their budgets differently and be more creative in generating income and public support. These actions and their results will, in turn, make future conditions in this park different from those in other major parks.

For readers who are card players, it may be helpful to think about history as being like the cards dealt early in a long game. There are many ways to play those early cards, and how it is done has a big effect on the rest of the game. But, the cards dealt should guide the player's strategy, and knowing what cards are out and which ones are left in the deck can be a big advantage to a skillful player. Similarly, understanding and paying attention to the history of their agencies, resources, and society in general can make a thoughtful outdoor recreation professional even more effective today.

Periods of Outdoor Recreation History

The history of outdoor recreation resources in the United States can be best understood in terms of six broad and overlapping eras. These periods weave together two important dimensions of the history of outdoor recreation and draw on two important sources with which outdoor recreation professionals should be familiar. The first is the history of federal land ownership and policy. The history of the public lands administered by the federal government is a key consideration for outdoor recreation resource management, because much of this land is natural, relatively undeveloped, and open to the public, making it particularly appealing for many forms of outdoor recreation. In terms of federal land history, we draw heavily on the outstanding work of Marion Clawson (1983). He proposed that since the early 1800s there have been six overlapping eras or phases in terms of federal land ownership and management in the United States: acquisition, disposal, reservation, custodial management, intensive management, and consultation and confrontation. The main activities of all of these six periods still continue in the United States today in one form or another.

The second important dimension of the history of outdoor recreation is the history of parks and recreation itself. In this regard we have drawn on many sources. A particularly important one, however, is the work of Galen Cranz (1982) who investigated the history of the role of city parks in America. Such areas represent a major source of opportunities for outdoor recreation even though they are generally more developed and less natural than federal lands. The forces and responses he presents apply well beyond urban environments and are ones that all outdoor recreation professionals should consider. In general, Cranz concluded park planners and policy makers responded in different ways based on their perceptions of "what cities have been, can be, and ought to be" and that these perceptions have become increasingly positive and optimistic (pp. 232, 242). He identified four sets of ideas about what urban parks were and what they could accomplish, and notes that these are commonly "layered" together in present parks:

1. The Pleasure Ground: 1850–1900
2. The Reform Park: 1900–1930
3. The Recreation Facility: 1930–1965
4. The Open-Space System: 1965 and After

Drawing on these and other sources, we believe the history of outdoor recreation resources in the United States can be best understood in terms of the following six broad and overlapping periods:

1. **Frontier:** From the first permanent European settlements in the 1500s and 1600s to the "closing of the frontier" in 1890.
2. **Acquisition:** From the signing of the U.S. Constitution in 1782 to the purchase of Alaska in 1867.
3. **Transfer and Disposal:** From the first federal disposal of public domain land in 1802 to the Taylor Grazing Act in 1934.
4. **Reservation:** From the creation of Yellowstone National Park in 1872 to the Taylor Grazing Act in 1934.
5. **Custodial Management:** Mainly from the Transfer Act of 1905 to the completion of the Outdoor Recreation Resources Review Commission (ORRRC) report in 1962.
6. **Confrontation and Partnership:** Mainly from the completion of the ORRRC report in 1962 and continuing to the present.

With obvious variations in dates and durations, these same broad periods apply to many other nations as well. The characteristics of these periods are covered in more detail next, followed by an annotated time line of the most important events in the history of outdoor recreation and outdoor recreation resources in the United States.

Frontier Period

A frontier is the region between settled and unsettled lands. From the perspective of the European colonists of North America, the frontier era began with the first permanent settlements founded in St. Augustine, Florida in 1565; Jamestown, Virginia in 1607; Santa Fe, New Mexico in 1610; and the Pilgrims at Plymouth in 1620. These first settlements by Europeans came quite late compared to those of most other nations. Prior to this time, the native peoples of North America depended completely on the natural world around them, and in many cases had elaborate spiritual systems based on nature. The colonists brought with them new attitudes toward the natural environment, which in general were oriented toward conquering nature and turning wilderness into profitable lands.

In general, the backgrounds of the early European colonists of North America included a stark distinction between ruling classes and working classes that influenced their recreation as well. The ruling classes were characterized by privilege, often enjoying considerable free time and access to manicured outdoor gardens, spectator sports, and hunting as sport. The working classes had far less free time, although they did enjoy festivals, drinking, and dances. The backgrounds of both of these classes were rooted in ancient Greek and Roman traditions. Although these ancient cultures valued outdoor facilities for games, athletics, spectacles, and circuses, and their upper classes enjoyed country villas and estates that often included rich gardens and hunting grounds, there was little outdoor recreation as we know it today. Wild areas were usually regarded with dread, because of real and imagined dangers. Many of the former Roman estates became monasteries or hunting grounds reserved for Kings and nobility during the Middle or Dark Ages (AD 476–1492). This is why hunting is still called the sport of kings in some circles. The Renaissance (AD 1400–1600) saw a rebirth of Greek and Roman ideals among the elite in Europe, but there was still little outdoor recreation as we know it today. The popular recreation of the time included drinking, pubs, gambling, and blood sports. (See Cross, 1990 for a thorough history of leisure since 1600.)

Although courage, individualism, resourcefulness, and love of freedom were admirable aspects of the frontier experience in North America, it was not a time of responsible attitudes toward natural resources. In terms of natural resources, the frontier era was generally a time of waste, exploitation, conquering nature, and a pervasive attitude that natural resources were unlimited. For example a group of Kentucky hunters bragged that they killed 7,941 squirrels in 1797, and in one ring hunt of a 40-square-mile frontier area, hunters killed 60 bears, 100 turkeys, 25 deer, and an even larger number of smaller animals and game birds (Cross, 1990, p. 46). Although passenger pigeons had been so plentiful that they darkened the sky during their annual migrations, they became extinct because of overhunting. The last wild one was killed in 1890 and the last one in captivity died in 1914. Market hunting of commercially valuable wildlife by professional hunters contributed to the killing of an almost unbelievable amount of wildlife during this period. For example, the estimated 30 to 75 million bison in North America were nearly hunted to extinction for food, profit, and sport. Frontier people typically felt that when land, timber, wildlife, or other resources were exhausted, there was always more available farther west.

Some people of the period did realize, of course, that natural resources were not unlimited, and several actions attempted to counter the waste and excess of the times. These included the establishment of Boston Commons (1640); the Great Pond Act, which reserved bodies of water 10 acres and larger for public fishing, hunting, and navigation (1640); and the first game protection laws and forest preserves (19th century). The frontier period in the United States ended with the census of 1890, which declared that there was no frontier remaining in the country. This official "closing of the frontier" marked an important change in the way people looked at resources.

Acquisition Period

The acquisition period, as the name suggests, was the era when the lands that would eventually make up the United States as we know it today were acquired and consolidated. This period stretched from the signing of the U.S. Constitution in 1782 to the purchase of Alaska in 1867. The sources of these lands included wars with England (for the original 13 colonies), Native American peoples, Mexico, and others; as well as land purchases, treaties, and cessions (e.g., Louisiana Purchase from France, Florida from Spain, cession from Mexico for southwestern territories, purchase of Alaska from Russia in 1867). By 1867, these acquisitions totaled 80% of the current land mass of the United States, with most of the rest being the original 13 colonies. The federal public lands originally acquired through war, purchase, treaty, and cession that have never left federal ownership are called *public domain*. Figure 3.2 (p. 44) and Table 3.1 (p. 45) present the sources of lands used to create

---

Key Figures of the Acquisition Period

Thomas Jefferson
Led acquisition of the Louisiana Purchase

Meriwether Lewis and William Clark
Explorers of western North America

William Seward
Secretary of State who led the purchase of Alaska, referred to as "Seward's Folly"

ACQUISITIONS

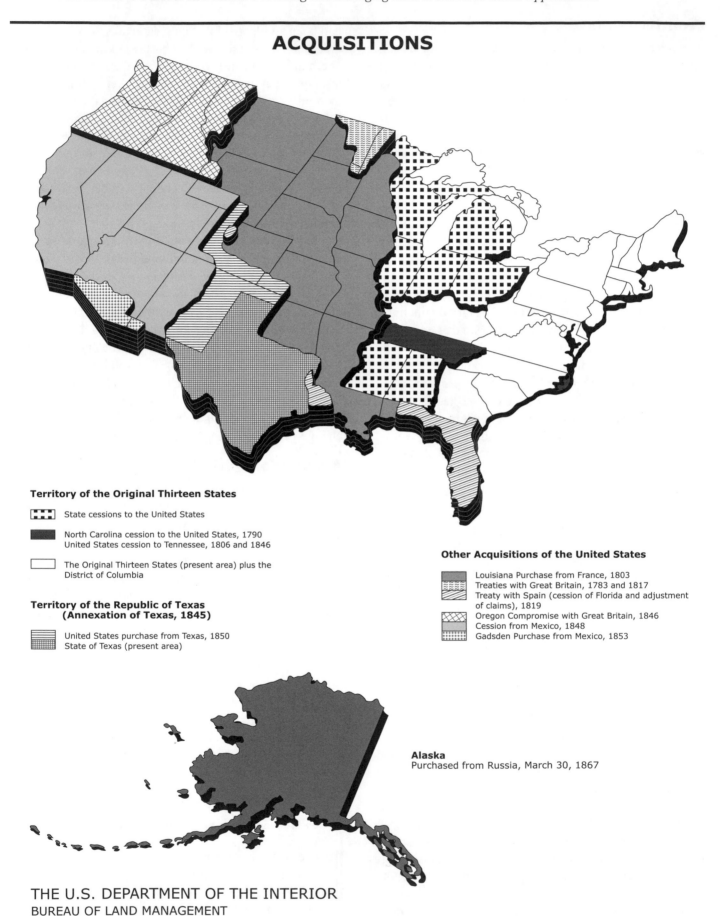

Territory of the Original Thirteen States

State cessions to the United States

North Carolina cession to the United States, 1790
United States cession to Tennessee, 1806 and 1846

The Original Thirteen States (present area) plus the
District of Columbia

**Territory of the Republic of Texas
(Annexation of Texas, 1845)**

United States purchase from Texas, 1850
State of Texas (present area)

Other Acquisitions of the United States

Louisiana Purchase from France, 1803
Treaties with Great Britain, 1783 and 1817
Treaty with Spain (cession of Florida and adjustment
of claims), 1819
Oregon Compromise with Great Britain, 1846
Cession from Mexico, 1848
Gadsden Purchase from Mexico, 1853

Alaska
Purchased from Russia, March 30, 1867

THE U.S. DEPARTMENT OF THE INTERIOR
BUREAU OF LAND MANAGEMENT

Figure 3.2   Acquisitions of the U.S. public domain, 1781 to 1867. Source: Bureau of Land Management (1999, p. 4)

the United States. The acquisition period is most often though of in terms of large remote federal lands, but there are many related trends in urban areas throughout the last half of the 19th century. According to Cranz (1982), this was the "pleasure ground era" for city parks when large tracts of land began to be protected and developed for urban parks. The best example is the $5 million purchase of hundreds of acres beginning in 1853 for the creation of Central Park in New York City. Central Park now makes up 6% of the total land area of Manhattan. In general, urban park planners of the day felt these parks could have a refining effect on people and designed them to be antidotes to the evils of urban life. They saw them as pieces of the country created for those in the city. Cranz sees this movement as an outgrowth of the romantic period, which among other things romanticized nature. This philosophy was influenced by American transcendentalists like Thoreau and Emerson, for whom "nature—attunement with it, contemplation of it, immersion in it—was thought to train the spirit" (p. 7). The urban parks of the time were, therefore, often designed for unstructured, passive activities, and commercial enterprises were resisted. According to renowned designer Frederick Law Olmsted, such parks should create conditions opposite from those found in normal urban life. By the end of the 19th century unstructured recreation activities such as racing, ice skating, bicycle riding, horse riding, walking, and carriage driving were very popular in these urban parks.

Transfer and Disposal Period

Even as lands were being aggressively acquired to form the United States, large parts of the public domain were being transferred from federal administration and "disposed" (i.e., sold, traded, granted) for purposes related to various federal policies, particularly promoting economic growth and settlement. This period of active land transfer and disposal stretched mainly from the first major federal land grant in 1802 until the Taylor Grazing Act in 1934. The first federal grant of public domain land to a state was to Ohio in 1802. Public domain land was transferred, often rapidly and in large areas, until 1934, when President Roosevelt ended most transfers of public domain land with the Taylor Grazing Act, which ended the grazing homesteading program in the lower 48 states. This act created "grazing districts" and various grazing controls on about half the remaining unappropriated and unreserved public domain. During the transfer and disposal period, land was granted to create new states beyond the original 13 colonies and to build railroads, roads, and canals. It was also granted or sold to homesteaders and veterans of military service and sold to private enterprises for timber and mineral production. Even many of today's "land grant" universities are located on lands the federal government gave to states to promote higher education during this period. Table 3.2 presents the scope of various categories of public domain land disposals.

Table 3.1   Origin of current federal lands and waters in the United States (in millions of acres)

Total Land and Water Area of the United States   2,316

Never Public Domain			Public Domain			
Original States	305	(13.2%)	State Cessions	(1781–1802)	237	(10.2%)
Texas	170	(7.3%)	Louisiana Purchase	(1803)	530	(22.9%)
Total	**475**	**(20.5%)**	Red River Basin	(1782–1817)	30	(1.3%)
			Cession from Spain	(1819)	46	(2.0%)
			Oregon Compromise	(1846)	183	(7.9%)
			Mexican Cession	(1848)	339	(14.6%)
			Purchase from Texas	(1850)	79	(3.4%)
			Gadsden Purchase	(1853)	19	(0.8%)
			Alaska Purchase	(1867)	378	(16.3%)
			Total Public Domain		**1,841**	**(79.5%)**

Data from Bureau of Land Management (1999, p. 3) and Clawson (1983, p. 26)

Table 3.2   Disposal of federal public lands, 1781 to 1998 (in millions of acres)

Disposal to states (for schools and other institutions, swamp reclamation, railroads, roads, canals)	328	(28.7%)
Granted or sold to homesteaders	288	(25.2%)
Granted to railroad corporations	94	(8.2%)
Granted to veterans for military service	61	(5.3%)
Sold (under timber and stone, timber culture, and desert land laws)	36	(3.1%)
Confirmed as private land claims	34	(3.0%)
Other (unclassified sales and mineral entries, scrip locations, townsites)	303	(26.5%)
Total Federal Land Disposed	**1,144**	**(100%)**

Source: Bureau of Land Management (1999, p. 5)

Reservation Period

Toward the end of the frontier period and in the midst of the transfer and disposal period, it became obvious to many federal policy makers that some public domain had unique and special values and should be set aside rather than disposed of. This period saw special lands reserved for a variety of purposes, including parks, forest and wildlife reserves, and national monuments. The period began with the creation of Yellowstone National Park in 1872. This was the first national park in the United States and arguably the first national park in the world. Although examples of reservations of public domain for various purposes occurred later (e.g., the Wilderness Preservation Act of 1964, the Alaska National Interest Lands Act of 1980) and still occur today, the reservation period as an important policy direction also ended with the Taylor Grazing Act of 1934.

This period saw many remarkable examples of reserving special parts of the public domain. In addition to setting aside Yellowstone, nearly two dozen other national parks had been created from existing federal lands by 1934, including Sequoia (1890), Yosemite (1890), Mount Rainier (1899), Crater Lake (1902), Mesa Verde (1906), Glacier (1910), Rocky Mountain (1915), and Grand Teton (1929). The Forest Reserve Act of 1891 used public domain to create the first permanent system of federal land reservations in the United States. These reserves contained prime timber and recreation opportunities—the beginning of what would later became the National Forest System, now managed by the USDA Forest Service. It is important to realize, however, that neither the creation of the early

national parks nor the first forest reserves reversed the policy of transfer and disposal of the public domain, which was going on at the same time. In fact, the creation of Yellowstone National Park was an isolated incident at the time and the Forest Reserve Act was never actually debated by Congress. It was a last minute provision to an appropriations bill passed just before a Congressional recess (see Clawson, 1983).

These pioneering land reservations for national parks and forest reserves are the early fruits of what is commonly known as the *conservation movement*. The conservation movement is usually described as having three "waves." The first wave corresponds to the presidency of Theodore Roosevelt (1901–1909), who used the Antiquities Act of 1906 and other authorities to set aside large numbers of national monuments and other natural areas (Zinser, 1995, p. 31). Among these efforts was his work with Gifford Pinchot to set aside over 100 million acres of public domain as forest reserves, later to become national forests. (We discuss the second and third waves in the following sections.)

Custodial Management Period

From the earliest days of the reservation period, too little money, personnel, expertise, and political will were available to effectively manage the federal lands set aside as national parks, forest reserves, and other reserved places. Lands were often reserved with little or no provision for caring for them. The first park managers in Yellowstone National Park were soldiers, because the National Park Service did not exist until 44 years after Yellowstone's creation in 1872. Problems with poaching, theft of artifacts, and even illegal homesteading became so great that Congress resorted to sending in the U.S. Cavalry in 1886 to protect the park. Not until the Transfer Act of 1905 gave the Bureau of Forestry (later to be renamed the Forest Service) control of the Forest Reserves (soon to become the National Forests) did a period of systematic management begin on any of the reserved lands.

This period is referred to as custodial management, because roads, cars, recreation equipment, and science related to resource and recreation management were primitive by today's standards. The levels of outdoor recreation use and even the popularity of extended outdoor vacations were also quite low during this period.

The custodial management period was characterized by the creation of the government agencies charged with land and natural resource management. In many cases, these agencies also provided outdoor recreation opportunities. In addition to the Forest Service assuming responsibility for the Forest Reserves, many other federal resource management agencies and efforts were created or formalized during this period. Examples include the Bureau of Reclamation (1902), the Bureau of Biological

---

Key Figures of the Reservation Period

Frederick Law Olmsted
Earliest landscape architect and influential park designer

John Muir
Founder of the Sierra Club (1892)

John James Audubon
Naturalist

George Perkins Marsh
Naturalist and author of *Man and Nature: Or Physical Geography as Modified by Human Action* (1864)

George Catlin, Thomas Cole, and Albert Bierstadt
Artists

Ralph Waldo Emerson, James Fennimore Cooper, and Henry David Thoreau
Authors

Theodore Roosevelt
U.S. President from 1901 to 1909 and pioneering conservationist

Gifford Pinchot
First Chief of the U.S. Forest Service

Stephen Mather
First Director of the U.S. National Park Service

Survey (1905; predecessor of the U.S. Fish and Wildlife Service), the National Park Service (1916), the Bureau of Land Management (through combination of the General Lands Office and the U.S. Grazing Service in 1946), and many state park and forest agencies. Extensive federal public works programs were also established during the depression in the 1930s (e.g., Civilian Conservation Corps, Works Progress Administration). These programs created jobs and accomplished huge amounts of conservation-related work on public lands. This period also saw continued growth of the park, forest, and wildlife refuge systems these agencies manage. The "New Deal" years (1933–1939) of Franklin D. Roosevelt's presidency during the custodial management period are often referred to as the second wave of the conservation movement and even the "golden age" of conservation by some (Zinser, 1995, p. 32).

The situation in urban parks began to change during this time as well. Cranz (1982) called the period from 1900 through 1930 the "reform park era" for urban parks. The large city parks created as natural "pleasure grounds" began to be used more as a location for organized recreation activities designed to "reform" the masses. The pleasure grounds landscape architects "gave way to reform park organizers, play leaders, play directors, and efficiency-minded experts in recreation" (Cranz, 1982, p. 61).

> Generally, for its advocates, the reform park was a moral defense against the potential for chaos that they perceived in this new abundance of free time, just as the pleasure ground had been as antidote to the old lack of free space. (Cranz, 1982, p. 62)

The reform efforts were directed especially toward reforming activities for children and closely tied to the playground movement. Urban parks provided an organized scheme for recreation—not just a nature-oriented setting in opposition to urban life. Athletics, swimming and bathing, dancing, arts and crafts, gardens, and playgrounds became more common in urban parks during this period. In many ways, natural beauty gave way to utility in this era. The quiet and serene pleasure ground often became a noisy organized reform park both visually and in terms of activity. From 1930 through the mid-1960s, urban parks entered a period that Cranz referred to as the

---

Key Figures of the Custodial Management Period

Gifford Pinchot
First Chief of the U.S. Forest Service

Stephen Mather
First Director of the U.S. National Park Service

F. D. Roosevelt
Initiator of the Civilian Conservation Corps and other public works efforts during the Great Depression.

"recreation facility era" when city parks lost much of their idealistic fervor and began to be seen (and planned and run) as expected public services. Stadiums, athletic fields, playgrounds, pools, beaches and parking became more prominent as did the importance of ease of maintenance. Urban park design became repetitive and stagnant during this time.

The management of federal land gradually became less custodial and more intensive as this period matured. A turning point came in the 1950 federal fiscal year, the "first year in modern times that the federal lands as a whole produced greater gross revenues than their total expenditures, including investment expenditures" (Clawson, 1983, p. 37). Pressures to manage the federal lands for timber, minerals, grazing, wildlife, recreation, and tourism gradually increased throughout the custodial management period and the number of people visiting federal lands for recreation increased rapidly as well, particularly beginning in the 1950s.

Confrontation and Partnership Period

The year 1962 saw perhaps the single most important event in the history of outdoor recreation in the United States: the completion of the Outdoor Recreation Resources Review Commission (ORRRC) report. ORRRC was created by an act of Congress in 1958. It was chaired by Laurance Rockefeller and charged with studying the demand for outdoor recreation and the supply of outdoor recreation resources needed to meet that demand through the end of the 20th century. ORRRC began its work in 1958 and made its recommendations to Congress in 1962 in the form of a 27-volume report that led to some of the most significant outdoor recreation and environmental legislation ever enacted in the United States. That legislation and other forces of the period from 1962 through the present have led to unprecedented partnerships for outdoor recreation, as well as levels of conflict and confrontation not seen before. ORRRC was the first significant acknowledgment that providing opportunities for outdoor recreation was a legitimate responsibility of the federal government, and it served to greatly heighten awareness and concern about outdoor recreation. It ushered in so many major initiatives in the 1960s that some consider that to be outdoor recreation's greatest decade (Jensen, 1995). What is typically called the third wave of the conservation movement corresponds with the first decade or so of this period. It is associated particularly with the flood of new environmental legislation proposed and enacted in the 1960s and 1970s (Zinser, 1995, p. 34).

The confrontation and partnership period of outdoor recreation history differs from prior eras in important ways. As noted earlier, the six major periods overlap, and activities characteristic of most past periods still continue to some extent. For example, land has been acquired to protect or expand national park units, like the Appalachian National Scenic Trail (acquisition), the Alaska National Interest Lands Act of 1980 formally granted large areas of public domain to native peoples (transfer and disposal), and numerous large Wilderness areas have been designated on existing federal lands (reservation). However, now major new forces affect outdoor recreation. Clawson (1983, pp. 40–56) identified three of these major new forces.

A Flood of New Laws

The 1960s and 1970s were decades of social unrest, an increasing role for the federal government in attempting to solve social issues, an increasing political activism, and a younger population. These factors and more helped lead to the passage of major new federal lands legislation that had major implications for outdoor recreation and its management. During the 1960s and 1970s these included the Multiple Use–Sustained Yield Act, National Wilderness Preservation Act, Classification and Multiple Use Act, National Trails System Act, National Wild and Scenic Rivers Act, National Environmental Policy Act (NEPA), TransAlaska Pipeline Act, Endangered Species Act, Forest and Rangeland Renewable Resource Planning Act (RPA), National Forest Management Act (NFMA), and Federal Land Policy and Management Act (FLPMA, pronounced "FLIP-ma").

Increased Public Participation

Public involvement in public land management and allocation decisions increased greatly after the passage of the National Environmental Policy Act (NEPA) in 1969. That act and other legislation mandated public participation. In addition, the general public was, and continues to become, better educated, more widely traveled and experienced, and more vocal than ever before.

Increased Confrontation

Lawsuits affecting public lands are far more common since the late 1960s. This is due, in part, to the more specific requirements of the new legislation related to federal lands (e.g., Environmental Impact Statement requirements under NEPA). Lack of compliance with these more stringent regulations can now be more easily challenged by individuals and special interest groups. Such suits can be expensive, time-consuming, and have far-reaching effects.

During the first part of this period (through 1980), federal funding for outdoor recreation and natural resource management generally increased. This and rapidly increasing outdoor recreation use made the 1960s and 1970s important growth years for outdoor recreation. The single most significant funding mechanism was the federal Land and Water Conservation Fund (LWCF). Established in 1965, the LWCF provided billions of dollars in federal and state leveraged money for outdoor recreation resource planning, and for acquiring and developing outdoor recreation resources. It also established the Statewide Comprehensive Outdoor Recreation Planning (SCORP) process by requiring states to have a current SCORP to be eligible to receive federal matching funds. Funding for the LWCF comes from several sources, notably from federal fees charged for offshore oil and gas leasing, the sale of surplus federal military properties, and from special appropriations from the U.S. Congress. The total amount available from the LWCF varies from year to year, but recent Congresses have generally appropriated much lower levels than formerly.

Another significant event at the federal level during this period was the President's Commission on Americans Outdoors from 1985 through 1987. President Reagan established this Commission (sometimes referred to as ORRRC–II or PCAO) with a similar charge to that of ORRRC. Presidential commissions frequently have less impressive results than Congressional ones, and this is certainly true when comparing PCAO with ORRRC. Although chaired by Lamar Alexander, former Tennessee governor and two-time presidential candidate, PCAO had few tangible outcomes. Its most important legacies were to call public attention to the importance of outdoor recreation and outdoor recreation resources and to call for a "prairie fire of local action" among citizens to protect significant recreation resources close to where they live. PCAO also emphasized establishing protected greenways and called for greater reliance on volunteerism to support outdoor recreation efforts.

In some ways the situation in urban parks was more complex than on federal lands during this period. Although some urban parks were declared national historic landmarks and there was some federal investment in them (e.g., the Urban Park and Recreation Recovery Program or UPARR), there was generally an urban crisis of crime and middle-class flight from inner cities, which affected parks as well. The public increasingly saw urban parks as unappealing and unsafe places. To counter this, some urban park managers began to transform their parks into places where "anything goes" in terms of creative programming and publicity (e.g., pop concerts, special event "happenings"). Cranz (1982) called the period from 1965 to 1980 the "open space system era," which began to see an increasingly comprehensive idea of what the city should be. In the mid-1960s, municipal and federal programs began to characterize urban parks as "open spaces," and in 1965 the American Institute of Park Executives reconstituted itself and changed its name to the National Recreation and Park Association (NRPA). Cranz saw this as a symbolic merger of urban parks and the recreation programming that takes place in those parks. Up until this point, urban park managers tended to promote the nature-oriented pleasure ground philosophy, whereas recreation programmers ascribed more to reform park ideals.

Partnerships among public sector outdoor recreation providers and between public sector providers and private and nonprofit sector groups became increasingly important as this period has progressed. Dramatic increases in these arrangements came, in large part, because of the significant reductions in federal funding available for outdoor recreation, which corresponded to the beginning of the Reagan administration in 1980. These reductions in public dollars forced federal providers to seek new partners and to increase their use of creative approaches to providing services. These included far greater use of contracts, concessions, cooperative agreements, and user fees. Of course, partnerships can do more than simply accomplish recreation resource management tasks in more economical ways. Recently, there has been a widespread trend for public sector parks and recreation agencies to form collaborative partnerships with stakeholders to assure stakeholder desires are considered. This has been one of the most significant changes in outdoor recreation resource management during this period. Confrontation, especially when it involves injunctions and other litigation by stakeholders, is extremely expensive and inefficient. Working as partners better serves park and recreation agencies and their diverse customers. We will elaborate on the topic of collaborative partnerships in greater detail in Chapters 9, 13, and 17.

Significant Events in the History of Outdoor Recreation

This timeline presents important outdoor recreation resources related events and places them in the context of the six overlapping periods of outdoor recreation history just discussed. Figure 3.3 (p. 50) illustrates the six periods graphically.

1782　U.S. Constitution establishes federal government and authorities to acquire public lands

1803　Louisiana Purchase
Five hundred thirty million acres purchased from France; at less than five cents per acre, this was one of the best real estate bargains in history

1804　Public domain land granted to Ohio
First major federal "disposal" of public domain land

1804–　Lewis and Clark Expedition
1805　"Corps of Discovery" ordered by President Jefferson to explore and establish U.S. presence in the western half of North America

1853–　Land for Central Park purchased
1856　First major purchase of land for an urban park

1867　U.S. purchase of Alaska from Russia
Another great land bargain at roughly two cents per acre

1872　First national park established
Yellowstone National Park established as "a pleasuring ground for the people"

1873　Adirondak and Catskill Forest Preserves established in New York

1876　Appalachian Mountain Club established in Boston

1886　U.S. Cavalry sent to Yellowstone National Park to protect area from abuses

1889　North Carolina's Pinehurst and other golf resorts established

1890　U.S. frontier declared closed in official U.S. census report

1890　Passenger pigeons became extinct in the wild

1890　Yosemite National Park established

1891　Creation Act
Created original National Forest Reserves, later to become National Forests; this is the first *system* of reserved lands in the United States

1892　Sierra Club established

1902　Bureau of Reclamation established

1905　Bureau of Biological Survey established
Predecessor of the U.S. Fish and Wildlife Service

1905　Transfer Act
Transferred responsibility for the Forest Reserves to the Bureau of Forestry; these soon became the National Forests and USDA Forest Service, respectively

1906　Antiquities Act
Gave President power to establish National Monuments on existing public lands; motivated in part by looting and destruction of archeological sites in the southwest

1911　Weeks Act
Legislation enabling the federal government to *purchase* lands for national forests; used mainly in the eastern United States where there was very little original public domain (in fact, none in area of original 13 colonies)

1916   National Park Service Act
Created the National Park Service with Stephen Mather as first director

1916   Mt. Mitchell State Park
First state park in North Carolina

1924   White House Conference on Outdoor Recreation
Convened by President Coolidge

1936   Civilian Conservation Corps
Depression era jobs program with 3.5 million workers, many building parks, park facilities, and trails

1937   Appalachian Trail completed
Two-thousand–mile hiking trail initiated by volunteers in 1922

1937   Pittman-Robertson Act
Excise tax on sporting guns and ammunition; receipts used for wildlife management

1946   Bureau of Land Management
Created through combination of the General Lands Office and U.S. Grazing Service

1950   Dingell-Johnson Act
Excise tax on fishing equipment; proceeds used for fisheries management programs

1956   Fish and Wildlife Act
Established the U.S. Fish and Wildlife Service

1956   National Park Service "Mission 66"
Ten-year effort to improve and refurbish national parks in preparation for NPS 50th anniversary

1957   USDA Forest Service "Operation Outdoors"
Five-year USFS improvement effort

1960   Multiple Use–Sustained Yield Act
Officially added outdoor recreation (along with timber, watershed, range, and fish and wildlife) as one of the multiple uses of National Forests

1958–   Outdoor Recreation Resources Review
1962   Commission (ORRRC)
Congressional Commission established to examine supply and demand for outdoor recreation through the end of the 20th century and recommend ways to meet outdoor recreation needs

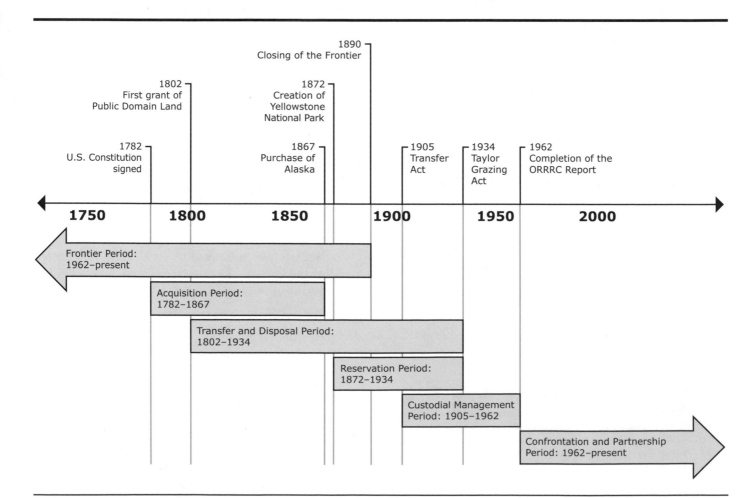

Figure 3.3   Six major periods in outdoor recreation history

1963 Bureau of Outdoor Recreation (BOR)
New federal bureau established within the Department of Interior to focus solely on planning for and assuring adequate supplies of outdoor recreation resources nation wide

1964 The Wilderness Act
Legislation that set up the National Wilderness Preservation System

1964 Classification and Multiple Use Act for Bureau of Land Management
Gave recreation more recognition

1965 Land and Water Conservation Fund Act (LWCFA)
Established large source of funding for planning, acquiring and developing outdoor recreation areas

1968 National Trails System Act
Established National Trail System and first inclusions into that system

1968 National Wild and Scenic Rivers Act
Established National Wild and Scenic Rivers System and first inclusions into that system

1969 National Environmental Policy Act
Established environmental standards and "NEPA" approval process, including Environmental Assessments and Environmental Impact Statements for developments on public land

1970 First Earth Day (April 22)
Nationwide celebration and awareness raising event initiated and founded by Senator Gaylord Nelson

1973 Endangered Species Act
Established threatened and endangered species program

1974 Forest and Rangeland Renewable Resources Planning Act
Required USDA Forest Service to make a comprehensive analysis of the nation's renewable natural resources and develop a national plan for the Forest Service every five years

1977 Accreditation of first undergraduate Parks and Recreation Program—National Recreation and Parks Association accredits North Carolina State University Department of Parks and Recreation (department established in 1947)

1976 National Forest Management Act (NFMA)
Improved management planning framework for USDA Forest Service; required updated management plans for every national forest; recognized recreation as an important use

1976 Federal Land Management and Policy Act
Requirements for BLM very similar to those for USDA Forest Service from the NFMA

1978 Bureau of Outdoor Recreation (BOR) becomes Heritage Conservation and Recreation Service. HCRS retains BOR responsibilities plus new roles

1980 Alaska National Interests Land Conservation Act
Granted large tracts of land to Native Americans in Alaska and made huge additions to federal lands managed by several agencies; essentially doubled the size of the National Park System.

1980 President Reagan takes office
Comes to office on platform of states' rights and reducing "big government;" budget cuts affect many federal agencies

1981 HCRS eliminated
Secretary of Interior James Watt eliminates only U.S. agency focused on outdoor recreation at the federal level

1985– President's Commission on Americans Outdoors
1987 Presidential commission with similar charge to that of ORRRC

Historical Perspectives on Outdoor Recreation Participation

One need not be an historian to know that outdoor recreation participation has changed dramatically through the six periods of history presented here. This applies both to what people have done for outdoor recreation as well as their levels of participation. Simply put, the number of outdoor recreation pursuits and levels of participation in them have expanded tremendously and continue to do so. Some activities and experiences, like hunting, fishing, and outdoor exploring, were originally engaged in for survival reasons and gradually transformed into outdoor recreation for most participants today. Similarly, horseback riding, hiking, canoeing, trail running, and other activities we now know as common recreation pursuits were necessary means of transportation for our ancestors. Other activities emerged much later partly or completely for outdoor recreation reasons, including mountain biking, snowboarding, scuba diving, hang gliding, and skydiving. No doubt new activities and experiences will continue to be developed as creative people figure out new ways to enjoy natural environments, often by designing or adapting new technologies for recreational purposes.

Current participation levels in outdoor recreation in general and trends in particular recreation activities will be presented in the next chapter. From the historical perspective, however, it is important to understand that outdoor recreation participation began increasing noticeably during the reservation period and much more rapidly after that. Increases in outdoor recreation participation during the reservation period included the small but increasing numbers of people who had the needed time and money to visit and enjoy the newly established parks in the United States. Outdoor recreation use began to increase much more rapidly after World War II and especially during the 1950s. This can be attributed to many factors, including increasing free time and prosperity, better transportation, and a desire among many to see more of the country. These increases prompted Mission 66 and Operation Outdoors during the custodial management period. Although there are few reliable national outdoor recreation use statistics prior to the 1960s, visitation to the U.S. national park system gives one indication of the dramatic increases that

began in the middle of the 20th century and continue in many areas today (Figure 3.4). Remember that some of the use increases reflected in Figure 3.4 are due to the increasing number of national parks available and the growth in the number of potential park visitors.

More recent indications of the growth in outdoor recreation participation come from national recreation studies, including the National Survey on Recreation and the Environment (NSRE). The overall outdoor recreation participation rates in the United States increased from 89% to 94.5% from the 1982–1983 to the 1994–1995 surveys (Cordell et al., 1999, p. 221). These are the estimates of the number of Americans ages 16 years or older who participated in any type of outdoor recreation during the previous 12 months. (Some of this increase is likely due to a longer list of recreation activities being included in the later survey.) Available figures for particular outdoor recreation activities also show significant increases in participation from 1960 through the mid-1990s (Table 3.3). With the exception of hunting, horseback riding, and

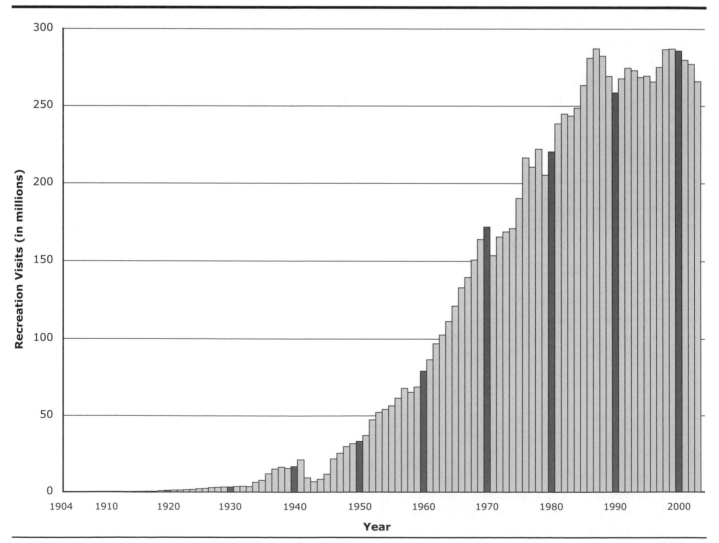

Figure 3.4   U.S. national park system recreation visitation from 1904 to 2003. Data source: National Park Service (2003, 2005)

sailing, participation grew greatly during these 35 years. The nine activities shown in Table 3.3 are the only ones where long-term data is available in the NSRE. More detailed current participation in a much broader range of activities will be presented in the next chapter.

Outdoor recreation in wilderness areas has also increased markedly during the last four decades. Interestingly, most of the increases came during the 1960s and 1970s. Use of wilderness leveled off in the 1980s, and even declined in some areas, before beginning to increase again in the 1990s (Cole, 1996; Lucas, 1985; Roggenbuck & Lucas, 1987).

Summary

In this chapter we presented an overview of the history of outdoor recreation in the United States organized around six overlapping periods based on important federal land policies. The frontier period was one of exploration and occupation characterized by wasteful practices and attitudes that resources were inexhaustible. The United States acquired and consolidated the lands that would eventually make up the nation during its acquisition period and transferred and sold off many of them for purposes such as creating new states, homesteading, and economic development during the transfer and disposal period. The reservation and custodial management periods were particularly important for outdoor recreation because they included setting aside special land areas for particular purposes and creating federal agencies to manage them for these purposes. These included the beginnings of our present national park, national forest, and national wildlife refuge systems. Our current period of history is that of confrontation and partnership characterized by a vast number of new laws related to natural resources and recreation, increased public participation and volunteerism, and increased lawsuits and other confrontation related to natural areas and natural resources. The history of outdoor recreation itself has been one of increasing levels of participation and expanding numbers and styles of recreation activities. Participation began to boom soon after World War II and continues to grow and expand today. The next chapter will present current trends related to outdoor recreation and its management including more detail on current types and levels of outdoor participation.

Literature Cited

Bureau of Land Management. (1999). *Public land statistics 1998*. Washington, DC: U.S. Government Printing Office.

Campbell, C. (1960). *Birth of a national park in the Great Smoky Mountains*. Knoxville, TN: University of Tennessee Press.

Clawson, M. (1983). *The federal lands revisited*. Washington, DC: Resources for the Future.

Cole, D. (1996). *Wilderness use trends, 1965 through 1994*. USDA Forest Service Research Paper (INT-RP-488). Ogden, UT: USDA Forest Service, Intermountain Research Station.

Cordell, H. K., Betz, C. J., Bowker, J. M., English, D. B. K., Mou, S. H., Bergstrom, J. C., et al. (1999). *Outdoor recreation in American life: A national assessment of demand and supply trends*. Champaign, IL: Sagamore.

Cordell, H. K. and Overdevest, C. (2001). *Footprints on the land: An assessment of demographic trends and the future of natural lands in the United States*. Champaign, IL: Sagamore.

Cranz, G. (1982). *The politics of park design: A history of urban parks in America*. Cambridge, MA: MIT Press.

Cross G. (1990). *A social history of leisure since 1600*. State College, PA: Venture Publishing, Inc.

Jensen, C. (1995). *Outdoor recreation in America* (5th ed.). Champaign, IL: Human Kinetics.

Lucas, R. (1985). Recreation trends and management of the Bob Marshall Wilderness Complex. In *Proceedings*

Table 3.3   Participation trends in selected outdoor recreation activities from 1960 to 1995

Activity	1960		1983		1995	
	Millions	Percent	Millions	Percent	Millions	Percent
Swimming	61.3	47%	99.7	53%	118.0	59%
Bicycling	13.0	10%	60.2	32%	63.3	32%
Fishing	43.1	33%	64.0	34%	63.3	32%
Camping	13.0	10%	38.9	21%	58.5	29%
Snow Skiing	2.6	2%	16.9	9%	26.2	13%
Hunting	20.9	16%	22.6	12%	20.6	10%
Horseback Riding	11.7	9%	16.9	9%	16.2	8%
Canoeing/Kayaking	2.6	2%	15.0	8%	17.5	9%
Sailing	3.9	3%	11.3	6%	10.6	5%

Source: Cordell and Overdevest (2001, p. 197)

of the 1985 National Outdoor Recreation Trends Symposium, Vol. II (pp. 309–316). Atlanta, GA: U.S. National Park Service.

Marshall, R. (1933). The forest for recreation and a program for forest recreation. In *A national plan for American forestry*. A report prepared by the Forest Service, U.S. Department of Agriculture in response to S. Res. 175 (72nd Congress). Washington, DC: U.S. Government Printing Office.

National Park Service (2003). Public Use Statistics Office. Retrieved January 9, 2003, from http://www.aqd.nps.gov/stats

National Park Service (2005). Public Use Statistics Office. Retrieved January 21, 2005, from http://www.aqd.nps.gov/stats

Roggenbuck, J. and Lucas, R. (1987). Wilderness use and users: A state-of-knowledge review. In *Proceedings, National wilderness research conference: Issues, state-of-knowledge, future directions* (pp. 204–245; General Technical Report INT-220). Ogden, UT: USDA Forest Service, Intermountain Research Station.

Zinser, C. I. (1995). *Outdoor recreation: United States national parks, forests, and public lands*. New York, NY: John Wiley & Sons.

Chapter 4
Social and Technological Forces Affecting Outdoor Recreation

Every cause is a lost cause unless we defuse the population bomb. Ehrlich (cited in McPhee, 1971, p. 84)

Learning Objectives

1. Identify the most important current trends affecting outdoor recreation.
2. Explain how each trend might affect the future provision of outdoor recreation opportunities.
3. Identify which trends will likely present the greatest opportunities and challenges for outdoor recreation providers and explain why.

Understanding the social and technological context is essential for understanding outdoor recreation. This applies to understanding outdoor recreation participation as well as how planners and managers can best provide outdoor recreation opportunities today and forecast what they will need to provide in the future. The purpose of this chapter is to introduce the key trends and forces affecting recreation and to discuss their implications for our profession.

Social and Technological Trends and Forces

Many factors affect participation in outdoor recreation and the provision of outdoor recreation opportunities, including

- users' and potential users' incomes, mobility, ages, free time, education, occupations, preferences, and past participation
- availability and location of natural areas and recreation-related facilities
- population levels and growth
- patterns of land ownership, agency policies, and regulations

Needless to say, tremendous changes in most of these factors in the past 50 years directly or indirectly affected outdoor recreation. To make the following overview more manageable and useful, the key trends and forces are organized into ten distinct groups presented from the broadest to the ones most specifically focused on outdoor recreation. Our selection of categories draws on those presented by

Godbey (1997), the President's Commission on Americans Outdoors (1987), and others. The most important forces and trends within each category are presented, and some of the likely implications of these trends for outdoor recreation and outdoor recreation managers are discussed. The ten groups of important forces and trends are

1. population changes
2. technological innovations
3. shifts in economic strengths and weaknesses
4. increased accountability of institutions and leaders
5. changes in transportation
6. concern for the environment and its effects on health
7. greater emphasis on partnerships
8. increasing pressure on public recreational resources
9. changes in recreation and leisure in general
10. changes in outdoor recreation participation in particular

Population Changes

Population size and composition have important implications for outdoor recreation. Some of the most important population-related trends are described here.

Trends

Growing Populations

Today's world population is nearly *four times* the estimated 1.6 billion people who existed in 1900. World population is now estimated to be 6.27 billion, having reached what demographers call the "day of 6 billion" on October 12, 1999. Although the annual rate of growth has decreased slightly to 1.3% (U.S. Census Bureau, 2002), the world population it is still growing rapidly, especially in developing nations. The population of the United States is approximately 290 million (U.S. Census Bureau, 2003). There is now one birth every 8 seconds, one death every 13 seconds, and one international migrant arriving (net) every 29 seconds in the United States. U.S. population growth in the 1990s was the largest of any decade in U.S. history (U.S. Census Bureau, 2001b). Population increases are caused by two basic factors: (a) birth rates that exceed death rates and (b) people, on average, are living longer. Life expectancy in the United States has increased from 47 years in 1900 to nearly 77 years in 2000 (Kane, 2002). According to many experts, the current worldwide growth rate is not sustainable in terms of the planet's natural resources.

Growing evidence suggests the actual number of *households* is a critical and often overlooked factor related to resource use and overall land pressures. Each household, whether it is made up of one person or ten, requires space and other resources to construct and maintain (e.g., refrigerator, stove, heating and cooling system; minimum energy and water consumption). If the number of households grows more rapidly than overall populations, as it has in many parts of the world, the amount of resource use per person will generally increase. Even in areas where overall populations are declining, such as Italy, Greece, Portugal, and Spain, the number of households is still growing rapidly (Liu, Dally, Ehrlich & Luck, 2003).

Aging Populations

Median ages are increasing overall. The median age in the United States increased from 32.9 years in 1990 to 35.3 in 2000. Figure 4.1 shows the age distributions in the United States for 1990 and 2000 (U.S. Census Bureau, 2001d). Two things are important to note in the figure. The first is the bulge in the 35- to 54-year-old category. This bulge is the aging Baby Boom generation (those born from 1946 through 1964), which now represents 28% of the U.S. population. By 2030, one in every five Americans will be 65 years old or older (Kane, 2002). The other thing to notice in Figure 4.1 is the far larger number of females than males in the older age categories.

Increasing Diversity

The racial and ethnic composition of the population of the United States and other countries is continually shifting. Caucasian is still the most common race in the United States at 75%, but that proportion continues to shrink. People of Hispanic or Latino origin are now the largest minority group in the United States at 12.5%. Blacks or African Americans make up 12.3% of the U.S. population (U.S. Census Bureau, 2001a). Note that the federal government considers race and Hispanic origin to be separate and distinct concepts and the data for these different categories are determined by different questions in the census.

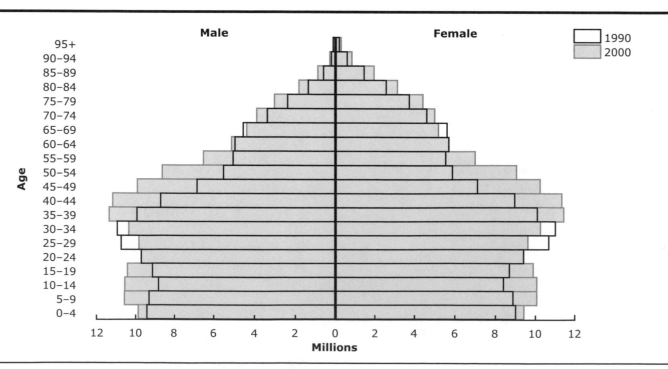

Figure 4.1   Population by age and sex in 1990 and 2000. Source: U.S. Census Bureau (2001d)

Urbanizing and Suburbanizing Continue

There are now 14 "mega-cities" in the world with populations over 10 million (Gartner & Lime, 2000). By 2000, the proportion of people in the United States who live in metropolitan areas increased to a remarkable 80%. Although all regions of the country continue to grow, the fastest growing regions continue to be the west followed by the south. Over half the people in the United States live in the ten most populous states, led by California at 12% (U.S. Census Bureau, 2001b).

Decreases in Traditional Families

Only 52% of U.S. households include married couples. A total of 16% of households are headed by a single parent (12% by the female and 4% by the male). Over a quarter of all households (26%) in the United States are now made up of just one person, while only 3.7% of households include more than two generations living together (U.S. Census Bureau, 2001c). Figure 4.2 presents a comparison of U.S. household types for 1990 and 2000. It illustrates that the proportion of traditional married-couple households has declined while all other categories of households have become more common.

Implications for Outdoor Recreation

All people need food, clean water, and shelter to live. They also need a host of other resources, space, leisure, recreation, and contact with natural environments to live well. As world and regional populations continue to increase, these necessities become more scarce and, therefore, more

valuable. Because many of these essential resources are located on lands and waters now available for outdoor recreation, the pressures on these areas will inevitably increase. Careful planning and political resolve will obviously be needed to preserve special places and conserve natural and heritage/cultural resources, including settings for outdoor recreation. As stated at the beginning of this chapter, "Every cause is a lost cause unless we defuse the population bomb" (Ehrlich, cited in McPhee, 1971, p. 84). This may well be true in the case of high-quality outdoor recreation resources.

There are several possible implications of the aging U.S. population. Although older people are more active than ever, they are still less likely to participate in many outdoor activities than their younger counterparts. However, older citizens are much more likely to vote. Will this cause outdoor recreation to become a lower funding priority for voters and government decision makers as the population ages? It may be prudent for outdoor recreation resource managers to more actively reach out to older citizens and those who will be older voters in the near future. Approximately half of all crime is committed by people under 25 years old. As the population ages, will levels of crime decrease? If so, will people be more likely to visit parks, especially large urban parks, if they become less fearful of crime?

Easy access to large natural areas is becoming more difficult for many urban and suburban residents. Will lack of easy access motivate these people to make the extra effort needed to visit large natural areas? Or will they lose

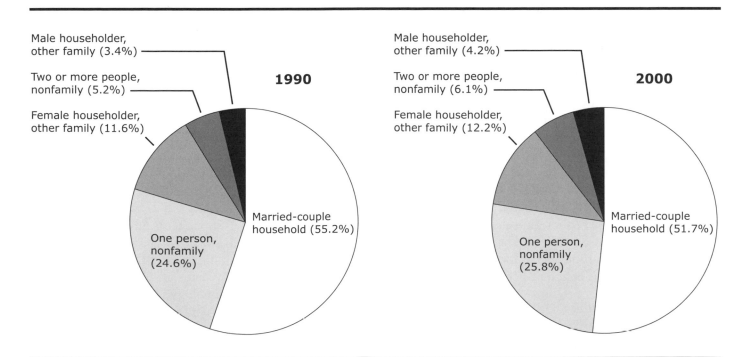

Figure 4.2   Households by type in 1990 and 2000. Source: U.S. Census Bureau (2001c)

interest in more difficult to reach settings and the outdoor recreation experiences available there because they feel uncomfortable in those environments or unskilled at certain outdoor recreation activities?

Different cultures perceive and use outdoor recreation settings in different ways. As our clientele become more diverse, managers need to better understand different cultures and in some cases even new language skills to communicate and interact with their visitors.

Technological Innovations

Technology advanced at an astonishing rate during the last 50 years. These advances relate to outdoor recreation in three primary ways: (a) innovations changing how people communicate and live, (b) innovations changing how we manage recreation resources, and (c) innovations changing how users engage in outdoor recreation.

Trends

Innovations Changing How People Communicate and Live

We can communicate more rapidly, and in some respects better, than ever before. Cell phones, pagers, the Internet, e-mail, Internet-capable personal data assistants, and fax machines make it possible to get in touch instantly, stay in touch, and transfer vast quantities of information at amazing rates.

Innovations Changing How We Manage Recreation Resources

Recreation and natural resource management have been revolutionized by an array of relatively new technologies. These include geographic information systems, powerful computer hardware, specialized computer software, laptops and other portable computers, remote sensing technology, the Internet, distance education, digital imaging, new wildlife tracking technologies, and high-tech communications devices. Many senior recreation and resource managers began their careers before any of these innovations existed. All of these tools enable managers to do more in less time with better results than ever before. In addition, there have been great advances in the science-based technologies and approaches for managing outdoor recreation resources, as described in Chapters 12 and 13.

Innovations Changing How Users Engage in Outdoor Recreation

The types of outdoor recreation activities and styles of participating in these activities continue to expand and diversify. This is due in part to technological innovations.

Some of these innovations have created entirely new types of activities, such as snowmobiling, mountain biking, personal watercraft use, all-terrain vehicle use, snowboarding, and geocaching. Mountain biking, for example, was virtually unknown until the late 1970s, and now about 5% of the U.S. population (roughly 14 million people) participate annually (Roper Starch Worldwide, Inc., 2000). Other technologies have made new styles of participating in outdoor recreation activities possible. Lightweight camping gear, continually refined since the 1960s, makes it possible for more people to take longer trips deeper into the backcountry. New, better, and safer rock climbing and mountaineering equipment helped to create new climbing styles like sport climbing, bouldering, aid climbing, multiday big wall climbing, and competitive climbing on artificial climbing walls. In addition, some technological innovations are causing changes in outdoor recreation engagements in much broader ways. GPS units make it possible for outdoor recreationists to pinpoint their exact position almost instantly and cell phones make it possible for users to communicate with the rest of the world from ever deeper parts of the backcountry whenever they wish.

Implications for Outdoor Recreation

Technological innovations have profound implications—some practical and others more philosophical—for outdoor recreation and outdoor recreation management. Increasing types and styles of recreational use increase the potential for user conflicts. New uses will frequently require new facilities or modifications to existing ones. And without exception, planners and managers will need to be diligent and proactive to anticipate user needs and preferences, and in some cases, to determine whether certain new uses are even appropriate in particular settings. Sometimes new policies and regulations or new interpretations of existing ones will be required regarding new user technologies.

Philosophical questions regarding new technology will become more frequent and probably more difficult. For example, what level of technology is appropriate in the wilderness and how will new technologies affect people's outdoor recreation experiences? Are cell phones acceptable in the backcountry? in the wilderness? Are they acceptable only if the ringer is turned off? Should they be banned altogether because they destroy the real or perceived isolation, solitude, and self-reliance that many people seek from outdoor recreation? More pragmatically, cell phones and GPS technology in combination can greatly aid emergency response when necessary and increase users' confidence (even when not warranted) and comfort levels. But these tools can, of course, also burden managers with trivial requests and tempt users to do things and go places beyond their abilities because "We can always just call for help if we get into trouble."

New technologies also aid and revolutionize outdoor recreation management, often enabling us to do our jobs better and more easily than before, as explained in Chapters 12 and 13. However, the skills managers will need will be radically different from those of even ten years ago and will be even more radically different ten years from now. It will no longer be possible to complete one or even two college degrees and expect to have all the skills that will be needed for an entire career in the recreation resource management professions. Continuing education will be essential at all levels. Agencies and universities will need to stay abreast of new technologies and invest more in research and development. They will need to use creative ways to train their employees, certainly including online courses and live distance education, and in the near future through media and in formats yet to be developed.

Shifts in Economic Strengths and Weaknesses

The strength and nature of the economy, whether local, state, national, or global, affects outdoor recreation participation and outdoor recreation management in many ways.

Trends

Transforming Economies

The economies of the United States and other industrialized nations continue to transform from a dependence on manufacturing to greater dominance of high technology, services, and information. In general, the economic sector has grown steadily, with occasional fits and starts like the Pacific Rim recession that began in the mid-1990s and the bursting of the high-tech bubble and bullish stock markets of the 1990s. Generally, steady economic growth has been good news for outdoor recreation, because users have had more discretionary income for recreation pursuits and strong national economies made it possible for governments to invest in natural resource areas and agencies. However, a persistent gap exists in wealth between the rich and poor, which means that all nations and all people within each nation do not benefit equally. In many places, including the United States, the gap between the rich and poor is widening. Some countries see this gap as one of the greatest dangers the world now faces (Pew Research Center for the People and the Press, 2002).

Increasing Debt Levels

Of course, prosperity sometime comes at a price, and increasingly, the price of prosperity is debt. Paying interest on the "debt bubble" caused by borrowing can be a staggering impediment for nations, corporations, and individuals. When a large amount of any budget is spent servicing debt, less money is available for other priorities, such as protecting and managing recreation areas or, in the case of users, actually visiting these areas. The federal debt in the United States recently stood at over $6.3 trillion (U.S. Treasury Department, 2002), which amounts to $22,000 for each person in the country. At the individual level, savings rates have been falling overall. Except for a handful of nations in eastern Asia, the average amount that individuals saved fell from 1984 to 1995 (World Bank, 1999).

Implications for Outdoor Recreation

If individuals and nations are, in fact, living above their means, some level of "belt-tightening" lies ahead, particularly if the economic downturn of the early 2000s continues. If so, outdoor recreation participation patterns will change and agencies and their managers will be even more challenged by tighter budgets. This could accelerate the current trend toward user fees for recreation services and access to outdoor recreation areas. If fees continue to increase, there will be a point beyond which a growing segment of the population could be priced out of participating. Policy makers could accept this as unfortunate or could consider ways to mitigate the effects on poorer users, such as sliding fee scales or free or reduced-fee coupons for some patrons.

Widening gaps between the rich and poor could also lead to demand for more luxurious accommodations and other facilities that are far beyond the means of huge segments of a country's population. This could also lead to pressures to create facilities in public parks that may not be consistent with the purposes of the areas. This is particularly true of ecotourism providers in developing nations.

Increased Accountability of Institutions and Leaders

Organizations in the public, private, and nonprofit sectors at all levels are being held more accountable than ever before by their constituents, stockholders, and members. This is due to many forces, which taken together will affect how we manage outdoor recreation resources.

Trends

Shifts in Political Power Closer to the People

Beginning most profoundly with the Reagan administration in the 1980s, policies and programs were designed to decentralize many government decisions and resource allocations from the federal level to the state and local levels. Mandated public involvement and the importance of building local support for agency decisions and actions vested greater power and influence in groups away from headquarters and closer to the park and recreation areas themselves. Certainly top-level leadership still continues to direct the fleet, but the captains of the ships, the rest of the crew, and the passengers themselves have more say than ever before.

Interest Groups More Politically Aware and Effective

People are becoming more actively involved in the issues and causes they care about. This is especially true at the local level and when decisions affect places that are particularly important to users and neighbors. The rapid growth of "Friends of the…" groups and increasing memberships of many mainstream interest groups are cases in point. To be sure, a huge segment of the population is still apathetic (as embarrassingly low voter turnout rates indicate) but the vocal and actively involved minority is growing and in many ways becoming more effective. Protests, lawsuits, fundraising campaigns, petition drives, and other actions related to natural resource and recreation resource issues are on the rise.

General Mistrust of Corporations and Government

Some scholars believe that relatively high levels of trust in government in the United States began to decline most dramatically during the Vietnam War era and with the Watergate scandal and cover-ups of the Nixon administration. Currently, when asked their biggest concerns, government corruption is Americans' second biggest after crime (Roper Starch Worldwide, Inc., 2000). Historians may well look back to the collapse of Enron, the corporate scandals at WorldCom, Tyco, and others, and the questionable accounting practices of the early 2000s as a similar turning point for the private sector. Just as the Baby Boom generation remembers the government scandals of the 1960s and 1970s, generations X and Y will likely remember recent corporate irresponsibility for many decades.

Implications for Outdoor Recreation

There is a political maxim that "all politics are local." As this becomes more true in terms of outdoor recreation and natural resource issues, some of the roles of our professions are changing and new skills will be required as a result. Planners and managers will need more formal training and experience in communications, conflict management, community organizing and development, negotiations, and legal issues than they did before. Proactive planning and data-based decision making will be increasingly important, both to make the best possible decisions and to document adherence with appropriate procedures and best practices. Working with and, in particular, listening to formal interest groups and less organized constituents will be crucial. This will be especially true before conflicts arise and increasingly important to avoid confrontations and associated litigation rather than simply reacting to them after the fact.

Changes in Transportation

How, where, and how long people participate in outdoor recreation is affected by the available transportation infrastructure, the fixed and variable costs of travel, and attitudes about travel in general. All these factors are in constant flux.

Trends

Greater Mobility

The biggest change in transportation in recent decades, of course, is that we are far more mobile than ever before. This is true for both domestic and international travelers. This is certainly a key factor in the surge of international visitors to the United States, many of whom are drawn here by natural resource areas in general and outdoor recreation in particular. Between 1987 and 1997, for example, international travel to the United States grew 66% to 46.2 million visitors. Canada, Mexico, Japan, the United Kingdom, and Germany were the leading sources of these visitors (O'Leary, 1999).

Concerns About Travel

In opposition to our greater mobility are recently heightened concerns about travel. In the wake of the terrorist attacks on the United States in 2001 and unrest in many parts of the world, travelers have become much more concerned about where they travel to and how they get there. Use of air travel, in particular, dropped dramatically after the 9/11 attacks, as did travel to the Middle East. Other areas where internal unrest, violent revolutionary movements, and drug-related crime are common face similar problems.

Fluctuating Energy Availability and Cost

Demand for outdoor recreation that occurs more than a few miles from people's homes overwhelmingly depends on car travel in the United States, which is affected to some extent by the price of gasoline. Gasoline prices have risen sharply since the first OPEC oil embargo in the 1970s. Since then gasoline prices have been much less stable and have been dependent, in large part, on volatile world political and economic conditions. These forces and associated instability will almost certainly continue.

Public Interest in Bicycling and Walking

Surveys indicate that far more people would bike to work if safe facilities were available, and most people would walk more if there were safe, secure places to do so (U.S. Department of Transportation, 1994). Many bicycle and pedestrian facilities are built with transportation in mind, but obviously these same facilities can be very beneficial for outdoor recreation purposes as well. Relatedly, there has been dramatic growth in the importance of public sector bicycle and pedestrian funding programs as illustrated by the federal Intermodal Surface Transportation Efficiency Act of 1991 (ISTEA) and then the 1997 Transportation Efficiency Act for the 21st Century (TEA-21) grant programs. These have provided significant funding for intermodal infrastructure and have been very helpful for trail and greenway development, particularly in urban and suburban areas.

Implications for Outdoor Recreation

With the exception of outdoor recreation trips very close to where people live, virtually all outdoor recreation trips involve transportation infrastructure, vehicles, and fuel. Changes in any of these factors affect access to and demand for outdoor recreation. The net balance of payments from tourism is becoming an important economic consideration for states, regions, nations, and outdoor recreation professionals. Tourism is the biggest generator of foreign exchange and provider of other types of economic benefits in many countries and ranks near the top in many others. Assuring decision makers and voters are aware of these economic roles recreation and tourism play should be an important priority for managers and outdoor recreation advocates.

Outdoor recreation opportunities and participation can be very sensitive to changes in transportation.

Based on public interest in pedestrian and bicycle transportation and the relative availability of funding for intermodal projects, managers should explore more bicycle, pedestrian, and mass transit options within their areas and between areas, even if they fall under the jurisdictions of different management agencies. Similarly, agencies should reach out more to commercial travel partners (e.g., airlines; railroad, bus, and ferry providers). These partners typically have a far more direct impact on the "travel to" and "travel back" phases of the total recreation experience than do resource managers.

Concern for the Environment and Its Effects on Health

Concern for one's health and the natural environment in general continue to be high. From the first Earth Day in the United States in 1970, to the 1992 worldwide "Earth Summit" in Rio De Janeiro, to the United Nations World Summit on Sustainable Development (WSSD) in Johannesburg ten years later, there has been no lack of concern about the environment. Although there have been great successes, the overall record on fruitful policy and actions resulting from environmental and health concerns has been mixed. However, two trends in particular will have implications for outdoor recreation resource management.

Trends

Increasing Concern for Personal Health and Safety

In terms of health, safety, and the environment, people have always tended to be most concerned about the things that affect them most directly. When asked about their biggest concerns in 2000, crime topped the list for Americans. Pollution of air and water was the biggest concern for 22%. This was up 7% from just the year before (Roper Starch Worldwide, Inc., 2000). Air and water quality are also big concerns internationally. Experts believe atmospheric pollution is leading to changes in climate and rainfall patterns and crop damage that could be causing several hundred thousand premature deaths from respiratory diseases. In parts of Asia, atmospheric pollution resulting from forest fires, burning of agricultural wastes and fossil fuels, industrial emissions, power stations, and inefficient wood and cow dung cookers is particularly problematic (United Nations Environment Programme, 2002). In addition to concerns about personal health related to pollution, people around the world are most concerned about disease, hatred, weapons, and the gap between the rich and poor. Figure 4.3 (p. 62) presents the ratings of various dangers facing the world from the perspectives of 38,000 people in a representative sample of 44 nations.

Increase in Radical Groups and Ecoterrorism

There have been a small but increasing number of protests, "tree sitters," and incidents of ecological sabotage ("ecotage" or "monkey wrenching") directed at things the perpetrators believe are harming the environment. Attacks have been made against ski area facilities, logging equipment, new housing developments, animal testing operations, and roadside billboards. Militant individuals and groups like Earth First!, Earth Liberation Front (ELF), People for the Ethical Treatment of Animals (PETA) and others advocate various forms of "direct action" as tactics. Ecoterrorism is illegal and some actions (like arson) could be deadly.

Implications for Outdoor Recreation

Public pressure and necessity have led to legislation and increasing funding for environmental protection and cleanups (e.g., clean air regulations, Superfund sites). Such funding will strain budgets but will lead to cleaner parks and perhaps healthier visitors. Some such programs could provide opportunities for creative piggybacking for outdoor recreation agencies. For example, disaster relief funding after floods and hurricanes could protect river corridor flood plains that are also critical wildlife habitats and potential locations for greenway trails and a wide variety of outdoor recreation opportunities. Similarly, pollution control funding could be directed to providing river buffers as filtration zones that could be used for some recreation purposes as well.

Ecoterrorism is a problem that could become serious, and potentially dangerous, for managers and visitors.

Earth First's slogan is "No compromise in defense of Mother Earth!" It seems likely that ecoterrorists, who claim to take great lengths to avoid injuring anyone, will eventually cause the deaths of innocent people. Managers and law enforcement have been vigilant and will need to be more so. Managers also need to do more to keep people from being lured into some protestors' destructive and dangerous activities. Actively involving people in decision making at the local levels, making greater attempts to understand exactly what is leading some people to resort to terrorism, and raising public awareness of and attitudes against such behavior seem like logical steps. Internationally, working to curb disease, violence, and inequality are extremely important priorities. Recreation resource managers need to be creative in designing complimentary programs to contribute to addressing these problems.

Greater Emphasis on Partnerships

Trends

The public, private, and nonprofit sectors are reaching out to one another and cooperating more than ever before. This is partly due to financial necessity (e.g., to prevent the very high costs of litigation and to accomplish work more economically) and partly because cooperation can be a more effective long-term strategy to achieve complicated and sometimes controversial resource management objectives. The increases in the use of contracts, concessions, cooperative agreements, and memoranda of understanding

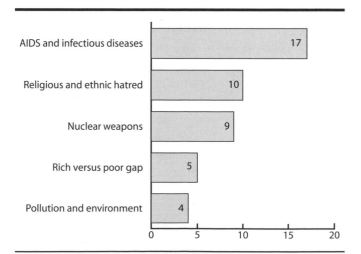

Figure 4.3   Number of countries rating various problems as the first or second greatest dangers in the world. Source: Pew Research Center for the People and the Press (2002, p. 47)

In general outdoor recreationists and citizens have increasing concerns about their health and personal safety.

that have taken place over the last two decades will almost certainly continue. New and even more creative partnerships will be developed as well.

Implications for Outdoor Recreation

Partners can tremendously increase our ability to accomplish outdoor recreation and resource management objectives if we are skilled facilitators and build and nurture these relationships for the long term. Some predict that "stakeholder management" will become the key park management (Machlis, 2003). Working effectively with partners and other publics will require that new and existing managers have strong organizational skills and the training and experience in coalition building that has more traditionally been found in community development professionals. This type of training will need to be developed and improved both within agencies and at universities where the next generation of recreation resource managers are being prepared.

One of the advantages of partnerships, particularly those with volunteers and nonprofits organizations, is that the citizens involved in the activities become more aware of the challenges agencies face and more sophisticated in helping to address them. This may create both opportunities and challenges. This might create opportunities, because these people may get to understand the agencies and their constraints better and become more vocal and credible advocates supporting agency positions. This might create challenges, however, in that these more involved and more informed citizens may become less tolerant of agency actions that they see as not in the best interests of the resources or their communities. In other words, some of the partners may develop a sense of ownership that could translate into support as well as challenges for some agency positions and programs.

Increasing Pressure on Public Recreational Resources

All outdoor recreation depends on the availability of natural areas of one sort or another. If such areas are not available in reasonably accessible locations, too few outdoor recreation opportunities will be readily available. Two trends, in particular, are affecting the availability of natural areas for outdoor recreation.

Trends

Less Land Available as Development Accelerates

Growing populations, and the associated increasing number of homes needed to accommodate them, require land and other resources for homes, businesses, roads, and schools. More people and growing communities mean greater pressures to develop remaining natural areas. This is a direct pressure in the sense that land is needed for places to locate these developments. There is also an indirect pressure as well, because growing populations require additional resources, such as timber, minerals, food, energy, and water. Because these and many other natural resources come in large part from the relatively undeveloped natural areas of the planet, these demands also put pressure on the lands currently available for outdoor recreation. These direct and indirect land pressures affect both private and public lands, including parks and outdoor recreation areas.

Recreation Use Increasing on Existing Public Lands

Increasing numbers of people and changing recreation patterns have translated into greater recreation use pressure on existing outdoor recreation resources. This trend will almost certainly continue. In some places, however,

Outdoor recreation providers increasingly rely on partnerships such as joint efforts with volunteer groups.

Many outdoor recreation areas, such as this park in South Korea, are experiencing dramatic increases in use.

the most popular and accessible outdoor recreation areas are becoming intensely overused while other areas have flat or even decreasing levels of use.

Implications for Outdoor Recreation

As some areas become more heavily used, visitor impacts on natural resources have the potential to become much more severe. Managers will have to be diligent in educating the public and managing use and resources to keep these areas from being "loved to death." Greater demand for a shrinking amount of land will continue to drive up the price of land. These economic pressures have been acute in rapidly growing and very desirable areas and will become even more so. As land prices increase it becomes more difficult for park agencies to purchase land for new parks and outdoor recreation areas. Planners and managers will need to be even more sophisticated, diligent, politically astute, and business-like to compete with the private sector for the land with the greatest outdoor recreation potential and to resist pressures to overdevelop existing park and natural resource areas. Figure 4.4 shows the earth at night, and gives some indication of the current extent of human development.

Changes in Recreation and Leisure in General

The amount of free time people have and how they choose to use it are obviously critical factors affecting recreation participation in general as well as outdoor recreation in particular. Several trends in this regard are important for outdoor recreation professionals to consider.

Trends

If We Have More Free Time, We Use It in Sedentary Ways

The average amount of free time for adults ages 18 to 64 in the United States increased from about 35 hours per week in 1965 to nearly 40 hours in 1985. However, this did not necessarily translate into more outdoor recreation participation. In fact, nearly all of the six hours of free time gained during the period was devoted to increased TV watching, which accounted for 15 hours of all free time per week in 1985 (Godbey, 1997). In 1985, only 2.2 hours of free time per week was used for "recreation/sports/outdoors" (Robinson & Godbey, 1997). More troubling still is the fact that the amount of free time Americans have may actually have started to *decrease* on average (Schor, 1992).

There have obviously been large increases in the amount of time some people spent surfing the Internet in the past decade, but it is still unclear whether this is cutting into TV time or into other time, like that previously devoted to outdoor recreation. Evidence also suggests although upper and upper middle-class people are better off financially, many of them have far less free time than other segments of the population. Some are in effect becoming money rich but leisure poor.

Figure 4.4   Earth at night in 2000 (NASA, 2005) Data courtesy Marc Imhoff of NASA GSFC and Christopher Elvidge of NOAA NGDC. Image by Craig Mayhew and Robert Simmon, NASA GSFC)

In terms of outdoor recreation participation and management, it is hard to exaggerate the importance of peoples' unobligated time. Lack of time is consistently given as the most important constraint to outdoor recreation participation. In a recent study of trail and greenway use in North Carolina, for example, lack of time was by far the biggest reason people gave for why they used trails less than they wanted (Moore, Siderelis, Lee, Ivy & Bailey, 1999). This is consistent with research regarding constraints to recreation generally. For example, the 1994–1995 National Survey on Recreation and the Environment asked people who had not participated in recreation to explain why. Lack of time was the most common reason. Table 4.1 puts this in perspective with the other reasons for nonparticipation in the United States.

Increased Rushing and Stress

Even if some people have more free time, few seem to be living more "leisurely" lives as a result. Most studies indicate we feel more stressed and rushed than ever. In fact, 38% of Americans report that they "always" feel rushed (Godbey & Graefe, 1993). We are becoming a culture of instant gratification. E-mail, cell phones, pagers, the Internet, and fast food all contribute to an expectation we should be able to get the things we want quickly, if not instantly. As a result, we tend to do more things at once, and generally do them more quickly. We alternate between talking on the cell phone, jotting notes on the PDA's to-do list, and drinking coffee, all while listening to the radio as we sit in traffic during our daily commutes. Women, in particular, engage in such "time stacking" to meet job demands as well as home responsibilities. In general, the pace of life continues to accelerate, helping to increase our rushing and stress, and fragmenting our time. This fast pace is not limited to North America. In fact, the United States may not be the most rushed, as Americans tend to assume. Levine (1997) estimated the overall pace of life in 31 countries by measuring walking speed (how fast pedestrians walked a 60-foot distance downtown), work speed (how fast a postal worker took to complete a standard request to purchase a stamp) and clock accuracy (the accuracy of public clocks in each country) in at least one major city in these countries. Table 4.2 shows the resulting rankings, from fastest pace of life (1) to slowest (31).

Increased Concern About Life Satisfaction and Quality of Life

As explained in Chapter 2, more people have become increasingly concerned about the quality of their lives, and have realized that while some accumulation of material goods is necessary, these goods are not sufficient for life satisfaction. Therefore, much more attention is now being given to good nutrition, stress management, preventing substance abuse, practicing preventive medicine, establishing social networks of friends, desiring local amenities near where they live, and enjoying those amenities during their leisure.

Implications for Outdoor Recreation

The amount of free time available to the average American seems to be decreasing. Even those who have more free time are not generally choosing to use that new-found time to increase their outdoor recreation participation. It is not clear what role feelings of increased stress and rushing play versus the fragmenting of free time into smaller periods. Regardless, lack of time is a major constrain to outdoor recreation participation.

Providing outdoor recreation opportunities close to where people live and work is important to give them a chance for outings during their more fragmented time and

Table 4.1   Reasons for not participating in recreation

Reason for Not Participating	Percent of General Population Giving Reason
Lack of time	63.8
Lack of money	42.5
Personal health	28.2
No companion	28.1
Outdoor pests	27.7
Inadequate information	21.1
Crowded activity areas	20.5
Inadequate facilities	16.8
Inadequate transportation	14.8
Personal safety concerns	14.0
Poorly maintained areas	14.0
No assistance for physical condition	13.7
Pollution problems	13.0
Household member with disability	6.0
Other reason	19.4

Source: Johnson (1999, p. 266)

Table 4.2   Ranking of pace of life for 31 countries

1. Switzerland	17. Canada
2. Ireland	18. South Korea
3. Germany	19. Hungary
4. Japan	20. Czech Republic
5. Italy	21. Greece
6. England	22. Kenya
7. Sweden	23. China
8. Austria	24. Bulgaria
9. Netherlands	25. Romania
10. Hong Kong	26. Jordan
11. France	27. Syria
12. Poland	28. El Salvador
13. Costa Rica	29. Brazil
14. Taiwan	30. Indonesia
15. Singapore	31. Mexico
16. United States	

Source: Levine (1997)

for more frequent escapes from the pressures of work and life. Similarly, linking people with outdoor recreation opportunities, especially ones close to where they live and work, is important. This can be done in many places through greenways, better bicycle and pedestrian infrastructure, and improved public transportation. Getting it done is another situation where stronger partnerships with transportation planners and providers would be advantageous. Money-rich but leisure-poor visitors will likely be willing to pay more for convenience (e.g., pay higher fees for last-minute reservations, pay surcharges for convenient information or planning assistance via the Internet). As explained in Chapter 2, growing public concern about quality of life directly impacts recreation resources management, because that concern stimulates more demand for recreation opportunities and related amenities.

Changes in Outdoor Recreation Participation in Particular

The final major force or trend affecting outdoor recreation and its management is the changing face of outdoor recreation participation. The most telling trends in this area involve changes in overall participation and changes in participation in particular activities.

Trends

Levels of Outdoor Recreation Participation Increasing Overall

As noted at the end of Chapter 3, outdoor recreation in general began to explode in popularity after World War II. Since then there have been periods when growth slowed, but overall, participation has steadily increased. By 1994–1995, it was estimated that 94.5% of Americans ages 16 or older participated in outdoor recreation annually (Cordell et al., 1999, p. 221). The percentage of people who frequently participate in outdoor recreation has increased dramatically in recent years. In 1994, 50% of Americans participated in outdoor recreation at least once a month. By 2000, 78% of Americans participated at least monthly (Roper Starch Worldwide, Inc., 2000, p. 23). Between 1999 and 2000, participation increased across all income levels and all age groups. The largest increase during that period was among people ages 60 years and older (Roper Starch Worldwide, Inc., 2000, p. 24).

Changing Participation Rates in Various Outdoor Recreation Activities

People participate in myriad outdoor recreation activities for a vast range of reasons. Table 4.3 includes the most recent estimates of what people in the United States cur-

rently do for outdoor recreation. It includes results from the two most recent and most comprehensive national studies. The 2000 data (first column) are from Roper Starch Worldwide, Inc. (2000) and were prepared for the Recreation Roundtable. These findings are based on 1,986 in-person interviews in people's homes and included Americans ages 18 or older. The 2000–2001 data (second column) and trends from 1994–2001 (third column) are from Cordell, Betz, Green, and Mou (2004), which used National Survey on Recreation and the Environment (NSRE) data. The NSRE is the latest in a series of national recreation surveys conducted since 1960. The 2000–2001 NSRE data are from a sample of approximately 50,000 Americans ages 16 or older. Accurately estimating the outdoor recreation behavior of 290 million Americans is not a simple task. So it should be no great surprise to find differences in the activity participation estimates developed through the two surveys. These differences are due partly to the different study methods employed, different samples, different age groups, and varied activity definitions and groupings examined. We include both results for comparison purposes. The activities in the table are arranged according to the percent change in people participating from 1994–2001.

According to these and other national studies, walking is the outdoor recreation activity participated in by the most Americans. According to the 2000–2001 NSRE study, the next most popular are visiting beaches and watersides, visiting nature centers, picnicking, and sightseeing. The Roper Starch results vary somewhat, indicating that after walking, swimming, picnicking, campground camping, and bicycling are the outdoor recreation activities that most Americans choose. Perhaps most interesting from a planning point of view are the changes in the number of people participating from 1994 to 2001 (last column in Table 4.3). The vast majority of the 49 activities examined had participation increases of at least 10% over the period, and three (i.e., kayaking, snowboarding, and personal watercraft use) were up by over 100%. Notice that many of the activities growing the fastest are physically demanding and require specialized equipment and skills. Only four activities decreased in the number of people participating: sightseeing, waterskiing, orienteering, and windsurfing. If the trends in percent participating are examined from 1983 through 2000, the biggest gaining activities were backpacking, hiking, snowmobiling, and walking. Over that period, only waterskiing and hunting lost participants overall (Cordell & Overdevest, 2001, p. 218). Cordell, Betz, Green, and Mou (2004) found some participation differences in terms of gender, race, urban versus rural residents, and region of the country, but there were far more similarities across these groupings than differences.

Table 4.3 Percent of U.S. adults participating in various outdoor recreation activities and percent change from 1994 to 2001 (results from two different national surveys)

Activity	Percent participating 2000 (Roper Starch)	Percent participating 2000–2001 (NSRE)	Percent change 1994–2001 (NSRE)
Kayaking[1]	5	3.46	185.66
Snowboarding	2	4.88	134.76
Personal watercraft use	5	9.53	119.33
Viewing or photographing fish		24.77	96.79
Snowmobiling	2	5.55	70.22
Ice Fishing		2.92	59.49
Sledding		14.65	56.18
Viewing wildlife	16	44.68	55.80
Backpacking	9	10.68	53.78
Day hiking[2]	19	33.25	51.80
Canoeing[1]	5	9.73	50.65
Bicycling	24	39.49	50.00
Horseback riding	5	9.68	47.99
Mountain climbing		6.03	46.52
Running or jogging	18	34.53	43.54
Coldwater fishing		13.58	42.77
Ice skating outdoors		6.87	42.69
Surfing		1.68	40.39
Developed camping[3]	26	26.38	38.71
Rafting		9.54	36.63
Driving off-road	7	17.46	36.50
Walking for pleasure[4]	57	82.97	35.32
Visiting archeological sites		20.91	30.71
Viewing birds/birdwatching	16	32.38	30.61
Big game hunting		8.41	28.92
Cross-country skiing	2	3.82	27.59
Rock climbing	4	4.32	26.86
Primitive camping[5]	8	16.01	24.75
Golfing	13	16.86	23.73
Small game hunting		7.23	21.43
Picnicking	36	54.49	20.91
Warmwater fishing		22.61	20.87
Migratory bird hunting		2.36	20.05
Saltwater fishing		10.35	18.99
Sailing	2	5.11	16.60
Swimming in lakes, streams[6]	39	41.74	16.58
Visiting nature centers		57.12	16.29
Visiting historic sites		46.20	13.91
Rowing	2	4.39	13.59
Motorboating	9	24.39	13.17
Downhill skiing	4	8.53	10.52
Snorkeling or scuba diving	3	7.26	9.25
Visiting beach or waterside		60.87	6.73
Anadromous fishing		4.41	6.21
Caving		4.34	0.33
Sightseeing		51.77	-0.49
Waterskiing	4	8.15	-0.63
Orienteering		2.00	-9.36
Windsurfing		0.82	-18.60

[1] Kayaking and canoeing were combined in the Roper Starch study.
[2] Simply called "hiking" in Roper Starch.
[3] Combines "campground camping—tent" and "campground camping—RV" in Roper Starch.
[4] Called "walking for fitness/recreation" in Roper Starch.
[5] Called "wilderness camping" in Roper Starch.
[6] Simply "swimming" in Roper Starch.

Sources: 2000 data are from Roper Starch Worldwide (2000, p. 31); 2000–2001 data and trends from 1994–2001 are from Cordell, Betz, Green, and Mou (2003) using National Survey on Recreation and the Environment (NSRE) data.

Implications for Outdoor Recreation

To provide the appropriate outdoor recreation opportunities in the appropriate places, we must understand our users and potential users. The most basic information is anticipating how many people are going to participate, what they will want to do, and what they hope to experience. Although projecting past trends cannot necessarily predict future use levels, there is every reason to believe that participation in outdoor recreation will continue to grow as will the number and styles of popular activities. Recent growth has been particularly strong in activities that are strenuous and require specialized equipment and skills. As participation in and diversity of outdoor recreation pursuits grow, there will be increasing use pressure on finite natural areas. It will be more important for planners to identify and to protect areas that can still be acquired for outdoor recreation and other purposes. Expanding uses will continue to escalate the potential for crowding, conflict, and environmental impacts in recreation settings. Managers need to be proactive in a number of ways to minimize these potential problems. We need to anticipate new and evolving activities as quickly and accurately as possible. We need to work with and through users and user groups to improve cooperation, sharing, and responsible use. We need to plan and manage carefully to assure that a wide range of opportunities are available as close as possible to where people live and work. We must also better understand the constraints to participation and work to minimize them as much as possible.

Of course growing numbers of users and increasing numbers and styles of recreation experiences also present important opportunities for planners and managers. The huge and growing number of outdoor recreation participants could represent a potent political block and an army of active volunteers for agencies and managers. Working to educate and constructively involve customers is an investment that could bring huge returns in terms of positive public opinion, support, and resources in the long run.

Summary

In this chapter we discussed the social and technological context of outdoor recreation and its management. We presented the most important trends and forces in ten groups: population changes, technological innovations, shifts in economic strengths and weaknesses, increased accountability of institutions and leaders, changes in transportation, concern for the environment and its effects on health, greater emphasis on partnerships, increasing pressure on public recreational resources, changes in recreation and leisure in general, and changes in outdoor recreation participation, in particular. We then described

some of the rapid and profound changes occurring in each of these areas that have important implications for our field now and in the future. We concluded, in every case, that planners and managers will need to broaden their perspectives and roles to be able to anticipate change and take advantage of tremendous opportunities. This will require new ways of thinking, new training and resources, and new partners, because each trend will continue to influence the amount of individual and social benefits that can be realized from use of outdoor recreation opportunities. One of the most important forces facing outdoor recreation is escalating and changing pressures on the finite amount of land and water available. We will examine these natural resources in more detail in the next chapter which begins Part II of this text.

Literature Cited

Cordell, H. K., McDonald, B. L., Teasley, R. J., Bergstrom, J. C., Martin, J., Bason, J., et al. (1999). History of outdoor recreation and nature-based tourism in the United States. In H. K. Cordell et al., *Outdoor recreation in American life: A national assessment of demand and supply trends* (pp. 219–321). Champaign, IL: Sagamore Publishing.

Cordell, H. K. and Overdevest, C. (2001). *Footprints on the land: An assessment of demographic trends and the future of natural lands in the United States.* Champaign, IL: Sagamore Publishing.

Cordell, H. K., Betz, C. J., Green, G. T., and Mou, S. (2004). *Outdoor recreation for 21st century America.* State College, PA: Venture Publishing, Inc.

Gartner, W. C. and Lime, D. W. (2000). *Trends in outdoor recreation, leisure and tourism.* New York, NY: CABI Publishing.

Godbey, G. (1997). *Leisure and leisure services in the 21st century.* State College, PA: Venture Publishing, Inc.

Godbey, G. and Graefe, A. (1993, April). Rapid growth in rushin' Americans. *American Demographics, 15*(4), 26–28.

Johnson, C. (1999). Participation differences among social groups. In H. K. Cordell et al., *Outdoor recreation in American life: A national assessment of demand and supply trends* (pp. 248–268). Champaign, IL: Sagamore Publishing.

Kane, R. L. (2002). *Healthy aging: Preventing disease and improving quality of life among older Americans.* Centers For Disease Control and Prevention. Retrieved January 5, 2002, from: http://www.cdc.gov/nccdphp/aag/aag_aging.htm

Levine, R. (1997). *A geography of time: The temporal misadventures of a social psychologist*. New York, NY: HarperCollins.

Liu, J., Dally, G. C., Ehrlich, P. R., and Luck, G. W. (2003). Effects of household dynamics on resource consumption and biodiversity. *Nature.* Retrieved from http://www.nature.com

Machlis, G. (2003, February). The fates of parks in modern America: Five trends that will shape our future. *Parks and Recreation*, 64–70.

McPhee, J. (1971). *Encounters with the Archdruid*. New York, NY: Farrar, Straus and Giroux.

Moore, R. L., Siderelis, C., Lee, J., Ivy, M. I., and Bailey, G. (1999). *1998 North Carolina State Trail and Greenway Survey*. Raleigh, NC: North Carolina Department of Environment and Natural Resources, Division of State Parks.

National Aeronautics and Space Administration. (2005). Earth's City Lights. Retrieved January, 20, 2005, from http://visibleearth.nasa.gov/cgi-bin/viewrecord?5826

O'Leary, J. (1999). International tourism in the United States. In H. K. Cordell et al., *Outdoor recreation in American life: A national assessment of demand and supply trends* (pp. 294–298). Champaign, IL: Sagamore Publishing.

Pew Research Center for the People and the Press. (2002). *What the world thinks in 2002: How the publics view their lives, their countries, the world, and America*. Washington, DC: Author.

President's Commission on Americans Outdoors. (1987). *Americans outdoors: The legacy, the challenge*. Washington, DC: Island Press.

Robinson, J. P. and Godbey, G. (1997). *Time for life: The surprising ways Americans use their time*. University Park, PA: The Pennsylvania State University Press.

Roper Starch Worldwide, Inc. (2000). *Outdoor recreation in America 2000: Addressing key societal concerns*. Washington, DC: The Recreation Roundtable. Retrieved from http://www.funoutdoors.com

Schor, J. (1992). *The overworked American: The unexpected decline of leisure*. New York, NY: Basic Books.

U.S. Census Bureau. (2001a). *Overview of race and Hispanic origin*. Retrieved from http://www.census.gov/prod/2001pubs/c2kbr01-1.pdf

U.S. Census Bureau. (2001b). *Population change and distribution*. Retrieved from http://www.census.gov/prod/2001pubs/c2kbr01-2.pdf

U.S. Census Bureau. (2001c). *Households and families: 2000*. Retrieved from http://www.census.gov/prod/2001pubs/c2kbr01-8.pdf

U.S. Census Bureau. (2001d). *Age: 2000*. Retrieved from http://www.census.gov/prod/2001pubs/c2kbr01-12.pdf

U.S. Census Bureau. (2002). *Birth, death, and net migration rate, and rate of natural increase and growth rate: 1998*. Retrieved January 20, 2003, from http://www.census.gov/mso/www/pres_lib/poptrnd/sld008.htm

U.S. Census Bureau. (2003). *PopClocks*. Retrieved January 13, 2003, from http://www.census.gov/main/www/popclock.html

U.S. Department of Transportation. (1994). *The national biking and walking study: Transportation choices for a changing America* (FHWA-PD-94-023). Washington, DC: U.S. Department of Transportation, Federal Highway Administration.

U.S. Treasury Department. (2002). *The debt to the penny*. Retrieved December 5, 2002, from http://www.publicdebt.treas.gov/opd/opdpenny.htm

United Nations Environment Programme. (2002, August). *Regional and global impacts of vast pollution cloud detailed in new scientific study*. Retrieved August 12, 2002, from http://www.unep.org/Documents/Default.asp?DocumentID=259&ArticleID=3103

World Bank. (1999, January–March). Why do savings rates vary across nations? *World Bank Policy and Research Bulletin, 10*(1), 1.

Part II

Outdoor Recreation Resources and Providers of Outdoor Recreation Opportunities

Chapter 5
Land and Water Resources for Outdoor Recreation

I recognize the rights and the duty of this generation to develop and use the natural resources of our land; but I do not recognize the right to waste them or rob, by wasteful use, the generations that come after us. (Theodore Roosevelt, 1910)

Learning Objectives

1. Identify who owns and manages the major categories of land and water available for outdoor recreation.
2. Discuss the relative quantities and availability of these outdoor recreation resources.

Outdoor recreation experiences result from activities that occur in and depend on a natural environment. As pointed out in Chapter 2, some recreation experience/benefit gestalts uniquely depend on the natural settings in which certain types of outdoor recreation occur. Thus, all outdoor recreation depends on the availability of natural and relatively natural settings. Such settings are at the heart of what are referred to as outdoor recreation resources. In Chapter 1 we noted the importance of defining outdoor recreation resources broadly to include any natural resources or related facilities that make outdoor recreation possible, such as land, water, vegetation, wildlife, air, minerals, mountains, forests, trails, marinas, picnic facilities, campgrounds, forest roads, and historical, cultural, and archeological resources. At the most basic level, however, none of these broader resources can exist without the land and waters where they are located. This chapter presents an overview of these most basic outdoor recreation resources in terms of types, scope, availability, and adequacy.

Types of Outdoor Recreation Resources

Only things we value are actually "resources" to us (Wellman, 1987). Viewed this way it is clear that outdoor recreation settings have become important resources in much of the world because of their popularity and scarcity. This is particularly true in more economically developed nations, where the relative scarcity and strong demand for outdoor recreation settings will likely assure they remain valuable resources.

Outdoor recreation depends on natural areas. The natural environment (as opposed to the built environment) is that part of our surroundings where the landscape and ecological processes have not been altered drastically by human activity. For instance, typical state parks (even ones where the forests are second growth) would be natural environments, while athletic fields would not. The athletic field may be more natural appearing than the typical commercial shopping area, but both are part of the built environment rather than the natural environment. There is obviously a continuum of naturalness from untouched wilderness areas at one extreme to completely altered and built-up settings at the other. Between these extremes are many settings where some parts are natural and some radically altered and unnatural. A typical golf course would be an example, where the fairways, greens, and bunkers are altered from their natural form, but the various fairways may be separated from one another by relatively natural landscapes.

Outdoor recreation can and does occur in virtually every natural and semi-natural setting in every part of the earth's biosphere (i.e., the area of life on the planet). This includes land (or lithosphere), water (or hydrosphere), and air (or atmosphere). Outdoor recreation occurs in all three major climactic zones (i.e., polar, temperate, and tropical) and in all environments (i.e., biomes or ecosystems) within all climactic regions (i.e., tundra, taiga, mountains, temperate forest, chaparral, desert, and tropical rainforest). It is not difficult to call to mind examples of outdoor recreation that take place throughout forests, prairies, rock faces, glaciers, and other terrestrial areas or marine settings from rivers and streams to lakes and oceans. Outdoor recreation also takes place in natural settings that may not come immediately to mind. For example, outdoor recreation takes place underwater in the case of scuba diving, above the earth in hang gliding and sky diving, and even under the earth in spelunking. Because of the diversity and scope of recreation settings and resources, many attempts have been made to classify them into distinct types.

One of the earliest attempts to classify recreation resources was by Clausen and Knetsch (1966) nearly four decades ago. They separated outdoor recreation areas into three broad types depending on naturalness, size, and relative location. Although little used today, their categories are useful as a starting point.

1. **Resource-based areas:** large, remote, natural areas such as typical national parks, national forests, federal wildlife refuges, and so forth.

2. **Intermediate areas:** areas having characteristics somewhere between those of resource-based and user-oriented areas in terms of access, remoteness, and naturalness. Examples would include many county and state parks as well as regional open-space systems.

3. **User-oriented areas:** areas relatively close to and accessible to where users live and work that are generally small in size with physical characteristics that are not too demanding. Examples would include most city parks and playgrounds.

Recreation resources are sometimes classified by geographic region. For example the 1974 Forest and Range-land Renewable Resources Planning Act (RPA) requires the USDA Forest Service to make periodic reports (now done every five years) of the renewable natural resources of the United States, including outdoor recreation and wilderness resources. The most recent RPA assessment classified resources into four geographic regions: North, South, Rocky Mountains/Great Plains, and Pacific Coast (Cordell et al., 1999, p. 32).

Other classifications make use of more generic resource types such as *land-based resources* and *water-based resources*. The most recent RPA report, for example, makes comparisons across the following types of resources (Cordell et al., 1999, p. 167):

- local facilities
- open space
- great outdoors
- wildlife land
- state and private forests
- western land
- camping areas
- other federal land
- large water bodies
- whitewater
- flatwater
- lowland rivers
- developed winter
- undeveloped winter

Another important distinction among natural areas is based on level or type of protected status. In much of the world the term *protected areas* is used to describe land or water areas where some legal protection is in place to protect the natural environment and associated resources. The World Conservation Union (IUCN) recognizes six categories of protected areas based on the level and type of human use appropriate in that area (UNEP World Conservation Monitoring Centre, 2003a).

- **Category Ia:** Strict nature reserve (protected area managed mainly for science)
- **Category Ib:** Wilderness area (protected area managed mainly for wilderness protection)
- **Category II:** National park (protected area managed mainly for ecosystem protection and recreation)
- **Category III:** Natural monument (protected area managed mainly for conservation of specific natural features)
- **Category IV:** Habitat/species management area (protected area managed mainly for conservation through management intervention)
- **Category V:** Protected landscape/seascape (protected area managed mainly for landscape/seascape conservation and recreation)
- **Category VI:** Managed resource protected area (protected area managed mainly for the sustainable use of natural ecosystems)

From the perspective of outdoor recreation planning and management, the first classification system to receive

Public "protected areas" as they are termed in most of the world can be classified based on purpose and types of protected status.

wide use in the United States was the one recommended in the summary volume of the Outdoor Recreation Resources Review Commission (1962). It proposed the following six classes of recreation settings:

1. High-density recreation areas
2. General outdoor recreation areas
3. Natural environment areas
4. Unique natural areas
5. Primitive areas
6. Historic and cultural sites

This classification system was used widely in the United States in the 1960s and 1970s, before another classifications system, known as the recreation opportunity spectrum (ROS) replaced it. The ROS system is popular and still used widely, because it takes into account not only the physical setting, but also the managerial setting and social setting as well and focuses particular attention on the types of recreation experiences that can be achieved in particular settings. (The ROS is discussed in detail in Chapter 12.)

One of the most common classifications of outdoor recreation lands and water, however, is based on the type of organization that manages the area. The most basic breakdown of this type simply distinguishes among areas owned and/or administered by public, private, or nonprofit organizations. This distinction is important from policy, planning, management, and administration perspectives and will be a basic distinction used throughout this text.

Public Sector

The public sector is comprised of tax-supported agencies of government at all levels. These agencies manage land for myriad purposes, but ultimately for the benefit of the citizens each particular public sector agency serves. Examples of public sector outdoor recreation resources include national parks, national forests, state recreation areas, and city parks.

Private Sector

From the purely economic perspective, the private sector is comprised of business enterprises and is sometimes referred to as the for-profit sector. Private sector organizations hold and manage land for many reasons, including to generate a profit for their owners and investors. Examples of private sector outdoor recreation resources include natural and semi-natural resort areas, timber and mineral company lands, private hunting reserves, and many private ski areas. Private sector lands also include lands owned by private individuals.

Nonprofit Sector

Although public sector agencies are in one sense nonprofit organizations as well, we use the phrase "nonprofit sector" to refer to the third distinct type of provider of outdoor recreation opportunities. The nonprofit sector is made up of nongovernmental organizations (NGOs). The nonprofit sector is sometimes called the independent, quasi-public, or charitable sector by NGOs in the United States. In the United States these are charitable, religious, scientific or educational organizations that have been declared tax-exempt by the Internal Revenue Service under the 501(c)3 provisions of the federal tax code. The YMCA and YWCA, Appalachian Trail Conference, most churches that operate camps, Boy Scouts and Girl Scouts of America, and nonprofit land trusts such as The Nature Conservancy and the Trust for Public Land are examples of nonprofit sector groups that own land that might be available for outdoor recreation.

Two important clarifications relate to these sectors that outdoor recreation professionals and their publics need to keep in mind. First, the land under the jurisdiction of public sector agencies is not owned by those agencies. It is "public land" in the sense that it is owned by the public. In other words, the citizens of a particular nation, state, city, or other jurisdiction are the landowners of those public lands and have associated rights and responsibilities. Those citizens, through their representatives in government, delegate the management and administration of that land to a particular agency. It is more accurate, therefore, to speak of national parks, National Park Service administered lands, or Park Service managed areas, rather than Park Service owned areas or government-owned land. The former phrases and the words "public lands" remind users and voters that they share the responsibility for the health of public lands and also remind us as managers that we are managing those lands in trust for all citizens. Second, it is important not to confuse "public land" with land open for public use. There are many examples of public sector managed areas not open to public access of any kind (including recreation), such as most military bases and some natural areas set aside for scientific research. Likewise, public sector areas are not the only ones open to public use. A great deal of land owned and administered by the private and nonprofit sectors is available for public recreation, but this does not make it public land.

Scope of Outdoor Recreation Resources

The Global Perspective

According to the most recent comprehensive tally, there are 30,350 protected areas worldwide covering more than 3.2 million square kilometers. This is an area larger than the United States, Canada, or China. If marine protected areas are excluded, 7.28% of the world's land area has some form of protected status (UNEP World Conservation Monitoring Centre, 2003b). These areas range in size from vast desert wildlife refuges to tiny isolated ocean islands. Nearly one third (30%) of the protected land area is in World Conservation Union (IUCN) Category II (i.e., national park) while 27% is in Category VI (i.e., managed resource protected area). Table 5.1 presents the number and extent of world protected areas by region. The regions are organized based on the number of square kilometers in protected status.

The United States Perspective

Through good fortune, the foresight of leaders and activists before us, and the diligence of current natural resource and recreation professionals, the United States has a large and diverse estate of protected natural lands and waters. The remainder of this chapter will introduce these actual and potential outdoor recreation resources in terms of their availability and adequacy.

Availability of Outdoor Recreation Resources

Determining accurately who owns and manages all the recreation lands and waters in the United States is a daunting task. The area is vast and land is constantly being bought, sold, transferred, and subdivided. The lands that comprise the United States are distributed roughly as shown in Figure 5.1, with nearly 60% being privately held and most of the remainder controlled by public sector agencies, primarily the federal government (Jensen, 1995). Data on lands owned or managed by the nonprofit sector are particularly difficult to identify and inventory at the national level. Nonprofit lands are included with the private sector total shown in Figure 5.1.

The percentages shown in Figure 5.1 are just a starting point when trying to understand the availability of outdoor recreation settings. First of all, public access is allowed on only a portion of the land managed by organizations from any of the three sectors in the United States. For example, when estimating the amount of land managed by the federal government available for outdoor recreation, a figure of 28% of the total U.S. land area is more accurate (Cordell et al., 1999, pp. 40–43). This figure excludes land managed by the Department of Defense, the General Services Administration, and miscellaneous agencies that do not typically provide outdoor recreation opportunities. The 28% figure includes only lands managed by the principal land managing agencies of the federal government (discussed in more detail in Chapter 6). The portion of federally managed land open to public recreation is somewhat smaller still, because about a quarter of national wildlife refuge lands and some lands at other special sites do not permit use by the general public. In addition, some public land is "land locked" by surrounding private land, meaning that the public agency does not have permanent legal rights across that adjacent private land to provide adequate public access to the lands it manages. By one estimate 14% of land managed by the Forest Service and Bureau of Land Management does not have adequate public access for various reasons (U.S. GAO, 1992). Similarly, not all

There are over 30,000 protected areas worldwide including this one in China. (Photo by Yu-Fai Leung)

Table 5.1   Number and extent of world protected areas by region

World Commission on Protected Areas Region	Number of Protected Areas	Square Kilometers Protected
North America	6,711	4,083,806
South America	1,437	1,838,826
Africa (Eastern/Southern)	927	1,318,615
Australia/New Zealand	5,882	1,109,024
North Africa/Middle East	542	1,037,576
East Asia	1,078	883,681
Africa (Western/Central)	343	755,836
North Eurasia	648	657,935
Europe	9,325	603,601
Southeast Asia	1,524	518,864
South Asia	719	212,924
Caribbean	579	108,637
Central America	384	86,049
Pacific	152	13,113
Antarctica	99	3,788

Source: Green and Paine (1997)

state and municipal lands are open or accessible to the public, and some Native American lands are not available to the general public for recreation.

The outdoor recreation situation on privately owned lands is more complex. Private sector landowners, whether individuals, partnerships, or corporations, can usually determine if and under what conditions other people may enter their property for any purpose, including outdoor recreation. Not surprisingly, only a portion of private land in the United States is open for public recreation. The most recent comprehensive study of outdoor recreation on private lands in the United States, completed in 1995–1996, shed some light on how accessible private lands are for public outdoor recreation. The National Private Land-owner Survey (NPLOS) examined rural tracts of private land 10 acres in size or larger (Teasley, Bergstrom, Cordell, Zarnoch & Gentle, 1999). Some form of access to non-owners was allowed on about half of the tracts studied, often by knowing the owner, asking permission, or leasing the land. At least some nonfamily members were allowed to recreate on the properties of 48% of the owners and about 15% of the owners had at least some of their land completely open to outsiders. About 29% of the owners, however, had closed some or all of their land to all outsiders (i.e., those not in their household). Access by the public to rivers and streams that flow though private lands is also problematic. Some states permit use of those waters for recreation by wading or boating from a public access point. Other states have laws declaring that, while the water is publicly owned, the stream bottom is privately owned. So, recreational users can float those rivers and streams but must not touch the bottom unless they have permission from the owners. Private sector providers of outdoor recreation opportunities are discussed in detail in Chapter 7.

Nonprofit sector lands are perhaps the most diverse in terms of public access. For example, most lands and outdoor recreation facilities owned by church camps or nonprofit clubs are available for members only, but may sometimes be used by nonmembers if they rent the facilities for a specific purpose. Nonprofit land trusts protect and hold land for many reasons. For example, The Nature Conservancy (TNC) one of the best known of the over 1,200 land trusts in the United States, has protected millions of acres of ecologically important land in the United States and 28 other countries since its inception in 1951 (The Nature Conservancy, 2003). These efforts have been carried out with many partners and do not always result in TNC actually owning or managing the protected lands. Many TNC preserves allow open public recreation, but some may be visited only as part of guided field trips. Still others are closed to the public or reserved for scientific research. Some nonprofit organizations, on the other hand, have the primary purpose of providing public access to natural areas.

Another important distinction in understanding the availability of outdoor recreation settings for public use is the fact that a particular owner may not control all the rights to a particular piece of land. Land ownership is best viewed as a bundle of rights that includes development rights, mineral rights, timber rights, access rights, and many more. An owner who has title to all the rights of a particular property is said to own that property in fee simple. Mixed ownership of these multiple rights can blur the distinction between public and private sector land, as in the case when private individuals or enterprises are granted use of public land areas for grazing or mineral extraction.

Adequacy of Outdoor Recreation Resources

Whether the amount of land available for outdoor recreation is adequate or not is a question with many answers. These answers generally depend on the values and priorities of who is asked.

Jensen (1995, pp. 48–49) used standards recommended by the National Recreation and Park Association to look at the relative availability of outdoor recreation areas by classification. He estimated another half million acres of user-oriented areas are currently needed and another 5 to 10 million acres of intermediate areas are needed in the eastern seaboard and densely populated areas. He felt there currently appears to be sufficient acreage of resource-oriented areas nationwide, but rightly points out that adequacy based on total acreage alone is misleading for several reasons. Particularly because almost no prospect of

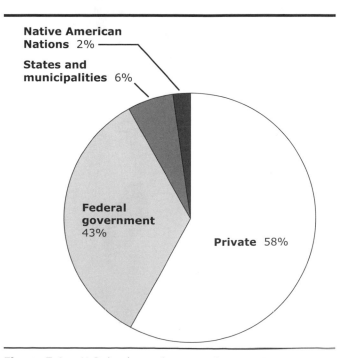

Figure 5.1 U.S. land area by type of jurisdiction

increasing this acreage exists and the existing resource-oriented areas can only accommodate a certain amount of use.

There are several important points to consider regarding the adequacy of the supply of natural areas for public outdoor recreation.

There is a finite and shrinking amount of potential outdoor recreation areas. Will Rogers' was right when he joked, "Land—they ain't making it anymore." The amount of natural land is fixed and when it is removed from its natural state for other purposes, regardless how important and appropriate, it is "gone." In some places, like many oceanfront communities, there is already no more available. Even the proportion of private land in the United States accessible for outdoor recreation appears to be decreasing. Between 1986 and 1996, for example, the proportion of private landowners allowing recreation access for people they did not know decreased from 25% to 15% (Teasley, Bergstrom, Cordell, Zarnoch & Gentle, 1999).

Outdoor recreation settings are in high and increasing demand. The most accessible and highest quality outdoor recreation areas are frequently under heavy pressure (from users, potential development, resource extraction, pollution, and so forth) and can only accommodate a certain amount of use before impacts reach unacceptable levels. These pressures will almost certainly increase on all outdoor recreation lands in the future and be very intense in many areas. Figure 5.2 shows where the most intense population pressures on public lands are expected to be through 2020 and Figure 5.3 shows where recreation demand pressures will be most severe for the same period.

Outdoor recreation lands and waters are not well-distributed geographically. The vast majority of publicly managed land is in western states (Figure 5.4, p. 80). This is particularly problematic in terms of population densities since most of the people in the United States live in the eastern half of the country. Only 7% of the federally managed land in the United States is in the eastern regions

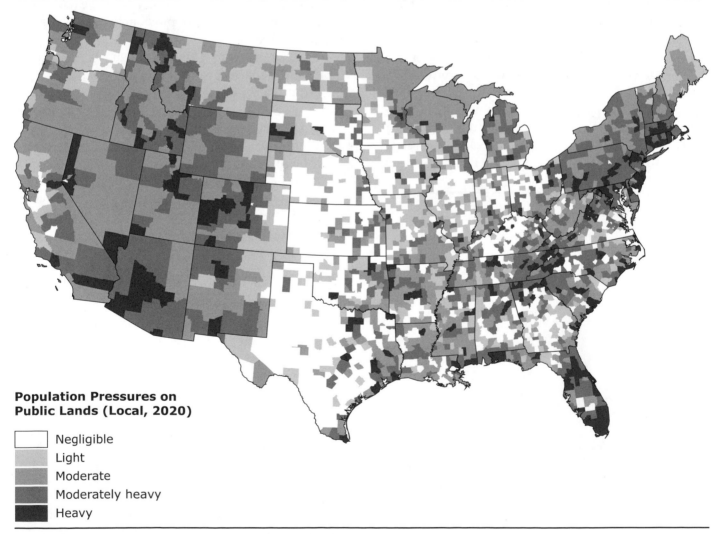

Population Pressures on Public Lands (Local, 2020)

- ☐ Negligible
- ☐ Light
- ☐ Moderate
- ☐ Moderately heavy
- ■ Heavy

Figure 5.2   Projected population pressures on public lands in 2020. Source: USDA Forest Service, 2004a

of the country, where 75% of the population lives (Betz, English & Cordell, 1999). Beginning in earnest with the President's Commission on Americans Outdoors (1987), there have been many calls to provide more outdoor recreation opportunities close to where people live and work, especially in and around urban centers.

Current use of existing outdoor recreation areas is uneven. People tend to use local and state public lands close to their homes for their outdoor recreation (President's Commission on Americans Outdoors, 1987). Because most trips are short, they choose the most accessible and highest quality areas easily available to them. In general, this leads to very heavy use in the best areas close to population centers but light use in other less accessible and less popular sites.

What does all this mean for outdoor recreation resources? Cordell and Overdevest (2001) conducted an extensive analysis of trends in the United States and how they will likely affect natural lands. They reached four primary conclusions:

1. Americans care about the natural environment.

2. Social changes in the next 100 years will be dramatic and unprecedented. Most important among these changes will be dramatic increases in population size, age, diversity, and urbanization, as well as significant transitions in rural areas and changes in leisure and recreation.

3. Some of the most rapid growth and development will occur in places where we still have substantial amounts of natural land. Development of natural lands will continue, at an accelerated rate; public lands will experience increasing recreation and resource use pressures, especially for water for agricultural uses; and pressures on wildlife, wildlife habitat, water resources, and wetlands will increase.

4. Acting on Americans' concern about the environment must happen promptly. If we are to arrest the loss of natural lands, Cordell and Overdevest (2001) believe there must be concerted action now. They

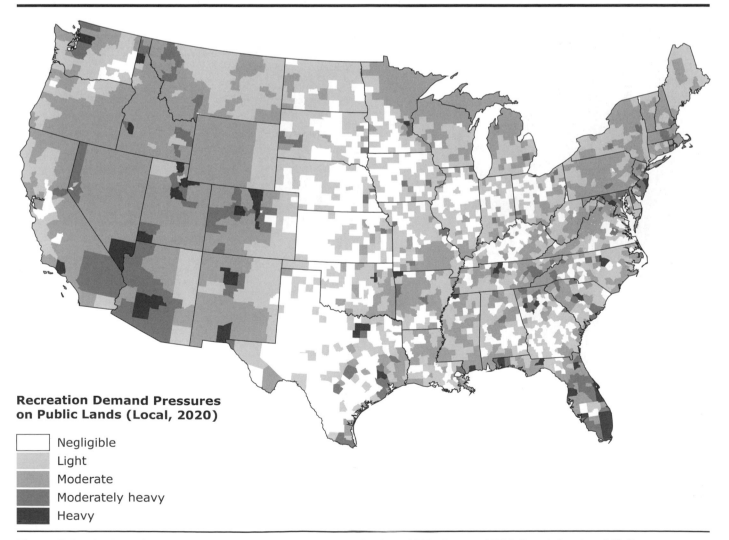

Recreation Demand Pressures on Public Lands (Local, 2020)

- Negligible
- Light
- Moderate
- Moderately heavy
- Heavy

Figure 5.3   Projected recreation demand pressures on public lands in 2020. Source: USDA Forest Service, 2004b

advocate focusing attention on the parts of the country where there are still relatively abundant natural lands, but where the trends indicate that demand and development pressures on those lands will be greatest. They identify these "hot spots" and call for collective action from all levels of the public sector and broad involvement of other organizations and publics. They also identify education as key and call for more accurate and timely information about issues facing natural areas for decision makers and citizens.

We agree with these conclusions and acknowledge the tremendous challenge of balancing economic growth with preserving and conserving natural areas and the resources located there. This is what sustainability is all about, and the future of outdoor recreation opportunities depends on the protection of natural areas and practicing sustainable management of all our land and water resources.

Summary

This chapter provided an overview of the natural and relatively natural settings on which all outdoor recreation depends. It began by pointing out the myriad environments and settings where outdoor recreation occurs and reviewing the many ways these types of settings can be categorized and organized. It then looked at outdoor recreation resources from a global perspective followed by a more detailed look at the situation in the United States, particularly in terms of the availability and adequacy of outdoor recreation resources. We concluded that although there are now vast areas of land available for outdoor recreation and the potential for more, there are also tremendous pressures on these lands and challenges that will almost certainly continue to increase. There is reason for optimism about the continued availability of high-quality outdoor recreation settings, but swift and decisive action at many levels and by many partners will be needed if these high-quality settings are to continue to be available

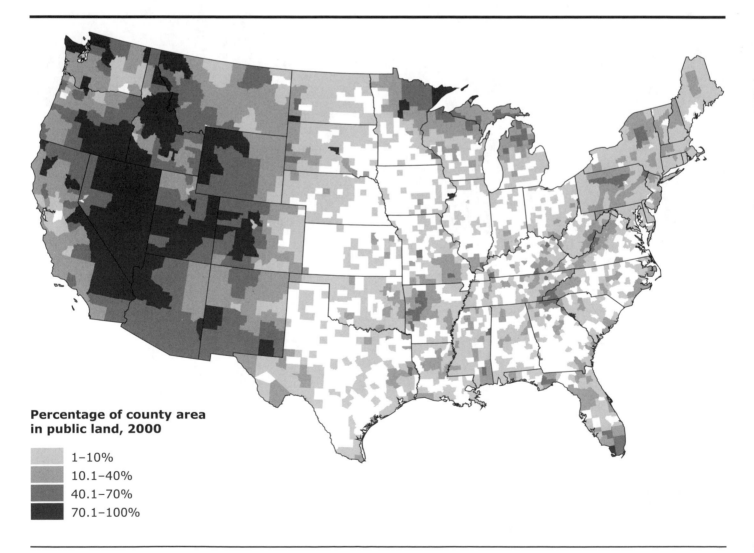

Percentage of county area in public land, 2000

- 1–10%
- 10.1–40%
- 40.1–70%
- 70.1–100%

Figure 5.4   Percentage of county area in public land, 2000. Source: USDA Forest Service, 2004c

in sufficient quantities and locations to meet growing demand. In the next five chapters, we look more closely at the organizations that provide outdoor recreation opportunities, beginning with public sector providers at the federal level.

Literature Cited

Betz, C. J., English, D. K., and Cordell, H. K. (1999). Outdoor recreation resources. In H. K. Cordell et al., *Outdoor recreation in American life: A national assessment of demand and supply trends* (pp. 39–182). Champaign, IL: Sagamore Publishing.

Clausen, M. and Knetsch, J. L. (1966). *Economics of outdoor recreation.* Baltimore, MD: Johns Hopkins Press.

Cordell, H. K., Betz, C. J., Bowker, J. M., English, D. B. K., Mou, S. H., Bergstrom, J. C., et al. (1999). *Outdoor recreation in American life: A national assessment of demand and supply trends.* Champaign, IL: Sagamore Publishing.

Cordell, H. K. and Overdevest, C. (2001). *Footprints on the land: An assessment of demographic trends and the future of natural lands in the United States.* Champaign, IL: Sagamore Publishing.

Green, M. J. B. and Paine, J. (1997, November 24–29). *State of the world's protected areas at the end of the twentieth century: From islands to networks.* Paper presented at IUCN World Commission on Protected Areas Symposium, Albany, Australia.

Jensen, C. (1995). *Outdoor recreation in America* (5th ed.). Champaign, IL: Human Kinetics.

Outdoor Recreation Resources Review Commission. (1962). *Outdoor recreation for America* (Summary Volume). Washington, DC: U.S. Government Printing Office.

President's Commission on Americans Outdoors (1987). *Americans outdoors: The legacy, the challenge.* Washington, DC: Island Press.

Roosevelt, T. (1910). Speech given in Osowatomie, Kansas, August 31, 1910.

Teasley, R. J., Bergstrom, J. C., Cordell, H. K., Zarnoch, S. J., and Gentle, P. (1999). Private lands and outdoor recreation in the United States. In H. K. Cordell et al., *Outdoor recreation in American life: A national assessment of demand and supply trends* (pp. 183–218). Champaign, IL: Sagamore Publishing.

The Nature Conservancy (2003). *Conservation results that speak for themselves.* Retrieved May 27, 2003, from http://nature.org/success/results.html

UNEP World Conservation Monitoring Centre (2003a). *1997 United Nations list of protected areas.* Retrieved April 2, 2003, from http://www.unep-wcmc.org/protected_areas/data/un_eintro2.htm

UNEP World Conservation Monitoring Centre (2003b). *1997 United Nations list of protected areas: Analysis of listed protected areas.* Retrieved April 2, 2003, from http://www.unep-wcmc.org/protected_areas/data/un_eanalysis.htm

USDA Forest Service. (2004a). Population pressures on public lands (Local, 2020). Athens, GA: USDA Forest Service, Recreation, Wilderness, Urban Forest, and Demographic Trends Research Group. Retrieved December 23, 2004, from http://www.srs.fs.usda.gov/trends/plpop.html

USDA Forest Service. (2004b). Recreation demand pressures on public lands (Local, 2020). Athens, GA: USDA Forest Service, Recreation, Wilderness, Urban Forest, and Demographic Trends Research Group. Retrieved December 23, 2004, from http://www.srs.fs.usda.gov/trends/plrec.html

USDA Forest Service. (2004c). Percentage of county area in public land cover, 2000. Athens, GA: USDA Forest Service, Recreation, Wilderness, Urban Forest, and Demographic Trends Research Group.

U.S. GAO (1992, April). *Federal lands: Reasons for and effects of inadequate public access.* Briefing report to the chairman, Subcommittee on National Parks and Public Lands, Committee on Interior and Insular Affairs, House of Representatives (GAO/RCED-92-116BR). Washington, DC: U.S. General Accounting Office.

Wellman, J. D. (1987). *Wildland recreation policy: An introduction.* New York, NY: John Wiley & Sons.

Chapter 6
Public Sector Providers

Caring for the land and serving the people. (Mission of the USDA Forest Service, 1999)

Learning Objectives

1. Explain the role and importance of the public sector in providing outdoor recreation opportunities.
2. Describe the key differences among the federal agencies that provide outdoor recreation opportunities.
3. Appreciate and explain how the differing purposes of public sector agencies affect their provision of outdoor recreation opportunities.

We have emphasized that outdoor recreation depends on natural environments and have also pointed out the counterintuitive fact that outdoor recreation professionals do not produce outdoor recreation per se. They provide outdoor recreation opportunities users can take advantage of to generate their own experiences and other important benefits. Like the USDA Forest Service, we define *outdoor recreation opportunities* as "the availability of a real choice for a user to participate in a preferred activity within a preferred setting, in order to realize those satisfying experiences which are desired" (USDA Forest Service, 1982, p. 4). Myriad organizations from the public, private, and nonprofit sectors can and do provide these outdoor recreation opportunities. This purpose of this chapter is to clarify what an outdoor recreation provider is and to introduce some of the major public sector providers.

Public Sector Providers of Outdoor Recreation Opportunities

An outdoor recreation provider can be broadly defined as any organization, enterprise, or individual that directly or indirectly provides outdoor recreation opportunities. Although there can be, and typically are, many components of an outdoor recreation opportunity, the essential and most basic one is the physical setting itself. All outdoor recreation requires a natural or semi-natural setting. Whether it is a vast, pristine wilderness or a small, highly modified urban park, a natural setting must be available if there is to be outdoor recreation of any kind. Conceptually, an organization that makes a natural setting available for recreation can be referred to as a *setting provider.* Of course, many outdoor recreation experiences also involve specialized equipment, facilities, information, or other services, which may or may not be provided by the setting

provider. Figure 6.1 (p. 84) illustrates how providers of outdoor recreation settings, equipment, facilities, and other services interact to make outdoor recreation opportunities available. In practice, of course, most providers operate in partnership and collaboration with others to provide outdoor recreation opportunities. The partners not directly responsible for the setting itself can be referred to as *associated providers* of outdoor recreation opportunities. These partners may manufacture, sell, or otherwise produce and provide the equipment, facilities, services, programming, expertise, and information needed for outdoor recreation experiences to occur. Associated providers are frequently private or nonprofit sector organizations, whereas the providers of outdoor recreation settings and the facilities located there are most often public sector land managing agencies. There are, of course, many exceptions to this general rule, which we will point out in the next several chapters. The purpose of this chapter is to introduce the major public sector providers of outdoor recreation opportunities. We begin with federal level public agencies in the United States, and then discuss state, regional, county, and municipal agencies.

Public sector agencies play a crucial role in providing outdoor recreation opportunities in most nations, including the United States. This is due in part to the sheer volume of opportunities they provide and in part to the nature of those opportunities. About 40% of all the land in the United States is controlled by the public sector. About a third of the total land in the United States is managed by various federal agencies alone. Since only about half of private landowners open their land to people outside the owners' families, and only about 15% of private owners allow access to anyone who wants it (Teasley, Bergstrom, Cordell, Zarnoch & Gentle, 1999), public lands provide the vast majority of outdoor recreation opportunities for most Americans. Perhaps more importantly, a remarkable number of special places are included in this public land "estate," including national parks, forests, monuments, wildlife refuges, wilderness, and recreation areas; state parks and forests; regional, county, and municipal parks and open space; and many more. Most of the remote and primitive settings as well as many of the natural areas close to major metropolitan areas are the responsibility of public sector providers. This is particularly true of the lands and waters managed by federal outdoor recreation providers. We begin with the major federal land managing agencies that provide opportunities for outdoor recreation and then address the federal water project agencies.

Federal Recreation Providing Agencies

To the uninitiated, federal agencies in general can be a confusing collection of mysterious acronyms. This can be true even when the discussion is limited to the major federal agencies that manage land and water resources and provide outdoor recreation opportunities in the United States. Many outdoor recreation users do not know (or even care) which agency is managing the lands they are visiting. However, each of these agencies was created for a specific and distinct purpose and each manages the lands under its jurisdiction accordingly. Naturally these differences affect the outdoor recreation opportunities available on the lands they manage.

To begin, it is important to recognize that none of the federal land and water managing agencies in the United States is identified as an "outdoor recreation agency" per se. Instead, each one exists within one of three cabinet level departments and has broader purposes. However, each one we will be discussing provides outdoor recreation opportunities as one of their important purposes, and in the case of USDA Forest Service lands, recreation is the "dominant use" (Dombeck, 1997). Because these agencies report directly to cabinet level departments, they are technically at the "bureau" level, but only three of the major ones we will discuss actually have that term in their name. Regardless of the agency name, which federal department each one exists within dictates, more or less, the broad purposes of the agencies within it, particularly in terms of each agency's primary focus of management. When considering the primary focus of how lands and waters are managed, there are three broad possibilities:

1. **Preservation** is management directed toward protecting natural and cultural/historic resources indefinitely, with on-site use permitted to the extent that it does not deplete or cause irreversible damage to those protected resources.

2. **Conservation** is management directed toward the wise and sustainable use of resources over the long term. Many uses may be allowed, but only in ways designed to avoid depletion and irreversible damage and only after long-term benefits are judged to justify the costs to resources and society.

3. **Exploitation** is management directed toward extracting the maximum economic gains from resources. This approach is often associated with a short-term focus, commercial enterprises, and non-renewable resources.

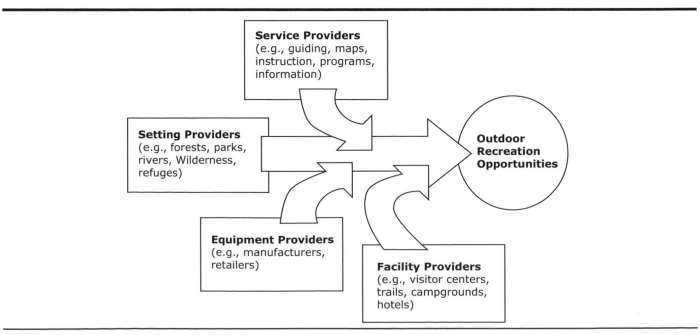

Figure 6.1   Interrelationships of different types of outdoor recreation providers

In general, the agencies within the Department of Agriculture have a primary management focus of conservation of natural resources while providing for the wise and sustainable use of those resources (e.g., crops, timber, minerals, domestic livestock, water) for the public good. In contrast, some of the agencies of the Department of Interior, with some exceptions, tend to have a primary management focus of preservation. For example, the National Park Service is charged with the long-term protection of resources and special places while providing for uses compatible with that protection. Table 6.1 presents six major federal recreation opportunity providing agencies organized by department, along with each agency's primary focus of management. Recognize, however, that these management generalizations are just that. For example, the primary focus of management of the USDA Forest Service and Bureau of Land Management is conservation.

However, each of these agencies also manage large areas of their lands as designated Wilderness for the purpose of preservation.

Table 6.2 presents a comparison of these various federal agencies in terms of some key outdoor recreation-related statistics. The agencies are presented in order by the level of outdoor recreation use that occurs on the lands they manage. The level of outdoor recreation use is presented in both recreation visitor days (RVDs), units of 12 person hours of recreation (e.g., 1 person staying 12 hours or 12 people staying 1 hour each), and recreation visits (a single visit to the area by one person regardless of length of stay) where data are available. These and other ways of quantifying outdoor recreation participation will be further discussed in Chapter 15.

Most of the figures in Table 6.2 are estimates of things that are changeable and/or very difficult to quantify

Table 6.1   Major federal outdoor recreation opportunity providing agencies and their parent departments

Department	Agency	Primary Focus Of Management
Department of Agriculture	USDA Forest Service (USFS)	Conservation
Department of Interior	National Park Service (NPS) Bureau of Land Management (BLM) U.S. Fish and Wildlife Service (FWS) Bureau of Reclamation (BOR)	Preservation Conservation Preservation and conservation Conservation
Department of Defense	U.S. Army Corps of Engineers (CoE)	Water projects

Source: Based, in part, on Dennis, 2001, p. 48

Table 6.2   Comparisons of major federal land managing agencies in the United States

Agency	Millions of Recreation Visits in 1996	Millions of RVDs[a] in 1996	Millions of Acres Managed	Number of "Areas" Managed	Annual Budget[b] (in billions)	Number of Employees in 2003[c]
USDA Forest Service	859.2	341.2	191.6	155 national forests and grasslands	4.7	32,000
U.S. Army CoE	375.7	212.0	11.6	500 projects	4.6	35,250
National Park Service	265.8	104.3	83.2	388 units	2.7	20,505
Bureau of Land Management	58.9	72.8	267.6	700 administrative sites	2.0	10,916 (2002)
Bureau of Reclamation	38.3	27.3	6.5	600 dams and reservoirs	1.1	5,634 (2002)
U.S. Fish and Wildlife Service	29.5	N/A	90.5	879 refuges	2.0	8,908

[a] An RVD (recreation visitor day) is an accumulated 12 hours of recreation use by one or more persons.
[b] For 2003 federal fiscal year.
[c] Estimates of the total number of agency employees, not just those working in outdoor recreation.

Sources: Stenger (1999, pp. 282–283) for recreation use data; Betz, English, and Cordell (1999, p. 41) for acres managed; U.S. Department of Interior (2003b) and agency websites for remainder

accurately. Therefore, the figures should be used for broad comparisons only. Figure 6.2 shows the locations of the major federal public land areas across the United States.

The remainder of this section presents a brief summary of each of the major federal public sector land and water managers that provide outdoor recreation opportunities. That discussion is divided into three subsections. The first focuses on federal land managing agencies. The next examines federal agencies that focus on developing and managing "water projects" and the final subsection looks at other federal agencies that are involved in outdoor recreation.

Federal Land Management Agencies

USDA Forest Service

Mission: The agency's mission is to ensure, for present and future generations, the long-term health, diversity, and productivity of the land. The phrase "Caring for the Land and Serving People" captures the essence of this mission. (*1998 Report of the Forest Service*)

The USDA Forest Service (USFS) is a multiple-use agency (as opposed to single or limited-use agency). In the broadest sense it is a *conservation*-oriented agency as opposed to a *preservation*-oriented one. When compared to the other major federal land managing agencies, the USFS receives more outdoor recreation use than any of the others and, with the exception of the Bureau of Land Management, is responsible for managing the most land as well. As set forth in the Multiple-Use Sustained Yield Act of 1960, the USFS manages the lands under its jurisdictions for the following primary uses: timber, range (grazing), water, fish and wildlife, and recreation. As set forth in it goals under the 1993 Government Performance and Results Act, the USFS operates to ensure sustainable ecosystems, to provide multiple benefits for people within the capability of those ecosystems, and to ensure organizational effectiveness.

The USFS is headed by its "Chief," its traditional shorthand for its "Chief Forester." The Chief reports to the Department of Agriculture's Under Secretary for Natural Resources and Environment who, in turn, reports directly to the Secretary of Agriculture on the President's Cabinet.

The Department of Agriculture also oversees the nation's crop and domestic livestock programs, cooperative extension service, food stamps, and much more, making the USFS context one of wise and sustainable use of resources and the production of important products for people.

The Forest Service is an agency rich in history and tradition. The following key historical events helped to establish the context for the USFS today:

- Congress establishes the Division of Forestry in 1886.

- Forest Reserve Act of 1891 authorizes the President to establish Forest Reserves.

- Organic Act of 1897 provides additional protections for Forest Reserves, and authorizes and funds development for minerals, water, and timber.

- Transfer Act of 1905 transfers responsibility for the Forest Reserves to the Bureau of Forestry, which are soon renamed to become the National Forests and the USDA Forest Service, respectively, with Gifford Pinchot as its first Chief Forester. The Transfer Act also moves Forest Reserves from the Department of Interior to the Department of Agriculture.

- Operation Outdoors begins in 1957 as a five-year USFS effort to improve recreation facilities available in the National Forest System.

- Multiple-Use Sustained Yield Act of 1960 further clarifies the uses of national forest lands. This is the first congressional mandate that the Forest Service should provide outdoor recreation opportunities.

- Forest and Rangeland Renewable Resources Planning Act of 1974 (RPA) mandates long-range forest assessments be developed and updated periodically.

- National Forest Management Act of 1976 requires the Forest Service to develop, and periodically revise, functionally integrated resource management plans for each national forest and national grassland.

Gifford Pinchot, the first Chief of the Forest Service, designed the agency to be a decentralized, on-the-ground, focused operation. His intent was that rangers would have the authority to take actions within defined limits and according to specified policies and procedures. These were spelled out in a *Use Book*, which Pinchot assured was small enough to fit in the ranger's hip pocket (Clawson, 1983, p. 33). Organizationally, the USFS remains quite decentralized. Its basic structure includes the Washington Office (WO) headquarters in Washington, DC, and nine geographic regions. Each region has a Regional Office (RO) headed by a Regional Forester. Because of various consolidations over the years there is no R-7 and the Alaska Region is actually R-10. There are 155 national

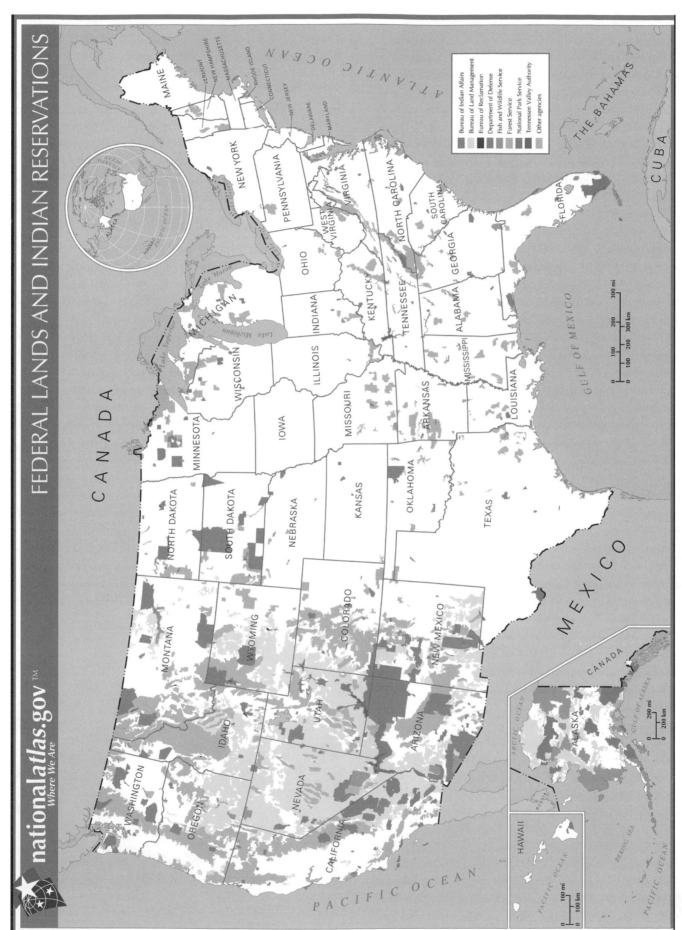

forests each headed by a Forest Supervisor who reports to the appropriate Regional Forester. The Forest Supervisors' Offices are often referred to as SOs. The 155 national forests are further divided into a total of 666 districts. These USFS districts are the smallest, and in many ways the most important, administrative units in the agency. A District Ranger heads each district.

To make such a large decentralized organization effective, the USFS still uses a version of Pinchot's original pocket-sized *Use Book*. Now commonly called the "regs," this modern-day version of the *Use Book* has expanded to over 30 linear feet of manuals, specifications, and procedures to give guidance for managing "by the book." Like many organizations, the USFS utilizes a structure with two types of positions: line and staff. Line positions are ones in the chain of command that have the authority to make policy decisions, issue directives and execute legal and financial contracts at the level appropriate to that position. Line positions are held responsible for the results of decisions made. The chain of command in this line begins with the District Ranger and moves up though the Forest Supervisor, the Regional Forester, and ultimately to the Chief. Staff positions, on the other hand, offer advice, assistance, services, reports, and other types of support. There are staff officers supporting each level in the chain of command. Recreation is one of many staff functions in the USFS, along with range management, timber management, public information, engineering, fire management, personnel, and civil rights. The name of the recreation staff in the USFS headquarters is the Recreation, Heritage and Wilderness Program Staff Group.

The USFS classifies its resources and programs into broad areas or functions. The three primary ones are the National Forest System, Research and Development, and State and Private Forestry.

The National Forest System (NFS)

The 191.8 million acres under USFS jurisdiction are extremely diverse. The lands managed are classified into the following types of areas:

- National Forests
- National Grasslands
- National Scenic Areas
- National Recreation Areas
- National Trails
- National Wild and Scenic Rivers
- National Monuments

These last four classifications are not unique to the USFS. These same classifications are used by other federal agencies, such as the National Park Service and Bureau of Land Management. It is also important to note that the USFS is responsible for managing about 17% of all designated Wilderness areas in the United States.

Research and Development (R&D)

The USDA Forest Service operates eight Research Stations around the country, representing the largest forest research program in the world. Research on outdoor recreation and outdoor recreation management are important areas of research carried out by scientists at these research stations and associated universities.

State and Private Forestry (S&PF)

This function encourages the conservation and wise management of forests on private lands, state lands, and in urban areas. Much of this work is accomplished by USFS personnel who provide technical assistance to other agencies, organizations, and individuals.

The other USFS functional areas have less direct focus on outdoor recreation and include Business Operations Programs and Legislation, and Office of the Chief Financial Officer. The major program areas of the USFS are shown in Figure 6.3.

An important aspect of Forest Service operations is the use of nationwide initiatives to direct this large and decentralized organization. These periodic initiatives typically come from the Washington Office and serve to focus attention on important, timely issues. Examples of recent USFS initiatives include the following:

The Recreation Agenda (2000): Established guidance to help meet the needs and expectations of forest recreation users while protecting the health and integrity of the land (USDA Forest Service, 2000). The Recreation Agenda set forth five key areas of concentration for recreation efforts:

1. improving the settings for outdoor recreation

USDA Forest Service areas receive more outdoor recreation visits and recreation visitor days (RVDs) than areas managed by any other U.S. federal agency.

2. improving visitor satisfaction with facilities and programs

3. improving educational opportunities for the public about conservation, land stewardship, and responsible recreation

4. strengthening relationships with private entities and volunteer-based and nonprofit organizations

5. establishing professionally managed partnerships and intergovernmental cooperative efforts

The Natural Resource Agenda (1998): As a national strategy for planning and managing USFS resources, the Natural Resource Agenda focused attention on watershed restoration and maintenance, sustainable forest ecosystem management, forest roads, and recreation.

New Perspectives for Managing the National Forest System (1992): Redirected USFS operations and programs to an ecosystems management approach and moved the

agency toward a more equal, locally established balance among the multiple uses of the National Forest System.

The Year of the Sweet Smelling Toilet (1990): Not all initiatives have significant national policy implications. This initiative was a systemwide effort to respond to customer concerns about pit toilet odors and sanitation. It resulted in a far better pit toilet design now being used systemwide.

Current Challenges Facing the USDA Forest Service

The Forest Service has had a long and proud history of managing the vast national forest and grassland system and providing opportunities for outdoor recreation. Like all land managing agencies, of course, the USFS does face difficult challenges. Many of these stem from the fact that the USFS manages very diverse resources for a wide variety of mandated uses, including producing timber and other commodities for the nation. Inevitably, controversies

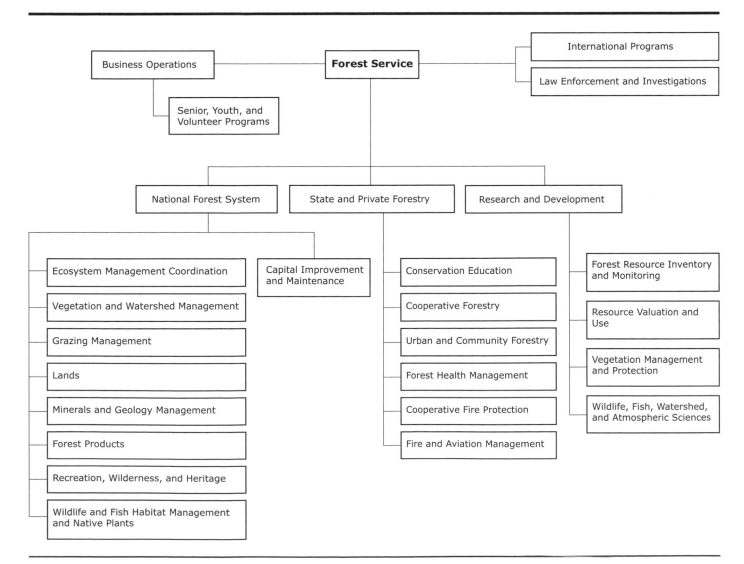

Figure 6.3 Major program areas within the USDA Forest Service. Source: Schuster and Krebs (2003, p. 3)

develop related to the differing priorities that different publics attach the USFS managed resources. Such differences have led to increased litigation of USFS decisions and expensive legal battles. Among the more visible of these controversies are ones revolving around the following:

- timber harvest practices and quantities (e.g., below-cost timber sales)
- old-growth forests
- endangered species protection (e.g., the spotted owl in the Pacific northwest)
- roads versus trails priorities and expenditures
- fire management practices

National Park Service

Mission: The National Park Service preserves unimpaired the natural and cultural resources and values of the National Park System for the enjoyment, education, and inspiration of this and future generations. The Park Service cooperates with partners to extend the benefits of natural and cultural resource conservation and outdoor recreation throughout this country and the world. (National Park Service, 2003a)

The primary purpose of the National Park Service (NPS) is preservation of the nation's most special places. In that sense the NPS operates under what has been called a "single-use" or "limited-use" concept (Jensen, 1995) as opposed to a multiple-use concept as is the case with the Forest Service. As enacted by the National Park Service Organic Act of 1916, areas administered by NPS are established:

> to conserve the scenery and the natural and historic objects and the wildlife therein and to provide for the enjoyment of the same in such manner and by such means as will leave them unimpaired for the enjoyment of future generations. (National Park Service Organic Act, 1916)

The Park Service, too, has a rich and important history. Some of the key historical events for NPS include the following:

- Yellowstone becomes the first national park in the world in 1872.

- The Antiquities Act of 1906 authorizes the President to establish national monuments.
- The Organic Act of 1916 creates the National Park Service with Stephen Mather as its first Director.
- "Mission 66," begun in 1956, sets out to refurbish NPS areas in preparation for the agency's 50th anniversary
- General Authorities Act of 1970 clarifies the authorities needed to include all the diverse areas administered by the NPS into one National Park System.
- The size of the National Park System doubles in size with passage of the Alaska National Interest Lands Conservation Act of 1980.

The National Park Service administers a relatively small land area, but that area is unique, extremely diverse, and irreplaceable. The NPS manages what are often referred to as the natural and cultural "crown jewels" of the United States. At last count there were 388 units of 19 different types encompassing 83 million acres, of which nearly 60% is located in Alaska. There are now National Park System units in every state except Delaware that range in size and character from Yellowstone and the Grand Canyon to the Blue Ridge Parkway, the Washington Monument, Gettysburg, and the Clara Barton National Historic Site. NPS units are created either by an act of Congress or, in the case of national monuments, a Presidential proclamation. To be included in the National Park System an area must be of national significance, be suitable and feasible for inclusion, and not be more appropriately managed by some other organization. However, the President can designate national monuments and Congress can establish park areas that do not fully meet these criteria (National Park Service, 1999b).

The NPS was reorganized in 1995 and 1996. At that time its ten regions were consolidated into seven to improve efficiency. In this process about 25% of employee positions in the Washington office were eliminated. The seven NPS regions report directly to the Director of the NPS, who in turn reports to the Secretary of the Interior. Some regions have grouped their units into "clusters" based on similarity of ecosystems rather than simple geographic boundaries. Figure 6.4 shows the location and distribution of the NPS regions.

Each of the major units has a superintendent who reports to the appropriate region. The NPS also operates various "national program centers" that support NPS operations. These include the following, which have particular relevance for outdoor recreation:

- National Center for Recreation and Conservation
- Natural Resource Center

- Interpretive Design Center
- Cultural Resources Center
- Partnership Service Center

Each NPS unit is classified as one of the following types (National Park Scrvice, 2003b). The current number of units by classification is summarized in Table 6.3

National Parks are generally large natural places with a wide variety of resources. Hunting, mining and consumptive activities are not normally allowed (e.g., Yellowstone, Great Smoky Mountains, Grand Canyon, and Everglades National Parks).

National Monuments are generally a single nationally significant resource. Typically much smaller and less diverse than national parks, National Monuments can be set aside by Presidential proclamation from lands owned or controlled by the government and may be landmarks, structures or other objects of natural, historic or scientific interest (e.g., Devil's Tower, Booker T. Washington, Fossil Butte, Statue of Liberty National Monuments).

Table 6.3   Number of National Park System units by classification

International Historic Site	1
National Battlefields	11
National Battlefield Parks	3
National Battlefield Site	1
National Historical Parks	41
National Historic Sites	77
National Lakeshores	4
National Memorials	29
National Military Parks	9
National Monuments	75
National Parks	56
National Parkways	4
National Preserves	18
National Recreation Areas	18
National Reserves	2
National Rivers	5
National Scenic Trails	3
National Seashores	10
National Wild and Scenic Rivers	10
Parks (other)	11
Total	**388**

Source: National Park Service (2002)

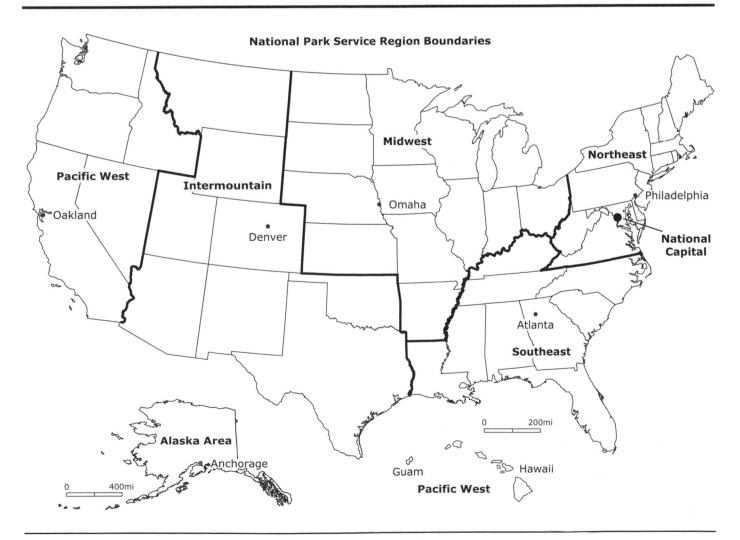

National Park Service Region Boundaries

Figure 6.4   Location of NPS regions. Source: National Park Service (2005)

National Preserves are areas with characteristics similar to national parks, but where Congress continues to permit hunting, trapping, or oil/gas exploration and extraction (e.g., Denali and Big Cypress National Preserves).

National Memorials are units that commemorate a significant historic person or episode (e.g., the Lincoln Memorial, Mount Rushmore, and USS Arizona National Memorials).

National Historic Sites are usually single historical features directly associated with its subject (e.g., Ford's Theater, Frederick Douglass, Golden Spike, and Frederick Law Olmsted National Historic Sites).

National Historic Parks are generally historic parks that extend beyond single properties or buildings (e.g., Minute Man, Nez Perce, and Klondike Gold Rush National Historical Parks).

National Battlefields include National Battlefield Sites, National Battlefield Parks, and National Military Parks. All preserve and commemorate important military actions (e.g., Antietam National Battlefield, Richmond National Battlefield Park, and Gettysburg National Military Park).

National Seashores are Atlantic, Pacific, and Gulf coastal areas. Some are developed, some primitive and hunting is sometimes allowed (e.g., Cape Hatteras, Padre Islands, and Point Reyes National Seashores).

National Lakeshores are much like National Seashores, but located on the Great Lakes (e.g., Apostle Islands and Indiana Dunes National Lakeshores).

National Parkways are slow-speed scenic touring roads with parkland paralleling the roadway. National Parkways often connect cultural sites (e.g., Blue Ridge Parkway, George Washington Memorial Parkway).

National Rivers are National, Wild, Scenic, and Recreation Rivers that fall under this category of protected segments of nationally significant rivers (e.g., New River Gorge National River, Missouri National Recreation River, Rio Grande National Wild and Scenic River).

National Trails are National Scenic and National Historic Trails authorized under the National Trails System Act of 1968 (e.g., Appalachian and Pacific Crest National Scenic Trails; Santa Fe, and Lewis and Clark National Historic Trails).

National Recreation Areas are areas close to major population areas and often centered on large reservoirs, which combine scarce open space with preservation of significant historic and natural resources. National Recreation Areas (NRAs) are located where they can provide outdoor recreation for large numbers of people (e.g., Gateway, Golden Gate, and Delaware Water Gap National Recreation Areas).

The units are not the only areas of focus or activity for the NPS. The NPS also operates numerous programs that extend well beyond the lands actually under the agency's jurisdiction (National Park System Advisory Board, 2001). Some of the programs most relevant to outdoor recreation include the following:

- Land and Water Conservation Fund State Assistance Program
- Federal Lands to Parks Program
- Wild and Scenic Rivers Partnership Program
- Urban Park and Recreation Recovery Program
- Hydropower Recreation Assistance Program
- American Battlefield Protection Program
- Cultural Resources
- Historic Landscape Initiative
- National Historic Landmarks Assistance Initiative
- National Heritage Areas Program

Many of the NPS programs that frequently focus on lands outside of traditional park unit boundaries are part of its National Center for Recreation and Conservation (NCRC). The NCRC fulfills the mandates of the Outdoor Recreation Act, Land and Water Conservation Fund Act, Wild and Scenic Rivers Act, National Trails System Act, and Urban Park and Recreation Recovery Act. The center provides various kinds of support and technical assistance to the field through grant programs such as the Land and Water Conservation Fund Program, and Urban Park and Recreation Recovery Program. It also operates other programs, including the following:

- Rivers, Trails, and Conservation Assistance Program
- Wild and Scenic Rives Act Coordination
- Nationwide Rivers Inventory
- Rivers Conservation Information/Outreach

The National Park Service manages the "Crown Jewels" of U.S. public lands like Yellowstone National Park.

- Federal Lands-to-Parks Program
- Long-Distance Trails Program
- Recreation Information/Coordination

Current Challenges Facing the National Park Service

The National Park Service has had a long and proud history of preserving special places and providing opportunities for outdoor recreation. Like all land managing agencies, of course, NPS does face vexing challenges.

Preservation versus use dilemma. The Organic Act of 1916, which established the NPS, stated the NPS is to

> conserve the scenery and the natural and historic objects and the wildlife therein and to provide for the enjoyment of the same in such manner and by such means as will leave them unimpaired for the enjoyment of future generations. (NPS Organic Act, 1916)

This legal charge sets up a tension for NPS in terms of how it manages the irreplaceable areas under its jurisdiction. Preserving special places and making them available for public use can require a delicate balance because certain types and levels of use can damage the very resources the agency is charged to protect. Like other "limited-use" agencies that emphasize preservation, the NPS tends to be more restrictive in managing outdoor recreation that occurs in its units. The NPS generally interprets its mission to mean that outdoor recreation is an appropriate use if it does not compromise the integrity of the resources where it takes place. The results of a recent national survey indicate Americans are supportive of the NPS emphasis on protection and preservation (see Table 6.4).

Pressures on park resources. There have been steady and significant increases in use of the National Park System for much of its history, and unintentional damage and willful violations are both on the rise. Overall, resource violations increased 123% over the five-year period ending in 1998 (National Park Service, 1999b). Poaching, cutting trees, theft and damage of Native American artifacts and Civil War relics, and other resource issues have become serious problems for some units. For example, studies show that park visitors have illegally removed approximately 12 tons of petrified wood from Petrified Forest National Park (National Park Service, 1999b). The American public is apparently pessimistic about whether damage and deterioration of park resources will be successfully addressed anytime soon. When asked to look 25 years into the future, 54% believed the condition of National Parks would worsen (Haas & Wakefield, 1998).

Observers point to several factors related to increasing pressures on park resources. First, there has been a rapid expansion of the National Park System, but not a corre-

sponding increase in budget appropriations. For many units, an increasingly large portion of the budgets has been directed toward "visitor services" rather than resource protection. A related issue is sometimes referred to as *undeserving units*. Critics feel many NPS units are not the kind of natural or historic "crown jewels" the Park Service was originally intended to manage. These so-called *orphan parks* are sometimes established by political pork barrel (also called *park barrel*) maneuvering rather than formal studies of potential units and subsequent authorization by Congress. Critics believe less deserving units drain funding from the most important units in the system, thereby contributing to an overall decline in resource protection. Serious pressures on park resources are challenges that are not likely to go away because they are, in many ways, inherent in the NPS mission to preserve resources and simultaneously provide for the public enjoyment of them.

Other important NPS challenges and opportunities. Other challenges and opportunities facing the NPS have been identified by the NPS and concerned observers. These include

- the role of private enterprise in the parks and concessions reform
- repair and maintenance backlogs
- park user fees and entrance fee reform
- the transfer of "surplus" military lands into the National Park System
- science and research needs
- maintaining biodiversity
- inadequate ranger pay, housing, and training
- impacts from adjacent development and pollution sources
- buffers for park boundary areas

Table 6.4 Percent of people listing each of the following as a "very important" reason for having national parks

Preserve America's most significant places for future generations	88%
Protect wildlife habitat	78%
Preserve natural ecosystems	73%
Protect air and water quality	73%
Provide opportunities to experience natural peace and the sounds of nature	72%
Preserve our country's culture and history	70%
Educate people about nature, history and culture	69%
Preserve historic buildings and sites	66%
Demonstrate environmentally sound management practices	53%
Provide recreational opportunities	49%
Conserve natural areas for research and scientific study	46%
Provide income for tourist industry	14%

Source: Haas and Wakefield (1998)

To address these challenges and to better accomplish their important mission, the National Park System Advisory Board (2001, p. 9) recommended, among other things, that the NPS do the following:

- Embrace its mission as educator and become a more significant part of America's educational system by providing formal and informal programs for students and learners of all ages inside and outside park boundaries.

- Encourage the study of America's past by developing programs based on current scholarship, linking specific places to the narrative of history, and encouraging a public exploration and discussion of the American experience.

- Adopt the conservation of biodiversity as a core principle in carrying out its preservation mandate and participate in efforts to protect marine as well as terrestrial resources.

- Advance the principles of sustainability, while first practicing what is preached.

- Actively acknowledge the connections between native cultures and parks, and assure that no relevant chapter in the American heritage experience remains unopened.

- Improve the service's institutional capacity by developing new organizational talents and abilities and a workforce that reflects America's diversity.

In terms of outdoor recreation, in particular, the NPS Advisory Board (2001, pp. 9, 23) recommended the NPS should

- Advocate for outdoor recreation and open-space conservation and the considerable public benefits they provide.

- Encourage collaboration among park and recreation systems at every level (i.e., federal, regional, state, and local) to help build an outdoor recreation network accessible to all Americans.

- Encourage collaboration among public and private park and recreation systems at all levels to build a national network of parks and open spaces across America.

Bureau of Land Management

Mission: It is the mission of the Bureau of Land Management to sustain the health, diversity and productivity of the public lands for the use and enjoyment of present and future generations. (Bureau of Land Management, 2003)

As noted in Chapter 3, large portions of the original public domain lands in the United States have been "disposed" to various entities, such as homesteaders, states, railroad companies, and veterans; reserved for various public purposes, such as national parks, reservations for native peoples, military bases, and wildlife refuges; or transferred to other agencies, such as the Forest Service and Bureau of Reclamation. The BLM manages the lands that remain of the original public domain after more than 200 years of dispositions and reservations. As a result the BLM is sometimes unflatteringly and unfairly referred to as the manager of the "lands that nobody wanted." This disparaging nickname is unfortunate and inaccurate. In fact, the BLM manages more land than any other federal agency, and the lands under BLM jurisdiction are often outstanding and extremely valuable for many purposes, including outdoor recreation.

Historically, the BLM and its current mission have been molded by many significant events, including the following:

- Formation of the General Land Office (GLO) in 1812

- Establishment of the U.S. Grazing Service to manage the public rangelands through the Taylor Grazing Act of 1934

- Creation of the BLM in 1946 with the merger of the General Land Office and the U.S. Grazing Service. This is quite late compared to the other major land managing agencies in the United States.

- Official sanction of a multiple-use mission for the BLM provided by the Classification and Multiple Use Act of 1964

- Unified legislative mandate for the BLM provided by the Federal Land Policy and Management Act of 1976 (FLPMA)

An excellent history of the BLM is available from the agency (Bureau of Land Management, 1988).

The BLM now manages the largest amount of land of any of the federal agencies in the United States (see Table 6.2, p. 85). Nearly all BLM managed land is located in 12 western states and much of it is arid or semiarid. Because of the ways that public domain lands were disposed, reserved, and transferred, however, BLM lands are often scattered and disconnected parcels, sometimes making effective management (and even access) challenging. BLM manages land under numerous federal laws. The most comprehensive is the Federal Land Policy and Management Act of 1976 (FLPMA), which states that "…the public lands be retained in Federal ownership, unless as a result of the land use planning procedure provided in this Act, it is determined that disposal of a particular parcel will serve the national interest…"

The BLM manages lands under a multiple-use philosophy much like that of the U.S. Forest Service. In fact, many of the multiple uses noted here are shared between BLM and the Forest Service. BLM manages its lands for the following multiple uses:

- range
- fish and wildlife
- watershed
- timber
- recreation
- wilderness
- soil conservation
- minerals
- cultural resources (e.g., Native American sites; mining sites; cabin, railroad, and pony express sites, other historic resources)

Organizationally the BLM is structured in a decentralized manner with its headquarters in Washington, DC, where its Director is located. The BLM is generally structured into two administrative levels below the Director. There are 12 state offices, each of which is headed by a State Director, with field offices reporting to the appropriate State Directors. Figure 6.5 (p. 96) illustrates the organizational structure the BLM uses to accomplish its mission. Recreation is part of the BLM's Renewable Resources and Planning function along with programs such as fish, wildlife and botany; rangeland resources; wild horses and burros; and forest and woodland management.

Outdoor recreation participation on BLM-managed lands increased dramatically in recent years, and the agency responded by increasing its emphasis on providing a wide range of recreation opportunities. Hunting, fishing, mountain biking, off-highway vehicle driving, camping, hiking, boating, recreation vehicle use, hang gliding, birding, and visiting natural and cultural heritage are particularly popular at BLM sites. BLM has become a leader in providing opportunities for mountain biking, in particular. The agency classifies some of its lands as either "special recreation management areas" or "extensive recreation management areas." The latter are areas managed in a custodial manner to allow for maximum user freedom.

The BLM has numerous initiatives and programs to accomplish its multiple-use mission. Examples of current and recent initiatives and programs include the following:

- **National Landscape Conservation System (NLCS)** designed to help protect remarkable and rugged landscapes located on BLM lands, such as National Monuments, congressionally designated National Conservation Areas, and other areas with important scientific and ecological characteristics.

- **Wild Horse and Burro Adoption Program**

- **National Backcountry Byways Program** in partnership with *Popular Mechanics* magazine and others

- **Watchable Wildlife Programs**

- Participant in **TREAD Lightly!**, a minimum impact education program for motorized recreation, carried out in partnership with other agencies and groups.

As the population of the American west continues to grow, and more people seek outdoor recreation opportunities, it is likely the BLM will place greater emphasis on managing its settings for the high-quality outdoor recreation experiences they can provide.

U.S. Fish and Wildlife Service

Mission: The U.S. Fish and Wildlife Service's mission is working with others, to conserve, protect and enhance fish, wildlife, and plants and their habitats for the continuing benefit of the American people. (U.S. Fish and Wildlife Service, 2003a)

From the earliest days, fish and wildlife management in the United States has been primarily a state-level function, with states enacting and enforcing the vast majority of hunting and fishing regulations. However, the federal government cooperates and provides critically important national fish and wildlife programs and resource areas. These national programs and areas are the responsibility of the U.S. Fish and Wildlife Service (FWS). The FWS oversees national programs related to migratory birds and threatened and endangered species and operates the

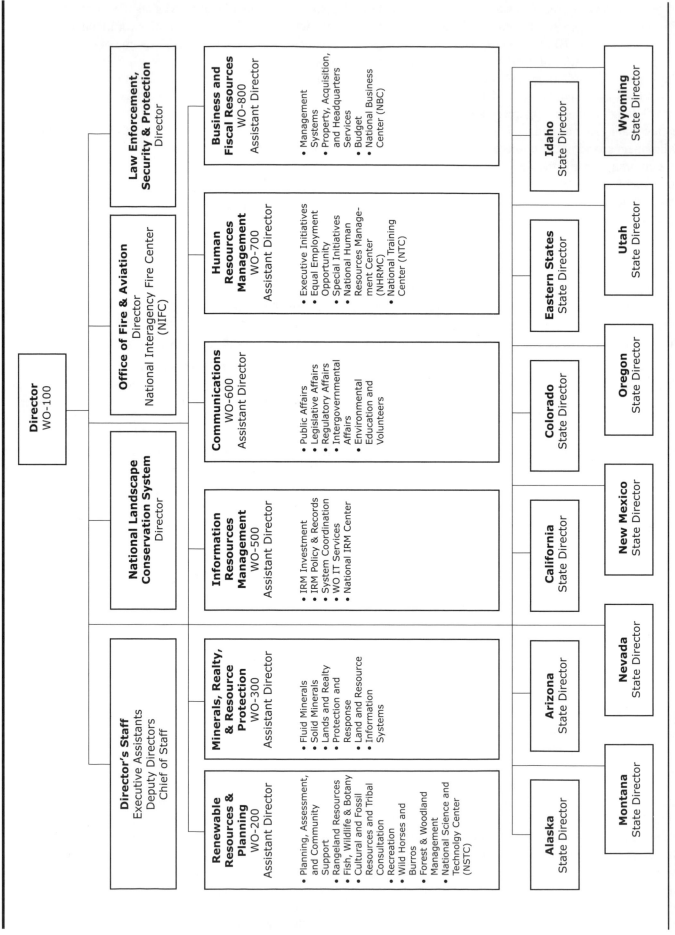

Figure 6.5   Bureau of Land Management organizational structure. Adapted from Bureau of Land Management, 2003b

extensive system of national wildlife refuges. The FWS can be thought of as preservation-oriented—protecting fish and wildlife and their habitats are the agency's highest priorities. It is also a conservation-oriented agency by virtue of its orientation toward the wise and sustainable use of fish and wildlife resources over the long term. Providing fish- and wildlife-oriented outdoor recreation opportunities is an important focus for the FWS, but only when these opportunities are compatible with the agency's preservation and conservation efforts. Those opportunities include hunting and fishing, observing wildlife and fish, hiking, and many more.

The FWS came into being as a result of public concerns over threats to animal and fish populations caused by overhunting, overfishing, habitat destruction, market hunting and pollution. Some of the significant historical events related to the FWS include the following:

- Bureau of Fisheries created (1871).
- Bureau of Biological Survey created (1885).
- Boone and Crockett Club established by Teddy Roosevelt (1888).
- Lacey Act of 1900 creates the first federal wildlife regulations in the United States and makes it illegal to transport illegally killed game across state lines.
- President Roosevelt establishes first national wildlife refuge at Pelican Island off the coast of Florida (1903).
- Bureau of Biological Survey created (1905).
- Migratory Bird Hunting Stamp Act of 1934 requires waterfowl hunters to purchase "duck stamps," the proceeds from which help fund migratory bird conservation efforts.
- Pittman-Robertson Act of 1937 establishes excise taxes on guns and ammunition to help fund wildlife conservation efforts.
- Bureau of Fisheries and Bureau of Biological Survey combined to form the U.S. Fish and Wildlife Service (1940).
- Dingell-Johnson Act of 1950 establishes excise tax on fishing equipment to help fund fish conservation efforts.
- Fish and Wildlife Coordination Act of 1958 requires "equal consideration" to fish and wildlife needs on water resource development projects.
- Endangered Species Act of 1973 established endangered and threatened species programs and prohibits possession, sale, and transport of these species or their parts.

The FWS is organized into seven geographic regions with over 700 field offices, plus a headquarters in Washington, DC. The responsibilities of the FWS most closely related to outdoor recreation are outlined next.

Manage Federal Wildlife Refuges and Fish Hatcheries

The FWS manages the National Refuge System, comprised of 538 Refuges, 37 Wetland Management Districts, and 50 Coordination Areas (U.S. Fish and Wildlife Service, 2003b). More than half of the total acreage of this system is in Alaska. The estuaries, wetlands, big game habitats, and other areas protected in this system are essential for habitat conservation for many species, including those listed as threatened or endangered. The FWS also operates 89 national fish hatcheries. Where compatible with the fish and wildlife purposes of these refuges, wildlife-oriented outdoor recreation is an important use of the National Refuge System. About a quarter of FWS lands are not open for recreational use (Betz, English & Cordell, 1999, p. 41).

Protect and Increase Populations of Threatened and Endangered Species

An essential role of the FWS is to manage the threatened and endangered species program established by the Endangered Species Act of 1973. This involves determining which species of plants and animals should be listed and establishing recovery plans to attempt to restore healthy populations of these species. An endangered species is one at the "brink of extinction on all or significant part of its range" while a threatened species is "likely to become endangered in the foreseeable future." There are a total of 987 species listed as endangered in the United States (388 animals and 599 plants) and a total of 276 listed as threatened (129 animals and 147 plants). All told there are a total of 1,263 threatened or endangered species (517 animals and 746 plants) that the FWS is working to protect and restore (U.S. Fish and Wildlife Service, 2003c). Since 1985 over a dozen species have recovered sufficiently to be "delisted" by the FWS.

Manage the Nation's Migratory Bird Program

Although states play the central role in wildlife management in the United States, some roles are most appropriate for the federal government because they affect and require the coordination of more than one state. The two primary examples are protecting threatened and endangered species and managing migratory birds. The FWS takes the national leadership role for the United States in partnering with the many nations, states, provinces, and other organizations that affect the flight paths of migratory landbird, shorebird, and waterbird species. The FWS is authorized by more than 25 conventions, treaties, and laws to ensure the survival of more than 800 species of migratory birds and their habitats. They accomplish this through population monitoring, assessment, and management; habitat conservation; permits and regulations (e.g., hunting regulations, "duck stamp" program); and consultation, cooperation, and communication (U.S. Department of Interior, 2003a).

Study Federal Water Development Projects

The FWS plays an important role in assuring water development projects do not adversely affect fish and wildlife populations. They accomplish this through involvement in water resources development project planning, permitting, and licensing for projects constructed by federal agencies or permitted under the U.S. Army Corps of Engineer's Regulatory Program. This FWS role extends beyond federal lands to include involvement in the licensing process for nonfederal hydropower projects. By studying the effects of proposed projects on fish and wildlife and attempting to mitigate any negative effects, the FWS assures new water resources projects enhance fish and wildlife populations whenever possible.

U.S. Fish and Wildlife Service activities related to each of these roles affect outdoor recreation opportunities either directly or indirectly. The FWS provides wildlife-oriented outdoor recreation opportunities directly through its National Refuge System and indirectly through its role in conserving fish and wildlife and their habitats. Fish and wildlife-oriented recreation is extensive indeed. According to the 2001 National Survey of Fishing, Hunting, and Wildlife-Associated Recreation, over 82 million U.S. residents ages 16 years or older hunted, fished, or watched wildlife in 2001. This recreation, including observing, feeding, or photographing wildlife, generated a total of $108 billion in spending in 2001. This figure represents $28 billion for trips, $64 billion for equipment, and $16 billion for other related items. Wildlife watchers alone spent $38 billion on their trips, equipment, and related items (U.S. Fish and Wildlife Service, 2003d).

Federal Water Project Agencies

Each of the federal agencies discussed in this section manages very large land areas as well as the bodies of water located within those land areas. The following three federal providers of outdoor recreation opportunities manage land and water resources, but their primary focus is on lakes and reservoirs and the lands immediately adjacent to them. While outdoor recreation is not the primary purpose of these water "projects" (as they are referred to by these agencies), outdoor recreation is a huge and growing use there.

According to the National Recreation Lakes Study Commission (1999) 1,782 lakes in the United States hold 50 acre-feet or more of water created by federal dams. Although there are actually 11 different federal agencies that develop and manage water resources in the United States, most of the federal lakes are managed by the U.S. Army Corps of Engineers (537), the Bureau of Reclamation (288), and the U.S. Forest Service (268). Outdoor recreation (e.g., boating, camping, swimming, fishing, hiking) is one of the important and very popular uses of these lakes and, in most cases, federal lake managing agencies develop recreation facilities as part of their lake projects. The commission reports that every year, federal lakes receive 900 million visits and generate $44 billion in economic impacts. They also estimate that federal lake use is increasing at 2% annually.

While a number of federal lake providers are important providers of public outdoor recreation opportunities, it is important to realize that providing recreation opportunities is not the primary purpose for any of them. There are significant similarities among many of these agencies—so much so in fact there are occasionally proposals that some of them should be combined into a single federal reservoir agency. There are important differences, though, in terms of function and geography that make these agencies distinct. So far, their differences have been sufficient

Federal water projects like this U.S. Army Corps of Engineers lake are very popular for boating and fishing experiences.

U.S. Army Corps of Engineers areas serve many purposes including providing outdoor recreation opportunities.

to justify their status as independent agencies. Three of the federal lake managing agencies focus primarily on water resources and are particularly important in terms of outdoor recreation. They are the U.S. Army Corps of Engineers, Bureau of Reclamation, and Tennessee Valley Authority.

U.S. Army Corps of Engineers

US Army Corps of Engineers ®

Mission: The mission of the U.S. Army Corps of Engineers is to provide quality, responsive engineering services to the nation including: planning, designing, building and operating water resources and other civil works projects...[1] (U.S. Army Corps of Engineers, 2003a)

The U.S. Army Corps of Engineers (USACE or CoE) is part of the Department of Defense. Its original focus was entirely military and can be traced to George Washington's chief engineer's work on the construction of the fortifications at Bunker Hill during the American Revolution. The mission and scope of this unique agency has evolved substantially to include exploring, surveying, mapping, dredging, and providing for river navigation, as well as constructing, maintaining, and in some cases operating canals, forts, jetties, piers, locks, levees, lighthouses, bridges, buildings, monuments, roads, dams, and recreation facilities. In fact, the CoE constructed roads, bridges, and aqueducts in Yellowstone National Park. Some of the significant historical events that have shaped the evolution of the Corps of Engineers include the following (U.S. Army Corps of Engineers, 2003b):

- Congress creates a separate CoE in 1779.
- Rivers and Harbors Acts of 1890 and 1899 require that dam sites and plans be approved by the CoE before construction.
- Flood Control Act of 1928 expands role of the CoE in flood control.
- Flood Control Act of 1936 puts the CoE firmly into the reservoir construction business. The Act also requires that a potential project's economic benefits must exceed its costs and specifies other conditions that must be met before the Corps can begin certain projects.
- Flood Control Act of 1944 establishes a multipurpose approach for the CoE including authority to provide recreation facilities.

- Federal Water Projects Recreation Act of 1965 mandates that the CoE (and Bureau of Reclamation) "give full consideration to recreation and fish and wildlife as purposes in federal water resource projects."

The CoE is organized into eight geographic Divisions based on watershed boundaries. There are 41 Districts that report to the Divisions, which in turn report to agency headquarters in Washington, DC. The CoE is responsible for over 500 water resources projects, most (although not all) of which are located in eastern and midwestern states. These CoE projects have varying combinations of the following purposes:

- flood control
- hydroelectric power generation
- providing for navigation
- irrigation
- recreation
- fish and wildlife

Organizationally, recreation is part of the Directorate of Civil Works within the CoE, which includes other programs, such as water resource development, flood control, navigation, infrastructure, and environmental stewardship. The CoE has seen tremendous growth in demand for recreation and is one of the nation's largest providers of outdoor recreation opportunities. The agency operates more than 2,500 recreation areas (e.g., camping areas, beaches, boat ramps, marinas) at 463 projects (mostly lakes). They also lease an additional 1,800 sites (over 40% of the total sites at CoE projects) to state or local park and recreation agencies or other partners. CoE sites receive about 360 million visits a year and they estimate 25 million Americans (about 1 in 10) visit a Corps project at least once a year. The Corps is an active partner in the National Water Safety Program (U.S. Army Corps of Engineers, 2003c).

Bureau of Reclamation

Mission: The mission of the Bureau of Reclamation is to manage, develop, and protect water and related resources in an environmentally and economically sound manner in the interest of the American public. (Bureau of Reclamation, 2003)

The Bureau of Reclamation (BOR) is part of the Department of Interior and operates exclusively in 17 western states. The BOR is a water management agency, best known for its dams, reservoirs, power plants, and canals. Originally established as the Reclamation Service through the Reclamation Act of 1902, it was named for its initial purpose of "reclaiming" arid and semi-arid lands by providing water for irrigation. The BOR has constructed over 600 dams and reservoirs, the best known of which are Grand Coulee Dam on the Columbia River and Hoover Dam on the Colorado. These dams store water for irrigation, hydroelectric power generation, flood control, and municipal, residential, and industrial uses. BOR reservoirs and their associated lands are important resources for fish and wildlife, outdoor recreation, and other benefits. All of these activities and benefits are important for the economic development of the western states.

The BOR is organized into five geographic regions—Great Plains, Lower Colorado, Mid Pacific, Pacific Northwest, and Upper Colorado—which report to the agency's Washington Office. Like the U.S. Army Corps of Engineers, the BOR relies heavily on partnerships with other agencies and other cooperators for the management of its outdoor recreation facilities and resources. These partnerships frequently involve leases and other agreements to transfer responsibilities to other public agencies or private businesses. For example, some of the largest reservoirs created by BOR dams are managed by the National Park Service. These include Glen Canyon National Recreation Area at Lake Powell (created by Glen Canyon Dam) and Lake Mead National Recreation Area at Lake Mead (created by Hoover Dam).

BOR areas currently have about 350 campgrounds and 308 recreational sites, and the agency has seen steady increases in levels of recreation use (U.S. Department of Interior, 2003b).

Tennessee Valley Authority

Mission: The Tennessee Valley Authority achieves excellence in public service for the good of the people of the Tennessee Valley by supporting sustainable economic development, supplying affordable, reliable power, and managing a thriving river system. (Tennessee Valley Authority, 2004a)

The Tennessee Valley Authority Act of 1933 created the Tennessee Valley Authority (TVA) to provide flood control, navigation, and electric power for the Tennessee Valley region. The TVA was an innovative part of President Roosevelt's New Deal for stimulating the nation's econ-

omy during the Great Depression in that it was designed to be "a corporation clothed with the power of government but possessed of the flexibility and initiative of a private enterprise" (Tennessee Valley Authority, 2004b). Unlike the other federal providers, TVA is a federal government corporation or quasi-public agency. TVA is also one of the nation's largest public power companies.

The TVA built and operates a system of 49 dams in the 41,000-square-mile Tennessee River watershed for flood control, navigation hydroelectric power generation, recreational opportunities, and regional economic development. It also owns and operates coal-fired and nuclear power plants. Although TVA has received subsidies from the federal government for much of its history, all of its programs are now paid for through power revenues (Tennessee Valley Authority, 2004c).

The TVA plays a critical regional role in providing outdoor recreation opportunities. TVA reservoirs and the 290,000 acres of land surrounding them are extremely popular for waterskiing, boating, windsurfing, fishing, swimming, hiking, nature photography, picnicking, birdwatching, and camping. The TVA provides public recreation areas, campgrounds, day-use areas, boat launching ramps, and property for private vacation homes. Water releases from TVA dams on the Ocoee River in southeastern Tennessee make it one of the region's best boating rivers and an excellent site for the mile-long Olympic whitewater course (Tennessee Valley Authority, 2004d).

Before leaving the federal lake providing agencies as a group, it is important to note that their role in providing outdoor recreation was examined by a Presidential commission in the late 1990s (National Recreation Lakes Study Commission, 1999). While concluding federal lake recreation is significant and beneficial nationally, the commission felt there was room for improvement. It concluded that although recreation is an authorized use at federal lakes, "It has not been treated as a priority, or often even as an equal, with other reservoir uses" (p. 9). Specifically, the commission felt federal lake recreation management needs improvements in terms of unified policy direction, leadership, planning, coordination, maintenance funding, flexibility, and partnerships. They also proposed a "national recreation lake system" was feasible and could be beneficial. They suggested that such a system be tested on a small scale in the form of a "lake demonstration program." To better realize the full potential of outdoor recreation at federal lakes, this commission recommended the following:

1. Make recreation a higher priority at federal lakes.

2. Energize and focus recreation leadership for federal lakes.

3. Advance federal lake recreation through demonstration and reinvention.

4. Create an environment for success in federal lake recreation management.

5. Identify and close the gap between recreation needs and services. (p. 11)

Other Federal Agencies Involved in Outdoor Recreation

The seven federal level public sector providers of outdoor recreation opportunities described above are the most significant in terms of land and water acreage managed and overall magnitude of public use for outdoor recreation. Other federal agencies and programs are important in this regard, even though their roles are more narrowly focused and they receive less recreation use than the agencies noted earlier. In some cases these other recreation-related federal agencies manage no land or water for outdoor recreation at all. Some of these agencies are described next.

Bureau of Indian Affairs (BIA)

The Bureau of Indian Affairs (BIA) is responsible for the government-to-government relationships between the United States and the 562 federally recognized Native American groups. Among many other activities, the BIA provides technical assistance and partial funding to assist native peoples to administer and manage the 55.7 million acres of reservations and other lands held in trust by the United States The largest area is the Navaho Reservation in Arizona, New Mexico, and Utah. These lands provide outdoor recreation opportunities for resident Native Americans and many Native Nations encourage tourism and fee-based outdoor recreation, such as hunting and fishing, on their lands for economic development and other purposes.

Federal Highway Administration (FHWA)

The FHWA is one of 13 agencies within the U.S. Department of Transportation. In addition to a wide range of federal highway programs and administration of all federal highway funds, the FHWA administers the Transportation Equity Act for the 21st Century (TEA-21). Enacted in 1998, TEA-21 (and its predecessor, the Intermodal Surface Transportation Efficiency Act, or ISTEA) authorized the federal surface transportation programs for highways, highway safety, and transit. Included among these programs are the Transportation Enhancements Program, the Bicycle Transportation and Pedestrian Walkways Program, the Recreational Trails Program, and the National Scenic Byways Program. All of these have provided important assistance for outdoor recreation. The Transportation Enhancements Program, for example, provided approximately $300 million for transportation "enhancements" annually since 1991. These enhancements include transportation-related trail, greenway, rail-trail, and historic preservation projects.

National Oceanic and Atmospheric Administration (NOAA)

The National Marine Sanctuary Program of NOAA operates 13 National Marine Sanctuaries (NMS) that together have an area nearly equal to the size of New Hampshire and Vermont combined. These preserved sites range from the Florida Keys NMS and Channel Island (California) NMS to the Hawaiian Island Humpback Whale NMS. Although regulations apply, recreation is encouraged at most Marine Sanctuaries.

U.S. Department of Labor

Since 1964 the U.S. Department of Labor has operated the Job Corps program. Job Corps is a residential training and work experience program for young adults between the ages of 16 and 25. Not unlike the Civilian Conservation Corps (CCC) during the Great Depression, Job Corps often focuses on outdoor recreation related projects in partnership with other agencies. The U.S. Forest Service, for example, operates 18 Job Corps Civilian Conservation Centers across the nation.

U.S. Geological Survey (USGS)

The USGS is the primary science agency for the Department of the Interior. As such, USGS provides a wide range of essential services and knowledge to outdoor recreation providing agencies and the general public. Its primary focus areas are natural hazards, resources, the environment, and information and data management. Its mapping and geographic information programs alone make it an important resource for outdoor recreation managers and users.

Department of Defense

Morale, Welfare, and Recreation (MWR) programs provide recreation programming for military personnel and their families. Some of these opportunities are for outdoor recreation in its many forms. Limited public outdoor recreation use is also allowed on lands and waters located on some military bases.

State Outdoor Recreation Providing Agencies

According to the 10th Amendment of the U.S. Constitution, states have any power not given to the federal government by the Constitution or specifically prohibited therein.

The authority to operate parks, recreation, and conservation programs is an example of a right that states can, and typically do, exercise. In most states this takes the form of providing state parks, state forests, state natural areas, and state fish and wildlife areas; enacting and enforcing most hunting and fishing regulations and state environmental regulations; and enabling municipal and county park and recreation programs through any required state legislation. These functions are all important for outdoor recreation in the United States.

Some of the important historical events that have helped shape the role of the states in providing outdoor recreation opportunities include the following:

1641   Great Ponds Act guarantees public access to lakes greater than ten acres in Massachusetts Bay Colony.

1885   First successful state forest preserve established in New York.

1864   Congress grants lands of Yosemite Valley and Mariposa Grove to state of California.

1890   Yosemite National Park created

1898   Pennsylvania establishes forest preserves.

1906   Yosemite Valley and Mariposa Grove lands returned to federal control and added to Yosemite National Park.

1911   Illinois and Indiana establish the first state park agencies.

1921   National Park Service Director, Stephen Mather, organizes the first state parks conference, in part to encourage states to help extend NPS efforts they did not have the resources to undertake.

1948   Amendments to the federal Surplus Property Act make it possible to convert federal property to state parks and recreation at 50% of their appraised value.

1965   Land and Water Conservation Fund created. Its "state side" funding provisions and State Comprehensive Outdoor Recreation Plan (SCORP) requirement provide a major boost to state park programs.

The scope of state lands is extensive. By one estimate, approximately 5% of all the land in the United States (some 78 million acres) is controlled by the states (Jensen, 1995). There is tremendous variation in the purposes for which different states manage their lands and how they organize their agencies to do so. However, most states structure their agencies to include at least a state park agency, state forestry agency, and state fish and wildlife agency. All of these contribute to the range of available outdoor recreation opportunities for state residents and visitors, but the most important in terms of outdoor recreation is typically a state's park system. In fact, relative to their total size, state parks play an extraordinary role in outdoor recreation. In 1995, state parks received about 686 million day visits and 59 million overnight visits (Landrum, 1999). This is more outdoor recreation visits than provided in 1996 by any of the federal providers except the U.S. Forest Service, even though the combined area of state parks is smaller than that of the U.S. Forest Service, Bureau of Land Management, U.S. Fish and Wildlife Service, or National Park Service (McLean, Chavez & Hurd, 2000).

Using one of the early classification systems for outdoor recreation resources noted in Chapter 5, most state parks were broadly considered "intermediate areas" as opposed to "resource-based areas," or "user-oriented areas." Of course state parks are extremely diverse and range from small historic sites to vast primitive areas. The National Association of State Park Directors (NASPD) classifies the types of areas administered by state park agencies into eight distinct categories (McLean, 1999):

1. State Parks
2. State Recreation Areas
3. State Natural Areas
4. State Historic Areas
5. State Environmental Education Sites
6. State Scientific Areas
7. State Forests
8. State Fish and Wildlife Areas

Figure 6.6 presents the relative abundance of each type in terms of total acreage in the United States and Figure

There are over five thousand state park, recreation, and natural areas in the United States. This site is in a state park near an urban area in North Carolina.

6.7 presents the number of areas for each type. Both of these tabulations are based on 1995 figures.

In terms of acreage alone, Alaska, California, Texas, and New York have the largest areas set aside as state parks. In terms of the number of state parks, New York, Pennsylvania, California, and Massachusetts have the most extensive systems. Alaska, of course, is an exception. Because over half of all state park land is in Alaska, New York, and California, the configuration of state park lands in those states have a large affect on the totals presented in Figures 6.6 and 6.7.

According to the National Association of State Park Directors (NASPD; 2003), state parks generally provide close-to-home outdoor recreation opportunities and the vast majority of visitors use them for day trips. A sampling of overall state park facilities status for 2002 and visitation figures from NASPD (2003) include the following:

- 4,114 trails encompassing 32,225 miles of trails
- Almost 210,000 campsites ranging from multiple hookups to primitive
- 6,592 cabins and cottages
- 124 lodges in 25 states with 6,695 rooms
- 127 golf courses
- 31 ski slopes
- 311 marinas
- 300 swimming pools
- 97 stable operations
- 323 million visitors to fee areas

- 435 million to nonfee areas
- 59 million campers
- 2.4 million lodge guests
- 3.9 million cabin guests
- 17.7 million campsites rented

In spite of the broad array of facilities and services provided by state park agencies and the huge number of visitors served, the average share of the state budgets allocated to state park agencies in the United States is only about 0.25% (NASPD, 2003).

Regional and County Outdoor Recreation Providing Agencies

Regional and county agencies and lands are critically important in providing outdoor recreation opportunities, because along with municipal agencies they tend to provide the areas and opportunities most accessible to where people live and work. In fact, as the nation's urban and suburban areas continue to expand into previously natural areas, the roles of regional, county, and municipal outdoor recreation providers becomes more important. This is true not only in terms of providing opportunities for current use but also in planning for and protecting adequate resources for rapidly increasing future needs.

County agencies frequently provide outdoor recreation opportunities on the lands they manage. This can

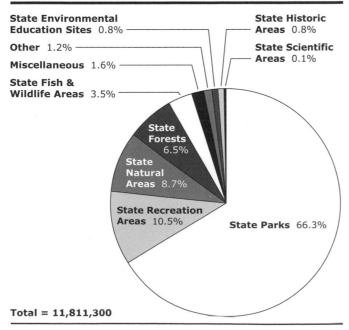

Figure 6.6   State acreage by category
Data source: McLean, D. (1999, p. 109)

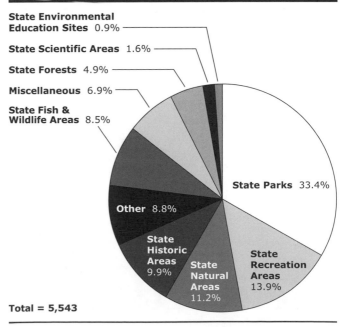

Figure 6.7   Number of state areas by category
Data source: McLean, D. (1999, p. 109)

vary from highly developed and modified areas to completely natural open space settings. Counties sometimes also play a critical role in guiding development through a wide range of regulations (e.g., zoning) and programs aimed at guiding development and protecting resources. In some parts of the country, where county and municipal boundaries and services do not effectively meet citizens' needs, regional agencies or "special districts" are also created for a number of purposes (Dennis, 2001). Such multijurisdictional agencies frequently provide outdoor recreation and open space areas and programs and do so in more efficient ways than county or municipal governments could acting alone. The following regional park agencies from around the United States are examples of this approach and give some indication of the variety and broad distribution of regional park agencies:

- Allegheny Regional Asset District (county containing Pittsburgh, Pennsylvania)
- City of San José Regional Parks (California)
- East Bay Regional Park District (eastern San Francisco Bay area, California)
- Fox Valley Park District (Illinois)
- Greater Huntington Park and Recreation District (West Virginia)
- Huron-Clinton Metropolitan Park Authority (Michigan)
- Jekyll Island State Park Authority (Georgia)
- Maryland National Capital Park and Planning Commission
- Northern Virginia Regional Park Authority (Arlington, Fairfax, and Loudoun Counties, and the Cities of Alexandria, Falls Church, and Fairfax)

- Palisades Interstate Park Commission (Hudson River Valley of New York and New Jersey)
- Pearl and Leaf Rivers Rails-to-Trails Recreational District (southern Mississippi)
- San Bernardino County Regional Parks (California)
- Three Rivers Park District (suburban Minneapolis–St. Paul metro area)

Municipal Outdoor Recreation Providing Agencies

The role of municipalities in providing outdoor recreation opportunities and services is too often underestimated or overlooked entirely. This might be because the most visible park and recreation resources in many communities are highly developed facilities. However, most municipalities provide a wide variety of recreation areas and services that range from community centers to more nature-oriented open space areas, many of which can provide opportunities for high-quality outdoor recreation experiences. As noted earlier, the recreation opportunities provided by county and municipal agencies are essential in that they are the opportunities closest to most people's homes and workplaces. Local government also has the most immediate and direct effects on how growth and development are planned for and managed, which in turn have profound influences on the availability of outdoor recreation opportunities.

Because municipalities range from small rural communities to large metropolitan areas, generalities are difficult and can be misleading. It is clear, however, that the most effective local governments, whether small or large, consider parks, open space, and other potential outdoor

Regional and county park and recreation agencies are extremely important providers of outdoor recreation opportunities in many parts of the United States.

Municipal agencies provide a tremendous variety of outdoor recreation opportunities from the large open space of Central Park in New York City to greenway trails like this one in Vermont.

recreation resources to be part of the infrastructure of their communities, just like roads and utilities, and plan accordingly. The benefits of city park systems are receiving increased attention and include community revitalization, community engagement, economic development, improved physical and mental health, reduced crime, and an overall increase in quality of life (City Parks Forum, 2003). As noted in Chapter 2, the existence of nearby amenities is one of the top five most important contributors to people's perceived quality of life or satisfaction with their lives. The relatively autonomous nature of municipal government also makes it possible for each to provide the most locally appropriate combinations of opportunities for their residents. These combinations may emphasize organized recreation programming or sports in some communities, winter recreation facilities in others, or trails, greenways, and open space in still others.

Municipal park and recreation systems have a much longer history than most people realize. The Boston Common, for example, created in 1634 as a pasture area for grazing visitors' livestock, is considered to be the nation's oldest city park. Major city parks in New York, Michigan, Pennsylvania, and New Jersey are all over a century old.

City parks are now an expected resource in most cities. Although the approaches and emphases vary considerably, municipal agencies will continue to be important providers of outdoor recreation opportunities. Table 6.5 presents comparisons of the city park and open space programs in 25 U.S. cities. The cities are presented in order from the most densely populated to the least based on 1990 census data for land area and 1996 census data for population size.

Summary

This chapter introduced and described the major outdoor recreation providers from the public sector. We defined an outdoor recreation provider broadly as any organization, enterprise, or individual that directly or indirectly provides outdoor recreation opportunities. We began with descriptions of providers at the federal level and moved on to discuss those at the state, regional, county, and municipal levels. The major federal providers included USDA Forest Service, National Park Service, Bureau of Land Management, U.S. Fish and Wildlife Service, U.S. Army Corps of Engineers, and Bureau of Reclamation. Remember the

Table 6.5 Comparisons of city park and open space programs in 25 U.S. cities

		Park and Open Space Acres per 1,000 Residents[a]	Park and Open Space as Percent of City Acreage[a]	Park-Related Expenditures per Resident[b]
High-Density Population	New York	7.2	26.8	$44
	San Francisco	10.3	25.4	$95
	Chicago	4.3	8.0	$114
	Boston	8.7	15.7	$96
	Philadelphia	7.2	12.4	$47
	Miami	3.6	5.8	$36
	Baltimore	7.5	9.8	$47
	Los Angeles	8.5	10.0	$35
Medium-Density Population	Detroit	5.9	6.6	$63
	Minneapolis	16.0	16.2	$153
	Cleveland	5.8	5.9	$72
	Pittsburgh	7.8	7.7	$54
	Seattle	11.8	11.5	$164
	St. Louis	9.6	8.5	$73
	Cincinnati	21.4	15.0	$130
	Portland, OR	26.2	15.8	$136
Low-Density Population	San Diego	30.8	17.4	$83
	Denver	11.4	5.8	$103
	Houston	12.5	6.3	$42
	Dallas	21.3	10.0	$47
	Atlanta	7.8	3.7	$63
	Phoenix	31.5	13.6	$69
	Tampa	10.8	4.4	$99
	Indianapolis	17.7	5.7	$32
	Kansas City, MO	30.2	6.7	$92

[a] Includes lands owned by city, county, regional, state, and federal agencies located within city boundaries
[b] Agency operating budgets plus capital budgets, excluding zoos, stadiums, museums, and aquariums

Source: Harnik (2000)

purpose of an agency, and the mission of its parent department in the case of federal agencies, have important implications for how the agency approaches outdoor recreation opportunities. This is most evident in terms of whether the agency has a preservation focus or a conservation focus. In the next several chapters we move beyond the public sector to consider the roles of the private and nonprofit sectors in providing outdoor recreation opportunities and then discuss partnerships among the three sectors.

Literature Cited

Betz, C. J., English, D. K., and Cordell, H. K. (1999). Outdoor recreation resources. In K. Cordell et al., *Outdoor recreation in American life: A national assessment of demand and supply trends* (pp. 39–182). Champaign, IL: Sagamore.

Bureau of Land Management. (1988). *Opportunity and challenge: The story of BLM*. Washington, DC: U.S. Government Printing Office.

Bureau of Land Management. (2003a). *BLM facts*. Retrieved December 27, 2003, from http://www.blm.gov/nhp/facts/index.htm

Bureau of Land Management. (2003b). *Bureau of Land Management organizational structure*. Retrieved December 27, 2003, from http://www.blm.gov/nhp/directory/BLM_Org_Chart.pdf

Bureau of Reclamation. (2003). *Mission statement*. Retrieved December 23, 2003, from http://www.usbr.gov/main/about/mission.html

City Parks Forum. (2003). *Briefing papers*. Retrieved January 6, 2004, from http://www.planning.org/cpf/briefingpapers.htm

Clawson, M. (1983). *The federal lands revisited*. Washington, DC: Resources for the Future.

Dennis, S. (2001). *Natural resources and the informed citizen*. Champaign, IL: Sagamore.

Dombeck, M. (1997, April 8). Presentation to USDA Forest Service Regional Foresters and Research Station Directors, Washington, DC.

Haas, G. and Wakefield, T. (1998). *National parks and the American public: A national public opinion survey on the national park system*. Washington, DC: National Parks and Conservation Association.

Harnik, P. (2000). *Inside city parks*. Washington, DC: Urban Land Institute.

Jensen, C. (1995). *Outdoor recreation in America* (5th ed.). Champaign, IL: Human Kinetics.

Landrum, N. (1999). America's state parks—An end-of-century assessment. In H. K. Cordell et al., *Outdoor recreation in American life: A national assessment of demand and supply trends* (pp. 112–115). Champaign, IL: Sagamore.

McLean, D. (1999). State park systems in the United States. In H. K. Cordell et. al, *Outdoor recreation in American life: A national assessment of demand and supply trends* (pp. 107–112). Champaign, IL: Sagamore.

McLean, D. , Chavez, D., and Hurd, A. (2000). *State parks: A diverse system*. Bloomington, IN: Indiana University, Department of Recreation and Park Administration, State Park Information Resources Center. Retrieved from http://naspd.indstate.edu/research.html

National Association of State Park Directors. (2003). *State park facts*. Retrieved from December 23, 2003, from http://naspd.indstate.edu/statistics.html

National Park Service. (1999a). *How national park units are established*. Retrieved February 7, 2001, from http://www.nps.gov/positions.htm

National Park Service. (1999b) *National park resources in peril*. Retrieved January 6, 2004, from http://www.doi.gov/pfm/ar4nps.html

National Park Service. (2002). *National park service statistical abstract 2002*. Washington, DC: National Park Service, Public Use Statistics Office.

National Park Service. (2003a). *The National Park System—Caring for the American legacy*. Retrieved December 23, 2003, from http://www.nps.gov/legacy/mission.html

National Park Service. (2003b). *Designation of national park system units*. Retrieved December 23, 2003, from http://www.nps.gov/legacy/nomenclature.html

National Park Service. (2005). *National Park Service headquarters*. Retrieved February 3, 2005, from http://www.nps.gov/legacy/regions.html

National Park Service Organic Act, 16 U.S.C. § 1 (1916).

National Park System Advisory Board. (2001). *Rethinking the national parks for the 21st century*. Washington, DC: National Geographic Society.

National Recreation Lakes Study Commission. (1999). *Reservoirs of opportunity: Report of the National Recreation Lakes Study Commission*. Retrieved from http://www.doi.gov/nrls/findings/nrls-summary.pdf

Schuster, E. G. and Krebs, M. A. (2003). *Forest Service programs, authorities, and relationships: A technical document supporting the 2000 USDA Forest Service RPA Assessment* (Gen. Tech. Rep. RMRS-GTR-112). Fort Collins, CO: U.S. Department of Agriculture, Forest Service, Rocky Mountain Research Station.

Stenger, R. (1999). Trends in visits to federal areas. In H. K. Cordell et al., *Outdoor recreation in American life: A national assessment of demand and supply trends* (pp. 282–284). Champaign, IL: Sagamore.

Teasley, R. J., Bergstrom, J. C., Cordell, H. K., Zarnoch, S. J., and Gentle, P. (1999). Private lands and outdoor recreation in the United States. In H. K. Cordell et al., *Outdoor recreation in American life: A national assessment of demand and supply trends* (pp. 183–218). Champaign, IL: Sagamore.

Tennessee Valley Authority. (2004a). *Providing power in the public interest*. Retrieved January 1, 2004, from http://www.tva.gov/abouttva/index.htm

Tennessee Valley Authority. (2004b). *A short history of TVA: From the new deal to a new century*. Retrieved January 1, 2004, from http://www.tva.gov/abouttva/history.htm

Tennessee Valley Authority. (2004c). *Frequently asked questions about TVA*. Retrieved January 1, 2004, from http://www.tva.gov/abouttva/keyfacts.htm

Tennessee Valley Authority. (2004d). *Recreation*. Retrieved January 4, 2004, from http://www.tva.gov/river/recreation/index.htm

U.S. Army Corps of Engineers. (2003a). *Who we are*. Retrieved December 31, 2003, from http://www.usace.army.mil/who.html

U.S. Army Corps of Engineers. (2003b). *Brief history*. Retrieved December 31, 2003, from http://www.hq.usace.army.mil/history/brief.htm

U.S. Army Corps of Engineers. (2003c). *Services for the public*. Retrieved December 31, 2003, from http://www.usace.army.mil/public.html

USDA Forest Service. (1982). *ROS users guide*. Washington, DC: USDA Forest Service.

USDA Forest Service. (1999). *1998 report of the Forest Service*. Washington, DC: USDA Forest Service. Retrieved from http://www.fs.fed.us/pl/pdb/98report/index.html

USDA Forest Service. (2000, December). *The recreation agenda* (FS-691). Washington, DC: USDA Forest Service.

U.S. Department of the Interior. (2003a). *A blueprint for the future of migratory birds*. Washington, DC: U.S. Department of Interior, Fish and Wildlife Service, Migratory Bird Program. Retrieved July 31, 2003, from http://migratorybirds.fws.gov/mbstratplan/mbstratplan.pdf

U.S. Department of the Interior. (2003b). *Orientation website data tables*. Retrieved from January 1, 2004, from http://www.doiu.nbc.gov/orientation/tables_all.cfm

U.S. Fish and Wildlife Service. (2003a). *Who we are*. Retrieved December 31, 2003, from http://www.fws.gov/who

U.S. Fish and Wildlife Service. (2003b). *How are lands classified within the refuge system?* Retrieved from December 27, 2003, from http://refuges.fws.gov/faqs/index.html

U.S. Fish and Wildlife Service. (2003c). *Species information: Threatened and endangered animals and plants*.

Retrieved December 27, 2003, from http://endangered.fws.gov/wildlife.html#Species

U.S. Fish and Wildlife Service. (2003d). *National survey of fishing, hunting, and wildlife-associated recreation*. Retrieved December 30, 2003, from http://federalaid.fws.gov/surveys/surveys.html

U.S. Geological Survey. (2005). Federal Lands and Indian Reservations [printable map]. Retrieved January 19, 2005, from http://nationalatlas.gov/fedlandsprint.html#United%20States%20(50%20States)

Endnote

1. The Corps' mission goes on to include other elements related to military facilities design and construction and management support for other federal agencies within and beyond the Department of Defense.

Chapter 7
Private Sector Providers

We support continuation of our national legacy of quality outdoor experiences on America's lands and waters in a manner that sustains the long-term ecological integrity of natural resources and the economic well being of communities....We desire to contribute to the fulfillment of the purposes for which the natural areas where we work were designated. (From the "Code of Ethics & Professionalism" of America Outdoors, an association representing active private sector travel outfitters and tour companies, 2004)

Learning Objectives

1. Describe the importance of the private sector in providing outdoor recreation opportunities.
2. Explain the six primary ways the private sector is involved in providing outdoor recreation opportunities and give examples of each.

When most people think about outdoor recreation opportunities, their first thoughts are of national forests, national parks, state parks, and other large, relatively remote lands managed by public sector agencies. In reality, though, there would be very little outdoor recreation as we know it today without the involvement of the business enterprises of the private sector. These enterprises range in size from huge multinational corporations to individual entrepreneurs who organize, promote, manage, and assume the risks for business ventures. The private sector is involved in providing outdoor recreation opportunities in six primary ways:

- providing private land and facilities for public outdoor recreation
- providing outdoor recreation equipment and supplies
- providing guiding, outfitting, and information
- providing support services
- operating commercial ventures on public lands
- providing donations and other support

Providing Private Land and Facilities for Public Outdoor Recreation

As noted in Chapter 5, about 58% of the land in the United States is privately owned. (This 58% includes lands managed by providers from the nonprofit sector, addressed in the next chapter.) From the perspective of actual and potential outdoor recreation opportunities, two important considerations relate to this vast area of private land. The first is the *type* of private owner and the second is the primary *reason* the private owners hold their land. The types of private owners can be broadly grouped into two categories: individual owners and corporate owners. Some individual and corporate owners allow outdoor recreation use of their undeveloped lands and some develop their lands with facilities and other improvements specifically for outdoor recreation purposes.

Individual Owners

The vast area of private land in the United States is available for the owners' use, and a portion of private owners open their land for public outdoor recreation. The best source of information on undeveloped and relatively undeveloped lands held by individual private owners is the National Private Landowner Survey (NPLOS), which examined rural tracts of private land ten acres or larger (Teasley, Bergstrom, Cordell, Zarnoch & Gentle, 1999). The NPLOS found private landowners hold property for many reasons, including wanting to live in a rural environment, enjoying owning greenspace, as an estate for their heirs, wildlife preservation, and generating income. Some of the ways landowners generate income from their property is through grazing livestock, sharecropping, harvesting timber and pulpwood, and leasing their land to businesses and hunters. About 70% of private owners recreate on their own land.

Private lands obviously represent a significant source of current and potential public outdoor recreation opportunities as well. The NPLOS found some form of access to nonowners was allowed on about half of the tracts studied. At least some nonfamily members were allowed to recreate on the properties of 48% of the owners and about 15% of the owners had at least some of their land completely open to outsiders. The most common forms of outdoor recreation that occur on these private lands nationally are hunting, hiking, fishing, off-road vehicle driving, target shooting, and birdwatching.

There have been important changes, however, in private land ownership, and even more significant changes are likely on the way. Taken together, these changes paint a mixed picture for outdoor recreation on lands owned by private individuals.

Broad Public Access to Individually Owned Private Land Appears to Be Decreasing

Between 1986 and 1996 the proportion of private landowners allowing open recreation access for anyone wishing to use their land decreased from 25% to 15% (Teasley et al., 1999). On one hand, 15% of the private land in the United States open for public access is a very large area indeed. On the other hand, if the amount of open private land is decreasing, perhaps rapidly, we are losing important outdoor recreation opportunities.

Big Changes Are Coming in Private Land Ownership

More important than existing owners closing their land is the fact that vast areas of private land in the United States are on the verge of a dramatic shift in ownership. Much of this land is now owned by the parents of baby boomers. In 2005, the baby boomers were between 41 and 59 years old. If we assume these boomers were born when their parents were 25 years old, on average, their parents are now between 66 and 84 years old. The vast majority of these aging landowners are retired or will be soon. Many will be selling their land to help make other retirement dreams come true, and some who do not live on that land now will be moving there in retirement. However, the biggest change is that the boomers will be inheriting this land at a very rapid rate over the next two decades, as the average lifespan in the United States is now 77. These new private landowners may well have very different priorities and attitudes than their parents did. Some will certainly sell their newly acquired land or subdivide it and sell a portion. Others will build new homes there, and some will simply hold their land for nostalgic reasons or as an investment. In addition, some may sell or donate their property to nonprofit land trusts or government agencies. It is difficult to tell now precisely what this massive land redistribution will mean. It is not difficult, however, to deduce dramatic changes are coming for the vast private land estate in the United States and the outdoor recreation that depends on it.

Corporate Landowners

Most people do not realize the extent of land owned and managed by corporations in the United States. These land holdings vary tremendously in size from one corporation to another and the corporate landowners have many different reasons for holding land. Typically, generating a profit for owners and investors now or in the future is one of the most important reasons. Large corporate owners range from forestry and wood products companies, such as Weyerhaeuser, Boise Cascade, International Paper, and Georgia-Pacific, to energy companies, mining companies, agricultural corporations, real estate investment companies, and many others. Some of these enterprises own vast amounts of undeveloped land. For example, the Weyerhaeuser Company alone owns 7.2 million acres of forestlands in North America and manages another 0.8 million acres of leased forestland. This is an area nearly the size of New Jersey and Connecticut combined. Some private corporate landowners allow and even encourage public recreation on their lands. A corporation might provide outdoor recreation opportunities to the general public for many reasons, including the following:

Good Public Relations and Community Relations

Most companies want to be good neighbors, and allowing people to hunt, fish, and hike on their lands is an excellent way to show people the company cares. This is especially true if such public recreation uses have been allowed for generations, particularly if they were allowed before the company took ownership of the land. Of course public recreation is only allowed when it does not conflict with operations that are higher corporate priorities.

Regulatory Requirements

In some cases private companies are actually required to provide public recreation opportunities. The Federal Energy Regulatory Commission (FERC), for example, requires private hydroelectric and nuclear power generating companies to be licensed. As part of the licensing requirements, these companies may be required to provide public boating, fishing, or other recreation on or around their lakes.

Income Generation

Some corporate landholders integrate recreation into their business plans to generate income. Charging for special hunting and fishing permits, leasing land for home sites for private cabins or camps, even leasing lands to entrepreneurs who build trail-and-hut systems and charge fees for their use are a few of the many ways this has been done successfully.

Private Lands Developed for Outdoor Recreation

It is common for private lands to be bought and developed specifically for private sector outdoor recreation enterprises. These can, of course, be owned and operated by corporations, individual entrepreneurs, or partnerships of many kinds. Such outdoor recreation businesses may be the owner's sole enterprise or supplement other business operations. Some of the most common examples of this type of outdoor recreation enterprise on private lands include

- alpine ski areas and resorts
- beach resorts
- developed campgrounds (e.g., Kampgrounds of America)
- ecotourism resorts
- guest ("dude") ranches
- motocross, ATV, and BMX courses
- mountain resorts
- nordic ski areas
- private camps
- private marinas
- private mountain biking areas
- shooting preserves, and rod and gun clubs
- trout farms and other private fishing areas
- vacation farms
- water parks

Providing Outdoor Recreation Equipment and Supplies

Providing land and facilities for outdoor recreation is obviously not the only or even the most important way the private sector is involved in providing outdoor recreation opportunities. The business of manufacturing and selling recreational equipment and supplies is essential for most kinds of outdoor recreation and is carried out almost exclusively by the private sector. The variety and scope of equipment and supplies manufactured for outdoor recreation is staggering. It is difficult to identify any outdoor recreation experiences that do not require (or at least typically involve) some sort of equipment or supplies provided by private sector enterprises. A few examples of recreation equipment and supplies include

- all-terrain vehicles (ATVs)
- ammunition

- backpacks
- bait and tackle
- batteries
- binoculars
- boats
- cameras
- camouflage clothing for hunting
- campfire wood
- camp stoves
- canoes
- compasses
- decoys for waterfowl hunting
- dehydrated camping food
- film
- fish finders
- GPS units
- hang gliders
- hiking boots
- horse trailers and tack
- hunting and fishing equipment
- maps and guidebooks
- mountain bikes
- off-highway vehicles (OHVs)
- outdoor and other specialty clothing (e.g., Gore-Tex jackets, polypropylene underwear)
- personal watercraft (PWC)
- recreation vehicles (RVs)
- ropes and rock climbing/mountaineering gear
- skis
- sleeping bags
- snowmobiles
- spotting scopes (for birding or hunting)
- sunscreen
- surfboards
- tents
- trail running shoes

The aforementioned equipment and supplies (and many others) are sometimes purchased and used exclusively for outdoor recreation (e.g., most PWCs and fishing rods), but others are used for outdoor recreation as well as other uses (e.g., hiking boots for a backpacking trip and for walking to class on a slushy December day, a recreational vehicle used for trips to national parks during the summer, football tailgating in the fall, and housing extra family members while still parked in the driveway during a family reunion). The multiple-use nature of most outdoor recreation equipment makes it hard to accurately account for the economic impact of the outdoor recreation industry or even to communicate broadly and effectively with private sector outdoor recreation providers. However, it is clear that the scope and breadth of private sector involvement in providing outdoor recreation opportunities is huge. Following are just a few examples of the many manufacturers and suppliers exclusively or partly in the business of providing outdoor recreation equipment and supplies (along with examples of the types of products they produce).

- Arctic Cat (snowmobiles and ATVs)
- Black Diamond (climbing, mountaineering, and backcountry equipment and apparel)
- Bombardier Recreational Products (snowmobiles, watercraft, boats, and ATVs)
- Buck (knives and other outdoor products)
- Bushnell (binoculars, spotting scopes, rifle scopes, and other optics)
- Cabela's (hunting, fishing, and outdoor gear)
- Camelback (water containers for outdoor and other uses)
- Cannondale (mountain bikes and outdoor clothing)
- Coleman, Inc. (stoves, lanterns, tents, and other outdoor equipment)
- Columbia (outdoor clothing)
- Dagger (kayaks and whitewater canoes)
- Eastern Mountain Sports (EMS; outdoor equipment and apparel)

- Eddie Bauer (outdoor apparel and gear)
- Honda (motorcycles, ATVs, and personal watercraft)
- Kelty (backpacks and other outdoor gear)
- L.L. Bean (outdoor gear and apparel)
- Lowe Alpine Systems (backcountry and mountaineering equipment and apparel)
- Mountain House (dehydrated food for backcountry and other uses)
- Old Town Canoe (canoes, kayaks, and boating accessories)
- Patagonia (outdoor apparel and gear)
- Perception (kayaks and other recreational boats)
- Petzl (climbing equipment, headlamps, and other backcountry gear)
- Recreational Equipment, Inc. (REI; outdoor recreation equipment and apparel)
- Remington (sporting firearms and ammunition)
- Sierra Designs (outdoor clothing and equipment)
- Suunto (compasses, altimeters, and underwater dive computers)
- The North Face (outdoor equipment and apparel)
- Winchester (sporting firearms and ammunition)
- Winnebago Industries (recreational vehicles)

Providing Guiding, Outfitting, and Information

The tangible private sector contributions to outdoor recreation in terms of equipment, supplies, and lands are extensive and easy to see. The outdoor recreation services

Virtually all outdoor recreation experiences rely in some way on equipment, supplies, and information provided by the private sector.

The private sector provides outdoor recreation equipment and supplies through many means including retail outlets like this REI store in Seattle.

provided by this sector are less tangible, but no less significant. Perhaps the most obvious private sector outdoor recreation services are providing guiding, outfitting, and information.

Guiding and Outfitting

Guiding and outfitting can be distinct services, but frequently are provided by the same enterprise and are often purchased and used together by customers. An outfitter is an individual or company that provides the services, equipment, and supplies needed for a particular trip. In a fully outfitted trip a paid outfitter/guide stays with the group for the duration of the trip. In a partially outfitted trip, the customers use the outfitter's equipment, supplies, transportation services, training, and/or trip planning, but actually take the trip on their own. Of course it is possible to hire a guide only and not have the trip otherwise outfitted.

America Outdoors, a national association of outfitters and guides, represents about 550 professional companies in the United States that provide a wide variety of trips, vacations, and other services. They estimate their member companies provide recreation services and equipment to over two million people annually (America Outdoors, 2003). Following is a partial list of the kinds of private sector outfitters and guides and an example of each:

- Whitewater rafting—Wilderness River Outfitters (Idaho, Montana, and Alaska)
- Canoeing—Northwoods Wilderness Outfitters (Michigan and Wisconsin)
- Kayaking—Rios Ecuador Rafting and Kayaking Adventures (Ecuador)
- Horseback riding and horsepacking—Diamond R Expeditions (Montana)
- Camping—Canadian Wilderness Canoe and Camping Outfitters (Ontario, Canada)

Whitewater guiding and outfitting services are provided almost exclusively by the private sector.

- Hiking—A Walk in the Woods (Great Smoky Mountains National Park)
- Fishing—Tahoe Fly Fishing Outfitters (California)
- Llama packing—Lander Llama Adventures (Wyoming)
- Bike touring—Hudson Trail Outfitters, Ltd. (Maryland, Virginia, and Washington, DC)
- Guest ("dude") ranches—Kay El Bar Guest Ranch (Arizona)
- Birding—Birding Escapes (Costa Rica)
- Photography—Dreamride (Utah)
- Snowmobiling—High Country Snowmobile Tours (Wyoming)
- Four-wheel driving—4X4 New Zealand, Ltd. (New Zealand)
- Mountain biking—Western Spirit Mountain Biking Tour Company (Utah)
- Hunting—Backcountry Outfitters (Colorado)
- Ecotourism—EcoTurismo Yucatan (Mexico)
- Mountaineering—Mountain Odyssey (Wyoming)
- Rock climbing—Active Africa Adventures and Touring (South Africa)

Information

Perhaps the biggest and most commonly underestimated type of outdoor recreation service provided by the private sector, however, is information. A huge amount, although certainly not all, of the information used by people planning and engaging in outdoor recreation is provided by the private sector. The information may take the form of maps and guidebooks, how-to books and videos about a particular activity, magazine articles, documentary films, Web sites, works of fiction, photographs, paintings, and many more. The information may serve to train or inform current participants, to inspire or motivate prospective participants, to help people remember or reminisce about at particular trip or place, or to act as a supplement or substitute for actual participation, such as films or adventure books for "armchair mountaineers." Taken together, information is a huge part of outdoor recreation and a great deal of it is provided by or through the businesses and entrepreneurs of the private sector. The following examples of the many book titles and magazines available at outdoor recreation retail stores may give a feel for the breath and scope of the private outdoor recreation information industry:

Books

- *50 Selected Climbs in Grand Teton National Park*
- *Backcountry Cooking*
- *Best Bike Rides in the South*
- *Canoeing and Camping: Beyond the Basics*
- *Canoeing Basics*
- *Caribbean Hiking*
- *Conditioning for Outdoor Fitness*
- *Fifty Favorite Climbs*
- *GPS Made Easy*
- *Hiking Trails of the Smokies*
- *Kayaking Made Easy*
- *Mountaineering: The Freedom of the Hills*
- *Orienteering*
- *Sleeping Bag Yoga*
- *The Complete Walker IV*
- *The Essential Cross-Country Skier*
- *The Ultimate Guide to Trail Running*
- *Walking the Appalachian Trail*
- *Women and Thru-Hiking on the Appalachian Trail*
- *Into Thin Air: A Personal Account of the Mount Everest Disaster*
- *50 Hikes in the Mountains of North Carolina*
- *Mountain Biking for Mere Mortals*

Magazines

- *American Snowmobiler*
- *Backpacker*
- *Birder's World*

- *Blackpowder Hunting*
- *Climbing*
- *Field and Stream*
- *Fly Fisherman*
- *Four Wheeler*
- *Mountain Bike Action*
- *Outdoor Life*
- *Outside*
- *Paddler Magazine*
- *Sea Kayaker Magazine*

Many other services provided by the private sector relate to outdoor recreation information and expertise. Businesses and entrepreneurs that provide classes, consulting, contracting, trip planning, software design, public speaking and presenting, rock climbing lessons, training for hunting dogs, photography, and other creative arts all provide information-related services that support outdoor recreation in one way or another.

Providing Support Services

Private enterprises in communities near outdoor recreation areas frequently provide important support services for outdoor recreation participants. The support services in these communities, sometimes referred to as "gateway communities" or "host communities," are especially important to tourists from outside the local area in which they recreate. Important goods and services provided by those local businesses include the following:

- lodging
- groceries
- gasoline, oil, maintenance, and repair services for vehicles
- laundry services
- meals in restaurants
- medical services
- hunting and fishing licenses
- processing of fish and game
- other goods and services needed locally

Even entrepreneurs who take freelance photographs of river rafting outfitters' clients provide a form of support service.

Studies have shown a significant share of the total trip expenses of tourists are made up of the costs of these locally purchased goods and services, as well as the costs of similar goods and services bought when the tourists

Information produced by the private sector, like these products available at a nature center, can greatly enhance outdoor recreation experiences.

are in transit between their places of residence and the outdoor recreation areas. Those expenditures, therefore, comprise a significant proportion of the contributions of tourism to local and regional economies, as discussed in Chapter 19 on the Economics of Outdoor Recreation. Because of their effects on the total satisfaction realized from an outdoor recreation outing, these local businesses are increasingly recognized as important associated "providers" of outdoor recreation opportunities. Many public park and recreation agencies now view such private enterprises as significant partners and involve them as collaborating partners in the outdoor recreation resource planning and management processes, as explained in Chapter 13.

Operating Commercial Ventures on Public Lands

The first private sector role addressed in this chapter related to lands owned by private individuals and businesses. We now move to the role of the private sector in providing commercial facilities and operations on public land. Under appropriate conditions and with necessary approvals, most outdoor recreation facilities and enterprises can be located in any appropriate setting regardless of whether the land there is private, public, or nonprofit. (The criteria for and mechanics of these arrangements are covered in Chapter 17.) In theory, any of the facilities or services mentioned earlier could be provided by the private sector on public land. Common examples of facilities the private sector often provides on public land through contracts or other special agreements include the following:

- developed campgrounds
- alpine ski areas and ski resorts
- gift and book shops
- restaurants and other food and beverage operations
- equipment rental operations
- hotels
- retail camp stores

These and many other kinds of facilities and services are provided on some public lands and can be operated by private, public, or nonprofit sectors. When operated by private businesses, these operations are generally referred to as "special uses" or "concessions." They provide services and products the public sector determined are needed and appropriate, but the public agency cannot provide itself or chooses not to provide for any of a number of reasons. The private owners of commercial enterprises operating on public lands are charged a fee, typically based on a percentage of their gross revenues generated from

their operations that take place on those lands. Examples of private outdoor recreation operations and services that can occur on public lands include the following:

- guiding and outfitting
- transportation services (e.g., bus services for visitors at Denali National Park)
- ecotourism trips into national parks
- photography "safaris" (e.g., Kruger National Park in South Africa)
- guided hikes (e.g., Inca Trail in Peru)
- construction and facility renovation
- maintenance of facilities

Private sector operations and services that benefit outdoor recreation, such as contractors who build, renovate, and in some cases maintain and operate recreation facilities, are becoming increasingly important. For example, the 50 companies that belong to the Professional Trailbuilders Association are private sector businesses that contract with many federal, state, and local land managing agencies and others to design, build, and reconstruct trails of all kinds (Professional Trailbuilders Association, 2005).

Some of the commercial operations taking place on public lands are ones most people are not aware of. Special-use permits are available and usually required for commercial filming and still photography on public lands. This includes creating products for sale, such as films, videotapes, television broadcasts, or documentaries of participants in sporting or recreation events created for profit-making purposes. Private individuals can also receive permits to build and occupy private recreation cabins on some public lands and even to rent certain lookout towers.

Commercial ventures on public lands are sometimes controversial. The locations and levels of commercial operations are sometimes contested, and sometimes "pirates" try to make illegal profits from providing recreation services illegally on public lands. For example, an unethical individual river "guide" with no special-use permit might try to charge customers for bootleg river trips and pretend they are "just a group of friends boating together" if confronted by river managers or legitimate outfitters.

Providing Donations and Other Support

Finally, the private sector supports outdoor recreation by providing donations and other support, such as cost sharing, which directly or indirectly helps to provide outdoor recreation opportunities. Private individuals donate a tremendous amount of money and volunteer time to outdoor recreation–related causes and projects. Many corporations, both outdoor recreation–related and others, also make charitable donations to causes they feel are important. A significant portion of this corporate support and corporate giving is directed to conservation of natural resources in general and outdoor recreation in particular. For example, Recreational Equipment, Inc. (REI) has an active grants program whereby its employees nominate organizations, projects, and programs to receive funding or equipment donations. They also organize and support many community service programs. For over ten years, the Conservation Fund has funded projects and made awards related to greenways across the United States. These efforts have been funded by donations from Dupont and Kodak. Some corporations also make in-kind donations of equipment and expertise that are very important for outdoor recreation providers. Some match charitable contributions that their employees make to nonprofits and some even donate their employees' time to worthy nature-oriented causes.

Cost sharing by private enterprises involves sharing with a public or nonprofit organization part of the cost of a particular structure or service that helps to facilitate outdoor recreation opportunities. Some type of plaque or sign frequently recognizes the cost-sharing donor, or the donor might remain anonymous. In either case, cost sharing by private enterprises is particularly important to all public park and recreation agencies in times of fiscal hardship, which seem ever present. Opportunities can then be provided that could not be provided without cost sharing.

Of course, in many cases the boundaries among these six private sector roles blur. A private entrepreneur may have his or her base of operations on private property, but make most of his or her income by taking customers into a nearby National Forest through a special-use permit. The same company might produce books, maps, and other information for sale in its store where they also sell outdoor gear and supplies purchased from major manufacturers. An entrepreneur might also work with a freelance photographer to take and sell photographs to clients and could even use some of the profits to provide charitable donations to a nonprofit organization to help protect local recreation settings important to his or her business.

Summary

The organizations and individuals of the private sector play a significant role in the provision of outdoor recreation opportunities. They do this primarily by providing private land and facilities for public outdoor recreation; providing outdoor recreation equipment and supplies; providing guiding and outfitting services, and information; providing support services; operating commercial ventures on public lands; and providing donations and other support. These roles frequently overlap, but taken together, the role of the private sector is essential for outdoor recreation as we know it. The private sector frequently works with and through the other sectors to support outdoor recreation.

Literature Cited

America Outdoors. (2003). *The national association of America's outfitters & guides*. Retrieved June 25, 2003, from http://www.americaoutdoors.org/aboutao1.htm

America Outdoors. (2004). *Code of ethics & professionalism*. Retrieved September 29, 2004, from http://www.americaoutdoors.org/ethics.htm

Professional Trailbuilders Association. (2005). *PTBA goals and activities*. Retrieved February 24, 2005, from http://www.trailbuilders.org/about.html

Teasley, R. J., Bergstrom, J. C., Cordell, H. K., Zarnoch, S. J., and Gentle, P. (1999). Private lands and outdoor recreation in the United States. In H. K. Cordell et al., *Outdoor recreation in American life: A national assessment of demand and supply trends* (pp. 183–218). Champaign, IL: Sagamore.

Chapter 8
Nonprofit Sector Providers

Volunteer organizations, with the assistance of providers,[1] develop a community spirit and pride of accomplishment at the grass roots. The local level is where efforts to encourage volunteering should be strongest. (President's Commission on Americans Outdoors, 1987, p. 104)

Learning Objectives

1. Describe the importance of the nonprofit sector in providing outdoor recreation opportunities.
2. Explain the primary ways the nonprofit sector is involved in providing outdoor recreation opportunities and give examples of each.

Working independently or in partnership with other providers, nonprofit organizations are vital in directly or indirectly providing outdoor recreation opportunities. The purpose of this chapter is to introduce readers to the role and importance of nonprofit organizations in outdoor recreation.

Overview of the Nonprofit Sector

The nonprofit sector is comprised of nongovernmental organizations that are not part of the private (for-profit) sector. The nonprofit sector is sometimes referred to as the quasi-public, nongovernmental, volunteer, or even the independent sector in the United States. Such groups are typically referred to simply as nongovernmental organizations (NGOs) in the rest of the world. Some people confuse the nonprofit sector with the other two sectors because they know that public sector agencies do not exist to make a profit, that private sector enterprises sometimes make no profit for a period of time, and that nonprofit sector organizations often charge fees to help cover their costs. However, the nonprofit sector is distinct from the public and private sectors, and it plays a large and unique role in providing outdoor recreation opportunities in the United States and many other countries.

In the United States, technically a "nonprofit" is any one of many types of organizations recognized as tax-exempt under the Internal Revenue Service (IRS) code (Internal Revenue Service, 2003). There are two types of nonprofits particularly relevant to outdoor recreation. The most important are those classified under IRS section 501(c)3. These are groups organized and operated exclusively for specific purposes that the IRS considers tax-exempt and include charitable, religious, educational, and scientific organizations. The other relevant category is comprised of organizations classified as tax-exempt because they promote pleasure, recreation, and other similar non-profit purposes as defined by the IRS. Examples include amateur hunting, fishing, tennis, swimming, and other sports clubs, as well as country clubs. Both classifications of organizations are exempt from certain taxes, and more importantly, donations to 501(c)3s are tax-deductible, which provides an additional economic incentive for individuals and corporations to support them. Both of these categories of nonprofits receive favored tax treatment, because federal and state governments want to encourage certain activities in the public interest. Conservation and directly or indirectly providing outdoor recreation opportunities are usually among these public interest activities.

Another important distinction of the nonprofit sector is its reliance on volunteer labor. Although many nonprofits hire professional paid staffs, they typically carry out most of their operations through volunteers. Certainly large numbers of volunteers work directly with public-sector agencies, including public outdoor recreation providers, but the nonprofit sector depends far more on the time and talents of volunteers. A large number of nonprofit organizations are operated completely by volunteers.

Scope and Types of Nonprofit Organizations Involved in Outdoor Recreation

A large number and variety of nonprofit organizations are involved in providing outdoor recreation opportunities. For example, an online search of the *Conservation Directory*, maintained by the National Wildlife Federation, yielded names of over 2,000 nonprofit organizations (National Wildlife Federation, 2003). Some nonprofit groups own land and may directly provide opportunities by opening their lands to outdoor recreation and by providing any needed facilities and improvements. Nonprofits are more frequently indirect providers of outdoor recreation, however. Some exist primarily to conserve natural resources or even to provide outdoor recreation opportunities, while in other cases these are secondary objectives or even unintended outgrowths of other activities. Nonprofits involved in providing outdoor recreation opportunities can be broadly grouped into the following seven types:

- professional groups and associations
- land protection organizations
- conservation, preservation, and environmental organizations
- user group associations
- public education organizations
- camps and social and recreation clubs
- foundations

Professional Groups and Associations

Nearly every profession has one or more professional associations that supports, advocates, and attempts to advance that profession and its practitioners. The leisure professions are no exceptions. The most prominent international professional association for parks and recreation in general is the World Leisure and Recreation Association (WLRA). In terms of outdoor recreation, the International Union of Forest Research Organizations (IUFRO) is prominent and very active. IUFRO is a nonprofit, nongovernmental, international network of forest scientists formed in the late 19th century. Its objectives are to promote international cooperation in forestry and forest products research. It is organized into six divisions, then into study groups by subject matter. One of its largest study groups focuses on outdoor recreation, tourism, landscape planning and management, and nature conservation research (IUFRO, 2003). Outdoor recreation professionals worldwide also advance their field through gatherings such as the International Symposium on Society and Resource Management (ISSRM) and conferences and publications sponsored by nonprofits such as the George Wright Society.

Many nations also have recreation-related professional associations. Several exist in the United States, the largest being the National Recreation and Park Association (NRPA) with over 21,000 members. As the professional association for the leisure professions in the United States, NRPA monitors legislation and lobbies at all levels, often through affiliated organizations. NRPA also accredits college and university leisure studies and park and recreation programs, develops and monitors professional standards, and certifies leisure professionals according to its criteria. It organizes national and regional conferences, regular educational training "schools," national information and educational campaigns, and award programs. Many of these NRPA activities have direct or indirect effects on the provision of outdoor recreation opportunities. Among NRPA's "branches" is the National Society for Park Resources (NSPR), which focuses on the aspects of the profession closely related to outdoor recreation. The National Association of Recreation Resource Planners (NARRP) is another national organization of outdoor recreation professionals and others involved in recreation resource planning and management.

Numerous other professional groups and associations are involved indirectly in making outdoor recreation possible. The National Association for Interpretation (NAI), for example, represents and supports the profession of interpretation, which works to promote and improve visitor understanding at parks, zoos, museums, nature centers, historic sites, and related settings. The Resort and Commercial Recreation Association (RCRA) serves professionals in that important specialty. Nonprofit associations of private sector groups are also involved in outdoor recreation. The American Recreation Coalition (ARC), for example, is a national coalition of more than 100 prominent private sector recreation companies and recreation-related associations. It has been particularly effective in lobbying in the political arena for support for outdoor recreation. The Professional Trailbuilders Association represents dozens of private trail designers, consultants, and contractors, and America Outdoors (2003) represents adventure travel outfitters, tour companies, and outdoor educators. All of these and many other professional groups and associations are important indirect providers of outdoor recreation opportunities.

Land Protection Organizations

Some nonprofit organizations provide important settings for outdoor recreation through protecting undeveloped lands, waters, and other natural resource areas. The most common nonprofits of this type are land trusts. A land trust is "a nonprofit organization that, as all or part of its mission, actively works to conserve land by undertaking or assisting direct land transactions—primarily the purchase or acceptance of donations of land or conservation easements" (Land Trust Alliance, 2003). Land trusts and other nonprofit land protection organizations operate in many ways and for many reasons. Some focus only on ecologically significant areas, like wetlands, river corridors, or habitats of endangered species. Others focus on lands related to certain periods of history, like U.S. Civil

War battlefields, or lands facing particular pressures, like farmland threatened by urban or suburban sprawl. Some trusts target limited geographic regions, while others work nationally or internationally. Some obtain land with the intent of holding and managing it themselves, and others prefer to purchase and hold only the development rights or related easements and then have other organizations actually hold and manage the lands under those restrictions.

From the perspective of outdoor recreation, there are two important things to remember about nonprofit land protection organizations. First, some land trusts open their properties to public use and encourage outdoor recreation, while others limit or prohibit public recreation. Second, this segment of the nonprofit sector is growing very rapidly in size and importance. The amount of land protected by local and regional land trusts (excluding national trusts) increased 226% between 1990 and 2000, and the number of local and regional land trusts increased 42% during the same period to 1,263 (Land Trust Alliance, 2003). Selected examples of nonprofit land trusts include the following:

- Trust for Public Land (national)
- The Nature Conservancy (international)
- Little Traverse Conservancy (Michigan)
- San Juan Preservation Trust (Washington)
- Appalachian Trail Conference Land Trust (regional)
- Triangle Land Conservancy (North Carolina)
- Civil War Preservation Trust (national)

Conservation, Preservation, and Environmental Organizations

The large number of nonprofit conservation, preservation, and environmental organizations have important effects on the protection and management of natural resources and on the outdoor recreation opportunities provided at those areas. Many of these groups are active in advocacy at the local, regional, and national levels and have various environmental and public policy agendas. Their lobbying can affect public policy as well as the budgets and practices of land and recreation management agencies. Some of these groups are also directly involved in public service efforts both on and off of public lands. For example, Trout Unlimited, Ducks Unlimited, the Rocky Mountain Elk Foundation, and the Student Conservation Association are all well-known for their conservation projects and educational efforts, and many conservation groups organize and operate volunteer "service trips." On the other hand, relationships between some environmental organizations and public land managing agencies can be contentious. It is common for some such groups to vigorously oppose agency policies and to pursue long and costly litigation against agency actions.

Selected examples of nonprofit conservation, preservation, and environmental organizations, and paraphrases of their purposes include the following:

- American Rivers: Protecting and restoring rivers nationwide
- Greater Yellowstone Coalition: Preserving and protecting the greater Yellowstone ecosystem and the unique quality of life it sustains
- National Audubon Society: Conserving and restoring natural ecosystems, focusing on birds, other wildlife, and their habitats
- Rails-to-Trails Conservancy: Creating a nationwide network of public trails from former rail lines and connecting corridors
- Sierra Club: Exploring, enjoying and protecting the wild places of the earth
- Student Conservation Association: Changing lives through service to nature
- Trout Unlimited: Conserving, protecting and restoring North America's trout and salmon fisheries and their watersheds
- Wilderness Society: Protecting America's Wilderness

User Group Associations

Some nonprofit organizations focus on the needs and interests of particular outdoor recreation user groups. They are commonly involved in advocacy by trying to influence legislation that impacts their activity and its participants. They educate participants, promote a positive image of their activity, and work to assure that areas continue to be available for people to participate. They may also be active in public service work to improve or to repair outdoor recreation areas and facilities important to their members. For example, the American Hiking Society

Nonprofit organizations, like the Adirondack Mountain Club, have been and continue to be instrumental in preserving and managing outdoor recreation opportunities.

sponsors a "National Trails Day" and operates dozens of "Volunteer Vacations" to build, repair, and maintain trails across the United States each year. Volunteers for Outdoor Colorado organizes extensive service projects and operates a large "volunteer clearinghouse" to involve citizens in enhancing the public lands and outdoor recreation opportunities across their state.

Selected examples of nonprofit user group associations, and paraphrases of their purposes include the following:

- American Birding Association: Inspiring people to enjoy and protect wild birds
- American Council of Snowmobile Associations: Advancing efforts to promote the expansion of responsible snowmobiling
- American Hiking Society: Speaking for America's hikers and the trails they love
- Boone and Crocket Club: Addressing issues related to hunting and wildlife
- Good Sam Club: Making recreation vehicle (RV) use safer and more enjoyable
- International Mountain Bicycling Association: Creating, enhancing and preserving trail opportunities for mountain bikers worldwide
- Quail Unlimited: Dedicated to the wise management of America's wild quail as a valuable and renewable resource
- The Access Fund: Conserving climbing areas and keeping them open

Public Education Organizations

Some nonprofits focus primarily on public education related to issues or areas of concern to their constituents. Their scope, messages, and approaches vary, but a large number of these groups have direct or indirect effects on outdoor recreation or the resources it depends on. Some, like TREAD Lightly! and Leave No Trace, educate and inform the public directly about outdoor recreation skills and responsible use. Others, like Outward Bound, use outdoor recreation as a means to accomplish broader educational objectives. Sometimes these organizations focus on a particular type of outdoor recreation setting, such as the Wilderness Education Association (WEA), while others direct their efforts toward particular populations, like Elderhostel for older adults or groups serving at-risk youth. Over 70 national park cooperating associations, friends groups, and interpretive associations (e.g., Eastern National) operate bookstores, develop educational materials, and run other educational programs at national parks across the United States (Association of Partners for Public Lands, 2003).

Selected examples of nonprofit public education organizations, and paraphrases of their purposes include the following:

- Association for Experiential Education (AEE): Developing and promoting experiential education
- Eastern National: Providing quality educational products to America's national parks and other public trusts
- Leave No Trace: Promoting and inspiring responsible outdoor recreation through education, research, and partnerships
- National Outdoor Leadership School (NOLS): Teaching people the skills to comfortably and responsibly lead others in the backcountry

User group associations, like this equestrian club in Florida, are important outdoor recreation providers.

Nonprofit organizations are extremely important in terms of educating recreation users.

- Outward Bound USA: Providing adventure-based programs to inspire self-esteem, self-reliance, concern for others, and care for the environment.
- TREAD Lightly! Emphasizing responsible use of off-highway vehicles, other forms of backcountry travel, and low-impact principles for all recreation activities on public and private lands
- Wilderness Education Association: Promoting professionalism in outdoor leadership to improve outdoor trips and enhance conservation of the wild outdoors
- Wilderness Inquiry: Sharing outdoor adventure with anyone who has an interest in enjoying and exploring the outdoors, including people with disabilities

Camps and Social and Recreation Clubs

As noted earlier, the IRS recognizes certain charitable, religious, educational, pleasure, recreation, and other similar organizations as nonprofit. A large number of these groups are directly involved in providing outdoor recreation opportunities for their members and other populations they serve by operating social and recreational clubs or providing camps. Amateur hunting and fishing clubs (sometimes called private rod and gun clubs), church and youth camps, fly fishing clubs, orienteering clubs, and four-wheel drive clubs are just a few of many examples.

Organized camping, in particular, is a vast area of nonprofit outdoor recreation involvement in its own right. The American Camping Association (ACA) estimates there are more than 12,000 camps in the United States, and that nonprofit organizations run 75% of them. ACA also estimates that more than ten million youth are served in some way by camps every year (American Camping Association, 2003).

Selected examples of nonprofit camps operators and social and recreation clubs include the following:

- Big Horn Mountain Flyfishers (Wyoming)
- Boy Scouts of America
- Breakaways 4WD Club of SA, Inc. (Australia)
- Camp Fire USA
- Girl Scouts of the USA
- Manchester Bow Hunters Club (New Hampshire)
- Mount Washington Rod & Gun Club (Maryland)
- United Church Camps, Inc.
- YMCA/YWCA

Foundations

Nonprofit foundations make monetary grants and provide other forms of support that advance the purposes and interests of their founders and supporters. Foundations, as well as other grant makers and benefactors, are actively involved in natural resource protection and management as well as supporting groups that provide outdoor recreation opportunities. Their philanthropy may take the form of donating money, equipment, materials, supplies, expertise, and other resources for a wide variety of purposes. A foundation might make a one-time donation to enable a local land trust to purchase a particular piece of property, give a series of annual grants for a trail club to create a low-impact recreation education program, make a donation to start a nonprofit organization to operate outdoor adventure programs for young people with disabilities, or even donate a fleet of vehicles to enable a conservation organization to expand its operations. There are far more foundations in operation than most people realize. According to The Foundation Center (2003) there are more than 70,000 private and community foundations in the United States. A significant number of these make important grants for conservation, recreation, or natural resource related purposes.

Selected examples of nonprofit foundations that directly or indirectly support outdoor recreation or conservation of natural resources include the following:

- Doris Duke Charitable Foundation
- Ford Foundation
- Mary Reynolds Babcock Foundation
- National Park Foundation
- New Hampshire Charitable Foundation
- Peter Jay Sharp Foundation
- Richard King Mellon Foundation
- Z. Smith Reynolds Foundation

Obviously, there can be significant overlap among the seven broad types of nonprofits, and many groups do not fit neatly into a single category. For example, a national association promoting and supporting a particular type of outdoor recreation activity may also function as a land trust to protect land for people engaged in that activity. It may also function much like a foundation by offering grants to other groups that promote, provide opportunities for, or even conduct research related to that outdoor recreation activity.

Summary

Many thousands of nonprofit organizations involve themselves directly or indirectly in providing outdoor recreation opportunities. Taken together and supported by small armies of volunteers, these organizations make tremendous contributions locally, regionally, nationally, and internationally. Nonprofits are often direct providers of outdoor recreation settings, although they are most frequently indirect providers of recreation opportunities. They operate on public, private, and nonprofit land and are frequently creative, flexible, and responsive in accomplishing their stated purposes or serving their members or constituents. Although they often overlap, outdoor recreation related nonprofit organizations can be broadly grouped into seven categories: professional groups and associations; land protection organizations; conservation, preservation, and environmental organizations; user group associations; public education organizations; camps and social and recreation clubs; and foundations. Each of these types of nonprofits has a distinct and important role. The nonprofit sector frequently teams up with partners in the private and public sectors to support outdoor recreation. Such partnerships across the three sectors are the focus of the next chapter.

Literature Cited

American Camping Association. (2003). *Enriching lives through the camping experience*. Retrieved July 17, 2003, from http://www.acacamps.org/aboutaca.htm

America Outdoors. (2003). *The national association of America's outfitters & guides*. Retrieved June 25, 2003, from http://www.americaoutdoors.org/aboutao1.htm

Association of Partners for Public Lands. (2003). *Serving America's people and public lands*. Retrieved July 17, 2003, from http://www.appl.org

Internal Revenue Service. (2003). *Publication 557—Tax exempt status for your organization*. Washington, DC: Department of the Treasury.

International Union of Forest Research Organizations. (2003). *IUFRO Unit 6.01.00—Forest recreation, landscape and nature conservation*. Retrieved June 27, 2003, from http://iufro.boku.ac.at/

The Foundation Center. (2003). *Foundation finder*. Retrieved July 2, 2003, from http://lnp.fdncenter.org/finder.html

Land Trust Alliance. (2003). *National land trust census*. Retrieved June 27, 2003, from http://www.lta.org/aboutlta/census.html

National Wildlife Federation. (2003). *Conservation directory*. Retrieved June 27, 2003, from http://www.nwf.org/conservationdirectory/

President's Commission on Americans Outdoors. (1987). *Americans outdoors: The legacy, the challenge*. Washington, DC: Island Press.

Endnote

1. The President's Commission used the word "provider" in a narrower sense than the authors. The authors prefer to make it clear that nonprofit organizations are very often direct providers of outdoor recreation opportunities as well.

Chapter 9
Partnerships Among Outdoor Recreation Providers

We recommend that partnerships be formed among private for-profit and nonprofit entities and public agencies to enhance recreation resources, services and facilities. (President's Commission on Americans Outdoors, 1987, p. 189)

Learning Objectives

1. Explain what outdoor recreation partnerships are, why they can be beneficial, and whom they involve.
2. Describe successful outdoor recreation partnerships and give examples.
3. Know the differences among the seven most common mechanisms used to create partnerships for providing outdoor recreation opportunities.
4. Describe how to create an outdoor recreation partner organization using hands-on field projects.

This chapter describes partnerships and cooperation among outdoor recreation providers from all three sectors by answering four basic questions:

1. *What* are partnerships?
2. *Why* is it beneficial to form and to nurture partnerships?
3. *Who* can and should be involved in partnerships?
4. *How* can partnerships be created and nurtured?

The closely related topic of planning and managing outdoor recreation using a collaborative approach will be addressed in Chapter 17.

What Are Partnerships?

Partnerships involve cooperation among public agencies, nonprofit organizations, and/or private sector enterprises in providing outdoor recreation opportunities. Partnerships among stakeholders can take many forms and represent an increasing blurring of the traditional roles of the three sectors as described in the previous three chapters. A partnership could be something as simple as a public sector agency recruiting a group of volunteers from a local conservation organization to help with a specific project for part of a day. Or it could be as sophisticated as a public agency formally delegating a major ongoing responsibility to a group of qualified private and nonprofit partners. The mechanisms for operating partnerships are quite varied and range from informal agreements to long-term binding contracts, cooperative agreements, leases, and other agreements among partners, as will be described later.

A classic partnership for providing outdoor recreation opportunities involves partners from each of the three sectors. This is because each sector can typically bring different strengths and resources to the collaboration. The roles of each partner can vary, of course, but a classic partnership typically involves the following roles for each partner:

- **Public sector land management agency.** Provides expertise, authority, and the actual outdoor recreation settings. The public agency can also provide funding and other resources in many cases.

- **Nonprofit volunteer organization.** Provides volunteers, resources, expertise, energy, and political support.

- **Private sector sponsor.** Provides funding, other resources, expertise, political support, and people.

A classic partnership of this kind can be visualized as a three-legged stool with the seat of the stool being the partnership (and the management objectives accomplished through it) supported equally by the three partners (see Figure 9.1, p. 124).

In practice, of course, partnerships come in many shapes, sizes, and flavors. Many of the examples of outdoor recreation providers presented in the previous two chapters were also illustrations of partnerships between a private or nonprofit provider and a public sector agency. Regardless of their size or purpose, however, most successful partnerships have a number of common characteristics:

- **Broad-based participation.** Successful partnerships typically involve entire organizations and many individuals from those organizations. This assures ongoing participation and enables broader access to the unique strengths and resources of each of the partners.

- **Clearly identified roles for all partners.** The process of explicitly identifying the partners' respective roles and agreeing on them is very important. Clearly identifying the roles for all partners assures each partner is involved in the most appropriate way.

- **Written agreement.** Formalizing the partnership relationship assures there is no confusion about who is responsible for what. The best way to do this is to document the agreement in writing.

- **Delegation of real responsibility to partners.** Having meaningful responsibilities for each partner to fulfill can be much more motivating than if their tasks seem trivial or unconnected with important outcomes. The strongest partnerships are ones where each partner is responsible for important aspects of the overall operation.

Countless examples of large and small partnerships provide outdoor recreation opportunities by exhibiting the

Figure 9.1   Classic partnership as a "three-legged-stool" formed and supported by a public sector land management agency, nonprofit volunteer organization, and private sector sponsor

characteristics noted here. The following three should help to illustrate the potential of partnerships among the three sectors. Notice each has the classic "three-legged stool" participation of partners from the public, private, and nonprofit sectors all working toward common goals.

Management of the Appalachian Trail

The nonprofit Appalachian Trail Conference (ATC) and its member clubs work in very close partnership with the National Park Service and other public sector providers and private sponsors to maintain and manage the 2,168-mile long Appalachian Trail (AT). Benton MacKaye proposed the AT in a 1921 article in *Journal of the American Institute of Architects*. The first section of the trail was built in New York in 1923, and the entire trail opened 14 years later in 1937, with most of the planning and construction being done by volunteers. The trail travels through 14 states and crosses the lands of a complicated collection of federal, state, and local agencies as well as nonprofit organizations. Since its formation in 1925, the ATC has been dedicated to building, protecting, and managing the Appalachian Trail for public outdoor recreation use (Appalachian Trail Conference, 2003).

Originally, about three quarters of the AT was on state and federal public lands. By the 1960s large portions of the trail still located on private land were threatened with closure as development expanded into what had been the most remote areas of the east. With the help of persistent lobbying by ATC and others, the National Trail System Act was passed in 1968, leading among other things to a major National Park Service effort to permanently protect the AT and a corridor of land around it. Since then, the AT has been a part of the national park system. Protecting and managing what was essentially a 2,100-mile "linear park" brought with it daunting challenges. The NPS made the logical decision to form and nurture a partnership with ATC and others to carry out the AT-related provisions of the Act and its amendments rather than attempt to do so alone. This partnership involved NPS, the USDA Forest Service, various state agencies acquiring the trail lands (a buffer corridor averaging 1,000 feet wide), and ATC continuing and expanding it traditional roles in trail management. As of mid-2003 less than 14 miles of the entire trail had yet to be protected.

The partnership approach along the AT worked so well that in 1984 the NPS formally delegated responsibility for managing the AT corridor lands to the ATC. These responsibilities included planning, maintenance, land stewardship, construction, management planning, management, safety, monitoring and much more. With some exceptions (law enforcement being the most important one), the day-to-day management of the AT remains the responsibility of ATC, its member clubs, and their volunteers.

The ATC has evolved into a confederation of 31 non-profit clubs and is itself a volunteer-based nonprofit with about 50 year-round and seasonal staff. The ATC mission is "the preservation and management of the natural, scenic, historic, and cultural resources associated with the Appalachian Trail, in order to provide primitive outdoor recreation and educational opportunities for Trail visitors."

ATC's member clubs have a combined membership of about 125,000 people throughout the eastern United States, and each year more than 5,200 volunteers from the ATC and its member clubs donate over 176,000 hours of physical labor on the AT. To support these efforts, nearly 90 corporations and 27 foundations have made gifts to the ATC; 44 of these are ATC corporate members.

Making the AT available to the multitudes of users who seek outdoor recreation there each year is a huge undertaking that involves a large number of national, state, regional, and local partners from the public, nonprofit, and private sectors. All of these work, in one way or another, through the very successful and sophisticated partnership between the National Park Service, Appalachian Trail Conference, and many others. Each of the various partnership mechanisms presented later in this chapter are used in one way or another among the many partners involved in the AT partnership. This partnership has been a model for many others.

National Park Visitor Information Through Cooperating Associations

Providing outdoor recreation and park-related information is commonly accomplished through partnerships. This may be by deliberately planned cooperation, as when an agency contracts with a private firm to create a publication or nature center display. Or it might not be due to deliberately planned collaboration, such as when publicly generated and available data is used by a private enterprise to produce maps and guides sold to the public to generate a profit. In some cases all three sectors are involved in partnerships to provide information. "Cooperating" or "interpretive" associations in national parks are an excellent example of this type of cooperation. The National Park Service contracts with these nonprofit associations to provide educational materials at many park visitor centers. These associations typically stock materials they produce as well as ones developed by private sector publishing companies.

Beginning at Yosemite National Park in 1920, national park cooperating associations have provided agency-approved information, such as publications, maps, videos, programs, and merchandise, to park visitors. This has proven to be a very effective and efficient way to provide information and services to visitors. It is also a means of generating income for parks, since a portion of revenues from cooperating association sales is used to support additional interpretation, education, and visitor service programs. In 2002 National Park Service cooperating associations provided $26.5 million in funding back to the national parks. There are now 65 national park cooperating associations serving NPS units across the nation. All are founded for educational purposes, governed by volunteer boards of directors, and operated under formal agreements with their agency partners (Parks & History Association, 2003). The largest national park cooperating association is Eastern National, founded in 1947 and now operating in more than 130 national park units and other public trusts. Eastern National operates book and gift shops in visitor centers, such as the Jamestown Glasshouse in Colonial National Historic Park, and the electric map and Cyclorama at Gettysburg National Military Park (Eastern National, 2003). Other cooperating and interpretive associations include the Alaska Natural History Association, Grand Canyon Association, Yellowstone Association, and Devils Tower Natural History Association (Association of Partners for Public Lands, 2003).

National Park Support Through the National Park Foundation

The National Park Foundation (NPF) is the congressionally chartered nonprofit partner working specifically with U.S. national parks. The NPF raises private funds, makes grants, and increases public awareness of national parks. The NPF was chartered in 1967 and launched by a $1 million grant from Laurance Rockefeller (the former Chair of the Outdoor Recreation Resources Review Commission). NPF receives no federal appropriations and over the past seven years raised $148 million in contributions and made $137.7 million in grants and program support to U.S.

Many outdoor recreation-related opportunities and services would not be possible without cooperation and partnerships among the three sectors.

national parks. Recent major private sector contributors to the National Park Foundation include General Electric, American Airlines, Discovery Communications, Ford Motor Company, Kodak, and *Time* magazine (National Park Foundation, 2003).

Why Form Partnerships?

Partnerships like the ones described here can be extremely beneficial. They are often entered into by public land managers for reasons such as the following:

Extend limited resources and improve management. Partners can bring important skills and energy the agency might not otherwise have at its disposal. A bigger and more talented team can accomplish more than the agency could on its own. Active partners can reduce costs, increase revenues, and help the agency do more with less. This can make it possible for the agency to better meet the challenges created by increasing outdoor recreation use and other demands.

Provide public input. An actively involved public can provide important input for land managers in a non-adversarial manner.

Educate the public. By getting actively involved in actual management activities, partners learn first hand about agency objectives, challenges, issues, and constraints. In so doing, they often develop a new respect and appreciation for the agency and their personnel. Using partnerships to build a better informed public constituency is a very important benefit often overlooked or underappreciated.

Increase public "ownership" and build support for the agency and its objectives. The "sweat equity" developed as partners work together on behalf of a public land area often fosters a new sense of "ownership" for public land resources. Such efforts can improve public perceptions of an agency, increase commitment and support for the agency and its objectives, and dramatically reduce any feelings of "us versus them" that can exist between public agencies and the people they serve.

Avoid or minimize costly litigation. Partners who are actively and meaningfully involved in addressing important land management challenges are much less likely to resort to lawsuits against the agency to accomplish their goals.

Meet regulatory or procedural mandates. Collaborative management is a very effective and appropriate approach in most cases. It is also required in planning and management frameworks like the beneficial outcomes approach to leisure (BOAL), because local stakeholders are the most knowledgeable and have vested interests in the success of agency actions (see Chapter 13).

Team Up With Whom?

The first question that comes to mind for many outdoor recreation managers when they begin to consider partnerships of any kind is, "With whom could we be teaming?" The potential partners available to most public sector land managers can be organized into four groups.

Other Public Sector Agencies

Other federal, state, regional, county, and local agencies are all important potential partners. Partnerships among agencies are particularly important when adjoining land areas are managed by different agencies or when nearby agencies have strengths or resources needed by their counterparts.

Individual Volunteers

Every year tens of thousands of individuals volunteer to assist public agencies in providing outdoor recreation opportunities. Many do so independently and with no formal agreements with their agency partners. Others do so more formally through established volunteer programs like Volunteers-In-Parks (VIP) for the National Park Service, and Volunteers in the National Forests (VIF) for the U.S. Forest Service. Such programs give agencies authority and assistance in recruiting volunteers to serve the agency essentially as unpaid employees. In many cases, agencies can pay VIP and VIF volunteers' expenses, provide training, and cover volunteers for liability and worker's compensation claims. From the agency perspective, the biggest disadvantage of relying on individual volunteers is that the agency must recruit, train, and supervise its volunteer workforce itself.

Volunteer programs organized and managed by public sector agencies are a growing type of partnership.

Nonprofit Sector

An important advantage of partnering with an organized nonprofit group is they can frequently provide much of their own recruiting, training, and supervision. As noted in Chapter 8, there are literally thousands of nonprofit organizations involved in one way or another in conservation or outdoor recreation. Each of these groups is a potential partner for an outdoor recreation provider. It may be helpful to consider potential partners based on the categories of nonprofit organizations as presented in Chapter 8. Those categories and examples of likely partnerships that a public agency might form with such an organization include the following:

- **Professional groups and associations** team up to provide expert training, project advice, interns, and experienced volunteers.

- **Land protection organizations** work together to protect adjacent lands, inholdings, and viewsheds; provide political support for agency land acquisition budget requests; and collaborate in land-use planning and protection strategies.

- **Conservation, preservation, and environmental organizations** collaborate on environmental monitoring and restoration projects; team up to protect adjacent lands, inholdings, and viewsheds; and provide coordination with other like-minded organizations.

- **User group associations** team up to provide user education among people participating in "their" outdoor recreation activity, to carry out hands-on improvement or restoration projects in areas popular with their user group, and to generate political support for actions supporting their activity and favorite places.

- **Public education organizations** partner to carry out interpretive and educational programs, to produce educational materials, to conduct research, and to monitor recreation use.

- **Social and recreation clubs and camp operators** team up to carry out "service projects," to build or maintain trails, and to sponsor special events.

- **Foundations** provide expertise, funding, and other resources for any of the partnerships noted here or for other agency efforts; work together to conduct research, to organize marketing campaigns, or to coordinate public education efforts.

Private Sector

Similarly, any private sector enterprise is also a potential partner for agencies providing outdoor recreation opportunities. Potential private sector partnerships based on the private sector categories used in Chapter 7 include the following:

- **Providers of private land and facilities for public outdoor recreation** team up to extend outdoor recreation opportunities into lands adjacent to those managed by the agency, or to assist with monitoring of boundaries and viewsheds.

- **Providers of outdoor recreation equipment and supplies** collaborate to offer classes, clinics, and safety courses to visitors and staff; provide discounted equipment and supplies for agency personnel; and operate equipment rental operations.

- **Providers of guiding, outfitting, and other services** team up to provide value added services for area visitors, assist with educating visitors (both customers and noncustomers), and help to monitor backcountry areas and conditions.

- **Operators of commercial ventures on public lands** partner with private enterprises to provide lodging, meals, and other services and products to visitors; to assist with educating visitors (both customers and noncustomers); and to provide income and other resources for areas operations.

- **Providers of donations and other support** from the private sector can be invaluable in donating funding, equipment, services, supplies, expertise, and other forms of support for one-time and ongoing agency needs.

There are, of course, many types of outdoor recreation partnerships entered into for a variety of reasons and to accomplish many different purposes. Their form and operation are limited only by the needs and creativity of those involved. One thing, however, is clear: Partnerships have been and will continue to be an efficient and effective way to provide outdoor recreation opportunities. The ability to form and nurture partnerships are skills that will be increasingly required of all outdoor recreation professionals.

How to Create and Nurture Partnerships

There is usually little doubt that partnerships among organizations from the public, private, and nonprofit sectors, can be a very effective and appropriate approach to providing outdoor recreation opportunities. The more pressing question is usually: *How* do I go about creating effective partnerships? The following section attempts to answer this question.

Mechanisms for Establishing Partnerships

A partnership is simply cooperation among recreation providers and other stakeholders. As will be detailed in Chapter 13, we use a broad definition of the word *stakeholder* to include any person or group that affects or is affected by (to any managerially relevant degree) the recreation opportunities being produced. Therefore the potential partner might be another public agency, nonprofit organization, and/or private sector enterprise. Or it could be groups of unorganized individuals who affect or are affected by the outdoor recreation opportunity provider's actions.

Mechanically, agencies can use a number of means to build and to maintain partnerships among organizations and with stakeholders. The following are seven common approaches for establishing partnerships. The list is arranged roughly from the least formal options to the most formal and sophisticated ones.

Informal agreements. Informal "handshake agreements" have been used, sometimes very effectively, to reach understandings between outdoor recreation providing partners on everything from where to locate a new trail to granting permission for new recreation activities on public lands. While informal agreements can be quick and easy, they have the obvious disadvantages of being prone to misunderstanding, difficult to enforce, and limited by how long those particular individuals are in their present positions of authority, and how long they remember their "agreement."

Existing agency volunteer programs. As noted earlier, many public agencies have formally established programs for involving volunteers in their operations. Examples include the Volunteers in the National Forests (VIF) program of the U.S. Forest Service and the Volunteers-In-Parks (VIP) program of the National Park Service. The VIF and VIP programs are very similar in that they each provide a structured way for individuals or organized groups of volunteers to become involved in a wide variety of tasks on behalf of the agency. Volunteers enrolled in the VIF or VIP program are considered federal employees for tort claims and injury compensation. While volunteer service does not provide other federal employment benefits, it is creditable work experience. The benefits of these programs to the agencies are significant. In fiscal year 2003, for example, 122,000 volunteers donated 4.5 million hours to national parks at a value of $77.3 million. (National Park Service, 2003, 2005). In fact, many federal agencies now cooperate in volunteer recruiting and provide an interagency Web portal with searchable information about volunteer opportunities nationwide (http://volunteer.gov/gov, 2003). Adopt-A-Trail programs run by many states and nonprofit organizations are another example of existing volunteer programs used to form partnerships to help provide outdoor recreation opportunities.

Memoranda of understanding. A memorandum of understanding (MOU) is a written agreement between two parties that typically describes in broad terms who has various responsibilities in which situations. For example, a public land manager may enter into a memorandum of understanding with nearby police or fire departments to clarify who has primary responsibility for a particular area of public land. Memoranda of understanding tend to be rather general in scope, but extremely important in assuring each partner considers what its appropriate role is and commits, in writing, to carry out that role.

Cooperative agreements. Cooperative agreements are typically more formal, specific, and detailed than memoranda of understanding. Cooperative agreements more clearly define the roles and responsibilities of each partner. A state park system might use a cooperative agreement to spell out the roles and responsibilities of a statewide hiking club willing to maintain and manage particular trails in particular state parks. The cooperative agreement would clearly describe the various tasks each partner was responsible for and how often they would be carried out.

Contracts. Like any legal document, contracts between outdoor recreation providers are legally binding agreements that commit each partner to perform very specific tasks and/or to provide specific services or products within some specified timeframe. Public land managers would use a contract to enter into an agreement with a partner, for example, to construct a new trailhead and parking area or to clean the rest rooms in a system of public campgrounds for a specified time period.

Concession agreements. A concessionaire is a private or nonprofit organization that operates a business on public land. A concession agreement is a specialized contract spelling out the terms of operation for the private concession. The National Park Service, for example, uses concession agreements with private corporations to authorize them to operate facilities like Yellowstone Lodge in Yellowstone National Park. Such agreements clearly specify the length and the terms of the contract, including the fee that the concessionaire will pay the agency for the right to operate the business there.

Special-use permits. Many agencies utilize special-use permits to authorize a partner to undertake a relatively unique operation within that agency's jurisdiction. Many of the major alpine ski areas operated by private corporations in Colorado, for example, are located on National Forest lands and must be authorized by special-use permits. Some agencies also require special-use permits for guides and outfitters that provide services like whitewater rafting or hunting trips on public lands. The U.S. Forest Service uses special-use permits, after a very specific approval process, to grant permission for the partner to operate these and many other special uses on public lands.

Other special uses include private cabins, communications towers, commercial filming and still photography, research, water transmission, and agriculture. There are currently over 72,000 special-use authorizations of 200 types on the National Forests and Grasslands alone (U.S. Forest Service, 2003).

It is important to remember these descriptions are general. Each of the approaches introduced for establishing a partnership is appropriate for different situations. Also recognize some agencies define the mechanisms slightly differently and may use them in situations other than those described here.

Typical concessions agreements, special-use permits, and some contracts involve more demanding terms than the other partnership mechanisms, because a private business is being given a form of regulated monopoly to profit from their use of public land and/or property. To successfully enter into these agreements, the private applicant usually must demonstrate at least the following:

- A demonstrated public need and demand exists for the services and/or facilities being proposed. In other words, an applicant's desire and ability to generate a profit is not sufficient.

- The proposed services and/or facilities are consistent with the agency's land management objectives for the area where they would be located. This includes consistency with the appropriate recreation opportunity spectrum (ROS) class where applicable.

- The business operator has sufficient experience, capital, and bonding (i.e., performance insurance) against business failure so the agency will not be financially responsible for lack of or inadequate performance on the part of the operator in carrying out the terms of the agreement.

- The public land in question is the *best* choice for the proposed operation and/or facility. This often means demonstrating that the same operation could not be adequately carried out on nearby private land.

Although the particular terms vary greatly, concession agreements and special-use permits typically specify that the private operator pay a percentage of their gross revenue back to the agency. This amount is often around 2% to 3%, which many critics feel is too low. Concession reform bills are periodically introduced before the U.S. Congress and are usually contentious.

Creating and Nurturing Nonprofit Groups for Partnerships

Most agencies desiring strong partnerships for providing outdoor recreation opportunities do not have a ready-made partner waiting in the wings asking to help. Sometimes this means the agency has not been creative enough in attempting to identify potential partners. It might be helpful to review the categories of private and nonprofit providers presented in Chapters 7 and 8 to be more systematic and focused in trying to identify potential collaborators. In some cases, however, there really are very few potential partners available. In such cases, the agency needs to consider helping to create a partner organization. This is a long-term investment, but one that can be well worth the effort. While at first helping to create a new organization might seem outside the normal responsibilities of a public land managing agency, it is consistent with the reality that meeting land management objectives can sometimes be most effectively accomplished through community development and facilitation activities carried out beyond the boundaries of public land. Whether led by agency staff, private citizens, or some combination, the basic steps in creating such a group are as follows (adapted from Moore, LaFarge & Martorelli, 1987; Moore, LaFarge & Tracy, 1992).

Find a key leader. This might be an agency staff member, a member of an existing group, or an unaffiliated local outdoor recreation or conservation enthusiast. This person's role is to lead the effort and to facilitate the creation of the new partner organization. He or she might not have a long-term role in the new group, but should feel strongly the new group is needed and have enough time to get things rolling.

Cultivate local support. The key leader first networks with as many relevant stakeholders as possible to informally and formally discuss the issues and assess the needs. If this networking is encouraging, he or she should pull together a steering committee of those most appropriate and most interested and work with the steering committee to identify a broad mission for the new group.

Sponsor hands-on, action-oriented projects. The most important step in creating the new partner organization is to sponsor projects that recruit new people interested in the things the new organization will be about. These projects should be

- fun, interesting, and rewarding

- successful

- highly visible and well publicized

- manageable (usually 50 to 150 volunteers depending on the tasks and the number of skilled leaders available)

- clearly committed to high-quality results
- ambitious but achievable
- clearly useful
- well-supervised and safe
- rich in pizzazz

The last characteristic, pizzazz, is the least tangible, but one of the most important ingredients for an effective project of this type. Good projects are ones that catch potential volunteers' attention when they see a recruiting poster at a local park or capture their interest when they hear about them from a friend or land manager. Since the point of these projects is to recruit new people who want to become active working in or for a particular recreation area (and not just talking about it), the projects must be selected and planned to appeal to this type of person: chopping up and carrying out old aircraft wreckage from a Wilderness area or planting 1,000 new trees in a devastated area will, litter cleanups and minor park repair efforts will not.

Build single projects into an ongoing program of projects. Use each of the initial projects very carefully and deliberately as recruiting tools to find interested and committed new volunteers. Integrate these new volunteers into the steering committee and involve them in choosing, planning and carrying out future projects. A "5% rule" for converting 5% of all project participants into new leaders is a good target.

Build the program of projects into a self-sustaining organization. After there is momentum in running successful projects, begin to address important organizational concerns such as incorporation and bylaws. It may seem counterintuitive, but addressing these organizational concerns too soon can suck the enthusiasm out of the people interested in working on projects. Do so only after there

is a strong sense that the group's efforts are fun and worthwhile enough to warrant formalizing the structure to make more action possible.

Volunteers for Outdoor Colorado (VOC) is an organization deliberately created using this approach. VOC celebrated its 20th anniversary project season in 2003 along with its 200th project. Its volunteer contributions to public lands in Colorado have had an estimated value of $10 million dollars (Volunteers for Outdoor Colorado, 2003). For a more complete description of the process of creating and nurturing potential partner organizations using hands-on, action-oriented projects, see Moore, LaFarge, and Tracy (1992) and Moore, LaFarge, and Martorelli (1987).

Summary

This chapter introduced the important and growing use of partnerships to provide outdoor recreation opportunities. We began with a description of the classic partnership as a "three-legged stool" supported equally by a public sector land management agency, a nonprofit volunteer organization, and a private sector sponsor. We then discussed the common characteristics of successful partnerships: broad-based participation, clearly identified roles, written plans, and delegation of real responsibility to partners. Next, we presented the numerous reasons why providers should consider forming partnerships: provide public input, educate the public, increase public "ownership" and build support for the agency and its objectives, avoid or minimize costly litigation, extend limited resources and improve management, and meet regulatory or procedural mandates. We then reviewed with whom recreation providers should consider partnering. The final part of this chapter addressed the question of how to form partnerships. It introduced seven mechanisms for establishing partnerships and discussed an approach for creating and nurturing groups for partnerships when no appropriate ones currently exist. We now move beyond the United States and look at outdoor recreation and outdoor recreation opportunities and management from other parts of the world.

Literature Cited

Appalachian Trail Conference. (2003). *What is ATC?* Retrieved November 28, 2003, from http://www. appalachiantrail.org/about/atc/index.html

Association of Partners for Public Lands. (2003). *APPL members directory*. Retrieved June 30, 2003, from http://www.appl.org

Eastern National. (2003). *Mission and purpose*. Retrieved June 30, 2003, from http://www.easternnational.org

Carefully designed volunteer programs can be an effective means of creating and nurturing nonprofit organizations for long-term partnerships.

Moore, R. L., LaFarge, V., and Martorelli, T. (1987). *Organizing outdoor volunteers*. Boston, MA: Appalachian Mountain Club.

Moore, R. L., LaFarge, V., and Tracy, C. (1992). *Organizing outdoor volunteers* (2nd ed.). Boston, MA: Appalachian Mountain Club.

National Park Foundation. (2003). *National Park Foundation*. Retrieved October 14, 2003, from http://www.nationalparks.org/aboutUs/aboutus-factsheet.shtml

National Park Service. (2003). *National Park Service: Partnering and managing for excellence*. Washington, DC: U.S. Department of the Interior, National Park Service. Retrieved from http://www.nps.gov/accompreport2003/pdf/npsdocu15web.pdf

National Park Service. (2005). *Volunteers-In-Parks*. Retrieved February 23, 2005, from http://www.nps.gov/volunteer/

Parks & History Association. (2003). *About cooperating associations*. Retrieved December 1, 2003, from http://www.parksandhistory.org/about/coop.asp

President's Commission on Americans Outdoors. (1987). *Americans outdoors: The legacy, the challenge*. Washington, DC: Island Press.

U.S. Forest Service. (2003). *Obtaining a special-use authorization with the forest service: The application process*. Retrieved June 27, 2003, from http://www.fs.fed.us/recreation/permits/broch.htm

Volunteers for Outdoor Colorado. (2003, Fall). Celebrating 20 Years of VOC Projects! *Trail Breaking News, 20*(3), 10–11.

Volunteer.Gov/Gov. (2003). *Building America's Communities of Service*. Retrieved December 20, 2003, from http://volunteer.gov/Gov

Chapter 10
Outdoor Recreation Opportunities From Selected Countries Around the World[1]

There is just one moon/And one golden sun/And a smile means friendship to ev'ryone/Though the mountains divide/And the oceans are wide/It's a small world after all. (From the Disney theme song "It's a Small World," by Richard M. and Robert B. Sherman, 1963)

Learning Objectives

1. Understand the vast scope of outdoor recreation opportunities throughout the world.
2. Describe the general characteristics of outdoor recreation resource management in the countries reviewed in this chapter.
3. Appreciate the tremendous worldwide economic and social contributions of outdoor recreation.

As acknowledged in the preface, this text has by necessity focused on outdoor recreation in the United States. However, we emphasized the contents of the text have relevance to any country in the world despite the differences among them. Those differences include how one country in contrast to another values leisure, the amount and quality of their park and recreation resources, and how they manage those resources. The factors that influence these differences include a country's level of economic development; the amounts of public land available; the number and types of public, nonprofit, and private-sector outdoor recreation providing organizations; the types of governmental philosophies and practices adopted; and the prevailing social mores and values related to leisure in general and to outdoor recreation in particular. For example, in some countries nude bathing on public beaches is accepted while in others it is not. Also, some subcultures do not have a word for the English word "leisure" as it was defined in Chapters 1 and 2 of this text, despite the fact that the definition (or close approximations of it) is widely accepted in most counties.

Other factors also influence recreation-related differences among countries, such as levels of personal disposable income, time available for leisure, types and costs of transportation facilities available, commitments of national and local governments to funding parks and recreation programs, and the amounts and types of college/university training in leisure, especially outdoor recreation. For example, in many less economically developed countries no formal education opportunities exist in outdoor recreation or nature-based tourism. Of course, the factors that influence the availability of outdoor recreation opportunities can also differ greatly among states and regions within the United States, as well as among political subdivisions in other countries.

Like the United States, most countries have public, nonprofit, and private-sector outdoor recreation providers who manage a variety of resources. They provide recreation opportunities, including parks, recreation areas, wilderness, cultural/historic resources, nature reserves, greenways, recreational/scenic highways, and specially designated areas, such as protected watersheds. Therefore, we believe all of the concepts, principles, management systems, and definitions presented in this text are relevant to and applicable in any country. They can be applied directly in more developed countries by recreation professionals by using current advances in their profession as well as serve as guides in other countries where such professionalism is just beginning.

As indicated by its title, this chapter presents an overview of the outdoor recreation opportunities provided and enjoyed in selected parts of the world. We apologize to readers from those countries not explicitly discussed here. But, it would be arrogant for us to assume we could describe outdoor recreation resources, management, and use for all the countries of the world. We simply do not have the experiences and knowledge to do so adequately. Thus, our purpose here is to provide an overview of outdoor recreation and related opportunities provided in selected countries to encourage a wider worldview and to acknowledge some of the many excellent and unique things happening around the world in terms of providing outdoor recreation opportunities. No attempt was made to present comparable information for each of the selected countries according to a list of characteristics, such as types of public agencies that manage the outdoor recreation resources, numbers and types of protected areas that have been designated, types of historic/cultural resources available, physiographic characteristics, or types of fauna and flora present. The reader will find some of these characteristics are discussed more for some countries than for others.

The United States has learned a great deal from its world neighbors, just as we hope this text will help others to profit from what we have learned in the United States. We strongly encourage each reader to actively explore what other countries are doing. It is a rich and rewarding, sometimes humbling, learning experience. One excellent source of additional useful information is Hendee and Dawson (2002, pp. 49–95), who discuss wilderness areas and management in many different countries and the recreational uses of those special areas.

For the following sampling and overview of outdoor recreation opportunities, the selected countries are grouped by broadly shared geographical locations, such as western Europe and the Scandinavian countries. We start with Canada because of its many similarities to the United States.

Canada

As does the United States, Canada comprises a large and varied land area that extends from the Atlantic to the Pacific, with four maritime provinces on the Atlantic side, the prairie provinces in the middle, the mountainous province of British Columbia on the western edge, and the territories and Arctic Region to the North. Canada has allocated considerable public land and water to the provision of outdoor recreation and related amenity services. As in the United States, the federal agencies of Canada are major providers of outdoor recreation opportunities, particularly through Parks Canada, a part of Environment Canada overseen by the Minister of the Environment. Its National Parks Branch manages about 32 million acres of national parks, making it one of the largest park systems in the world. Most of that area is in the prairie and mountain provinces. The National Historic Parks and Sites Branch manages historic and other resources, such as designated canals and rivers.

Each of the provinces of Canada also offers a variety of outdoor recreation opportunities, especially in provincial parks. Unlike in the United States, the provinces manage the "Crown Lands," equivalent to the public domain lands in the United States (discussed in Chapters 3 and 12), managed by the Bureau of Land Management, a federal agency. Therefore, each Canadian province has more public land available for outdoor recreation than the individual states of the United States.

The variety of outdoor recreation opportunities and services provided and facilities managed in Canada are very similar to those of the United States. There are also many universities in Canada that offer courses and degree programs in outdoor recreation, and overall there is a very high degree of professionalism in the provision of outdoor recreation opportunities there.

Latin America

This category includes all the countries of North, Central, and South America in which the Spanish or Portuguese languages are dominant. This group of countries is offered together in this general overview of outdoor recreation around the world, because they share several rather distinctive characteristics regarding outdoor recreation resources and participation in outdoor recreation activities. Of course, there are differences among these countries, but each of the Latin American countries tends to share the following characteristics to a greater or lesser extent.

While wide differences exist in the degree of economic development and in per capita income among the Latin American countries and within different regions of a particular country (e.g., Mexico), most of these countries are not among the most economically developed in the world. Chapter 4 pointed out levels of economic development and personal disposable income are important variables affecting public, private, and nonprofit investments in outdoor recreation and tourism resources as well as the level of citizen participation in leisure opportunities. That is reflected to widely varying degrees in the Latin American countries and significantly affects the number of outdoor recreation opportunities available and the relative amount of participation in such, especially those opportunities not easily accessible from one's home.

Despite the fact most citizens of the Latin American countries do not enjoy high per capita incomes, larger numbers of them now own personal automobiles. That increased mobility, as well as use of mass transit, has permitted more people to access and to enjoy outdoor recreation opportunities.

Although the federal and state governments of most Latin American countries do not have the fiscal resources to invest in outdoor recreation at the levels many other countries do, in general they are doing quite well with the funds they have. Most, if not all Latin American countries have national parks and other areas set aside for conservation and preservation. However, many of the publicly managed areas, such as national parks, cultural/historic sites, and natural resource conservation areas are managed under a philosophy that strongly recognizes the needs of local indigenous people. Part of this philosophy stems from the recognition that limited fiscal resources do not allow for the intensive management that might otherwise be practiced elsewhere. Put simply, local resources must often be used by the local indigenous people for purposes other than recreation, such as for supplying fuel wood, grazing domestic livestock, using wildlife and fish for food, and agriculture and private enterprises. Therefore, these many multiple uses are frequently found in the national parks and other dedicated resource protection and conservation areas. The extent of such uses of conservation areas varies from country to country and strongly relates to the fiscal resources available. For example, Chile has a system of many well-developed and managed national parks; Equador has its world famous and strictly regulated Galapagos Islands; and Peru, Costa Rica, and many other countries take pride in and aggressively protect their special natural and cultural areas.

Throughout the Latin American countries, ecotourism has grown rapidly during the past two decades. While common now in many countries, ecotourism has been particularly important in helping to attract and retain tourists' dollars in local communities rather than having that money going to large corporations with headquarters in other countries. Costa Rica, for example, has been an international leader in ecotourism.

While all countries display both group and individualistic patterns of recreation participation, research has shown group-oriented recreation participation is generally more popular with Latin American people than with most ethnic groups. This can take the form of large extended family outings or many friends and associates gathering for a picnic, barbecue, or celebration of a local festival.

Recreation and especially tourism in the Latin America countries is strongly influenced by and oriented to cultural/ historical resources and traditions, whether visits to Mayan ruins, celebrating and understanding the lives of the Aztecs and Incas, or exploring the influences of the early Spaniards. While the recreation and international tourism of

Ecotourism and outdoor recreation in areas, like this protected area in Costa Rica, can be important sources of economic and environmental benefits for developing nations.

many countries is also oriented to cultural history and heritage, this seems particularly so in Latin America. Examples elsewhere include tourists pursuing learning and appreciating the Native American Indian cultures in the United States and Canada, the significance of folk dance and costume to Scandinavian and many other countries, visits to sites of military battles and sacrifice, symbolism of significant historic/heritage resources such as the Liberty Bell at Independence Hall in the United States, and statues of and memorials to famous leaders in national capitals and renowned artists in Rome and Florence. Nevertheless, recreation, and especially tourism, in Latin America is strongly influenced by and oriented toward historical and cultural resources and traditions.

The British Isles and Western Europe

We combine England, Wales, Scotland, and Ireland with the western European countries, because those countries share many common historical and cultural roots and current practices regarding the availability, character, management, and use of outdoor recreation and related amenity resources.

Much change has occurred in Europe since the end of World War II, especially as a result of the formation and expansion of the European Union and the break up of the USSR in the early 1990s. For example, ten countries were admitted to the European Union in 2004. Nevertheless, to limit our scope, we arbitrarily focus on those countries with similar histories, especially in terms of their cultures, systems of governance, and derivations of language. Our focus is mostly on the Netherlands, Belgium, Germany, France, Italy, Austria, Luxembourg, Switzerland, Spain, and Greece. We consider Denmark later with the Scandinavian category even though it shares many common characteristics of the just-mentioned countries.

The cultural history of the British Isles and western European countries extends back thousands of years longer than does the "European" history of the "New World." That history significantly influenced the evolution and current orientations of those countries toward nature-based and cultural/heritage resource based recreation. Specifically, early use of nature for recreation was largely reserved for the nobility/aristocracy who had private, manicured gardens and mansions often set in spacious "parks." These estates were comprised of large tracts of green/open space, with hunting and fishing for the prized species reserved for the landed gentry, while the masses could hunt for rabbits and other small animals. Over time, the general population gained more access to nature for recreation. According to Ibrahim and Cordes (1993, pp. 222–227), the industrial revolution, with its structuring of work and nonwork time, lead to discussions about the need for constructive uses of free time by the masses. So by the late 19th century, "...the middle class was on the rise, a class that was bent on imitating the aristocracy, which traditionally lived in the country and enjoyed open space." For example, the fight of the working class in Britain for the right of access to open space from the 1850s to the present is an important part of British social history. Other characteristics of this group of countries are discussed next.

The British Isles and countries of western Europe have been settled with relatively high population densities for hundreds of years. In fact, they have some of the highest population densities per square kilometer of any nation, with the Netherlands being one of the most densely populated countries in the world. Therefore, unlike the United States and Canada, the federal/state governments did not have as many large blocks of public lands they could allocate to outdoor recreation or related amenity and conservation purposes.

Despite the high population densities of these countries and the demands on the natural resource base for housing, transportation, centers of settlement, agriculture, and other uses, each of these countries values and appreciates their natural and cultural/heritage resources. They have also found innovative ways to assure their citizens access to the countryside. England is an interesting case in point. Ibrahim and Cordes stated that Great Britain's

> first national park was established in 1950...[after] the National Parks and Countryside Act was passed...[in 1947, and] national parks represent one tenth of the land area of England and Wales. Most of those parks are still predominantly privately owned. (1993, pp. 223–224)

In addition to the national parks, the British Isles have many lands open to public use for recreation managed by the Forestry Commission. There are also many smaller sites used heavily for recreation, such as Historic Buildings (e.g., castles, estates) and gardens managed by the National Trust. Sidaway (1996, p. 217) stated, "...25% of Britain is protected in...[these ways]." Scotland has lagged somewhat, but now has national parks as well.

In addition to the British Isles, each of the western European countries has also taken actions to protect resources, such as national parks, conservation areas, cultural/historic sites, and nature-based outdoor recreation areas. Sidaway summarized these efforts succinctly:

> Although some legislation to protect nature had been enacted in most countries of the EU within the first 25 years of this century, the protection of

natural resource areas has taken markedly different forms. Belgian, Denmark, the former West Germany, Luxembourg, and Britain have given greater emphasis to landscape protection (i.e., measures to control development within cultural landscapes, which may or may not be largely in private ownership). These countries, together with the Netherlands, have well over 10% of their land area designated for landscape or nature protection.... The degree of protection afforded to designated areas varies considerably in each country, as do the criteria by which these areas are selected. However, it is probably fair to say that the protection of cultural landscapes is both an older tradition and based on a holistic concept of "natural beauty," which included wildlife and nature. (1996, pp. 217–218)

Given the relative scarcity of public lands that can be allocated to outdoor recreation and related amenity uses such as nature conservation, many of these countries have also relied on nonprofit organizations to sponsor and maintain such areas. This is often done by nature conservation organizations that frequently have large and active memberships, such as the National Trust and The Royal Society for the Protection of Birds in Britain and Natuurmonumenten and Provinciale Landscappen in the Netherlands.

Lastly, tourism is very important to the economies of each of these countries. It depends highly on the cultural/historic resources those countries protect as well as the natural resource base. Tourism is increasingly seen as a key factor in rural development.

Scandinavian Countries

The Scandinavian countries considered here include Denmark, Finland, Norway, and Sweden (and exclude Iceland, Greenland, and the Faeroes Islands). These countries share the same approximate geographical location in the world, some common cultural characteristics, similar climates, many topographic features, and most importantly their approaches to the provision and use of outdoor recreation opportunities. Most of these countries are sparsely populated, with the estimated 2003 populations as follows:

Sweden	8.5 million
Denmark	5.4 million
Finland	5.2 million
Norway	4.5 million
Total	*23.6 million*

We mention these populations, because these four countries combined have a land and interior water area much larger than Germany, France, and the Netherlands combined, with those three western European countries having a total 2003 population estimated to be 158.7 million. Reunala (1996, p. 225), when considering only Finland, Norway, and Sweden, stated, "There are fifteen to twenty times more forest land per inhabitant than in Central Europe." He continues:

> Scandinavians have always depended on forests, [and mountains and shorelines] and they have gained a livelihood from them in innumerable ways. Finland is the most forested and most forest dependent of the three countries.… Northern Sweden is much like Finland, but southern Sweden [and Denmark] is, historically and culturally, closer to central European in agricultural traditions. Norway is characterized by its orientation to the sea, fishing, and high, treeless mountains. For Norwegians nature means mountains, forests, and sea.… Forests cover more than two thirds of the land of Finland and of Sweden. In Norway, the percentage is lower, 27%, because of treeless mountains. Forests are mainly coniferous.… In southern Sweden, as in Denmark, hardwood forests of beech and oak are also found. On average hardwoods comprise 10 to 20% of the stands. (pp. 125, 226)

Denmark, at the southern edge of the Scandinavian Peninsula and partially attached to western Europe, forms more of a transition zone to mainland Europe, where hardwoods comprise more than 35% of the forest stands, which cover only 11% of the total area.

The citizens of Scandinavia have a long tradition of using their forests for many purposes, including recreation, but compared with most other countries of the world, they have a special fondness for their mountains, forests, and other open spaces. Reunala (1996, p. 230) stated, "The strong cultural traditions attached to the forests are easy to see in all art forms. Scandinavian music, literature, painting, cinema, architecture, and popular arts all reflect the importance of forests." This attachment is particularly evident in the unique Scandinavian concept of what has historically been called "every man's right." As explained by Reunala, regarding Finland, Norway, and Sweden, this is

> …a traditional common right of access to all forests. Everyone is free to walk, ski, pick berries and mushrooms, and even stay overnight in any forest with the condition being that no damage is done and the owner is not disturbed. Free access exists not only in publicly owned forests but also

in forests owned by private families and industrial corporations.

> This free access strengthens the feeling that forests are common national property, important for everyone.…Common right of access to privately owned land is especially important, because only about 25% of the forest area is in public ownership. When all forests are open for recreation, the need for specially managed recreation forests is not as important as in many countries, and therefore good recreation opportunities can be offered with little investment. Because of the abundance of forests, recreational use is frequently so dispersed it does not cause inconvenience to the owner. (1996, pp. 229–230)

Regarding "every man's right," Denmark forms a link between sparsely populated Scandinavia and more densely populated continental Europe. This is evidenced by the rules that govern public access to the countryside in Denmark. For example, it is believed "every man's right" has applied in Denmark historically, as in the rest of Scandinavia. This was the case until a 1782 act forbade access by all unauthorized persons to the national (i.e., Royal) forests. Legally, but not in practice, this situation prevailed until the first Nature Conservation Act of 1917 reestablished access to public forests (only one year after the U.S. National Park Service was created). An amendment in 1969 established a legal right of access to private forests. This is significant, because in Denmark private forests receive a large share of the 75 million annual visits made to forests by its adult population (Jensen & Koch, 2004).

According to Reunala (1996, p. 230), "Two thirds of Scandinavian forests are owned by private families…[in Finland] nowadays most often by ordinary urban families who have inherited forest property." In Norway, most private owners of forests do not live in cities. However, in the Scandinavian countries, private forests and other open-space lands receive much use for recreational purposes. For example, in Finland, many have nearby, generally modest, and highly used cabins, frequently on the shores of lakes. In fact, 45% of Finns have access to a vacation home on a regular basis, and 16% of Finnish households own a vacation home.

Reunala (1996, p. 231) makes a particularly interesting point when he refers to the findings of an earlier study that disclosed "…three out of four Finns feel the forest is a womb-like environment. The forest seems to be a lost paradise, a protecting place, where one can feel safe, free, and relaxed." A popular saying in Finland is "one goes to the forest to rest in the lap of Mother Nature." In Denmark, Jensen and Koch (1997) found "silence," in the 1970s as well as the 1990s, was the highest "forest preference score" out of 100 different scores (or values) that could have been recorded.

Despite the Scandinavian right of common access, the growth of the environmental movement since the 1960s put pressure on public agencies and forest industries to set aside more lands as protected areas, wilderness, and nature reserves. For example, nature restoration and forestation has been put high on the agenda in Denmark. As Reunala (1996, p. 228) summarized, "For almost thirty years, conflicts between production and protection values of forests have been regular issues on the public scene." The conflicts, however, have not come to a level as seen in the United States (e.g., "tree occupants" attempting to prevent logging).

Lastly, it is important to note that for decades each of the four Scandinavian countries have had scientists who specialize in research on outdoor recreation. They contributed substantially to the international literature; supervised national household surveys on participation in outdoor recreation activities in their countries to identify and quantify citizen preferences for outdoor recreation activities, settings, experiences, and benefits; and worked closely with practitioners to provide desired and high-quality outdoor recreation opportunities.

Japan, South Korea, and Taiwan

Since the middle of the 20th century, these three Asian countries have made great progress economically, which has significantly affected their citizens' orientation to nature-based recreation. Japan, roughly the size of California, is densely populated, with at least 85% of its estimated 2003 population of 127.2 million people living on about 15% of the land area, of which about 70% is mountainous. For most of its history, the primary orientation to nature of the Japanese centered on manicured gardens (both large and small) and art, such as nature scenes on silk screens. Common nature-based outings consisted mostly of walks in the forest to gather mushrooms or other native plants. Today, much of the outdoor recreation in Japan remains passive, and there is not the high level of facility development (e.g., campgrounds, visitor centers, RV parks) found in the United States and Canada. In the affluent 1980s and 1990s, many Japanese enjoyed the outdoor recreation opportunities provided by other countries as well. For example in the 1990s, at least 5% of the total visitors to Grand Canyon National Park in the United States were from Japan. Japan itself is an important international tourist destination, more so for its beautiful gardens and interesting cultural sites (especially shrines) than for nature-based recreation.

Korea, in contrast to Japan, has many more colleges and universities that teach natural resource related disciplines, such as forestry and outdoor recreation. Like Japan, Korea is a very mountainous country. It possesses excellent opportunities for hiking and other outdoor pursuits. Its Forest Service promotes outdoor recreation, and many forms are less passive than those popular in Japan. There are national parks, some high-end nature-oriented resorts, several areas demonstrating historical culture, and many areas centered on native crafts.

Taiwan also has colleges and universities that offer programs and/or courses in outdoor recreation. It has natural parks and conservation areas that are popular places for outdoor experiences. Like Japan and South Korea, Taiwan is a mountainous country with large numbers of people living in a very small flat area. It also has some beautiful mountains and coasts that provide outdoor recreation opportunities.

Protected areas, like this one in South Korea, are particularly important sources of outdoor recreation opportunities for densely populated nations.

Like other protected areas around the world, this one in China provides many important benefits, including those associated with outdoor recreation participation. (Photo by Yu-Fai Leung)

Africa

Many African nations do not have a strong orientation to outdoor recreation as that concept is understood in other countries. In fact, some of the native tribes/subcultures of several countries of Africa do not have a word that can be accurately translated as "leisure."

The general lack of a strong orientation toward outdoor recreation in much of Africa has to do with many of the factors noted in the introduction to this chapter, especially levels of economic development. Many of the characteristics noted for the Latin American countries apply to African nations as well. Especially important are wide variations in per capita income, a need to use many resources (including some in protected areas) to meet the basic needs of indigenous peoples, and a growing emphasis on ecotourism.

Egypt is renowned for its outdoor cultural sites, and large numbers of tourists from many countries visit annually. Major protected areas in countries such as Kenya, Tanzania, Botswana, and South Africa attract significant international visitation interested in wildlife, both for watching and for hunting. South Africa has been a leader in the international wilderness movement. It also boasts the greatest concentration of transboundary protected areas in Africa. Virtually all of these areas are open to visits for outdoor recreation pursuits, and they allow fairly free movement across international boundaries. While the wild animals of south and east Africa often require recreationists to use motor vehicles or guided recreation services, there are places where one can backpack and trek into the wilderness on foot, especially in mountainous areas. The countries of west Africa have been slower to establish

In addition to protecting significant national resources, protected areas in nations like South Africa have become important attractions for international visitors.

parks and protected areas, but countries such as Gabon have recently made major moves in this direction. For example, in 2003, it established 13 national parks covering about 20% of that country's land. Some of these parks are along the coast and others are interior. One of the goals for these parks is to tap into high-end ecotourism.

In southern Africa, the citizens of European descent share many of the outdoor recreation customs and traditions of the British Isles and western Europe from which their ancestors came. For most of the indigenous population, however, outdoor recreation as it is known and practiced in western Europe is not yet a high priority.

New Zealand and Australia

New Zealand and Australia are each important destinations for an increasing number of international tourists, especially from the United States, Canada, the British Isles, Asia (mostly Japan, China, and Korea), and western Europe. Each have many attractive qualities, including being relatively safe, disease-free, and stable countries offering a welcome respite from the winters of the northern hemisphere. Equally important, the citizens of both of these countries have strong outdoor orientations. But like the counties that comprise the British Isles and western Europe, these two countries differ from one another greatly in their geography, fauna and flora, types of recreational opportunities provided, organizations that provide those opportunities, and how the basic resources are managed. Their differences stem from the different sizes of the two countries, the characteristics of the aboriginal inhabitants and their customs and present influences on the provision of outdoor recreation opportunities, their history of settlement and development by Europeans and the cultural influences of such, and how their public outdoor recreation agencies are organized and function. Neither country is as densely populated as the British Isles and the western European countries, with New Zealand's estimated population in 2003 being about four million and Australia's being about 20 million. The outdoor recreation related characteristics of each of these two countries will be described next.

New Zealand

New Zealand comprises two major islands, the North and South Islands. Although much smaller than Australia, it is very diverse as reflected by the geyser and volcanic regions of the North Island, the snowcapped Southern Alps, and extensive beech forests and native rain forests of the South Island. Except for forested areas and high mountain areas, the overall environment is pastoral with agricultural production, including sheep and dairy cattle husbandry, fruit production, and viticulture being major industries. In the last decade, the diversity and unique natural attributes of New Zealand combined with a long tradition of outdoor recreation participation led to the development of a thriving tourism industry. Tourism is now the country's major earner of foreign exchange.

Prior to the passage of the Conservation Act in 1987, which created the Department of Conservation (DOC), the federal/state public lands of New Zealand were managed primarily by two agencies, the Department of Lands and Survey and the New Zealand Forest Service. In 1987, the commercial forest lands were placed under the management of a quasi-public/private organization, and the remaining conservation and recreation lands were placed under the management of DOC. The DOC administers those lands in cooperation with the native Iwi Maori people, who settled New Zealand from Polynesia, starting in the 12th century. The rights of the Maori, including their right to own land, were formally recognized in the Treaty of Waitangi in 1840. The Maori own and administer their own lands as well as lands administered in conjunction with DOC that provide important recreation opportunities.

The chief administrative officer of the DOC is the Director General, who serves under the Minister of Conservation. There are three regional directors, and those three regions are divided into a total of 13 conservancies, each headed by a Conservator. The conservancies are further divided into areas headed by Area Managers. These managers reflect a high degree of professionalism, as indicated by DOC having adopted modern science-based management systems, such as the Recreation Opportunity Spectrum system described in Chapter 12.

The lands administered by DOC comprise about one third of the total land and interior water area of New Zealand. DOC's important managerial functions cover national parks and conservation parks (formerly called *forest parks*), reserves and conservation areas, protected indigenous forests, some protected inland waters and wild and scenic rivers, indigenous/native wildlife, noncommercial freshwater fisheries, historic places on conservation land, marine reserves, Crown pastoral leases, and protection of marine mammals on offshore islands set aside for conservation.

In addition to the many outdoor recreation opportunities provided by the DOC in cooperation with the Maori, significant opportunities are also provided by regional councils, such as the Auckland Regional Council, which administers a very large forested area and seacoast near Auckland, as well as by local municipalities and councils.

Because of the attractiveness and diversity of the New Zealand landscape and because it is surrounded by water, a wide variety of outdoor recreation opportunities are provided. Particularly attractive are the high-quality freshwater fishing, pleasant climate, rare and unusual fauna (e.g., the flightless kiwi bird), the variety of national parks (some with active volcanoes and geysers), the hot springs, and the very popular "tracks" (i.e., trails), such as the 54 kilometer Milford Track (with huts for overnight stays) in the Fiordland World Heritage Area of southwestern New Zealand.

Australia

In contrast to the narrow latitudinal extent of New Zealand, Australia is a continent with lush tropical forests in the north, an extensive dry interior, and the mountainous Antarctic beech rain forests of Tasmania in the far south. While New Zealand is characterized by its rather wet, pastoral, mountainous, and forested landscapes, Australia is most typically represented by its extensive, dry, red "outback" inhabited by a diversity of fauna including the kangaroo and emu, beautiful sun-drenched beaches and the coral splendor of the Great Barrier Reef, its aboriginal culture, and the laid back attitude of its citizens.

While Australians do enjoy the countryside, the *Crocodile Dundee* movies promoted the inaccurate perception that Australians are a universally rugged people prone to extended "walkabouts" in the "outback." In fact, Australia has historically been one of the most urbanized countries/ continents of the world. The majority of the population is concentrated along the coasts in the southeast in the major cities of Brisbane, Sydney, and Melbourne, and on the west coast in Perth. The vast interior of the country and much of the coastline remain sparsely populated. So, most of the "walkabouts" are to beaches or urban parks near home and not in the outback.

Unlike the United States, Australia is highly decentralized, with much governmental responsibility vested in the seven political states: Queensland, New South Wales, South Australia, Victoria, Tasmania, Western Australia, and Northern Territory. Each state has its own park system supplemented by a federal system of high-profile national parks and world heritage sites, including the Great Barrier Reef Marine Park and Kakadu, Uluru, and Fraser Island Cooloola National Parks. The aboriginal people and state and federal governments comanage many of these areas. This system of protected areas is a major focus for outdoor recreation for both domestic and international tourism. Each state has its own forest service, which in addition to maintaining responsibility for overall timber management also provides a broad spectrum of motorized and nonmotorized recreation opportunities.

For many citizens of Australia, much of their outdoor recreation was historically oriented to the country's beautiful coastal areas with sandy beaches. That has changed somewhat in the past decade, because of Australia's location under the "hole in the ozone layer." Concerns about sun-related cancers reduced use of the beaches somewhat and changed how those beaches are used. Nevertheless, Australia's coasts and related recreation and its cultural history, traditions, attractive climate, and geographical and biophysical diversity with unique animals such as the kangaroo, koala, Tasmanian devil, and dingo remain strong drawing cards to the citizens of Australia and to tourists from many other countries.

Summary

The focus of this chapter was to present an overview of the provision and use of outdoor recreation and related amenity opportunities in selected countries of the world. We have not attempted to present an even discussion comparing one country directly with other countries along several specified dimensions, such as types of public agencies that manage outdoor recreation resources or specific types of opportunities provided. Instead, we presented an international outdoor recreation smorgasbord to stimulate the reader to learn more about what has been happening, and is happening in countries other than the United States. We could not present an overview of all countries, but hope what we provided was instructive and motivates the reader to learn more from other sources, especially from personal experience.

Throughout this text, emphasis has been on outdoor recreation professionalism, and the concepts and principles related to such have been influenced by the fact that both authors are Americans. Hopefully, this chapter reinforced the meaning of another stanza from the song "It's a Small World" quoted at its outset: "There's so much that we share/That it's time we're aware/It's a small world after all." As stated at the beginning of this chapter, practically all of the concepts and principles presented in this text have application to the management and use of outdoor recreation resources in every country of the world, because many of those concepts and principles have resulted from sharing among leisure professionals from many countries.

Literature Cited

Hendee, J. and Dawson, C. (2002). *Wilderness management: Stewardship and protection of resources and values* (3rd ed.). Golden, CO: Fulcrum Publishing.

Ibrahim, H. and Cordes, K. (1993). *Outdoor recreation.* Boston, MA: McGraw-Hill.

Jensen, F. and Koch. N. (1997). *Friluftsiliv i skovene* [Outdoor recreation in the Danish forest] 1976/77–1993/94 (Research Series No. 20). Horsholm, Denmark: Danish Forest and Landscape Research Institute.

Jensen, F. and Koch, N. (2004). Twenty-five years of forest recreation in Denmark and its influence on forest policy. *Scandinavian Journal of Forest Research* (Suppl. 4), 1–10.

Sherman, R. M. and Sherman, R. B. (1963). It's a small world (after all). Written for the 1964 Pepsi-Cola/Disney exhibit at the World's Fair.

Sidaway, R. (1996). Current environmental issues in urban western Europe and their relevance to a new land management ethic. In B. Driver, D. Dustin, T. Baltic, G. Elsner, and G. Peterson (Eds.), *Nature and the human spirit: Toward an expanded land management ethic* (pp. 215–223). State College, PA: Venture Publishing, Inc.

Reunala, A. (1996). Cultural and spiritual forest values in Scandinavia. In B. Driver, D. Dustin, T. Baltic, G. Elsner, and G. Peterson (Eds.), *Nature and the human spirit: Toward an expanded land management ethic* (pp. 225–233). State College, PA: Venture Publishing, Inc.

Endnote

1. Appreciation is expressed to the following for their helpful comments on this chapter: Perry Brown (United States), Roger Mannell (Canada), Dan Turnquist (Mexico), Juan Carlos Rivera-Montes (United States, formerly of Honduras), Roger Sidaway (Scotland), Aarne Reunala and Tuija Sievanen (Finland), Frank Jensen (Denmark), Oystein Aas (Norway), Chris Jenkins, (New Zealand), Elery Hamilton-Smith (Australia), and Norm McIntyre (Canada, formerly of both New Zealand and Australia).

Part III

Managing Outdoor Recreation Opportunities

Chapter 11
Policy Development, Management, Administration, and Planning

...decisions often involve risk and must be done in a thoughtful yet decisive manner.
(Edginton, Jordan, DeGraaf & Edginton, 1995, p. 286)

Learning Objectives

1. Describe the four decision processes (i.e., policy development, management, administration, and planning) that guide the direction of all public agencies and other organizations that provide outdoor recreation opportunities.
2. Explain not only how these four decision processes differ but also how they complement, supplement, and interact with one another.
3. Explain why different policies lead to different approaches to managing outdoor recreation resources.
4. Help the reader to decide whether he or she wishes to specialize in outdoor recreation policy development, management, administration, or planning.

Outdoor recreation professionals work for a variety of recreation and tourism organizations in the public, private, and nonprofit (nongovernmental) sectors of society. Each of these providers of outdoor recreation opportunities uses the same four decision processes to establish and guide their actions: policy development, management, administration, and planning. They determine which types of outdoor recreation opportunities will be provided, as well as where, when, in what amount, at what quality of service, for whom, and at what price.

The types of opportunities provided by different parks and recreation (P&R) organizations vary greatly because of the different purposes and responsibilities of those providers. For example, the opportunities provided by the U.S. Department of the Interior (USDI) National Park Service (NPS) differ from those of the USDA Forest Service (USFS), which differ from those of the Vail Ski Corporation, which differ from those provided by The Nature Conservancy. Nevertheless, the characteristics and purposes of each type of decision process are similar across providers, though the outcomes of those decisions differ.

This chapter describes the general characteristics and purposes of the four decision processes that guide the provision of outdoor recreation opportunities. The overview should increase understanding of how these decision processes differ, how they supplement and complement each other, and how they interact. Such understanding will alert outdoor recreation students to the fact that different skills and training are needed to specialize either in policy development, management, administration, or

planning. More detailed training and understanding can, and should, be obtained from the many sources and academic courses that concentrate on each type of decision process. For example, many colleges and universities offer courses on each of these decision processes and options to major in one of them at the undergraduate and graduate levels.

Several problems have frequently impeded students gaining an adequate understanding of the four decision processes. First, too few academic programs present a synoptic overview of these four decision processes, especially how they complement and supplement each other. Second, and more problematic, many texts tend to group these four decision processes under the general rubric of management. This causes confusion because the four processes do differ in their purposes and the types of skills they require. For that reason, the authors of this text believe students of outdoor recreation should understand the unique characteristics and purposes of each of these four decision processes.

Outdoor recreation professionals should also know what professional skills are needed to carry out each type of decision process and how each type of decision interacts with the others. This is true for two related reasons. First, all outdoor recreation professionals need to have a basic understanding of the four decision processes to perform effectively within any organization. Otherwise, they will get confused by the wide differences between the policies and managerial rules and regulations that exist for their organization and other organizations that provide outdoor recreation opportunities on similar lands. Second, such confusion is also common among people who visit outdoor recreation areas managed by different organizations. They wonder why certain rules and regulations are enforced by one provider and not by another. These customers, frequently with agitation, confront the managers with questions. Why do other providers offer services such as hot showers, while your organization does not? Why do you charge different entrance and use fees? Why? Why? Why? These many questions are posed to managers who reply too frequently, "It is just our policy," which is not an adequate answer. The reasons for these differences need to be explained clearly to those users.

Differences exist among providers because of their different policies and the various management strategies and administrative procedures they develop based on those policies. But, we iterate that despite these different organizational goals and orientations, the four decision processes used by each organization are quite similar (at least in countries having a democratic republic form of government).

The primary purpose of this chapter is to increase basic understanding of the characteristics of the four decision processes. That understanding will help students of outdoor recreation:

1. to decide whether they want to specialize in policy development, management, administration, or planning

2. to cope with the confusion caused by the wide variety of different policies and managerial rules and regulations they are sure to confront if they go to work within a public P&R agency or other providers of outdoor recreation opportunities

3. to be one step ahead of their professional associates who do not have that understanding

4. to be better prepared to answer customers' questions about why there is such wide variation in the policies and managerial actions of the agencies and organizations who manage the outdoor recreation areas they visit

5. to better appreciate the science-based management systems described in the next two chapters, developed explicitly to meet specific policy directives

We will now describe those general characteristics and the purposes of each of the four decision processes.

Definitions of the Four Decision Processes

To begin differentiating the four decision processes, we give perhaps overly simplistic definitions of each. We depart from the normal convention of describing planning before management, and put planning last, because planning is necessary for policy development, management, and administration. In that sense, planning is always first. But, it is easier to understand what planning is after one understands the nature and scope of the other three decision processes for which planning is done.

Policy Development

Policy development (frequently called *policy making*) is the creation and refinement of the guiding policies of an organization. A policy is generally a broad guide for the actions of the people subject to that policy. Some people find it useful to view policies as broad "standing decisions." Being broad, policy directives generally do not provide much detail about how the policy should be implemented, just as the statement "honesty is the best policy" does not specify what does or does not constitute honest behaviors. Similarly, policies that mandate that an organization consider the special needs of people challenged by disabilities, implement equal opportunity requirements, and protect employee civil rights do not specify in detail how these policies should be implemented. More broadly, the same can be said for many policies that have been written into the Constitution of the United States, especially the Bill of Rights, which over time has been subjected to many different interpretations by federal courts.

Management

In contrast to policy development, management decisions must establish very specific guidelines about what can and cannot be done, and those decisions must be made within the guidelines for action set by the established policies. Specific and explicit managerial directives, therefore, are developed to provide clear and exacting guidelines for actions that will be taken to assure that policy guidelines are met. Those managerial actions are implemented to meet management objectives that are refined and determined by the decision process of management planning. One can see that management must be closely integrated with policy and planning decisions. Put simply, policies generally establish broad guidelines. Then, specific managerial actions are taken to meet managerial objectives established during management planning so that the policy goals will be realized. For example, a policy of most football teams is to win games. Game plans are developed and practiced to enable the team to achieve that goal. Two managerial objectives would be to make touchdowns and to avoid serious injury to the players.

Administration

Administration is concerned with those activities necessary for policy makers, managers, and planners to operate effectively, efficiently, responsibly, and legally, as well as to be treated fairly and properly. Administrative decisions typically include those related to personnel management, budgeting, performance reporting, maintenance of buildings, support services (e.g., electricity, plumbling), and maintenance of vehicles.

Planning

Guidelines and recommendations for policy, managerial, and administrative decisions are expressed in various types of plans. *Planning,* therefore, is the decision process that prepares different types of plans, such as policy, managerial, and administrative plans. For example, management plans provide very specific direction for taking clearly delineated managerial actions. Such plans specify clear management objectives, the actions needed to meet those objectives (frequently called *management prescriptions*), and the desired results (or desired future conditions) once the approved plan is implemented. Implementation of the management prescriptions then helps assure that the management objectives and the policy directives toward which those objectives are oriented will be realized.

When thinking about how these four decision processes interrelate in an organization, it might be helpful to visualize them as the interconnected parts of a tree as in Figure 11.1. All four processes must be supported by a solid "root system" of policy. The straight "trunk" of planning effectively guides each of the four processes and therefore the entire organization. The "vascular system" of administration flows through every part of the tree, providing the needed resources to keep the organization healthy and functioning efficiently. Finally, the many distinct "branches" of management reach out to accomplish the organization's purposes, supported by policy, guided by planning, and nourished by administration. Each of these four decision processes will be described in some detail in the remainder of this chapter. The following discussion will draw most of its examples from the public-sector providers of outdoor recreation opportunities, but will draw from private-sector organizations and nonprofit providers as well.

Descriptions of the Four Decision Processes

Policy Development

Three characteristics of policy development with which outdoor recreation professionals should be familiar directly affect the provision of outdoor recreation opportunities.

First, policies are hierarchical in nature. Policies developed at higher administrative levels of any organization set the boundaries on any policy that can be developed at lower levels.

Second, different organizations that provide outdoor recreation services adopt different policies to meet the purposes for which those organizations exist. In the public sector, those purposes would be to meet the legislative mandates or executive orders that created those agencies.

Third, managerial and administrative decisions are generally guided by broad policy directives. In some instances, however, the policies are very specific and must be followed with little interpretation. Several of the approaches (i.e., systems) used to manage outdoor recreation and related amenity resources were developed to meet policy directives that clearly specify that particular managerial action be taken. Professional outdoor recreation planners and managers must understand the nature and requirements of those policies before they can understand

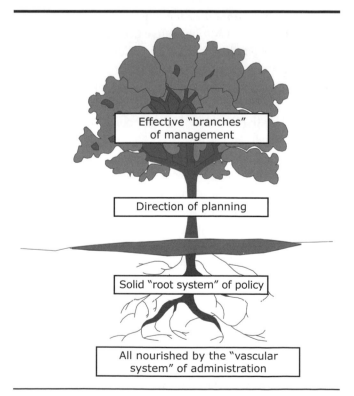

Effective "branches" of management

Direction of planning

Solid "root system" of policy

All nourished by the "vascular system" of administration

Figure 11.1 One way to visualize the interrelationship of policy development, management, administration, and planning processes within an organization

and apply those management systems properly. In particular, they must have this understanding before they can explain clearly to their recreating customers what those policies are, especially why those policies were established and how they influence the managerial actions they guide.

Policy Making Is Hierarchical

Policy making in all private and public agencies is hierarchical, with broader, more encompassing policies established at higher levels and more specific policies set at lower levels, but always within the boundaries of the policies set at the higher levels. Put differently, there are higher to lower levels of management and administration in any organization, and policies set at higher levels establish the boundaries for policies that can be set at the lower tiers. Employees of any organization need to understand this hierarchical nature of the purpose and function of policies.

We will illustrate the hierarchical nature of policies first by looking at the public sector. As we learned in elementary and secondary school, most countries that operate as a democratic republic have three branches of government: the executive, the legislative, and the judicial. In the United States those branches are the Office of the President, the U.S. Congress, and the Supreme Court, which in many other countries are called the Office of the Prime Minister, the Parliament, and the Supreme Court. The policy directives established by the U.S. Congress are the laws it passes, and the President establishes policy by executive orders and administrative decrees. The Supreme Court issues legal decisions when policy directives by the U.S. Congress, the executive branch of government, or lower branches of government (e.g., a law passed by a state legislature) are contested. Those judgments (i.e., policy decisions) by the Supreme Court become the practiced law of the land.

Policy making by legislative bodies, such as members of the U.S. Congress, is a very complex, time-consuming, and often controversial process, because it is directed toward achieving reasonable compromise among people holding different interests and values. Reasoned debate, bartering, and sometimes coercion are required to achieve such compromise. The guiding philosophy is that such reasonable compromise through a participative policy-making process is far better than settling of differences through armed conflict or by a dictator whether benevolent or not. Fortunately, there are checks and balances in the policy-making process, such as the ability of a majority of the citizens to vote periodically to retain or remove their elected policy makers in the executive and legislative branches of the government. Each of the three branches also serves as checks and balances for the other two.

The policy directives established at the top of the policy-making hierarchy determine the boundaries within which all lower levels of an organization can set policies and operate. For example, within the executive branch of the U.S. government the next level below the President is the U.S. Cabinet. It includes the cabinet-level departments, some particularly relevant to the provision of outdoor recreation opportunities, especially the Department of Agriculture and the Department of the Interior. In other countries, the cabinet level of policy making is referred to as ministries, not departments. The major responsibility of the heads of cabinet-level departments or ministries is to make and implement policies consistent with what the President or Prime Minister wants.

The third level of public policy making in the executive branch is at the level of the heads of agencies within cabinet departments or ministries. Examples include the Director of the NPS, the Director of the USDI Bureau of Land Management (BLM), and the Chief of the USDA Forest Service in the United States, and the Director General of the Department of Conservation in New Zealand. There are two major policy-related tasks for these top-level agency officials. First, they must interpret the higher level policies relevant to the missions and responsibilities of their agencies. Those responsibilities are assigned to an agency by the highest levels of policy making, especially the enabling legislation of the U.S. Congress that created the agency. Some policies set by the U.S. Congress, the Office of the President, and/or the U.S. Supreme Court apply to all agencies of the U.S. government at this third level of policy making. Generally, however, most of those policies do not relate directly to the provision of outdoor recreation opportunities by a particular federal land management agency. Some of the policies do, however, especially ones related to the funding made available to operate the land management agencies.

The second task, after interpreting the relevancy to agency functioning of all higher level policies, is to develop agency-level policies needed to meet assigned agency responsibilities. By necessity, such agency-level policies are more specific than the higher level policies relevant to the agency. Such policy making is done with the aid of professional policy analysts who work within functional divisions of each agency. They generally work at the headquarters of the agency (e.g., Washington, DC, in the United States, Wellington in New Zealand). For example, within the USFS the functional division responsible for outdoor recreation is called the Recreation, Heritage, and Wilderness Resources Staff Group. The directors of such staffs recommend policy guidelines to the heads of their agency (e.g., the Chief of the USFS) who must approve all agency policy directives.

Below the heads of the agencies, the policy-making hierarchy continues down through the so-called "line officers" of an agency (similar to the chain of command in the military), which below the Chief of the USFS are the Regional Foresters, Forest Supervisors, and District Rangers. At the lower or field levels, much less attention is devoted to policy making, and lower-level policies are generally more action specific to give clear direction for the managerial decisions made at those lower levels of the organization.

At these lower levels of an agency (or private or non-profit organization), most of the policy directives have their major impact. Those lower or field levels implement management plans developed to realize the social values and goals toward which the policies were oriented. Put differently, higher levels in the policy-making hierarchy, such as Congress or Parliament, are primarily concerned with policy making, while administratively lower, field-level units are much less concerned with policy making and devote most of their attention to effecting management actions designed to address policies set for them at higher administrative levels.

Hierarchical policy development can also be traced through public P&R agencies that exist at the state and local levels of government, but there will be fewer levels in these hierarchies. For example, a municipality will typically range only from a city council down to operating departments in city government. Such policy-making hierarchies also exist for large corporations as well as for small business enterprises and nonprofit organizations. In a large tourism industry, the highest policy makers would be the Board of Directors and the CEO, and the manager of specific on-the-ground opportunities for tourists (e.g., the director of a tour) would be equivalent to the field-level managers of a public land management agency described previously.

Lastly, on the hierarchical nature of policies, it should be pointed out that while most top-level policies are usually very broad, many are quite specific and not subject to refinement at lower levels to make them operational. Examples within the federal government of the United States are policies that employees cannot use government property for their personal use (except as clearly specified, such as when and how much government phones and credit cards can be used) and specific prohibitions against sexual harassment in the workplace.

Policies Differ Within and Among Different Public Agencies and Other Providers

Chapters 5 through 10 describe the different public agencies and private and nonprofit organizations that provide outdoor recreation opportunities in the United States. The more limited purpose of this section is to show why these many different providers of outdoor recreation opportunities often have such varied policies, especially in the United States.

Different types of providers of outdoor recreation opportunities exist in most countries, but no other country has as many different providers as the United States does, especially at the national or federal level. Included at that level are the NPS, the BLM, the Bureau of Reclamation, and the FWS in the U.S. Department of the Interior; the USDA Forest Service; and the U.S Army CoE within the Department of Defense (see Chapter 6).

As mentioned, each federal land management agency has specific functional responsibilities defined and mandated by its enabling legislation, and those responsibilities related to outdoor recreation vary among agencies. For example, the BLM has different responsibilities than the NPS or the FWS or the USFS. Because federal agency responsibilities related to outdoor recreation differ, so will the policies they develop to meet those assigned responsibilities. Although close cooperation often occurs between the recreation, wilderness, and cultural/heritage resource staffs of different federal land management agencies, many of their policies still differ, sometimes considerably because of the agencies' different responsibilities.

To function effectively, outdoor recreation professionals with federal agencies need to understand why those policy differences exist. For example, the USFS and BLM are multiple-use agencies that provide both commodities (e.g., timber, range, mineral, water-related products) and noncommodities (e.g., recreation-related services). In contrast, the NPS is oriented much less to the production of commodities. Instead, it manages the nation's truly unique resources for preservation as well as recreational enjoyment so long as that recreational use does not impinge adversely on preservation. Because of these different functional responsibilities, the outdoor recreation policies of the NPS differ from those of the USFS. As a case in point, the NPS typically imposes more rules and regulations on recreational use, while the USFS allows more autonomy to its visitors. In addition, the developed, as contrasted to more remote campgrounds, of the NPS tend to have much higher densities of campsites per unit of area than do USFS campgrounds, which tend to have much more space between campsites and be more natural in appearance because of vegetative screening. Likewise, the policies of the USFS differ from those of the BLM, which differ from those of the FWS, which in turn differ from those of the CoE.

This potentially perplexing profusion of public P&R agencies with different recreation-related policies is made even more confusing by the existence of many other non-federal public P&R agencies with their different policies. For example, each of the 50 states (as well as most political subdivisions, such as states and provinces, in other countries) has a public P&R agency as well as other state agencies that, while having other primary responsibilities, also provide outdoor recreation opportunities. Examples include the state or provincial fish and wildlife agencies that provide opportunities for hunting, fishing, and viewing wildlife, and agencies primarily concerned with managing timber products, such as state and provincial forestry departments that also offer outdoor recreation opportunities.

In addition, to the state-level agencies, there are county and regional P&R authorities such as the Huron-Clinton Metropolitan, Cleveland, and Adirondack Mountains regional P&R authorities. And the large number of providers extends to nonprofit organizations, such as The Nature Conservancy, the Rocky Mountain Elk Foundation, the Appalachian Mountain Club, and land trusts that provide outdoor recreation opportunities. Each has its specialized policies. Likewise, many private P&R enterprises, including ski corporations and ecotourism enterprises, have their own specialized policies.

Much confusion is also caused by the fact that the many providers of outdoor recreation opportunities do so for different reasons. Most public P&R agencies do so as a public service, but many of those agencies have different legislatively mandated responsibilities. In contrast, private tourism firms have to make a profit, so their policies are influenced accordingly. Still other organizations, especially nonprofit organizations, provide outdoor recreation opportunities to promote particular interests for particular clienteles (e.g., The Nature Conservancy, the Appalachian Mountain Club, private rod and gun clubs).

The purpose of these many providers of outdoor recreation opportunities differs, as does the emphasis on particular types of opportunities provided. Some providers more than others emphasize ecotourism, ecosystem sustainability, protecting the stability of local communities, promoting health and fitness, environmental awareness, nurturing the social networking of senior citizens, providing primitive types of outdoor recreation opportunities in wilderness areas, or providing playgrounds for children.

In summary, because their policies determine the types of managerial actions that can be taken, those actions also differ both within and among the public agencies and other organizations that provide outdoor recreation opportunities. So, until important policy differences are understood and communicated by professional managers, it is understandable that visitors frequently have difficulty understanding why they can do some things at some areas but may not do the same things at others.

Specific Policies Require Specific Managerial Actions

Because most policies establish broad guidelines for actions, managers and administrators must interpret how to act to meet the purposes of those policies. In contrast, some policies are very narrow and explicit, and the required course of managerial or administrative action is clearly mandated by the policies. Such policies frequently relate to matters of purchasing, use of an organization's funds and other resources, or personnel issues. The policies of concern here are those that dictate particular actions that may or may not be taken regarding management of outdoor recreation resources.

Most public agencies, private enterprises, or nonprofit organizations that provide outdoor recreation opportunities have adopted one or more approaches to management, hereafter called *management systems*. Those systems direct outdoor recreation resource planning and management activities. Each of these systems was developed, refined, and implemented within the policy guidelines of the public P&R agencies using the system. Many graduates of outdoor recreation programs will be using these management systems, helping to refine them, and even developing new and improved systems. Outdoor recreation professionals need to understand why each system was developed, especially if the systems were developed to meet specific policy directives.

Several of the outdoor recreation resource planning and management systems described in the next two chapters of this text were developed explicitly to meet very specific requirements of particular federal laws (i.e., policies) passed by the U.S. Congress. For example, the recreation opportunity spectrum (ROS) system was developed to meet the requirement of the 1976 National Forest Management Act (for the USFS) and the 1997 Federal Land Management and Policy Act (for the BLM) that those two agencies develop and implement functionally integrated resource management plans.

Even when a particular act does not require development of a specific management system, that act may lead directly to the development of such systems. For example, the wilderness opportunity zoning (WOZ) management system was developed to guide management of areas designated as Wilderness within the National Wilderness Preservation System created by the Wilderness Act of 1964. The WOZ, like the ROS, was developed because no applicable system existed. The policy provisions of the Wilderness Act determined what wilderness managerial actions the WOZ system could recommend and guide.

The ROS and WOZ management systems cannot be understood unless one understands the policies that led to their development. For example, the Wilderness Act allows for only "primitive" types of recreation opportunities and for exclusion of "mechanized" types of use, so management must conform to those policies. Therefore, the WOZ system must conform as well. (For more details about specific and important outdoor recreation policies see Wellman, 1987, 2004.)

In summary on policy development, it is important to understand and to appreciate that higher level policy directives generally serve as broad guides for action, those policies become more specific and functionally detailed at lower levels within an organization, and all the policies determine what managerial actions can or must be taken. A practicing outdoor recreation professional must understand these influences of policy development on outdoor recreation resource management, administration, and planning. That knowledge will facilitate better appreciation of why and how the different approaches to outdoor recreation resource planning and management discussed in the next two chapters have been influenced by different policies. But first, we must also have a working understanding of the managerial, administrative, and planning processes.

Management

Management, in contrast to policy development, is the decision process within which specific actions are taken "on the ground" to achieve policy goals. Another useful way to view management is to realize that managerial decisions serve two purposes:

1. producing goods (e.g., cars on a production line, pulpwood or logs for saw timber from a forest) or services (e.g., recreation opportunities)

2. protecting something to assure its sustainability (which would in part constitute providing a stewardship service)

Understand that when we refer to an outdoor recreation opportunity as a "service" we do so in the economic sense. That means that an outdoor recreation opportunity is not intangible. An outdoor recreation opportunity is a combination of a physical setting and the various other elements needed for the user to produce their outdoor recreation experience.

Regarding the first purpose of management being producing goods and services, few people have problems with the idea that goods or commodities are produced. Some leisure scientists, however, have objected to the word *production* when it is applied to the delivery of services, including leisure services.

The authors of this text have no problem with the generalization that leisure services are provided by what has been called the *leisure services delivery system.* But from a managerial perspective there is a very important reason to adopt the view that professional managers produce outdoor recreation opportunities. The reason is that professional

outdoor recreation resource planners and managers must understand the "recreation opportunity production process" (described in detail in Chapter 13). Only then can they understand the cause-and-effect relationships among the components of that production process. They must understand what inputs (e.g., land, labor, capital, visitor preferences) are needed to produce the recreation services or outputs (e.g., recreation opportunities), the probable beneficial, and negative outcomes or impacts that result from the production and use of outdoor recreation opportunities in different recreational settings. Put simply, the words "producing recreation opportunities" require clear professional understanding of all aspects of the leisure service delivery system just as a medical doctor or educator must understand clearly all aspects of their delivery of medical or educational services.

At one level, differentiating between *providing* and *producing* recreation opportunities involves semantics and nuances. Within a managerial perspective, these are very important nuances, however. For example, administrators of too many outdoor recreation organizations have failed to recognize and require the types of professional knowledge and skills needed to plan and manage resources to produce outdoor recreation opportunities. For that reason, people without those necessary skills have too often been put in positions for which they were not professionally qualified. This has been done frequently in public agencies when budget cuts required terminating positions in nonrecreation functions, such as timber management. Instead of laying off those employees, they would often be given positions in recreation under the false assumption that if the person ever camped or hiked, they would know how to manage outdoor recreation. That erroneous logic is the same as that which would say that if a person has even been ill, they are qualified to be a medical doctor. This too common approach defies and demeans the concept

USDA Forest Service manager orienting members of a volunteer organization in California. The group is an important stakeholder and partner.

of professionalism in the recreation field that is emphasized in this text.

The concept of managing to produce recreation opportunities within the idea of a recreation production process is described in detail in Chapter 13, because it is fundamental to the beneficial outcomes approach to leisure and to benefits-based management on which that chapter focuses. Suffice it to say here that the authors of this text believe that (a) both goods and services are produced, whether the services are recreational, medical, educational, or otherwise in nature; and (b) to be a professional manager requires professional knowledge, and demonstration of knowledge about how recreation opportunities are produced attests to the possession of such needed knowledge.

Beyond producing a good or service, the other stated dimension of management was "protecting something." That protection might be sustaining ecosystems; protecting a cultural/historic site or artifact; or helping to assure the safety of visiting customers from dangerous animals, poisonous plants, hazardous features of a site, or adverse impacts of extreme weather conditions.

Much detail could be provided here on specific tasks required in the management of outdoor and related amenity resources. (Because that detail is given in Chapter 13 where benefits-based management is reviewed, it will not be repeated here.) Briefly, management is a logical decision/resource allocation process that includes assisting planners, developing a management plan, working collaboratively with relevant stakeholders, accomplishing clear management objectives by implementing prescribed management actions, and applying standards to monitor implementation of those prescriptions. In a nutshell, management can be viewed simply as getting something relatively concrete done, while policies are developed to provide general guidance on what that something will be.

Other texts have been written on recreation resource planning and management in general and outdoor recreation resource planning and management in particular. See, for example, Edginton, Hudson, and Lankford (2001), Hammitt and Cole (1998), Jubenville and Twight (1993), Kraus and Curtis (2000), and Torkildsen (1992).

Administration

As stated earlier, administrators do those basic activities necessary for policy makers, managers, and planners to function efficiently, legally, and responsively. Those administrative actions are extremely important and cover a host of endeavors that keeps policy makers, planners, and managers on track and performing within organizational policies. Included are all tasks related to personnel matters, such as recruitment, hiring, and on-the-job training. In addition, administrators monitor all policies regarding equal and fair employment and organizational privileges,

rights, safety, health and life insurance, retirement, and other benefits. Also within administration are fiscal management functions involving preparing annual budgets; tracking and documenting revenues and expenditures; and preparing, entering into, and administering contracts. Other important administrative tasks are maintaining the physical plant or facilities, which includes communications, electric power, heating, air conditioning, sanitation and water supplies, parking lots, and motor pools.

Essentially, administration is concerned with all those extremely important "housekeeping" responsibilities that assure policy makers, planners, and managers can do their jobs effectively, efficiently, and responsibly. Generally, administrators do not make allocation decisions about which outdoor recreation opportunities will be provided, in what amount, when, for whom, or of what quality. Outdoor recreation resource managers make these decisions. However, when the budget of a field-level management unit precludes hiring a full-time administrator, the manager and clerical personnel usually bear the administrative responsibilities. Although administration has distinct responsibilities requiring specialized training and skills, it interacts with the other three decision processes described in this chapter. Administrators must understand the policies within which they operate and must know what the planners and managers they serve are doing and why.

Planning

Planning largely determines what policy, managerial, and administrative decisions will be made. As such, there is policy planning, management planning, and administrative planning to guide the actions of administrators (e.g., budget planning). Planning is a logical and systematic process pursued to define and refine organizational policies and goals, to set directions for managerial actions, and to guide administrative decisions. Policy planning is directed toward policy development, administrative planning is directed toward administrative matters, and management planning is directed toward management (i.e., the production of goods and services or the protection of something).

Each type of planning can be broad in scope, such as to develop an overall policy regarding user fees or to develop policies about use of mountain bikes in certain areas. Similarly, management planning can be broad or narrow in scope. For example, comprehensive multiple-use plans for a large area are more general than plans for subunits of that area or plans for specific uses. Thus, there are various levels of detail and specificity among plans for a new administrative building, a picnic area, an interpretative plan for a particular site, a hazard reduction plan, or a fire prevention and suppression plan.

Planning is frequently done by a multidisciplinary planning team. Typically, such a team includes professional personnel of the agency or organization who have disciplinary training in the functional areas relevant to the planning tasks. Thus, a management planning team for a relatively large nature-based recreation area or complex might include landscape architects, economists, foresters, ecologists, and specialists with training in recreation, range, fisheries, timber, cultural/heritage resource, and wildlife management. In contrast, the team for developing an interpretive plan for a nature trail might comprise only an interpretative naturalist and the manager of the area in which the nature trail is located.

Planning teams generally include relevant policy makers, managers, and administrators, depending on whether policy, management, or administrative planning is being done. Most planning teams in public agencies now include representatives of managerially relevant stakeholders who work as collaborative partners with the planners and managers, as elaborated in Chapter 13.

The literature on planning shows different types of plans serve different purposes. Included are master plans that lay out overall managerial directions, strategic plans that define and describe the overall short-term and long-term goals and objectives of an organization, and advocacy plans that promote or protect the values and interests of a particular group of people. For example, nonprofit organizations such as the Rails-to-Trails Conservancy, the International Mountain Bicycling Association, and land trusts make and implement various plans for their organizations to protect and promote the values inherent to the group they represent. Put simply, these different types of plans exist to define the most efficient, accountable, responsive, and effective ways to accomplish the goals or purposes of an organization.

Just as the four decision processes discussed in this chapter require different professional skills, different professional skills are also required to do planning of different types, especially where multidisciplinary expertise is needed. For that reason, there are academic course offerings on planning in colleges and universities. Many texts have been written on the subject, such as one by McLean, Bannon, and Gray (1999), and texts on recreation management also consider planning.

Summary

It is important for any recreational professional, including an outdoor recreation professional, to understand the nature of and purposes served by the four distinct but interrelated decision processes of policy development, management, administration, and planning. They then understand more completely the policies and managerial rules and regulations of an agency or organization that provides outdoor recreation opportunities, why selected managerial actions are taken by the organization for which they work, and why other organizations take different managerial actions and have different rules and regulations. This knowledge should enhance one's professional productivity, effectiveness, and job satisfaction.

An equally important purpose of this chapter was to provide insight into the different career options that exist for specialization within outdoor recreation. As we have emphasized, the skills required for policy development, management, administration, and planning are quite different. Some people are better suited to be policy makers, others managers or administrators, and still others planners. Too many outdoor recreation professionals (and other professionals) who study to be managers end up in planning and are ineffective at it. Managers are trained in how to accomplish tasks and produce recreation opportunities "on the ground" according to prescribed approved courses of action that have little ambiguity. Planning, on the other hand, is concerned with determining the best course of action that managers should follow from among many possible courses of action for meeting agency/organizational goals. While managers typically work with clear direction and little ambiguity, planners must be more tolerant of uncertainty and ambiguity and be comfortable with considering many "what if" questions related to the many different ways that an organization's goals might be realized. Their job is somewhat like playing a chess game that demands attention be given to many contingencies, and many complex feedback and feed-forward loops must be understood and considered. In this sense, planning is like the policy formulation process, which always concerns compromising among competing interests and values to achieve an acceptable solution, at least in the short run. So, just as many people who study management do not make good planners, many people who

USDA Forest Service planners evaluating managerial policies options for a National Forest in Arizona.

study planning do not make good managers. Not only does the public agency or other organization and its customers suffer from these mismatches of skills and personal dispositions but also the professionals suffer by not being as professionally satisfied as they might be.

The next chapter provides more detail about the management of outdoor recreation and introduces some of the most established management systems in our field.

Literature Cited

Edginton, C. Hudson, S., and Lankford, S. (2001). *Managing recreation, parks, and leisure services*. Champaign, IL: Sagamore.

Edginton, C., Jordan, D., DeGraaf, D, and Edginton, S. (1995). *Leisure and life satisfaction: Fundamental perspectives*. Dubuque, IA: W. C. Brown Communications, Inc.

Hammitt, W. E. and Cole, D. N. (1998). *Wildland recreation: Ecology and management* (2nd ed.). New York, NY: John Wiley & Sons.

Jubenville, A. and Twight, B. W. (1993). *Outdoor recreation management* (3rd ed.). State College, PA. Venture Publishing, Inc.

Kraus, R. G. and Curtis, J. C. (2000). *Creative management in recreation, parks, and leisure services* (6th ed.). Boston, MA: McGraw-Hill.

McLean, D. D., Bannon, J. J, and Gray, H. R. (1999). *Leisure resources: Its comprehensive planning* (2nd ed.). Champaign, IL: Sagamore.

Torkildsen, G. (1992). *Leisure and recreation management*. London, England: E & FN Spon.

Wellman, J. D. (1987). *Wildland recreation policy: An introduction*. New York, NY: John Wiley & Sons.

Wellman, J. D. and Propst, D. B. (2004). *Wildland recreation policy: An introduction* (2nd ed.) Malabar, FL: Krieger Publishing Co.

Chapter 12
Evolution of Science-Based Management of Outdoor Recreation Resources

While the goal of the recreationist is to obtain satisfying experiences, the goal of the recreation resource manager becomes one of providing the opportunities for obtaining these experiences. By managing the natural resource setting, and the activities which occur within it, the manager is providing opportunities for recreation experiences to take place. (USDA Forest Service, 1982, p. 5)

Learning Objectives

1. Explain the evolution of management of outdoor recreation resources.
2. Understand the significance of the Outdoor Recreation Resources Review Commission to current management of outdoor recreation resources.
3. Describe the basic characteristics of the science-based approaches to outdoor recreation resource management widely used today in many countries.
4. Appreciate the tremendous progress that has been made in the professional management of outdoor recreation resources, especially since 1960.

Chapter 3 presented a summary of the historical context of outdoor recreation in the United States by describing six periods: Frontier, Acquisition, Transfer and Disposal, Reservation, Custodial Management, and Confrontation and Partnership. This chapter expands Chapter 3 by focusing solely on the management of outdoor recreation resources, especially the evolution of scientifically credible management systems in the United States. By focusing on management of outdoor recreation resources, and to a lesser extent on policies that guide that management, this chapter elaborates a theme of Chapter 11 that management is "where the rubber hits the road" with respect to the provision of outdoor recreation opportunities. In addition, this chapter illustrates that Santayana's well-known quotation— "Those who cannot remember the past are condemned to repeat it"—is relevant to management of outdoor recreation resources. Too many recreation professionals still manage as they "always have" in the past without incorporating new professional knowledge. In the process, they have been "condemned" to not take advantage of the new and better management practices described in this chapter.

A special focus of this chapter and Chapter 13 is the evolution of ever-improving approaches to the management of outdoor recreation resources, facilitated by the tremendous advances in scientific knowledge about leisure and recreation since 1960. As such, this chapter also reinforces the theme of Chapter 2 that professionalism must be based on scientific knowledge. This chapter traces how enhanced professionalism in outdoor recreation resource management in the United States evolved through four periods toward the use of better science-based management systems that have incrementally led to more effective, efficient, cost-effective, responsive, and accountable management, and also to better protection of basic natural and cultural/heritage resources.

To emphasize the critical role of scientific knowledge in enhancing professionalism, the phrase *science-based management systems* is used frequently in this chapter. Those words are a common shorthand to denote an approach to management that has scientific credibility, because it is based on the results of research as well as good judgment, and not mostly on intuition. In the past, too many approaches to managing outdoor recreation resources were mostly intuitive, in large part because the needed research had not yet been done. It is emphasized that our use of the words "science-based" in no way implies a technocratic or authoritative approach in which the technically trained manager does not work with collaborating stakeholders and associated providers who both affect and are affected by the recreation opportunities provider. This is not to deny the critical role of professional technical expertise; it is to deny exclusion of affected and affecting persons and organizations from participating in outdoor recreation resource management planning.

Different Periods of Management and the Approaches Used Therein

The evolution of improved outdoor recreation resource management in the United States will be traced through four periods: settlement, custodial management, low priority management for outdoor recreation, and overtly managing for outdoor recreation. While our focus here is on the United States, similar periods of evolution of outdoor recreation resource management can be found in many other countries, especially since the 1960s when many nations entered the period of overtly managing for outdoor recreation. In fact, many countries now use science-based management systems.

Most use of outdoor recreation opportunities in the United States has occurred, and continues to occur, on public lands. But as Chapters 7, 8, and 9 pointed out, increasing numbers of opportunities for outdoor recreation continue to be provided by nonprofit and private-sector organizations. For example, during the past several decades, there have been trends toward more private ownership of land for second homes, ecotourism has increased, more private firms that own large tracts of land and water (e.g., timber and mining companies) opened their lands for outdoor recreation use, and many nonprofit organizations, such as The Nature Conservancy, offered opportunities for outdoor recreation. By and large private and nonprofit providers generally do not manage their lands for recreation as the dominant use. Therefore, the systems for managing outdoor recreation resources described in this chapter and Chapter 13 were developed primarily to help public agencies. Nevertheless, those systems can be used by private and nonprofit providers of outdoor recreation opportunities as well. Each of the four periods of management for the United States will now be described.

Settlement

This period nationwide began with the arrival and settlement of Europeans in the United States in the 1600s, and ended in the middle to late 1800s. The end of that period varies from one region of the United States to another because of the westward pattern of human settlement. It ended earlier in the eastern and later in the western regions.

The most essential characteristic of this period was the settlement and use of the country's resources, mostly for the purposes of one's own choosing. The land management orientation of federal and state authorities during this period could best be described as laissez faire, or "hands off." Early outdoor recreational pursuits outside the villages and cities were similar to what is today called adventure recreation and would include hunting, fishing, trapping,

exploring, and orienteering—both for fun and for extrinsic rewards such as food, pelts, minerals, and finding land to settle. This laissez faire attitude is reflected by the ways in which about one half of the original public domain lands owned by the United States government were transferred to private/corporate ownership. Dennis (2001, p. 83) pointed out in his excellent text that the General Land Office (GLO) was created in the U.S. Department of the Treasury in 1812 to help administer and dispose of the public domain lands. The creation of the GLO was necessary because of the mushrooming total size of that public domain, particularly after 530 million acres were added by the Louisiana Purchase in 1803. Under many land laws passed by the U.S. Congress, the GLO disposed of just over one billion acres of the public domain by sales and grants of land to promote development and settlement. Included were sales and grants to railroad and canal companies and to private individuals (for homesteads) and lands assigned to Native Americans. A primary reason for the sales and grants of this public land was to stimulate economic growth and development of the nation. An important second reason was for the lands to be settled and developed by the private sector to deter other countries from occupying and claiming them. Approximately three quarters of a billion acres of the original public domain remain in federal ownership. They now comprise lands reserved/withdrawn to create national parks, national forests, grasslands, wildlife refuges, and military bases; acreage purchased by the federal government later; and the residual public domain lands now administered by the USDI Bureau of Land Management (BLM). In total the lands now under federal agency administration constitute about one third of the surface area of the United States. As just stated, a larger acreage was transferred to private ownership (see Chapter 3).

It is difficult to generalize about this period from the perspective of the entire United States because of regional variations in the degree of human settlement noted earlier. Some villages and cities had commons, such as the Boston Common created in 1634 as a common forage area for livestock. Boston Common evolved into one of the best-known urban parks and green spaces in the United States. Other cities, such as Washington, DC, had malls and reflecting pools with ducks, fish, and other wildlife that afforded opportunities for outdoor recreation. Many towns had turkey shoots and other forms of outdoor recreation. Even prior to the early 1900s, some state legislatures acted to constrain a laissez faire orientation to outdoor recreation. For example, several states had established laws regulating hunting of some species of wildlife by 1800.

The little outdoor recreation resource management that did exist during this period was not based on the results of scientific research, and except occasionally at the local level was seldom driven by explicitly stated outdoor recreation related policy directives. Certainly, countries hundreds or even thousands of years older than the United States made progress toward the purposeful management of resources for outdoor recreation long before the Pilgrims landed at Plymouth Rock or Jamestown was established.

In some of these countries, opportunities were available only to the rich and landed gentry, such as on private hunting preserves managed by game tenders. But many other opportunities for outdoor recreation, particularly in or near centers of human settlement, were more publicly available. Even in those countries, the management that was done for outdoor recreation was not science-based earlier than or during the dates of this period simply because that knowledge did not exist.

Custodial Management

From a nationwide perspective in the United States, this period of management of lands for outdoor recreation overlapped the end of the period of settlement, beginning around the middle 1800s and ending in the 1930s and 1940s. Again, we are dealing with general dates, because nationwide there was a transition period of several decades into this period. Some regions made that transition earlier than others, and some public lands were still being managed custodially much later. For example, the GLO was transferred to the U.S. Department of the Interior (USDI) when it was created in 1849. That is probably the best date to mark the beginning of the period of custodial management of the public domain. Certainly this period of custodial management was underway by the late 1890s, and evidence of it was very clear at the time of the presidency of Theodore Roosevelt, credited with influencing the first so-called conservation movement in the United States in the early 1900s. Interestingly, this period was ending about the time of the presidency of Franklin D. Roosevelt who influenced strongly the second conservation movement. The transition out of the period of custodial management was essentially completed when the GLO and the U.S. Grazing Service (which both practiced custodial management) were combined to form the Bureau of Land Management (BLM) in 1946. The BLM became responsible for managing the residual public domain lands and retains that role to this day.

The focus of custodial management was more on protection and improvement of natural resources than on their development for use. Examples included reforestation, prevention of wildfires, prevention of overgrazing of range lands by livestock, and prevention of damage to watersheds. The early management of the national forests and grasslands reflected this orientation.

Although the U.S. Congress authorized the Secretary of the Interior to create forestry reserves out of the public

domain in 1891, funds were not appropriated for any management of those reserves until the Forest Management Act of 1897. Those reserves remained under the administration of the GLO in the USDI until they were transferred to the Division of Forestry in the U.S. Department of Agriculture, a feat engineered by Gifford Pinchot, who headed that division and was a close friend of President Theodore Roosevelt. In 1906, Pinchot changed the name to the U.S. Forest Service (USFS) and became its first chief. Within weeks after Pinchot became the first Chief of the U.S. Forest Service, he issued his *Wise Use* books. They reflected that Pinchot was one of the first professionally trained foresters in the United States by laying out the first, but still very general, principles of multiple-use management of natural resources in the United States. Multiple-use management means managing for several different uses of the land of which one or more uses can be dominant instead of managing for just a single use such as production of timber, pulpwood, minerals, forage for domestic livestock, water, or recreation. Those *Wise Use* books and Pinchot's orientation to management started what has come to be called the "scientific school of forestry" in the United States. It was in reality a technocratic approach guided largely by the technical training of forest managers (Hayes, 1955). Although Pinchot advocated utilization via conservation (in contrast to preservation or exploitation), the early decades of management by the USFS reflected custodial management.

Some, but relatively little, managerial attention was devoted to outdoor recreation before the 1930s. To be sure, there were forward-thinking employees of the USFS and National Park Service (NPS) who recognized the social significance of recreational uses of the national forests and parks before then (e.g., Albright, Carhart, Marshall, and Mather). Nevertheless, recreation was not recognized as a primary use of the national forests, national parks, or other major public land areas during the period of custodial management. No science-based management of outdoor recreation resources existed during this period, because, as explained in Chapter 2, there was no relevant scientific knowledge available until the 1960s.

A similar pattern of custodial management can be traced through the early histories of other public land management agencies in the United States, especially at the federal level. For example, when Yellowstone National Park was created in 1872, no federal money was appropriated for its management for several years, and the U.S. Cavalry was the first "managerial" presence there, with its purpose being to protect park resources. Such custodial management was typical of other national parks as they were established, and the orientation of the National Park Service (NPS) when it was created in 1916. Early management of the parks was oriented toward protecting and sustaining the natural, cultural, and historic resources and not toward promoting recreational use. Similarly, the USDI Bureau of Reclamation, created in 1902, built many dams for generation of hydroelectric power and to provide water for irrigation. Most of the recreation opportunities at the reservoirs created by that bureau are now managed by state and local units of government and receive high use, especially day use. But early management of those bodies of water and surrounding lands was custodial.

Low Priority Management for Outdoor Recreation

This period started in the early 1930s and ended about 1960; it is the shortest period described here. But again, there were different starting dates in different regions of the country.

As mentioned previously, the early 1930s began what has been called the second conservation movement in the United States. That movement was spawned for many reasons, including the dust storms in the lower Midwest, concerns about overgrazing of public range lands, and growing demands on land and water resources because of growing populations. Thus, in the 1930s there was a transition from mostly custodial management of the public lands to this next period in which outdoor recreation was slowly but surely being recognized by public land management agencies as an increasingly important use. Nevertheless, recreation during this period generally received less attention and was of lower priority to the public land management agencies than were other uses.

The U.S. economy expanded rapidly after World War II, and demands for all goods and services, especially automobiles and houses, increased accordingly. As a result, pressures increased on many public land management agencies to provide the raw materials needed to meet those demands. For example, the USFS was under pressure from the U.S. Congress to produce lumber and pulpwood for homes, other structures, and paper. Likewise, pressures increased on the BLM for it to meet demands for gas, oil, uranium ore, coal, other minerals, and forage on the public lands for domestic livestock. The U.S. Bureau of Reclamation was pressured to provide more hydroelectric power and water to irrigate arid lands. The Civil Works Division of the U.S. Army Corps of Engineers was also expected to help meet growing demands for hydroelectric power, flood control, and improvement of the channels of navigable rivers. These pressures came from the U.S. Congress, high officials in the office of the President, and interest groups representing pulp and timber, grazing, mineral, electrical energy, and other interests.

Despite the pressures of public land management agencies to focus on uses other than outdoor recreation, recreational use continued to increase after the end of

World War II. In addition, two other factors slowed movement into the period of overtly managing for outdoor recreation. First, the agencies were under pressure from the U.S. Congress to generate revenues for federal and state treasuries, and outdoor recreation then could not complete with timber and mineral products in doing so. At that time the federal agencies had extremely limited authority from the U.S. Congress to levy recreation entrance and use fees. So, those agencies tended to emphasize other uses that would return funds to government treasuries. Second, and probably most important, was the fact that land managers at that time had much better professional training in forestry, range management, game management, fisheries management, geology, petroleum engineering, watershed management, and civil engineering than they did in management of outdoor recreation resources. This lack of clear understanding of how to manage for outdoor recreation caused public policy makers and land managers to focus on the types of management for which they had been trained, which was not outdoor recreation. That situation is understandable, because few colleges and universities offered courses in, much less opportunities to major in, outdoor recreation before 1960. The outdoor recreation courses that were offered did not have the backing of scientific research that other natural resource professions did at that time.

As mentioned, several visionary and unusually perceptive employees of the public land management agencies (e.g., Carhart and Marshall) did recognize that more agency attention needed to be devoted to outdoor recreation and related amenity values. While they exerted considerable influence, it came only after a time lag, and had its major impacts near the end of this period in the late 1950s. It was then increasingly reflected in agency programs and initiatives that recognized the growing demands for outdoor recreation opportunities. Examples include *Mission 66*, the ten-year program initiated by the NPS (1956) to increase expenditures for improvement of facilities and *Operation Outdoors* of the USDA Forest Service (1957), which addressed the lack of facilities and other resources to accommodate rising recreational use. For example, the preface of *Operation Outdoors* states:

> Recreation facilities built in the 1930s have been deteriorating under the heavy wear and tear. In recent years the overflow of people has gone into unimproved areas where there are no sanitary facilities and no fireplaces.... This situation has been building up rapidly and no letup is in sight...

The growing recognition that public land management agencies needed to better understand and accommodate outdoor recreation was reflected in the early 1960s by the USFS creating cooperative outdoor recreation units jointly with several universities. That agency helped to staff and fund those units for many years, with the objective being to create more interest in outdoor recreation in schools and colleges of forestry and natural resources. Those projects stimulated more research on outdoor recreation, created more and better courses on outdoor recreation, and trained undergraduate and graduate students on how to better accommodate outdoor recreation uses and values once they went to work for an outdoor recreation resource management agency.

Overtly Managing for Outdoor Recreation

As with the other periods, this one started earlier in localized areas of the eastern part of the United States, but generally it started nationwide around 1960 and it continues today. The beginning of this period marks a significant turning point in the history of managing public lands for outdoor recreation and related amenity values. At that time outdoor recreation was beginning to be recognized as an important and highly valued use of public lands. That recognition continued to increase and in 1997 Mike Dombeck, then Chief of the USFS, stated that recreation had become the dominant use of the national forests (Dombeck, 1997).

Even though it had become apparent that outdoor recreation had emerged as an important use of public lands in the United States by 1960, overt (i.e., purposeful) management to accommodate rapidly increasing participation in outdoor recreation activities was still novel and frequently without clear policy guidelines from top administrative levels of the responsible public land management agencies. This situation did not reflect lack of concern as much as it did lack of needed professional knowledge. As explained in Chapter 2, there was a dearth of scientific knowledge about outdoor recreation to guide management at this time and of opportunities to get academic training in outdoor recreation resource planning and management. Practically all early approaches to overtly managing for outdoor recreation reflected some combination of intuition and judgment. In retrospect, given the challenges facing them, early planners and managers of outdoor recreation resources did a remarkably good job in their time.

The very significant things that have happened, and are still happening, to outdoor recreation resource management during this period will be described in detail in the remainder of this chapter and in Chapter 13. The remaining discussion in this chapter has two parts. The first describes significant legislation ("policies" in the vernacular of Chapter 11) that had profound impacts on overtly managing for outdoor recreation. The second reviews the science-based systems that have been and are still being used to manage outdoor recreation opportunities. It shows how those systems have become better as scientific research about leisure in general, and outdoor recreation in particular, have incrementally advanced professional knowledge and its application to those management systems.

Significant Legislation

ORRRC and Its Impacts

After World War II the United States needed to accommodate the rapidly increasing demands for outdoor recreation opportunities, while also understanding how to reduce negative environmental impacts of such use. Because of these needs, the U.S. Congress created the Outdoor Recreation Resource Review Commission (ORRRC) in 1958. The ORRRC issued its report in 27 technical volumes plus a summary volume in 1962. Those reports and the recommendations therein that have been implemented since are probably the most significant events in the history of outdoor recreation in the United States for the reasons outlined here.

The ORRRC led to creation of the USDI Bureau of Outdoor Recreation in 1963. Until it was eliminated in 1981, the Bureau of Outdoor Recreation promoted and coordinated many important outdoor recreation programs. Probably most significant was administration of the Land and Water Conservation Fund (LWCF), which was created by the Land and Water Conservation Fund Act (LWCFA) of the U.S. Congress in 1965 and amended several times after that. That act was recommended by the ORRRC to be "a federal grants-in-aid program....To stimulate and assist the states in meeting the demand for outdoor recreation" (ORRRC, 1962, p. 10). The LWCFA substantively influenced management of outdoor recreation resources in the United States in several ways:

1. It allowed for funds from the LWCF (garnered in the U.S. Treasury from revenues from entrance and use fees at federal recreation areas, royalties from permits to private enterprises to drill for off-shore oil, sales of surplus military properties, and special appropriations from the U.S. Congress) to be distributed by the Bureau of Outdoor Recreation to federal, regional, state, and municipal recreation agencies for the acquisition and development of outdoor recreation facilities and resources.

2. It provided much broader authority from the U.S. Congress for federal agencies to charge entrance and use fees for recreation than had existed before (see Driver, Bossi & Cordell, 1985).

3. It required that states prepare and submit State Comprehensive Outdoor Recreation Plans (SCORPs) to the Bureau of Outdoor Recreation before they could qualify for grants from the LWCF.

Prior to the ORRRC reports, no widely used system existed for inventorying and classifying outdoor recreation resources as to the potential of different types of land and water to provide various types of outdoor recreation opportunities. The ORRRC proposed such an inventory and system, known as the Bureau of Outdoor Recreation Area Classification Plan (ACP). The ACP used general characteristics of different types of lands to classify them as either

Class I: High-Density Recreation Areas

Class II: General Outdoor Recreation Areas

Class III: Natural Environment Areas

Class IV: Unique Natural Areas

Class V: Primitive Areas

Class VI: Historic and Cultural Sites

Although the ACP system for classifying outdoor recreation resources was not based on systematic research, it was a logical approach that filled the vacuum that continued to exist until the early 1980s, when the recreation opportunity spectrum (ROS) system replaced it.

A significant impact of the ORRRC reports is that they stimulated rapid acceleration of research on outdoor recreation in particular and on leisure in general. For example, most of the 27 technical volumes produced by the ORRRC were detailed reports of studies about outdoor recreation conducted by respected scientists located throughout the United States. Particularly important were the ORRRC's nationwide studies of outdoor recreation demand and supply and the factors that contributed to them. Equally and probably more significant to stimulating ongoing development of a scientific body of knowledge about outdoor recreation were the literally hundreds of studies done in the 1960s across the United States to help the states develop the SCORPs they needed to qualify for grants from the LWCF. Scientists in research institutions, especially colleges and universities, did many of those studies which then had a ripple effect that spread rapidly and stimulated more research on outdoor recreation that went beyond the needs of the SCORPs. For example, leisure scientists expanded the scope of their studies, graduate students whose education was funded totally or in part from funds for the SCORP studies became more interested in research on outdoor recreation, and professors who had not engaged in leisure/recreation research before became interested in such because of their direct or indirect involvement in the SCORP studies. Put simply, the ORRRC reports and the SCORP studies that resulted and continue today were a major stimulus for the rapid acceleration of research on outdoor recreation in the 1960s, and as such marked the beginning of professionalism in outdoor recreation. In combination with events that occurred during the period of low priority for outdoor recreation management, the ORRRC reports and the impacts of its recommendations—especially the creation of the Bureau of Outdoor Recreation and passage of the LWCFA (and its requirements for SCORPs)—rapidly moved the United States into the period of overtly managing for outdoor recreation.

Other Significant Legislation

The same forces that lead the U.S. Congress to pass legislation that created the ORRRC in 1958 also prompted it to pass several other acts that promoted overt management for outdoor recreation. Particularly important were the 1960 Multiple Use and Sustained Yield Act (MUSYA) for the USFS and the similar, but much more limited, 1964 Classification and Multiple Use Act (CMUA) for the BLM. Those acts mandated the USFS and BLM to give full consideration to all uses of the public lands they administered and not just to the uses that had previously been emphasized (i.e., timber by the USFS, mining and grazing by BLM). While those two acts did have educational value and caused some improvements in managing overtly for recreation, they did not influence the USFS and BLM as much as the U.S. Congress intended them to. Instead, it took the 1976 National Forest Management Act (NFMA) for the USFS and the 1976 Federal Land Management and Policy Act (FLMPA) for the BLM to really move those agencies to truly implement management that considered the economic and social values of all uses of the public lands, including use for outdoor recreation. Specifically, those 1976 acts demonstrated that the American public, through their congressional delegations, were serious about environmental concerns, including better accommodation of demands for outdoor recreation opportunities. A major stimulus for the passage of those acts was considerable litigation by groups dissatisfied with the existing managerial practices of those two agencies, especially the USFS.

Other legislation also influenced the movement toward overt management for outdoor recreation, but most of it did not have the impact of the acts just discussed. Probably most notable was the Wilderness Act of 1964, which created the National Wilderness Preservation System. That system now includes over 105 million acres of Wilderness in the United States designated under provisions of the 1964 Act and its amendments. That act would not have been passed without the support of many citizens who never visited those areas. Nor would it have been passed if it had not, in part, defined wilderness as offering "…outstanding opportunities for solitude or a primitive and unconfined type of recreation."

Other legislation relevant to overtly managing for outdoor recreation include the Clean Air and Clean Water Acts at the beginning of this period, the Threatened and Endangered Species Act of 1973 and its subsequent amendments and reauthorization in 1988, the 1969 National

Environmental Policy Act (NEPA), and legislation that authorized creation of national scenic and recreational rivers and trails as well as scenic byways. This legislation and its impacts have been significant in that it incrementally reoriented managerial practices toward overtly managing for outdoor recreation.

We will now examine the role of the results of scientific research in promoting overt management for outdoor recreation resources by better defining the demands for outdoor recreation opportunities and by facilitating the development of improved management systems to meet those demands.

How Advancements in Knowledge Have Facilitated Better Management Practice

Chapter 2 documented great advances in scientific knowledge about leisure since 1960. As that knowledge has improved, so has the delivery of leisure services, including outdoor recreation opportunities. An excellent example of the relationship between research and management is the incremental improvement in knowledge about recreation demands and the accompanying development of new managerial approaches to accommodate those demands. Recreation demands can be envisioned as existing within a "recreation demand hierarchy" (Driver & Brown, 1978). That hierarchy includes three related types, or levels, of demands for different types of recreation opportunities (Figure 12.1):

1. demands for opportunities to engage in desired activities

2. demands for opportunities to realize desired experiences as well as desired activities

3. demands for opportunities to realize additional benefits beyond satisfying experiences

Those demands are hierarchical in that each higher level of demands also includes the demands reflected by the lower level(s). Thus, there is increasing complexity associated with attempts to define, understand, research, and managerially accommodate each type of demand as one moves from the less complex Level 1 demands for recreation activity opportunities through the Level 2 demands to realize satisfying recreation experiences to the much more complex Level 3 demands to have opportunities to realize benefits other than those associated with the Level 2 demands. Remember that Chapter 2 defined three types of benefits of leisure with the third type being the realization of satisfying psychological recreation experiences. Level 3 demands focus on the other two types of benefits (other than realizing satisfying experiences).

Most P&R resource management still focuses on the Level 1 demands and to a lesser extent on the Level 2 demands. This is understandable, because as explained in Chapter 2, most scientific understanding of the Level 3 demands for the other benefits of recreation has been gained since about 1985. Therefore, most managers could not understand and accommodate this demand as well as they could the Level 1 and 2 demands, about which more knowledge existed. The remainder of this chapter describes science-based managerial approaches for accommodating the Level 1 and 2 demands. Chapter 13 will then focus on accommodating the Level 3 demands by applying benefits-based management.

It is quite helpful to understand the evolution of science-based approaches and the overt management of outdoor recreation resources in order to realize that the states of knowledge about the three levels of recreation demand have strongly influenced the goals and orientations of P&R management over time. Thus, until about 1980, management focused on Level 1 demands for recreation activity opportunities (herein called *activity-based management*, or ABM), because leisure research had not produced a body of knowledge to overtly manage for Level 2 demands for satisfying experiences (called *experience-based management*, or EBM). Since about 1980, EBM has gained credibility and is now applied widely. As more research was done on the benefits of leisure during the past 15 to 20 years, *benefits-based management* (BBM)

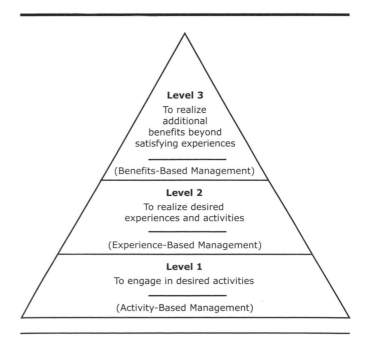

Figure 12.1 Hierarchy of demands for recreation opportunities

has begun to gain acceptance to supplement ABM and EBM to meet Level 3 demands. The essential characteristics of ABM and EBM, and the general characteristics of BBM, will now be outlined here to contrast it with ABM and EBM. BBM will be described in detail in the next chapter where it can be discussed more thoroughly as an important part of a new paradigm about leisure called the *beneficial outcomes approach to leisure* (BOAL).

Activity-Based Management

The principle characteristics of activity-based management (ABM) include the following:

- It is simplistic and defines recreation only as the human behavior of participating in a recreation activity, just as eating and sleeping are human behaviors.

- By just describing and documenting counts of people participating in different types of recreation activity, ABM says nothing about how the recreationists are affected or impacted by the provision of the activity opportunity.

- ABM is supply oriented and focuses mainly on facilities or resources. It gives little attention to the demand side of management other than the demands for specific activity opportunities (i.e., Level 1 demands).

- Other than for their demands for activity opportunities and for facilitating attributes of recreation activity settings, ABM defines the user inputs to the recreation production process in much the same terms as it does the outputs of that process. Specifically, user inputs (other than their demands for activity opportunities and for facilitating attributes of recreation activity settings) are defined as users coming, and user outputs are defined as users going, so the inputs are essentially the same as the outputs, and we do not know what the impacts of participation are. By analogy, hospitals need better measures of their social contributions than just counts of the patients coming and leaving, because they also need to know what happened to the patients while they were in the hospital and before they left.

- ABM provides too little opportunity to consider the quality of the recreation activity opportunities provided or used. It does require consideration of the specific attributes of the recreation settings necessary for activity opportunities to be created. But it does not explicitly require experiential understanding of why those attributes are needed and desired.

- Under ABM, management objectives, prescriptions, guidelines and actions are oriented only to the provision of outdoor recreation activity opportunities.

It is fair to say that until recently, the vast majority of recreation resource management was primarily ABM. In addition, it is professionally embarrassing to say that a great deal of P&R resource management still remains primarily ABM.

Experienced-Based Management

Experience-based management (EBM) builds on, *but does not replace,* ABM. In other words, ABM is necessary but not sufficient for the management of outdoor recreation resources. The essential characteristics of EBM include the following:

- It is much more complex then ABM, because it defines recreation as a psychological state in experimental terms (as explained in Chapters 1 and 2) and not just the behavior of participating in a recreation activity.

- It requires understanding of both supply and demand factors, including information from the customers about the types of experience opportunities that they desire.

- It focuses on the types of psychological experiences that the customers desire to realize, so it is customer driven. This contrasts with ABM, which provides little focus on the customers' demand and expectations other than for activity opportunities and the attributes of the recreation settings necessary for those activities.

- EBM provides a better basis for understanding and improving the quality of recreation opportunities provided and the experiences actually realized from using those opportunities. It does so because it

Considering the activity engaged in is only the beginning of effective management of outdoor recreation resources.

requires analyses and evaluations of user satisfactions in experiential terms. It also requires relating preferences for experiences both to activity opportunities and the attributes/features of the recreation settings necessary for those activities and experiences to take place. Therefore, it requires very specific delineation of setting attributes that both add to and detract from the quality of specific types of recreation experiences, such as realizing solitude or applying and testing one's outdoor skills.

- Under EBM, management objectives explicitly state the types of recreation experience opportunities that will be provided, when, where, for whom, and in what amount. Then management prescriptions, guidelines, and standards are written to assure targeted experience opportunities will be delivered within the time frame proposed by the plan for which the experience opportunity management objectives have been written.

- Until recently, the applications of EBM focused on the on-site visitors/customers. But now EBM refers to all customers who realize satisfying psychological experiences from either the management or use of recreation and related resources. Thus, EBM covers the visitors to the outdoor recreation facilities, sites, and areas being managed, the residents of local communities who take pride in nearby amenities, and also the tax-paying owners of the public outdoor recreation resources who live more remotely than residents of local communities (even in large distant cities) but who still receive psychological stewardship-related satisfactions from just knowing that the resources are being protected.

- EBM is an important but limited type of BBM as outlined next. Recall that Chapter 2 defined the third type of benefit of leisure as the realization of satis-

fying recreation experiences. So if EBM addresses satisfying experiences, then EBM is a limited type of BBM—limited because BBM covers all types of benefits and not just that third type.

A good example of EBM is use of the recreation opportunity spectrum (ROS) system, which will be described shortly.

Benefits-Based Management

As mentioned previously, benefits-based management (BBM) will be considered in detail in the next chapter, so only the basics of how that approach helps meet Level 3 demands are outlined here.

- BBM considers not only psychological experiences but also psychophysiological and physiological ones, such as reduced tension and hypertension.

- BBM considers all types of benefits that result from the management and use of leisure resources, including benefits that accrue to individuals, to groups of individuals (extending from the family and other smaller groups, thorough communities to the nation at-large and beyond), and to the biophysical and cultural/heritage resources. As shown in Table 2.2 (p. 29), these benefits are commonly classified into the four groups of personal (psychological/psychophysiological), social/cultural, environmental, and economic.

- BBM considers not only immediate benefits but also long-term benefits.

- BBM requires that planners and managers collaborate with all affecting and affected stakeholders and associated providers on the types of benefit opportunities that should be provided.

- BBM recognizes that before recreation professionals can consider both the positive and negative impacts of recreation resource management and use, they must understand the nature and scope of those impacts

- BBM could not have been developed and implemented until sufficient research had been completed on the benefits of leisure.

Regarding the last characteristic of BBM listed, it should be iterated that the concept of a recreation demand hierarchy would have limited professional credibility had research not quantified the three levels of recreation demand. However, while that position is technically correct, it does not give just and deserved credit to the many forward thinking, sensitive, and responsive park and recreation (P&R) planners and managers who did a reasonably good job of intuitively and judgmentally practicing at

The experiences sought by visitors are an essential consideration in experience-based management systems like the ROS.

least limited ABM and EBM without the benefit of research results related to Level 1 and 2 recreation demands and on specific attributes of a recreation setting required for specific recreation activity and experience opportunities to be created. Similarly, P&R planners and managers practicing both ABM and EBM have considered benefits of leisure other than those realized from satisfying experiences. Their managerial orientations showed they knew, before science documented it, that leisure promotes mental and physical health, enhances family kinship, and facilitates learning of many types. Excellent examples of such recreation planners and managers go back to Frederick Law Olmsted, the father of landscape architecture and designer of Central Park in New York City, and many other highly successful parks who started these practices in the last half of the 1800s. We applaud the insights and orientations of these early professionals, and we firmly believe that good intuitions, judgments, and "art" are vitally important in any human endeavor, including planning and management of P&R resources. But, professions cannot be built on these alone, so we emphasize the need for science-based policy development and management.

Science-Based Approaches for Overtly Managing for Outdoor Recreation

This section describes the science-based management systems that have been and are still being used to manage outdoor recreation resources. It begins by clarifying what we mean by a science-based management system and how we use the word *system*.

What Does Science-Based Mean?

By a science-based management system we mean an approach to management that systematically integrates the best available scientific knowledge relevant to the purposes to which those management activities are directed. Thus, a science-based plan to control an infectious disease would require use of the best scientific knowledge available to control that disease. We quickly emphasize that in some instances science will point primarily in one direction to solve a particular problem. In other instances, there might be several almost equally useful solutions, so professional judgment is always needed. Therefore, in no way do we exclude good judgment or "art" in the management of outdoor recreation resources that also use the best scientific knowledge available. Put simply, reliance should not be mostly on judgment and intuition when reliable results of research can help guide professional decisions.

We also hasten to emphasize that in no way do we use the words "science-based" to denote a technocratic or authoritative approach in which the technically trained manager assumes and behaves as if he or she is all knowing about what needs to be done and therefore does not need to collaborate closely with the people who affect or are affected by policy and managerial decisions. Former Chief of the USFS, Jack Ward Thomas stated this need for openness as follows:

> …by definition, we are operating in the realm of risk and uncertainty [not certainty]. This means that resource management decisions will have both subjective and objective components…. There is a set of possible decisions that defines the range of alternative feasible allocations that can meet to varying degrees the competing biophysical and social objectives that must be considered when making allocation decisions. Each reflects a set of "value mixes," including judgments about what is fair for future generations. Thus, these decisions are in the realm of ethics whether we recognize it or not. (1996, p. xxiv)

Technocrats cannot know and allow for all the "subjective components" and "value mixes" involved in policy and managerial decisions, so the stakeholders that are affected must be involved in helping make those decisions. Fortunately, recent research has provided excellent guidance about how to form and to maintain collaborative partnerships with affecting and affected stakeholders (Wondolleck & Yaffee, 2000). Chapter 13 shows how results of that research is incorporated into BBM.

Science-based systems for managing outdoor recreation resources must be based on the results of research from many disciplines or professions, including forestry, wildlife and fisheries biology, range management, geology, psychology, social psychology, psychophysiology, physiology, sociology, economics, anthropology, communication science, environmental education, conflict management, political science, landscape architecture, management science (e.g., total quality management), marketing, and other ancillary disciplines, such as police protection, criminal justice, transportation, architectural design, and civil engineering related to structures and facilities. Each of these disciplines/professions has contributed science-based information that has advanced considerably the state of science-based management of outdoor recreation resources since 1960.

In sum, a science-based management system is simply one with reasonable scientific credibility. That concept is extremely important given the emphasis in this text on the fact that professionalism is based on understanding and keeping abreast of new scientific knowledge relevant to one's profession.

What Is a System?

Our use of the word *system* is drawn from general systems theory (Buckley, 1968). The relevant principles and concepts of that theory are explained in Chapter 13, but it will suffice here to say a system denotes a whole that functions as a whole because of the interdependencies of its parts. A management system, therefore, is a system that integrates and considers all of the relevant components and processes of that system that interact and interdependently constitute the whole system.

Examples of a nonsystems approach to management planning were the lands and resources plans developed for national forests and national grasslands by the USFS as required by the 1976 National Forest Management Act (NFMA). Those plans were developed for management units defined by the administrative boundaries of the national forests and grasslands. From an ecosystems perspective, the resulting plans did not reflect a holistic systems approach, because the functioning of natural ecosystems within and among those management units did not conform to arbitrarily established administrative boundaries. This oversight was corrected in 1992 when Dale Robertson, then Chief of the USFS, issued a directive stating that henceforth the USFS would practice sustainable ecosystem management (SEM), as elaborated in the discussion of SEM near the end of this chapter.

Relating Specific Science-Based Management Systems to ABM and EBM

Earlier in this chapter, the recreation demand hierarchy was used to show how research has advanced our understanding of recreation demand. It was explained that ABM, EBM, and BBM evolved from that research as three distinct science-based approaches to management. The remainder of this chapter gives brief descriptions of the most widely used science-based systems for managing outdoor recreation resources. These systems do one of the following:

1. clearly reflect either ABM or EBM (which must include ABM because EBM supplements but does not replace it)

2. mesh mostly ABM with some EBM (i.e., consider a limited set of experience opportunities but do not do so comprehensively enough to represent EBM as it was defined earlier)

3. mesh a focus on ABM with some EBM and very limited BBM by requiring consideration of some benefits, such as ones that accrue from protecting

and improving the basic recreation resources being managed

This may sound confusing, but it reflects the reality of the incremental professional advancement of outdoor recreation resource management from ABM through EBM to BBM. Because there is no one formal management system that can be called ABM, it will be described first and generally.

Generic Activity-Based Management

ABM has been applied for over a century to manage P&R resources, and unfortunately remains the most widely used approach. While little research was done prior to 1960 to guide ABM, a few studies focused on demands for activity opportunities, attributes of recreation settings needed to facilitate specific activity opportunities, and methods to measure recreational use. Less structured administrative studies also helped to provide needed information. By and large, though, until about 1960, ABM was based on the judgments of planners and managers, observations of the degree to which provided opportunities were actually used, and trial-and-error through providing activity opportunities and adjusting those supplies based on feedback from potential and actual users. Such sources of information remain important for implementing ABM today.

ABM is a necessary but insufficient approach that should be practiced in the planning and management of all P&R resources. It is an approach that should use all relevant scientific knowledge available. ABM is science-based to the extent it uses results of research on the following:

1. demands for recreation activities (e.g., camping, picnicking, hiking)

2. facilitating attributes of the recreation settings in which those activities occur

3. any related needs for information to implement ABM

Simple examples of required setting attributes considered by ABM include bodies of water having certain characteristics for safe and pleasurable swimming, for fishing of many types, for waterskiing, and for different forms of boating, or picnic areas having parking spaces, grills, tables, toilets, and safe play areas for children.

ABM can be implemented as a science-based approach, because there has been much excellent and useful research on the following:

- improving our objective understanding of the types of recreation activities most desired as well as not desired

- predicting demands for different activities by clearly defined "market segments" of customers with different characteristics

- estimating the economic value and impacts of the provision and use of recreation activity opportunities

- trends in choices for activities and how managers can best accommodate new or emerging uses (e.g., snowboarding, hang gliding)

- measuring the use of areas, sites, and facilities

- what types and amounts of use cause most adverse ecological impacts and ways to avoid or reduce such

- biophysical, social, and managerial features or attributes that contribute to or detract from overall satisfaction with particular activities within particular settings

Perhaps the best way to understand ABM is to remember it is necessary but insufficient. It is fundamental because planners and managers of P&R resources must understand recreation activities and the features or characteristics of the settings necessary for particular activities to occur. Although necessary, ABM is not sufficient by itself to assure effective, responsive, accountable, cost-effective, fair/equitable, and ecologically responsible planning and management. ABM does not explicitly require consideration of the types of satisfying experiences, as EBM does, or the additional types of benefits (beyond realizing satisfying experiences), as BBM does. A related and critical problem with ABM is that managers who practice it tend not to appreciate the relevance and importance of EBM and BBM. They then still hold the antiquated view that recreation is just a human behavior (like eating or sleeping) without recognizing and understanding that their broader professional responsibility of providing recreation activity opportunities is to provide opportunities for satisfying experiences and other benefits. It is difficult, if not impossible, to hold a customer orientation while relying primarily on ABM. When ABM is stripped to its bare bones, it says only that customers will be provided activities in which to participate and says nothing about the positive impacts that result. In contrast, both EBM and BBM require the impacts of management and use be understood, and management be directed overtly to them.

Despite the limitations of ABM, we reiterate that it is a needed and important part of planning and managing outdoor recreation resources, albeit not sufficient. It is, however, the major way outdoor recreation resources have been and continue to be managed in the United States and other countries. Unfortunately, ABM is not supplemented as much as it now can and should be by EBM and BBM.

The rest of this chapter reviews, chronologically, specific science-based outdoor recreation resource man-

agement systems and points out whether each one represents ABM, EBM, or a transition between ABM and EBM. Realize, of course, each of the individual science-based systems reviewed is much more complex and detailed than the brief overviews here might indicate. Courses that focus on outdoor recreation resource planning and management go into more detail, as do the references cited herein.

Visual Resource Management System

Two visual resource management (VRM) systems have received wide application. One was developed by the USFS and the other by the BLM. The one used by the USFS was developed and then applied in the early 1970s. The BLM VRM system was developed in the 1980s and is very similar to the USFS system. Because of those similarities and the fact that the USFS VRM system was developed first and has more documentation, this overview will concentrate on that system. Both systems were developed primarily by landscape architects (LAs) employed by the USFS and BLM in collaboration with other LAs and leisure scientists in colleges and universities.

Several converging forces spawned the need for the VRM system in the 1960s. One was the increasing use of natural areas by rapidly increasing numbers of people who became more aware of what they wanted to experience and better informed about what they could experience in outdoor recreation areas. As a result, more people were becoming concerned about unfavorable managerial activities, particularly the growing practice of clearcutting to harvest trees. In addition, the 1960 Multiple Use and Sustained Yield Act gave legal teeth to people's concerns about managing for all uses, and the 1969 NEPA required review by the public of all federal environmental projects. Therefore, the late 1960s saw considerable public opposition to ways scenic resources were being managed by

The quality of visual resources is critical to many outdoor recreation experiences. (Photo courtesy of NC Division of Tourism, Film and Sports Development)

the USFS and BLM. By the middle 1970s, considerable litigation against the USFS and BLM had been initiated in opposition to their lack of adequate protection of scenic resources. In response to these public sentiments, the VRM system was developed by the USFS, with the two prime movers in that effort being Burton Litton and Warren Bacon.

In the late 1960s and early 1970s, Litton and his associates conducted studies of people's responses to landscapes that had different configurations, including portions of forested areas that had been harvested using clearcutting and other less visually pleasing methods of harvesting trees (cf. Litton, 1968, 1972). That research documented the scientific bases of the VRM system. Not surprising, one finding was that people perceived the large square or rectangular clearcuts as unsightly. They apparently agreed with the axiom that "nature abhors a straight line." At the same time, the general public was expressing strong sentiments about the adverse scenic impacts of clearcutting trees. In response, Warren Bacon, a landscape architect with the USFS, took the lead role in developing the VRM system in the early 1970s. Soon after, he and his associates drafted a series of publications that described the VRM system in general (USDA Forest Service, 1974a, 1974b). Later publications provided guidance for protecting scenic values in the management of utilities (USDA Forest Service, 1975), rangelands and roads (USDA Forest Service, 1977a, 1977b), timber (USDA Forest Service, 1980), and recreation resources (USDA Forest Service, 1987) on public lands administered by the USFS. For a description of the BLM's similar VRM system, see USDI Bureau of Land Management (1986).

The VRM system considered many characteristics of particular landscapes that defined their scenic properties, such as the quality of the views, how sensitive the landscapes were to disturbance by humans, how subject they were to being seen and by how many people, and public opinion about the scenic qualities of the landscapes being evaluated. These landscape analyses were then integrated into recommendations about what degree of managerial alteration should be permitted. The classes of possible alteration ranged from Preservation, Retention, Partial Retention, and Modification, to Maximum Modification with criteria established for each of these VRM management objectives. An excellent description of the VRM, and related visual resource management concepts, is presented in Jubenville and Twight (1993, pp. 167–193).

As noted earlier, the categories of ABM, EBM, and BBM overlap. In fact, some perceptive managers intuitively managed for some satisfying experiences (EBM) while practicing ABM even before EBM emerged in the late 1970s, and some perceptive managers practicing EBM were also considering some benefits other than the real-

ization of satisfying experiences. Thus, there are transition periods between ABM and EBM, and between EBM and BBM. The visual resource management (VRM) systems clearly represent a transition between ABM and EBM because of its focus on aesthetic experiences. There is even limited BBM involved, because of the environmental benefits that accrue from the VRM systems' protection of basic scenic resources.

The VRM system used by the USFS was modified and changed to the Scenery Management (SM) system in 1995, which provides better inclusion of ecosystem analyses, constituency involvement, and EBM and BBM in scenery assessments and management. It is described briefly later in this chapter.

Impact Management Systems

Several impact management (often referred to as IM) systems are being used to prevent and/or reduce adverse physical, biophysical, and social impacts of recreational use. Those systems include limits of acceptable change (LAC; Stankey et al., 1985), visitor experience and resource protection (VERP; Manning, Lime & Hof, 1996), visitor impact management (VIM; Graefe, Kuss & Vaske, 1990), and visitor activity management process (VAMP; Graham, Nilsen & Payne, 1988; Parks Canada, 1991). These references do not necessarily reflect the times at which the systems were developed and first applied in the 1980s, but instead are the ones that best describe the systems.

The LAC, VERP, and VIM impact management systems are very similar and are oriented to the ends of preventing and/or reducing adverse impacts on the resources being managed and to determining appropriate levels and types of human use for particular recreation settings and activities. Each follow essentially the same analysis process:

1. Review existing management objectives of the area being evaluated.

2. Define key indicators of impacts.

3. Establish standards to be met to assure unacceptable levels of impact will not occur.

4. Compare the standards with existing conditions.

5. Identify probable causes of discrepancies found.

6. Select and implement management actions to reduce the discrepancies.

7. Monitor to assure the standards are being met.

To varying degrees, each system requires involvement by the affecting and affected stakeholders.

The LAC, VERP, and VIM systems have occasionally guided the overall management of large management units, such as a national park unit, but each one has normally either been implemented on a subpart of such a unit or integrated into the overall and larger management planning and management processes for a larger unit.

VAMP shares the same objectives of the LAC, VERP, and VIM systems and uses a process similar to these other three impact management systems. VAMP serves a much wider role when it is used to guide the entire planning and management processes of many parks and other areas (e.g., heritage rivers) administered by Parks Canada. Thus, VAMP is actually more than an impact management system. VAMP is no longer being used by Parks Canada as a distinct management planning system under the name of VAMP, but has now been integrated into a number of other guides and processes used by that agency.

To a very limited extent, the LAC, VERP, and VIM impact management systems have been used to assure provision of experience opportunities beyond those related to social density of users and avoiding evidences of unwanted human impacts on the physical and biophysical resources, but that has been the exception rather than the rule. Although they could do so, none of the impact management systems practice EBM to the degree they could, and instead their focus has been, and remains to be, on resource protection and social impacts. As such, these three impact management systems can be considered as transition systems between ABM and EBM with limited BBM involved because of the improvements and protection they provide to the physical and biophysical environments, just as the visual resource management system does. VAMP, however, did consider other types of experiences and other benefits but not as comprehensively as EBM or BBM does. As such, VAMP can be considered a transition system between ABM and EBM and to a limited extent BBM.

Each of these systems use results of scientific research on the impacts they address, such as the considerable

Impact management systems like LAC and VERP are used to identify, prevent, and manage adverse impacts of human use in places like backcountry campsites and trails. (Photo by Yu-Fai Leung)

amount of research on the social carrying capacities of outdoor recreation areas (abundantly cited in the previous references to each impact management system) and on the impacts of humans on biophysical resources (cf. Hammitt & Cole, 1998).

Recreation Opportunity Spectrum System

As mentioned, the visual resource management and the impact management systems represent important transitions from basic ABM to EBM by considering a limited set of experiences related to scenic enjoyment, solitude, and enjoying relatively natural environments not highly impacted by humans (Bacon, 1996). The recreation opportunity spectrum (ROS) system follows that trend set by the visual resource management and the impact management systems, but expands the concept of EBM much more. In fact, as will become apparent in the following review, the ROS system clearly represents EBM, because its focus is on the different types of recreation experiences and activities that can be realized in different outdoor recreation settings. It should be recognized, however, that the focus of the ROS system has been on recreation experiences realized by on-site users only. Since the ROS system was developed, EBM has been expanded to include experiences realized by off-site as well as on-site users, especially in the management of watchable wildlife programs (Manfredo, 2002). As such, the use of the ROS system is a more limited application than are more recent applications of EBM. Because the ROS system has been used more widely than the other management systems, it is described in more detail than the other systems in this chapter.

Outdoor recreation resource planners and managers and leisure scientists who worked closely together for several years in the late 1970s and early 1980s developed the ROS system. They represented a variety of professional backgrounds. Other professionals then helped refine the system later.

The ROS system has reasonable scientific credibility, because it is based on the results of considerable research in the 1960s and 1970s related to recreation experiences, especially on relationships between satisfying and unsatisfying experiences received and specific characteristics or attributes of the recreation settings in which those experiences are realized. Significantly, two of the leisure scientists who played a key role in the development and refinement of the ROS system had done or led a great deal of research on recreation experiences, and they were quite familiar with the research of other scientists on recreation experiences. That knowledge helped to assure the ROS had scientific credibility.

Chapter 11 mentioned that several acts of the U.S. Congress (i.e., policy directives) required the development of new management systems. The ROS system is a clear example of this, because it represents a direct link to policy. As mentioned earlier, the NFMA of 1976 for the USFS and the similar FLMPA of 1976 for the BLM mandated those two agencies to do functionally integrated management planning for all USFS national forests and grasslands and BLM resource areas and, in doing so, to assure citizen participation as mandated by the NEPA of 1969. "Functionally integrated" meant that all values and uses be given appropriate consideration and be integrated into resource management plans. This showed that the U.S. Congress was serious about those two agencies considering recreation and related interests and values. As also mentioned earlier, this message to consider all uses was also clear in the 1960 MUSYA for the USFS and the 1964 CMUA for the BLM. For example, the MUSYA required of the USFS that consideration "…be given to the relative values of the various resources, and not necessarily the combination of uses that will give the greatest dollar return or the greatest unit output." But, the 1976 NFMA and FLMPA were much stronger mandates to the USFS and BLM to overtly integrate outdoor recreation values into their resource management planning.

A major problem with implementing the outdoor recreation-related mandates of NFMA and FLMPA was that at the time those two acts were passed in 1976 no applicable scientifically credible outdoor recreation resource planning and management systems existed for meeting those mandates. At that time, field units of the USFS and the BLM were applying at least six different land inventory classifications and managing systems. For an overview of the systems being used then see Brown, Driver & McConnell (1978, pp. 76, 78).

To resolve this problem, in late 1976 the heads of the recreation, heritage, and wilderness resource staff groups of the USFS and BLM asked Bev Driver and Perry Brown to work with members of their staffs to develop an outdoor recreation resource planning and management system that would meet the mandates of NFMA and FLPMA. This request was made because research by Driver and Brown on recreation experiences and their relationships to attributes of recreation settings necessary to realize those experiences was well-received by many outdoor recreation resource planners and managers and the heads of the USFS and BLM recreation staff groups. In addition, the concept of a recreation opportunity spectrum had been written about by several leisure scientists and had gained wide acceptance (for a review, see Driver, Brown, Stankey & Gregoire, 1987, p. 202). So the time was ripe to develop a scientifically credible outdoor recreation resource planning and management system based on EBM and employing the concept of a recreation opportunity spectrum. Driver and Brown worked with teams of planners and managers in the USFS and BLM for three years to

develop and refine the ROS system. The results of those efforts are best described in the *ROS Users' Guide* (USDA Forest Service, 1982).

While the system described in the *ROS User's Guide* was being developed, pilot-tested in the USFS and BLM, and refined, Clark and Stankey (1979) were working on their version of a similar system, parts of which were integrated by Warren Bacon into a *ROS Primer and Field Guide* as a supplement to the *ROS Users' Guide* (USDA Forest Service, 1990).

Basic characteristics of the ROS system. The ROS system proposes a spectrum of recreation settings that range from urban areas to remote, undeveloped natural areas, and across that wide spectrum of recreation settings all types of desired outdoor recreation activity and experience opportunities can be realized. For practical reasons, the commonly used ROS system identifies six broad classes of such opportunities along the spectrum it envisions: Urban, Rural, Roaded Natural, Semi-primitive Motorized, Semi-primitive Nonmotorized, and Primitive, as illustrated in Figure 12.2 (p. 170).

The team of developers of the ROS system recognized that no spectrum, such as the electromagnetic spectrum, can be perfectly divided into discreet segments. By definition, the contiguous segments of any spectrum merge together at the edges of each segment. This is true of the ROS. But to make the concept of an ROS operable, six ROS classes or zones of outdoor recreation opportunity were identified. Different agencies in different countries have modified the ROS setting class names to meet their purposes. For example the New Zealand Department of Conservation uses the names Wilderness Remote, Nonmotorized Remote, Motorized Remote, Semi-natural Accessible, Rural, and Peri-urban. In addition, some users of the ROS system have added additional classes. These modifications do not violate the central concepts of an ROS.

The *ROS Users' Guide* (USDA Forest Service, 1982) describes the types of recreation activities and experiences that most probably can be realized in each of the ROS classes.

Figure 12.2 also presents some of the types of recreation experiences, or "indicators of experiences," that will most likely be realized in or near the two polar ends of the ROS. Examples of the likely experiences that can be realized in the other ROS zones are shown on page 8 of the *ROS Users' Guide* (USDA Forest Service, 1982).

One premise of the ROS system is that any experiences not mentioned in the *ROS Users' Guide* can also be realized somewhere along the ROS because of the breadth of the spectrum of recreation settings it covers. For example, the increasingly popular concept of an experience of "sense of place" can be realized in each of the ROS classes (Williams & Stewart, 1998). Many recreation activities, such as walking for pleasure, fishing, photography, and driving for pleasure can occur in most or all of the ROS classes, as can many experiences (e.g., enjoying nature, family togetherness, mental relaxation, stimulation, nature-based spirituality, risk taking). Nevertheless, some recreational activities and experiences are more dependent on particular ROS settings than are others. As one example, an opportunity to hike in a remote, undisturbed natural area to experience a sense of isolation and the need to rely on one's outdoor skills is more probable in the classes near the primitive end of the spectrum, but as such, opportunities for large-group affiliation cannot occur there.

The ROS system considers three types of interacting recreation setting components that make up the overall recreation setting: Physical, Social, and Managerial. The features of each component influence the types of outdoor recreation activity and experience opportunities that can be provided to meet the Level 1 and 2 demands explained earlier. The Physical recreation setting component is made up of the biophysical environment and includes fauna, flora, water, hills, geology, topography, climate, cultural/heritage sites, and all physical recreation facilities provided by management (e.g., roads, parking lots, buildings, picnic tables, marked-off camping spots, grills, bulletin boards, toilets, water faucets, boat ramps, docks). The Social setting component comprises the on-site users and their impacts. The Managerial setting component covers rules and regulations, the on-site presence of managerial and maintenance personnel, and the equipment they use.

Relationships between the characteristics or attributes of the Physical setting component and types of recreation activities and experiences that can be realized are commonly considered in planning of outdoor recreation resources. For example, remoteness from roads with motorized vehicles, total size of the remote area, evidence of past and current human activity (e.g., dams, railroads, timber harvesting, fences), and characteristics of the biophysical environment (e.g., vegetation, animals, water, geology, topography) are commonly considered in outdoor recreation site and project planning. The influences of the Social and Managerial setting components frequently receive less attention. However, they also strongly affect the types of recreation activities, and especially the types of experiences, that can be realized. Those influencing features of the Managerial setting component include managerial rules and regulations, services offered, fees charged, the on-site presence or absence of managerial personnel, and the equipment (e.g., power saws, tractors) they use and how, when, and where they use it. The same holds true for features of the Social setting component, such as the number of other users, their behaviors, and the things they bring with them (e.g., large RVs, noisy boom boxes, horses, pets) that have significant influences on the types of experiences that can be realized. Put more simply, the features of each of the three recreation setting components interact with one another to influence whether a specific type of recreation activity, experience, and experience gestalt (as explained in Chapter 2) can or cannot be

Primitive	Semi-primitive Nonmotorized	Semi-primitive Motorized	Roaded Natural	Rural	Urban

Solitude	Interaction With People
Challenge/Self-reliance	Comfort
Risk taking	Security
Outdoor skills	Competition
Undisturbed nature	Facilities
Self-directed	Programmed
Distance to overcome	Near to home

Figure 12.2 Some likely experiences for two polar end classes of the ROS system

realized. For that reason, the ROS system needed to consider each of the three types of settings components.

A ROS inventory is done by using easy-to-apply inventory criteria selected to simply define each recreation setting component. Those criteria were identified as being critical to facilitating different recreation activity and experience opportunities. Remoteness, Size, and Evidence of Humans are the three criteria used to define the characteristics of the physical setting component. To keep the ROS system simple, only Managerial Regimentation and Noticeability was selected to define the managerial setting component, and only one criterion (i.e., User Density) is used to define the Social setting component. These criteria are explained on pages 14–28 of the *ROS Users' Guide*. They are shown in Table 12.1, but only a few examples of the use of those criteria are given here.

Different "standards" are used to make the inventory criteria as quantitative as possible. For example, the Remoteness criterion is quantified by distances to the nearest boundary of the area from roads or railroads with motorized use, and different distance standards must be met for an area to be inventoried as qualifying for a particular ROS class. To illustrate, the boundaries of Primitive areas must be at least three miles from the nearest motorized road or railroad, Semi-primitive Nonmotorized areas must be less than three miles but at least one-half mile, and Semi-primitive Motorized areas must be within one-half mile of lightly used primitive roads (e.g., by ATVs) but not closer that one-half mile from roads heavily used by all types of motorized vehicles. There are no distance standards from motorized roads for the Roaded Natural, Rural, and Urban ROS classes. We should point out that the distinction between "primitive" and "heavily used" roads must be defined and located on maps by the agency that implements the ROS system as the USFS has done. The ROS system distance standards used to define Remoteness can be modified if the planner doing the inventory determines that certain features of the landscape exist to create the sense (i.e., experience) of remoteness required for a particular ROS class. For example, the distance standard for the Primitive and Semi-primitive Nonmotorized classes can be relaxed if a broad and roaring river, a

high cliff, or extremely dense vegetation exist to block the sounds and negate the psychological sense of nearness of a particular motorized road.

Total area in acres is the standard used to quantify the Size component of the physical setting. For example, to qualify as Primitive an area must be at least 5,000 acres. The standards for the Evidence of Human Activity criteria of the Physical setting component, however, are more descriptive than quantitative. A particular concern was whether those more qualitative/subjective criteria would cause different planners to come up with inconsistent results. If they did, the ROS system would not be useful because it would not give reliable, consistent results. This did not happen in several tests of the consistency of the results. In those tests, different planners would inventory and classify the same area, and this process was replicated several times using a different area each time. Those tests showed very consistent/reliable results among the different planners.

Although many additional inventory criteria and standards could have been included in the ROS system, only five were included to keep that system as simple as possible. That simplicity was necessary because those who developed and refined the ROS system were ever mindful of the fact that the major reason the existing outdoor recreation resource planning and management systems could not be applied to meet the requirements of NFMA and FLPMA was that they were too complex, and thus too costly and time-consuming to implement given existing agency budgets, personnel, and time constraints. It is relevant to note that not making the ROS system more complex has led to some criticisms of it. Most have been caused by insufficient understandings that the ROS system is not a system to guide outdoor recreation project and site planning, but instead is a system to identify and classify the outdoor recreation opportunities currently and potentially available on large tracts of land.

The common practice in making ROS inventories is to make a separate plastic/acetate or geographic information system (GIS) map overlay of the landscape being inventoried, for each of the five inventory criteria being applied. As such, there will be a separate acetate/overlay prepared for Remoteness, Size, Evidence of Human Activity, User Density, and Managerial Regimentation and Noticeability. Each overlay shows the boundaries of each ROS class that qualifies according to application of each inventory criteria and its standards. As such, each overlay will map the boundaries of separate land areas that qualify as Primitive to Urban, with the Urban zones being around places of human settlement and major developments such as an alpine ski areas. These five overlays define the existing recreation conditions of the area to which the ROS inventory is being applied.

Table 12.1   ROS setting components and inventory criteria

Setting Component	Inventory Criteria
Physical	Remoteness
	Size
	Evidence of Human Activity
Social	User Density
Managerial	Managerial Regimentation and Noticeability

Source: USDA Forest Service (1982, p. 14)

The next step of the ROS inventory/classification is to systematically integrate the information on each of the five overlays to make a composite or summary ROS overlay. This is necessary because while an area can qualify as a particular class, such as Primitive, for one inventory criteria, it might not for another. For instance, even though an area qualifies as Primitive by application of the Size criteria, it might not qualify as Primitive because there is too much Evidence of Human Activity, too much Managerial presence, and/or too much current use (i.e., User Density). Even one conflicting component will determine the proper classification. The end result of this process of integrating the information from the five overlays prepared for each inventory criteria is an overlay that shows a "summary" ROS classification of the area. That summary map shows the boundaries of the existing ROS zones that meet each of the five inventory criteria for each zone. Put differently, that final/composite overlay shows the existing recreation situation and maps the boundaries of each of the ROS classes identified by the ROS inventory. Figure 12.3 illustrates a basic ROS inventory map.

During the ROS inventory/classification process, narrative statements should be written to document any characteristics of each of the three setting components that might be useful when the ROS inventory is used later to make managerial allocation decisions. This should be done when each of the five inventory criteria is being applied. For example, assume the only reason an area could not be classified as a particular ROS class is that the density of current on-site use did not permit such a classification. In that case, those numbers of users could be reduced by a managerial allocation decision if more of that particular class of outdoor recreation opportunity was determined to be needed by demand analyses made during the rest of the planning process. Such a managerial possibility should be documented as part of the inventory of the existing condition.

Given this example, it is extremely important to understand that there is a difference between a resource inventory decision and a managerial allocation decision. The ROS inventory map and other documents show the existing recreation conditions of the areas inventoried. That information, along with other types of information (e.g., from demand studies; involvement of stakeholders; needs to accommodate other complementary, supplemental, or competing uses of the resources) are then used to make managerial allocation decisions reflected in the management plan for the area inventoried. Those allocation decisions may or may not managerially classify all or part of an area the same way as the ROS inventory described its condition before that allocation decision is made. The point is, the ROS inventory is only one informational input to the management planning process, especially of multiple-use planning that needs to integrate outdoor recreation values and uses with other ones related to timber, minerals, water, range forage, and production along with holistic sustainable ecosystems management. For example, a managerial decision might reflect the need to reduce or increase use over the user densities that existed in the ROS system inventory of the existing conditions. Or, it might reflect the need to reduce or increase the current amount of on-site presence of managerial personal, open or close roads for motorized use, or increase or decrease the number and/or types of on-site facilities.

This distinction between an inventory decision and a managerial allocation decision is an important one, because some people have incorrectly believed the ROS inventory documents what ROS zones should be created by management action and not what existed at the time the inventory was made. We iterate, the ROS inventory is only one informational input to the management planning process, especially of multiple-use planning that needs to functionally integrate all uses and the values of such.

In conclusion on using the ROS to inventory the existing recreation conditions of relatively large tracts of land, it should be mentioned that some ROS classes of recreation opportunities will not always be found in some areas. For example, because of more human settlement and development (especially of motorized roads) in the eastern United States, Primitive and Semi-primitive Nonmotorized areas are in shorter supply there than on national forests in the western United States. For this reason, when the ROS was first being used in the eastern United States, some of the USFS planners believed it would not be applicable there, because they erroneously believed they should be able to classify some land as qualifying for each of the ROS classes. Put simply, the ROS system was applicable in those situations because it inventoried what existed, not what the planners thought might or should exist.

In addition to inventory, the ROS concept has also been used widely in managerial allocation decisions to designate, by ROS classes, how particular areas will be managed. In this way, one area might be allocated to be managed as Roaded Natural, another as Primitive, and so on. Frequently those managerial allocations will change the designation of a particular area from the one given it as a result of the inventory conducted using the ROS system. For example, to meet public demands for more Primitive or Semi-primitive Nonmotorized opportunities, the managerial allocations might prescribe that some motorized roads be closed or the density of on-site use be reduced. Alternatively, public demands might be for other types of opportunities, so managerial decisions might prescribe opening more areas to motorized use or allowing increased use in areas that were classified during the inventory as being near the Primitive end of the ROS. Such

Example of a Basic ROS Inventory Map

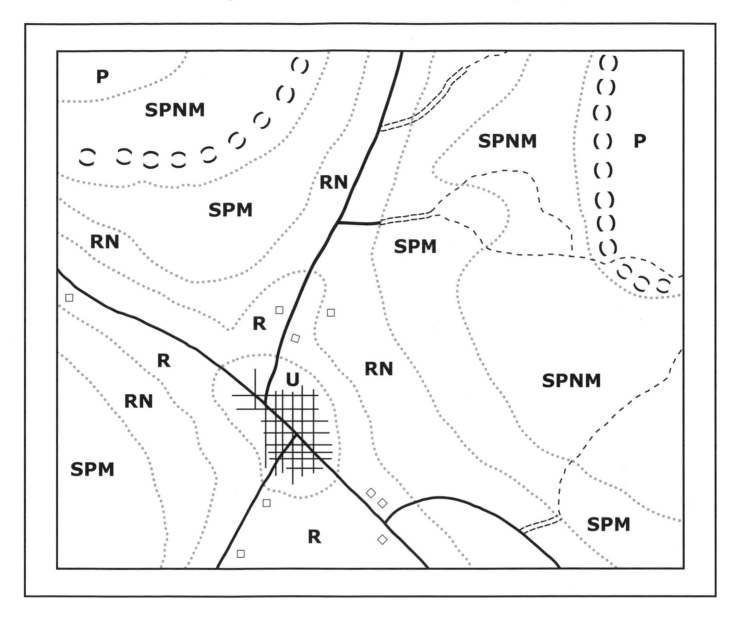

ROS Zones/Classes

U = Urban
R = Rural
RN = Roaded Natural
SPM = Semi-primitive Motorized
SPNM = Semi-primitive Nonmotorized
P = Primitive

Key

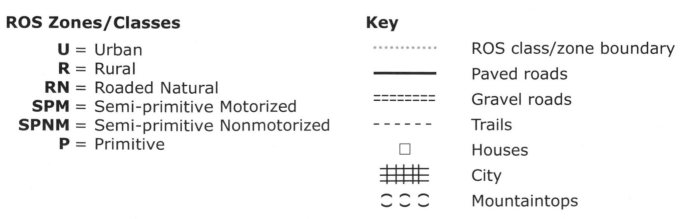

·············	ROS class/zone boundary
——	Paved roads
=======	Gravel roads
- - - - -	Trails
▢	Houses
▦	City
◠ ◠ ◠	Mountaintops

Figure 12.3 Example of a summary ROS inventory map

managerial allocations are frequently called *management prescriptions* in many resource management plans for the USFS and the BLM. When this happens, the ROS system inventory criteria become standards and guidelines to be applied during monitoring of plan implementation to assure that the types of outdoor recreation activity and experience opportunities targeted for provision in the management plan are being provided. Put differently, the same setting components, inventory criteria, and standards used to make an ROS inventory become managerial standards to be enforced during plan implementation. But even here, the distinction between an inventory decision and a managerial allocation decision still holds; they are two separate decisions (and uses of the ROS system).

Another use of the ROS is for impact assessment. This is when the ROS is used during monitoring of management plan implementation to determine what impacts a proposed change in the plan (e.g., a large timber harvesting operation, construction of new facilities) will have on the to-be-impacted ROS zone prescribed in the management plan allocation.

Lastly, the ROS concept has been used as a marketing tool to inform prospective outdoor recreationists about the numbers, sizes, and locations of the different ROS zones that have been mapped as part of the managerial allocation process after the ROS inventories have been done. This information is frequently provided in *Recreation Opportunity Guides* in field offices. Therefore, potential users can understand better which areas they can visit to engage in desired recreation activities and realize desired experiences.

Much of the research on which the ROS was based used the recreation experience preference (REP) scales presented in Appendix A and explained in Chapter 2 and several publications (Driver, 2003; Driver, Tinsley & Manfredo, 1991; Manfredo, Driver & Tarrant, 1996). But as mentioned, the results of other research on recreation experiences contributed to the scientific credibility of the ROS as well. See Chapter 2 for a discussion of that research or the many publications that have described the ROS, including Brown, Driver, and McConnell (1978), Clark and Stankey (1979), Driver, Brown, Stankey, and Gregorie (1987), and Driver (1990). The best description of how to implement the ROS is still the *ROS User's Guide* (USDA Forest Service, 1982) as supplemented by the *ROS Primer and Field Guide* (USDA Forest Service, 1990).

The ROS in a nutshell. The ROS system was developed to do the following things, which it has done with reasonable success:

- Move outdoor recreation resource management away from practicing ABM alone by supplementing ABM with EBM, because customers desire and expect

opportunities to realize satisfying experiences as well as to engage in activities.

- Provide a scientifically credible approach for helping to assure realization of the experience gestalts (described in Chapter 2) across a spectrum of settings that ranges from the central city to very remote landscapes that cover the imaginable range of desired and expected outdoor recreation activity and experience opportunities.

- Provide a guide for outdoor recreation inventory, management, and evaluation of impacts on recreation opportunities of alternative competing uses at the macrolevel of landscape analysis instead of at the site, facility, or project level of management planning.

- Incorporate the fact that the types of recreation activity and experience opportunities that can be realized, planned, and managed for depend not only on attributes or characteristics of the physical setting but also on social and managerial settings.

- Provide a system for planning and managing outdoor recreation resources that is reasonably easy to understand and implement, not too costly to implement (as other available systems are), and comprehensively covers all types of outdoor recreation resources and demands for outdoor recreation activity and experience opportunities.

- Meet all the mandates to the USFS and BLM of the 1976 NFMA and FLPMA.

- Meet the requirement that when outdoor recreation resource planners and managers apply the system in different regions of the USDA and BLM, they come up with reasonably consistent results (i.e., the system can be applied usefully in any location and to any type of landscape).

Responses to the ROS system. Overall, the ROS system has been well-received, but as with all innovations, there are supporters and detractors. The positive reception of the ROS system is indicated by the fact that it has been applied widely in the USFS and BLM, by several states in the United States, several provinces of Canada, and in quite a few foreign countries. Results of a survey by Anderson and Schneider (1993, p. 27) of 146 USFS managers and 24 university and USFS scientists revealed that the ROS system ranked

1. highest in terms of "recreation resource management innovations developed over the past 20 years that have improved outdoor recreation management."

2. high in terms of its contributions among the innovations considered (pp. 34–35), many of which were

process-oriented, such as to provide better information to visitors, to improve public involvement, and to improve use of computers in management.

3. first as a useful innovation voluntarily mentioned in the first round of the Delphi research method used in the survey.

There have been negative responses to the ROS system as well, which have generally been based on misunderstandings. For example, one argument was that the ROS considers too few dimensions of a recreation opportunity, which ignores the fact that the ROS system requires consideration of the five criteria to inventory the existing condition of the Physical, Social, and Managerial settings. Of course many other attributes of the settings could have been included, but they could not be and still keep the system simple. As explained previously, without its inherent simplicity, the ROS system would not have been used for the same reasons that the other available systems were not used; they were too complex and not cost-effective.

Another misunderstanding of the ROS system is that it was designed to meet the requirements of the 1976 NFMA and FLPMA and not to be a guide for outdoor recreation site and project planning. This misunderstanding is particularly evident in the critiques of the ROS system by Jubenville and Twight (1993, pp. 34–35) and Hultsman, Cottrell, and Hultsman (1998, pp. 275–276). For example, Hultsman, Cottrell, and Hultsman stated the ROS system is biased toward the Primitive end of the spectrum and that it discourages developed sites. Nothing ever written by people who developed the ROS system has implied that the ROS system considers recreation activities and associated experiences that can be realized in one ROS zone are somehow of higher social or moral value than are those that can be realized in another ROS zone. In fact, the team that developed the ROS system strongly disagreed with that position and carefully avoided implying it in the ROS system. If, in fact, "forest service personnel" (and others who use the ROS system) tend to "think, rustic, primitive, and small" as Hultsman, Cottrell, and Hultsman (1998, p. 275) stated, those biases can in no way be attributed to the ROS system. Put simply, the ROS system does not advocate a particular managerial allocation decision. Those decisions can place any type of development anywhere so long as demands for them, and other considerations considered during the managerial allocation decision process, dictate they need to be placed, and they can legally be placed, within the bounds of restrictive legislation such as the Wilderness Act of 1964. However, as explained earlier, once managerial allocations have been made, the inventory criteria and inventory standards of the ROS system can become monitoring standards to be used during plan implementation to assure any ROS class prescribed by the management plan will be managed to meet those prescriptions. Such use of those monitoring standards will assure delivery of the recreation opportunities targeted for provision by the managerial allocations. We iterate there is a difference between an inventory decision and a managerial allocation decision.

We elaborate some of these criticisms in part to clarify misunderstandings about the ROS system, but also to point out in this introductory text that any professional innovation will be misunderstood by some people—a topic to which we return briefly in the last chapter of this text.

The ROS system is far from a perfect system, and in some ways, it was a "grand punt" to help the USFS and BLM meet the requirements mandated by the 1976 NFMA and FLPMA. Despite its few misunderstandings and misrepresentations, the ROS system remains alive and well and is being used widely at the time of the writing of this text to optimize outdoor recreation choices for people in many countries.

Wilderness Opportunity Zoning System

The wilderness opportunity zoning (WOZ) system was developed to guide management of wilderness areas designated as part of the National Wilderness Preservation System established by the Wilderness Act of 1964. It came about as an unexpected result of a two-year collaborative research-demonstration project in the Maroon Bells Wilderness Area of Colorado. Participants in that project represented the Natural Resource Recreation and Tourism Department of Colorado State University, the Rocky Mountain Region (Region 2) of the USFS, and the Rocky Mountain and Intermountain Forest and Range Experiment Stations of the USFS. The WOZ system has been used widely by the federal agencies that manage the National Wilderness Preservation System, especially the USFS and BLM (see Haas, Driver, Brown & Lucas, 1987 for more details on the WOZ).

The WOZ system builds on the ROS system but is substantially different. It does not focus on recreation opportunities but instead on the mandates of how designated Wilderness should be managed as "representative ecosystems" that also provide "primitive types of recreation," as specified in the Wilderness Act of 1964.

The WOZ considers four zones of management within designated Wilderness: Transition, Semi-primitive, Primitive, and Pristine. Transition zones are the portions of many designated Wilderness areas that in some respects probably should not have been classified and approved as Wilderness because of their nearness to human developments. Therefore, the WOZ system designated those areas as transition zones because it is not possible for the federal agencies that administer all designated Wilderness areas to manage those transitions zones as "real" Wilderness as specified by provisions of the 1964 Wilderness Act such as being "untrammeled by man" and providing "opportunities for...primitive type of recreation." Those transition zones cannot meet these criteria unless the contiguous conflicting developments (which typically provide ready access to the transition zones by large numbers of people) are removed and/or very stringent limitations on use are imposed, neither of which has been socially acceptable or economically feasible. However, modest limitations on use have been imposed for some transition zones, and strict rules and regulations are normally enforced, such as not permitting use of open fires or overnight camping to minimize residual signs of human presence.

Opponents of designating transition zones say that such areas violate the provisions of the Wilderness Act. That statement is probably true, but it ignores the budgetary and political constraints facing the responsible managing agencies and the fact that such areas comprise an extremely small percentage of the total wilderness preservation system, which now exceeds 105 million acres. This debate continues.

At the other end of the WOZ spectrum, Pristine areas are remote and often include threatened and endangered species of flora and fauna and truly reflect the ideal of wilderness. Under the WOZ system, trails will not be built or maintained in those areas, and much lower levels of use are encouraged, illustrating that different rules and regulations and density of use criterion are frequently established for each zone.

It is difficult to classify the WOZ system as mostly ABM, EBM, or BBM, because it focuses on wilderness resources, not on outdoor recreation resources as the other management systems described in this chapter (except for sustainable ecosystems management). Nevertheless, the WOZ system does help to assure the provision of a spectrum of different types of wilderness-related recreation activity and experience opportunities that exist in each of the four WOZ zones. It also represents a BBM approach to some extent by its attention to protecting wilderness resources. It is science-based to the extent results of research on social carrying capacities, ecological impacts, forming and maintaining collaborative partnerships with affecting and affected stakeholders, and other relevant research are used to apply the WOZ system to wilderness management.

Meaningful Measures System[1]

The meaningful measures (MM) system is actually short for *meaningful measures for quality recreation management system*. Work started on developing it in the early 1990s. Its multiple purposes include the following:

- to provide high-quality outdoor recreation opportunities
- to be driven by visitor preferences and resource conditions
- to be tied to existing plans, programs, and other recreation management systems
- to make information on, and management of, outdoor recreation uniform nationwide
- to enable managers to set program priorities based on budget constraints through negotiation
- to track and to record all costs associated with these activities

It should be pointed out that the MM system is the only management system that explicitly requires consideration of costs. As such, it promotes cost-effectiveness of outdoor recreation resource planning and management.

The MM process addresses three basic management concerns relating to quality of outdoor recreation opportunities provided, management uniformity, and budgeting. It provides guidance for (a) how to provide quality service to the visitors, (b) how to compete effectively for funds in the budgetary process, and (c) how to establish expectations among peer units about uniformly managing outdoor recreation resources.

A team of USFS outdoor recreation resource planners and managers and several leisure scientists started to develop the MM system in the early 1990s, and incremental implementation in the USFS started soon after that. Although the original MM system is no longer being implemented under the name of MM, its concepts, principles, and analytical requirements have been integrated into other budget, management planning, and manager evaluation procedures of the USFS. Nevertheless, the original MM system remains a relevant science-based system for managing outdoor recreation resources. That original MM system is described next and that discussion draws heavily from Jaten and Driver (1996).

The MM system's essential characteristics include the following:

- accurate, reliable, uniform, and verifiable system for developing, recording, and reporting recreation use and cost data
- improved method for planning and implementing a field unit's annual recreation program of work, including coordinating the recreation program of

work of one field unit with contiguous field units, such as nearby ranger districts on a national forest

- provides clear and uniform standards of quality for outdoor recreation resource management throughout the entire USFS

- helps to assure clear, fair, and objective evaluations of the performance of outdoor recreation resource managers

The six steps for implementing the MM system are as follows:

1. Identify and inventory the measurable recreation facilities, sites, and areas (i.e., the infrastructure used to provide the outdoor recreation opportunities).

2. Establish standards of quality based on customer expectations.

3. Determine and level the costs of managing the inventory (in Step 1) to the standards of quality (in Step 2).

4. Prioritize work to be accomplished on an annual basis (i.e., the annual recreation program of work).

5. Develop budget and allocate the program of work.

6. Monitor, measure, and report actual management attainment.

Each step will now be briefly described.

Identify and inventory the recreation components. In this step, the management unit (which in the USFS is a ranger district of a national forest) must identify and inventory the location, type, economic value, and size of each recreation "component" being managed on that unit. In the USFS implementation of MM, those components were groups of outdoor recreation resources primarily distinguished by settings, developments, or designations identified as developed recreation (e.g., campsites and picnic areas), dispersed recreation (e.g., areas in which where there are few if any developed facilities for recreation but in which a variety of recreation activity opportunities exist), trails and trailheads, designated Wilderness areas, and recreation permits for special uses such as summer cabins. This inventory data will then be used during the remaining steps.

Establish standards of quality. For implementation of the MM system in the USFS, separate sets of standards of quality to guide outdoor recreation resource management were developed for four key indices of quality and separately for each of the different recreation components. These standards apply across the entire USFS. The indices of quality are given in italics and are followed by examples of only a few of the standards for the developed sites recreation component only. Standards preceded by an asterisk are called *drop-dead standards* and must be

met or the applicable area or facility must be closed until they can be met.

Health and Cleanliness

- ∗ Humans are free from unhealthy exposure to human wastes.

- ∗ Water systems and water served meet state and national standards.

- Graffiti is removed within 24 hours of discovery.

General Recreation Setting

- Recreation impacts to highly sensitive areas will be mitigated as needed.

- A vegetative management plan will be implemented.

- Scenery of the area is consistent with the scenery management objectives established for the area.

- Management of the area is consistent with the ROS objectives established for the area.

Safety and Security

- A documented site safety inspection is completed annually and high-risk conditions are corrected prior to use by the public.

- High-risk conditions that develop during the use season are corrected immediately.

- ∗ Electrical systems meet applicable state and national codes.

- Patrols for an appropriate level of law enforcement occur.

Responsiveness

- ∗ Facilities signed as accessible for people with disabilities must meet established guidelines.

- Site entrance is well-marked, easily found, and visitors feel welcome.

- Seasonal and temporary employees receive an appropriate level of "good host" training.

These key indices of quality are rather general, and a longer list of more specific indicators of quality could have been included in the MM system. They were not included to help keep the MM system simple and cost-effective to implement. But it should be remembered that each of the standards written for each of the key indices of quality, and for each recreation component separately, address a specific dimension of quality. Many of the standards apply to more than one recreation component. For example, the developed recreation sites, trails, and general recreation areas components each share an identical standard for the general recreation setting index of quality. That standard requires that "management activities are consistent with the ROS objective that has been set for the area." Similar standards exist for the scenic management objectives established for the area. In this way the ROS system and the scenery management system (described in the next section) are integrated with, and not replaced by, the MM system.

It should be noted the key indices of quality are similar to the "indicators" required by the LAC, VIM, and VERP systems described earlier, and that the USFS-wide national standards are the same types of standards required by those systems. The difference is that the standards of the MM system apply to management of all the USFS's outdoor recreation inventory, as defined in Step 1. That nationwide set of standards was developed for the MM system to enable uniform and consistent management application nationwide, to establish a foundation from which outdoor recreation infrastructure can be evaluated across regions, and to avoid the requirement of the LAC, VIM, and VERP systems to develop a relevant and separate set of indicators and standards each time any of those impact management systems are used. That is very time-consuming and can weaken the willingness of stakeholders to participate in collaborative management. The MM system, with its key indices of quality and standards applied uniformly across the USFS, prevents the need for those duplicative efforts.

Determine and level costs. This step has two parts:

1. Determine the costs of meeting the standards for each component inventoried in Step 1.

2. Compare the costs calculated by proximate management units to identify and resolve outstanding differences.

The first part requires that each field unit determine and record what it will cost to fully meet the requirement specified by each standard of quality for each recreation component managed by that unit. The second part of this step is to "level" the costs by resolving any discrepancies in the costs of meeting standards for a particular recreation component reported among proximate units (e.g., different ranger districts within a national forest). Any discrepancies among units must be justified and agreed to by all the unit managers. After costs are leveled by proximate units, the data are used for several purposes, including to estimate the backlog of capital investments needed to rehabilitate facilities, to make other needed improvements and developments, and most importantly to develop and prioritize the annual recreation program of work for each unit. It is through this process the MM system assures cost-effective and accountable operations both at the field level and at higher administrative levels to which the cost data are aggregated. None of the other outdoor recreation resource management systems described in this chapter or in Chap-

ters 13 or 14 explicitly consider the economic costs of providing outdoor recreation opportunities.

Prioritize work to be accomplished. This step integrates several factors to determine what the recreation-related priorities of the management unit are and how these priorities would change under different circumstances, including the following:

- customer preferences and demands
- customer demographic changes
- interests of other stakeholders
- budgetary constraints
- existing legal requirements
- directions from higher administrative levels and from legislature(s)
- actual and potential liabilities
- local cultural and historical factors
- recreation opportunities being provided by other agencies, nearby management units of the agency, and other organizations
- opportunities for cost sharing and other collaborative efforts, including use of volunteers
- economies of scale and the recreation opportunity "niches" that can best be filled by the management unit implementing the MM system

Additionally, a result of other provider opportunities and changing customer demographics might be that one or more elements of the outdoor recreation inventory will be scheduled to be upgraded, reduced, or eliminated to accommodate dynamic changes in customer preferences and thereby not manage either less used or unused inventory.

Develop budget and allocate the program of work. During this step, personnel from lower management units work with those in higher units (e.g., ranger districts work with the supervisor's office of a national forest) to determine which of the recreation priorities established in the preceding step are feasible and likely to be successful given budget and other constraints as well as other facilitating factors, such as cost sharing and other collaborative efforts between the management unit and outside partners. As a result of these deliberations, an annual recreation program of work is determined and budgets are negotiated and set to accomplish that work. The *program of work* establishes the recreation priorities that will be pursued by the management unit (e.g., a ranger district). That program of work specifies which components and their elements will be managed at what level of targeted quality, and if necessary which elements will be shut down because of low demand or limited operating funds available to the field unit. Because of ever-present budget constraints, each of the recreation components cannot always be managed at full or optimal quality, achieved when each of the standards for a component is met. Therefore, the MM system provides limited options for a unit manager to negotiate with the supervisor, in concert with customer preferences, to manage some recreation components or elements at less than full-standard quality so long as critical health- and safety-related (i.e., drop-dead) standards are achieved.

Monitor, measure, and report actual management attainment. Monitoring evaluates how and whether or not the manager is meeting customer preferences, expectations, and needs at the targeted level of quality (i.e., standard) to which any component of the recreation program is being managed. This step also ensures the system is working as designed. *Measuring* refers to internal agency assessments of whether the budget that was allocated for the program of work actually achieved the planned and targeted results. *Reporting* refers to documentation and reporting of attainment by management and of customer satisfaction. The results from this sixth and final step are analyzed together to determine whether

- Targets are higher or lower that customer expectations.

- Adjustments need to be made in the application of the standards by the management unit.

- The measurements or measuring criteria are accurate.

- There is a significant change in customer demographics to warrant changes in either management or the recreation inventory.

- The reporting targets are adequate for measuring trends in customer satisfaction (i.e., the delivery of public benefits over time) as a basis for management decisions.

Because the MM system adopts a management-by-objectives approach, a manager's performance can be evaluated in terms of clear and measurable performance objectives that define the types, levels, quantities, and qualities of service they have negotiated with their supervisors to produce. This is a significant advancement over the previous, frequently inequitable, and largely subjective practice of evaluating work performance.

From about 1994 until 2002, the USFS was implementing MM as a separate outdoor recreation resource planning and management system. However, the concepts, logic, and requirements of the MM system have recently been integrated into the regular "business cycles" of the USFS. For example, each year the USFS must report to the U.S. Congress the cost of bringing its recreation inventory up to fully maintained condition (MM Step 1). To report annual performance accomplishments, the USFS has adopted management standards (MM Step 2) for managing

the outdoor recreation inventory. To enable a better system of budget planning, that agency has developed the budget formulation and executions system to plan for the costs (MM Steps 3 and 5) of providing goods and services from the national forests and grasslands. To operate and to maintain the outdoor recreation program of work in a fiscally sound manner, several USFS management units are developing a broad-based system for evaluating which pieces of the recreation inventory are critical to their missions and special recreation-related niches. These efforts are generally in concert with the revision of each unit's resource management plan, which in the USFS is done for each national forest. In addition, the MM system helps to meet the requirements of 1993 Government Performance and Results Act that each federal agency measure outputs and outcomes of their managerial activities and report the progress made toward accomplishing them (MM Step 6).

MM is science-based, because most of the standards developed in Step 2 drew on the results of research. The customer satisfaction surveys it requires rely on systematic research designs, and its requirement of management by objectives draws from research from modern management science. Because the MM system integrates results of other management systems being used, especially the ROS and scenery management systems, it inherits the scientific credibility of those systems. Because it relies mostly on these other management systems and is itself more of a work planning, measurement-of-attainment, and reporting system, it is not as subject to being defined as ABM, EBM, or BBM as the other systems being described here are. Nevertheless, a review of all of the standards it developed and applies shows that it endorses and promotes ABM, EBM, and BBM. Other public P&R agencies have developed and applied systems similar to the MM system, but publications are not yet available to cite.

Scenery Management System

In 1995 the USFS issued its *Handbook for Scenery Management* (USDA Forest Service, 1995). Scenery management (SM) is a system that built on and improved the older visual resource management (VRM) system of the early 1970s (see pp. 166–167). The SM system retains the logic and many of the procedures of the VRM system, but provides for better incorporation and use of the ROS system, ecological analyses as part of sustainable ecosystems management (summarized next), and benefits-based management (described in the next chapter). It also provides for improved involvement of stakeholders (called *constituents* in the SM system) and incorporates scientific knowledge about visual/scenic resource management and establishment of collaborative partnerships with stakeholders that has been developed since the original VRM system was developed and refined in the 1970s. As was the

VRM systems that it replaced in the USFS, the SM system was developed using results of available relevant research, including recent research on landscape aesthetics, involving stakeholders, and ecosystem sustainability. Also, as did the VRM systems, the SM system promotes both ABM and EBM, and BBM to a limited extent via its use to improve and maintain scenic resources. The *Handbook for Scenery Management* describes how to implement the SM system (USDA Forest Service, 1995).

Sustainable Ecosystems Management

Sustainable ecosystem management (SEM) is not so much a management system as it is a philosophy or holistic orientation to management. SEM relates to all human uses and appreciation of physical and biological resources—all of "spaceship earth." Its concern is much broader than just the provision and use of outdoor recreation opportunities. For several reasons, however, it is appropriate to review SEM briefly in this chapter on outdoor recreation resource management systems. First, management and use of outdoor recreation resources do impact the basic biophysical and cultural/heritage resources and ecological processes on which provision of outdoor recreation opportunities depend. Second, outdoor recreation is now the dominant use of very large tracts of public lands, including parts of 105 million acres designated as Wilderness areas in part for their opportunities for "primitive types of recreation." In combination, the areas used for outdoor recreation cover parts of all natural ecosystems. Third, participation in outdoor recreation activities is the primary mode of learning about natural ecosystems for many people and improves existing understanding of such for others. (Environmental learning and related benefits of both on-site and off-site users were described in Chapter 2.)

Through their paintings and writings, artists, philosophers, politicians, and scientists (e.g., Catlin, Muir,

Considering and managing scenery, like this viewshed in a National Forest in Wyoming, are critical to providing high-quality outdoor recreation opportunities.

Thoreau, Theodore Roosevelt, Marsh) have promoted ecosystem sustainability for over 100 years in the United States, and others have done the same in many other countries. Also, scores of scientific texts and journals have been written about SEM and sustainable development of natural resources for several decades by authors in many countries.

In the past, many definitions have been given for sustainable development and ecosystems management. Currently, SEM is widely interpreted to mean an approach that integrates knowledge about natural ecosystems and needs of people in a way that serves human needs while maintaining diversity and productivity of natural ecosystems over time.

It is important to note that SEM (sometimes called *sustainable development*) is not equivalent with nonuse of resources, but instead allows use and recognizes that humans benefit from such use so long as the natural environment and ecological processes are sustained over time. Such sustainability is much easier to accomplish with renewable resources, such as fauna and flora, than it is with nonrenewable resources, such as minerals. Debates about SEM focus on both of these two types of resources, such as whether or not to protect threatened and endangered species of plants and animals or if technological advances will continue to provide relatively inexpensive sources of energy as the supplies of nonrenewable fossil fuels in the world are depleted. As they have for over 100 years, these debates continue to be economic, technological, political, philosophical, and moral.

It is difficult to accurately establish the date that SEM was first applied to actually guide land management instead of just being proposed as a philosophy. But it is clear that early withdrawals of lands from the federal public domain in the United States were in part related to the concept of SEM. For example, key areas of what is now Yosemite National Park (and the Mariposa Redwood Grove) were transferred by the U.S. Government to the State of California in 1864 with the stipulation those lands be held "inalienable for all times" (Dennis, 2001, p. 39). Twenty-two years later, California returned that area to the U.S. government to be added to Yosemite National Park. And it is clear that sustaining natural ecosystems was a primary reason for the creation of most of the national parks in the United States, including the first one, Yellowstone National Park, in 1872—over four decades before the NPS was created in 1916.

Other than the just-mentioned preservation of early parks, the next promotion of SEM was when the U.S. Department of the Interior created the Pelican Island National Refuge in 1903. That was done by direction of President Theodore Roosevelt. The preservation of that refuge was followed by the creation of over 50 additional wildlife refuges by Roosevelt and later by creation of the United

States Fish and Wildlife Service (FWS) in the U.S. Department of the Interior in 1956. But the seeds of the FWS existed under other names much earlier. It started when the U.S. Congress established the U.S. Fish Commission (USFC) in 1871 to study the decrease of the nation's food fish supply—a commitment to SEM as early as the period of custodial management. In 1905, the USFC became part of the Bureau of Biological Survey in the U.S. Department of Agriculture, which in 1939 was combined with the Bureau of Fisheries and in 1940 transferred to the U.S. Department of the Interior and named the Fish and Wildlife Service. In 1956, it became the U.S. Fish and Wildlife Service by an act of the U.S. Congress. This history of the FWS shows again that public policies and managerial practices evolve slowly but surely. In the case of the FWS, this evolution retained a strong commitment to SEM.

Other than creation of the U.S. Fish Commission in 1871 and establishment of the Pelican Island National Refuge in 1903, the first federal land management agency to practice SEM, at least to a limited degree, in the United States was the USFS. Although Pinchot's *Wise Use* books of 1906 can be criticized as not explicitly advocating SEM as that concept evolved to be interpreted today, Pinchot did promote sustainable development and lead the early USFS in that direction. As mentioned, after they were created later, the NPS and FWS also promoted the SEM concept as a fundamental part of their managerial practices.

Although the concept of SEM is not a new one to land management agencies, actually managing lands to promote SEM was not articulated as the core management philosophy of most land management organizations until the early 1990s. By analogy, it evolved just as the concept of multiple-use or functionally integrated management did. The previous discussion showed that the Multiple-Use and Sustained Yield Act of 1960 for the USFS did not get the same attention within that agency as did the 1976

Sustainable ecosystems management considers the interactions of all living organisms, including recreation visitors, with their environment.

NFMA, which followed the NEPA of 1969. Change in land management policies and practices generally take considerable time.

With perhaps the exceptions of the NPS and FWS and management of areas for a particular species, such as the grizzly bear in the Greater Teton–Yellowstone Area (a cooperative venture between the NPS, USFS, BLM, FWS, the states in which that land is located, and other organizations), the concept of SEM was more implicit than explicit to the actual management of most natural resources until the early 1990s. Put simply, the concept of SEM has evolved slowly to where it is today: recognized and practiced widely and overtly by many public, private, and nonprofit land management and outdoor recreation providing organizations.

As mentioned earlier, the 1976 NFMA and FLMPA for the USFS and BLM required that resource management plans be done by those two agencies. Years were spent developing those plans for the administrative units of those two agencies (i.e., National Forests and Resource Areas). But the arbitrarily established administrative boundaries of those management units had little to do with representing natural ecosystems. Later, the USFS and BLM recognized they needed to change to a holistic/ecosystem type of management and issued policy directives to do so in the early 1990s. On June 4, 1992, for example, Dale Robertson, then Chief of the USFS, issued an internal directive to Regional Foresters, Research Experiment Station Directors, and Area Directors of the State and Private Forestry branch of the USFS stating:

> …the Forest Service is committed to using an ecological approach in the future management of the National Forests and Grasslands. By ecosystem management, we mean that an ecological approach will be used to achieve the multiple-use management of the National Forests and Grasslands. It means that we must blend the needs of people and environmental values in such a way that the National Forests and Grasslands represent diverse, healthy, productive, and sustainable ecosystems.

This reorientation of the country's two largest land management agencies was soon followed by similar commitments by other federal and state land management agencies and by large pulp and timber companies that managed large areas of forested land. These new managerial orientations spawned considerable debate in the 1990s about what SEM is and is not, and many of those debates were as emotional as they were technical. For example, some ecologists suggested unrealistically that we should return natural ecosystems to the states and conditions of their existence before arrival of Europeans on the North American continent, which ignored the facts that natural succession made that impossible and that the Native Americans often used practices, such as use of wild fires, that significantly altered many natural ecosystems. People with commodity interests in the public lands feared that SEM would have unwanted economic consequences for them. And others proposed that humans should show less physical presence in natural ecosystems because that was "unnatural." In fact, many studies were done of the "Human Dimensions of SEM" (cf. Driver, Manning & Peterson, 1995; USDA Forest Service, 1994). Over time greater consensus has been reached and it is now generally accepted that SEM does not mean "no use" by humans but instead "wise use."

A good summary illustration of what SEM is about is shown in the two Venn diagrams of Figure 12.4. The left side of Figure 12.4 shows little integration of social needs, economic needs, and economic components, while better ecological sustainability is achieved when these factors of SEM are integrated as indicated on the right side.

Summary

This chapter traced the evolution of science-based management of outdoor recreation resources through four periods in the United States, starting with the period of settlement of the Europeans in the United States and ending with the period of overtly managing for outdoor recreation, which continues today. The discussion of that last period described three conceptual approaches to the management of outdoor recreation resources that evolved as the result of leisure-research improved management: activity-based management (ABM), experience-based management

(EBM), and benefits-based management (BBM). Much of this chapter then described briefly the scientifically credible systems that fall within the ABM and EBM categories, which have been and are still being used to manage outdoor recreation resources. The general characteristics of BBM were outlined, but it was not described in this chapter. The specifics of BBM will be covered in the next chapter, which should be considered a continuation of this one. The science-based management systems covered in this chapter were generic activity-based management and the systems known as visual resource management, limits of acceptable change, visitor experience and resource management, visitor impact management, visitor activity management process, recreation opportunity spectrum, wilderness opportunity zoning, meaningful measures, scenery management, and sustainable ecosystems management. We iterate that only a brief overview could be given of each of these systems and again refer the reader to the references cited for more information.

A major point of this chapter is how the remarkable advances in scientific knowledge about leisure, including outdoor recreation, during the past 40 years have led to improved management systems based on that knowledge. We in the leisure professions should take great pride in these professional accomplishments.

Literature Cited

Anderson, D. and Schneider, I. (1993). Using the Delphi process to identify significant recreation research-based innovations. *Journal of Park and Recreation Administration II, 1*, 25–36.

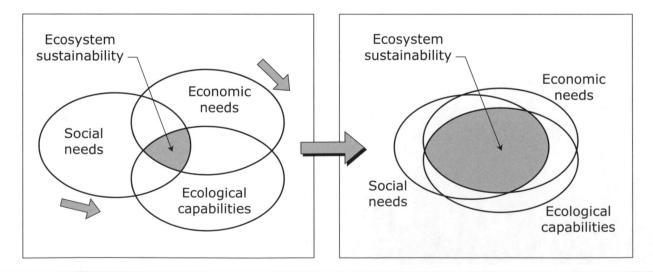

Figure 12.4 Sustainable ecosystem management (SEM) requires careful integration of social and economic needs with capabilities of the ecosystem itself as illustrated on the right. Source: Adapted from Kaufman and others (1994, p. 2)

Bacon, W. (1996). Multisensory landscape aesthetics. In B. Driver, D. Dustin, T. Baltic, G. Elsner, and G. Peterson (Eds.), *Nature and the human spirit: Toward an expanded land management ethic* (pp. 311–320). State College, PA: Venture Publishing, Inc.

Brown, P., Driver, B., and McConnell, C. (1978). The opportunity spectrum concept and behavior information in outdoor recreation resource supply inventories: Background and application. In G. H. Lund et al., *Integrated inventories of renewable natural resources: Proceedings of a workshop* (pp. 73–84). Fort Collins, CO: USDA Forest Service, Rocky Mountain Forest and Range Experiment Station.

Buckley, W. (1968). *Modern systems research for the behavioral scientist.* Chicago, IL: Aldine.

Clark, R. and Stankey, G. (1979). *The recreation opportunity spectrum: A framework for planning, management, and research.* (General Technical Report PNW-98). Portland, OR: USDA Forest Service, Pacific Northwest Experiment Station.

Dennis, S. (2001). *Natural resources and the informed citizen.* Champaign, IL: Sagamore.

Dombeck, M. (1997, June 24). Presentation made at the Public Lands Forum of the Outdoor Writers' Association of America, Greenefee, FL.

Driver, B. (1990). Recreation opportunity spectrum: Basic concepts and use in land management planning. In R. Graham and R. Lawrence (Eds.), *Toward serving visitors and managing our resources. Proceedings of a North American workshop on Visitor Management on Parks and Protected Areas* (pp. 159–183). Waterloo, Ontario, Canada: University of Waterloo, Tourism Research and Education Center.

Driver, B. (2003). Leisure experiences. In. J. Jenkins and J. Pigram (Eds.), *Encyclopedia of leisure and outdoor recreation.* London, England: Routledge Press.

Driver, B., Bossi, J., and Cordell, H. (1985). Trends in user fees at federal outdoor recreation areas. In *Proceedings, 1985 Outdoor Recreation Trends Symposium, volume I.* Clemson, SC: Clemson University, Department of Parks, Recreation and Tourism.

Driver, B. and Brown, P. (1978). The opportunity spectrum concept and behavioral information in outdoor recreation resource supply inventories: A rational. In G. H. Lund et al., *Integrated inventories of renewable natural resources. Proceedings of a workshop* (pp. 24–31; General Technical Report RM-55). Fort Collins, CO: USDA Forest Service, Rocky Mountain Forest and Range Experiment Station.

Driver, B., Brown, P., Stankey, G., and Gregorie, T. (1987). The ROS planning system: Evolution, basic concepts, and research needed. *Leisure Sciences, 9*, 201–212.

Driver, B., Manning, C., and Peterson, G. (1995). Toward better integration of the social and biophysical components of ecosystems management. In A. Ewert (Ed.), *Natural resource management: The human dimension* (pp. 109–127). Boulder, CO: Westview Press.

Driver, B., Tinsley, H., and Manfredo, M. (1991). The paragraphs about leisure and recreation experience preference scales: Results from two inventories designed to assess the breadth of the perceived psychological benefits of leisure. In B. Driver, P. Brown, and G. Peterson (Eds.), *Benefits of leisure* (pp. 263–187). State College, PA: Venture Publishing, Inc.

Graefe, A., Kuss, F., and Vaske, J. (1990). Visitor impact management: The planning framework. In *Volume two of a report examining visitor impact management for the national parks and other recreation lands* (pp. 83–96). Washington, DC: National Parks and Conservation Association.

Graham, R., Nilsen, P., and Payne, R. (1988, March). Visitor management in Canadian national parks. *Tourism Management, 44–61.*

Hammitt, W. E. and Cole, D. N. (1998). *Wildland recreation: Ecology and management* (2nd ed.). New York, NY: John Wiley & Sons.

Haas, G. E., Driver, B. L., Brown, P. J., and Lucas, R. L. (1987, December). Wilderness management zoning. *Journal of Forestry, 17–21.*

Hayes, S. (1955). *Conservation and the gospel of efficiency.* Cambridge, MA: Harvard University Press.

Hultsman, J., Cottrell, R., and Hultsman, W. Z. (1998). *Planning parks for people* (2nd ed.). State College, PA: Venture Publishing, Inc.

Jaten, A. and Driver, B. (1996). Meaningful measures for quality recreation management: Managing the recreation program of work at the site or project level. *Journal of Park and Recreation Administration, 16*(3), 43–57.

Jubenville, A. and Twight, B. W. (1993). *Outdoor recreation management: Theory and application* (3rd ed.). State College, PA: Venture Publishing, Inc.

Kaufman, M., Graham, R. T., Boyce, D. A., Jr., Moir, W. H., Perry, L., Reynolds, R. T., et al. (1994). *An ecological basis for ecosystem management* (General Technical Report RM-246). Fort Collins, CO: USDA Forest Service, Rocky Mountain Station.

Litton, B. (1968). *Forest landscape description and inventories: A basis for land planning and design* (Research Paper PSW 49). Berkeley, CA: USDA Forest Service, Pacific Southwest Experiment Station.

Litton, B. (1972). Aesthetic dimensions of the landscape. In. J. Krutilla (Ed), *Natural environments: Studies in theoretical and applied analysis* (pp. 262–291). Baltimore, MD: Johns Hopkins Press.

Manfredo, M. (Ed.). (2002). *Wildlife viewing: A management handbook*. Corvallis, OR: Oregon State University Press.

Manfredo, M., Driver, B., and Tarrant, M. (1996). Measuring leisure motivation: A meta analysis of the recreation experience preference scales. *Journal of Leisure Research, 28*, 188–213.

Manning, R., Lime, D., and Hof, M. (1996). Social carrying capacity of natural areas: Theory and application in the U.S. national parks. *Natural Areas Journal, 16*(2), 118–127.

National Park Service. (1956). *Mission 66*. Washington, DC: U.S. Department of the Interior.

Outdoor Recreation Resources Review Commission. (1962). *Outdoor recreation for America*. Washington, DC: U.S. Government Printing Office.

Parks Canada. (1991). *Selected readings on the visitor activity management process*. Ottawa, Ontario, Canada: Environment Canada.

Robertson, F. D. (1992, June–July). Forest Service Chief announces new ecosystem management policy for National Forests and Grasslands. *Nonpoint Source News-Notes, Issue 22*. Retrieved February 28, 2005, from http://www.epa.gov/owow/info/NewsNotes/issue22/nnd22.htm

Stankey, G., Cole, D., Lucas, R., Peterson, M., Frissell, S., and Washburne, R. (1985). *The limits of acceptable (LAC) system for wilderness planning* (General Technical Report INT-176). Ogden, UT: USDA Forest Service, Intermountain Forest and Range Experiment Station.

Thomas, J. (1996). Foreword. In. B. Driver, D. Dustin, T. Baltic, G. Elsner, and G. Peterson (Eds.), *Nature and the human spirit: Toward an expanded land management ethic* (pp. xxiii–xxv). State College, PA: Venture Publishing, Inc.

USDA Forest Service. (1957). *Operation outdoors. Part 1: Outdoor recreation*. Washington, DC: Superintendent of Documents.

USDA Forest Service. (1974a). *National forest landscape management, Volume I* (Agriculture Handbook 434). Washington, DC: U.S. Government Printing Office.

USDA Forest Service. (1974b). *National forest landscape management, Volume I. Chapter 1: The visual resource management system* (Agriculture Handbook 462). Washington, DC: U.S. Government Printing Office.

USDA Forest Service. (1975). *National forest landscape management, Volume II. Chapter 2: Utilities* (Agriculture Handbook 478). Washington, DC: U.S. Government Printing Office.

USDA Forest Service. (1977a). *National forest landscape management, Volume II. Chapter 3: Range* (Agriculture Handbook 483). Washington, DC: U.S. Government Printing Office.

USDA Forest Service. (1977b). *National forest landscape management, Volume II. Chapter 4: Roads* (Agriculture Handbook 484). Washington, DC: U.S. Government Printing Office.

USDA Forest Service. (1980). *National forest landscape management, Volume II. Chapter 5: Timber* (Agriculture Handbook 599). Washington, DC: US Government Printing Office.

USDA Forest Service. (1982). *ROS users guide*. Washington, DC: USDA Forest Service.

USDA Forest Service. (1987). *National forest landscape management, Volume II. Chapter 8: Recreation*. Washington, DC: U.S. Government Printing Office.

USDA Forest Service. (1990). *ROS primer and field guide*. Washington, DC: Author.

USDA Forest Service. (1994). *The human dimension in sustainable ecosystem management: A management philosophy*. Fort Collins, CO: USDA Forest Service, Rocky Mountain Forest and Range Experiment Station.

USDA Forest Service. (1995). *Landscape aesthetics: A handbook for scenery management* (U.S. Department of Agriculture Handbook 701). Washington, DC: USDA Forest Service.

USDI Bureau of Land Management. (1986). *Visual resource inventory* (BLM Manual Handbook 8410-1). Washington, DC: U.S. Department of the Interior.

Wilderness Act of 1964, 16 U.S.C. § 1131 et seq.

Williams, D. and Stewart, S. (1998). Sense of place: An elusive concept that is finding a home in ecosystem management. *Journal of Forestry, 96*(5), 18–23.

Wondolleck, J. and Yaffee, S. (2000). *Making collaboration work: Lessons from innovation in natural resource management*. Washington, DC: Island Press.

Endnote

1. Appreciation is expressed to Allen Jaten for his review of and contributions to this section. Jaten is past National Coordinator of the meaningful measures management system, and for many years he ably guided the improvement and implementation of that system in the USFS.

Chapter 13
The Beneficial Outcomes Approach to Leisure[1]

By focusing on the perceived needs of the community, benefits-based management both empowers and informs the clients of our park and recreation services…. If our aims are to truly make a difference in the lives of the communities we serve, then benefits-based management and community-based research are appropriate tools to be further developed. (William Borrie & Joseph Roggenbuck, 1994)

Learning Objectives

1. Explain why the beneficial outcomes approach to leisure (BOAL) was developed as an encompassing paradigm for leisure, including outdoor recreation.
2. Understand the evolution of the BOAL, its characteristics, and its advantages.
3. Describe the different applied uses of the BOAL, especially how benefits-based management or BBM (also called *beneficial outcomes management*) builds on and supplements the outdoor recreation resource management systems described in Chapter 12.
4. Understand how the BOAL can help to "reposition the image" or to correct inaccurate perceptions about the social contributions and roles of leisure, including outdoor recreation, in a society.
5. Appreciate the contributions of the BOAL and BBM to enhancing the professionalism of people who specialize in outdoor recreation.

Chapter 12 described four different periods of management of outdoor recreation resources in the United States, including the periods of settlement, custodial management, low-priority management for outdoor recreation, and overtly managing for outdoor recreation. In the discussion of the last period (which continues today), it was emphasized that advancements in scientific knowledge about leisure since 1960 improved the systems that evolved to guide management of outdoor recreation resources. That discussion described three different approaches to such management, identified as activity-based management (ABM), experience-based management (EBM), and benefits-based management (BBM). It was emphasized that ABM was not replaced by EBM but was supplemented by it, and that EBM was not replaced by BBM but was similarly supplemented and improved by it. The last part of that chapter reviewed science-based ABM and EBM systems that have been used to guide planning and management of outdoor recreation resources. It was pointed out that most of these systems are still being used today in the United States and other countries.

Chapter 12 ended with the explanation that BBM is the most recent system being used to manage outdoor recreation resources. The description of BBM was deferred to this chapter, because it needed to be explained within

the context of a new paradigm developed since EBM systems, such as the recreation opportunity spectrum (ROS) system, were first implemented in the early 1980s. That paradigm is the beneficial outcomes approach to leisure (BOAL) of which BBM (also called *beneficial outcomes management* by some leisure professionals) is only one specialized application.

This chapter begins by tracing the evolution of the BOAL. The first part describes current customer/client expectations of organizations, especially public park and recreation (P&R) agencies, that provide leisure services. Then, it shows that the responses of those providing organizations disclosed a need for the BOAL. This chapter continues by explaining other reasons why the BOAL was developed, how it evolved, its purposes, and its characteristics. That discussion reviews the specialized uses of the BOAL in leisure policy development, management, research, education, marketing, and "repositioning the image" about the real worth of leisure to a society, the needs for which were described by Crompton (1993) and Crompton and Witt (1998) as reviewed in Chapter 2. The chapter ends with a focus on BBM as a guide for managing outdoor recreation resources, because that focus is necessary to finish the discussion of such management systems begun in Chapter 12.

Changing Public Values and Recreation Agency Responses to Them[2]

On April 8, 1997, Mike Dombeck, then Chief of the USDA Forest Service (USFS), stated: "Today, society's priorities are shifting. Our management priorities must keep pace with…society's values" (Dombeck, 1997a). Those expectations, especially of public P&R agencies, are now much clearer and have been articulated strongly during the past 15 to 20 years. This means that society's values and expectations have changed and intensified since most of the systems for managing outdoor recreation resources discussed in Chapter 12 were developed. Those expectations and the providers' responses to them will now be reviewed, because the BOAL was developed primarily to help public, private, and nonprofit providers of leisure services meet the expectations of their customers.

Changing Public Values and Expectations

Following are the most significant changes in societal priorities, values, and expectations to which providers of outdoor recreations opportunities are now giving more attention.

Increased prominence of recreational uses and changing concepts of outdoor recreation. Earlier chapters of this text described and documented the rapidly increasing use of outdoor recreation opportunities in the United States since the end of World War II. That increasing use means that an ever-growing number of people have valued and formed personal opinions and expectations about outdoor recreation and those who provide opportunities for it. During the same time, the concept of outdoor recreation has broadened and certain dimensions of it have received more attention and consideration than formerly. These include the primitive types of recreation emphasized in the Wilderness Act of 1964, more use of outdoor recreation and related amenity resources to renew and nurture the human spirit (Driver, Dustin, Baltic, Elsner & Peterson, 1996), greater articulation of the importance of natural areas as special places and appreciation of a psychological sense of place (Bruns & Stokowski, 1999; Greene, 1999; Roberts, 1999; Williams & Stewart, 1998), and increased use of natural areas to learn about ecological processes, to nurture an environmental ethic, and to become more committed to sustainable development and use of natural and cultural/historic resources (Hammitt & Cole, 1998).

Widespread concern by people about the perceived quality of their lives and growing commitments of time and other personal resources toward maintaining and improving such quality. These concerns and introspec-tions, outlined in Chapter 2, are particularly relevant here because users of outdoor recreation opportunities have become very aware of what characteristics of outdoor recreation opportunities do and do not contribute to their perceived quality of life. As a consequence, many, if not most, users are now able to articulate rather clearly to providers of leisure services their desires for and expectations of those services, including the types of benefits they wish to realize and the undesirable impacts they wish to avoid. Users now know what characteristics of those opportunities and recreation settings are important to them and why. Just as recreation resource management evolved from ABM to EBM and is now evolving to BBM, so have the recreating customers become more consciously aware of their Level 1, 2, and 3 demands for recreation activity, experience, and benefits opportunities, as described in Chapter 12. Put simply, providers of outdoor recreation opportunities are now serving customers who are more astute and can articulate their preferences clearly.

There are growing public demands that all elected and professional public officials become more efficient, cost-effective, fair/equitable, responsive, and accountable and that public natural resource agencies sustain the biophysical and cultural/heritage resources they manage. These demands are particularly evident to public P&R agencies, but a customer orientation and efficiency of operations are expected of private and nonprofit providers as well.

Increasingly, the public demands that all affected stakeholders become involved in environmental decision making. This is a part of the demand that agencies become more responsive, but it is listed separately for emphasis because it is a critical part of the BOAL.

Increased and maintained concern about the condition of the biophysical environment, and in particular the lands administered by public agencies. For several decades, national surveys in the United States and other countries have documented that the public cares deeply about the biophysical environment and desires to see it protected and managed properly.

Responses of the Agencies

These changes in social values, priorities, and expectations have affected policy decisions and managerial practices of providers of outdoor recreation opportunities, especially public P&R agencies, in numerous ways.

More functionally integrated management. As explained in Chapter 12, there has been a reorientation of the perspective of multiple-use public land management agencies (e.g., the USDA Forest Service, the USDI Bureau of Land Management) away from focusing mostly on the commodity uses of the public lands they administer to a more balanced focus that recognizes the societal importance of recreation uses of the resources being managed. For example, in 1997 then Chief of the USFS Mike Dombeck stated recreation was the dominant use of the national forests (Dombeck, 1997b). This represented a major change for an agency that historically has emphasized the production of timber/wood products. These types of reorientations have required all public P&R agencies to develop and to apply more sophisticated and scientifically credible outdoor recreation resource management systems; to acquire more personnel with training in the social sciences to complement existing personnel trained in timber, range, fishery, watershed, and wildlife management; and to modify their budgetary processes to justify additional appropriations for recreation and related uses. Such changes are also apparent in many private and nonprofit providers as well as in the public P&R agencies.

Recreation resource management agencies have moved away from activity-based management (ABM), which focuses on supply considerations, as explained in Chapter 12. They have begun to widely adopt EBM approaches and are increasingly adopting BBM, which views the major goals of management as being to promote realization of positive outcomes and avoidance of negative outcomes, while protecting and improving the basic biophysical and cultural/historic resources being managed.

There has been widespread adoption of the total quality management (TQM) perspective. TQM requires a customer orientation, meaning information needs to be solicited not only on customers' preferences for specific recreation activity opportunities but also on their preferences for specific types of satisfying recreation experiences and other benefits. TQM has also stimulated more monitoring of the customer/client satisfactions with the outdoor recreation services delivered.

Many providers of recreation opportunities have substituted the word "customer" for the words "users" and "visitors." They are recognizing that both on-site and off-site customers (i.e., all stakeholders) must be involved in public policy-making and management decision processes. There has been greater recognition that no public, private, or nonprofit providing organization is ever the sole provider of outdoor recreation services at a particular site or area. A "customer orientation" is increasingly being applied to denote that sovereign customers are being served. Also, it is being recognized that multiple collaborating providers (e.g., other agencies, local communities, business enterprises, nonprofits, tourism agencies) significantly affect the type, quality, and amount of recreation opportunities that can be provided where, when, and for whom. Although this transition is not complete, it is progressing slowly but encouragingly.

There has been rather widespread movement away from a narrow interpretation of public involvement. In the past, providers tended to solicit input from customers only at a few selected steps of the resource planning processes. Today, providers are moving toward much wider development and maintenance of collaborative partnerships with all affecting and affected policy and managerially relevant stakeholders and associated providers. As a result, many providing organizations now recognize that both on-site and off-site customers (i.e., all stakeholders) must be involved in policy-making and management processes to increase the extent that they feel they have "ownership" in the allocation decisions made. This has helped to promote an improved atmosphere of trust and respect within which the customers believe they are an active part of decision processes. Especially significant here has been movement away from the philosophy that the professional managers are all-knowing technical experts who can technocratically determine the one "right" managerial allocation decision. A growing number of managers now recognize several acceptable right allocation decisions that differ in terms of which stakeholders' values and interests are to be or not to be accommodated, and to what degree (Wondolleck, 1996).

In addition to being more responsive to their customers, there has been a distinct trend toward more efficient, cost-effective, and accountable management by public agencies. Although public P&R agencies do not operate as profit-making firms, they have widely adopted business-like principles to assure more efficient and cost-effective operations. This greater accountability by agency and other provider personnel has enhanced the ability of higher administrative levels, stakeholders, and the general public to evaluate the performance of public agencies more objectively.

There has been widespread adoption of the philosophy of holistic sustainable ecosystem management. This has led to movement away from the development of management plans for land areas defined by administrative boundaries alone. As explained in Chapter 12, it is now widely recognized that ecological processes cross administrative boundaries.

To accommodate these changes, a growing number of providers have reevaluated and changed many of their goals as well as their managerial philosophies and practices. As only one example, many of them now practice sustainable ecosystems management as explained in Chapter 12.

The BOAL was developed explicitly to meet the needs of providers as they changed in the ways just noted. These agency responses will be related to the needs for the BOAL in the remainder of this chapter. Specifically, the BOAL was developed to help the providers become more responsive, accountable, equitable/fair, efficient or cost-effective, and to practice sustainable ecosystems management. For that reason, the BOAL is now receiving wider use as providers continue to respond to the changing expectations of their customers. For example, the BOAL is helping federal P&R agencies to meet the requirements of the 1993 Government Performance and Results Act that mandates use of better measures of performance to improve their accountability.

Evolution of the BOAL

Time Was Ripe for the Beneficial Outcomes Approach to Leisure

Wide use of the recreation opportunity spectrum (ROS) system since the early 1980s prompted increased understanding of and support for EBM. As previously mentioned, EBM itself was a limited type of BBM, because it focused on the third type of benefit of leisure defined by the BOAL (i.e., the realization of a satisfying recreation experience as defined in Chapter 2). Such use of EBM, along with increased research on the other benefits of leisure discussed in Chapter 2 caused much greater attention to be given to all the benefits of leisure. That attention, and customer expectations of organizations that provide leisure services, both facilitated and spurred development of the BOAL. Therefore, by the early 1990s, there was sufficient scientific knowledge about the benefits of leisure so that the basic concepts of the BOAL could be developed and applied with reasonable scientific credibility to improve on existing paradigms about leisure. The discussion of the evolution of the BOAL that follows draws heavily from Driver, Bruns, and Booth (2001).

The editors and coauthors of *Benefits of Leisure* (Driver, Brown & Peterson, 1991) met at Snowbird, Utah, in 1989 to preview near-final drafts of that text. Several administrators of public P&R agencies and other authors there expressed strong interest in the need for a paradigm about leisure oriented toward realization of benefits and the prevention of unwanted impacts. Their request led to a Benefits Application Workshop, held in Estes Park, Colorado, in May 1991. Thirty-five leaders and managers of federal, state, regional, and municipal P&R departments attended that workshop, as did another 35 leisure scientists and educators interested in the benefits of leisure who wanted to see more of the results of leisure research applied in leisure policy development and management. The participants were from the United States and Canada.

The basic ideas, purposes, and advantages of the BOAL were developed at that workshop, which at first focused on the management of P&R resources but soon expanded to a paradigm about leisure in general. For the following three reasons, those participants desired a systematic and scientifically credible approach to the delivery of leisure services that explicitly addressed the positive and nega-

tive outcomes of the management and use of recreation resources, which other available approaches (i.e., those described in Chapter 12) did not consider adequately.

First, top administrators of public P&R agencies needed better information about the social and other benefits of recreation so they could more accurately describe them with enhanced credibility to elected officials responsible for funding the delivery of publicly provided leisure services. Put simply, recreation was then still generally viewed by the legislators as merely "fun and games" (cf. Jordan, 1991) and as providing few benefits to society as a whole. Therefore, legislators believed that the users, not the taxpayers, should bear most of the costs of providing leisure opportunities. This erroneous perception that leisure was relatively trivial for society created regular funding crunches for top-level administrators of public P&R agencies. When proposing and justifying budget requests, they badly needed a scientifically credible benefits-oriented paradigm to provide better documentation that significant benefits of leisure to a society include but go beyond the benefits realized by individuals (e.g., the role of leisure in helping to prevent/reduce the rapidly increasing public costs of health care).

Second, the field-level planners and managers present at the workshop, while believing that conventional social, economic, and environmental impact assessments were useful, found those assessments were typically too general and provided inadequate specific guidance for managerial actions once the results of these assessments had been used to help guide basic resource allocation decisions. Also, although they understood the need to practice both ABM and EBM, they also realized the time was ripe to move into BBM to supplement ABM and EBM, and they needed guidelines on how to do so. In short, they wanted to know how to optimize the net benefits that would accrue from their planning and managerial actions. In particular, the field-level managers wanted to predictably know which types of positive outcomes their managerial actions could most effectively and responsibly provide and which negative outcomes or impacts of management could be minimized in cost-effective ways, while sustaining the basic biophysical and cultural/heritage resources they managed.

Third, the leisure scientists and university educators at the workshop desired to better understand the positive and negative consequences of leisure behavior, how the net benefits of such could be enhanced, and how they could work more closely with practitioners to facilitate better management. They were also all committed to creating a more accurate perception and understanding of the social values of leisure (i.e., reposition the image) in the minds of other people outside the leisure professions. They believed strongly that understanding and then articulating the benefits was the best way to do this.

In simple terms, the participants at the workshop recognized the need to go beyond managing just for recreation activity opportunities and opportunities to realize satisfying recreation experiences, and they rejected the idea that recreation was little more than "fun and games." The participants knew that production and use of leisure services were much more beneficial to individuals and to society than just "enjoyment." They understood that recreation

- improves one's physical and mental health
- advances understanding of the cultural history of a city, region, or nation
- promotes understanding and appreciation of natural ecological processes and natural and cultural/historic resources
- builds stronger families
- improves community stability and cohesion
- offers unique opportunities for renewal of the human spirit and development and testing of skills of many types
- affords quiet times for personal introspection and value clarification
- contributes greatly to local, regional, and national economic growth and stability

Nevertheless, the participants were strongly aware there was too little understanding of the tremendous benefits of leisure (including outdoor recreation) by the public and by legislators. It was frustrating to them that other social services (e.g., health, education, welfare, safety, sanitation, police protection), for which the positive outcomes were more widely understood, had much broader public appreciation and support. This frustration existed because leisure professionals had no systematically integrated means for

- comprehensively identifying the positive and negative impacts of outdoor recreation resource management and use
- prioritizing types of positive and negative outcomes that should direct P&R policy and managerial decisions
- managing deliberately to deliver targeted high-priority positive outcomes and prevent negative outcomes
- articulating and promoting those known but not widely understood social benefits of leisure

In particular, participants who represented provider organizations, especially public P&R agencies, needed better guidance for meeting their aforementioned needs:

- to be more accountable for their actions by being able to clearly articulate what they were doing and why they are doing it with the scarce funds they are allocated
- to be cost-effective/efficient/nonwasteful in their use of available funds, especially as fiscal stringency had increased in the public sectors of most countries
- to be responsive to customer/client interests, values, demands and needs, especially because in many countries customers (often known as *stakeholders*) now insist they be actively involved in a collaborative style of management
- to be equitable or fair
- to sustain the basic biophysical and cultural/historic resources and natural processes for which they are responsible

Why the Name of the BOAL Changed Several Times

At the 1991 Benefits Application Workshop and for a short time after, the BOAL was called benefits-based management (BBM), because its focus then was primarily on management. That title was soon abandoned, because administrators of P&R agencies saw that the paradigm was also relevant to leisure policy development. In addition, leisure scientists and educators soon started to use the BOAL to guide research and as a subject for instruction in academic classes. Also, many leisure professionals viewed themselves as having a central role in repositioning the image of leisure. Because the BOAL covered much more than just management, the name was first changed from BBM to the benefits approach to leisure (BAL; Driver & Bruns, 1999). But as the paradigm became better known, some people who did not understand the BAL objected to what they called its focus on benefits and argued inappropriately that it did not require consideration of negative impacts. To prevent those misinterpretations, the name was changed again from BAL to the net benefits approach to leisure (NBAL; Driver, Bruns & Booth, 2001). In retrospect, that change was a mistake for two reasons. First, it is impossible to quantify a net benefit of leisure, because incommensurate units of measurement are used to measure the many different types of benefits of leisure. One cannot compute total benefits by adding so many units of increased family harmony, to other different units of increased mental or physical health, to different measures of still other types of benefits and then attempt to quantify the net benefits by subtracting the total amount of all the measures all the different negative impacts. Put simply, while the concept of net benefits has intuitive and semantic appeal, it is inoperable and cannot be quantified as economists do by measuring all benefits and costs in the same (i.e., commensurate) monetary unit. Second, the term NBAL was not needed simply because the second type of benefit of leisure was adopted by the BOAL along with the definitions of the two other types of benefits given in Chapter 2. That second type of benefit was defined as the maintenance of a desired condition and thereby prevention of an *unwanted condition from occurring*, prevention of an *undesired condition from becoming worse*, or *reduction of the unwanted impacts of an existing undesired condition*. The words in italics clearly require that negative impacts be considered by the BOAL because it adopted that definition. We did not mention it in Chapter 2, but logically the last dimension of the definition just given should have been a part of the first type of benefit, defined in Chapter 2 as a change in a condition or state viewed as more desirable than a previous one. Reducing existing unwanted conditions falls within that definition. We purposefully did not make that inclusion so that the second definition would cover all the negative impacts that need to be considered by the BOAL.

The current name, the BOAL, was adopted for four major reasons. First, the word *outcomes* fits nicely with current requirements, such as the one of the 1993 Government Performance and Results Act that mandates agencies develop and use better measures of their performance in terms of outputs and outcomes. (Unfortunately, the act does not clearly define and distinguish between outputs and outcomes as measures of performance.) Second, the word *outcomes* is increasingly being used by service-providing agencies to distinguish between outputs (generally defined in terms of types of opportunities provided) and the positive and negative impacts or outcomes caused by the production and use of outputs (cf. United Way of America, 1996). For a brief time, some advocates of the BOAL used the simple name outcomes approach to leisure (Driver, 2003), to emphasize its positive and negative outcomes orientation. That was stopped because of the strong desires of users and advocates of the BOAL to retain the word *beneficial* in the title because of its semantic advantages given the ongoing uses of the BOAL to guide leisure policy development, to assist in repositioning the image, and to promote and guide additional research on the benefits of leisure. We reiterate that use of the word *beneficial* in the title of the BOAL should not be interpreted to mean the BOAL does not require comprehensive consideration of negative impacts or outcomes. Third, and perhaps most important, the word *outcomes* in the title denotes clearly that the BOAL is concerned with results. It views the ends of leisure policy and management decisions as the opportunities produced to realize positive outcomes and to avoid and/or reduce negative outcomes.

Fourth, the BOAL requires asking why any leisure service will be produced. That question can only be answered through consideration of likely outcomes. For each of these reasons, the name of the BOAL now includes the words beneficial and outcomes.

Additional Considerations Regarding the Evolution of the BOAL

In closing this section on the evolution of the BOAL, it should be pointed out that the concept of using leisure resources for the benefits they provide is not new. It goes back at least to Aristotle, who viewed the purpose of leisure as promoting contemplation, improved thinking, and excellence of the mind and soul, and thereby, nurturing people, who as better citizens would contribute more to a society. Since then, the basic argument underlying the parks and recreation movement in Great Britain, Canada, the United States, and other countries in the middle to late 1800s and early 1900s was that recreation and parks contribute greatly to human welfare. Among well-known civic leaders who articulated these social merits of parks and recreation were Frederick Law Olmsted (Olmsted & Kimball, 1970) and Jane Addams (1910). While the notion of managing recreation resources to realize benefits is not novel, a systematic, conceptually integrated, scientifically credible, and operational means of promoting and applying that approach did not exist until the BOAL was developed.

It is also pointed out that although the BOAL was developed to guide delivery of leisure services, it has now been extended to other areas of natural resource management, such as management of nature reserves (Driver, 1996) wildlife viewing programs (Manfredo & Driver, 2002), and other natural resource conservation efforts (Driver & Manfredo, 2003).

Lastly, it should be mentioned that people now widely recognize the basic idea of optimizing the realization of positive outcomes to a society and the minimization of negative outcomes should be the focus of all public agencies that provide social services, and not just those that provide leisure services.

Essential Characteristics of the BOAL

This section first describes the four general characteristics of the BOAL paradigm as it relates to all leisure and not just to outdoor recreation. It then describes briefly implementation of the BOAL to guide leisure policy development and management and to guide leisure research, education, marketing, and repositioning the image of the role of leisure in a society.

The BOAL Recognizes the Social Worth of Leisure

A fundamental premise of the BOAL is that when leisure is conceived broadly the value it adds to most societies equals or exceeds the value added by any other social service. Leisure is one of the largest economic sectors of many nations in the world. The BOAL also recognizes that too few people realize these tremendous social and economic contributions. Advocates of the BOAL believe the only way more people can be influenced to modify their inaccurate perceptions about leisure and be brought to understand its social importance (i.e., repositioning the image) is by commitment of all leisure professionals to understand the benefits of leisure and to articulate them clearly. The BOAL serves as a conceptual paradigm for doing this.

The BOAL Raises the Fundamental Question of Why

The fundamental question raised by the BOAL is: *Why* should any leisure service be provided? The answer to that question includes consideration of what has been done in the past. But the BOAL does not accept past actions, in and of themselves, as sufficient basis for continuing those actions. Instead, the why question is answered in terms of positive outcomes to be realized and negative outcomes to be avoided or reduced within the context of what the agency is legislatively mandated to do and what it can do feasibly within the constraints of its budget allocation and other available resources. To answer the why question in this manner, leisure policy makers and managers must understand what benefits should be provided and what unwanted likely negative impacts can be avoided or reduced in magnitude when providing a particular leisure service.

The BOAL Views Leisure Service Delivery Systems as a Production Process

The BOAL views the provision of leisure opportunities as a production process, or more technically as a service delivery system. However, it is easier to understand the concept of production if we refer to recreation *opportunities* instead of services. As explained in Chapter 12, recreation opportunities are commonly considered to be provided, and the word *providing* is used throughout this

text. But from a service delivery perspective, the concept of provision does not explicitly denote the need to understand all the cause-and-effect relationships that go into providing those services. For that reason, the BOAL uses the word *production* of recreation opportunities instead of *provision*. The people who developed and refined the BOAL, and other advocates of it, have learned it is instructive, and actually necessary for instructional purposes, to view the delivery of leisure services as a *recreation opportunity production process* or *system*. The word *system* is important, because the concept of the recreation opportunity production process inherent to the BOAL draws heavily on the basic concepts of general systems theory (GST; Buckley, 1968). Because understanding those basic principles and concepts of GST helps one better understand the BOAL, they will be reviewed here briefly. Analogies will be made to the recreation production system for each, and each will be elaborated in other parts of this chapter. The basic systems model is illustrated in Figure 13.1.

- A system is defined as a whole that functions as a whole because of the interdependencies of its parts. It will be shown that the whole of the leisure delivery system is comprised of many interdependent parts. In addition, most whole recreation opportunity production systems are conceived to be much larger within the BOAL than they are traditionally because of the broad way the BOAL defines stakeholders and associated providers, as explained shortly.

- Systems are hierarchical with many subsystems operating within a larger suprasystem. Campgrounds, picnic areas, playgrounds, parking lots, roads, sanitation systems, and water services are each subsystems of the larger recreation system being managed. Following the discussion in Chapter 11, recreation systems are also hierarchical administratively within a particular leisure service providing organization. That hierarchy ranges downward from the headquarters to the manager of an interpretive program at a recreation area.

- Systems have structure (e.g., campgrounds, land, water, historic sites, fauna and flora) and processes (e.g., interactions of managerial and collaborator

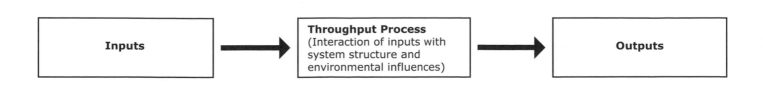

Figure 13.1 Basic systems model

actions to provide recreation opportunities and the use of those opportunities by customers to create satisfying experiences and other benefits for themselves). Most systems have evolved over time (e.g., the evolution of the science-based management systems discussed in Chapter 12), including the BBM system itself.

- Many systems are said to be *teleological,* defined loosely to mean they function to reach an end-state or accomplish a purpose. For example, cardiovascular systems, automobile production systems, stereo systems, and recreation production systems function to serve a particular purpose or purposes, with the targeted endstates of recreation systems being the realization of beneficial outcomes and the avoidance of undesirable outcomes. A fundamental requirement of the BOAL is that these functions must be understood clearly as well as the cause-and-effect relationships among the parts and processes of a recreation opportunity production system.

- Systems interact with their surrounding environments. For example, recreation systems are influenced by the weather and climate and what is happening near their boundaries (e.g., an out-of-control wildfire, unwanted noise entering the system). An important environmental influence on subsystems defined administratively is policy guidelines set at higher levels, as explained in Chapter 11. Other environmental influences are the policies of nearby providers of similar recreation opportunities, including the services they do and do not provide and the fees they charge.

- Normally, when a subsystem is viewed as a separate system, influences from the larger systems (of which the subsystem it is a part) are viewed as part of the surrounding environment of that subsystem. This is necessary for analysis because everything is in some way connected to everything else.

- Systems have positive and negative feedback mechanisms to influence whether the system will maintain its equilibrium (or homeostasis), move from one desirable steady state to another, or lose its desired functioning. Good recreation managers maintain constant flows of information to and from their customers about matters such as their satisfactions and dissatisfactions with the opportunities being provided. For example, maintenance of collaborative partnerships with stakeholders requires both to and from feedback.

- A characteristic important to the conceptualization of the recreation opportunity production process is that

systems are generally viewed to have three major components: inputs, throughputs, and outputs. Relations between these components and interactions with the environment of the system broadly outline basic system processes. The inputs are put into the system, and during the throughput process interact with the system structure and its environmental influences, and outputs are produced.

- Systems can be defined psychologically, physiologically, socially, physically, mechanically, and so on. For purposes of this text the basic system structure through which inputs are made and outputs result will be a physically defined recreation facility, site, or area.

We now discuss in some detail the systems components and processes shown in Figure 13.1 and how the BOAL expands that basic systems model to conceive the recreation opportunity production process. We begin by repeating a simple example from Driver and Bruns (1999) of a farmer managing a corn-producing system. The farmer inputs knowledge (e.g., the proper time to plant), labor (e.g., tilling the soil), seed, fertilizer, and perhaps irrigation water and chemicals to control weeds or the corn borer insect. The physical structure of the system is the cornfield and includes the soil as well as any weed seeds and corn borer larva. The environment inputs rain, wind, and sunshine. Through interaction of the rain or irrigation water, soil, temperature, seed, fertilizer, tilling, and any chemicals used during the throughput process, outputs are produced. Those outputs are corn kernels, corncobs, corn stalks, and weeds, with the weeds showing that not all outputs are desirable. Other undesirable impacts might be some erosion of the soil by wind or water. Similar simple conceptualizations can be made for many other types of systems, including recreation systems.

Figure 13.1 shows why the BOAL prefers use of the word *production* instead of provision. It denotes that managers must know what inputs are needed to produce particular outputs, and they must understand the interactions between the inputs, outputs, system structure, processes, and environmental influences for production to take place. In fact, many advocates of the BOAL believe the word *production* should be applied to all social services (e.g., medical professionals, teachers, ministers), because they produce and nurture opportunities for healthy living, learning, and maintenance and growth of personal spiritual/religious values, respectively—all in interaction with the customers served. Each of these professionals must input something to produce the opportunities mentioned.

It should be noted that the aforementioned example of producing corn as a production process did not include consideration of the beneficial or negative impacts or outcomes that resulted from the management of the cornfield. Nor did Figure 13.1 include *outcomes*. That omission will now be addressed, because the consideration of outcomes is central to the BOAL. In other words, it is not enough to produce recreation opportunities as outputs; one must define why they are being produced in terms of outcomes. If nothing else is remembered about the BOAL, this "why" question it raises must be.

Although previous papers on the BOAL (cf. Driver & Bruns, 1999; Driver, Bruns & Booth, 2001) used a modification of the basic systems model shown in Figure 13.1, that basic model of the BOAL recreation opportunity production process was expanded into its current form (Figure 13.2) for the following four reasons, with the last three being directly relevant to needs of organizations that provide leisure opportunities:

1. Early illustrations and terminology (Driver & Bruns, 1999) did not clearly differentiate between inputs, outputs, and outcomes in the same way that P&R practitioners do. Although technically correct in GST terms, that terminology caused confusion and needed to be changed. The current expanded BOAL has corrected this.

2. The term *output* has traditionally been used by managers of natural resources, including outdoor recreation resources, to refer to the physically defined things they produce from their managerial actions. Examples include numbers of campgrounds or picnic areas installed and/or maintained, acres of critical winter or summer habitat maintained for a species of game, watchable wildlife viewing platforms installed and maintained, huts installed or maintained along a trail, miles or kilometers of trail installed and/or maintained, numbers of interpretative talks given, and so on. Traditionally, these types of outputs were the ones that field-level managers received operating budgets to produce. In addition, annual performance evaluations were based primarily on the degree to which the managers produced the outputs budgeted for and targeted in annual plans of work, which was why those outputs were called *hard targets* by some public agencies. Such an approach

to recreation resource management, which focuses on the just mentioned types of outputs, did consider many negative impacts but tended to give little to no attention to the beneficial outcomes realized. Because earlier representations of the BOAL's recreation opportunity production process model did not use the word *output* consistent with the previous use of that word, the BOAL now defines outputs in terms of its common usage. It also assures an overt focus on outcomes, and it uses the word "outcomes" to denote *only* positive and negative outcomes or consequences.

3. More service-providing organizations now distinguish between the outputs produced and the positive and negative outcomes that result from the production and use of those outputs (cf. United Way of America, 1996). Because the concept of outcomes defined only as positive and negative impacts is increasingly being used and understood by service providers, the previous conceptualization of the BOAL needed to be expanded to be consistent with that movement and to make that explicit in its recreation opportunity production process.

4. The 1993 Federal Government Performance and Results Act and similar mandates in other countries require public P&R agencies to develop, adopt, and use better measures of performance, including better measures of outputs and outcomes. Those mandates use the words *outputs* and *outcomes,* but they fail to define or distinguish between them, as the BOAL now does. One reason the BOAL expanded its recreation opportunity production process was to help public P&R agencies meet these mandates.

Figure 13.2 illustrates the expanded BOAL model, which will now be explained.

The BOAL inputs are dedicated to the production of facilitating outputs. They are called *inputs* because they are put into a physically defined system, such as a recreation facility or area, from outside the boundaries of the system. Inputs by managers, contractors, and associated providers (e.g., concessionaires) include time/labor/effort, professional knowledge and skills, capital investments,

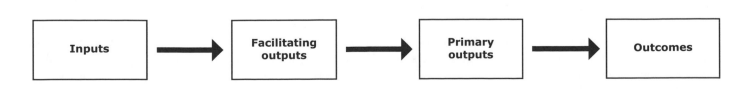

Figure 13.2 Expanded BOAL model of the recreation opportunity production process

information on customer and other stakeholder preferences, social norms and mores, regulations, fees or lack of fees, administrative vehicles, information brochures and maps, materials (e.g., for roads, parking lots, picnic tables, exhibits), sanitation and potable water systems, and so on. The customers and other stakeholders input their expectations, preferences, knowledge, past experiences, numbers of users (who contribute to on-site density), and the pets and other trappings the customers bring, including vehicles, equipment, radios, musical instruments, dance costumes, and electrical generators. The associated providers also input their services, prices, and regulations (e.g., use of easements across private lands). Inputs from the natural physical environment include weather, climate, and any other influences from outside the boundaries of the physical boundaries of the recreation facility, site, or area.

The *facilitating outputs* are any components of the recreation production system being managed that interact synergistically to produce opportunities for benefits to be realized. In the past, the facilitating outputs were always physical in nature and were identical to the outputs toward which most budget allocations and performance evaluations have been (and still are) oriented. Those physically defined facilitating outputs then (and now under the BOAL) included usable roads, parking lots, visitor centers, interpretative trails, bulletin boards, picnic and campground areas, tennis courts, swimming pools, play equipment for children, sanitary and potable water services, and opportunity guides. Also included under the BOAL are the administrative and social, nonphysical components of the recreation production system that influence opportunities to realize benefits. Administrative facilitating outputs include the regulations and the on-site presence of managers (which some customers desire for a sense of security). The social facilitating outputs include the numbers of on-site users, their behaviors, and the things they bring with them (e.g., pets, horses, boom boxes). Anything that facilitates the creation of primary outputs is a facilitating output. The name facilitating outputs is used by the BOAL to emphasize that production of these outputs is not the ends of outdoor recreation resource management but that these facilitating outputs are produced only to facilitate the realization of positive outcomes and prevention of unwanted impacts, which are the actual objectives of management. Unfortunately, other approaches to the management of outdoor recreation resources still commonly view the production of facilitating outputs as the ends of management in and of themselves, which is why traditional performance evaluations of managers tend to consider them alone.

The *primary outputs* comprise the opportunities created to provide benefits and/or to reduce negative impacts. Included are the recreation opportunities made available and all other opportunities to realize personal, economic, social, and environmental benefits. Most significant are the recreation opportunities produced for on-site and off-site customers to realize benefits. Those opportunities are produced by the facilitating outputs interacting with physical, social, and administrative components of the recreation system being managed. As said, administrative rules and regulations, the on-site presence of managers, and the numbers and behaviors of other users all influence the types of recreation opportunities produced.

Experience has shown that the benefits to on-site users of the recreation opportunities produced are relatively easy to visualize and attend to managerially once the BOAL is understood. Less so are the opportunities for benefits that accrue to

- local communities (e.g., contributions to host/gateway communities local economic stability, growth realized by host/gateway communities from tourism)
- remote off-site users (e.g., appreciative and stewardship benefits)
- society in general (e.g., reduced health care costs to society, reduced needs for general tax revenues to help cover those costs) that result from use of the recreation opportunities (i.e., primary outputs)

While off-site and on-site users realize most of the benefits, significant benefits also accrue that are not directly related to use of the recreation opportunities produced. Such "nonuse" benefits include

- benefits realized by employees of the providing organization (and its contractors) to gain an income as salary
- local economic benefits that result from the expenditures of that income
- improvements of the natural and natural/heritage resources related to producing the recreation opportunities for the on-site and off-site users

In sum, the primary outputs (i.e., benefit opportunities) include all opportunities to realize benefits and reduce negative impacts both on-site and off.

Under the BOAL, the word *outcomes* refers only to positive and negative impacts or consequences. To reiterate, the primary outputs, like the facilitating outputs, are not the ends of management; the ends are the positive and avoided or reduced negative outcomes that result from management and use of recreation resources. Put simply, the BOAL insists on a distinction between facilitating outputs, primary outputs, and outcomes.

We close this discussion of the BOAL's concept of the recreation opportunity production process by emphasizing that the word *production* is applied not only to the creation of facilitating and primary outputs but also to the production of positive outcomes. However it must be understood that while some positive and negative outcomes result directly from managerial actions and don't require use of the recreation opportunities produced, most of the positive and negative outcomes result from the use of the recreation opportunities by on-site and off-site customers. The critical point to understand is that the managers and associated providers do not produce most of the outcomes. Instead, the customers use the opportunities to produce satisfying experiences and other benefits for themselves and for other people who receive spin-off benefits. This point is very important, because some authors (e.g., More, 2002) erroneously suggested the BOAL advocates "engineering of experiences production." In fact, the BOAL only "engineers" recreation opportunities, not experiences, and does so by requiring that providers collaborate with stakeholders and associated providers to decide what types of recreation opportunities should be produced. Thus, under the BOAL, the customers engineer or produce the experiences for themselves through the ways they use the recreation opportunities provided. Such production of experiences by customers is a part of the total recreation production process, but the term *recreation opportunity production process* is purposely used by the BOAL to avoid past misinterpretations that the managers produce the benefits for the customers or that the BOAL endorses a mechanistic or technocratic approach to management. This important point will become clearer in the next section on collaborating with stakeholders and associated providers. Another important point is that the customers can significantly influence the nature of the primary outputs, or recreation opportunities, by the things they bring to the area, the number of customers present, their on-site behaviors, and the ongoing interactions of what they are doing and are motivated to do next based on what they have just experienced (i.e., the influence of the social component of the recreation setting as explained in the description of the ROS system in Chapter 12). Thus, on-site customers not only use recreation opportunities to produce benefits but also affect the recreation opportunity production process significantly for themselves and for others; they represent a part of the structure of the recreation production system described earlier. As such, the users don't just use the recreation opportunities provided, they mold them. This is particularly true in dispersed outdoor recreation areas where few developments for recreation are provided.

In review, the expanded recreation opportunity production process (or leisure services delivery model) inherent and central to the BOAL requires that leisure policy makers and managers be able to answer not only the question why but also what, how, for whom, in what amount, and when

the opportunities will be delivered. They must also understand the cause-and-effect relationships that exist within the expanded model of the recreation opportunity production process shown in Figure 13.2 (p. 193). To reiterate, that model of production makes those cause-and-effect relationships explicit and not implicit as they are under the concept of providing opportunities. This seems only reasonable and appropriate. Professionals who deliver medical, educational, welfare assistance, communication, transportation, and other social services must ask and answer the same questions. Before leisure professionals can attain the same degree of public recognition of the nature and importance of what they provide, they must stand ready and able to answer the same questions and to clearly articulate the reasons for their answers. That is an essential part of what professionalism and accountability is all about.

The BOAL Requires Establishing and Maintaining Collaborative Partnerships

In addition to recognizing the social worth of leisure, asking the why question that focuses on beneficial and unwanted outcomes from policy and managerial decisions, and viewing the delivery of leisure services as a production process or system, there are two other defining characteristic of the BOAL:

1. It requires building and maintaining ongoing collaborative partnerships with all affecting and affected stakeholders

2. It recognizes the important roles of associated providers who significantly influence the amount and quality of outdoor recreation opportunities that can be provided. (see Figure 6.1, p. 84)

Stakeholders

The stakeholders are the best source of information about the primary outputs (i.e., recreation opportunities) and positive and negative impacts toward which leisure policy and managerial decisions should be directed. For these reasons the BOAL requires that decisions about which outcomes will be targeted *must* be made through collaborative efforts between those stakeholders and the responsible providing organization, especially public P&R agencies. Put simply, the targeted outcomes cannot be chosen by provider personnel acting independently and technocratically. This is critical to remember, because the BOAL rejects any technocratic approach to the delivery of recreation opportunities, especially by public agencies. Under a technocratic approach, trained professionals behave as if they technically know what all customer values and preferences are and what managerial decisions are the right ones to make. So, with these all-knowing attitudes, they fail to solicit information from the stakeholders affected by their decisions. The BOAL, and the authors of this text, strongly disagree with this technocratic approach. We believe that recent movement toward establishing and maintaining collaborative partnerships with relevant stakeholders is the greatest advance in outdoor recreation resource management we have observed during our professional careers. For that reason we repeat (from Chapter 12) part of the statement made by Jack Ward Thomas (1996, p. xxiv), when he was Chief of the USFS, regarding natural resource management decisions: "…each reflects a set of 'value mixes,' including judgments about what is fair for future [and current] generations. Thus, these decisions are in the realm of ethics whether we recognize it or not." Those sentiments are also shared and reflected by Wondolleck (1996, p. 257), whose research concentrated on establishing collaborative partnerships. She wrote, "…there is simply no [one]…right answer that systematic technical analysis will uncover."

Put simply, while the BOAL recognizes the need for technical expertise and is based on professional understanding of science-based knowledge, it rejects a technocratic approach and *requires* active and ongoing involvement of affecting and affected stakeholders. For this reason, the BOAL adopts a much broader than normal definition of the word *stakeholder* to include any person or group that affects or is affected by (to any managerially relevant degree) the recreation opportunities being produced. Such stakeholders include on-site customers who directly receive amenity-related benefits by using the recreation opportunities, off-site customers who benefit from just knowing those resources are being protected, residents of local host/gateway communities, local landowners, members of environmental and other voluntary citizen supported organizations, and other relevant individuals and groups.

Although leisure professionals give much attention to the users and visitors who actually use the leisure services and opportunities provided, they tend not to think sufficiently about the nonusers, who for various reasons have left the market or who might become active users if certain conditions were met. Although these are difficult issues to address, the BOAL urges that leisure policy makers and managers be sensitive to the recreation-related needs and preferences of these current nonusers. This is particularly true for policy makers, planners, and managers working in the public sector.

More relevant customers that receive little attention are the off-site users who benefit from the management of recreation resources, but do not visit the recreation facilities, sites, or areas being managed. The BOAL requires that these off-site users be considered in leisure policy making and managerial decisions because of the leisure-related benefits they receive. They are important stakeholders and customers as well. There are two types of such off-site users. One type comprises those people who live near the recreation resources being managed, such as in local host/ gateway communities, or just down the street from a park in a city, but are not currently on-site users. The other type of off-site users are those who live much more remotely from the recreation resources being managed, but still realize stewardship and other appreciative benefits from learning about the protection and management of those resources from television, movies, books, other publications, and other media. Both types of off-site users pay tax dollars to support the management and protection of public P&R resources. As such, they are just as much the owners of those public resources as the on-site uses are.

Surveys show members of local gateway/host communities realize both beneficial and negative impacts from the management and use of nearby recreation and related amenity resources. Positively, such management and pro-

Stakeholder groups, like this volunteer cross country ski club in New Mexico, are important partners to involve in implementing the beneficial outcomes approach to leisure (BOAL).

Adjacent private landowners are too frequently overlooked when attempting to create collaborative partnerships with stakeholders.

tection helps maintain a local sense of place and contributes otherwise to local residents' overall perceived quality of life and all that entails (cf. Allen, 1991; Campbell, 1981; Marans & Mohai, 1991). Tourism also contributes significantly to the economic stability and growth of many local communities, which benefit both the on-site and off-site users residing there.

Members of local communities have also expressed concerns about how nearby public recreation/tourism developments and the associated influx of new visitors and residents and the ensuing community growth have negatively impacted local communities. Such changes can cause increased traffic congestion, increased crime, reduced neighborhood safety, and related problems. In some areas, local communities have deteriorated, as have adjoining natural resource landscapes, because of poorly and insensitively planned large-scale, unsightly, or otherwise incongruent tourism-related structures and uses. There has also been weakened community capability to protect local property rights and to maintain distinctive main streets and residential architecture, which has eroded the character, quality, and sense of place of many small-town rural landscapes. These negative impacts of development and use of nearby recreation resources has frequently complicated the task of nurturing or maintaining good relationships between the communities, the managers, and the users of those resources.

Several regional household surveys and at least one national study have established that the economic willingness of these off-site users to pay taxes for responsible public land management is sizable and exceeds by several orders of magnitude the on-site users' willingness to pay for such management (Loomis & Walsh, 1997, pp. 366–367). Furthermore, the number of off-site users equals or exceeds the number of on-site users. Basic principles of consumer economics state that if people have a willingness to pay, or expend their scarce personal resources, they must be receiving some type of utility or benefit. Given the large number of such off-site users and their expressed willingness to pay, it is reasonable to believe that the total benefits realized by these off-site customers probably exceed the total benefits realized by the relatively much smaller number of on-site users, to whom the greatest policy and managerial attention is usually given. The BOAL, in its quest for equity, requires that responsive public recreation policy makers and managers not forget that these off-site customers are every bit as much owners of public land as are the on-site users. Put simply, they are relevant (albeit too frequently forgotten) stakeholders, who should be involved in helping answer the basic why question. In addition, greater consideration of, and involvement by, these off-site users could play an important role in repositioning the image of leisure. In a nutshell, the

BOAL views customers as sovereign, and close collaboration with all managerially relevant stakeholders is required to protect and appreciate that sovereignty.

Associated Providers

The BOAL not only requires a broader than normal definition of "stakeholder" to include the off-site users but also expands the traditional concept of "service provider" beyond that of the providing organization responsible for managing the resources on which recreation opportunities are provided. It does this because of the influences associated providers have on the types, amounts, and quality of the total package of leisure services made available. Associated providers include the following:

- businesses that provide medical, lodging, laundry, and dry-cleaning services
- businesses that sell groceries
- business that sell hunting and fishing licenses
- automotive service stations
- tourist organizations that provide information, outfitters and guides, concessionaires, and tour operators
- local private landowners
- providers of leisure services that offer complementary, supplemental, and even competing leisure services
- public agencies, such as local sheriff and police departments, that frequently assist in law enforcement at recreation facilities and areas
- local public and private organizations that provide services such as electric power

Without the assistance of these associated providers, most recreation opportunities would have an altogether different character than those now being produced, and many

Associated providers like guides and outfitters are very important stakeholders.

opportunities would not exist at all. This is particularly true of outdoor recreation opportunities, which depend highly on local host/gateway communities.

All recreation providers that affect the character or availability of opportunities produced must be involved collaboratively, simply because of their profound influence. In addition, it is important to remember that the total recreation experiences realized by on-site users are multiphasic, encompassing trip planning, travel to the site, on-site engagements, travel back, and recollection (Clawson & Knetsch, 1966, pp. 33–36). Associated providers frequently affect several of these phases more than the responsible providing organization does. Furthermore, associated providers play an important role in communicating various messages about recreation area management and protection. They have an impact on the images the customers have about the providing organization, influence customer expectations and preferences, and promote a positive understanding of the social importance of outdoor recreation. In short, the BOAL recognizes the impossibility of attempting to produce opportunities for desired outcomes and minimizing undesired impacts without the collaboration of associated providers and acknowledges the many advantages of collaboration.

Summary of the BOAL's Requirement for Collaboration

Given that leisure policy development and management under the BOAL starts with answering the fundamental question, "Why should any leisure service be provided?" information from relevant stakeholders and associated providers is not only necessary, but *essential*. How to establish such collaboration is described in Chapter 17.

Within the context of general systems theory, stakeholders and associated providers each represent an integral part of the whole recreation system being managed because each affects the production of the recreation opportunities. That is why the boundaries of the entire leisure service delivery system extends considerably beyond the physical boundaries of the recreation facility, site or area being managed. Lastly, the foregoing discussion clarifies why the BOAL prefers use of the words *provider actions* instead of *managerial actions* and use of the word *customer* instead of *visitor* or *user*. The word *customer* is now widely applied to refer to the users of social services (United Way of America, 1996).

In concluding this section on the characteristics of the BOAL, it must be emphasized that the BOAL is sufficiently credible scientifically as a paradigm. It integrates results of research on leisure behavior, benefits of leisure, public policy development, modern management science, organizational psychology, personal choice theory, and methods for creating and maintaining collaborative part-

nerships with affected stakeholders. If the BOAL did not have a high level of scientific credibility, it justifiably would be suspect and would not have received wide and growing acceptance during the past decade of its development and refinement.

In a nutshell, the essential characteristics of the BOAL are that it requires

- professional understanding of the many benefits of leisure explained in Chapter 2
- collaboration with relevant stakeholders and associated providers
- understanding of the cause-and-effect relationships within the BOAL recreation opportunity production process shown in Figure 13.2 (p. 193)
- understanding of the likely positive and negative outcomes/impacts associated with the delivery of each leisure service provided
- opportunities for benefits and unwanted negative outcomes to be addressed overtly
- willingness and ability to work with leisure scientists to stay current on the latest relevant knowledge in the unusually rapidly advancing leisure professions (cf. Driver, 1999b)

Applying the BOAL Paradigm

As pointed out earlier, the earliest focus of the BOAL was on management, and the resulting management system was called benefits-based management (BBM). This soon expanded to cover leisure policy development, planning, management, research, education, marketing of leisure services, and repositioning the image of leisure. Each of these current applications of the BOAL will be reviewed briefly. Management applications will be given the most attention, because that has been the widest use of the BOAL so far. Also, that focus should help one better understand the broader BOAL paradigm.

Outdoor Recreation Policy Development Within the BOAL

Chapter 11 defined policies as guidelines that establish directions within which managerial and administrative actions must be taken to meet those policy mandates. As such, policies set the goals to be accomplished by an organization. That chapter also pointed out that different organizations that provide outdoor recreation opportunities have different goals. Therefore, each provider must evaluate what constitutes beneficial and negative outcomes in terms of its goals. A private-sector provider will tend to look at economic profits and losses, long-term growth, and maintenance of a favorable proportion of market share. A nonprofit provider will pursue policies oriented to their particular goals, as described in Chapter 8. In contrast, public P&R agencies define their organizational goals differently, because they exist to promote the general welfare. But each of these three types of providers use the same recreation opportunity production process inherent to the BOAL as shown in Figure 13.2 (p. 193). So in policy development, each must start by defining, at least generally, the types of positive outcomes they want to see realized by managerial actions and unwanted impacts or outcomes to be reduced or avoided. Then each must be cognizant of the inputs needed and their costs. Each needs to understand the preferences of the likely users of the recreation opportunities they provide. Thus, they need to have a customer orientation and involve their customers at least to some degree in their policy-developing processes.

Applying the BOAL by Implementing BBM on Outdoor Recreation Resources

Characteristics of BBM

As mentioned in Chapter 12, benefits-based management (BBM) builds on but does not replace activity-based management (ABM) or experience-based management (EBM). However, that chapter only mentioned a few of characteristics of BBM and did not outline all of them as it did for ABM and EBM. Those full characteristics of BBM are outlined here to distinguish it from and contrast it with ABM and EBM:

- BBM could not be developed as a science-based management system to supplement ABM and EBM before sufficient research was done on the benefits of leisure. (See Chapter 2 for a summary of the history of that research.)
- Whereas EBM considers only psychological experiences, BBM considers all types of experiences— physiological and psychological.
- BBM considers all types of benefits, including those to individuals, to groups of individuals (e.g., family, community, society at-large), and to the natural and cultural/heritage resources (i.e., sustainable development and use). Those benefits include personal (i.e., psychological and psychophysiological), social/cultural, environmental, and economic ones, as shown in Table 2.2 (p. 29).
- BBM considers benefits to both on-site and off-site users/customers. Although some recent applications of EBM, especially to watchable wildlife programs (Manfredo, 2002), have included consideration of the types of satisfying experiences realized by off-site users, most of the applications of EBM have focused on the on-site users alone.
- BBM considers not only immediate benefits but also long-term benefits.
- BBM makes the benefits of leisure explicit, not implicit.
- BBM adopts the recreation opportunity production process of the BOAL shown in Figure 13.2 (p. 193) and requires professional understanding of the cause-and-effect relationships among the components of that model.
- BBM provides a better basis than EBM for considering the quality of recreation opportunities because it requires a more explicit definition of the products being demanded and produced from the recreation opportunity production function. The cause-and-effect relationships that must be understood include the relationships that define the quality of the recreation opportunities produced.
- BBM provides information on benefits to justify programs in the policy arena and to help reposition the image of leisure, which ABM does not do and EBM does to a much more limited degree.
- BBM requires that recreation professionals understand both the positive and negative impacts of recreation resource management and use.
- Under BBM, management objectives are written that overtly and explicitly specify the types of opportunities for positive outcomes that will be provided, the negative impacts that will be minimized, and where and when the outcomes will be realized and in what amounts. Then, management prescriptions, guidelines, and standards are written to assure delivery of those targeted outcome opportunities.
- The why question is central to BBM, and it is much more complex than the why question raised by EBM because of the comprehensive coverage by BBM of benefits other than the realization of satisfying experiences. It assumes that if the why question cannot be answered adequately by outdoor recreation resource planners and managers, they are not performing as professionally as they should be.
- BBM requires the providing organization, especially public-sector agencies, to collaborate with all managerially relevant affecting and affected stakeholders and associated providers. As such, it requires information from the customers served about the types of benefit opportunities they desire to be provided and the negative outcomes they want reduced or prevented.

Each of the characteristics of BBM should be understandable given the foregoing description of the characteristics of the BOAL. A few of the features of BBM will be elaborated briefly, because they have particular significance relevant to management and were not elaborated previously for the broader BOAL paradigm.

A fundamental requirement of BBM as implemented within the BOAL paradigm is that once the targeted outcomes have been determined, clear and explicit management objectives must be written for each type of targeted outcome. Those management objectives must specify what each targeted outcome is and where, when, in what amount, and for whom the opportunities to realize that outcome will be delivered. Generally, these management objectives are geared to a specific site, facility, or area, but some might be much broader, even national, in scope. Then, for each such management objective, a set of *intended management actions* (frequently called *management prescriptions*) must be written to assure the management objective will be met. This means the Figure 13.2 inputs must be related to facilitating outputs, primary outputs, and targeted outcomes by prescribed managerial actions and by the customers' expected use of the primary outputs to create benefits for themselves. In addition, hopefully quantitative but certainly objective standards must be developed to assure, during implementation of the monitoring plan, the management prescriptions and thus the management objectives have been met. In flow diagram terms, it is easier to understand these cause-and-effect relationships if one views planning of a leisure service delivery system as going from the right to the left side of the recreation opportunity production process shown in Figure 13.2. The starting point is, therefore, decisions about what beneficial outcomes will be targeted and which negative outcomes will be prevented/reduced in impact. Then, decisions need to be made about what primary outputs, facilitating outputs, and inputs are needed to achieve the targeted outcome goals. From a management plan implementation perspective, one goes from left to right—from inputs to facilitating outputs and primary outputs to targeted outcomes. Put simply, the desired outcomes determine what will be done and why.

Under BBM, managerial performance must be evaluated primarily in terms of the positive outcomes facilitated and the negative outcomes prevented. This sharply contrasts with conventional approaches of evaluating performance, especially within public sector park and recreation agencies. In the past (and continuing in many instances today) performance has been (and still is) evaluated primarily in terms of numbers and types of facilitating outputs produced and numbers of users/visitors, but not in terms of the net benefits realized. This emphasis on facilitating outputs instead of on outcomes occurs for three reasons:

1. Providers of outdoor recreation opportunities do not understand the overriding BOAL paradigm and the changes in one's thinking or mindset required by it.

2. Production of the facilitating outputs comprise the largest part of the costs of producing outdoor recreation opportunities.

3. Headquarters of practically all public agencies require that subunits report their performance primarily in terms of the types and numbers of facilitating outputs (e.g., campsites) produced or maintained.

The obvious problem from the perspective of BBM and the BOAL is that such reporting in the past, and too frequently today, does not report what outcomes will be facilitated by production of those facilitating outputs and why. To reiterate, the BOAL views management of inputs and the production of facilitating outputs only as necessary means to the production of primary outputs (i.e., opportunities for benefits) necessary for the attainment of the explicitly defined and clearly articulated ends of capturing the targeted beneficial outcomes and preventing unwanted impacts/outcomes. Notice that the words *outcomes* and *impacts* are being used synonymously.

Steps for Implementing BBM

Space constraints prevent giving a detailed description of how to implement BBM. Because those steps have not been published in readily available publications, the most critical considerations for successfully implementing the BBM are outlined here. This discussion draws heavily from a recent report of the New Zealand Department of Conservation (2002).

Obtain supervisor's approval. Any field-level planner or manager who wants to implement BBM should have the approval of that approach by his or her immediate supervisor. It is desirable that BBM be endorsed by all levels of the agency for it to be effective. A staff member working in isolation will most probably encounter difficulty in implementing BBM.

Establish the planning team. The planning team is the group of people who develops a recommended management plan for a particular outdoor recreation facility, site, or area. It normally will be comprised of representatives of the providing organization, who will represent different relevant disciplines. Under the BOAL, it is critical that relevant stakeholders and associated providers be involved in all phases of the management planning and plan implementation process that utilizes BBM. Stakeholders and associated providers must be members of the planning team or at least regularly consult with it.

Understand BBM. All participants in the management planning and plan implementation process must understand BBM and the overriding paradigm of the BOAL.

Understand responsibilities and constraints. The roles and responsibilities identified as appropriate (and not appropriate) for the field unit that is taking the lead to implement BBM must be understood clearly to establish boundaries on what can and cannot be done. These roles and responsibilities are established by the legislation or other directives that govern the operations of the providing organization. The resources available to that organization to practice BBM must also be clearly understood. Similarly, the bounds of actions that the collaborating stakeholders and associated providers can reasonably take must be understood. These constraints, or likely boundaries on feasible and legal actions that can possibly be taken, will determine what positive outcomes can be targeted for realization and what negative outcomes the management plan will try to avoid. They will also help to define those outcomes that should receive the most attention. Stakeholders and associated providers need to understand clearly the constraints on the agency that prevent it from meeting everyone's preferences fully.

Understand opposition. Any opposition to using BBM within or outside the agency or by associated providers must be understood and considered as to its degree of impact before much work on implementing BBM is done.

Brainstorm current situation. A brainstorming exercise should take place in which members of the planning team identify and list the types of positive and negative outcomes or impacts currently being created by managerial actions and used by customers. This exercise should involve the collaborating stakeholders and associated providers. Then, each of these impacts should be defined as to what the impact was, its likely magnitude, where it occurred, and who or what was impacted. This brainstorming has proven to be very effective in helping all people involved understand more fully the nature and scope of BBM and the BOAL. The result of this brainstorming exercise is a definition of the current condition, which must be understood before desired future biophysical and social conditions can be visualized.

Brainstorm desired future conditions. A second brainstorming session of the planning team should take place to start preliminary visualizations of desired future biophysical and social conditions for the planning area. The purposes are

1. to identify what possible positive outcomes might feasibly be provided, and what negative ones might be avoided, given available agency and associated provider policies and resources

2. to begin to crystallize an image of what the desired overall composition, characteristics, and nature of the management unit, and its nearby landscapes and communities, will be like in the near future

3. to obtain information that will guide the demand studies that will be made in the next step

It is vital that the stakeholders and relevant associated providers be involved in this visualization process. Of course, professional judgment is important in brainstorming and listing the feasible outcomes that might be provided.

Define management zones and recreation niches. Most study/planning areas have distinctive subparts that represent niches for specific or closely related types of recreation activities and experiences. They might be water recreation related niches, historic/heritage sites, unusual special geological features, places with special types of fauna or flora, large remote areas, or places for cycling and group activities (e.g., picnicking, games, sports). These niches must be visualized to help facilitate dividing the planning area into logical subunits or management zones.

List and define possible outcomes. Both positive and negative outcomes/impacts must be defined explicitly and in terms of their likely magnitudes, and where and when the impacts will likely occur and on whom. Then, the planning team must recognize some outcomes that might be targeted might have impacts across jurisdictional (e.g., country, state, provincial) boundaries and that some are national in scale (e.g., providing opportunities for physical exercise to maintain and to improve people's health). It has been found useful in past applications of BBM that, when the possible and feasible outcomes are being brainstormed, a broad list of outcomes first be considered with each outcome then screened for relevancy and feasibility. Chapter 2 provides a list of possible positive/beneficial outcomes, as does *The Benefits Catalogue* (Canadian Parks/Recreation Association, 1997). This comprehensive checklist procedure helps to prevent the omission of relevant outcomes and helps to guide the demand studies that must be undertaken. Contrary to uninformed published opinion (e.g., More, 2002), those checklists are to be used only to trigger ideas about possible and feasible beneficial outcomes and not to dictate what beneficial outcomes should be targeted in every situation. The managers and the collaborating stakeholders and associated providers make that determination, not a checklist.

Analyze demands. Demand studies must be conducted to determine which types of positive outcomes are most desired and which types of negative outcomes are most important to avoid. The extent of these studies will vary from one application of BBM to another and might include systematic representative sampling of households, on-site user surveys, consultations with major user groups, use of focus groups, or special scientific studies of particular types of demands. Use should also be made of available secondary sources of data, such as economic, social, and environmental impact assessments. The planning team must recognize that some of the social outcomes that might be targeted apply across the entire agency, and some will be area or site specific.

Ranking and selecting outcomes. Some vision of what is desirable and possible should now be crystallized, and then more serious consideration must be given to the feasibility of what can be undertaken. This means the planning team must develop criteria for ranking the outcomes in terms of their priority and then select outcomes on which the plan will focus. This process will require use of the information acquired in the two previous steps, especially on demand and supply, and also include the best-available information about what the off-site customers desire. Here, the decision might be made to focus attention primarily on a subset of outcomes most critical to the agency's goals and responsibilities and in highest demand, such as those that will contribute most to realization of the desired future conditions. Much past experience in implementing BBM has shown there is a learning curve, and it is generally best for an agency to apply BBM incrementally and not try to be too comprehensive the first several times the approach is used. Thus, we recommend that at first the focus be on a few key outcomes to gain experience with implementing the approach.

Develop a preliminary plan. A preliminary plan to be implemented must now be prepared. That planning process should follow the normal approach in which the likely consequences of each proposed action must be evaluated, perhaps using social, economic, and environmental impact assessments and even special science-based studies that focus on particular issues.

Develop final plan. The plan to be implemented should now be prepared. This must include clear management objectives, setting prescriptions, and implementing actions (e.g., actions addressing management; marketing; monitoring/evaluation including standards, methods, and schedules). These statements must be written for each outcome targeted, or for each set of similar targeted outcomes. Here BBM differs considerably from earlier approaches to planning recreation and park resources. Too commonly, management objectives are vague and generally direct management actions toward what has been done in the past. In addition, too little attention is typically given to specifying clearly what settings are needed to provide particular recreation opportunities. Also, those outdoor recreation opportunities are commonly defined only as activity opportunities with little or no attention given to the types of satisfying experiences and other benefits that can be realized from those activities. In contrast, BBM does not accept that what has been done in the past should necessarily continue to be done. More importantly, under BBM, a set of clear management objectives must be written to explicitly define where, when, in what amount,

and for whom each type of "outcome opportunity" will be provided. Then, BBM requires the sometimes difficult task of clearly specifying the desired characteristics/features of the on-site settings, of the local host/gateway communities, and of the facilities and other resources of the associated providers necessary for the targeted outcomes to be delivered. Those setting prescriptions must be very precise and detailed for each management objective (or targeted outcome), and they must use information about the preferences of the collaborating stakeholders who represent the potential customers who will use the opportunities created in those settings. Those prescriptions for the on-site settings must consider the desired characteristics of the biophysical, social, and managerial settings that interact to create the overall on-site recreation setting. Once these setting prescriptions have been developed, explicit management actions (frequently called *management prescriptions*) must be developed and specified to show what actions must be taken to assure the settings will be managed as prescribed. These actions are needed to assure that the management objectives will be met. Lastly, sets of objective and quantifiable standards must be developed for each management prescription to guide plan implementation and to determine, during monitoring, if the management actions are being implemented properly so the management objectives will be met. Developing and clearly specifying these management objectives, setting prescriptions, management prescriptions, and implementing actions and standards is not an easy task, but they represent the most important parts of implementing BBM because they demonstrate professional understanding of what needs to be done as well as understanding of the cause-and-effect relations inherent to the recreation opportunity production process. In addition, implementing that process opens, or "sunlights" what is happening, so the stakeholders, associated providers, and most importantly the customers being served know what to expect. Also, following that process helps to ensure managerial responsiveness, accountability, and efficiency (or cost-effectiveness). It should be noted that past experience has shown some managers do not want to follow a process that requires them be explicit about their intentions because it pins them down—something BBM deliberately aims to achieve. Hopefully, more professional managers will replace them.

Prepare marketing plan. A marketing plan should be included as part of the management plan. It should identify how, where, in what amounts, and what types of activity and outcome opportunities will be made available. The primary purpose of the marketing plan is to inform the customers about the types and locations of the benefit opportunities being made available, as well as the negative impacts that management is attempting to avoid. It is not intended to overpromote what the agency is doing, but to provide useful information to customers. Again, it is important the stakeholders and relevant associated providers be actively involved in developing this marketing plan.

Prepare monitoring plan. The management plan should include a monitoring plan with detailed instructions and guidelines for monitoring and evaluating plan implementation. During plan implementation, monitoring and evaluation activities should be documented in writing, as should any corrective actions needed and taken.

Public review and revision. Once the plan has been prepared, it should receive wide public review and be revised as needed before being accepted as the plan that will be implemented.

Two Uses of BBM

BBM is currently being used in two slightly different ways:

1. to assure an array of benefit opportunities are being provided by a particular provider of recreation opportunities, with different organizations deciding how wide that array should be, given their own resources and responsibilities

2. to target and facilitate the realization of one or more, but only a few, specific types of benefits desired, such as to promote physical fitness, to increase understanding of the natural environment, or to increase understanding and appreciation of a particular cultural/heritage site or event

One example of this second type of use of the BBM is to prevent or resolve the social problems associated with at-risk youth, defined as young people who

- have problems with accepting social authority
- are delinquent
- abuse substances such as alcohol or other drugs
- are doing poorly in school
- have poor patterns of social interaction
- display social alienation or related issues

In the United States, about 70% of municipal P&R departments have programs targeted to at-risk youth, and they attempt to prevent those youth from becoming greater problems to themselves and/or to society. In most of these applications, public P&R agencies are cooperating closely with the justice, education, public welfare, and other relevant public agencies through recreation programming as an intervention strategy to help targeted youth (Hurtes & Allen, 2001; Witt & Crompton, 1996, 2002). It should also be mentioned that the two uses of BBM are sometimes combined so an array of benefit opportunities is targeted, of which particular subsets are emphasized. This might happen when a provider has a special "niche" for providing

certain benefit opportunities and/or because some types of benefits are deemed more important than are others.

Lastly on uses of BBM, we should raise the difficult but very important question of to what degree a public P&R agency should purposefully extend its reach beyond its normal interpretation of its administrative jurisdictions and responsibilities to consider how the leisure services it provides can better serve the general welfare in particular ways. For example, should particular social benefits of leisure be extolled more in political arenas? Examples could include the significant roles of leisure in

- promoting and maintaining physical and mental health and thereby reducing the rapidly rising cost of health care
- reducing social alienation and antisocial behaviors, such as crime, and the high social costs associated with such behaviors
- promoting a nonradical environmental ethic related to sustainable development and management of a nation's natural resources
- increasing understanding of the history of local, regional, and national places and events, which nurtures and maintains cultural mores/values; pride in communites, regions, and nations; and thereby promotes better citizenship

Certainly each of these social benefits of leisure now gets some attention, but each could, and perhaps should be given a lot more attention by P&R providers.

Other Applications of the BOAL

We have given an overview of how to apply the BOAL to leisure policy development and management via BBM. But as mentioned, the other uses of the BOAL are to guide leisure research, education, and marketing, and to reposition the image, for which the recreation opportunity production process is not as directly relevant as it is for policy development and management. That process is somewhat useful in helping to reposition the image of leisure because understanding it demonstrates an understanding not only of the nature and scope of the benefits of leisure described in Chapter 2 but also of what is involved in order for a society to gain those benefits.

As to the use of the BOAL in leisure education and research, it provides a model for teaching about leisure policy development and management, such as the critical importance of involving stakeholders and associated providers, and it helps to alert leisure scientists about the "holes" in our knowledge that need to be filled. It is also useful in explaining the need to reposition the image of leisure. Regarding marketing, the BOAL promotes marketing of leisure opportunities not only in terms of activity opportunities but also in terms of benefits opportunities, including experience opportunities, which goes well beyond the conventional approach that emphasizes places and activities.

Advantages of the BOAL

The BOAL offers many advantages over traditional approaches. The most important ones follow. (This section draws from Driver and Bruns [1999], which lists the benefits of the BOAL.)

Promotes greater public understanding and appreciation of the social significance of recreation. Chapter 2 argued that although leisure is one of the most important economic sectors and the most beneficial social service, it is not publicly recognized as such. A major reason for this paradox is that professionals in all the subdisciplines of leisure have not successfully or effectively articulated the social importance of leisure. One of the purposes of the BOAL is to provide a framework for promoting more widespread understanding of the important contributions of parks and recreation to improving humans' welfare. That knowledge helps to correct (i.e., reposition) the too frequent misperception that recreation is trivial and helps advance greater recognition of the real contributions of recreation to human happiness and productivity. Widespread understanding of the benefits of recreation will increase public support for recreation. Such support is necessary to any profession that delivers a social service that is highly dependent on public funding. In addition, this increased public understanding will facilitate more effective working relationships not only among the customers served and recreation professionals but also between leisure and other professionals.

Justifies allocations of public funds to parks and recreation in the policy arena. Policy makers need to compare the benefits and costs of alternative uses of public resources. These comparisons, which include but go beyond economic measures of benefits, have grown in importance as demands on public resources have increased and broadened in the face of increasingly stringent agency budgets. As a consequence, public officials, including those in P&R agencies, are being held more accountable. They must explain more explicitly how the public goods and services they provide relate to specific social needs, why those goods and services are being provided, and the likely desirable and undesirable impacts of production and use of those goods and services. The BOAL objectively defines those social needs and orients delivery of recreation services explicitly to them. As such, it makes policy decisions less subjective and public policy makers more responsive, accountable, and efficient.

Helps planners and managers to develop clearer management objectives. Once public policy decisions have allocated public resources to a particular type of recreation, information on benefits improves the ability of recreation planners and managers to define clear management objectives and prescriptions and then to establish more explicit standards and guidelines for meeting those objectives. Provision of exercise trails, opportunities for challenge, quiet places, sites for socialization (e.g., enhancing family kinship), and options to be free from specific everyday pressures are examples of the results of discrete management actions that can assure opportunities to realize specific types of benefits. Understanding of the outcomes of the leisure service delivery system facilitated by the BOAL helps to clarify the management actions needed. The BOAL requires such understanding.

Facilitates social interventions. Increasingly P&R agencies are being given social mandates to promote particular benefits—for example, environmental learning, increased physical fitness, and the many benefits associated with use of leisure programs to prevent a specific social problem, such as reduction in crime or substance abuse through various recreation programs, such as midnight basketball. While the BOAL itself is silent with regard to such social engineering, it provides guidance on how to meet social agendas.

Facilitates more meaningful recreation demand analyses. By focusing on ends rather than means (i.e., outcomes instead of just inputs and outputs), the BOAL makes explicit the different types of recreation demands (i.e., demands for activity, experience, and other benefit opportunities, as explained in Chapter 12). Thus, under the BOAL, the on-site and off-site customers can now better communicate their recreation-related demands to managers than they could when their demands were managerially interpreted only in terms of demands for activity opportunities.

Facilitates a collaborative style of management. More public P&R agencies are adopting a collaborative/ participatory style of policy making and management that actively involves a wide array of partners and stakeholders in the planning and delivery of leisure services. The BOAL rejects the common idea that a P&R agency is a sole provider, and it requires a collaborative style of decision making that necessitates forming partnerships with other providers who affect provision of recreation opportunities and with all other affecting or affected, or just interested, stakeholders. The BOAL provides a useful and effective framework for facilitating such a style of management.

Provides flexibility to managers. Practitioners appreciate the flexibility the BOAL affords them. It can be implemented incrementally, and it can be practiced at different degrees of comprehensiveness. For example, one agency and its collaborating partners might decide to focus on only one key benefit (e.g., improved physical fitness) or a selected group of the most significant and widespread benefits, while another agency and its partners might decide to look more comprehensively at a wider number of benefits (i.e., optimize an array of benefit opportunities).

Better identifies conflict and substitutes. Different customers desiring different types of benefits cause most conflicts among customers. The BOAL makes conflicting demands more explicit. It also facilitates better identification of complementary or noncompetitive demands and therefore affords better understanding of which recreation activities and settings are and are not substitutes one for the other.

Enhances the customers' choice processes and consumer sovereignty. The BOAL assumes the individual generally knows best what does and does not improve his or her personal welfare. Much of this knowing is derived from experiential learning by trial-and-error. Certainly each individual's personal knowledge is highly subjective and is mediated by social norms and mores and personal values, beliefs, and conditioning. Nevertheless, a considerable amount of each individual's personal knowledge comes from the factual sources of information outside the individual. Examples include research-derived information on the probable effects on an individual's personal welfare of the use of seat belts, the avoidance of excessive low-density lipid cholesterol in one's bloodstream, hypertension, overexposure to the sun, substance abuse (including tobacco and alcohol), failure to manage stress, physical inactivity, and poor nutrition. In a similar vein, the information on the likely beneficial (and detrimental) consequences of specific leisure activities required by the BOAL helps create more informed choices of leisure opportunities by citizens. In this way, human welfare is promoted, and the role of leisure opportunities in doing so is better understood and appreciated.

Facilities marketing. Because the BOAL makes the products of parks and recreation management explicit, the managing agencies can use this information to develop more explicit informational packages and recreation opportunity guides orientated to the specified types of activity, experience, and other benefit opportunities being made available where, when, in what amount, and of what relative quality. The BOAL also facilitates promotion of specific benefit opportunities if the agency has the social mandate/consensus to do so.

Enhances the rationality of recreation fee programs. Most, if not all, public recreation agencies must now consider implementing or increasing the entrance and use fees they charge. This is an emotion-laden issue in which the two-sided sword of equity cuts in both directions. One side says don't constrain access by charging fees, and the other says it is unfair for the nonuser to subsidize the costs of provision and maintenance of recreation opportunities for users. Some people argue that the users should pay their fair share of these costs, while other people expand this reasoning and say the beneficiaries and not just the users should pay. Their logic is that since recreation is a "merit good" (i.e., one that provides spin-off benefits from users to nonusers), it is only fair that those who receive these social benefits (e.g., enhanced local physical amenities) help to pay the costs of providing opportunities to realize those benefits. The BOAL helps to implement this beneficiaries-should-pay rationale because it requires identification and, to the extent possible, quantification of all benefits to all beneficiaries. Therefore, the BOAL helps to identify those beneficiaries to whom the costs can most fairly be apportioned either as user fees or as tax levies.

Advances knowledge. The scientific community is interested in knowledge about the benefits of leisure, because scientists and educators want to understand better what recreation is and how it contributes to human welfare. The BOAL motivates scientists and educators to attain this understanding. That understanding advances basic knowledge about recreation and thereby promotes better professional practice.

Facilitates additional research. Given that research is a building process, an understanding of the impacts of leisure behavior nurtures additional hypotheses and research about the positive and negative impacts of parks and recreation, including outdoor recreation.

Promotes better education. Better understanding of the benefits of recreation facilitates better formal training of students and on-the-job training of practitioners because of that improved knowledge base.

Increases pride in the profession. Lastly, and of subtle but vital importance, these advantages serve to increase the pride of recreation professionals in their fields and careers. This helps to make leisure professionals less defensive and allows them to take more pride in their socially important roles. It also causes more highly talented people to enter the leisure professions, a trend clearly apparent during the past 20 years, as the systematic body of knowledge about leisure behavior has increased.

Summary

This chapter continued the discussion of science-based management systems started in Chapter 12 and showed how benefits-based management (BBM; called beneficial outcomes management by some leisure professionals) expands and supplements the activity-based management and experience-based management approaches described in Chapter 12. It explained how BBM is only one specialized application of the beneficial outcomes approach to leisure (BOAL) that also covers leisure policy development, research, education, and marketing. The BOAL is also playing an important role in "repositioning the image" of the social roles of leisure, as called for by Crompton (1993) and Crompton and Witt (1998).

This chapter emphasized that leisure professionals must understand the BOAL regardless of their professional interests and orientations. Leisure professionals must focus on both the positive and negative outcomes/impacts that result from the management and use of leisure resources, including outdoor recreation and related amenity resources.

We close by repeating some central characteristics of the BOAL, which have been misrepresented in a few publications critical of the BOAL. Hopefully the following brief outline of those characteristics will be helpful in conveying what the BOAL is really about.

- The BOAL requires consideration of negative as well as positive impacts.

- The purpose of the BOAL extends considerably beyond helping administrators of public P&R agencies justify budget requests to legislators. It also guides leisure management, research, education, marketing, and repositioning the image of leisure.

- The BOAL's recreation opportunity production process refers *only* to producing opportunities to realize benefits. It does, however, cover the fact that customers affect the types of benefit opportunities provided, and some benefits accrue directly by the actions of managers and their associated providers without use of benefit opportunities by the customers.

- The BOAL opposes strongly the technocratic approach that managers produce all the benefits that accrue from use of the recreation opportunities provided. Most of the benefits are created by the customers through their use of the benefit opportunities provided.

- The BOAL opposes the technocratic approach in another way; it requires that collaborating stakeholders and associated providers help determine what opportunities will be targeted to realize benefits and to avoid negative impacts. It insists those decisions should not be made by the manager alone while acting independently of those collaborators.

- The BOAL facilitates interpretation and conceptualization of recreation experiences, including sense of place, the evolving ("lived") experience, and experiences realized by both the on-site and off-site users.

- The BOAL has acceptable scientific credibility as documented in Chapter 2.

- While different from conventional approaches and while insistent on and demanding of professionalism, implementing the BOAL it is not as difficult to implement as it might at first seem. In many past applications of the BOAL through BBM, the managers had surprisingly little difficulty in implementing BBM.

- Based on many implementations of BBM, it is apparent the customers served endorse it and have few problems understanding it.

The next chapter continues to address outdoor recreation resource management by focusing attention on understanding and managing the negative impacts of recreation use.

Literature Cited

Addams, J. (1910). *Twenty years at hull house*. New York, NY: MacMillan.

Allen, L. (1991). Benefits of leisure services to community satisfaction. In B. Driver, P. Brown, and G. Peterson (Eds.), *Benefits of leisure* (pp. 331–350). State College, PA: Venture Publishing, Inc.

Borrie, W. and Roggenbuck, J. (1994). Community-based research for an urban recreation application of benefits-based management. In Chavez, D. (Ed.), *1995 Proceedings of the Second Symposium on Social Aspects and Recreation Research*, February 23–25, San Diego, California (General Technical Report PSW-GTR-156; pp. 159–163). Albany, CA: USDA Forest Service, Pacific Southwest Research Station.

Bruns, D. and Stokowski, P. (1999). Sustaining opportunities to experience early American landscapes. In B. Driver, P. Brown, and G. Peterson (Eds.), *Nature and the human spirit: Toward an expanded land management ethic* (pp. 321–338). State College, PA: Venture Publishing, Inc.

Buckley, W. (1968). *Modern systems research for the behavioral scientist*. Chicago, IL: Aldine.

Campbell, A. (1981). *The sense of well-being in America: Recent patterns and trends*. New York, NY: McGraw-Hill.

Canadian Parks/Recreation Association. (1997). *The benefits catalogue*. Gloucester, Ontario, Canada: Author.

Clawson, M. and Knetsch, J. (1966). *Economics of outdoor planning*. Baltimore, MD: The John Hopkins Press.

Crompton, J. (1993). Repositioning recreation and park services: An overview. *Trends, 30*(4) 2–5.

Crompton, J. and Witt, P. (1998, October). Repositioning: The key to building community support. *Parks and Recreation*, 80–90.

Dombeck, M (1997a, June 24). Presentation to Public Lands Forum of Outdoor Writers' Association of America. Grenefee, FL.

Dombeck, M. (1997b, April 8). Presentation to USDA Forest Service Regional Foresters and Research Station Directors.

Driver, B. (1996). Benefits driven management of natural areas. *Natural Areas Journal, 16*(2), 94–99.

Driver, B. (1999a). Recognizing and celebrating progress in leisure studies. In E. Jackson and T. Burton (Eds.), *Leisure studies: Prospects for the twenty-first century* (pp. 523–544). State College, PA: Venture Publishing, Inc.

Driver, B. (1999b). Management of public outdoor recreation and related public amenity resources for the benefits they provide. In. H. Cordell (Ed.), *A renewable assessment for the Resources Planning Act outdoor recreation and wilderness demand and supply trends in the United States* (pp. 2–5, 27–29). Champaign, IL: Sagamore.

Driver, B. (2003). Benefits of leisure and managing to provide them. In. J. Jenkins and J. Pigram (Eds.), *Encyclopedia of leisure and outdoor recreation*. London, England: Routledge Press.

Driver, B., Brown, P., and Peterson, G. (Eds.). (1991). *Benefits of leisure*. State College, PA: Venture Publishing, Inc.

Driver, B. and Bruns, D. (1999). Concepts and uses of the beneficial approach to leisure. In. E. Jackson and T. Burton (Eds.), *Leisure studies: Prospects for the twenty-first century* (pp. 349–368). State College, PA: Venture Publishing, Inc.

Driver, B., Bruns, D., and Booth, K. (2001). Status and common misunderstandings of the net benefits approach to leisure. In *Trends 2000: Shaping the future. Contributed Papers for the 5th Outdoor Recreation & Tourism Trends Conference* (pp. 245–263). East Lansing, MI: Michigan State University, Department of Park, Recreation, and Tourism Resources.

Driver, B., Dustin, D., Baltic, T., Elsner, G., and Peterson, G. (Eds.) (1996). *Nature and the human spirit: Toward an expanded and management ethic*. State College, PA: Venture Publishing, Inc.

Driver, B. and Manfedo, M. (2003, April). The beneficial outcomes approach. *Urbanistica, 120*, 89–91.

Greene, T. (1996). Cognition and the management of place. In B. Driver, D. Dustin, T. Brown, G. Elsner, and G. Peterson (Eds.), *Nature and the human spirit: Toward an expanded land management ethic* (pp. 301–310). State College, PA: Venture Publishing, Inc.

Hammitt, W. E. and Cole, D. N. (1998). *Wildland recreation: Ecology and management* (2nd ed.). New York, NY: John Wiley & Sons, Inc.

Hurtes, K. and Allen, L. (2001). Measuring resiliency in youth: The resiliency attitudes and skills profile. *Journal of Therapeutic Recreation, 35*(4), 333–347.

Jordan, C. (1991). Parks and recreation: More than fun and games. In B. Driver, P. Brown, and G. Peterson (Eds.), *Benefits of leisure* (pp. 365–368). State College, PA: Venture Publishing, Inc.

Lewis, D. and Kaiser, F. (1991). Managerial needs for information on the benefits of leisure. In B. Driver, P. Brown, and G. Peterson (Eds.), *Benefits of leisure* (pp. 21–35). State College, PA, Venture Publishing, Inc.

Loomis, J. and Walsh, R (1997). *Recreation economic decisions: Comparing benefits and costs* (2nd ed.). State College, PA: Venture Publishing, Inc.

Marans, R. and Mohai, P. (1991). Leisure resources, recreation activity, and the quality of life. In B. Driver, P. Brown, and G. Peterson (Eds.), *Benefits of leisure* (pp. 351–363). State College, PA: Venture Publishing, Inc.

Manfredo, M. (Ed.). (2002). *Wildlife viewing: A management handbook*. Corvallis, OR: Oregon State University Press.

Manfredo, M. and Driver, B. (2002). Benefits: The basis of action. In M. Manfredo (Ed.), *Wildlife viewing: A management handbook* (pp. 43–69). Corvallis, OR: Oregon State University Press.

More, T. (2002). "The parks are being loved to death" and other frauds and deceits in recreation management. *Journal of Leisure Research, 34*(1), 52–78.

New Zealand Department of Conservation. (2002). Managing public conservation lands by the beneficial outcomes approach with emphasis on social outcomes (DOC Science Internal Series 52.). Wellington, New Zealand.

Olmsted, F., Jr. and Kimball, T. (Eds.). (1970). *Frederick Law Olmsted, landscape architect, 1822–1903*. New York, NY: Benjamin Bloom.

Roberts, E. (1996). Place and spirit in public land management. In B. Driver, D. Dustin, T. Baltic, G. Elsner, and G. Peterson (Eds.), *Nature and the human spirit: Toward an expanded land management ethic* (pp. 61–80). State College, PA: Venture Publishing, Inc.

Thomas, J. (1996). Foreword. In B. Driver, D. Dustin, T. Baltic, G. Elsner, and G. Peterson (Eds.), *Nature and the human spirit: Toward an expanded land management ethic* (pp. xxiii–xxv). State College, PA: Venture Publishing, Inc.

United Way of America. (1996). *Measuring program outcomes: A practical approach* (Item No. 0989). Washington, DC: Author.

Williams, D. and Stewart, S. (1998). Sense of place: An elusive concept that is finding a home in ecosystem management. *Journal of Forestry, 96*(5), 18–23.

Witt, P. and Crompton, J. (Eds.). (1996). *Recreation programs that work for at-risk youth: The challenge of shaping the future*. State College, PA: Venture Publishing, Inc.

Witt, P. and Crompton, J. (2002). *Best practices in youth development in public park and recreation settings*. Ashburn, VA: National Park and Recreation Association.

Wondolleck, J. (1996). Incorporating hard-to-define values into public lands decision making: A conflict management perspective. In B. L. Driver, D. Dustin, T. Baltic, G. Elsner, and G. Peterson (Eds.), *Nature and the human spirit: Toward an expanded land management ethic* (pp. 257–262). State College, PA: Venture Publishing, Inc.

Endnotes

1. Many people helped develop and refine the BOAL and BBM described in this chapter. Particularly notable are Larry Allen, Dorothy Anderson, Brian Hopkins, Kay Booth (New Zealand), Chris Jenkins (New Zealand), and Marty Lee. Most notable is the always smiling Don Bruns. Thanks Don, you are a true professional in all ways, not only professionally!

2. This section draws heavily from Driver (1999a).

Chapter 14
Negative Impacts of Recreation Use

Assure for all Americans safe, healthful, productive, and aesthetically and culturally pleasing surroundings. (One purpose of the National Environmental Policy Act of 1969)

Learning Objectives

1. Describe the types of negative impacts caused by outdoor recreation use.
2. Understand the interrelationships that can exist among different types of recreation impacts.
3. Explain the differences between formula-based and standards-based approaches for managing recreation impacts.
4. Describe the commonly used visitor impact management systems and the general processes for implementing them.

From the start of this text, we emphasized outdoor recreation and outdoor recreation resource management are inherently multidisciplinary. At the most basic level they involve interactions between people and natural and/or cultural/heritage recreation resources. Nowhere is this more apparent for managers than in understanding and managing the negative impacts of outdoor recreation use. While many publications use the phrase *recreation impacts* to refer to only negative or unwanted consequences of the management and use of recreation resources, we prefer to use the more accurate term *negative recreation impacts* since recreation also has a tremendous variety of *positive* impacts as explained in Chapters 1, 2, and 13. As such, negative recreation impacts are defined as any damage, intentional or otherwise, that results from outdoor recreation use. Sometimes referred to as user impacts, visitor impacts, recreation resource impacts, or ecological impacts, negative recreation impacts can affect any natural and cultural/heritage resource as well as the experiences of other recreation users. The purpose of this chapter is to introduce readers to the types of impacts commonly caused by recreation use and the various approaches that managers have at their disposal for preventing or minimizing those impacts.

Negative Recreation Impacts

Negative recreation impacts as discussed here are unwanted impacts to resources or experiences caused by recreation. There are numerous examples of resource and experience impacts caused by factors other than recreation, such as air and water pollution that drift or flow into a park from external sources. Other negative impacts can be caused by management actions or the lack of appropriate management actions. Examples include policies that detract from users' experiences, such as overly authoritative rules (conflicting with the perceived freedom essential for recreation); excessive or unwarranted entrance or use fees; inadequately trained managers and staff; inadequate information, facilities, or services; and unwanted impacts associated with the construction and maintenance or roads and other facilities. Professional recreation and natural resource managers are and should be concerned about all potential threats to recreation resources and visitor health and experiences. The focus of this chapter, however, is on the negative impacts caused by recreational use.

Negative recreation impacts are best thought of broadly as any undesirable changes to the resource base or experiences of other users caused by recreation use. Like the study and management of outdoor recreation generally, the study and management of negative recreation impacts can be approached from the standpoint of the natural resources or the people interacting with those resources. Ultimately, of course, both of these aspects can be best addressed in an integrated way. The discipline that focuses on recreation impacts to natural resources, in particular, is known as *recreation ecology* (Hammitt & Cole, 1998; Liddle, 1997). Recreation ecologists direct their attention to the degradation of soil, vegetation, wildlife, and water resources of an area caused by recreation use. Because all the elements of an ecosystem (including the humans that use them) are interrelated, the effective study and management of recreation impacts brings together many disciplines from the physical, biological, and social sciences.

These include soil science, hydrology, geography, biology, ecology, wildlife management, forestry, psychology, sociology, and social psychology. The term *carrying capacity* is also closely related to and has long been associated with the topic of managing recreation impacts. We will return to this concept and term latter in this chapter.

Categories of Recreation Impacts

The most common and important negative outdoor recreation impacts are impacts on soil, water quality, air quality, vegetation, wildlife, and the experiences of other visitors (i.e., social impacts). These types are sometimes organized into different categories, with the most basic distinction being that between ecological (sometimes referred to as environmental) impacts and social impacts. Sometimes distinctions are also made between physical (e.g., soil, water), biological (e.g., vegetation, wildlife), and social impacts. Regardless of the groupings, the key types are the same. Each is briefly introduced next.

Impacts to Soil

Soil is comprised of minerals, living and dead organic material, water, dissolved substances, and the air spaces between the solid particles (Hammitt & Cole, 1998). Each of these components can be adversely impacted by recreation use. Impacts to soil are most commonly due to trampling from people, horses and other stock, or the effects of tires from vehicles such as bicycles, ATVs, motorcycles, or four-wheel drive vehicles. Trampling typically

Soil erosion on trails is a destructive, and often obvious, negative impact of recreation use. (Photo by Reuben Rajala)

results in removal of leaf litter, loss of organic material, compaction, increased water runoff, and increased erosion (Manning, 1979). The eroded soils themselves may then cause additional damage when they are deposited elsewhere as sediment. These harmful processes can affect soils anywhere including trails, campsites, lakeshores, and riverbanks.

Impacts to Water Quality

Water is extremely important for outdoor recreation. It plays an immediate and direct role in recreation experiences like boating, fishing, skiing, and viewing scenery, and an indirect role in recreation by supporting flora and fauna and their habitats as well as for drinking and sanitation for recreation visitors themselves. Needless to say, outdoor recreation use can also adversely affect the water resources it so often depends on. Recreation impacts to water quality can be caused by such actions as

- improper disposal of human waste
- accidental "planting" of exotic aquatic species that change dissolved oxygen and nutrient levels in bodies of water
- chemical pollution from gasoline, oil, and coolants from boats and other motorized vehicles
- bathing in or near water sources and using nonbiodegradable soaps
- washing dishes in or near water sources

Water-based recreation activities can also cause other resource impacts. These include shoreline erosion from boat wakes, turbulence, and cutting action from propellers (Liddle, 1997), as well as litter related to swimming, fishing, and boating. Shoreline erosion and vegetation trampling are also common along lakes and streams frequented by anglers and other shoreline users.

Impacts to Air Quality

Recreation use can cause negative impacts to air quality. Such impacts are most often in the form of pollution from motorized vehicles, although campfire smoke can also be an air quality problem in some areas during particular climactic conditions. The source of vehicle exhaust may be recreation vehicles themselves such as boats, personal watercraft (PWC), or ATVs; automobiles and RVs used to access the recreation area; or even traffic simply passing through a natural area on a road selected, in part, for its scenery or wildlife viewing. Of particular concern have been snowmobiles and personal watercraft (PWCs), which until recently were all powered by two-cycle engines that burn a mixture of gasoline and oil. The ongoing controversy related to snowmobile use in Yellowstone National Park is a case in point. In other areas, vehicle emissions from park visitors combines with other atmospheric pollutions drifting in from other sources to make air quality a serious concern. Great Smoky Mountains National Park, for example, holds the dubious distinction of having some of the worst air quality in the National Park System, affecting visibility from park vistas, vegetation, and visitor health. Although most of the park's pollution is caused by the burning of coal, oil, and gas in upwind areas far outside park boundaries, emissions from park visitors' vehicles are one source (National Park Service, 2001). Reduced visibility in Grand Canyon National Park, mainly caused by electric power generating facilities in the four corners area, is another example.

Impacts to Vegetation

Recreation impacts to flora are often highly visible and dramatic. Vegetative impacts affect such things as which species are present in what proportions (i.e., species composition), the amount of ground cover, seed germination, and the condition of trees and plants. Vegetative impacts can be caused by a wide variety of behavior related to outdoor recreation, including

- trampling seedlings and groundcover
- gathering firewood
- tying horses to live trees
- carving initials in trees
- "planting" exotic plant species through horse and other stock manure
- placing gasoline lanterns on live trees
- gathering flowers and other parts of plants
- grazing horses and other pack stock
- improper disposal of human waste and garbage

Impacts to Wildlife

Viewing or hunting wildlife and viewing or catching fish are the primary goals of many outdoor recreationists and a welcome addition to the experiences of many others who visitor outdoor recreation areas. But negative recreation impacts on wildlife and their behavior are common. Knight and Cole (1995) identified six factors of recreation that can disturb wildlife:

1. the recreation behavior itself
2. how predictable the impact
3. how frequent the impact
4. the magnitude of the impact
5. when the impact occurs
6. where the impact takes place

Hammitt and Cole (1998) noted some wildlife-related recreation impacts are "selective" in that they affect only a particular species. A group of birders closely following a particular rare species is a selective impact. Other impacts are "nonselective" in that they affect the local species generally as when a group of mountain bikers or hikers use a particular trail and affect the behavior of all the nearby wildlife. Examples of impacts on wildlife caused by outdoor recreation include

- poaching of wildlife
- pursuing animals to photograph them
- damaging or destroying an animal's food supply
- camping near water sources in arid environments
- disrupting breeding by being in an animal's territory during mating season
- affecting an animal's nutrition and tolerance of people by feeding them
- bringing dogs or other pets into an animal's habitat

Motorized recreation vehicles, especially those using two-cycle engines, can dramatically degrade air quality.

Outdoor recreation use can cause serious vegetation damage, as in this fragile Wyoming meadow. (Photo by Reuben Rajala)

• chasing wildlife with off-highway vehicles (OHVs), snowmobiles or other means

Social Impacts

Soils, water, air, vegetation, and wildlife are not the only elements of an ecosystem that can be adversely affected be recreation use. The people visiting an outdoor recreation area can be impacted by other recreation users as well, most frequently in regard to the recreation experiences they hope to have there. Recreation impacts to visitors' experiences caused by the presence, behavior, or even evidence of other users are called *social impacts.* The most common examples of the social impacts of outdoor recreation are crowding and conflict.

To understand the social impacts of recreation use, it is important to remember why people engage in outdoor recreation. Recall that outdoor recreation is "goal-directed behavior," meaning simply that people engage in recreation to consciously or unconsciously satisfy certain needs or to meet certain goals. In other words, our motivations, needs, and desires for certain outcomes, rewards, or experiences drive our behavior. As elaborated in Chapter 1, all outdoor recreation visitors have motives for their outdoor recreation behavior and most have multiple motives, even for a single recreation engagement. This perspective is the basis of the "behavioral approach" to understanding outdoor recreation and providing high-quality opportunities for it. In addition to the motives for outdoor recreation engagements, the behavioral approach also focuses on the experiences that result. The quality of these recreation experiences is usually measured in terms of satisfaction (i.e., the extent to which visitors are able to achieve the experiences they desired).

Many factors can reduce the satisfaction someone experiences with their outdoor recreation, including bad weather, illness, not catching a fish or seeing an elk, inadequate facilities, and so on. A social impact occurs when the source of a visitor's dissatisfaction is the presence, behavior, or even evidence of other users. Although outdoor recreation research generally shows most outdoor recreation users are satisfied, social impacts can and do become serious problems. The most common of these social impacts are *perceived crowding* and *recreational conflict.*

Perceived Crowding

When people think about "crowded" places, they are more likely to recall a crowded sidewalk, party, or concert than a crowded outdoor recreation setting. But crowding frequently is a problem for outdoor recreationists and, therefore, is an ongoing concern for outdoor recreation managers. Recreation crowding has been the subject of dozens of scientific studies focused on recreation activities as varied as hunting, fishing, climbing, backpacking, tubing, rafting, canoeing, hiking, sailboating, and wildlife photography.

Recreation crowding has to do with more than simply the objective number of people present in an area or even the density of people present there. Because users' satisfaction with their recreation experiences involves their personal evaluations, recreational crowding includes a subjective element and is therefore frequently referred to as *perceived crowding.* Crowding in a recreation setting is best defined as a negative appraisal of the density of other people in an area (Kuss, Graefe & Vaske, 1990). In other words, when recreationists' experiences are negatively affected by the number or density of people present, they are experiencing crowding. It may be helpful to think of perceived crowding as the user's value judgment that there are simply "too many" people present in a particular situation at a particular time. Of course, what constitutes "too many" can vary greatly from person to person and situation to situation.

The situational and subjective nature of recreation crowding is illustrated by the results of a study at Buck Island Reef National Monument in the U.S. Virgin Islands (Graefe & Moore, 1991). One of the main attractions at this National Park Service unit is an underwater snorkeling trail, which most visitors access on "head boats" operated by commercial tour companies. Even though visitor numbers and densities were high on the underwater trail itself, users reported low levels of crowding there. This was because many users were inexperienced snorkelers and liked the assurance and increased safety of having others nearby. Visitors reported being much more crowded when they spent their lunch times on the nearby beach, however, even though the actual densities of other people there were far lower than on the underwater trail. The same people were apparently more sensitive to others on

Levels of crowding in outdoor recreation settings is dependent on many things, not simply the number or density of other people present.

the beach because they were expecting more solitude there and many wanted more privacy with their significant others than was actually available.

In fact, sensitivity to crowding and other social impacts of outdoor recreation varies from person to person, place to place, and situation to situation. More specific factors that affect levels of social impacts in general will be summarized shortly. (For excellent reviews and syntheses of research related to recreation crowding see Kuss, Graefe & Vaske, 1990 and Manning, 1999.)

Conflicts Among Users

Another common social impact of outdoor recreation is *recreation conflict.* As with crowding, conflict is not an objective state, but depends on individual interpretations of past, present, and future contacts with others (Jacob & Schreyer, 1980). Recreational conflict is also more than simple competition for limited recreation resources. Recreational conflict is best defined as "goal interference attributed to another's behavior" (Jacob & Schreyer, 1980, p. 369). In other words, conflict is a special type of dissatisfaction that occurs when one person cannot achieve the recreation experiences they desire because of the interference of other users. Examples could include the sounds of motorboats interfering with the experiences of back-country canoers, inconsiderate mountain bikers frightening trail hikers, large horseback groups making it difficult for mountain bikers to pass on a trail, or large groups of commercial rafters blocking rapids and otherwise spoiling the experiences whitewater kayakers. Recreational conflict has been found between cross-country skiers and snowmobilers, and hikers and motorcyclists, canoe paddlers and motorboaters, nonmotorized raft users and motorized raft users, mountain bikers and hikers, downhill skiers and snowboarders, hikers and horseback riders. However, it is important to realize such findings do not

Litter can be an obvious negative impact of recreation use, as this site in the Boston Harbor Islands illustrates. (Photo by Yu-Fai Leung)

imply that these pairs of activities are inherently incompatible. Conflict is an individual reaction and goal interference can occur among individuals involved in different activities, the same activity, or for reasons that may not be related to the "offending" user's activity at all, such as rude or unsafe actions.

Recreational conflict is sometimes broken down into two distinct types. *Interpersonal conflict* involves some sort of contact or encounter among the parties (at least visually), while *social-values conflict* need not involve contact at all. An example of social values conflict in a recreation setting would be nonhunters experiencing conflict simply by knowing that they must share the area with hunters or visa versa (Vaske, Donnelly, Wittmann & Laidlaw, 1995). Conflicts in outdoor recreation are sometimes "asymmetrical" or "one-way" as well. This occurs when one group dislikes contacts with another but the reverse is not true. For example, cross-country skiers tend to dislike encountering snowmobilers, but snowmobilers are not as unhappy about encountering cross-country skiers (Jackson & Wong, 1982; Knopp & Tyger, 1973).

With both recreation crowding and conflict, the same objective conditions might or might not produce social impacts. In general the dynamic is that people visit recreation areas with particular goals and expectations about the kinds of conditions and experiences they desire. When faced with threats to their ability to realize those experiences, they either experience the crowding/conflict or they may employ coping strategies to avoid the social impact. Crowding or conflict can then also result when the person's coping strategies are not successful. The most common coping strategies are substitution, redefinition of the experience, and rationalization (Manning, 1999).

Substitution occurs when a person chooses a different activity, place, or time for their recreation when they find the original conditions unacceptable. For example, a fly fisher who finds her favorite stream too crowded on a Saturday morning might decide to try another stream that morning, return to the same stream at a less crowded time, or put the rod away and go hiking instead. These are examples of place, time, and activity substitution, respectively. When recreation users choose, or are forced, to substitute alternatives for their preferred place, time, or activity, they are said to have been *displaced.*

Redefining the experience involves the person changing their recreation goal or their preference for a particular recreation opportunity. For example, if a camper hoping for solitude finds his preferred campsite occupied, he might consciously or unconsciously decide to enjoy the company of the other campers. He has, in essence, changed his recreation goal from solitude to social interaction, and therefore has not experienced crowding or conflict. This redefinition of the experience is sometimes referred to as *product shift* (Shelby, Bregenzer & Johnson, 1986; Shelby & Heberlein, 1986).

Rationalization occurs if a person feels they have so much invested in the outing (personally and/or financially) that they convince themselves (and perhaps others) they were satisfied anyway, even if the conditions fell far short of their hopes.

General Characteristics of Negative Recreation Impacts

The previous discussion should give some indication of the breath of impacts that outdoor recreation can have on soils, vegetation, wildlife, water, air, and recreation experiences. In fact, almost all recreation use causes some sort of impact. Some impacts are very subtle and imperceptible in the short term, while others are severe and quite obvious. The relationships among impacts and their dynamics can be quite complex, of course, and the better a manager's understanding of this complexity, the more likely it is the impacts can be managed effectively. After a thorough review of the scientific research related to recreation impacts, Graefe, Kuss, and Vaske (1990, pp. 1–2) came to the following five major conclusions and recommended that they be incorporated into any system for managing impacts. We have reworded the titles of their conclusions slightly and provide examples of each for clarification.

Impacts Are Interrelated

Environments and individuals do not respond to recreation use in a single, predictable way. Different impacts are frequently related with one another and often respond to recreation use in complicated ways. Recreation impacts can also be either direct or indirect (Graefe, Kuss & Vaske, 1990; Hammitt & Cole, 1998). For example, trampling by hikers on a steep trail will likely cause the direct impacts of soil compaction and erosion. That erosion, in turn, may cause increased runoff and sedimentation downhill that results in the indirect impact of sedimentation that can damage vegetation and decrease water quality. Or, consider the case of severe physical and biological impacts that then cause indirect impacts on users' recreation experiences when they are noticed. Evidence of other people, such as "beaten out" campsites, litter, badly eroded trails, initials carved in trees, and motorcycle tracks, can lead to feelings of crowding, conflict, or dissatisfaction in general, even without actually seeing the other users themselves.

Impact Levels Are Related to Use to Some Extent

Although most impacts are related in some way to the amount of recreation use an area receives, the relationships are usually not direct or linear. For example, steady increases in the number of people using an area will not usually cause equivalent increases in resource damage or social impacts. Most damage to soils and vegetation at campsites, for instance, occurs after relatively few groups use the site. After the initial impacts have occurred, addition groups cause less damage per group. Other factors such as tolerance to impacts and visitor preferences and expectations make use-impact relationships more complicated.

Tolerance to Impacts Varies

The way impacts relate to levels of use vary widely. These variations may be from species to species, ecosystem to ecosystem, or even from one person to another. For example, some plants and soils are hardy, some are fragile. Some users may feel crowded by meeting one other group in the backcountry, while others may not mind encountering dozens.

Influences Are Activity-Specific

Some types of recreation activities cause more or faster impacts than do others. Horses, bikes, walkers, and snowmobiles all affect resources differently. And often the *style* of use is even more important than the type of activity. For example, one irresponsible mountain biker can cause more physical damage and recreation conflict than many responsible ones combined.

Influences Are Site-Specific

The effects of recreation use depend on where and when the use takes place. Different areas of a recreation site are not equally susceptible to impact. As in the Buck Island Reef example noted earlier, the location of contact affects social impacts. Similarly, the level of physical and biological impacts can be related to such factors as slope, orientation to the sun, microclimate, vegetation type and density, and soil type. The time of year and time of day can be important, too. Trails are typically most fragile in the spring, for example, because of wetter soils.

What Factors Influence Levels of Recreation Impacts?

Research indicates many factors affect the severity of recreation impacts. Some of the most important ones are noted next with brief examples. Each applies in varying degrees to soil impacts, vegetation impacts, wildlife impacts, water quality impacts, air quality impacts, and social impacts. As noted previously, it is important to remember that impacts tend to be interrelated with one another and not necessarily related to increasing use in direct or linear ways. The same caveats apply to the factors noted here. They are often interrelated and generally do not affect the levels of impacts in linear or direct ways.

The following list of factors that influence levels of recreation impacts is based, in part, on summaries of the literature provided in Hammitt and Cole (1998), Kuss, Graefe, and Vaske (1990), Moore (1994), and Hendee and Dawson (2002). Some of the relationships described in these factors are supported by strong scientific evidence and others are only suggested by a few studies. Research on these relationships and factors is continuing.

Environmental durability. The ability of the resource elements to resist damage. Some species and ecosystems are more sensitive to recreation use than are others.

Environmental resilience. The ability of the resource elements to recover from damage. Some species and ecosystems are more resilient to damage caused by recreation use than are others.

Type of activity. Larger, heavier uses (e.g., motorized vehicles, horses) tend to cause more impacts than others. Nonmechanized users (e.g., hikers, cross-country skiers) tend to be more sensitive to contacts with others than are mechanized users.

Size of group. Larger groups tend to cause more damage to resources, in part, because they spread out more than smaller groups do. Members of smaller groups also tend to be more sensitive to the presence and behavior of others. Contacts with large groups generally cause greater social impacts than contacts with small groups.

Location of contact. Users generally have their lowest tolerance for contacts with others in remote wilderness areas. Tolerance for others tends to be highest at trailheads, lower on the trail, and lowest at campsites. Tolerance is probably lowest at campsites because people tend to want more privacy there.

Time of use. Some sites and species are more sensitive to impacts at certain time than others. Soils and vegetation can be more sensitive in wet springs than dry summers or frozen winters. Wildlife is more sensitive to disruption during breeding season and winter when their food is less available and their energy reserves are limited.

Length of stay. Groups that stay in the backcountry longer generally have more impact than ones that stay only a short time. Day hikers usually cause less impact than overnight campers and longer stay campers may cause more impacts, still, by "improving" their campsites to make them more comfortable.

User motivation. *Why* a user engages in their outdoor recreation can affect their sensitivity to contacts with others. For example, nature and solitude seekers tend to be less tolerant of contacts with others than are excitement, thrill, and social contact seekers.

User behavior. *What* other users do is often more important than *how many* there are. For example, one user cutting live trees for firewood will cause more vegetative damage than dozens who use camp stoves instead of campfires. Similarly, one inconsiderate camper playing a loud radio can cause more crowding and conflict than would many others who behave considerately. Properly educated users who behave responsibly can minimize nearly all of their impacts dramatically.

Type of user encountered. Users tend to be most tolerant of people who seem to be like themselves rather than different. The type of activity someone is engaged in is often the most visible cue others use to judge how alike they may be, although stereotypes based on visible cues can be quite inaccurate.

When the user first visited. Many users evaluate present conditions against their earliest visits to that site, making long-time visitors more sensitive in general than newcomers. This tendency is sometimes referred to as a *floating baseline* and may be related to the so-called *last settler syndrome* where some users want conditions and allowed uses to stay the same as when they themselves first used the site.

User preferences and expectations. Discrepancies between actual, expected, and preferred conditions or encounters can relate to feelings of crowding, conflict, or dissatisfaction in general.

User norms. Norms are essentially the unwritten "rules" that users hold related to how an area should be used and what conditions "should" be like there. Breaking these unwritten rules can lead to social impacts. For example, tubers may feel it is perfectly appropriate to drink and be boisterous on a particular river segment, while anglers might feel the same river segment should be used quietly and with more reverence. Differences in norms are likely an important factor in the social values conflicts mentioned earlier.

Number and density of others present. The number and density of others often have some relationship with recreation impacts, but the connections are usually weak and often indirect. Concentrations of users can cause more damage to a particular site than dispersed ones, although the same number of users dispersed in a fragile environment may cause more total impact than if they are concentrated in the most durable site available. Note that the number of others present in an area and the number of others actually seen can be quite different. The number of others seen can be affected by factors as simple as whether the others use brightly colored versus earth-toned clothes, tents, and equipment.

Level of user experience. Users who are more experienced or expert tend to be more sensitive than novices. This is probably due to the fact that more experienced users often have more refined needs and expectations than beginners. More refined needs and expectations are more easily disrupted by undesirable site conditions or social conditions.

Definition of place. Attitudes toward and perceptions of the environment can affect how sensitive users are to impacts. Those who are more attached to a particular place tend to be more sensitive to impacts there than are more casual visitors.

Level of tolerance. Individuals differ in how tolerant they are of others generally, and they bring these attitudes with them when they come to outdoor recreation settings.

Systems for Managing Negative Recreation Impacts

For many years this area of outdoor recreation management was almost universally referred to as *recreation carrying capacity*. It is really an adaptation of the carrying capacity concept borrowed from range and wildlife management that estimated the number of animals that a certain range could support long term within the limits of its soils, water, and vegetation (e.g., head of sheep per acre per month). The recreation carrying capacity concept is now over 40 years old and was originally defined as the "level of recreational use an area can withstand while providing a sustained quality of recreation" (Wagar, 1964, p. 3). Carrying capacity is now typically examined in two parts: *physical carrying capacity* and *social carrying capacity*. The important implication of all carrying capacity and recreation impact management systems is that a quality environment is necessary to provide quality recreation opportunities.

There are two basic approaches to assessing and managing recreation impacts: formula-based and standards-based.

Formula-Based Approaches

These are generally the early approaches based more strictly on the original range and wildlife management carrying capacity concept. They attempt to identify a maximum number of people an area can accommodate and still provide for healthy resources and reasonably high-quality recreation. However, a strict carrying capacity concept doesn't work well for outdoor recreation management because outcomes like recreation experiences are much harder to measure and much more complex than head of livestock per acre per month, and the inputs are much more varied and interrelated than the forage and water needed to raise healthy animals.

The system used to determine a carrying capacity for backcountry recreation in Yosemite National Park in the early 1980s is an example of a formula-based approach. The following formula was used to determine the maximum "people at one time" (PAOT) that the area was expected to sustain (Wagtendonk, 1983):

Carrying Capacity = A − (BA)

Where:

A= .01 x (total acreage of the zone) + 2 x (total trail mileage in the zone)

B = (relative uniqueness of the system + relative vulnerability of the system + relative resiliency of the system + ease of reparability of the system by man)/36

Each of the variables used in factor B were estimated and measured on a 0 to 9 point scale. These calculations were made for each backcountry zone and resulted in a carrying capacity for that zone in PAOT. This type of approach is almost never used today. Currently all major systems for managing recreation impacts are standards rather than formula-based.

Standards-Based Approaches

For years the most common management response to unacceptable recreation impacts was to restrict the amount of recreation use allowed in an area or to close it entirely. We now know the causes of recreation impacts are much more complex and interrelated than simply how many people use a particular area. Older formula-based approaches focused primarily on recreation use levels. However, the more sophisticated and appropriate approach is to focus on the level of impact, not just the number of people using the area. Standards-based approaches were designed to do just that.

Standards-based approaches to identifying and managing recreation impacts are systematic approaches to evaluate, manage, and monitor the recreation impacts themselves (rather than the number of people) and to keep the impacts within some appropriate, agreed on levels (i.e., standards). Standards-based approaches have all but replaced the older formula-based approaches. The most common examples of standards-based approaches in use today include the following:

Limits of Acceptable Change (LAC)

LAC was developed by USDA Forest Service scientists and is currently the most well-known and widely used of the standards-based approaches (Stankey et al., 1985). LAC has been used by the U.S. Forest Service and Bureau of Land Management for many years. Although LAC was originally designed to help manage wilderness resources, it is applicable to and has been used in many outdoor recreation settings and is currently being used in several countries outside the United States as well.

Visitor Experience and Resource Protection (VERP)

VERP is the most recent of the standard-based approaches. This relatively new approach was developed by university and National Park Service (NPS) scientists working in collaboration (Manning, Lime & Hof, 1996). Parts of the VERP process were designed to be integrated with requirements of the NPS general park planning process.

Visitor Impact Management System (VIM)

VIM was developed by University of Maryland scientists working with the nonprofit National Parks and Conservation Association in hopes that it would be adopted by the National Park Service (Graefe, Kuss & Vaske, 1990). This is one of the simplest of the four standards-based approaches, but it has not been widely adopted by any of the major land managing agencies.

Visitor Activity Management Process (VAMP)

As noted in Chapter 12, VAMP is a Canadian model (Graham, Nilsen & Payne, 1988; Parks Canada, 1991) that shares similar objectives with the LAC, VERP, and VIM systems and uses a similar process. However, VAMP frequently serves a much wider role in guiding the planning and management processes of entire parks and other areas administered by Parks Canada. VAMP is no longer being used by Parks Canada as a distinct management planning system under the name of VAMP, but has now

been integrated into a number of other guides and processes used by that agency.

Figures 14.1, 14.2, and 14.3 (pp. 218–219) give illustrations of the basic steps in the three standards-based recreation impact management systems just mentioned.

There are more similarities than differences among the three impact management systems illustrated. Each has similar orientations and steps and promotes active collaboration of the planners and managers with the stakeholders who either affect or will be affected by any managerial actions taken. The degree of such collaboration has varied from one application of these three systems to another, but in general it has been a part of the process. A difference among the systems is the extent to which they are used to help guide the overall management of an area as opposed to being applied more at the smaller recreation site or project level. The VAMP system is more integrated into management planning of much larger sites and reserves than are the other three systems. Regardless of the degree of such integration, of course, each of these impact management systems must be applied within the bounds of the policy directives guiding the agency.

As noted here and in Chapter 12, the LAC, VERP, and VIM impact management systems are similar in their steps and orientations. The eight steps of the VIM system are presented next in slightly more detail as an example of the logic and application of standards-based approaches in general (Graefe, Kuss & Vaske, 1990, pp. 9–27). The steps in the VIM process are as follows:

Preassessment database review. The goal of this first step is to identify and summarize information pertinent to the site and its purpose by means of a thorough review of all relevant sources of information about the area. These may include enabling legislation and other policy

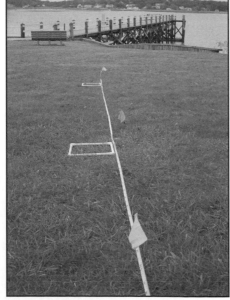

Impact assessment and management systems like limits of acceptable change (LAC) can employ many specialized techniques, such as vegetation transects. (Photo by Yu-Fai Leung)

Systematically measuring and recording the levels of selected impact indicators is an essential part of all standards-based approaches. (Photo by Yu-Fai Leung)

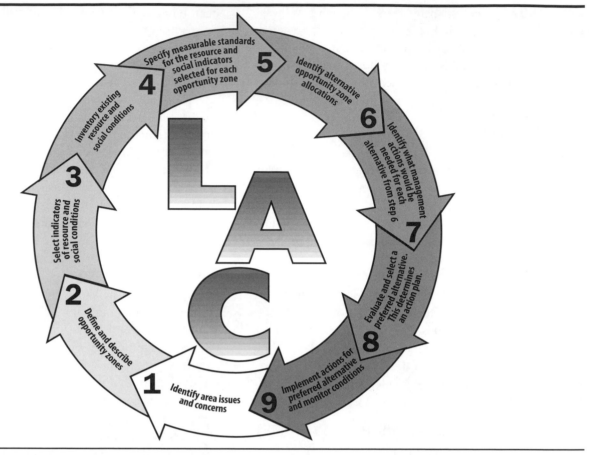

Figure 14.1   Steps of the limits of acceptable change (LAC) process.   Source: Stankey et al. (1985, Fig. 1, p. 3)

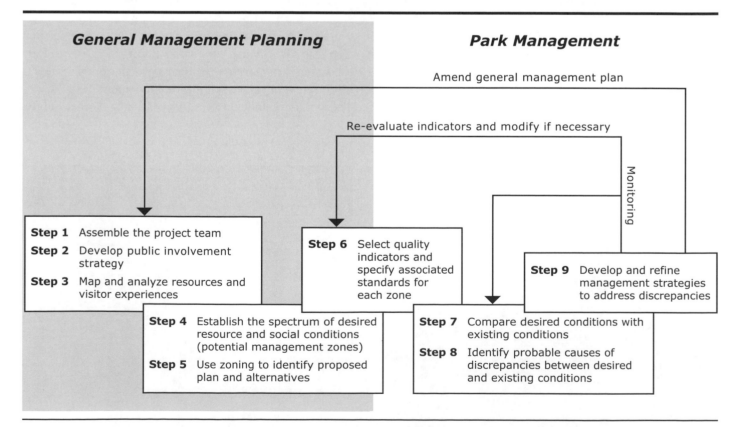

Figure 14.2   Steps of the visitor experience and resource protection (VERP) process.   Source: Hof et al., 1994, p. 11

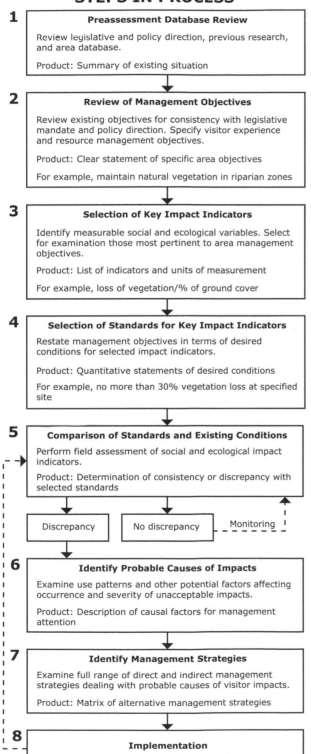

Basic approach: Systematic process for identification of impact problems, their causes, and effective management strategies for reduction of visitor impacts.

Conditions for use: Integrated with other planning frameworks or as management tool for localized impact problems.

STEPS IN PROCESS

1 **Preassessment Database Review**

Review legislative and policy direction, previous research, and area database.

Product: Summary of existing situation

2 **Review of Management Objectives**

Review existing objectives for consistency with legislative mandate and policy direction. Specify visitor experience and resource management objectives.

Product: Clear statement of specific area objectives

For example, maintain natural vegetation in riparian zones

3 **Selection of Key Impact Indicators**

Identify measurable social and ecological variables. Select for examination those most pertinent to area management objectives.

Product: List of indicators and units of measurement

For example, loss of vegetation/% of ground cover

4 **Selection of Standards for Key Impact Indicators**

Restate management objectives in terms of desired conditions for selected impact indicators.

Product: Quantitative statements of desired conditions

For example, no more than 30% vegetation loss at specified site

5 **Comparison of Standards and Existing Conditions**

Perform field assessment of social and ecological impact indicators.

Product: Determination of consistency or discrepancy with selected standards

Discrepancy | No discrepancy | Monitoring

6 **Identify Probable Causes of Impacts**

Examine use patterns and other potential factors affecting occurrence and severity of unacceptable impacts.

Product: Description of causal factors for management attention

7 **Identify Management Strategies**

Examine full range of direct and indirect management strategies dealing with probable causes of visitor impacts.

Product: Matrix of alternative management strategies

8 **Implementation**

Monitoring

Figure 14.3 Steps of the visitor impact management system (VIM) process. Adapted from Graefe, Kuss & Vaske (1990, Fig. 1, p. 10)

directives, agency mission statement, previous research, proceedings of meetings establishing the area, specific databases related to existing area conditions, and so forth. This step must also delineate the boundaries of the physical area to be evaluated.

Review of management objectives. Where management objectives exist for an area, they should be reviewed for consistency with all relevant legislative mandates and agency policy. If clear and specific visitor experience and natural resource management objectives do not exist, they should be established as part of this step. Specific objectives provide much better guidance for identifying and managing recreation impacts than do broad or vague ones, of course. This step is often the most important one in the process because clear objectives often do not exist. Examples of objectives from a VIM application for a popular trail in Glacier National Park (Graefe, Kuss & Vaske, 1990, p. 30) include the following:

1. to offer an opportunity for visitors to observe and experience an alpine ecosystem at close range through intimate contact provided by a trail structured to facilitate access to this area and to protect the fragile environment

2. to manage soil and vegetation resources by application of the carrying capacity concept to control ecosystem impacts at an acceptable level

3. to provide opportunities for visitors to fully experience the park's unique semi-wilderness areas without adverse impact on the resources

Selection of key impact indicators. In this step the measurable social and ecological variables most pertinent to area management objectives are identified. The best of these variables are then selected to serve as the key impact indicators. As much as possible, the impact indicators should be

• directly observable

• easy to measure

• directly related to area objectives

• sensitive to changing use

• amenable to management

It is almost always best to use multiple indicators and to include ones which target physical, biological, and social impacts. Examples of good indicators would be depth of trail erosion or the number of fire rings at a campsite.

Selection of standards for key impact indicators. This step involves the quantitative restatement of management objectives to reflect the desired conditions for selected impact indicators. Setting appropriate *measurable* maximum or minimum acceptable levels for each indicator is essential. Standards may be sophisticated measures, such as multi-item indices of water chemistry in parts per million, or more subjective visual ratings, such as low, moderate, or extensive levels of campsite deterioration based on specific criteria. Examples of standards, in terms of the examples given in the previous step, might be "no more than four inches of trail erosion depth" or "no more than a single fire ring at each campsite."

Comparison of standards and existing conditions. This step entails actually measuring the conditions of each indicator in the field and comparing them with the standards set for each. If the level of an indicator is found to be unacceptable, the process moves on to the next step. If not, its levels should be monitored as specified in the final step.

Identify probable causes of impacts. This step attempts to determine the most important causes affecting the occurrence and severity of any impacts found to be unacceptable in the previous step. To be useful to management, the causes identified need to be more specific than "too much use." Remember to consider all the possible factors that could affect impact levels identified earlier in this chapter, including

- spatial use patterns
- user behavior
- level of use
- time of use (e.g., day, week, season)
- type of use
- concentration of use
- length of stay
- size of group

Recognize there may be a need to gather more data to understand the causes of the impacts well enough to be able to address them effectively.

Identify management strategies. This step identifies the specific management strategies most likely to address the causes of the unacceptable recreation impacts. It is important to consider the full range of direct (e.g., regulations and restrictions) and indirect (e.g., less obtrusive) management options in this step. When identifying strategies, be certain to focus on the likely causes of the impacts and not on the impact conditions, which are actually the symptoms. Chapter 16 presents details on the many options for influencing visitor behavior.

Implementation. This step is when the previously identified management strategies are implemented to address the unacceptable recreation impacts identified earlier. Implementation should specify who, what, when, where, and how to actually carry out each strategy. Implicit in this step is the fact that the levels of each indicator must be monitored on an ongoing basis in the field to assess the effectiveness of the management strategies implemented and to track any trends in impacts. Monitoring also assures the strategies implemented are not also causing additional unanticipated problems.

Before leaving this discussion of managing recreation impacts it is important to point out two things. The first relates to the term *carrying capacity* itself and the second has to do with the perspective we should have when addressing recreation impacts in general. As noted earlier, the concept of carrying capacity and the term itself were borrowed from range and wildlife management and applied to the field of recreation resource management. Some people believe that term no longer fits with the current emphasis on standards-based approaches to managing recreation impacts and should be phased out. Their main objection is they feel the word *capacity* implies a maximum number, especially to members of the general public. Since the maximum numbers of people that resulted from the early formula-based approaches have given way to impact-oriented standards in the current standards-based approaches, they feel the term carrying capacity is inappropriate.

Others have adapted and updated the definition of carrying capacity and feel it is still the most appropriate term. For example, the authors of VERP define carrying capacity as "the type and level of visitor use that can be accommodated while sustaining the desired resource and social conditions that complement the purposes of the park units and their management objectives" (Hof et al., 1994, p. 11). Such a definition clearly emphasizes that resource and social standards are essential. Similarly, Hendee and Dawson (2002, p. 234) believe there has been an "evolving recognition of carrying capacity as a conceptual approach, derived from social and ecological judgments about appropriate wilderness conditions." It is important for outdoor recreation managers to be aware that the term carrying capacity is still commonly used, but that it can be misleading to the uninformed, particularly members of the general public who may wrongly expect that the process will always result in a maximum level of allowable use.

The second point to remember in terms of understanding and managing recreation impacts is that, in one respect, recreation impacts are problems of success. Outdoor recreation is popular—so popular that more people are participating and doing so in more diverse ways. These increasing use pressures can, in turn, cause increasing impacts on the environment and the experiences of others. This point is not intended to lessen the importance of doing everything we can to minimize recreation-related impacts to resources and experiences, including helping visitors to better understand their responsibilities. It is simply a reminder that the challenge of recreation impacts results, to some degree, from the sheer popularity of outdoor recreation itself.

Summary

This chapter introduced the concept of negative impacts of recreation use and presented information on systems currently used to identify and to manage such impacts. These impacts are best thought of broadly to be any undesirable changes to the resource base or experiences of other users caused by recreation use. The negative impacts of recreation use can be divided into six categories: soil impacts, water quality impacts, air quality impacts, vegetation impacts, wildlife impacts, and social impacts. Perceived crowding and recreation conflict are the most common social impacts of recreation use. In terms of recreation impacts overall, we presented and discussed five main conclusions based on Kuss, Graefe, and Vaske (1990): impacts are interrelated, impact levels are related to use to some extent, tolerance to impacts varies, influences are activity-specific, and influences are site-specific. We then reviewed over a dozen factors that appear to influence the levels of recreation impacts. Finally, the most important systems for managing negative recreation impacts that are commonly used today were introduced and discussed, including limits of acceptable change (LAC), visitor experience and resource protection (VERP), visitor impact management system (VIM), and visitor activity management process (VAMP). All of these systems are "standards-based" rather than "formula-based." In the next chapter we broaden our view from recreation impacts to address the important topic of how to actually gather data for managing outdoor recreation.

Literature Cited

Graefe, A. R. and Moore, R. L. (1991). Monitoring the visitor experience at Buck Island Reef and National Monument. In *Proceedings of the 1991 Northeast Recreation Research Symposium* (General Technical Report NE-160; pp. 55–58). USDA Forest Service, Northeast Forest Experiment Station.

Graefe, A., Kuss, F., and Vaske, J. (1990). *Visitor impact management: The planning framework*. Washington, DC: National Parks and Conservation Association.

Graham, R., Nilsen, P., and Payne, R. (1988, March). Visitor management in Canadian national parks. *Tourism Management*, 44–61.

Hammitt, W. and Cole, D. (1998). *Wildland recreation: Ecology and management* (2nd ed.). New York, NY: John Wiley and Sons.

Hendee, J. and Dawson, C. (2002). *Wilderness management: Stewardship and protection of resources and values* (3rd ed.). Golden, CO: Fulcrum.

Hof, M., Hammett, J., Rees, M., Belnap, J., Poe, N., Lime, D., et al. (1994). Getting a handle on visitor carrying capacity: A pilot project at Arches National Park. *Park Science, 14*(1), 11–13.

Jackson, G. R. and Wong, R. A. G. (1982). Perceived conflict between urban cross-country skiers and snowmobilers in Alberta. *Journal of Leisure Research, 14*(1), 47–62.

Jacob, G. and Schreyer, R. (1980). Conflict in outdoor recreation: A theoretical perspective. *Journal of Leisure Research, 12*, 368–380.

Knight, R. and Cole, D. (1995). Factors that influence wildlife responses to recreationists. In R. L. Knight and K. J. Gutzwiller (Eds.), *Wildlife and recreationists* (pp. 71–81). Washington, DC: Island Press.

Knopp, T. B. and Tyger, J. B. (1973). A study of conflict in recreational land use: Snowmobiling versus ski-touring. *Journal of Leisure Research, 5*(3), 6–17.

Kuss, F., Graefe, A., and Vaske, J. (1990). *Visitor impact management: A review of literature*. Washington, DC: National Parks and Conservation Association.

Liddle, M. (1997). *Recreation ecology: The ecological impact of outdoor recreation and ecotourism*. New York, NY: Chapman and Hall.

Manning, R. (1979). Impacts of recreation on riparian soils and vegetation. *Water Resources Bulletin, 15*(1), 30–43.

Manning, R. (1999). *Studies in outdoor recreation: Search and research for satisfaction* (2nd ed.). Corvallis, OR: Oregon State University Press.

Manning, R., Lime, D., and Hof, M. (1996). Social carrying capacity of natural areas: Theory and application in the U.S. national parks. *Natural Areas Journal, 16*(2), 118–127.

Moore, R. L. (1994). *Conflicts on multiple-use trails: Synthesis of literature and state of the practice*. Washington, DC: Federal Highway Administration.

National Environmental Policy Act of 1969, 42 U.S.C. § 4331(b)2 (1969).

National Park Service. (2001). *Air quality: Great Smoky Mountains National Park Management folio #2*. Gatlinburg, TN: Great Smoky Mountains Natural History Association and National Park Service.

Parks Canada. (1991). *Selected readings on the visitor activity management process*. Ottawa, Ontario, Canada: Environment Canada.

Shelby, B., Bregenzer, N., and Johnson, R. (1986). *Product shift as a result of increased density: Empirical evidence from a longitudinal study*. Paper presented at the First National Symposium on Social Science in Resource Management, Corvallis, OR.

Shelby, B. and Heberlein, T. (1986). *Carrying capacity in recreation settings*. Corvallis, OR: Oregon State University Press.

Stankey, G., Cole, D., Lucas, R., Peterson, M., Frissell, S., and Washburne, R. (1985). *The limits of acceptable change (LAC) system for wilderness planning* (Gen. Tech. Report INT-176). Ogden, UT: USDA Forest Service, Intermountain Forest and Range Experiment Station.

Vaske, J., Donnelly, M., Wittmann, K., and Laidlaw, S. (1995). Interpersonal versus social-values conflict. *Leisure Sciences, 17*, 205–222.

Wagar, J. (1964). *The carrying capacity of wildlands for recreation* (Forest Science Monogram No. 7). Washington, DC: Society of American Foresters.

Wagtendonk, V. (1983). *Carrying capacity determinations for the Yosemite backcountry*. Unpublished manuscript.

Chapter 15
Gathering Data for Managing Outdoor Recreation

Central Park is probably the most closely watched and monitored 843 acres on earth.
(Knowler, 1984, p. 162)

Learning Objectives

1. Explain how the various measures of outdoor recreational use differ.
2. Describe the major ways current and future recreational use can be estimated.
3. Describe techniques for measuring impacts to recreation resources.

In the previous four chapters we introduced the essential foundations for managing outdoor recreation resources and opportunities. Those discussions began broadly by differentiating among policy development, management, administration, and planning (Chapter 11). The discussion became more focused in Chapter 12 by reviewing the most widely used science-based systems for managing outdoor recreation resources. Chapter 13 then described the needs for and characteristics of the beneficial outcomes approach to leisure (BOAL) with special attention devoted to a growing application of the BOAL through benefits-based management. In Chapter 14, specific systems for managing recreation-related impacts to natural resources and visitor experiences were reviewed. In this chapter, we focus on how outdoor recreation professionals can obtain the types of data and other information they need to plan, implement, and monitor the types of decisions and managerial systems described in the previous four chapters. As emphasized in Chapters 1 and 2, professionalism in the management of recreation resources is based fundamentally on wise applications of the relevant body of science-based knowledge that defines and anchors the profession. As such, any effective policy development, planning, management, or administration effort must be based on accurate and timely information. This is particularly true when making outdoor recreation resource allocation decisions because of the many, often conflicting, uses and priorities such resources face and the dynamic and rapidly changing environments in which they exist.

In this chapter we turn our attention to gathering the information needed to make effective and efficient outdoor recreation decisions. This is not a new topic, of course, since as early as the 19th century, Fredrick Law Olmsted used careful observations of users' behavior to determine if park features were having the effects he desired. We can and should be even more diligent in gathering needed information and should do so by employing the best and most appropriate tools and techniques available.

Before we begin our discussion, however, it is important to place the material presented in this chapter within the proper context. Gathering information for approaching outdoor recreation professionally is an essential and ongoing process that can and should occur at all stages of policy development, planning, management, and administration. The types of information needed and the level of detail required will vary considerably at different times, but appropriate, timely, reliable, and accurate information is essential at all stages. For example, as master plans are being developed for new recreation areas, broad information about the roles of complimentary providers, the recreation opportunities available in nearby areas, and the preferences of existing and potential users is important. Once an area is developed and in use, much more targeted data about use patterns, resource impacts, and specific user concerns and desires become more valuable.

Also realize that gathering information for outdoor recreation-related decisions is an ongoing process. Certain decisions will require particular and highly specialized types of information. Gathering this information may lead to unexpected results that require asking new questions and gathering other information. This is important to keep in mind when reading this chapter and Chapter 16 (see Strategies for Managing Outdoor Recreation). For example, managers and planners attempting to reduce recreation conflicts on a popular trail should, among other things, gather information from users about the actual sources of conflict to determine the best management strategies. In so doing they could learn that the main problems are a lack of opportunities for unanticipated types of trail experiences and a lack of understanding of proper trail etiquette among some users. These findings should trigger additional research to see if and where those desired experiences could be provided and how best to target problem users to improve their trail behavior. Regardless of the strategies chosen to address these two challenges, ongoing monitoring (i.e., more data gathering) will be required to determine whether the management strategies implemented are being effective. In other words, the process of gathering the information needed for establishing policies and plans, implementing management strategies, and monitoring is ongoing.

The most important point related to the context of gathering information, however, centers on the careful planning of data gathering efforts. While reading the following sections about how to gather the information needed to make informed and professional outdoor recreation decisions, recognize that gathering information can be an expensive and time-consuming process and sometimes places burdens on recreation users. As such, it is very important to plan carefully so only the needed information and the correct information is gathered and obtained in the most efficient and effective manner possible. As a general rule, always be certain that each type of information being sought is truly necessary. Determine in advance precisely how that information will be used and in what form it is needed. Carrying out this step consciously and deliberately before beginning to gather the information often leads to refinements in the types of data being gathered and how it is obtained.

Because outdoor recreation and outdoor recreation management involve interactions between people and natural environments, we address information gathering related to both the human dimension and the natural resource dimension of outdoor recreation resource policy, planning, administration, and management decisions. We begin by addressing data needs related to the human aspects of outdoor recreation, with a discussion of how to estimate existing recreation use and how to forecast future use. We then present techniques for gathering information about the recreation users themselves. In the last part of the chapter we turn our attention briefly to data needs related to the outdoor recreation resources with information on how to measure recreation impacts on natural resources.

Estimating Recreation Use

Estimating existing and future outdoor recreation use falls under a broad topic area sometimes referred to as *demand studies*. Such use estimates are important because they are one gauge of the popularity of the outdoor recreation opportunities being provided in an area. They are necessary for determining trends in outdoor recreation use. However, it is very important to remember that simply knowing how frequently and intensely an area is used is not sufficient to determine how successful the area is being in providing the experiences and other benefits for which the area is being managed. This is related to the very important point made in Chapter 12: Activity-based management is necessary but not sufficient for the management of outdoor recreation resources. However, because estimating visitation is relatively straightforward and such estimates are often used directly or indirectly for budget requests and building other forms of agency and community support, it is an important skill for managers to master.

Units of Measure

The most basic aspect of estimating existing or future outdoor recreation use is to clearly understand the different units of measure involved in quantifying such use. The three most basic use measurement units are recreation visits, recreation visitor days, and recreation visitors.

- **Recreation visit:** one entry by one person for any part of a day regardless of length of stay. So, for example, a person visiting a particular park every day for one week has generated seven recreation visits that week, as would seven different people each visiting the park once during that week. Recreation visits are often referred to simply as the number of "visits."

- **Recreation visitor day (RVD):** recreation use that aggregates to 12 visitor hours. This could consist of 1 person for 12 hours, 2 people for 6 hours each, or any equivalent combination.

- **Recreation visitor:** a distinct individual who uses an area for recreation, regardless of their number of visits or length of stay.

As a simple example of how important it is to clearly understand the differences among these measures, consider a suburban couple that walks for an hour along a greenway trail near their home every day for a year. This annual use is 730 recreation visits (2 people times 365 visits per year), 60.8 RVDs (365 hours times 2 people divided by 12 hours per RVD), and 2 recreation visitors. The most common mistake related to these units, even among recreation professionals, is to be careless or confuse recreation visits with recreation visitors. If 5,000 different individuals use that same trail each year, each visiting an average of 20 times per year, that trail receives 100,000 *visits* annually. However, it has 5,000 *visitors* annually, not 100,000.

Other units of measure related to outdoor recreation that are less commonly used but sometimes tracked in particular areas include the following:

- **Activity occasion:** a single person participating in one recreation activity for any part of one day. For example, one visitor participating in whitewater rafting, hiking, and picnicking during a one-day trip to a popular river would be counted as three activity occasions. *Activity hours* are sometimes used as well.

- **Recreation visitor hour:** an accumulated 60 minutes of recreation use by one or more persons. This could be 1 person for an hour, or 2 people for 30 minutes each, etc. This measure can be used as a building block for RVDs depending on how the data is gathered and tabulated.

Which of these units of measure is used depends in part on the needs of the agencies in question and the nature of the outdoor recreation use their areas generally receive. For instance, RVDs better represent the amount of use when stays to as area are relatively long. Counting a week-long pack trip by a family of five as simply 35 recreation visits (5 visitors times 7 visits each) is accurate, but not as meaningful as 70 RVDs (5 visitors times 7 days times 24 hours per day, all divided by 12 hours per RVD). RVD as a measure of recreation use was developed by the USDA Forest Service and is still favored by them, in part, because of the longer stays their visitors often have. The National Park Service, on the other hand, favors recreation visits, partly because of the relatively short stays common in many parks. If our family of five visits Devil's Tower National Monument and stays an hour, it is more meaningful to account for that as five recreation visits rather than converting that to the equally accurate 0.42 RVDs (i.e., 5 person-hours of recreation divided by 12 hours per RVD). Five visits better represents the fact that these five people used the site and were all served in some way by National Park Service facilities and programs.

Actual Use Estimation Techniques

A relatively large number of approaches and devices can be used to estimate levels of recreation use. Each has strengths and weaknesses and most can be applied in a very rigorous way, involving careful and thorough sampling. However, each can also be applied in sloppy and casual ways that will yield inaccurate or misleading estimates. Which approach is used will depend on the agency's available resources and the purpose of the data collection. An expensive high-tech counting technique does not necessarily mean an accurate use estimate. Nearly 25 years ago, Knudson (1980, p. 399) identified five general classes of use estimates. Although the technology and sophistication of some of the tools available has advanced greatly, the classes of approaches remain essentially the same:

1. pure guess
2. observational estimates by administrators
3. growing statistics based on rough year-to-year comparisons
4. sampling procedures
5. pure count

In terms of actual use estimation techniques, a number of options vary considerably in terms of accuracy, expense, and ease of implementation. Each involves gathering data directly or indirectly, then estimating total use based on these data. The most common approaches used in outdoor recreation areas are presented next. See Yuan, Maiorano, and Yuan (1995) and Hollenhorst, Whisman, and Ewert (1992) for more detailed discussions of how to implement the following and other techniques as well as the advantages, disadvantages, and approximate costs of each.

Voluntary Registration or Permit Stations

Voluntary registration or permit stations that make some sort of appeal to users to provide various kinds of information are often placed at trailheads, campgrounds, or visitor centers. Because they are usually unstaffed and compliance is voluntary, not all users sign in or provide full information. Using voluntary registrations or permits alone can give some sense of use levels, but can be quite inaccurate if not adjusted for noncompliance. A review of a dozen studies involving unmanned voluntary trail registers between 1961 and 1981 found compliance rates varied widely and ranged from 20% to 89% (Krumpe & Lucas, 1986, p. 154). The value of voluntary registration system information can be greatly increased by using such

Voluntary trailhead registration stations like this one in a Wyoming National Forest can provide information for rough recreation use estimation.

systems in combinations with traffic counters or visual observation to determine registration or permit compliance rates that allow the counts to be adjusted to compensate for noncompliance. Using supplemental approaches with registrations or permits also allows other information to be gathered as well.

Mandatory Registration or Permits

Mandatory registration or permits issued by the managing agency or mandatory registration required before entry are more burdensome on visitors than voluntary or other indirect approaches and can be time-consuming for agency personnel. However, they can provide detailed and accurate information about use levels and users if compliance rates are high. They can offer the added advantage of serving as a means to educate users as well by providing important information to users during the process or at least including written information with the permit itself. It is generally not appropriate to implement a mandatory permit or registration system solely to gather use information, but adding questions to an existing permit system about users, their preferences, or travel behavior can help managers to gather valuable information that is not difficult or expensive to obtain. Some fee system receipts at recreation areas can be used in much the same manner as mandatory registration and permit system information.

Visual Observation

Visual observation involves having a person or persons observe recreation use in some way and record the information needed for estimating use. The accuracy of these approaches is greatly affected by the quality of the sampling design, the diligence and skill of the observers, and the complexity and dynamics of the recreation use at the particular site. For example, estimating use of a short loop trail with a single access point is much simpler than estimating use of an extensive dispersed recreation area with many dozens of access points. Although visual observation approaches can be time-consuming for agency personnel and must be done in ways that are sensitive to users' privacy, they have the important advantage of enabling the collection of much more information about use and users than simple counts. See Gregoire and Buhyoff (1999) and Yuan, Maiorano, and Yuan (1995) for excellent discussions of how to best design and carry out observation-based use estimations in recreation areas.

Traffic Counters

Traffic counters include numerous devices available specifically designed to sense and count traffic of various types. Counters are available for use on trails, roads, rivers, and other settings and can be adapted for counting virtually any type of outdoor recreation use where the users pass through a particular spot. Again, traffic counters are most effective if combined with some other counting technique. Some of the most common types of traffic counters are discussed next.

Pneumatic counters record the number of vehicles that drive over an attached rubber tube stretched across a section of road. The accuracy of use estimates based on these counters depends on being able to place the counters in appropriate locations and on having accurate estimates of the average number of people per vehicle. Because traffic counters simply tally the number of vehicles (or axles) that cross them, recreation managers must use other means to estimate how many of those vehicles are there for recreation rather than nonrecreation purposes like access by delivery trucks, travelers simply passing through the area, or even the normal activities of agency staff.

Inductive loop counters operate much like pneumatic traffic counters except that the sensor itself is a copper wire imbedded in a road or buried under a trail.

Pneumatic traffic counters at park access roads can form the basis of estimates of the number of recreation visits.

Inductive loop traffic counters use an electric sensor to record the number of passing vehicles.

The counter is triggered when a metal object passes through the electrical field created by the copper wire.

Seismic counter systems are devices connected to geophones or other seismic sensors buried at specific depths under trails or roads. They are activated by the vibrations caused by passing vehicles, horses, and others.

Pressure plate or floor mat counters can be buried under a trail to record the number of people stepping on that spot. Floor mat counters are similar, but more commonly used at the entrances to buildings such as visitor centers or ranger stations.

Optical counters use various kinds of light beams to detect and count traffic on trails, roads, rivers, building entrances and so forth. *Active infrared* counters send an invisible beam to a reflector and count the number of times the beam is broken by, say, a trail user. *Passive infrared* counters send a beam across the area of interest and records each time the beam reflects back to its source after bouncing off something passing by. Optical counters must be placed carefully to avoid counting, say, branches waving in the wind. Because such counters record anything that breaks the light beam, they cannot distinguish between recreation use and wildlife or pets, or the same visitor making more than one pass (e.g., multiple laps on a loop trail, several trips in and out of a dispersed use area by the same person).

Remote Sensing

Remote sensing approaches use various technologies to observe use unobtrusively and from some distance. Airplanes, helicopters, and tethered balloons equipped with cameras or other imaging devices have all been used for this purpose. Satellite imagery will likely be available at some future point for this purpose as well. However, all of these remote sensing approaches are currently very expensive and not commonly employed for estimating recreation use.

Camera Systems

Digital, 35mm, or video camera systems can be used to estimate use and gather additional information related to type of use and group characteristics. Although vandalism and theft of equipment are potential problems, cameras can be valuable, especially in relatively open areas and in combinations with other techniques. A common approach is to set the camera to record images at predetermined intervals. Users of these approaches must be especially sensitive to privacy issues. Cameras should not be used in campground areas (where greater privacy is expected) and equipment should be set slightly out of focus or at low resolutions to make it impossible to identify individuals from the images obtained.

Other Indirect Counts

Under certain conditions, predictive relationships can be found that enable use to be estimated from other relatively easy to obtain information. Yuan and associates (1995) offer the examples of monitoring water use through the water meter at a campground to estimate campground use, or monitoring park entrance totals, campground occupancy rates, and weather conditions to estimate trail use in dispersed area. Care and skill are needed initially to discover and understand the relationship, and periodic reevaluation and revisions are necessary. Once in place, however, these formulas can be very efficient means of providing at least rough estimates of use levels.

Each of the aforementioned methods for estimating recreation use has advantages and disadvantages that must be weighted before selecting the most appropriate one for any particular application. Some of the important factors to consider when choosing a method include cost, time, and other resources available; susceptibility of equipment to discovery and vandalism; ease of installation and operation; size; weight; lifetime of power source; ability to gather additional types of information; potential burden on visitors and their privacy; and the accuracy and reliability of the resulting data. The type of recreation area in question is also an important factor in selecting the most appropriate approach. Particularly important are whether it is a concentrated use area or dispersed use area, and whether it has limited access or multiple access points (Yuan, Maiorano & Yuan, 1995).

As noted in some of the previous examples, combining different techniques can provide better results than implementing single approaches alone. For example, voluntary registration systems used in combination with traffic counters or visual observations can improve the accuracy and scope of information that either can provide alone. Likewise, placing cameras near traffic counters can help establish how many of the counts are actually recreation users (as opposed to park staff or animals), how many RVDs are represented (by providing information to calculate lengths of stay), and other useful information, such as recreation activity types and group sizes.

Forecasting Future Recreation Use

Having accurate information about existing outdoor recreation use is important. Often, however, being able to forecast how much and what types of recreation use might occur at some point in the future is even more important. This is particularly true when recreation planners are attempting to determine how many recreation areas of various types will be needed, where they should be located, and what types of opportunities should be offered at each. Making these and other predictions about the future is referred to as *forecasting*. Loomis and Walsh (1997) summarized the most commonly used recreation forecasting approaches. They included the following, arranged roughly from the most basic to the most complex and sophisticated.

Informed Judgment Approach

Forecasting based on informed judgment incorporates the best information available, but ultimately relies on the best, sometimes subjective, insights of the planners and managers involved. It can be done systematically as in the Delphi technique (Moeller & Shafer, 1983) or less formally. Although this approach is frequently used, it is usually unreliable if used alone, especially if used to attempt to forecast long-term trends.

Resource Capacity Approach

In situations where there is more demand for an area than can be practically accommodated, the demand for future use can be roughly estimated to be equal to capacity. For example, the effect on total use of increasing the size of such an area's main parking area or the number of rooms at its main overnight facility can be easily predicted if planners can be confident that the area will continue to operate at 100% capacity under the new conditions.

Market Survey Approaches

Market assessments can be useful to predict short-term trends in outdoor recreation use. This is most often accomplished through household surveys of people's recreation intentions or interests or through test marketing (e.g., new programs, fees, or facilities) to gauge visitor and potential visitor reactions and behaviors.

Extension of Past Trends

One of the most commonly used outdoor recreation forecasting methods is simply to examine past trends and extend them to some particular point in the future. This technique is also called a *time series* approach because it utilizes a series of observations over time for a variable of interest, such as annual visitation to a particular park. If the factors that determined demand in the past continue to affect demand in the same ways in the future, this can be an accurate and efficient approach, particularly in the short run.

Regression Methods

Regression methods use mathematical models to predict changes in recreation use based on particular variables known (or assumed) to be related to outdoor recreation participation. For decades changes in population, per capita real income, total available leisure, and per capita travel have been among the variables used to help forecast changes in future recreation use (e.g., Clausen & Knetsch, 1966). Single variable regression methods use what is assumed to be the single most important explanatory variable alone to predict future use and multiple regression methods use a group of important variables together in hopes of making the model more accurate. When systematically and expertly applied, regression approaches and other related mathematical modeling techniques can be powerful tools for recreation planners.

Each of these and other approaches are appropriate in different situations. Notice, too, that some of them require accurate estimates of current or past use as a basis for forecasting future use levels. See Loomis and Walsh (1997) for a more thorough discussion of these and other approaches.

Gathering User Information

Estimating current use and projecting future demand for outdoor recreation are important, but those are not the only types of information needed for providing and managing outdoor recreation opportunities effectively and professionally. Managers should also have an understanding of who their visitors are, how they use available opportunities, what they like and dislike, and other related information. Examples of the types of information that are useful and sometimes essential for effective outdoor recreation management include visitor

- beliefs (e.g., what they believe their responsibilities as visitors are)
- attitudes (e.g., whether they feel a proposed fee program is justified)
- preferences (e.g., what kinds of settings and experiences they desire)
- use patterns (e.g., where visitors go in the area, when, and how long they stay)
- knowledge (e.g., visitor knowledge and understanding of low-impact use skills)
- behavior (e.g., what activities visitors engage in and how much money they spend in nearby areas)
- experiences (e.g., overall levels of visitor satisfaction, satisfaction with particular aspects of the recreation opportunities provided)
- perceptions of problems (e.g., levels of recreational crowding and conflict, unsafe conditions)

Outdoor recreation managers can obtain user information of the types just noted in a number of ways. Some of this information can be gathered through adaptations of the approaches noted earlier for estimating recreation use. For example, well-designed visual observation techniques can also be used to record the recreation activities in which visitors are engaged, group sizes, and some visitor characteristics, such as gender and broad age categories. Camera systems can give information about many of these variables as well. As noted earlier, permit and registration forms can be designed to include questions to gather important information on users and use, in addition to enabling estimates of numbers of users.

However, many types of user information, especially those related to beliefs, attitudes, preferences, knowledge, and experiences, require more sophisticated approaches. Many of these approaches require special skills and experience and can make ideal collaborative partnerships between managers and agency scientists, university faculty, or students. Several of these approaches are introduced next.

Analysis and Application of Secondary Data

Secondary data is available information gathered for purposes other than the particular need at hand. There are occasions, however, when secondary data can be very helpful in decision making beyond the scope of its original purposes. For example, recreation visitor studies conducted at other similar sites might help managers and planners to understand some characteristics or behaviors of visitors to their own site. Data gathered for broader purposes, such as a Statewide Comprehensive Outdoor Recreation Plan (SCORP), can often give insights to planners and managers of specific sites in that state. If, for example, a particular state's SCORP indicates "watchable wildlife" experiences

Well-designed and executed user surveys can be a very effective method of gathering user information.

are growing in popularity statewide and that a lack of large blocks of free time is an increasingly problematic constrain to recreation participation, planners and managers across the state should consider the possibility these things might also apply to the users of their particular sites, even if they cannot afford to systematically gather addition information about their own local users. Likewise, national census data or data from national studies such as the National Survey on Recreation and the Environment (NSRE) can help agency managers and planners in important ways, even though those data were not drawn exclusively from the users or potential users of that agency's sites. Information from industry, trade associations, retailers, and associations of recreation users can frequently give insights into trends and preferences of users and potential users as well.

User Surveys

Surveys of recreation visitors can be used to generate wide varieties of information for many outdoor recreation planning and management purposes. They have the advantage of being flexible enough to gather any and all of the types of information noted earlier and can be adapted to nearly any type of situation. But user surveys have several disadvantages as well. User surveys can be expensive and time-consuming, and considerable expertise is required to conduct user surveys that provide valid and reliable information in ways not overly burdensome to recreation users. This needed expertise extends to proper sampling, questionnaire design, data entry, analysis, and interpretation. Surveys typically require approvals of various kinds as well, with most agencies requiring internal reviews of all proposed user studies. Data-gathering efforts that use federal funds can also require Office of Management and Budget (OMB) review and approval. User surveys can take different forms and be conducted in various ways. The two most common types are interviews and written questionnaires. Interviews can be conducted on-site or off-site and can be either face-to-face or over the telephone. Written questionnaires can be used on-site, off-site, through the mail, or even over the Internet in some situations. A related technique is to ask visitors to record information in journals such as what they do, where they go, and what they like and do not like when in an area. As noted earlier, it is important to only gather information actually needed. Consider carefully, in advance, how the information from a planned user survey will used to assure that each question is actually needed and that it is asked in the proper way.

Unobtrusive Observation

Similar to the visual observation approach to estimating use noted earlier, this technique involves systematically watching and recording users' behavior at the site. Information, such as group size, mode of travel, what users bring with them, what they do, where they go, and how they interact with other users, can be determined this way. Making these observations unobtrusively, without interacting with the users, makes this information particularly valuable because it can reveal what is actually going on. Of course, such observations must be done in ways that are sensitive to users' privacy.

Focus Groups

Focus groups are semi-structured group interviews. They typically involve six to ten people discussing topics of interest to the sponsor in a facilitated question and answer format. It is possible to gather a great deal of information through well-designed and facilitated focus group sessions. Again, skill is required in selecting the proper participants, preparing the questions, facilitating the session, and interpreting the input received.

Techniques for Measuring Impacts to Recreation Resources

In Chapter 14 we introduced the major systems currently being used to identify and manage the negative impacts recreation use may be causing to natural resources and visitor experiences, including limits of acceptable change (LAC), visitor experience and resource protection (VERP), and visitor impact management (VIM). The successful application of these systematic approaches depends on having appropriate, accurate, and timely information about the impacts and the use dynamics causing them. This involves measuring existing impacts before and during applications of visitor impact management systems, and perhaps more importantly, monitoring impacts after these systems have been put in place in a particular area.

The techniques available for measuring particular site impacts vary tremendously and depend on which type of impact is being examined. Highly specialized approaches exist for assessing impacts to soils, vegetation, wildlife, water quality, and air quality and are beyond the scope of an introductory text. For example, sophisticated tools are available for measuring soil compaction, including "penetrometers" that determine the pressure needed to penetrate the soil with a probe and nuclear density testers costing thousands of dollars. These devices are equipped with a probe containing a nuclear source. After the probe is driven into the ground the amount of radiation reaching the meter above the ground is used to calculate soil density. Likewise, sophisticated protocols arc available to deter-

mine the presence and behavior of various wildlife species as well as make accurate measurements related to the other specialties noted previously.

More detailed information on specialized resource condition techniques can be found in the LAC, VERP, and VIM references provided in Chapter 14 as well as Hammitt and Cole (1998), Liddle (1997), and other sources. Many agencies also employ experts in specialized resource areas who can be called on to apply their skills and methods to particular recreation-related resources and impacts. However, the growing field of recreation ecology has refined several approaches to measuring and monitoring common recreation impacts. In general, the best natural resource assessment systems have the following characteristics (Graefe, Kuss & Vaske, 1990):

1. use multiple indicators
2. record each indicator separately
3. are as precise as possible (given the agency resources available, the number of sites to be monitored, frequency of measurement needed, and so forth)

Consistency is crucial when assessing and monitoring resource conditions. It is important to keep in mind that monitoring resource conditions is a long-term endeavor. The team that does the initial assessment will likely not be the only one that will be engaged in condition monitoring, particularly over the long term. Therefore, instructions about how indicators are measured must be clear and complete. For example, "the amount of trail erosion" is not measurable or replicable and will inevitably result in inaccurate and inconsistent data. Details such as "the depth of erosion at its deepest point relative to the undisturbed edges measured every 100 meters along the trail" provides much better guidance.

Measuring and monitoring impacts to recreation resources is important and can employ many different techniques. (Photo by Yu-Fai Leung)

The two most common recreation resources where recreation impacts have been assessed are backcountry campsites and trails. Several broad types of assessment approaches have been developed for each and are briefly introduced next.

Campground Assessment

Campground assessment techniques fall into the following three general types (Hendee & Dawson, 2002):

Photo Point Photography

Using photographs to document the overall condition of an area has been used for many years. The photos must be from an identifiable and relatively permanent landmark (e.g., boulder, metal pin) and include precise information that can be used to reproduce photo parameters as nearly as possible in future years (e.g., date, time of day, camera height above ground, compass bearings for the precise direction of each photo). Global positioning system (GPS) devices can now be used to document photo locations as well. Photo point photography can provide an excellent permanent visual record of a site for comparisons of overall conditions, but does not provide adequate information to be used alone for impact assessments.

Condition Class Systems

These are relatively fast and efficient field assessments that assign an overall condition score (often from 1 to 5) for each site. Conditions can be based on a number of variables, but commonly use factors such as loss of groundcover, vegetation loss, and visible erosion. Although these approaches can be very helpful in terms of the relative impacts across many sites, they are not very sensitive and may not provide information on the severity of particular impacts.

Campground Assessment Methods

These are detailed inventories of the conditions of campsites. Assessments can include measures of any number of variables and provide much more information, but at the cost of being more time-consuming and therefore more expensive. Such systems make and record measurements of multiple variables from the center point of each campsite, often in 16 compass point directions. The data is used for mapping each site and calculating values such as loss of ground cover area (e.g., area of the site's barren core, barren area as a percent of the overall campsite area), number of damaged trees within the campsite area, and presence of fire rings and other development.

Trail Condition Assessment

Trail condition assessment techniques fall into several broad categories as well (Hendee & Dawson, 2002; Marion & Leung, 2001):

Rapid-Assessment Approaches

Rapid assessment techniques involve gathering a limited amount of resource condition information at particular points along a trail rather than continuously for the entire trail. At fixed intervals, perhaps every 100 meters, key variables such as trail width, depth, and muddiness are measured and recorded. As the name implies, these approaches are fast, efficient, and valuable for determining the relative condition of different trail segments.

Trail Maintenance Assessments

These are much more detailed assessments of maintenance needs on particular trails. They focus on determining what maintenance activities are needed to correct or prevent trail problems such as erosion, widening, or muddiness. These approaches can be used to generate prescriptive work logs, which are essential for planning future maintenance needs and directing the efforts of trail maintenance crews and volunteers.

Trail Condition Assessments

These are detailed assessments of resource conditions along the entire length of a trail. They record more information than rapid-assessment approaches and are useful for developing accurate descriptions of resource conditions and identifying relationships between impacts and influential variables, such as slope and vegetation type. Condition assessments can be done at fixed intervals (e.g., every 100 meters), continuously for an entire trail segment (e.g., a census), or in the form of a problem assessment where every occurrence of a particular problem, such as erosion over a certain depth, is recorded by location.

Summary

This chapter introduced and described approaches for gathering the information needed for professionally planning and managing outdoor recreation resources and opportunities. Information gathering is an essential and ongoing process, and one that needs to be consciously and deliberately planned. Four main areas were discussed. The first was how to estimate recreation use, where we began by introducing the most commonly used units of measure: recreation visits, recreation visitor days (RVDs), and recreation visitors. We then introduced a number of techniques for estimating levels of existing recreation use, including voluntary and mandatory registration or permit systems, visual observation, five different types of traffic counters, remote sensing, and camera systems. The second area of discussion related to forecasting future recreation use, where we introduced the following as the most commonly used approaches: informed judgment, resource capacity, market surveys, extension of past trends, and regression methods. Gathering user information was the third area of discussion. The main approaches for gathering the many types of information noted here were analysis and application of secondary data, user surveys (e.g., interviews, questionnaires), unobtrusive observation, and focus groups. The final area addressed was how to gather the information needed to identify and manage the negative impacts recreation use may be causing to natural resources and visitor experiences. These kinds of information are essential for effectively applying the management systems described in Chapters 12, 13, and 14. General characteristics of assessment techniques were addressed and specific examples given in the areas of backcountry campsites and trails. The next chapter moves beyond the information needed for effective outdoor recreation planning and management and presents specific strategies for influencing and managing visitor behavior.

Literature Cited

Clausen, M. and Knetsch, J. L. (1966). *Economics of outdoor recreation*. Baltimore, MD: Johns Hopkins Press.

Graefe, A., Kuss, F., and Vaske, J. (1990). *Visitor impact management: The planning framework*. Washington, DC: National Parks and Conservation Association.

Gregoire, T. and Buhyoff, G. (1999). *Sampling and estimating recreational use* (PNW-GTR-456). Portland, OR: USDA Forest Service, Pacific Northwest Research Station.

Hammitt, W. and Cole, D. (1998). *Wildland recreation: Ecology and management* (2nd ed.). New York, NY: John Wiley and Sons.

Hendee, J. and Dawson, C. (2002). *Wilderness management: Stewardship and protection of resources and values* (3rd ed.). Golden, CO: Fulcrum.

Hollenhorst, S., Whisman, S., and Ewert, A. (1992). *Monitoring visitor use in backcountry wilderness* (PSW-GTR-134). USDA Forest Service, Pacific Southwest Research Station.

Knowler, D. (1984). *The falconer of Central Park*. Princeton, NJ: Karz-Cohl Publishing.

Knudson, D. (1980). *Outdoor recreation*. New York, NY: Macmillan Publishing.

Krumpe, E. and Lucas, R. (1986). Research on recreation trails and trail users. In *President's commission on Americans outdoors: A literature review*. Washington, DC: U.S. Government Printing Office.

Liddle, M. (1997). *Recreation ecology: The ecological impact of outdoor recreation and ecotourism*. New York, NY: Chapman and Hall.

Loomis, J. and Walsh, R. (1997). *Recreation economic decisions: Comparing benefits and costs* (2nd ed.). State College, PA: Venture Publishing, Inc.

Marion, J. and Leung, Y. (2001). Trail resource impacts and an examination of alternative assessment techniques. *Journal of Park and Recreation Administration, 19*(3), 17–37.

Moeller, G. and Shafer, E. (1983). The use and misuse of Delphi forecasting. In S. Lieber and D. Fesenmaier (Eds.), *Recreation planning and management* (pp. 96–104). State College, PA: Venture Publishing, Inc.

Yuan, S., Maiorano, B., and Yuan, M. (1995, August). *Techniques and equipment for gathering visitor use data on recreation sites*. Missoula, MT: USDA Forest Service, Technology and Development Center.

Chapter 16
Influencing and Managing Visitor Behavior

While nature is not a uniquely suitable setting, it seems to have a peculiar power to stimulate us to reflectiveness by its awesomeness and grandeur, its complexity, the unfamiliarity of untrammeled ecosystems to urban residents, and the absence of distractions. (Sax, 1980, p. 46)

Learning Objectives

1. Explain why outdoor recreation professionals should be concerned with understanding visitor behavior.
2. Describe the different types of visitor behaviors and motives.
3. Differentiate between direct and indirect approaches for managing outdoor recreation opportunities.
4. Describe the major strategies for managing and influencing visitor behavior.

As pointed out in Chapter 11, management involves taking specific steps to meet established objectives so policy goals can be attained. Boards of directors and CEOs manage corporations, heads of transportation departments manage highway systems, general managers and their coaching staffs manage professional sports teams, and managers of outdoor recreation resources manage the provision of outdoor recreation opportunities. Many management processes and skills are applicable across different management contexts. Most Fortune 500 CEOs, for example, are skilled and effective enough to manage many aspects of any large organization, regardless of what products or services it provides. However, managing outdoor recreation opportunities is unique in three very important respects.

First, managing the provision of outdoor recreation opportunities is different from other forms of management in that it involves integrating the management of two very different but related dimensions: people and natural environments. Therefore, providing and managing outdoor recreation opportunities involves blending natural resources management (as well as cultural and historic resources management) with the management of human use and its influences.

Second, the "products" of outdoor recreation resource management are quite different from those that result from most managerial processes. Outdoor recreation managers do not generate commodities like the mass-produced tangible outputs of manufacturing processes. Although professional outdoor recreation managers often provide services, that is not their primary role. Outdoor recreation managers work with their many partners to provide opportunities in natural environments and at cultural/historic sites that visitors may then use to "produce" their own outdoor recreation experiences. Chapters 1 and 2 described

recreation as an experience, and Chapter 13 detailed the recreation opportunity production process that leads to those experiences and other benefits. Therefore, in the strictest sense "outdoor recreation management" is a misnomer because we do not manage outdoor recreation per se. We actually manage the outdoor recreation opportunities rather than outdoor recreation itself. This generally involves managing the recreation setting as well as influencing and managing the behavior of visitors.

A third major distinction between outdoor recreation management and other types of management has to do with the nature of the outdoor recreation experiences that result from visitors' use of the opportunities provided by managers. Recall from Chapter 1 an essential element of outdoor recreation is perceived freedom. For most outdoor recreationists, satisfying experiences require freedom and spontaneity to be satisfying. This is hinted at in the quote at the beginning of this chapter, because nature can indeed stimulate us in unique and powerful ways. But this can only occur if management provides appropriate settings for the desired experiences and does so in ways not distracting or overly intrusive on visitors' freedom. Managing outdoor recreation opportunities in ways that allow for perceived freedom and spontaneity can be equally important for off-site users as well.

Other chapters in this text recognized these three unique characteristics of managing to provide outdoor recreation opportunities while at the same time protecting the basic resources from negative impacts and minimizing adverse impacts of users on each other. Chapters 12 and 13 described the available science-based management systems proven to be useful. Chapters 14 and 15 focused on managing to prevent negative impacts and gathering data needed by management, respectively. Chapter 18 will continue this emphasis in its discussion of managing special outdoor recreation resources. Each of these chapters recognizes the need to manage the basic resources as well as to influence and manage visitor behavior, but none concentrated specifically on visitor behavior as an essential managerial concern and responsibility.

The purpose of this chapter, therefore, is to introduce the most important proven techniques available for influencing and managing visitor behavior. Most of the early material on this topic focused on influencing and managing visitor behavior solely to prevent or to reduce negative impacts. That orientation probably stems from the fact that, until recently, outdoor recreation resource management did not adopt a behavioral approach like that presented in the outdoor recreation experience model described in Chapter 1. This caused the focus of management to be primarily on supply (mostly on the recreation resources) instead of on both supply and demand (especially the experiences desired by the users). Protecting the resources is certainly a very important concern, but managers also need to know how to influence and manage visitor behavior to facilitate and enhance the realization of satisfying recreation experiences by the visitors.

We begin with a discussion of why it is important to understand visitor behavior and move on to the types of behaviors that can be influenced. We then spend the bulk of the chapter introducing specific management strategies and discussing how to select the most appropriate ones for particular situations. Before we begin, two qualifications must be made. First, our focus here is on managing outdoor recreation opportunities for the on-site users, which we refer to herein as *users* or as *visitors*. However, many of the users of recreation and related amenity resources are off-site users who never actually visit the resources being managed, but nevertheless have expressed strong approval for protecting and managing those resources and, through their tax dollars, help to pay for such activities. Therefore, recreation, nature appreciation, and many other opportunities are being created and managed for off-site users as well as on-site users. We emphasized the importance of those off-site customers in Chapter 13. Second, some people object to the concept of managing people, such as visitors to recreation resource areas. We

recognize influencing and managing visitor behavior are almost always necessary to accomplish managerial goals, but must be done in ways sensitive to the unique needs of users, and in ways that allow users to have high-quality outdoor recreation experiences. This will become more clear later in this chapter when we discuss the *minimum tool rule* and the need to minimize visitor *burden* when managing outdoor recreation opportunities.

Understanding Why Visitors Behave the Way They Do

Providing high-quality outdoor recreation opportunities is the responsibility of outdoor recreation professionals and their many partners. In some respects, however, much of the long-term health of outdoor recreation resources depends on the behavior of the recreationists themselves. This in no way implies managers have only a minimal role. Managers must work diligently and proactively to provide opportunities for desired recreation experiences and to assure users behave responsibly to minimize the negative impacts of recreation on natural resources and the experiences of other users. It requires managers of outdoor recreation resources to influence and manage the visitors to some extent, with that amount varying from one situation to another. This requires that managers understand visitor behavior. To be able to select the most appropriate management strategies, managers need to know three key things about visitor behavior:

1. What types of satisfying experiences and other benefits are desired and expected by the users, and what dissatisfying experiences are not desired?

2. What relationships do the visitors perceive between the attributes of the social, biophysical, and managerial settings necessary for them to realize the satisfying recreation experiences desired?

3. Why do users behave the ways they do in outdoor recreation settings?

These three points are necessary to meet visitor preferences and to assure users have the least possible negative impacts on resources and other users.

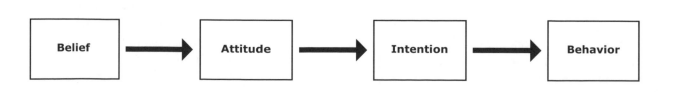

Figure 16.1 A theory of reasoned action for outdoor recreation behavior. Adapted from Fishbein & Manfredo, 1992, p. 32

In Chapter 1 we introduced a simple outdoor recreation experience model, which illustrated in the broadest sense that people's needs and desires motivate them to seek certain types of outdoor recreation experiences. Understanding these needs, desires, and experiences users seek helps planners and managers to provide the appropriate mix of settings to provide opportunities for these experiences. This is the basis of the recreation opportunity spectrum (ROS) as described in Chapter 12. But a broad understanding of motivations is not sufficient to guide managers in terms of specific strategies for managing outdoor recreation opportunities. For example, using the concepts illustrated in the outdoor recreation experience model, planners and managers might determine that users of a certain wilderness area seek opportunities for adventure, solitude, and challenge, and desire wild settings with few other people where they can hike and camp. Such information is essential to guide managers regarding the types of settings and other opportunities to provide. However, when users take advantage of the opportunities provided, they sometimes use the natural resources in responsible ways and sometimes they do not. For instance, some users dispose of their human waste appropriately and others do so in ways that pollute water and cause health and aesthetic problems. Similarly, some users are considerate around others, but some are not. Managers need more guidance than that provided by the outdoor recreation experience model to understand why people behave these ways to help them select the most appropriate management strategies for minimizing irresponsible behaviors and the negative impacts such behaviors cause, as well as to facilitate and enhance the realization of satisfying recreation experiences for visitors.

Specific outdoor recreation behavior is thought by many to have its roots in people's beliefs, attitudes, and intentions. For instance, the theory of reasoned action (Fishbein & Manfredo, 1992), as summarized in Figure 16.1, suggests our beliefs affect our attitudes, which affect what we intend to do, which in turn affects what we actually do in outdoor recreation settings. For example, if users of a particular park believe (i.e., belief) that the natural resources there are not fragile, they may feel (i.e., attitude) that how they use the resources there will have no negative impacts. Therefore, they may decide (i.e., intention) to ride their mountain bikes off trail that day, and then, in fact, do just that (i.e., behavior). The theory of reasoned action is important for outdoor recreation managers because it implies changing inaccurate beliefs and irresponsible attitudes may be the most effective ways to change some problem behaviors. This can aid in selecting management strategies.

Outdoor recreation researchers have also made progress in understanding what influences visitors' perceptions and satisfaction. In addition, research has helped improve our understanding of why people sometimes behave irresponsibly in outdoor recreation settings. Problem behaviors can cause unwanted impacts on the recreation resources as well as on other users, which reduce the satisfactions realized by those impacted users. Considerable research has been done on problem behaviors of recreation visitors. The first distinction typically made is whether the problem behavior is intentional or not (Knopf & Dustin, 1992). The common terms used to distinguish between these two basic categories of problem behavior are

Depreciative Behavior: any act that detracts from the social or physical environment (Clark, Hendee & Campbell, 1971)

Vandalism: a willful act of damage to the environment (Harrison, 1982)

Vandalism, therefore, is one type of depreciative behavior, characterized by being intentional rather than unintentional. Various types of intentional and unintentional problem behaviors have been identified. For example, Hendee and Dawson (2002) divided problem visitor actions into five types: illegal actions, careless actions, unskilled actions, uninformed actions, and unavoidable impacts. Others (Gramann & Vander Stoep, 1987; Vander Stoep & Gramann, 1987) identified six different types of depreciative behavior in park settings based on the apparent motives for the action: unintentional violations, releasor-cue violations, uninformed violations, responsibility-denial violations, status-confirming violations, and

Vandalism, as opposed to other types of depreciative behavior in general, involves willful damage.

willful violations. Table 16.1 blends depreciative behavior into nine general groupings and distinguishes between the intentional and unintentional ones. It also provides descriptions and possible examples of each type. This information can give valuable guidance to managers that they can use to help select the most appropriate strategies to address particular problems they might face.

Note there can be considerable overlap among the nine types. For example, it is possible a few park visitors remove native vegetation from public lands to save money on their home landscaping, not realizing this is against the law (i.e., material gain and uninformed). There are also situations where users are uninformed and unskilled regarding responsible outdoor recreation behavior. This would be the case when a person does not know that allowing bears to get to human food creates dangerous problems by habituating them to people and/or does not know the proper ways to store their food at campsites. We will return to these nine types of problem behaviors in the last section of this chapter where we discuss the most appropriate management strategies for influencing and managing visitor behaviors for particular situations.

Strategies for Managing Outdoor Recreation Settings and Influencing Visitor Behavior

Understanding why users do the things they do is an essential first step in determining the most appropriate management strategies to reduce or to eliminate particular problems in particular situations or to facilitate and enhance the visitors' experiences. Next, managers must consider the aspects of the recreation settings and recreation use they can influence. There are more options in this regard than most people realize. For example, Hendee and Dawson (2002, pp. 467–469) listed the following as elements of visitor use subject to management:

- amount and distribution of use
- redistribution of visitor use
- method of travel
- party size
- length of stay

Table 16.1   Types of problem behaviors in outdoor recreation settings

UNINTENTIONAL PROBLEM BEHAVIORS

Problem Type	Description
Unavoidable	Necessary behaviors that cause unintentional impacts which are essentially unavoidable byproducts of being in the area at all (e.g., soil compaction on trails, some displacement of wildlife, human waste)
Uninformed	Damaging behaviors engaged in because the user is not aware he or she is causing damage or behaving inappropriatly (e.g., skidding a mountain bike, hanging gasoline lanterns on trees in campgrounds, feeding wildlife, washing with soap in streams)
Unskilled	Depreciative acts caused by a lack of skill. In other words, when the user would have behaved responsibly if he or she had the proper skills to do so (e.g., selecting improper camping sites, storing food improperly in bear country, not properly disposing of human waste)

INTENTIONAL PROBLEM BEHAVIORS

Problem Type	Description
Careless	Behaviors the user knows are wrong or inconsiderate, but still engages in, often without really thinking about it (e.g., some littering, playing loud music at a campground)
Releasor-Cue	Problems involving users seeing others be irresponsible (or evidence of it like litter or graffiti) and concluding that they can do the same thing (e.g., short-cutting trail switchbacks because others obviously have, mountain biking on closed trails because the closure is posted but apparently not enforced, littering because management does not seem to care enough to clean it up). Such actions involve cues the user feels "releases" them from the responsibility to behave responsibly; could also be called "copycat" behavior
Responsibility-Denial	Behaviors the user knows are wrong, but rationalizes are acceptable in particular circumstances (e.g., not paying fees because "I already pay taxes that support this park")
Status-Confirming	Doing something to affirm formal or informal "membership" in some group that violates rules (e.g., "tagging" graffiti on public property to be one of the gang, riding a mountain bike on a wilderness trail closed to bikes to gain respect of irresponsible friends who do so too)
Protest	Deliberately engaging in problem behavior as a form of protest or revenge (e.g., using a motorized vehicle on a closed trail because "the closure is unfair," damaging facilities to "get back at them" for some management action seen as unjustified)
Material Gain	Breaking rules to obtain something of material value (e.g., illegally removing Native American artifacts from public lands to add to a private collection, poaching wildlife to sell on the black market)

Adapted from Hendee and Dawson (2002) and Vander Stoep and Gramann (1987)

- visitor behavior (e.g., where to camp, whether to build fires)
- visitor effects on the resource

The following are also things that managers can influence that relate to how visitors use outdoor recreation opportunities:

- user expectations
- user knowledge (e.g., about responsible, low-impact use)
- time of use
- season of use (e.g., wet spring vs. dry summer)
- level of individual and community support for management and its policies

According to the theory of reasoned action introduced earlier, the most effective ways to influence visitor behavior over the long term may be to change user beliefs, attitudes, and intentions.

The traditional (and one of the most fundamental) distinctions among the various strategies available to outdoor recreation managers is the extent to which they directly address visitors' behavior. At the most basic level, management strategies have traditionally been categorized as being either "indirect" or "direct" approaches (Hendee & Dawson, 2002, p. 472). Indirect and direct approaches are distinguished as follows:

Indirect management strategies attempt to influence user behavior indirectly rather than through regulations or restrictions. Indirect approaches tend to be more subtle than direct ones and compliance is not mandatory. Examples of indirect management approaches include information and education programs and physical alterations to settings

and facilities that attempt to encourage (rather than mandate) responsible behavior.

Direct management strategies are actions by management that directly affect what users can and cannot do. Direct strategies restrict or regulate user behavior through rules, regulations, area closures, zoning, requiring mandatory permits, and rationing.

It may be tempting to assume indirect strategies should be favored over more direct ones. However, this is not necessarily the case (Hammitt & Cole, 1998). Each of the two general approaches has advantages and disadvantages and most are highly effective in some situations but not in others. Therefore, selecting the most appropriate combination of management strategies needs to be done after considering many factors, which we will address in the

Assuring that visitors have accurate expectations can be an effective way of influencing outdoor recreation behavior.

Determining what methods of travel will be allowed in particular areas is an important aspect of managing outdoor recreation resources.

Some managers close trails when soils are very wet and, therefore, most susceptible to damage.

final section of this chapter. However, the indirect or direct distinction can be a useful starting point.

The remainder of this section introduces common outdoor recreation management strategies. It will be immediately apparent there is a great deal of overlap among many of the strategies. Some focus primarily on aspects of the natural resources and some focus more on visitor behavior, but most of them are directed at both. The indirect approaches are presented first followed by the direct approaches, along with short descriptions and examples of each. More detailed information about many of the following approaches is available from numerous other sources. Two excellent ones are Hendee and Dawson (2002) and Hammitt and Cole (1998).

Indirect Management Approaches

Many indirect approaches can be used to manage outdoor recreation opportunities and to influence user behavior. The four most common types—modifications of the physical setting, information and education programs, user involvement, and fees or other economic constraints—are introduced next.

Modifications of the Physical Setting

Modifying the physical setting can be a very effective way to manage or influence visitor behavior. It can be used to enhance the visitors' experiences through provision of desired features of the physical setting or by eliminating hazardous and bothersome features where appropriate. It can also be a very effective way to protect resources and to encourage visitors to behave responsibly without resorting to more heavy-handed approaches. This can be accomplished by careful initial design (e.g., locating new trails in the most durable locations) or by taking steps to correct problems that have already occurred (e.g., eliminating shortcut trails at switchbacks and rehabilitating damage there using natural materials and native plantings). A

Physical modifications like this pedestrian-only trail entrance in New Mexico are a type of indirect management approach.

few examples of setting modifications that can be effective and appropriate in particular situations include the following:

- "Harden" vulnerable sites by installing native rock steps on eroded trails, subtle natural barriers around fragile areas, hard surfacing on heavily used frontcountry trails, or vandal-resistant materials for facilities.
- Relocate campsites, trails, and other facilities away from fragile areas to the most durable sites available, then rehabilitate the damaged areas.
- Protect natural resources by using waterbars and other drainage control devices on trails.
- Clean up, rehabilitate, and aggressively maintain sites to minimize problems caused by releasor-cues such as litter and vandalism. Be aware that these approaches may be treating symptoms rather than actual causes, however (Hendee & Dawson, 2002).
- Manage design capacity. For example, limit the size of parking areas or campgrounds near fragile areas or expand the size of ones located at durable sites, or keep some access roads and facilities primitive to discourage use there.
- Design and construct improvements to positively influence behavior. For example, use trail surfaces that encourage or discourage particular uses, locate facilities in ways that screen out undesirable sights and sounds, provide long sight distances in frontcountry areas to enhance feelings of safety, and design trails so there are no switchbacks to shortcut.

When using approaches that modify physical settings, it is important the site modifications be as subtle and natural-appearing as possible to minimize distractions from the naturalness of the setting. This is essential for settings toward the more primitive end of the ROS, but important for any outdoor recreation setting.

Information and Education Programs

A second very popular indirect approach is the use of information and education (I&E) programs. These are efforts that attempt to inform, educate, and/or influence visitors, potential visitors, or other publics. They may utilize many different means (e.g., ranger programs, brochures, videos, radio spots, billboards) and may be directed at beliefs, attitudes, knowledge levels, or behaviors. Among many other objectives, I&E programs can be designed

- to inform users of what types of recreation settings, activities, and experiences they can expect
- to improve their understanding or appreciation of an issue or topic

- to teach them the skills they need to best enjoy their outings
- to minimize their negative impacts to resources and other users

I&E programs can be directed at things such as where to camp, how to minimize impacts to natural resources, how to interact with other users to minimize recreation conflicts, or how to properly dispose of human waste in the back-country. The specific ways I&E efforts could be used to help manage outdoor recreation opportunities and behavior are almost limitless. The following are just a few examples:

- Promote low-impact and other responsible use practices (e.g., Leave No Trace principles of outdoor ethics, TREAD Lightly).

- Encourage less damaging timing of use (e.g., not during early spring in places where soils are wet and plants are most vulnerable, not during nesting seasons for rare or endangered birds).

- Encourage dispersal or concentration of recreation use. Which of these distinct approaches is most appropriate depends on many factors. In general, where use is light and resources relatively hardy, dispersing use can reduce total impacts. Where use is heavy or resources are fragile, however, concentrating use (e.g., encouraging users to stay on trails and to use only designated campsites) can reduce total impacts.

- Encourage or discourage use of particular locations. This might involve encouraging visitors to use impact-resistant sites (Hendee & Dawson, 2002), not to camp near water sources or areas frequented by endangered species, or to stay on designated trails. It could also involve redistributing use by various other indirect means (e.g., informing users of more lightly used areas, not promoting heavily used or fragile sites, promoting alternative sites)

- Help users form accurate expectations of the conditions they are likely to encounter at particular sites or help them match their desires and preferences to the most appropriate settings available.

- Influence user beliefs, attitudes, or intentions. As suggested by the theory of reasoned action, this can be the best way to influence behavior over the long term. For example, help users to understand that certain resources and places are particularly susceptible to impacts, help them to realize they must share responsibility for the sustainability of the natural and historic resources there, and help them to resolve to behave in ways that minimize their impacts.

These examples should give some sense of the adaptability of I&E approaches. It is also important to note any of these examples (and many others) could also be implemented as a direct strategy simply by formalizing it into a rule or regulation that users must comply with while in the area.

Planning and implementing effective I&E programs involves more than simply conveying information to users, however. It is important to consider who says what, how, and to whom. In other words, the source, message, channel, and receiver factors that together make up the context of persuasion must also be addressed (Ajzen, 1992, pp. 6–8).

- **Source factors** relate to the person(s) or organization that is the source of the message—the characteristics of the communicator, such as apparent credibility, similarity to the receiver, and level of authority.

- **Message factors** refer to the content of the message as well as the order of the "arguments"—whether the presentation is one- or two-sided, emotional versus nonemotional.

- **Channel factors** are the means used to communicate the message, including face-to-face, writing, audio, and audiovisual.

- **Receiver factors** relate to the person(s) or group(s) being targeted by the communication.

- **Situational factors** relate to the context of the communications attempt, such as whether there are distractions present and whether the receivers are "forewarned" of the message.

Some I&E campaigns employ tangible reinforcement like rewards or patches, but most do not. In general, I&E

Innovative means of providing users with information and education, like this interagency effort in Washington, can be effective ways of influencing visitor behavior.

efforts can be designed to utilize either a "central route to persuasion" or a "peripheral route to persuasion" (Roggenbuck, 1992).

Central route to persuasion messages are designed to be carefully considered by the recipient with the objective of changing the beliefs and attitudes causing a particular behavior. If successful, the new beliefs and attitudes can lead to long-term improvements in behavior. Such approaches can only be effective if the recipients have the time, desire, and ability to process the message. An example of using the central route to persuasion would be a thoughtful and compelling informative brochure mailed to people applying for backcountry permits that explains why it is important to store food properly in bear country and illustrates how to do so.

Peripheral route to persuasion messages are designed for situations where visitors cannot or will not carefully process the information. Peripheral messages are generally designed to put a simple concept into users' minds that may sway behavior without needing to affect beliefs or attitudes. Repetition of the message, using a credible source to communicate it, and using an approach that gains the person's attention are important to the effectiveness of this approach. A peripheral route approach to reduce trail conflicts involving aggressive mountain biking might use an attention-grabbing poster showing a national mountain biking champion with the caption, "I share the trail, you should too!"

Both central route and peripheral route approaches can be effective if well-designed and used in the appropriate situations. Comprehensive I&E campaigns will use central route appeals in some situations and peripheral route ones in others to address the same issue. An example of an I&E

campaign promoting responsible use of outdoor recreation resources are the Leave No Trace Principles of Outdoor Ethics (Leave No Trace Center for Outdoor Ethics, 2004):

1. Plan ahead and prepare.
2. Travel and camp on durable surfaces.
3. Dispose of waste properly.
4. Leave what you find.
5. Minimize campfire impacts.
6. Respect wildlife.
7. Be considerate of other visitors.

Specific details regarding these principles and other information related to responsible outdoor recreation use are available from the Leave No Trace Center for Outdoor Ethics (2004) and others.

User Involvement

Involving individual users in management activities or forming partnerships with user organizations can also serve to inform and educate. Such efforts can be designed to function as a special form of intensive hands-on information and education program in addition to providing other benefits like those discussed in Chapter 9. Volunteer program participants, for instance, often gain new understanding and appreciation of the issues faced by park managers. In that way user involvement can function much like I&E programs using the central route to persuasion. Other examples might include mobilizing hiking clubs to help repair trail damage or starting a peer education program where snowmobile organization members distribute information to other snowmobilers about how to minimize their impacts on wildlife. In each case, the volunteers involved can improve their understanding and appreciation of natural resource issues related to recreation and of the challenges faced by managers.

Simple, easy-to-remember messages like this "IMBA Triangle" of trail sharing, are examples of the peripheral route to persuasion.

Peer education efforts, like this volunteer trail patrol on a popular greenway trail in California, can be very effective in meeting certain management objectives.

Fees or Other Economic Constraints

Imposing entrance or other use fees can affect the number of users who visit an area, the number of times they come, and the particular settings they choose. Fees are generally considered an indirect approach because in most cases they do not directly attempt to restrict what visitors do (Hendee & Dawson, 2002, p. 486). Of course if fees are required and there are no reasonable substitute sites that do not require payment of fees, this approach is much like a direct strategy.

Direct Management Approaches

As noted earlier, direct management strategies restrict, regulate, and/or directly affect user behavior in some other way. Direct approaches are common and can be quite effective if diligently enforced. Such approaches typically involve rules and other restrictions along with appropriate enforcement. We have grouped the most commonly used direct management approaches into seven general types: rules and regulations in general, and restrictions on party size, length of stay, activities allowed, timing of use, location of use, and use levels.

Rules and Regulations in General

Any rule or regulation that restricts or facilitates visitor behavior in some direct way is a direct approach. For example, rules closing campground gates after 10:00 p.m. can influence the visitors' sense of security, and rules regarding keeping dogs on leashes and not making loud noises enhance the quality of the recreation experience. Other rules may mandate no littering, no camping, or no swimming, or may set legal hunting seasons and bag limits. Again, any of the objects of I&E programs introduced earlier could also be the basis of a direct strategy simply by making the I&E guideline a rule or regulation. Conversely, any of the direct approaches noted here could also be converted into a guideline and encouraged through a variety of indirect strategies.

User fees are one type of indirect management strategy.

Restrictions on Party Size

As noted in Chapter 14, larger groups generally cause more damage to resources and the experiences of others than do smaller groups. This is partly because larger groups tend to spread out more than small ones. Direct approaches are sometimes used to require that groups be relatively small. A common regulation in designated Wilderness areas requires that groups have no more than eight people in them. However, as noted in Chapter 10, members of some subcultures tend to prefer to recreate in groups. Managers should understand and accommodate these preferences in appropriate settings and to the extent feasible.

Restrictions on Length of Stay

Groups that stay in the backcountry longer generally have more impact than ones that stay only a short time. Day hikers usually cause less impact than overnight campers and longer-stay campers often cause more impacts by "improving" their campsites to make them more comfortable. Longer-stay users can also displace shorter term ones when space (e.g., number of legal campsites) is scarce. Therefore, some managers limit the length of stay allowed in campsites or other areas to a maximum number of nights per visit.

Restrictions on Activities Allowed

Managers of outdoor recreation areas frequently restrict certain activities. For example, hunting is allowed only in some areas at some times, and only certain activities are permitted on particular trails. Use of motorized and mechanized equipment is illegal in designated Wilderness areas. Even access alternatives may be restricted using direct strategies. Denali National Park, for example, requires visitors to certain parts of the park to ride on buses during certain months of the year to reduce traffic on the main park road for a number of reasons.

Restrictions on Timing of Use

Modifying the time when use is allowed can protect natural resources and alleviate crowding/congestion as well. Such strategies can be based on season of year, day of the week, or time of day. For example, some ski areas offer night skiing in part to reduce congestion during the day time. Excessive resource damage can be reduced by prohibiting the most damaging uses in the spring when soils are wet and plants are most vulnerable. Alternatively, all human uses of a particular area could be banned during particular sensitive seasons. This is done on certain ocean beach and dune areas during the nesting season for endangered shorebirds like the piping plover. Day-of-week activity restrictions have been used in places like the trails at Tsali Recreation Area in North Carolina to reduce conflicts. During each day of the week, bikes are allowed only on particular trail loops and horses on others. These allowable uses are then switched on subsequent days. Time-of-day restrictions have been used on some very popular trails by allowing bicycles only between certain hours to provide safer more enjoyable walking conditions at other times. Requiring "quiet time" between 10 p.m. and 8 a.m. in a campground is another example of a direct approach based on a time-of-day restriction.

Restrictions on Location of Use

Direct approaches can be used to direct use to or from particular sites for various reasons. Such rules may apply generally within an entire jurisdiction (e.g., no camping within 100 feet of any body of water) or only to particular sites within the area. For example, certain campsites might be permanently closed because they are particularly fragile, or temporary closures could be used to allow heavily impacted areas to regenerate. General regulations can also be used to require concentration of use (e.g., camping only in designated areas). Restrictions on location of use are essentially zoning. Some applications of the previous two categories are actually various types of zoning as well. Although based on different criteria (i.e., type, time, and location of use) each can be used to restrict uses to only certain allowable zones.

Restrictions on Use Levels

Restriction on use levels are limits placed on the number of users allowed in a particular area. Such rationing of use could be based on total people at one time (PAOT) or limits at certain access points, campsites, or other locations. Restrictions on use level could be accomplished in a number of ways. Hammitt and Cole (1998, pp. 256–264) noted the following five general alternatives:

- request (reservation)
- lottery (selection based on chance)
- queuing (first come, first serve)
- price (fee system)
- merit (proof of skill or knowledge proficiency; e.g., watching a backcountry skills video before receiving a backcountry camping permit)

Dustin (1977, pp. 135–136) added the following as additional ways that use could potentially be limited or rationed:

- geographic quotas (e.g., use of a formula allowing certain numbers of users per day from predetermined zones of origin, such as 500 local, 500 within state, and 500 out-of-state users)
- frequency of visit (e.g., allow each person a specified number of visits per season, or other time period, without other constraints).

- time rationing (e.g., pay at the end of a visit for the time spent in the park). This approach could be modified to allow each user a certain amount of time per season.

Each of these approaches for restricting use levels favors some class of user. For example, reservation systems favor those willing and able to plan their trips in advance, and fee systems have less impact on those most able to pay. Of course, some of the approaches could be used in combination to create more equitable overall systems of rationing use. For example, many areas allow a portion of campsites to be reserved in advance, but hold some each day that can be obtained on a first come, first serve basis for those less willing or able to plan in advance.

Naturally, the many indirect and direct outdoor recreation management strategies introduced here can be used in combinations and are almost always more effective when they are. In fact, comprehensive campaigns that use multiple strategies can be quite adaptable and effective. For example, the following 12 principles for minimizing conflicts on multiple-use trails (Moore, 1994, pp. 1–2) are an example of a comprehensive approach for managing outdoor recreation opportunities because they blend a variety of direct and indirect approaches to address a single challenge:

1. **Recognize conflict as goal interference.** Do not treat conflict as an inherent incompatibility among different trail activities, but instead as goal interference attributed to another's behavior.

2. **Provide adequate trail opportunities.** Offer adequate trail mileage and provide opportunities for a variety of trail experiences. This will reduce congestion and allow users to choose the conditions best suited to the experiences they desire.

3. **Minimize number of contacts in problem areas.** Each contact among trail users (as well as contact with evidence of others) has the potential to result in conflict. As a general rule, reduce the number of user contacts whenever possible.

4. **Involve users as early as possible.** Identify the present and likely future users of each trail and involve them in the process of avoiding and resolving conflicts as early as possible—preferably before conflicts occur.

5. **Understand user needs.** Determine the motivations, desired experiences, norms, setting preferences, and other needs of the present and likely future users of each trail. This "customer" information is critical for anticipating and managing conflicts.

6. **Identify the actual sources of conflict.** Help users identify the specific tangible causes of any conflicts they are experiencing. Get beyond emotions and stereotypes as quickly as possible, and get to the roots of any problems that exist.

7. **Work with affected users.** Work with all parties involved to reach mutually agreeable solutions to the specific issues. Users who are not involved as part of the solution are more likely to be part of the problem, now and in the future.

8. **Promote trail etiquette.** Minimize the possibility that any particular trail contact will result in conflict by actively and aggressively promoting responsible trail behavior. Use existing educational materials or modify them to better meet local needs. Target these educational efforts, get the information into users' hands as early as possible, and present it in interesting and understandable ways (Roggenbuck & Ham, 1986).

9. **Encourage positive interactions among different users.** Trail users are usually not as different from one another as they believe. Providing positive interactions both on and off the trail will break down barriers and stereotypes and build understanding, good will, and cooperation. This can be accomplished through a variety of strategies, such as sponsoring "user swaps," joint trail-building or maintenance projects, filming trail-sharing videos, or forming trail advisory councils.

10. **Favor light-handed management.** Use the most light-handed approaches, as opposed to heavy-handed ones (Cole, Peterson & Lucas, 1987), that will achieve area objectives. This is important to provide the freedom of choice and natural environments that are so important to most trail-based recreation.

11. **Plan and act locally.** Whenever possible, address issues regarding multiple-use trails at the local level. This allows greater sensitivity to local needs and provides better flexibility for addressing difficult issues on a case-by-case basis.

12. **Monitor progress.** Monitor the ongoing effectiveness of the decisions made and programs implemented. Conscious, deliberate monitoring is the only way to determine if conflicts are indeed being reduced and what changes in programs might be needed. This is only possible within the context of clearly understood and agreed on objectives for each trail area.

Choosing the Most Appropriate Management Strategies

Recall from the beginning of this chapter that outdoor recreation management is different from other types of management in several important respects. It involves integrating the management of two very different but interrelated dimensions: people and natural environments. The "products" are unique in that they are actually outdoor recreation opportunities in natural environments that visitors can use to "produce" their own outdoor recreation experiences. Perceived freedom is usually an important element of the experience. These essential aspects of outdoor recreation management must be kept in mind when considering the most appropriate combinations of management strategies for a particular situation.

Outdoor recreation managers can influence many aspects of the recreation setting and users' behavior to accomplish their objectives. Just because they can do so, of course, does not mean it is always appropriate. Over the years a number of factors have been suggested for evaluating the appropriateness of outdoor recreation management strategies. We build on these and suggest outdoor recreation managers consider at least the following: protection of resources, facilitating and enhancing satisfying recreation experiences, consistency with management objectives, likely effectiveness, available resources, and level of visitor burden.

Protection of Resources

Because outdoor recreation depends on natural settings, management strategies must help protect (or even help restore) the natural and historic resources of the area. This does not mean strategies with some negative impacts on resources must be rejected. It simply implies implementation of the strategy should have a net positive impact on the natural resources of the area. For example, building a developed campsite destroys some natural resources, but could still have a net positive effect if encouraging (or requiring) users to camp there reduces negative impacts that would have been caused elsewhere. This requires understanding the vulnerability of various hisoric and natural resources in general and those of the area in question in particular.

Facilitating and Enhancing Satisfying Recreation Experiences

In addition to protecting the basic resources, a second overriding purpose of management is to facilitate and enhance the realization of satisfying recreation experiences. This must be kept in mind when selecting and implementing any strategy to influence or manage visitor behavior.

Consistency With Management Objectives

Any management strategy implemented must be consistent with the management objectives of the area, including overall management objectives (e.g., high priority of wildlife-related objectives in National Wildlife Refuges) and recreation-specific objectives. For example, in settings classified as Primitive by the recreation opportunity spectrum (ROS), human-constructed structures and unnatural building materials are not appropriate. Lists of objectives should also include guidance about what types of recreation experiences are appropriate for that setting. For example, providing outstanding opportunities for self-reliance, challenge, and solitude are objectives in many wilderness areas. A mix of management strategies that overly restrict visitors in such areas would be less appropriate than it might be in an urban open space area because of the different experiences opportunities typically provided and sought there. Also remember, in addition to protecting the basis resources, a second overriding management objective is to facilitate and to enhance the realization of satisfying recreation experiences as noted previously.

Likely Effectiveness

Hammitt and Cole (1998, pp. 222–224) suggest evaluating management actions based on effectiveness and visitor burden. Selecting the strategies most likely to be effective should involve an explicit evaluation process on the part of the manager. Considerable research and experience exists to guide this process, particularly in terms of the factors related to the negative environmental impacts of outdoor recreation use as discussed in Chapter 14. That each management strategy effectively addresses the objectives for which it is designed is critically important. Of course, determining whether a particular management strategy is effective or not requires several things. First, management objectives must be written down and worded in specific and measurable ways. Second, managers must have a clear understanding of the problem itself and what is causing it. Finally, determining a strategy's effectiveness also requires explicit and ongoing monitoring of the applicable conditions to determine what effect the strategy is having over time. These essential concerns should be familiar from the various impact management systems discussed in Chapter 14.

Having a clear understanding of the problem and what is causing it is a part of this process frequently given too little attention. For example, a manager might jump to the conclusion that crowding and certain negative environmental impacts are caused by too much use and too quickly consider placing restrictions on use levels. More careful observation and interaction with users could reveal reports of crowding were due in large part to a litter problem that gave the impression to many users the area must be very heavily used. The most effective strategy might be a creative information and education campaign and more diligent enforcement of littering rules.

As noted earlier in this chapter, a particularly helpful tool in choosing the most effective management strategies can be to attempt to clearly understand why visitors are behaving irresponsibly. For example, while I&E programs can be very effective in some situations, they can be completely ineffective in others. This is often due to why the user is engaged in the behavior in the first place. Roggenbuck (1992, pp. 164–166) and Hendee, Stankey, and Lucas (1990) proposed the potential for persuasion (typical of indirect approaches like I&E efforts) to reduce various types of depreciative behavior varies depending on the type of problem behavior and its motive. Their advice is summarized in Table 16.2.

These predictions are based partly on the assumption that people involved in uninformed, unintentional, and unskilled violations would attempt to behave more responsibly if they realized that the behavior they were engaged in is causing problem and they had the skills to behave more responsibly.

Table 16.3 presents possible management responses for different types of problem behaviors based on the categories presented earlier in Table 16.1. It also provides examples of types of management strategies generally effective for different types of situations.

Available Resources

Managers must consider the resources at their disposal when considering any action. Levels of funding, staffing, time, equipment and materials, and expertise are all important in determining what management strategies are realistic options. For example, hiring full-time backcountry rangers to perform I&E activities and basic backcountry

---

Table 16.2 The potential of persuasion to reduce depreciative behavior depending on type and motive of the behavior

Type of Behavior	
Uninformed	Very High
Unavoidable	Low
Unskilled	High
Careless	Moderate
Illegal	Low
Willful Violations	Low
Motive for Behavior	
Unintentional	High
Uninformed	Very High
Releasor-cue	Low
Responsibility denial	Moderate
Status-conforming	None

Sources: Roggenbuck (1992, pp. 164–166) and Hendee, Stankey, and Lucas (1990)

monitoring might be prohibitively expensive for some agencies but not others. Likewise, some agencies have access to capable and reliable volunteer organization partners that can implement and monitor management strategies while others agencies do not.

The resources available to managers often have the most impact on how the various indirect and direct strategies introduced earlier might actually be implemented, communicated, and monitored. Some of the most common options are noted next, roughly in order from the most expensive for managers to the least. Remember, a more expensive approach may be the better choice if that approach is necessary to effectively accomplish the management objective.

- agency field personnel (e.g., backcountry rangers, wilderness rangers, paid "ridgerunners" or caretakers, trail crews, maintenance staff)

- individual volunteer programs (e.g., unpaid personnel recruited, trained, and supervised by the agency to carry out some of the responsibilities of the agency personnel)

- volunteer organization partners (e.g., conservation groups undertaking rehabilitation of damaged resources, user groups carrying out I&E programs related to park resources or activities)

- mass media (e.g., public service announcements about agency initiatives, articles or television specials about area resources, educational programs promoting responsible use)

- peer education programs (e.g., equestrian club members informing other riders how to minimize impacts to natural resources, mountain bike club members informing other riders how to reduce trail conflicts)

Realize that all of these approaches require agency staff time and often full-time positions to be effective. Volunteer programs must be coordinated and managed and media campaigns must be designed and implemented, often by an agency public information officer.

Level of Visitor Burden

Hammitt and Cole (1998, pp. 222–224) and Cole, Peterson, and Lucas (1987) suggested evaluating management actions based on a concept they refer to as *visitor burden*. This relates, in part, to attempting to maintain visitors' perceived freedom, but goes beyond that to include other dimensions of how burdensome management actions might be. They identify six factors that affect how heavy-handed management actions are, including

1. freedom of choice (i.e., directly regulating vs. indirectly influencing)

2. subtlety (i.e., how aware users are they are being "managed")

3. where management occurs (i.e., on-site vs. off-site)

4. when management occurs (i.e., visitors aware of action only after arrival vs. during trip planning)

5. number of visitors affected (i.e., total number of visitors affected by the action)

Table 16.3   General management responses for different types of problem behaviors

UNINTENTIONAL PROBLEM BEHAVIORS

Problem Type	Possible Management Responses
Unavoidable	Locate use in most durable sites, other indirect approaches, and reduce use levels when necessary
Uninformed	I&E programs using both central and peripheral routes to persuasion and other indirect approaches
Unskilled	Education programs directed at improving the deficient skills, particularly using the central route to persuasion

INTENTIONAL PROBLEM BEHAVIORS

Problem Type	Possible Management Responses
Careless	Education about the problem and its causes, persuasion, and enforcement of appropriate rules
Releasor-Cue	Actions to eliminate or reduce the cue (e.g., litter, graffiti), education, persuasion, and enforcement of appropriate rules
Responsibility Denial	Education about the reasons for the requested responsible behavior, persuasion, and enforcement of appropriate rules
Status-Confirming	Peer education particularly using the central route to persuasion, and active enforcement of appropriate rules
Protest	Education, persuasion, active enforcement of appropriate rules, and other direct approaches
Material Gain	Rigorous enforcement of appropriate rules, other direct approaches, and possibly user involvement in peer education and monitoring

Adapted and expanded from Hendee and Dawson (2002, p. 463)

6. importance of activity that is forgone (i.e., users asked to give up a very important activity vs. an unimportant one)

Based on these factors, the least burdensome management strategies (and therefore most desirable in terms of visitor burden) would be ones that

- indirectly influence users
- are subtle enough that visitors are not aware of them
- do not control activities on-site
- visitors are aware of during their trip planning
- affect as few visitors and possible
- only cause visitors to forgo relatively unimportant aspects of their experiences

Conversely, an example of the most burdensome strategy possible for reducing damage caused by irresponsible gathering of firewood might be for campers looking forward to enjoying a campfire and cooking their dinner on it to arrive at a very popular campsite and be informed by a backcountry ranger that fires are now illegal and punishable by a fine and possible arrest.

As noted earlier, it might be tempting to assume indirect strategies should always be favored over more direct ones. The previous discussion should clarify why this is not necessarily the case. Each of the two general approaches has advantages and disadvantages and most are highly effective in some situations but not in others. Therefore, selecting the most appropriate combination of management strategies needs to be done after considering at least the aforementioned factors. That said, however, it is typically more desirable to use indirect rather than direct approaches if the indirect ones also protect natural and historic resources, are consistent with management objectives, will likely be effective, and are feasible based on the resources available to managers. This is because indirect approaches are generally less burdensome on visitors, and regulations cost managers time and resources to inform and enforce (Hendee & Dawson, 2002, p. 472).

The so-called *minimum tool rule* (Hendee & Dawson, 2002) attempts to provide general guidance in selecting management strategies in this regard. The minimum tool rule simply suggests managers start with the least intrusive approaches likely to be effective and escalate to more intrusive ones only if necessary. So, when indirect techniques are likely to be effective (and meet the other criteria noted), they should be tried first. Regulations and enforcement will, of course, be needed in many situations, because there will always be some who will not or cannot be influenced by the other more light-handed approaches. When direct approaches are used,

however, it is important to communicate to visitors the reasons they are necessary, their desired results, and to consistently and impartially enforce the rules.

Minimum Tool Rule: "Apply only the minimum tools, equipment, device, force, regulation, action or practice that will bring the desired result" (Hendee & Dawson, 2002, p. 201)

For example, in some areas there are few if any restrictions placed on day hiking. Effective indirect approaches may be employed to inform and educate users about minimum impact skills. A mixture of indirect and direct approaches is often used for overnight backcountry use, however, because of the greater potential negative impacts camping and related activities can have. There might even be a variety of different mixes of these approaches employed to manage backcountry camping within the same park or forest. In Great Smoky Mountains National Park, for example, backcountry camping is allowed only at designated areas (i.e., concentrated use). Some areas are rationed, but others are not to allow somewhat greater user freedom in some areas. The reasons these more direct approaches are necessary are communicated to users when they receive their required backcountry camping permits.

Summary

This chapter introduced and described the major strategies available for managing outdoor recreation opportunities and influencing user behavior. We emphasized the importance of understanding what visitors desire, how they behave, and why problems occur—especially the reasons visitors might behave irresponsibly. Next we introduced the two broad categories of outdoor recreation management strategies—the more subtle indirect and the restricting or regulating direct approaches. The bulk of the chapter introduced various management strategies, including the indirect approaches of modifications of the physical setting, I&E programs (either through a central or peripheral route to persuasion), user involvement, and fees or other economic constraints. Specific direct management approaches were also presented, including rules and regulations in general, restrictions on party size, length of stay, activities allowed, timing of use, location of use, and use levels. The chapter concluded with a discussion of how to choose the most appropriate management strategies for particular situations, with a focus on protecting natural resources, facilitating and enhancing satisfying recreation experiences, consistency with management objectives, likely effectiveness, available resources, and level of visitor burden. In the next chapter we elaborate on one of the most powerful overall approaches managers can use to accomplish their natural resource and recreation experience objectives—creating collaboration partnerships and cooperation among recreation providers and other stakeholders.

Literature Cited

Ajzen, I. (1992). Persuasive communication theory in social psychology: A historical perspective. In M. Manfredo (Ed.), *Influencing human behavior: Theory and applications in recreation, tourism and natural resources management* (pp. 1–27). Champaign, IL: Sagamore.

Clark, R., Hendee, J., and Campbell, F. (1971). Values, behavior and conflict in modern camping culture. *Journal of Leisure Research, 3*(3), 143–159.

Cole, D., Peterson, M., and Lucas, R. (1987). *Managing wilderness recreation use: Common problems and potential solutions* (General Technical Report INT–230). Ogden, UT: USDA Foreset Service, Intermountain Research Station.

Dustin, D. (1977). *Gaming-simulation in the college classroom: An assessment of Quagmire, a recreation resource management game.* Unpublished doctoral dissertation, University of Minnesota.

Fishbein, M. and Manfredo, M. (1992). A theory of behavior change. In M. Manfredo (Ed.), *Influencing human behavior: Theory and applications in recreation, tourism and natural resources management* (pp. 29–50). Champaign, IL: Sagamore.

Gramann, J. and Vander Stoep, G. (1987). Prosocial behavior theory and natural resource protection: A conceptual synthesis. *Journal of Environmental Management, 24*, 247–257.

Hammitt, W. and Cole, D. (1998). *Wildland recreation: Ecology and management* (2nd ed.). New York, NY: John Wiley & Sons.

Harrison, A. (1982). Problems: Vandalism and depreciative behavior. In G. Sharp (Ed.), *Interpreting the environment* (2nd ed.; pp. 473–495). New York, NY: John Wiley & Sons.

Hendee, J. and Dawson, C. (2002). *Wilderness management: Stewardship and protection of resources and values* (3rd ed.). Golden, CO: Fulcrum Publishing.

Hendee, J., Stankey, G., and Lucas, R. (1990). *Wilderness management* (2nd ed.). Golden, CO: Fulcrum Publishing.

Knopf, R. and Dustin, D. (1992). A multidisciplinary model for managing vandalism and depreciative behavior in recreation settings. In M. Manfredo (Ed.), *Influencing human behavior: Theory and applications in recreation, tourism and natural resources management* (pp. 209–261). Champaign, IL: Sagamore.

Leave No Trace Center for Outdoor Ethics. (2004). *Leave No Trace principles.* Retrieved March 15, 2004, from http://www.lnt.org/TeachingLNT/LNTEnglish.php

Moore, R. L. (1994). *Conflicts on multiple-use trails: Synthesis of literature and state of the practice.* Washington, DC: Federal Highway Administration.

Roggenbuck, J. (1992). Use of persuasion to reduce resource impacts and visitor conflicts. In M. Manfredo (Ed.), *Influencing human behavior: Theory and applications in recreation, tourism and natural resources management* (pp. 149–208). Champaign, IL: Sagamore.

Roggenbuck, J. W. and Ham, S. H. (1986). Use of information and education in recreation management. In *A literature review, the President's commission on Americans outdoors* (pp. 59–71). Washington, DC: U.S. Government Printing Office.

Sax, J. (1980). *Mountains without handrails: Reflections on the national parks.* Ann Arbor, MI: University of Michigan Press.

Vander Stoep, G. and Gramann, J. (1987). The effect of verbal appeals and incentives on depreciative behavior among youthful park visitors. *Journal of Leisure Research, 19*(2), 69–83.

Chapter 17
Collaborative Planning and Management

A new style of environmental problem solving and management is under development in the United States. Government agencies, communities, and private groups are building bridges between one another that enable them to deal with common problems, work through conflicts, and develop forward-thinking strategies for regional protection and development.
(Wondolleck & Yaffee, 2000, p. 3)

Learning Objectives

1. Describe why collaboration emerged to replace the technocratic approach to resource planning and management.
2. Understand the general characteristics and essential ingredients of collaborative partnerships.
3. Know the major barriers that need to be overcome to practice collaborative planning and management.

This chapter briefly reviews the evolution of a collaborative style of planning and management (CPM), outlines the characteristics and essential ingredients of such a style, explains why that style emerged to replace the technocratic approach, which did not adequately consider and involve relevant stakeholders, and describes significant barriers to collaboration. In this introductory text, no attempt is made to describe CPM in great detail. Rather, the purpose is to introduce the reader to CPM and to provide references to significant publications that describe it in more detail.

Gray (1985, p. 912) defined collaboration as "...the pooling of...tangible [personal] resources, such as interaction, money, labor, [time], etc....by two or more stakeholders, to...solve a set of problems which neither can solve individually." Although it is possible to consider a public land manager to be a stakeholder in the broadest sense, we will continue to use the following definitions established in Chapter 13:

- **Managers** are the providers of outdoor recreation opportunities, and as professionals they maintain, improve, and protect the basic natural and cultural/heritage recreation resources being managed.

- **Associated providers** comprise all the individuals or organizations (e.g., local businesses, other tourist organizations) who influence the amount, type, and quality of goods and services produced, including outdoor recreation opportunities. They exert this influence in many ways but primarily by the support services they provide (e.g., lodging, food, laundry, automotive, film, hunting and fishing equipment and licenses, guided tours, outfitting).

- **Stakeholders** are the on- and off-site customers who either affect or are affected by resource allocation decisions, such as the provision of outdoor recreation opportunities.

Therefore, for the purposes of this text a *collaborative style of planning and management* (CPM) is one in which resource managers work collaboratively with the customers (i.e., stakeholders) they serve as well as with the associated providers to solve a set of problems which none of them can solve individually. To simplify the discussion in this chapter, reference will often be made to collaboration between managers and stakeholders. Recognize, however, that the most effective CPM involves managers, stakeholders, and associated providers.

CPM has been practiced most by public agencies that manage "common property" resources, such as public lands, although it is also practiced by some nonprofit sector land managers. Thus, public agencies predominate in using CPM, with some nonprofit organizations using it generally with smaller groups of stakeholders. Compared to common property stakeholders, the stakeholders of nonprofit lands tend to have fewer conflicting interests and values because they are more often supportive of the mission, goals, and actions of the nonprofit organizations. In such situations, the resource allocation decisions tend to be less complex and less divisive. In contrast to public and nonprofit providers of outdoor recreation opportunities, private sector providers tend to rely mostly on market research to identify customer/client preferences, values, and interests, so they practice CPM much less.

It is important to understand the distinction between a CPM as discussed in this chapter and partnerships among recreation opportunity providers as presented in Chapter 9. Partnerships reflect cooperation among public agencies, nonprofit organizations, private sector enterprises, and private individuals in providing outdoor recreation opportunities. In that sense a partnership is a means of providing a particular opportunity or service. This could be as simple as two organizations working together for a single weekend to rehabilitate a damaged campsite or as sophisticated as the hundreds of organizations that work together formally to maintain and manage the 2,200-mile Appalachian Trail on an ongoing basis. In contrast, CPM as presented in this chapter is an approach to planning and managerial decision making. It is most often used to bring relevant stakeholders and associated providers together with managers to collaboratively make complex planning and management decisions. There can obviously be a great deal of overlap between CPM and partnerships. The groups involved in CPM are working as partners, and ongoing partnerships in providing outdoor recreation opportunities are often an outgrowth of CPM. Similarly, stakeholders and associated providers that have worked as partners with an agency become important players when a CPM approach is employed.

Brief History of Collaborative Planning and Management

The literature on CPM views it as a relatively new style of management developed and refined since 1985 as an alternative to technocratic decision making (explained in Chapter 13). In one sense this view is correct, but in another sense at least some of what is now referred to as CPM was practiced much earlier than the 1980s.

The "new style of management" view of CPM is correct when applied to complex resource allocation decisions that impact many different individuals (and organizations) who have different interests in, and hold strong opinions about, those decisions. Because such complex resource allocation decisions that have wide impact are now the rule rather than the exception, CPM emerged to accommodate the complexity and many competing and conflicting vested interests of the parties that will be affected by those decisions. Those types of complex resource allocation decisions that have wide impacts and frequently require a CPM are the ones considered in this chapter.

Although this chapter focuses on the recent role of CPM in guiding complex resource allocation decisions that affect many stakeholders who hold diverse interests and values, it is only fair to point out that smaller scale CPM has been practiced in the United States since at least

the early 1900s. During that period, there was not as much complexity, and a much smaller number of stakeholders with competing interests were involved or impacted. In addition, field-level managers with public land management agencies then had much fewer regulatory and procedural mandates with which to contend. Therefore, they had more discretion and were able to spend most of their time working one on one with their stakeholders to determine what their values and interests were and how reasonable compromises could be made. In addition, those field-level managers generally lived and worked in small rural communities, were well-known, were often active in the civic affairs of those communities, and were frequently leaders in their communities. At that time, collaboration melded itself well with a technocratic approach to management and did so until about the 1950s. The technically trained managers were generally respected professionally by their stakeholders, and especially because most of the stakeholders then had direct, frequent, and informal access to the managers.

As explained in Chapter 4, social, economic, and technological changes accelerated after World War II. Competition increased on public lands for raw materials to feed a growing economy and demands for amenity uses such as outdoor recreation. Public concerns about the natural environment grew as media outlets communicated messages related to growing concerns about the health of the natural environment (e.g., Rachel Carson's *Silent Spring*). The 1960s and 1970s also brought much environmental legislation and the beginning of the "environmental movement" with the first Earth Day in 1970. These and other factors gradually changed the nature of most natural resource allocation decisions from ones having relatively limited complexity and scope of impacts to ones that were much more complex and impacted a much larger array of stakeholders. In addition, passage of the National Environmental Protection Act of 1969 (NEPA) prompted federal land management agencies to be more concerned about public involvement. Similar laws were passed soon after that by many state legislatures.

After passage of the NEPA in 1969, the technocratic approach to natural resource management started to wane. This does not mean that technical/professional expertise was no longer needed then. Instead, it means that stakeholders wanted a greater say in the management of the resources administered by public agencies (and nonprofit organizations). It also means that many of the stakeholders now had considerable relevant technical expertise and political clout and used it to challenge the technocratic approach used previously.

The first steps toward CPM involved what was typically called public involvement, and gained momentum in the 1970s after passage of the NEPA. That was a progressive step that both educated the managers and caused stakeholders to want to be more involved than early public involvement processes permitted. The problem remained that the agencies were reluctant to share their decision-making responsibilities, while still wanting public input into allocation decisions. The upshot was that most of the early public involvement efforts solicited public (i.e., stakeholders) input only during a few of the steps of the resource planning and allocation process, but did not solicit such input at other critical steps of that process. Specifically, public input was generally solicited only at two of the many steps of the resource planning process: (a) early on when the key issues, concerns, and goals of the planning effort were defined and (b) after agency planning personnel had systematically evaluated alternative courses of feasible action and had selected the preferred or recommended plan of action, which was then submitted for public review and comments.

While involvement of the public at even these two steps of the management planning process represented considerable progress over approaches used before, it was still limited, primarily because the stakeholders were not involved at other important steps (including envisioning desired future conditions, making demand analyses, formulating and evaluating alternative feasible courses of action, plan implementation, monitoring, and revision). As such, agency managers viewed the stakeholders as providing useful information, but not as joint allocation decision makers. The stakeholders, therefore, did not feel "ownership" of those decisions. In fact, the word *stakeholder* was seldom used before the middle to late 1980s. Overcoming these problems led to a more refined and interactive CPM.

Broadly, CPM can be compared with the technocratic approach and early public involvement efforts as follows:

- **Technocratic/authoritative allocations.** Characterized by technically/professionally trained planners and managers making the allocation decisions with little consultation with the affecting and affected stakeholders. This has been called *top-down planning,* in which the few decide for the many (USDA Forest Service, 1993, p. 1).

- **Public involvement.** Reflected by the first, but limited, attempts at collaboration in which "stakeholders" were invited to have input at only a few of the many steps of the resource management planning, plan implementation, and plan-revision processes. The stakeholders involved were not true partners in actually making the allocation decisions. As such, they did not feel ownership in the allocation decisions made.

- **Collaborative management.** This is the process in which stakeholders are active and ongoing collaborators with the agency planners, managers and associated providers throughout the entire resource management planning and plan implementation processes. They help make, implement, and monitor the actual allocation decisions, which helps them feel personal ownership of the results of those decisions.

A big problem in the past has been that managers have been conditioned by the organizations (especially public agencies) for which they work to believe they could not and should not share with their stakeholders the responsibilities vested in those managers' official positions. Chapters 6 and 11 explained that within any public land agency an administrative hierarchy extends downward from heads of agencies to field-level managers responsible for managing a particular management unit. For example, the managers of a ranger district within the USFS or of a resource area within the BLM are the lowest level line managers of those two land management agencies. Recall that the term *line manager* is a military concept (i.e., line officer) that defines and designates who answers to whom within an organization's chain of command and who will be held responsible for the results of decisions made. For example, at the top, the Chief of the USFS and the Director of the BLM have considerably more administrative authority and responsibility for the operations of those agencies than do a district ranger in the USFS or manager of a resource area for the BLM at the lowest line levels. Such hierarchical authorities and responsibilities exist within all public, nonprofit, and private organizations that provide outdoor recreation opportunities.

The relevant point is that field-level managers, with whom most CPM can occur, are bound by the limited responsibilities they have been delegated. Nevertheless, those managers are acutely aware they are legally and organizationally responsible for the decisions they make. Given this situation, those managers have been very reluctant to, and often believed they could not, share their official responsibilities with their stakeholders, which is a critical requirement of CPM. Fortunately, the agencies have learned that while managers are ultimately legally responsible, they can formally share responsibilities with interested and willing stakeholders. This is now being done by use of legal documents, such as memoranda of understanding, letters of mutual agreement, cooperative agreements, and some of the other formal mechanisms introduced in Chapter 9, which delineate clearly the delegated responsibilities of individual stakeholders or groups of stakeholders. In this way important responsibilities are now being shared with stakeholders and associated providers in many successful CPM efforts.

In review, under the technocratic/authoritative style, little to no responsibility was shared with stakeholders, and under the public involvement model, responsibility was seldom shared, and if so, to a very limited degree. In contrast, under CPM considerable responsibility is shared under mutual agreements.

The remainder of this chapter briefly describes the characteristics of CPM. The purpose is to provide an overview that will facilitate basic understanding of CPM. An excellent reference for additional information on CPM is Wondolleck and Yaffee (2000), with other useful sources being USDA Forest Service (1993) and Beldin, Russonello & Steward Research and Communication (2001).

Reasons Why Collaborative Planning and Management Was Needed

This section draws heavily from Wondolleck and Yaffee (2000, pp. 5–18), and the personal experiences of the authors of this text, to explain reasons why a collaborative approach was needed. Specifically, why was CPM needed to replace the conventional technocratic top-down approach to resource planning and management in situations involving much complexity and when many different parties holding conflicting values and interests would be affected by that planning and management? The key reasons CPM was needed follow.

Growing mistrust. For several decades, there has been a growing general mistrust of government in the United States and many other countries. Several factors have contributed to that mistrust and include disagreements about needs for and the conduct of the Vietnam War, the Watergate scandal, concerns about the quality of natural environments, and greater awareness of how public decisions were being made in a technocratic way with little consultation with the people affected by those decisions. Other factors, such as increases in population levels and improvements in worldwide communications, also contributed to widespread feelings of not having control over one's life and of being disenfranchised. These factors combined to increase public alienation and mistrust of government, which has been reflected by decreased participation in civic activities, such as voting. One aspect of these feelings was the belief that public agencies were not performing adequately or being held accountable in managing common property resources, such as the public lands. Stakeholders wanted a change and to have a greater role in those managerial decisions.

Cost of litigation. Starting in the 1970s, after passage of the NEPA, stakeholders as private individuals or through the environmental groups to which they belonged began taking legal actions against public land management agencies to stop or to delay the implementation of management plans, or parts of them with which they disagreed. For example, all but a few of the resource management plans completed by the USFS in the 1980s, to meet requirements of the 1976 National Forest Management Act, were held up in courts because of litigation by stakeholders who represented a wide range of interests and concerns. This litigation was very costly to the federal agencies and to stakeholders. Among the costs were those of preparing and defending the different positions legally, opportunities forgone because of court-issued stays on implementing proposed management actions being contested, and simply responding to threats of litigation and appeals. The agencies recognized a new style of management was needed that would reduce stakeholder opposition. The old approaches were simply not working, and the customers' favorable images of public agencies deteriorated as mistrust of them grew.

Growth in numbers of concerned stakeholders. As documented in Chapters 3, 4, and 12, use of outdoor recreation opportunities grew rapidly since the end of World War II. As the sheer number of these and other stakeholders increased, so did the number who articulated dissatisfaction with the existing approaches to management.

Increased complexity and more knowledgable stakeholders. The complexity and accompanying risk and uncertainty of natural resource allocation decision increased greatly after the end of World War II, and especially after the mid-1960s. Demands expanded for more and newer types of goods and services dependent on those natural resources. Environmental pollution became a larger concern and a more complex problem to solve. Growth in domestic and international tourism added new managerial concerns. Advances in science and technology disclosed new managerial issues to be addressed. As demands on finite nonrenewable resources increased, so did concerns about resource and ecological sustainability. Along with this increasing complexity, relative scarcity, and widespread dissatisfaction with approaches being used to management public resources was a growing number of concerned and motivated stakeholders with diverse and competing interests who were incrementally becoming more aware of, and concerned about, environmental management. Particularly significant was that many of these stakeholders were rapidly developing technical and analytical expertise, which they applied to successfully challenge the technical analyses made by agency managers to justify their proposed resource allocation decisions. Both parties—the managers and the stakeholders—came to realize the best approach was to share their interests and skills collaboratively to cope with increasing complexity, relative scarcity, and larger numbers of stakeholders being impacted.

Characteristics of Collaborative Planning and Management

Successful CPM efforts share many common characteristics. According to Wondolleck and Yaffee (2000, pp. 24–41) and USDA Forest Service (1993), general characteristics of CPM include the following:

- CPM emerges from those affected by resource allocation decisions.
- CPM recognizes and honors the full spectrum of values of the managers and managerially relevant stakeholders and associated providers.
- No one is excluded from the table, and all participants are considered to be equals with power dominance highly discouraged.
- The process begins with sharing information and building trust.
- The common problem is defined and agreed on.
- Participants educate one another, explore their differences, discover common ground, and build mutual understanding.
- Participants envision a future compatible with their diverse values and interests, make compromises, and then create an action plan to get there by coordinated effort. Responsibilities for doing so are shared by all the participants.
- The participants mobilize resources needed for the agreed on actions to be taken.

- Stakeholders work with managers to implement and monitor implementation of the proposed actions to which they have mutually agreed.
- Collaboration generally creates the fastest, least costly, and most democratic results.
- The collaboration process, by definition, results in measurably fewer litigations.

Essential Ingredients of Collaborative Planning and Management

Beyond the general characteristics noted here, there are also specific, essential ingredients of successful collaborative efforts. A list of those ingredients identified by Wondolleck and Yaffee (2000, pp. 24–41), Belden, Russonello & Steward Research and Communications (2001, pp. 7–10), and the authors of this text, include the following:

- There must be a group leader trained/skilled in mediation/group decision making. Not everyone has those skills and/or the personality to use them effectively.
- Meetings should be held at times and places reasonably convenient for the participants to attend.
- While the CPM process takes time, the impression must not be left that it will go on indefinitely and closure will not be reached.
- All participants must be treated as equals.
- One or more participants cannot take advantage over other participants.

Private sector providers, like marina operators, can be important collaborators in both planning and management.

Volunteer organizations often share land managers' values, interests, and goals and can make excellent collaborators.

- The collaborative process must start by focusing on shared values, interests, and goals, not on disagreements. This is of critical importance to prevent one or more participants from pushing and locking into (and frequently exaggerating) entrenched positions. Much research on group decision making has documented that members of adversarial groups almost always share a much larger number of common beliefs and values than they would have imagined before they get to know and understand one another. It has also been found that a person representing other like-minded people (i.e., a representative of an organization) will almost invariably exaggerate the strength of that organization's true position(s) to make her or his case seem even stronger. If strong personal beliefs are pushed or exaggerated early in the CPM process, it is very difficult to get the proponents of those beliefs to compromise meaningfully later, which defeats the basic purpose of CPM. To iterate, focus first on common values, beliefs, and interests; handle disagreements later after trust, understanding, and some friendships (and this is an extremely important word) have been established.
- Participants must agree on shared goals and desired outcomes.
- The focus must be on outcomes, not process.
- If there is an overriding facilitating or constraining mandate for any participants to achieve a particular outcome, all participants must understand what that mandate (or mandates) is (are). Such mandates include laws and agency administrative decrees governing what the managers can do, set positions of stakeholders representing themselves, and firm policies of the organizations to which the other stakeholders belong and represent. For example, the Wilderness Preservation Act of 1964 sets some clear (as well as some unclear) boundaries on what managerial actions can be applied in designated Wilderness areas.
- An attitude and demeanor of tolerance and patience must be promoted and maintained.
- The CPM process requires the building of trust and mutual respect in all ways possible.
- Talk "facts," not rhetoric, to the extent possible.
- Stress that collaboration results in better and less costly outcomes for all participants.
- Promote learning from one another for all participants.
- Promote an atmosphere of flexibility, admit mistakes, and avoid defensiveness.

- Be positive, optimistic, and constructive.
- Assign responsibilities for implementing the recommendations.
- Encourage participants to mobilize resources needed to help implement the recommendations.
- Promote stakeholder pride in, and ownership of, the decisions and recommendations made.
- Clear and time-bounded actions and responsibilities must be assigned and accepted.
- Means for monitoring and documenting success or lack thereof must be developed and accepted.
- Full credit must be given to all participants for their contributions.
- If appropriate, and means exist to do so, use the media to inform "outsiders" of the composition of the CPM team, its purposes, the efforts made, the recommendations agreed on, and planned actions to achieve those recommendations.

Hard-to-Remove Barriers of Collaborative Planning and Management

The previous list of specific essential ingredients for successful CPM also discloses significant barriers that can arise if those specific ingredients are not present. However, there are some less specific and harder to remove barriers, which are described in Wondolleck and Yaffee (2000, pp. 51–68) as "obstacles to effective collaboration." Those hard-to-remove barriers, along with other obstacles identified, follow.

Institutional entrenchment. Managing organizations generally find it difficult to change their ways of operating. Thus, resource management agencies that always operated technocratically with structured rules, regulations, and processes have difficulty adopting an open collaborative approach in which they have to use new methods and share decision authority and responsibilities.

Lack of familiarity. Even when a managing organization is willing to try collaboration as a new approach, it might lack sufficient understanding of how to do so. For example, when the federal natural resource managing agencies in the United States started to practice "public involvement," very few professional employees in those agencies possessed the requisite skills in conflict management, mediation, or group decision making. In fact, few had training in the social sciences, other than resource economics. They had studied to become foresters, wildlife/fisheries/range managers, hydrologists, geologists, and so on. So, few professional natural resource managers had (or still have) formal training or experience in conflict management and mediation.

Lack of organizational support. At times, field-level managers who desired to work collaboratively have been told by their supervisors not to do so. This is often because of concerns that they should not "give up" any of their delegated authorities and managerial responsibilities that were vested to the positions they held. Fortunately, such situations are becoming uncommon. As one example, the USFS now proudly acknowledges it practices "collaborative stewardship," establishes hundreds of meaningful partnerships, and shares with many local stakeholders its responsibilities for planning and management for which the USFS managers still remain ultimately responsible. Nevertheless, some remnants of the earlier orientation that discourage CPM still exist.

Insufficient resources. Collaborative efforts take time and can cost money for supplies, transportation, fees for consultants, and so forth. These constraints can serve as serious barriers both for managers and stakeholders.

Conflicting goals. While collaborative management is about achieving reasonable understanding, agreement, and compromise among parties with different and frequently conflicting interests, some goals are quite difficult to change—especially when the parties attempting to collaborate do not have the power or influence to change the goals set at higher administrative levels of the organizations they represent. For example, the USFS was long under pressure from the U.S. Congress and/or the Office of the President to "get out the cut" (i.e., sell timber products) and a field manager could do little about it. Similarly, many field managers have worked closely with local chapters of national environmental organizations to reach acceptable compromise on a particular management problem only to find that the national offices of those organizations would litigate against such management actions. That created significant barriers to future collaboration.

Lack of incentive. Collaboration requires commitments by both managers and stakeholders. Sometimes these commitments are weakened when neither side perceives collaborating will be worth the time and effort required. It is important not to discourage participants by leaving the impression the process will take a very long time, which can be a significant disincentive.

Lack of trust. Closely related to the previously mentioned barriers, and frequently an important part of having sufficient incentive to collaborate, is a lack of trust between the managers and the stakeholders, especially where strongly held differences of opinion have persisted for a considerable time.

In-group rigidities and differences in attitudes. Just as stakeholders and managers hold both similar and different values and interests, so do the different stakeholders. A real barrier to achieving successful collaboration exists when one or more of the stakeholders are so set in their attitudes, have such vested interests in the management issue, do not want to relinquish a power position they have, or for other reasons do not want to cooperate with the other stakeholders. Put simply, differences among the stakeholders can be a barrier to collaboration no matter what the position(s) of the managers might be. Parties who desire to work together must be aware of these barriers or obstacles to collaboration. While they are frequently difficult to overcome, many successful collaboration efforts have done so.

Summary

Collaborative planning and management (CPM) is an approach where resource managers work collaboratively with the customers (i.e., stakeholders) they serve, as well as with their associated providers, to solve a set of problems none of them can solve individually. CPM is closely related to partnerships among providers of outdoor recreation opportunities as discussed in Chapter 9, although in the broadest sense, the partnerships described there are providers, and CPM is an essential approach to making the often complex and contentious decisions that face resource and recreation managers. This chapter traced the development of CPM, which replaced the limited public involvement approach, which had replaced the technocratic approaches used by most public agencies prior to the 1960s. We then outlined the reasons why CPM was needed, presented its general characteristics and specific ingredients, and identified the most difficult to remove barriers to implementing CPM. This chapter demonstrated that a collaborative approach to planning and management is needed and such an approach is effective. In spite of the barriers to CPM and the ongoing commitment required to make it work, CPM is the best alternative in the long run. The next chapter discusses management of some special types of outdoor recreation resources and opportunities.

Literature Cited

Belden, Russonello & Steward Research and Communications. (2001). *Collaborative process: Better outcomes for all of us.* Dillon, CO: Meridian Institute. Retrieved from http://www.merid.org/showproject. php?ProjectID=21

Gray, B. (1985). Conditions facilitating inter-organiza-
    tional collaboration. *Human Relations, 38,* 912.
USDA Forest Service. (1993, September). *The power of
    collaborative planning: The report of a national
    workshop* (FS-553). Washington, DC: Author.
Wondolleck, J. and Yaffee, S. (2000). *Making collabora-
    tion work: Lessons from innovation in natural resource
    management.* Washington, DC: Island Press.

Chapter 18
Management of Special Outdoor Recreation Resources: Wilderness and Trails

Peering at a wilderness area from a tramway station, however, is not a wilderness experience...
The opportunity can and should be offered as a choice, to be accepted or rejected; but it
should not be falsified or domesticated. (Joseph Sax, 1980, p. 63)

Learning Objectives

1. Explain the differences between sociological wilderness and designated Wilderness.
2. Explain the most important principles of wilderness management.
3. Describe the various types of trails and greenways.
4. Give examples of the benefits that result from protecting wilderness, trails, and greenways.

As pointed out in Chapters 5 and 10, outdoor recreation can and does occur in virtually every natural and semi-natural setting imaginable in every part of the earth's biosphere (i.e., land, water, and air) and in all climactic zones and environments. The diversity of settings and classes of opportunities that outdoor recreation professionals are called on to understand, plan, and manage is much more diverse than variations based on different environments and climates alone, however. A brief sampling of the types of outdoor recreation settings and classes of outdoor recreation opportunities includes the following:

- designated Wilderness areas
- scenic byways and other scenic roadways
- trails
- greenway corridors
- rivers and lakes
- seashores and other coastal areas
- cultural, historical, and archeological sites and resources
- developed and backcountry campgrounds
- picnic areas
- visitor centers
- swimming areas
- interpretive sites and facilities
- threatened and endangered species and their habitats
- wetlands
- hang gliding takeoff and landing areas

- cliffs, crags, and other rock climbing and mountaineering settings
- caves
- tropical and alpine environments
- coral reefs and other underwater resources (where scuba diving and snorkeling are popular)
- motorized recreation areas (e.g., for ATV, snowmobile, personal watercraft, motorcycle, four-wheel drive, and other motorized uses)
- hunting and fishing areas
- winter recreation areas

Several earlier chapters of this text emphasized that outdoor recreation professionals must focus on both the

Cultural and historical resources and events can be important parts of outdoor recreation experiences, as these American Revolution reenators along the Overmountain Victory National Historic Trail in North Carolina illustrate.

natural resource dimensions and human dimensions of natural places like those noted here. Obviously this can be a daunting task. Fortunately, most outdoor recreation professionals work in partnership with other experts and have direct responsibilities that relate to only a few subsets of the aforementioned classes of settings and the particular managerial challenges and responsibilities they pose. But the applicable subset of settings an outdoor recreation manager may have responsibilities for (and therefore need skills related to) can be far greater than most people realize. The recreation staff of a large national forest, for example, might be responsible for administering opportunities for boating and developed camping at lower elevations and serious mountaineering in high peaks. They could be responsible for lakes popular with swimmers and waterskiers in the summer and ice fishers and ice skaters in winter. Their jurisdiction likely includes forests frequented by birders in spring, mountain bikers in summer, hunters in fall, and cross-country skiers and snowmobilers in winter. Add a popular rock climbing crag, a Class V whitewater river segment, an endangered species habitat and proximity to an urban area, and the importance of breadth and depth of skills and experience for every outdoor recreation professional becomes much more obvious.

The primary purpose of this book is to introduce readers to the essential body of knowledge needed to be effective outdoor recreation professionals. The focus, therefore, has been on presenting the most important principles and concepts related to outdoor recreation policy, planning, management, visitor behavior, benefits desired and realized, and natural resource management that apply to the provision of outdoor recreation opportunities in general. Such principles and concepts are applicable across all of the types of settings and classes of opportunities

outdoor recreation professions are typically called on to manage. There are, however, some particular types of settings so common and with such specialized management issues that all outdoor recreation professionals need more specialized working knowledge about them. Primary among these are wilderness areas and trails, greenways, and rivers. The purpose of this chapter is to provide more information on these important outdoor recreation settings and to describe the basic concepts of professionally managing them and the many outdoor recreation opportunities that exist there.

Wilderness Areas

Readers not interested in wilderness recreation or not expecting to be responsible for wilderness management might be tempted to think this section is not applicable to them. Not true. As will become clear shortly, "wilderness" means many different things to different people, some general and relative and some very focused and even legally specified. From a broad perspective, however, all outdoor recreation managers need to be familiar with wilderness recreation and the principles of wilderness management, because they should be looking at outdoor recreation settings and opportunities as existing along a spectrum from urban to primitive like that used in the recreation opportunity spectrum (ROS). The primitive end of the spectrum is always "wilder" than the urban end regardless of whether it is wilderness or not. Although not every outdoor recreation manager and planner will be responsible for truly wild and primitive settings, they all need to understand what motivates people to seek such settings, the types of experiences both on- and off-site users typically

Outdoor recreation facilities, like this backcountry campground in Great Smoky Mountains National Park, have unique management issues.

Fragile environments and potentially dangerous activities can make climbing and mountaineering resources particularly challenging for managers. (Photo by Aram Attarian)

expect, and the importance of people having a wide variety of choices to meet their individualistic outdoor recreation related preferences. The manager also needs to know what constitutes a more primitive setting and how to manage such settings to assure those desired types of opportunities continue to be available. Most importantly, they need to assure wilderness/primitive recreation opportunities are provided somewhere reasonably accessible to their visitors.

Before proceeding, we need to acknowledge the tremendous contributions to the field of wilderness and wilderness management made by of a number of authors. The definitive work on wilderness management is the third edition of *Wilderness Management: Stewardship and Protection of Resources and Values* by John Hendee and Chad Dawson (2002). Along with its first (1978) and second (1990) editions by John Hendee, George Stankey, and Robert Lucas and their collaborating coauthors and reviewers, *Wilderness Management* is an essential resource. Another very important reference to those interested in wilderness is *Wilderness and the American Mind* by Roderick Nash (2001). We have drawn heavily from these sources in preparing this section and encourage readers to seek them out for a thorough treatment of this important subject.

What Is Wilderness?

The term *wilderness* can mean many things depending on the person asked and the context. Wilderness is a relative term best viewed along a continuum from what is sometimes referred to as sociological wilderness at one extreme (Hendee & Dawson, 2002) to legally designated Wilderness at the other extreme as illustrated in Figure 18.1. *Sociological wilderness* is a culturally defined concept meaning anything that people happen to think wilderness is. In other words, whatever someone thinks is "wild" is the basis of what wilderness is to them. That could mean a rugged mountain range to one person, the

bottom of the ocean, a suburban park, the undeveloped banks of a river flowing through an urban area, or even outer space to others. *Legally designated Wilderness*, on the other hand, is a specific area that has been officially and legally designated as Wilderness. In the United States this means Congress has designated the area as Wilderness under the Wilderness Act of 1964 (or related acts and amendments) to be a part of the National Wilderness Preservation System, which is currently made up of over 105,000 million acres of such legally designated areas in the United States. For simplicity, these legally designated Wilderness areas are sometimes referred to as "big-*W*" Wilderness or designated wilderness (as opposed to "little-*w*" wilderness for sociological wilderness). There are specific requirements that must be met for an area to qualify to become legally designated big-*W* Wilderness, and the area must then be managed in ways that conform to the relevant legislation, as will be discussed shortly.

Legally designated Wilderness is a relatively new development in a long evolution of meanings and attitudes toward wild natural areas. Historically, wilderness was often thought of as a place of dread and unknown and in some biblical references even a place of punishment and penitence (Hendee & Dawson, 2002; Nash, 2001). In fact, our word *wilderness* actually comes from the Old English term wild-deor-ness meaning "place of untamed beasts" (Nash & Hendee, 2002). As late as the 1600s, credible people reported seeing dragons in the "wilderness" of the European Alps.

Gradually, however, wilderness became a place of inspiration and purification. This was partly due to the increasing scarcity of wild places (McCloskey, 1966; Nash, 2001). These more positive connotations were reflected in the literature of transcendentalists like Thoreau and Emerson and in the arts. For example, the paintings of the Hudson River School artists and western painters such as George Catlin portrayed wild areas as much more beautiful

High alpine environments are very popular for outdoor recreation and require special management attention.

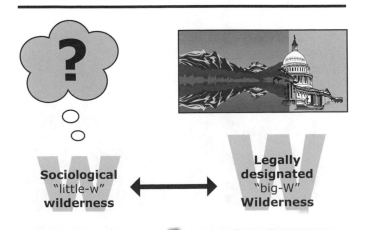

Figure 18.1 Wilderness continuum

and nurturing than had their predecessors. However, the steady westward expansion of the U.S. population during the 19th century was rapidly transforming what had been a vast, nearly untouched wilderness. By the end of that century, large undeveloped wilderness areas were disappearing. The official U.S. census of 1890 declared there was no longer a frontier in the United States.

There were, of course, important voices in the late 19th and early 20th century that began to call for the protection of wild places, including John Muir, President Theodore Roosevelt, and the first National Park Service Director, Stephen Mather. The first steps to protect wild areas as wilderness per se, however, were pioneered by the USDA Forest Service (USFS). Through the vision and leadership of Arthur Carhart, Aldo Leopold (of *A Sand County Almanac* fame), and others, the USFS instituted its L-20 Regulation in 1929 to provide various protections to large natural areas. This was the first systematic effort to protect and to guide management of selected large areas in their wild and natural state. The agency expanded and strengthened protection and management of such areas in 1939 when Bob Marshall developed its U (for "unroaded") regulations, which applied to areas of 100,000 acres in size and larger.

Broad, systematic, nationwide protection of wild areas as Wilderness, however, was not achieved until the passage of the Wilderness Act of 1964. The Wilderness Act created designated Wilderness (i.e., the National Wilderness Preservation System) in the United States and was the result of a prolonged campaign by wilderness advocates that took eight years and 66 different bills. The first of these bills was written in 1956 by Howard Zahniser of the Wilderness Society, generally considered to be the father of the Wilderness Act. President Johnson signed the Wilderness Act into law in 1964, creating the National Wilderness

Legally designated Wilderness areas have been set aside for particular purposes, among them their public use and enjoyment *as wilderness.*

Preservation System (NWPS) with over 9 million acres of "initial inclusions." The Eastern Wilderness Areas Act followed in 1975, which applied specifically to land east of the 100th meridian. The NWPS now includes areas in 44 states and comprises over 105 million acres in 662 separate areas (Wilderness.net, 2004) from Fire Island near New York City to large parts of the Aleutian Islands in Alaska. Just over 4% of U.S. land mass has now been designated as Wilderness, with over half of the total acreage being in Alaska. Approximately 2% of the land area of the lower 48 states is now designated Wilderness (Hendee & Dawson, 2002, p. 511).

According to the Wilderness Act of 1964, designated Wilderness is specifically defined as follows:

> A wilderness, in contrast with those areas where man and his own works dominate the landscape, is hereby recognized as an area where the earth and its community of life are untrammeled by man, where man himself is a visitor who does not remain (*Wilderness Act of 1964*, Pub. L. No. 88-577, Section 2c).

The word "untrammeled" was chosen quite deliberately and means something different than "untrampled." Untrammeled means "not subject to human controls and manipulations that hamper the free play of natural forces." (Hendee & Dawson, 2002, p. 615).

The Wilderness Act of 1964 established "initial inclusions" (mainly USFS areas already managed as primitive by that agency) and a process for reviewing other areas for possible inclusion in NWPS. It was enacted in part "…to assure that an increasing population, accompanied by expanding settlement and growing mechanization, does not occupy and modify all areas within the United States…leaving no lands designated for preservation and protection in their natural condition" (*Wilderness Act of 1964*, Pub. L. No. 88-577). To accomplish these and other purposes, the Act specifies that areas must have the following characteristics to qualify for designation:

- be natural (i.e., substantially unaffected by human influences)
- offer "outstanding opportunities for solitude or a primitive and unconfined type of recreation"
- generally be at least 5,000 acres in size; that is, an area of approximately 7.8 square miles (e.g., a square about 2.8 miles on a side)
- may contain ecological, geological, scenic, or other features of scientific, educational, or historic value

Designated Wilderness is intended to provide and/or protect a variety of values. According to Hendee and Dawson (2002, pp. 7–12) they the result from four distinct historical themes used to advance the cause of wilderness preservation over the years. These four historical wilderness themes and the values associated with them include the following:

Experiential. This theme emphasizes the experience of wilderness as valuable in its own right. This argument asserts the experiences available in wilderness, such as freedom, solitude, adventure, character building, natural beauty, personal growth, restoration, healing, and value clarification, are inherently worthwhile and justify the protection and continued availability of wild areas.

Scientific. This theme argues wilderness is essential because of its value to science as an untouched living laboratory. Such areas can improve our understanding of the workings of the natural world, provide baseline data unavailable in other areas, help gauge environmental degradation of nonwilderness areas, and preserve yet-to-be-discovered organisms and compounds.

Symbolic and spiritual. The importance of wilderness in offering a sense of stability, simplicity, self-imposed limits on technology and growth, and opportunities for connecting with the natural world is the basis of this theme. Although the value of wilderness in the spiritual growth of individuals and societies is more difficult to document and quantify than many other benefits, it is extremely important to a very large number of people.

Economics. Nature-based tourism and recreation generate significant levels of direct and indirect economic benefits for nearby communities and the regions where they are located (see Chapter 19). Such benefits are the basis of this theme in advocating for the protection of wilderness.

It is important to note although the NWPS is a large and important nationwide resource, there is no single agency responsible for its management. Four different federal agencies are responsible for particular Wilderness areas depending on their locations. They are (in descending order based on number of Wilderness acres managed):

- National Park Service
- USDA Forest Service
- U.S. Fish and Wildlife Service
- Bureau of Land Management

When the vast designated Wilderness areas in Alaska are excluded, most wilderness acreage is managed by the USDA Forest Service, followed by the National Park Service, Bureau of Land Management, and U.S. Fish and Wildlife Service (Hendee & Dawson, 2002, p. 609). Nine individual states have their own wilderness preservation programs as well.

Management of Wilderness

At first, it may seem logical that Wilderness areas should not be managed at all, that the objective of keeping as area "untrammeled" (i.e., not subject to human controls and manipulations that hamper the free play of natural forces) might require a completely hands-off approach on the part of managers. This is not the case. The Act specifies that Wilderness

> …shall be administered for the use and enjoyment of the American people in such manner as will leave them unimpaired for future use and enjoyment as wilderness, and so as to provide for protection of these areas, the preservation of their wilderness character, and for the gathering and dissemination of information regarding their use and enjoyment as wilderness.

In some ways, "wilderness management" (or even wilderness "administration" as in the Wilderness Act) might appear to be a classic paradox (Nash, 2001). Wilderness implies the free play of natural forces while "management" indicates at least some level of control by humans. However, the wording regarding these areas' use and enjoyment "as wilderness" are absolutely critical for management. Management intervention is frequently required to assure designated Wilderness areas remain available "as wilderness." But such management intervention must always be sensitive to and consistent with the concept of designated Wilderness and the requirements of the Act. The irony is it is generally the people in Wilderness areas that necessitate management action rather than the natural processes themselves.

To guide management of designated Wilderness areas, the Act prohibited some uses there. The following (with some exceptions) are specifically prohibited in Wilderness areas:

- use of motorized vehicles, motorized equipment, or motorboats
- use of mechanized transport (e.g., bicycles)
- permanent and temporary roads
- aircraft landing
- commercial enterprises
- structures or installations

Some exceptions to these bans were allowed in the Act, often as necessary compromises to enable passage of the Act. The most notable exceptions are the following:

- These and other prohibitions are in place "except as specifically provided for in this Act…and, except as necessary to meet minimum requirements for the administration of the area for the purpose of this

Act." In other words, some specific exceptions were made and wilderness managers are allowed to make exceptions if necessary for management of the area as wilderness. However, these exceptions would need to be justified on grounds more compelling than simple convenience or even cost savings.

- Uses of particular Wilderness areas if these uses were well-established prior to the signing of the Act in 1964 (e.g., wilderness appropriate commercial activities, such as guiding and outfitting, aircraft landing, motorboating, grazing).

- Mining and mineral extraction if the application for lease was filed before 1984

- Fire, insect, and disease control

- Water resource development (e.g., a dam, reservoir, transmission lines) if the President feels it is in the public interest

- Some commercial services (e.g., wilderness appropriate guiding and outfitting) are allowed "to the extent necessary for activities which are proper for realizing the recreational or other wilderness purposes of the areas" (Wilderness Act of 1964, 16 U.S.C. § 1133)

Wilderness managers use a number of specialized approaches to plan and manage Wilderness areas. For example, the wilderness opportunity zoning system (WOZ) is applied in many wilderness areas to help guide wilderness planning and management. The WOZ is similar to the recreation opportunity spectrum (ROS), and both systems of management were described in Chapter 12. The difference is the ROS focuses only on the management of resources to provide outdoor recreation opportunities, while the WOZ focuses on management of designated Wilderness areas to met the broader purposes of the Wilderness Act. It establishes criteria to classify and manage different areas within a particular wilderness as Transition/portal, Semi-primitive, Primitive, or Pristine (Haas, Driver, Brown & Lucas, 1987).

Because of the complex nature of wilderness management, however, general principles can serve as valuable guides. Such principles may also be most helpful to those who may be managing primitive areas not actually designated as wilderness. Hendee and Dawson (2002, pp. 191–206) offer 13 very useful principles of wilderness management, which provide a framework to guide the management of wilderness areas. These principles can provide excellent guidance not only for the management of designated Wilderness areas, but also for any lands toward the more primitive end of the ROS system managed by any agency or organization. Their 13 principles (and brief explanations of each) follow.

1. **Manage wilderness as the most pristine extreme on the environmental modification spectrum.** The "environmental modification spectrum" describes a continuum of environments from the "paved to the primeval" (Nash, 2001)—in other words, environments completely modified at one extreme to those completely wild and primeval at the other. Designated Wilderness is, of course, characterized by naturalness, solitude, and minimum modifications to the environment. This first principle emphasizes wilderness areas should be managed to maintain these distinctive characteristics relative to their adjacent lands. From the perspective of the ROS, wilderness is part of the Primitive class.

2. **Manage wilderness comprehensively, not as separate parts.** Wilderness is characterized by the natural relationships among all the parts of its ecosystems. This includes land, water, wildlife, vegetation, and geology as well as cultural resources. All of these elements and more are parts of the wilderness whole. The interrelationships among them and other parts must be managed comprehensively.

3. **Manage wilderness, and sites within, under a nondegradation concept.** The level of naturalness varies from one wilderness to another and even within different parts of the same wilderness. This principle highlights the importance of maintaining current levels of environmental conditions if they are at or above minimum standards. If not, conditions should be restored to minimum standards.

4. **Manage human influences—A key to wilderness protection.** The stewardship of wilderness areas depends on effective management of human use and its influences. The negative impacts of recreation must be controlled to maintain the wilderness character. This might involve use of one of the impact management systems presented in Chapters 12 and 14, such as WOZ, LAC, VIM, or VERP.

5. **Manage wilderness biocentrically to produce human values and benefits.** Wilderness is designated to protect its resources and to provide wilderness-related benefits (including enjoyment) for people. Biocentric (emphasizing environmental integrity) rather than anthropocentric (i.e., human-oriented) management is essential. Wilderness-related values and benefits, rather than the many other benefits these areas could produce, should be emphasized. Providing opportunities for high-quality wilderness experiences is certainly one appropriate focus for wilderness managers.

6. **Favor wilderness-dependent activities.** Almost all outdoor recreation activities and experiences could conceivably occur in wilderness, but some experiences (e.g., some experience gestalts as described in Chapter 2) can only occur in wilderness. For example, while fishing is possible in any body of water containing fish, the solitude and challenge of fishing in a remote, hard-to-access alpine lake may only be possible in certain wilderness areas. "Wilderness-dependent" activities and experiences should be favored in wilderness areas.

7. **Guide wilderness management using written plans with specific area objectives.** Effective management of areas as wilderness depends on having formal plans with specifically stated objectives and explanations of how those objectives will be accomplished.

8. **Set carrying capacities as necessary to prevent unnatural change.** Wilderness areas can only receive limited levels of negative impacts and still retain the qualities that make them wilderness. Impact management systems, such as WOZ, LAC, VIM, and VERP, should be used to monitor and manage negative physical, biological, and social impacts in wilderness areas.

9. **Focus management on threatened sites and damaging activities.** Some activities are more damaging than others, some sites within wilderness areas are more fragile than others, and popular and heavily used sites within wilderness areas receive more negative impacts than others. These uses and sites should receive more management attention and action than others rather than assuming across-the-board management actions or restrictions are necessary.

10. **Apply only the minimum tools, regulations, or force to achieve wilderness-area objectives.** As noted in Chapter 16, the so-called *minimum tool rule* advocates managers to "apply only the minimum tools, equipment, device, force, regulation, action or practice that will bring the desired result" (Hendee & Dawson, 2002, p. 201).

11. **Involve the public as a key to the success of wilderness management.** Public involvement, volunteerism, and partnerships are essential in developing and implementing wilderness plans and carrying out wilderness management activities.

12. **Monitor wilderness conditions and experience opportunities to guide long-term wilderness stewardship.** Ongoing monitoring of biological, physical, and social conditions in wilderness areas is essential for their management as wilderness. This is particularly true given the importance of wilderness in terms of science and environmental monitoring. Monitoring must be explicitly guided by clear objectives related to what and how data will be gathered, evaluated, and compared.

13. **Manage wilderness in relation to management of adjacent lands.** Wilderness areas do not, of course, exist in a vacuum. Activities and conditions outside wilderness boundaries affect activities and conditions within the wilderness and vice versa. Wilderness managers must be aware of these effects and develop and cooperate with many partners to minimize the negative effects originating outside wilderness boundaries. This applies to both public and private land adjacent to wilderness, although different approaches may be needed in each case.

Wilderness Use

As noted in Chapter 3, outdoor recreation in Wilderness areas is very popular and has increased markedly during the last four decades. The most rapid increases in use came during the 1960s and 1970s. Use of Wilderness leveled off in the 1980s (and even declined in some areas) before beginning to increase again in the 1990s (Cole, 1996; Lucas, 1985; Roggenbuck & Lucas, 1987). Hendee and Dawson (2002) predicted Wilderness use will continue to increase at a rate of about 2% per year. That would mean Wilderness areas would have been receiving about 19 million visitor days of recreation annually in 2001 and will be receiving a projected 23.5 million visitor days of recreation annually by 2010.

According to Hendee and Dawson (2002, pp. 372–411) most Wilderness visits are short (often day trips), group sizes are typically from two to four people, and hiking is the most common activity (with exceptions in some areas, of course). In most Wilderness areas, summer is the heaviest use season. Compared with the general population in the United States, wilderness users tend to be younger and more highly educated and have slightly higher incomes. Although use by females in increasing, the majority of Wilderness users are male.

Hendee and Dawson (2002, pp. 504–512) also pointed out the number of acres that could be added to the NWPS in the United States is ultimately quite limited—perhaps only another one million acres beyond the roughly 105 million acres that have been designated so far. However, in spite of the fact that much of the NWPS has likely already been established, they predict that Wilderness will become increasingly important in the United States and internationally. The United States is only one of nine nations that have a designated wilderness preservation system, created either by law or administrative mandate. There have been a series of World Wilderness Congresses, the most recent being (the 7th) in South Africa in 2001 and (the 8th) in Alaska in 2005. There is every reason to be optimistic about the future of public interest in wilderness.

It is possible that as societal values change, there might one day be renewed suggestions that some areas of wilderness be designated as so-called "no rescue wilderness." These have been proposed as areas where visitors would have the opportunity (and responsibility) to be completely self-reliant, to the point of understanding that no rescue operation would be mounted if they ran into trouble (McAvoy & Dustin, 1981, 1983). For some, no rescue wilderness is a natural extension of the intent of the Wilderness Act to provide unique opportunities for freedom, solitude, adventure, character building, and personal growth. For others the concept seems immoral or impractical. So far, there are no wilderness areas with an official no rescue policy.

Trails and Greenways

Another extremely common category of outdoor recreation opportunities all outdoor recreation professionals should have a working knowledge of is trails and greenways. Trails are one of the most common and popular types of resources available for outdoor recreation. They provide opportunities for many activities, a wide variety of experiences, and access to many other settings. The purpose of this section is to provide working definitions of trails and greenways, to describe their types, and to provide an overview of the extent of the systems of trails and greenways in the United States. The section borrows from and builds on a review paper by Moore and Shafer (2001). Other valuable references related to trails and greenways interested readers can access include the following:

- *Trails for the Twenty-First Century: Planning, Design, and Management: Manual for Multi-Use Trails* (Flink, Olka & Searns, 2001)

- *Appalachian Trail Design, Construction, and Maintenance* (Birchard & Proudman, 2000)

- *The Complete Guide to Trail Building and Maintenance, 3rd edition* (Demrow & Salisbury, 1998)

- *Lightly on the Land: The SCA Trail-Building and Maintenance Manual* (Birkby, 1996)

- *Greenways for America* (Little, 1990)

Trail and Greenway Definitions and Types

Trails and greenways and other types of linear outdoor recreation opportunities are almost always complementary and very closely related, but although they are frequently confused, they are not the same thing. The confusion between trails and greenways is due to overlapping terms, careless use of terms, the many types of trails and greenways that exist, and the relatively new and rapid development of greenways as a type of protected area. It is important to understand the distinctions between trails and greenways to effectively plan for, protect, develop, and manage them from the many perspectives for which they are important, such as outdoor recreation, transportation, environmental health, economic benefits, and conservation. The following discussion attempts to clarify the distinction between trails and greenways and to provide a basic understanding of each for outdoor recreation professionals.

Trails

There are many different types of trails and many working definitions of what trails are. Dictionaries commonly define a trail simply as a "beaten path." A nationwide task force of trail organizations and government agencies defined a trail in more useful detail as, "a linear corridor, on land or water, with protected status and public access for recreation or transportation" (American Trails, 1990, p. 2). Axelson and colleagues (1999) defined trails as paths of travel for recreation and/or transportation within a park, natural environment, or designated corridor, not classified as a highway or street. While there is no universal legal definition of a trail in the United States, one of the best, used for national recreation trails, is

> ...a travel way established either through construction or use which is passable by at least one or more of the following, including but not limited to: foot traffic, stock, watercraft, bicycles, inline skates, wheelchairs, cross-country skis, or off-road recreation vehicles such as motorcycles,

This recreational greenway trail in Tennessee, like many others, provides a wide variety of outdoor recreation opportunities close to where people live and work. (Photo by National Park Service)

snowmobiles, ATVs, and 4-wheel drive vehicles. (National Park Service, 2004a)

Trails can be classified into a number of different types. The National Recreation and Park Association (NRPA) categorizes trails as (a) those incorporated in greenways, (b) park trails, and (c) connector trails (Mertes & Hall, 1996). Moore and Ross (1998) grouped trails into the following five broad overlapping types:

Traditional backcountry trails. These trails typically have a narrower tread than other types, have a natural tread surface, and provide for multiple recreational uses in more remote parts of parks and recreation areas. These narrow, natural trails are sometimes referred to as "single-track" trails.

Recreational greenway trails. Recreational greenways are natural corridors of open space that contain a trail. The term is sometimes used to refer to the corridor and sometimes to the actual trail within it. In either case, the greenway corridor is often in contrast to urban or suburban development adjacent to it. It is more precise and preferable to use the term *recreational greenway* to refer to the natural corridor that contains a trail, and to refer to the trail within the greenway corridor as a *greenway trail.*

Multiple-use trails. These trails are characterized by a wider, hardened tread suitable for higher densities of use and multiple trail activities. Multiple-use trails (also called *multi-use trails*) can be located in any environment, but the term is commonly used to refer to trails located in recreational greenways. Ryan (1993) referred to the multiple-use trail as "a modern public space" that "invites many different types of users…to share a trail corridor collectively" (p. 5).

Water trails. Water trails are a concept growing in popularity. Water trails are simply navigable rivers, streams, lakes, or other bodies of water that provide users with opportunities to float, paddle, or motor along a designated water route. Camping facilities are often provided along water trails to make multiday trips possible.

Rail-trails. Rail-trails are abandoned or unused railroad lines that have been converted into trails for recreation and/or transportation purposed. Rail-trails are being created at a rapid pace and are increasingly popular recreation facilities in the United States. Because of the rich history of rail and water transportation in the modern settlement and growth of the United States, rail-trails and water trails often contain significant historic and cultural features as well.

Trails have been and continue to be built for many reasons, particularly for recreation and transportation. Native peoples built and used trails as transportation and commerce routes long before colonists arrived from Europe. Many of their historic routes became the colonists' bridle paths, stage roads, and later the paved highways still in use today.

Greenways

Greenways are a much newer development than trails and are somewhat more difficult to define. This is due, in part, to the many functions that greenway corridors serve. Planners, landscape ecologists, and recreation professionals all define greenway resources relative to their particular perspectives. In general, a greenway is a linear open space corridor that follows some natural or human-made feature. Little (1990, p. 1) provided a comprehensive definition of greenways, which is often used as a starting point. He defined greenways broadly as

Rivers, including this recreational "water trail" in Ohio, can be extremely important multipurpose natural resources. (Photo by Paul Labovitz, National Park Service)

Rail-trails, like this one in Iowa, are a rapidly growing and increasingly important category of outdoor recreation resources in the United States.

- a linear open space established along either a natural corridor, such as a riverfront, stream valley, or ridge-line, or overland along a railroad right-of-way converted to recreational use, a canal, a scenic road, or other route
- any natural or landscaped course for pedestrian or bicycle passage
- an open-space connector linking parks, nature reserves, cultural features, or historic sites with each other or with populated areas
- locally, certain strips of linear parks designated as a parkway or greenbelt

Little also identified the following five major types of greenways:

- urban riverside greenways
- recreational greenways
- ecologically significant natural corridors
- scenic and historic routes
- comprehensive greenway systems or networks

Greenways also serve much broader purposes than simply providing locations for trails and other outdoor recreation opportunities. Most important among these is probably the protection of ecological resources located in a natural corridor. Greenways have been described as "nature's superstructure" (Fabos, 1995) and "geneways" for their role in providing species habitat and natural migration routes. Landscape ecologists have focused on the value of greenways in providing better regional connectivity (Bueno, Tsihrintzis & Alvarez, 1995; Dramstad, Olsen & Forman, 1996) and protecting habitat (e.g., Baschek & Brown, 1995; Hellmund, 1993). Some greenways located in ecologically sensitive corridors exclude trails because of the potential for negative impacts due to human use (Baschek & Brown, 1995; Hellmund, 1993). Some consider greenways to be an important part of "green infrastructure" that should be planned into communities as purposefully as we now plan other kinds of infrastructure, such as roads and water, electric, and sewer systems (GreenInfrastructure.net, 2004).

In reality, greenways can be many things, including recreational corridors, areas for managing storm water and runoff, routes for transportation, habitats for wildlife, and opportunities for alternative economic development (Shafer, Scott & Mixon, 2000), as well as corridors of protected open space managed for conservation. Greenways can be publicly, privately, or nonprofit owned and managed and are often the results of partnerships among these three sectors.

Current Scope of Trail and Greenway Systems

Pioneering individuals and organizations have left a rich and diverse collection of trails in many parts of the world. In the United States, early mountain trails were often developed out of a fascinating mix of exploration, scientific curiosity, adventure seeking, and commercial opportunism (Waterman & Waterman, 1989). Mountain guides in New Hampshire, for instance, began building trails in the early 19th century to facilitate a growing tourist trade based on mountain scenery. Their clients would likely be called ecotourists today. Following the early efforts of explorers, guides, and outfitters, the principal forces in creating trails at different times and in different areas have been volunteers and nonprofit organizations, federal programs like the Civilian Conservation Corps, and the full spectrum of government agencies from town councils to the USDA Forest Service and many others.

Building on this heritage, there are now actually two distinct but sometimes interconnected and overlapping systems of trails and greenways in the United States. The first and best known is the National Trail System (NTS), authorized by the National Trail System Act of 1968. This and later amendments authorized an official system of "national trails" in the United States. There are three important types of "national trails" officially established under the authorities of the National Trails System Act (National Park Service, 2004a).

National Scenic Trails. National Scenic Trails are primarily nonmotorized continuous routes 100 miles long or longer with outstanding recreation opportunities. National Scenic Trails must be designated by an act of Congress. The Appalachian, Continental Divide, and Pacific Crest Trails are examples of National Scenic Trails.

The Appalachian National Scenic Trail, or AT as it is often called, is one of the best known trails in the world. (Photo by Craig Evans)

National Historic Trails. National Historic Trails commemorate historic routes of travel significant to the entire nation. They follow routes used for purposes such as exploration, migration, or military travel and must be established by act of Congress. National Historic Trail designations are mainly used to identify the route, its artifacts, and remnants and are generally not intended to create trails that can be traveled on foot. Many are marked motor routes on existing roads with visitor centers, interpretive signs, and occasional connecting trail segments. The Lewis and Clark, Santa Fe, Iditarod, and Mormon Pioneer Trails are examples of National Historic Trails.

National Recreation Trails. National Recreation Trails (NRTs) are existing, typically shorter, regional and local trails that provide maximum recreation potential, especially near population centers. Any combination of trail uses can be allowed. National Recreation Trails can be designated by the Secretary of Agriculture or the Secretary of the Interior.

There are currently 23 National Scenic and National Historic Trails authorized (8 scenic and 15 historic). These long national trails will total more than 40,000 miles in length if completed (National Park Service, 2004a). However, only a portion of this total now exists as actual off-highway trail mileage. There are also over 800 National Recreation Trails with a combined mileage of more than 10,000 miles available for public use (Chavez, Harding & Tynon, 1999; National Park Service, 2004a). The National Recreation Trails range in length from less than one mile to 485 miles (American Trails, 2004). The National Trail System is indeed extensive and impressive and will become even more so. It is also highly varied, including long and remote wilderness routes, multiple-use urban greenway trails, and commemorative historic trails. However,

National Historic Trails in the United States are often commemorative, with only portions being available for more traditional outdoor recreation use.

the official National Trail System was never intended to and will never meet all trail needs in the United States.

Augmenting, often predating, and almost certainly far exceeding the mileage of the designated National Trail System is another national system of trails comprised of all the other trails and greenways in the United States. These routes include local trail networks as well as individual trails. Many of these trails are not yet connected to others and some will never be. With the exception of ones that have received recognition as National Recreation Trails, they are not part of the National Trail System. These trails provide important outdoor recreation opportunities developed by public agencies, nonprofit organizations, volunteers, private enterprises, and enthusiasts in local communities. For example, there are now over 1,200 rail-trails, found in every state, totaling over 12,500 miles and estimated to attract around 100 million users per year (Rails-to-Trails Conservancy, 2004a, 2004b). A number of organizations, notably the nationwide nonprofit Rails-to-Trails Conservancy (RTC), are actively working to promoting rail-trail conversions.

The designated National Trail System consists of existing and proposed long-distance routes that crisscross the country (see Figure 18.2, p. 268). In contrast, former Chief of the National Park Service Recreation Resources Assistance Division, Bill Spitzer, likened the configuration of the "system" of other trails in the United States to "star bursts" of local trails that may or may not be connected to the National Trails.

The extent of trail resources that exist today is extremely difficult to gauge accurately for a number of reasons. These include the vast number of trails in the United States, differing criteria for what should and should not be included in trail inventories, and the many different public agencies, private enterprises, nonprofit organizations, and private individuals involved in providing trail opportunities. Specifically, a huge number of people and organizations plan, build, and maintain trails in the private, nonprofit, and public sectors at all levels, including public land managers, trail user groups, nonprofit land trusts, private landowners, guides and outfitters, and myriad less formal clubs and interest groups. Often overlooked are the people who build, maintain, and use trails on their private land holdings.

Trail and greenway use is also difficult to tabulate accurately, because what are commonly thought of as "trail activities" might or might not actually occur on trails, and most large-scale studies focus on participation in particular recreation activities not where the activity takes place. There seems little doubt, however, that trails are extremely popular and heavily used. During 1994–1995, for example, an estimated 68.3% of Americans ages 16 or older participated in nonmotorized "trail/street/road

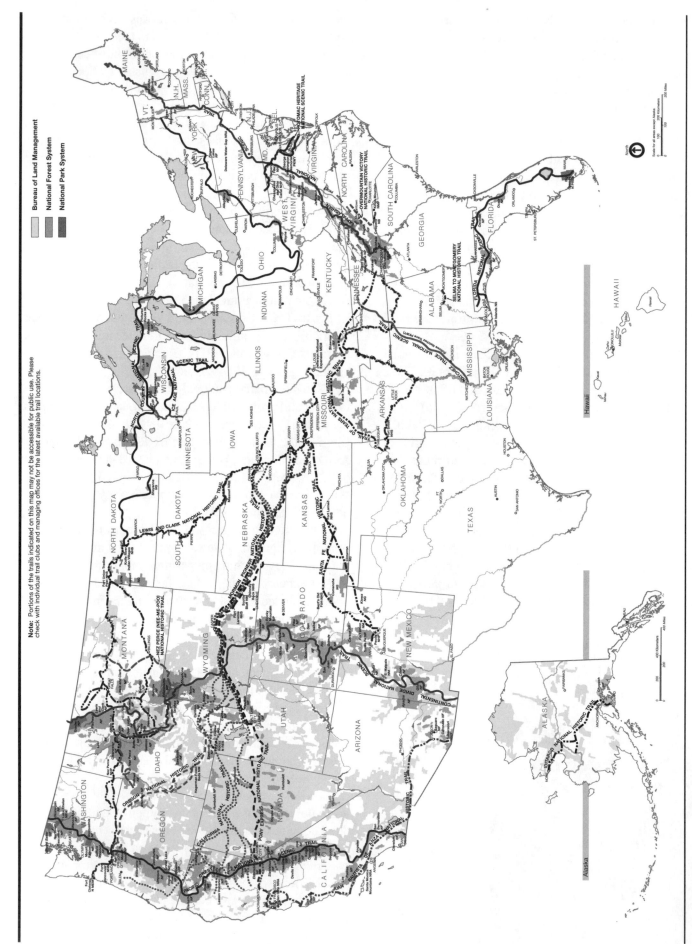

Figure 18.2 Map of the U.S. National Trail System. Adapted from National Park Service, 1998

activities" as defined in the National Survey on Recreation and the Environment. This means 136.9 million people in the United States walked, ran, jogged, or biked during that period. The same study found walking was the most popular outdoor recreation activity in the nation, with two thirds of the population participating in the previous 12 months (Cordell et al., 1999, pp. 221–223). A 1998 study in North Carolina found 32% of state residents had used a trail in the past 12 months and another 22% wanted to but were unable for some reason (Moore, Siderelis, Lee, Ivy & Bailey, 1999). A similar study in South Carolina found 33% of residents had used a pedestrian trail during the past 12 months (University of South Carolina, 1992). In Texas, 70% of statewide respondents had walked for pleasure and averaged 106 days a year in which they engaged in the activity (Goldbloom, 1992). It also appears that trail use is increasing significantly. The number of Americans ages 16 or older participating in activities typically engaged in on trails increased dramatically between the 1982–1983 and 1994–1995 surveys examined by Cordell and colleagues (1999, p. 239). For example, the percentage of people engaged in hiking increased by 93.5% between the two surveys, the percentage backpacking was up 72.7%, the percentage off-road driving was up 43.8%, and the percentage cross-country skiing was up 22.6%. Among activities typically engaged in on trails, only horseback riding dropped (10.1%) between the two surveys.

Trail and Greenway Benefits and Current Policies

Part of the surge in popularity of trails and greenways is due to the fact that they offer a particularly wide range of benefits both to those who use them and to the wider communities where the corridors are located. Personal benefits of trail use have been researched in many places and with different user groups. Exercise and fitness and the appreciation of nature are often benefits users report as being especially important in relation to trails (East Bay Regional Park District, 1997; Goldbloom, 1992; Moore & Ross, 1998; Shafer, Lee & Turner, 2000). People commonly use trails and greenways with family members and friends, and therefore receive social benefits through the development and maintenance of relationships. Sharing trails and greenways with neighbors and other community members who walk, ride, or skate may also provide social benefits.

As multiple-use corridors, greenways in particular can be extremely beneficial for users and nearby areas. Commonly touted benefits of greenways include the following:

- outdoor recreation opportunities
- transportation alternatives
- open space and ecological protection
- wildlife habitat (especially in urban and suburban areas)
- economic development (e.g., tourism spending, as amenities that attract corporate relocations, enhancements of nearby property values)
- locations for utility easements
- enhanced community pride
- pollution mitigation (e.g., natural filtration of runoff)
- environmental education opportunities
- improved health and fitness for users
- historic preservation opportunities

There have been a number of important policies and initiatives regarding trails and greenways in the United States since the passage of the National Trails System Act in 1968. The President's Commission on Americans Outdoors (1987) promoted trails and greenways and spoke of the need to develop such resources through citizen-driven initiatives. The President's Commission recommended, in particular, access to outdoor recreation should be available at the local level and suggested networks of trails and greenways were important ways of doing this. At the state level, nearly every state in the United States now has a state trails program and/or a bicycle and pedestrian coordinator for related issues.

Since 1991, however, federal transportation policy has likely had more far reaching implications for greenway and trail development than any other park or open space initiatives. The Intermodal Surface Transportation Efficiency Act (ISTEA) of 1991 began a new era of transportation policy that made hundreds of millions of dollars available for transportation projects designed to increase the viability of bicycling and walking as modes of transportation. This money has been used for everything from purchasing greenway corridors and developing multiple-use trail facilities to constructing rail-trails in rural areas and pedestrian bridges over highways. The primary stipulation of ISTEA and its successors has been that funded projects enhance the surface transportation system in the United States. Many trail and greenway projects do so, and therefore qualify for funding. The ISTEA legislation also created the National Recreational Trails Program that has allocated millions of dollars to trail projects that do not have to be directly linked to surface transportation. These grants encourage public-private partnerships and can supply funds for up to 80% of a trail project. The ISTEA legislation was reauthorized in 1997 as the Transportation Equity Act for the 21st Century (TEA-21), helping to further institutionalize the importance of trails and greenways as components of community infrastructure.

Although no official national standards propose how many trails or greenways there should eventually be in the United States, there have been attempts to provide some guidance. For example, a nationwide task force of trail organizations and government agencies proposed there should be a trail within 15 minutes of every American (American Trails, 1990, p. 2). The National Recreation and Parks Association's (NRPA) "Open Space Standards" offer a rough guideline that there should be one mile of bicycle/jogging trail for every 2,000 people in a community (Flink, Olka & Searns, 2001, p. 13).

Rivers

Another important category of linear outdoor recreation resources that often overlaps with and is almost always complimentary with trails and greenways is rivers. As noted earlier, water trails are an important and growing category of outdoor recreation resource, and rivers often form the backbone of greenway corridors. However, rivers and streams are also important sources of outdoor recreation opportunities even when they are not designated as official water trails or comprise part of a wider greenway corridor. An extremely important river recreation resource is the National Wild and Scenic Rivers System as created by the National Wild and Scenic Rivers Act of 1968.

The National Wild and Scenic Rivers Act of 1968 mirrors the National Trails System Act in many respects, but focuses on nationally significant rivers and their immediate environments. To be included in the National Wild and Scenic Rivers System, river segments (i.e., sections) must have outstanding scenic, recreational, geologic, fish and wildlife, historic, cultural, or similar values. Congress must designate the river segments included in the system. They are categorized as one of the following three types depending on their characteristics:

Wild River segments must be free-flowing (i.e., have no dams or other impoundments) and be unpolluted (or restorable to an unpolluted condition). These segments are managed primarily for preservation and enhancement. Wild rivers and their corridors can also offer outstanding outdoor recreation opportunities.

Scenic River segments are also free-flowing, but are more accessible by roads than wild rivers. Scenic rivers are managed for maintaining natural and scenic features. Like wild rivers, scenic rivers can be extremely popular for river-related outdoor recreation.

Recreational River segments have high recreational potential and good access. They are managed to maintain the environment and accommodate river-related outdoor recreation.

As of 2002 there were more than 180 river segments in 41 states totaling over 11,000 miles in the National Wild and Scenic Rivers System (5,351 wild, 2,457 scenic, and 3,495 recreational; National Park Service, 2004b). This extensive national system of river segments is managed by a variety of federal agencies, including the following:

- National Park Service
- USDA Forest Service
- Bureau of Land Management
- U.S. Fish and Wildlife Service
- U.S. Army Corps of Engineers

A number of states have wild and scenic river programs as well.

Summary

This chapter introduced and described two categories of outdoor recreation resources common enough and with issues unique enough that all outdoor recreation professionals should have more than a basic understanding of them: wilderness resources and trails, greenways, and rivers. We clarified the difference between sociological wilderness and legally designated Wilderness, described the National Wilderness Preservation System (NWPS) in the United States created by the Wilderness Act of 1964, and related the basics of managing wilderness resources, including 13 Principles of Wilderness Management offered by Hendee and Dawson (2002, pp. 191–206). We turned next to trails and greenways, starting with important definitions and distinctions among the different types of these important linear recreation resources. We presented an overview of the current scope of trail and greenway systems in the United States and a description of the most important aspects of both the National Trails System and the less formal system of other trails nationwide. We then briefly discussed the benefits and current policies related to trails and greenways and ended with a short summary of river resources, another very important linear outdoor recreation resource. In the next chapter we present important concepts regarding the economics of outdoor recreation—an essential tool for understanding and valuing the many benefits of outdoor recreation settings and participation.

Literature Cited

American Trails. (1990). *Trails for all Americans: The report of the National Trails Agenda Project.* Washington, DC: U.S. Department of the Interior, National Park Service.

American Trails. (2004). *National recreation trails program.* Retrieved June 25, 2004, from http://www.americantrails.org/nationalrecreationtrails/default.htm

Axelson, P., Chesney, D., Galvan, D., Kirschbaum, J., Longmuir, P., Lyons, C., et al. (1999). *Designing sidewalks and trails for access: Part I* (FHWA-HEP-99-006). Washington, DC: U.S. Department of Transportation.

Baschek, L. and Brown, R. (1995). An ecological framework for the planning, design and management of urban river greenways. *Landscape and Urban Planning, 33*(1–3), 211–226.

Birchard, W. and Proudman, R. (2000). *Appalachian trail design, construction, and maintenance* (2nd ed.). Harpers Ferry, WV: Appalachian Trail Conference.

Birkby, R. (1996). *Lightly on the land: The SCA trail-building and maintenance manual.* Seattle, WA: The Mountaineers.

Bueno, J., Tsihrintzis, V., and Alvarez, L. (1995). South Florida greenways: A conceptual framework for the ecological reconnectivity of the region. *Landscape and Urban Planning, 33*(1–3), 247–266.

Chavez, D., Harding, J., and Tynon, J. (1999). National recreation trails: A forgotten designation. *Journal of Forestry,* (97)10, 40–43.

Cole, D. (1996). *Wilderness use trends, 1965 through 1994* (USDA Forest Service Research Paper INT-488). Ogden, UT: Intermountain Research Station.

Cordell, H. K., Betz, C. J., Bowker, J. M., English, D. B. K., Mou, S. H., Bergstrom, J. C., et al. (1999). *Outdoor recreation in American life: A national assessment of demand and supply trends.* Champaign, IL: Sagamore.

Demrow, C. and Salisbury, D. (1998). *The complete guide to trail building and maintenance* (3rd ed.). Boston, MA: Appalachian Mountain Club.

Dramstad, W., Olsen, J., and Forman, R. (1996). *Landscape ecology principles in landscape architecture and land use planning.* Washington, DC: Island Press.

East Bay Regional Park District. (1997). *Iron Horse Regional Trail trail use study.* Available from the East Bay Regional Park District, 2950 Peralta Oaks Court, P.O. Box 5381, Oakland, CA 94605-0381.

Fabos, J. (1995). Introduction and overview: The greenway movement and uses of potential greenways. *Landscape and Urban Planning, 33,* 1–14.

Flink, C., Olka, K., and Searns, R. (2001). *Trails for the twenty-first century: Planning, design, and management manual for multi-use trails* (2nd ed.). Washington, DC: Island Press.

Goldbloom, A. (1992). *The 1991 Texas trails study.* Available from the Texas Parks and Wildlife Department, 4200 Smith School Road, Austin, TX 78744.

GreenInfrastructure.net (2004). *What is green infrastructure?* Retrieved July 3, 2004, from http://www.greeninfrastructure.net

Hass, G., Driver, B. L., Brown, P., and Lucas, R. (1987, December). Wilderness management zoning. *Journal of Forestry,* 17–21.

Hellmund, P. (1993). A method for ecological greenway design. In D. Smith and P. Hellmund (Eds.), *Ecology of greenways: Design functions of linear conservation areas* (pp. 123–160). Minneapolis, MN: University of Minnesota Press.

Hendee, J. and Dawson, C. (2002). *Wilderness management: Stewardship and protection of resources and values* (3rd ed.). Golden, CO: Fulcrum Publishing.

Hendee, J., Stankey, G., and Lucas, R. (1978). *Wilderness management.* Washington, DC: USDA Forest Service.

Hendee, J., Stankey, G., and Lucas, R. (1990). *Wilderness management* (2nd ed.). Golden, CO: Fulcrum Publishing.

Little, C. (1990). *Greenways for America.* Baltimore, MD: The Johns Hopkins University Press.

Lucas, R. (1985). Recreation trends and management of the Bob Marshall Wilderness Complex. In *Proceedings of the 1985 National Outdoor Recreation Trends Symposium, Vol. II* (pp. 309–316). Atlanta, GA: U.S. National Park Service.

McAvoy, L. and Dustin D. (1981, March). The right to risk in wilderness. *Journal of Forestry,* 150–152.

McAvoy, L. and Dustin, D. (1983). In search of balance: A no-rescue wilderness proposal. *Western Wildlands, 9*(2) 2–5.

McCloskey, M. (1966). The Wilderness Act: Its background and meaning. *Oregon Law Review, 45*(4), 288–321.

Mertes, J. and Hall, J. (1996). *Park, recreation, open space and greenway guidelines.* Reston VA: National Recreation and Park Association.

Moore, R. and Ross, D. (1998). Trails and recreational greenways: Corridors of benefits. *Parks and Recreation, 33*(1), 68–79.

Moore, R. and Shafer, S. (2001). Trails and greenways: Opportunities for planners, managers, and scholars. *Journal of Park and Recreation Administration, 19*(3), 1–16.

Moore, R., Siderelis, C., Lee, J.-H., Ivy, M., and Bailey, G. (1999). *1998 North Carolina State trail and greenway Survey.* Raleigh, NC: North Carolina Department of Environment and Natural Resources, Division of State Parks.

Nash, R. (2001). *Wilderness and the American mind* (4th ed.). New Haven, CT: Yale University Press.

Nash, R. and Hendee, J. (2002). Historical roots of wilderness management. In J. Hendee and C. Dawson, *Wilderness management: Stewardship and protection of resources and values* (3rd ed.; pp. 31–47). Golden, CO: Fulcrum Publishing.

National Park Service, Harpers Ferry Center. (1998). *National Trail System map and guide* [printable map]. Retrieved February 2, 2005, from http://www.nps.gov/hfc/carto/nps-trails.htm#

National Park Service. (2004a). *National trails system—General information.* Retrieved June 25, 2004, from http://www.nps.gov/nts/nts_faq.html

National Park Service. (2004b). *River mileage classifications for components of the National Wild & Scenic Rivers System.* Retrieved July 3, 2004, from http://www.nps.gov/rivers/wildriverstable.html

President's Commission on Americans Outdoors. (1987). *Americans outdoors: The legacy, the challenge.* Washington, DC: Island Press.

Rails-to-Trails Conservancy. (2004a). *Accomplishments.* Retrieved June 30, 2004, from http://www.railtrails.org/about/accomp.asp

Rails-to-Trails Conservancy. (2004b). *1,000 great rail-trails: A comprehensive directory* (3rd ed.). Guilford, CT: Globe Pequot Press.

Roggenbuck, J. and Lucas, R. (1987). Wilderness use and users: A state-of-knowledge review. In *Proceedings—National Wilderness Research Conference: Issues, state-of-knowledge, future directions* (General Technical Report INT-220; pp. 204–245). Ogden, UT: USDA Forest Service, Intermountain Research Station.

Ryan, K. (Ed.). (1993). *Trails for the twenty-first century: Planning, design and management manual for multi-use trails.* Washington, DC: Island Press.

Sax, J. (1980). *Mountains without handrails: Reflections on the national parks.* Ann Arbor, MI: University of Michigan Press.

Shafer, S., Lee, B., and Turner, S. (2000). A tale of three greenway trails: User perceptions related to quality of life. *Landscape and Urban Planning, 49,* 163–178.

Shafer, S., Scott, D., and Mixon, J. (2000). A greenway classification system: Defining the function and character of greenways in urban areas. *Journal of Park and Recreation Administration, 18,* 88–106.

University of South Carolina. (1992). *Public attitudes on recreation trails and related activities.* Columbia, SC: University of South Carolina, Institute of Public Affairs.

Waterman, L. and Waterman, G. (1989). *Forest and crag: A history of hiking, trail blazing, and adventure in the northeast mountains.* Boston, MA: Appalachian Mountain Club.

Wilderness Act of 1964, 16 U.S.C. § 1131 et seq.

Wilderness.net (2004). *Wilderness fast facts.* Retrieved June 10, 2004, from http://working.wilderness.net/win/index.cfm?fuse=NWPS&sec=fastfacts

Chapter 19
Economics of Outdoor Recreation[1]

...however praiseworthy one's objectives may be they are rarely, if ever, achieved without costs, and resources and budgets are never so plentiful that consideration of economic efficiency can ever be ignored with impunity. (Brazer, 1970, p. 129)

Learning Objectives

1. Understand and appreciate the scope and relevance of the principles and methods of economics to parks and recreation management in general and to outdoor recreation in particular.
2. Explain how economists define the word *value,* how economic values of publicly provided outdoor recreation opportunities are measured, why commensurate economic measures of value are useful, and why measures of value other than economic ones are needed to complement and supplement economic measures.
3. Understand the magnitude of the economic benefits generated by outdoor recreation opportunities supported by public, nonprofit, and private organizations.
4. Explain what is meant by a public, a nonmarket, and a merit good or service, and describe how these types of goods or services relate to economic valuations of outdoor recreation and to recreation entrance and use fees.
5. Understand the rationales given for and against imposing recreation entrance and use fees for publicly provided recreation opportunities and the techniques that can reduce adverse responses to such fees.
6. Describe and give examples of commonly accepted means of financing publicly provided recreation opportunities, including outdoor recreation opportunities, other than by charging entrance and use fees.

Many texts have focused on the economic valuation of natural resources within which outdoor recreation has received extended treatment (cf. Champ, Boyle & Brown, 2003; Decker & Goff, 1987; Johnson & Johnson, 1990; Peterson, Driver & Gregory, 1988; Peterson & Randall, 1984; Peterson, Swanson, McCollum & Thomas, 1992). Still other texts have focused on the economics of leisure (Crompton, 1999, 2000) or outdoor recreation in particular (Loomis & Walsh, 1997). In addition, hundreds of scientific papers on the economics of outdoor recreation have been published in refereed journals and proceedings of technical conferences and workshops. Many colleges and universities offer majors in natural resource economics as well as courses specifically on the economics of outdoor recreation. Therefore, this chapter can only give an overview of the economics of outdoor recreation.

In providing an introduction to outdoor recreation, the major sections of this chapter attempt to

- review the general characteristics of the academic discipline of economics
- explain how misunderstandings of economics have caused some people to underappreciate its contributions to outdoor recreation resource policy development, planning, and management

- describe the economic concepts of value and benefit
- describe the concept of public, merit, and nonmarket (or unpriced) goods or services
- describe various methods used to estimate the economic values and benefits of outdoor recreation
- review arguments both in favor of and opposed to recreation entrance and use fees
- describe techniques for reducing opposition to fee increases
- review methods/means commonly used to finance outdoor and other recreation developments and maintenance

General Characteristics of Economics

It is important the reader understand that economics, like many other disciplines or academic fields of study, offers a wide variety of options to specialize in particular subareas. While each specialization is guided by a set of overriding theories and principles of the parent discipline, each is distinct. For example, within the parent discipline of psychology, one can specialize in experimental, clinical, social, organizational, environmental, developmental, or personality psychology. Similarly, a person can specialize in one of many of the subareas of leisure, such as history and philosophy, programming, interpretation, therapeutic recreation, commercial recreation, recreation economics, outdoor recreation, adventure recreation, tourism (e.g., international, domestic, ecotourism), sports management, or recreation resource planning and management. In the same way, the discipline of economics includes many specializations, such as public finance, money and banking, fiscal and monetary policy, international trade, management of securities, developmental economics, agricultural economics, and natural resource economics—a major focus of which has been the economics of outdoor recreation.

The most telling characteristic of economics is that it is the only academic discipline that focuses explicitly on allocation of scarce resources. Of course, other disciplines, such as political science and marketing, are concerned with allocating scarce resources, but it is not their central focus. Despite advances in technology, all resources are scarce either in a finite (i.e., limited supply) sense or because the resources have many competing uses to meet different human demands and needs and are therefore relatively scarce for any particular use. This unique focus on the allocation of scarce resources defines the primary contribution of economics and highlights the need for economic analyses by private, public, and nonprofit organizations. Many people who are critical of economists do not recognize and understand this focus of economics and the need for economic analyses.

The focus of economics on the efficient and equitable allocation of competitive/rival (and therefore relatively scarce) resources caused it to be called the "dismal science." In the late 18th and early 19th centuries Thomas Malthus described social problems, such as poverty, hunger, disease, and other misery, that accompany rapidly increasing levels of human population while the resources and technology needed to feed and otherwise sustain those populations would remain essentially finite or fixed. After Malthus, practically all economists emphasized that finite, as well as relatively scarce, resources ought to be allocated judiciously. Economists continue to do so today despite differing opinions about the roles of new technology and increased productivity in helping humans continue to realize streams of benefits from the development and use of limited to very scarce natural resources. Put simply, while most of us would like to have unlimited resources, we do not. So the expertise of economists is needed to help guide the allocations of the scarce resources that do exist.

Economists have contributed useful information to decisions regarding the allocation of scarce outdoor recreation resources in two primary ways: (a) the development of their concept of economic efficiency, which is probably the most central of all principles of economics; and (b) the guidance they provide for estimating the economic impacts of tourism on designated locations by economic impact analyses (EIAs). EIAs will be reviewed in a later section of this chapter, but first we will introduce economic efficiency and its relevance to publicly provided outdoor recreation opportunities.

To economists, *economic efficiency* means not only that the economic benefits of a private or public investment will exceed the costs of providing those benefits but also that the maximum net economic benefits will be realized. Economists use some type of monetary unit (e.g., dollars) to measure economic benefits and costs. Therefore, an investment that shows, say, twice as many economic benefits as economic costs is economically efficient, and the same investment that shows three times as many benefits as costs is even more efficient. As reviewed later, economists have a longstanding body of theory and practice to depict how the net benefits of investments can be maximized.

In addition to efficient allocations, economists are also concerned about an entirely different concept called *equity* or *distributive equity* (i.e., fairness of allocation decisions), usually covered under the topic of welfare economics and public finance. All the applications of economic theories, principles, and methods, in one way or another, are concerned with economically efficient allocations of scarce resources and frequently with the distributive equity of the economic benefits and costs that result from those allocations. Included in these two economic concerns about the allocation of all scarce resources are economic goals related to

- promoting national, regional, and local economic growth and stability
- obtaining fair but not excessive (i.e., "unearned") economic returns (i.e., profits) from privately invested funds
- realizing both economically efficient and fair collections and allocations of public tax dollars
- maintaining fair trade practices with other countries
- preventing large international trade deficits
- regulating the economic growth of a nation through sound monetary and fiscal policies
- assuring those who benefit from the provision of publicly provided goods and services pay their share of the economic costs of providing them
- preventing private firms from gaining monopolistic controls and power
- regulating trade in securities such as stocks and bonds

The authors of this text believe too many recreation professionals tend to view the discipline of economics, including the economics of outdoor recreation, with overly critical eyes. We believe these unfavorable perceptions of economics, particularly in recreation and other amenity economics, stem mostly from a lack of adequate understanding of

- the basic concepts, principles, methods, and applications of economics to outdoor recreation policy, planning, and management decisions
- how economics provides a unique type of information regarding the efficient and equitable allocation of scarce recreation and amenity resources
- the advantages of the use of one common unit (e.g., dollars) to measure both the benefits and costs of investments
- how economic information on benefits and costs, while tremendously useful, is only one type of information needed in recreation resource policy development, planning, and management decisions
- the fact that economic criteria and information seldom dominate recreation resource allocation decisions

We have all witnessed, and often objected to, inappropriate levels of commercial development of recreation and open spaces for private economic gain. We know too that many economists have promoted the virtues of a free-enterprise economy without giving enough attention to the social problems as well as benefits of such. In addition, many of us who have visited other countries have been chastised because of their perceptions of the greed and materialism evidenced by too many people and companies in the United States. Nevertheless, these are not the realms of recreation economists and the public decisions they influence. For example, most recreation economists realize, and write about, both the uses and limitations of economic analyses. Practically all of them are concerned with distributive equity as well as economic efficiency. We need to remember that in most societies the political, social, and economic pendulums tend to swing in directions that effectively counteract the excesses of every discipline.

Given economics is the only discipline that focuses on allocating scarce resources, recreation professionals should have at least a basic understanding and appreciation of the many contributions economics can play in park and recreation policy development, planning, and management decisions. To create or advance such a basic understanding, the remainder of this chapter provides an overview of a number of important topics, each of which has received much more extensive and thorough treatments in the literature cited earlier, as well as in special courses on natural resource and recreation economics. The topics to be addressed include the following:

- how economists define economic value and economic benefit
- what is meant by a public, nonmarket (or unpriced), and merit good or service and how each relates to the economics of recreation
- how economists measure the economic value and benefits of recreation
- how economists measure the regional and local economic impacts of tourism
- the economic significance of recreational travel and tourism-related industries
- the impacts of recreation and related amenity resources on nearby property values and on property tax revenues
- rationales for and against levying recreation entrance and use fees and means of reducing public opposition to such fees
- means for financing outdoor recreation opportunities other than by entrance and use fees

Economic Concepts of Value and Benefit

One reason many leisure professionals do not adequately appreciate the relevancy and contributions of economics to the park and recreation field is they do not understand that the narrow and highly specialized way in which economists define economic value and economic benefits and why they do so. Many leisure professionals also do not understand that most economists recognize information about economic value and economic benefit can and should be used as only one of several types of technical information needed in recreation resource policy and management allocation decisions. To clarify these misconceptions, one must understand the very specialized ways in which economists define *economic value* and *economic benefit* and how they propose information about those values be obtained and used. A useful way to begin is to contrast economists' concepts of the word *value* with other definitions of that word:

- Ethicists and moralists talk and write about political, social, and personal *values* tied to concepts about what is right or wrong, desirable or undesirable, just or unjust, or fair or unfair.
- Artists use the word *value* to refer to the intensity or darkness of colors.

- The phrase *aesthetic value* refers to the visual and other sensory pleasantness of an object or scene.

- The word *value* is also used to refer to those beliefs that people hold dear. Included are one's political orientation, respect for and love of one's country and its symbols (e.g., flags, banners, uniforms, statues, monuments); cherishing one's family and kin, one's spiritual and religious beliefs, and other deep and abiding preferential judgments about what a person treasures deeply.

- Mathematicians use the word *value* to designate a magnitude, such as the value of pi (π) as 3.141592+.

- Nutritionists and others use the word *value* to denote the function of, or purpose served by, an object, such as the value of a diet low in cholesterol, the value of physical exercise, or the value of oxygen to the brain.

- Some environmental philosophers use the words *intrinsic value* to refer to the value of an object they say is inherent to it and worth pursuing regardless of, or independent of, the usefulness or utility of that property or characteristic to humans. For example, it has been proposed that the genetic information that has accumulated and been stored in the DNA of any living species over many years of evolution has intrinsic value in and of itself (Callicott, 1985).

Like other disciplines, economists use the word *value* within several contexts. At a general level, some of the most commonly referred to economic values include

- values of stocks and bonds

- recreation entrance and use fees

- monetary expenditures made to get to and use recreation areas (e.g., costs of transportation, lodging, fuel for lights, food)

- secondary economic impacts of tourist expenditures on regional and local economies

- increased property values and tax revenues caused by proximity of nearby lands to recreation and other amenity resources

Despite these everyday types of economic value, economists technically use the words *economic value* in a much more narrowly specified way, founded on longstanding theories of economic consumption and production, which focus on voluntary exchange within free, competitive, and open markets in which consumers are viewed as sovereign (i.e., each consumer is best qualified to decide what is best for him or her). As such, economic value in exchange is generally defined as the amount of money (or other goods and services having monetary value if bartered) a person is willing to give up (i.e., willingness to pay) to get a par-

ticular good or service. Environmental economists also recognize another type of exchange value that reflects the amount of monetary compensation required by a person to give up a possessed good, object, or right, such as to sell one's land under the right of eminent domain or to relinquish other court-mandated orders that permit a public agency to change existing environmental conditions for an individual. This *exchange value* is called "willingness to accept compensation" rather than willingness to pay.

Brown (1984) called exchange values "assigned values," and because not all personal values are reflected in monetary exchange, distinguished them from *held values*. According to Brown, held values reflect a person's enduring beliefs about what is or is not preferable and relate to all human choice decisions and not only economic ones. For example, those held values reflect comparative preferential judgments about whether one particular system of beliefs or a good or service is better or worse or more or less preferable or desirable than other beliefs, opinions, goods, or services. This introspection is the basis of the perceived personal utility or satisfaction derived from those things or acquiring particular goods and services. The concept of personal utility (which to economists is equivalent to economic benefits) is at the center of recreation economics as elaborated shortly. However, it is important to note here, while Brown proposes held values are the basis of assigned (i.e., exchange) values, they are not equivalent. This is especially true for goods and services, such as education and much recreation, where the value to society in general is greater than the exchange values actual users of those services are willing to pay. This will be discussed in a later section of this chapter, but first it is important the reader understand two types of assigned values: exchange value and use value.

Economists recognize two types of Brown's assigned economic values: value in exchange and value in use. For example, potable water can often be purchased relatively inexpensively in a market, and can be taken at no economic cost from a free flowing, remote, wild river. In contrast to this zero or low exchange value, such potable water is indispensable to human life, so its use value is very high. The value in use is, therefore, considerably higher than the value in exchange. Economists believe this situation exists for most goods and services, and people are not willing to pay more in exchange for a good or service than its set exchange price. They would be foolish to do so. Therefore exchange value does not measure the magnitude of the total benefits realized from the good or service purchased. This brings us to the economists' concepts of utility and consumer surplus.

Economists use the word *utility* to refer subjectively to the satisfaction a good or service provides a person through its utilization. Specifically, the perceived personal utility or satisfaction one realizes from the use of a good or service is the reason why people willingly engage in economic transactions. Such utility is based on the person's held values discussed earlier. Furthermore, and vitally important, economic demand theory proposes although a person can gain more utility from use of a particular good or service than he or she must pay in exchange to acquire that good or service (i.e., use value is larger than exchange value), that person will never pay more for a particular unit or amount of a good or service than the expected amount of utility he or she expects to realize from that good or service. The question is whether a good or service offers more perceived utility than the money one must give up to get it.

To economists, utility is an unquantifiable abstraction, so they do not attempt to identify, define, and measure the various types and amounts of utility people derive from a particular good or service. Instead, they assume reasonably rational consumers will expend their scarce resources in such a way that a dollar's worth of money will purchase at least a dollar's worth of utility. So, dollars (or other personal resources exchanged) serve as proxy measures of utility for purposes of quantification. In contrast, scientists who have researched many of the subjectively appraised benefits of leisure described in Chapter 2 have attempted to identify and quantify the many different types of utility of leisure engagements. They segment that utility, or benefit, into the categories shown in Table 2.2 (i.e., personal, social, economic, and environmental benefits, p. 29) to identify the points of impact or realization of the benefits. In a nutshell, the objective of the research summarized in Chapter 2 was to try to identify the beneficial (i.e., desirable) consequences or changes recreation produces in people's lives or in society as a whole. Economists, on the other hand, try to measure what people are willing to pay to get those consequences or changes or what they require in compensation to be willing to give them up. As explained by Randall (1984) and Driver and Burch (1988), both Chapter 2 and the economists' approach to defining and measuring the benefits of recreation and other amenities are needed in resource allocation decisions, especially decisions where nonmarket forces guide the allocations, such as in the case of publicly provided goods and services, which typifies the provision of most outdoor recreation opportunities.

Economic demand theory proposes that for most goods and services there is incrementally decreasing marginal utility realized from purchasing or acquiring an additional unit of a particular good or service. Therefore, consumers will be willing to pay less for each additional unit of most goods or services because of the incrementally reduced utility they realize from each additional unit. One can question the degree to which there is diminishing marginal value for some goods and services, such as for prescribed medicines, and essential goods, such as salt in one's diet. But much research on economic behavior supports the proposition that most goods and services show diminishing marginal utility or use value over a set period of time. Such diminishing marginal utility (i.e., reduced utility from each additional unit) explains why economic demand curves slope downward to the right. More significantly, the economists' concept of utility directly relates to their concept of economic benefit and net benefit—critical to economists' valuation of outdoor recreation opportunities as elaborated shortly.

The example in Table 19.1 illustrates the points just made and introduces the additional concept of consumer surplus, which must be understood to appreciate how economists value outdoor recreation resources, sites, and services. Table 19.1 shows the total utility, marginal utility (i.e., economic benefits), and consumer surplus realized by a hypothetical recreationist during one year. It shows that six trips were made to the same recreation site for which the entrance fee and cost of transportation was $10 per trip. Remember that economists do not attempt to quantify types and units of utility realized but use monetary units, such as dollars to do so, which is reflected in Table 19.1.

Notice the total utility and marginal utility realized for the first trip were valued at $60. Notice particularly there was a $10 decrease in marginal utility for each additional trip until trip six, which reflects diminishing marginal utility. Note also the marginal utility for trip six was $10, which is equal to the cost of the trip. Therefore, a prudent person would not take a seventh trip because of diminishing marginal utility, because the entrance fee and transportation costs of $10 is $10 more than the zero marginal

Table 19.1 Total and marginal utility and consumer surplus realized for each trip per year, with cost per trip of $10

Number of Trips	Total Utility (Dollars)	Marginal Utility	Consumer Surplus
1	$60	$60	$50
2	$110	$50	$40
3	$150	$40	$30
4	$180	$30	$20
5	$200	$20	$10
6	$210	$10	$0
7	$210	$0	-$10

utility that would be received from that trip. Table 19.1 also illustrates the economists' concepts of total and net benefit. Given that a prudent person would only take six trips, the total utility (i.e., benefit) would be the sum of all the marginal benefits, or $210. The net benefits (total benefits minus total costs) would be $210 minus $60 (the costs of the six trips), or $150. Thus, the $60 spent on entrance fees and transportation represents the previously mentioned exchange value, and the $210 represents the use value.

The data in Table 19.1 can be plotted as a demand curve for the hypothetical recreationist with marginal utility per trip plotted on the vertical (y) axis and number of trips plotted on the horizontal (x) axis. Typical of demand curves, the curve will slope downward to the right, reflecting diminishing marginal utility per trip (see Figure 19.1).

Using these concepts, we can now describe the concept of *consumer surplus* (CS), which economists recommend as the appropriate measure of the economic benefits of publicly provided recreation opportunities, because prices for such are not disclosed by exchanges made in open and competitive market transactions between producers and consumers. Put simply, the total CS is the total utility (i.e., monetary value of the good or service) minus the total costs of the trips. So, CS for each trip diminishes directly with diminishing marginal utility, as illustrated in Table 19.1. In that case, total CS is $150, which is equivalent to the net benefits and is sometimes called *net willingness to pay*. When the aforementioned demand curve is plotted (Figure 19.1), that CS would represent the area under the demand curve and above a horizontal line representing the $10 cost per trip. The word *surplus* is used in CS to denote an economic surplus of benefits to the consumers for which they did not have to pay.

Having defined these concepts, we can now explain why recreation economists, as well as other environmental economists, view CS, or net economic benefits, as the appropriate measure of the economic value/benefit of publicly provided recreation opportunities, as well as the appropriate measure of all services provided by a public agency for which competitive market prices have not been established. The following explanation will be overly simplistic and assumes goods and services produced by private enterprises are exchanged in open, competitive, and undistorted markets that anyone can enter. Distorted markets exist when one or a few producers have unusual market power, such as in the case of monopolistic or oligopolistic control. The following paragraphs emphasize the fundamental points regarding the economists' recommendation that consumer surplus is the appropriate measure of the economic benefits of publicly provided recreation opportunities

For goods and services exchanged in open, competitive, and undistorted markets, exchange value (or price) is determined by interactions of large numbers of producers and large numbers of consumers of a particular good or service in such a way that (a) the producers must receive a price (i.e., revenue) that covers their costs of bringing the good or service to market plus a fair profit, and (b) no one producer or consumer can significantly affect the price. The results of those competitive market transactions are commonly net benefits, or total benefits/revenue minus total costs. Economists view such transactions to be the most efficient if they maximize net benefits, which occurs when price is set at the point where the increasing marginal cost curve intersects the deceasing marginal revenue curve. If the marginal (i.e., extra) cost for the next good produced is greater than the extra (i.e., marginal) revenue gained from that extra good, it would not be produced, because it would reduce net revenue. If the marginal cost of an additional unit of a good or service is larger than the utility a customer perceives he or she would realize from purchasing that additional unit, it will not be consumed because the marginal cost is greater than the marginal utility of that additional unit of the good or service. So the consumer would be foolish to buy that additional unit. Economists call these types of changes in costs and utility for an additional (i.e., marginal) unit of a good or service *marginal changes* (cf. McCollum, Peterson & Swanson, 1992, pp. 28–29). Economists emphasize that in open competitive, and undistorted markets, no one producer/supplier and no one consumer can influence such a marginal change very greatly or at all, simply because each single producer and

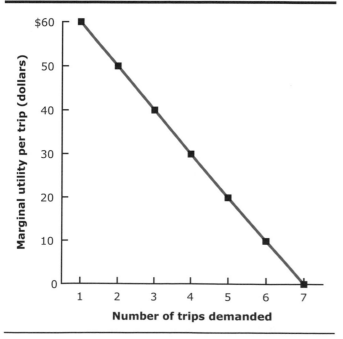

Figure 19.1   Demand curve for recreation trips by a hypothetical recreationist

customer is only one of a large number of producers and consumers acting independently. The exception is when market distortions exist, such as with a monopoly, which is why monopolies are controlled by governmental regulations. A vitally important point to remember within the context of this discussion is that a very large public provider of outdoor recreation opportunities (e.g., USDA Forest Service, National Park Service, U.S. Army Corps of Engineers) can and does significantly affect the number of opportunities provided and the prices charged in the way of entrance and use fees. In the language of recreation economists, they can make large "nonmarginal" (i.e., more than just a little extra) changes in qualities provided and prices charged. Furthermore, they do not necessarily set prices where marginal revenue is equal to marginal cost, so economically efficient allocations (i.e., net economic benefits) are seldom realized. Thus, some other measure of net economic benefits, such as consumer surplus, is needed to evaluate the economic efficiency of those public allocations, a point to which we will return shortly.

Although there is usually some consumer surplus associated with goods and services exchanged in open, competitive, and undistorted markets, the amount of such may be comparably small for nonessential goods and services (i.e., in comparison with the CS realized from publicly provided services) because of the need of consumers to reveal their willingness to pay in their interactions with the producers in establishing the market price. For example, few private providers of the outdoor recreation opportunity described in Table 19.1 could cover their costs and make a reasonable profit by charging an entrance fee of only $10, so the necessary higher fee would reduce considerably the consumer surplus shown for that hypothetical example. Even if the CS of marketed goods and services is large, that is irrelevant to economic valuations of publicly provided outdoor recreation opportunities simply because the intent with public goods and service is to determine the net benefits to society from those public investments. This is not the goal of private markets, which instead is to operate in economically efficient ways so that the private firms can optimize the net benefits to themselves, not to society as a whole. For example, if recreation opportunities are being provided at a privately operated campground, the investments in the campground are private capital, not public funds. Therefore, the efficiency of that investment is a concern of the private investor, not of a public park and recreation agency. Nevertheless, recreation economists do evaluate the economic impacts of the private-sector recreation and tourism-related industries for reasons other than determining the economic efficiency of the expenditures of public agencies that manage recreation and related amenity resources. Some of those evaluations are described in the section of this chapter on economic

impact analyses. Other economic analyses attempt to document the size and scope of recreation and tourism-related industries, including those that manufacture and distribute recreation clothing, equipment, and other facilitating supplies. As emphasized in Chapter 2, these leisure-related enterprises are big business in the United States and other countries.

In contrast with goods and services exchanged in open, competitive, and undistorted markets, most publicly provided goods and services are provided by public agencies, which generally do not attempt to cover all their costs of provision, or to gain a profit by prices charged/revenues received. So, price is not usually set at where actual marginal costs intersect actual marginal willingness to pay (i.e., revenue). Therefore, most of the actual economic benefits to society are received as consumer surplus. Thus, measures of consumer surplus (i.e., net economic benefits to society) are needed to compare the total economic benefits with total economic costs to determine if the public investments are economically sound or not. Many people who do not understand economists' thinking question whether consumer surplus is the appropriate measure of the benefits. They do not understand that if the recreationists do not have to pay a price that represents their actual willingness to pay, they then retain that money to use to purchase other goods and services. In that sense, consumer surplus is equivalent to a monetary gift in the amount of the consumer surplus. While this description of consumer surplus is accurate, that does not mean that gift should be made. A public agency must practice financial efficiency and decide how much of its operating costs must be recovered in the form of fees (a topic addressed later in this chapter).

Public agencies exist to serve the public, and many different rationales are given and adopted for public agencies to subsidize the provision of goods and services at less than the costs of providing them. For example, the good or service might be judged so meritorious to a society the citizens are willing to subsidize its provision by their tax dollars. Or, there may be an equity issue, such as providing service to underprivileged members of society. Public education has long been the prime example of a merit good. But economic valuation of recreation opportunities is not concerned with these political and social judgments. Instead, it is concerned only with providing outdoor recreation policy makers, planners, and managers with reasonably accurate and reliable data about the net economic benefits of either developing a new or changing (including possibly closing down) a particular type of outdoor recreation resource, site, or service. Public agencies can and do charge a wide variety of entrance fees. Therefore, a single public agency, unlike a single private producer, can significantly influence the prices it charges and the amounts of service it provides, and changes in those amounts can cause large/nonmarginal changes. Therefore, some facsimile of market prices must be used to create demand curves for outdoor recreation opportunities so that measures of consumer surplus can to be used to estimate the net economic benefits realized by society from proposed and existing recreation resources, sites, and services.

Put simply, the primary purpose for estimating consumer surplus is to determine if the existing or proposed public recreation development can and will offer net benefits to society at least equal to or greater than the level of public investment needed, or equal to or greater than the net benefits that could be realized from alternate uses of those natural resources, such as for mining or timber production. The purpose is not to determine what fees should be charged. But it must be said that, with ever-increasing costs of public provisions of outdoor recreation opportunities, fees have needed to be raised in nearly all countries, and measures of consumer surplus has provided guidance about what might be viewed as fair and equitable fees. But, in only one instance of which we are aware have attempts been made by public providers of outdoor recreation opportunities to set prices to cover the total costs of public provision of outdoor recreation opportunities, a practice that the authors of this text oppose for reasons given in a later section, Recreation Entrance and Use Fees (p. 293).

In review, recreation economists consider consumer surplus to be the appropriate measure of the net economic benefits to society of recreation opportunities—and of all publicly provided services such as resource preservation actions. It is called surplus because benefits are realized for which the recreationist would be willing to pay if she or he had to but does not have to because the price charged for each unit is less than this willingness to pay (WTP) except for the last unit purchased, where the price (i.e., exchange value) is equal to the WTP (or use value for that unit). Also relevant to the economics of outdoor recreation and related amenities is the fact that people are sometimes required by government to sell or give up certain goods, services, and/or rights they possess. Examples include a public agency exercising its right of eminent domain to acquire private property or to change amounts of polluting substances allowed in the air, ground, or water. In those instances, environmental economists recommend that willingness to accept compensation (WTA) is the appropriate measure of the economic benefits that will be forgone by the private individuals affected. Both WTP and WTA measure economic benefits, either gained (via WTP) or foregone (via WTA).

Remember the economists' definition of a benefit of recreation differs from the definition of a benefit of leisure given in Chapter 2. Each measure of benefits is used for different purposes as well as used to complement and supplement one another (see Driver & Burch, 1988). We also emphasize one of the great advantages of economic analyses is that both benefits and costs are measured in the same commensurate units (i.e., dollars or some other monetary unit). This commensurability enables benefit-cost analyses and other types of economic analyses, which compare the benefits and costs of allocating scarce resources to alternative uses or compare the benefits and costs of developing or not developing a particular project (called "with" and "without" evaluations). In addition, using the same monetary metric helps to facilitate secondary impact analyses of tourist expenditures, the contribution of amenity resources to increased values of nearby properties, and to facilitate evaluating alternative means of financing recreation opportunities—all topics considered later in this chapter. As mentioned in Chapter 2, the different implied and explicitly stated benefits discussed there cannot be summed simply because they are not measured by the same or commensurate metrics. One cannot add units of better mental or physical health to different units used to quantify increased learning of many types, enhanced local community cohesion and stability, reduced health care costs, and so on. Instead, each category of benefit must be considered and weighed separately in leisure policy development and in park and recreation resource planning and management decisions. The advantages of the commensurability of economic metrics are obvious, as are the measures of benefits given in Chapter 2—both are needed to guide the allocation of outdoor recreation resources. For example, sailors used to die of scurvy because they did not have vitamin C and did not know they needed it. The Chapter 2–type of "nutritional" benefit of vitamin C is it that promotes and preserves good health. The economic benefit of vitamin C is what people are willing to pay for it. One of the limitations of economic value is that people are not willing to pay for things they do not know they need.

Public, Merit, and Nonmarketed Goods and Services

Exchange value in open, competitive, and undistorted markets reflects customers' willingness to pay (WTP) and suppliers' willingness to accept compensation (WTA). But, when such markets do not exist for nonmarket or "unpriced" goods and services provided by public agencies, then net benefits, or consumer surplus, is the correct measure of the economic benefits of recreation. Because most outdoor recreation opportunities are provided by public agencies, they fall within the context of nonmarket goods and services. This section briefly reviews why such goods and services are provided by public agencies. Specifically, it describes why all goods and services are not exchanged in fair and competitive private markets. Sometimes these concepts are discussed under the title of *market failures* or *market imperfections*. The major reasons the public sector provides many goods and services and regulates the provision of others are outlined next.

The large capital investments needed to acquire, develop, and maintain land and other resources necessary to provide recreation and related amenities, plus the associated annual operating costs, dissuade provision of many types of recreation opportunities by the private sector. However, as demands have increased for some types of outdoor recreation in the past several decades (e.g., camping), the private sector has increasingly provided more of those types of opportunities as now evidenced by the large number of private campgrounds and RV parks.

Many outdoor recreation opportunities are so-called *public goods* or services for two reasons. First, there is no way to exclude users who do not pay an exchange price for using the opportunities, so there is little to no incentive for private investors to provide those opportunities. The economic costs of excluding nonpaying users are greater than the economic benefits that would gained by a private investor. Open spaces in cities, large tracts of land with many access points, and fireworks displays in cities are examples of instances where no excludibility occurs. Second, many public goods and services are nonrival in production, in that consumption by one individual does not diminish the amount that can be consumed by other people (e.g., nonpolluting use of air, enjoyment and appreciation of ecological diversity), or the good or service does not become rival until congestion occurs (e.g., campsites, hiking trails, many hunting and fishing places, scenic overlooks). Private markets are based on competition and rivalry for the resources needed to produce goods and services. So, if anyone can consume a good or service without diminishing its supply, that good or service resembles in some ways a free good or service, which causes consumers not to be willing to pay the exchange value that a private provider needs for profitability.

Only public provision can prevent monopolistic control that would be likely if some nationally and internationally significant resources (e.g., Grand Canyon or Yellowstone National Parks) were controlled and operated by private enterprises, with resultant charging of excessive prices that would create an unfair, or unearned, profit. This reason for public provision usually relates to other rationales, such as public subsidization of merit goods or services as described next.

The public sector provides or partially subsidizes the provision of some goods and services because they are viewed as being meritorious. In other words, the use/consumption of them provides benefits to society in general. The logic is that consumption of merit goods and services results in advantages, or beneficial spin-off consequences, or benefits to other people beyond the ones doing the consuming. Education is the classic example. The Universal Education Act requires youth to remain in school until a certain age because the consensus of citizens of the United States was that society needs an educated populace (a concept proposed not only by Benjamin Franklin but also by Aristotle) to function effectively and fairly. Citizens also believe that some fundamental level of education is needed to enhance the productivity of that nation's citizens. Most other countries have similar legislation and values regarding public support of education. Because of the spin-off benefits to a society at large, there has been a large amount of subsidization of education by public agencies via tax dollars. The public-finance rationale for such subsidization by public revenues is that if people other than those who consume educational services also benefit, then they should help pay the costs. The only feasible way they can do so is by paying tax dollars to support public subsidization of education. Provision of universal medical care is also viewed as a merit service in many countries. There are merit good aspects of many leisure services, including museums, zoos, symphony orchestras, operas, arts, recreation services, and outdoor recreation. Each of these amenities is partially subsidized in most countries of the world, with the amount of subsidy varying greatly among amenity services and among countries. We will return to the concept of merit goods later in this chapter when recreation entrance and user fees are discussed.

Public provision/partial subsidy also occurs for another reason closely related to the merit good/service criterion, which focuses on preventing or reducing external *diseconomies* (i.e., negative impacts). This rationale for public intervention is the other side of the merit-good coin and is oriented toward the prevention of external diseconomies, or unwanted (including unfair and unjust) impacts, which might accompany the production and/or consumption of a good or service. Examples include governmental regulation of air and water pollution, establishing speed limits, and creating public wildlife reserves to protect certain species of fauna, such as the endangered whooping crane.

Government also intervenes by exercising its right of eminent domain and by supplying goods and services, or regulating private production of such goods and services, to ensure quality in essential things and to promote public health and safety.

Other reasons for governmental intervention in the affairs of the private sector include the following:

- to regulate international trade and immigration

- to establish needed quarantines of diseases and insects
- to provide for national defense
- to oversee trading in securities such as stocks and bonds
- to regulate banking
- to establish and implement national monetary and fiscal policies
- to levy and collect taxes
- to do other tasks the private sector cannot effectively do or has been judged by social consensus should not do

A lot of time has been devoted here to explaining the basic concepts of recreation economics. The purpose was to give the reader a better understanding of some basic principles of economics so the following discussions of how economists value outdoor recreation opportunities can be better understood. With such an understanding of these basic economic concepts and methods recreation professionals will gain a better appreciation of

1. the contributions of economics to leisure policy development and to park and recreation planning and management decisions
2. what types of economic information are useful for outdoor recreation
3. why other types of information about the preferences, demands, and values of outdoor recreationists and other measures of the benefits of recreation (e.g., those provided in Chapter 2) are also needed to complement and supplement economic measures

Measuring Economic Values

In the previous section, different types of economic values were outlined; the concepts of public, nonmarket (or unpriced), and merit goods were discussed; and net willingness to pay (or consumer surplus) was described as the recommended measure of the economic benefits of outdoor recreation opportunities. This section gives an overview of the most common techniques for measuring the benefits and costs of outdoor recreation opportunities. The three parts of that discussion focus on measuring consumer surplus, the economic impacts of tourism, and additional measures of the economic value of outdoor recreation opportunities.

Measuring Consumer Surplus

As emphasized in the preceding discussion, natural resource and recreation economists recommend measuring consumer surplus (i.e., net economic benefits) to estimate

the economic value of unpriced, publicly provided goods and services, including public-sector natural resource preservation efforts. In review, consumer surplus is the benefit or utility a recreationist realizes for which they do not pay. Technically it is the total benefit realized minus the costs of engaging in the recreation opportunity being evaluated. Different recreation economists compute these costs differently, with some including travel costs, entrance and recreation use fees, and other costs (e.g., opportunity costs of salaries foregone while recreating). This section provides an overview of the two major methods economists use to measure the consumer surplus benefits of recreation and related amenities (e.g., scenic beauty, air quality, water quality, wilderness preservation, ecological diversity).

The two methods most commonly used to estimate consumer surplus of public-provided goods and services are the contingent valuation method (a type of stated preference) and the travel cost method (a type of revealed preference). Each method has its own corresponding economic theories and procedures and each has variations, refinements, and nuances favored by different adherents to particular variations, applications, or even basic methods. Extensive literature is available on these two methods and variations within each (cf. Champ, Boyle & Brown, 2003; Loomis & Walsh, 1997), and it is not the purpose of this text to describe their variations in detail.

Contingent Valuation Method

The contingent valuation method (CVM) uses surveys to measure the consumer surplus associated with recreational use. It has also been used to determine the economic benefits associated with preservation of natural resources. Resource economists segregate preservation values into existence values, option values, and bequest values. *Existence values* relate to a willingness to pay for protection of a resource that the person does not plan to ever use, but values the protections of and therefore derives stewardship-related benefits. *Option values* (grouped with existence values by some environmental economists) reflect willingness to pay for protection of a resource to maintain its existence so the option will exist in the future to use it. *Bequest values* relate to a willingness to pay so one's children, grandchildren, significant others, and/or future generations can use and enjoy the resources being protected. Some economists use *moral values* to refer these protection-related values.

In the typical CVM, a representative sample of people from a relevant population is asked to report its maximum willingness to pay, contingent on hypothetical changes in recreation opportunities or resources, thus the name contingent valuation. As described by Loomis and Walsh (1997, p. 160):

Contingent valuation methods use simulated (i.e., hypothetical) markets to identify values similar to actual markets, if they existed. The reliability of the estimates depends, in part, on the care with which the interviewer describes the nature of the hypothetical market; the change in the recreation activities or resources to be valued; the time period for which the valuation applies; the method of hypothetical payment; and the type of value question asked.

The hypothetical change being evaluated might be a need

- to obtain more revenue from increased fees to cover the costs of keeping an existing recreation facility open or a service provided
- to add a new recreation facility, such as a boat dock or campground
- to obtain a license to hunt a specific game animal for which numbers of licenses are quite limited
- to realize a change in environmental protection such as reduced air or water pollution
- to increase acreage of designated Wilderness areas by a stated amount

Methods of hypothetical payment used in past CVM studies included maximum willingness to pay increased costs to visit a recreation site and willingness to pay increased taxes to realize specific proposed public-sector preservation-related actions. Space constraints here preclude providing more details about how to implement CVM and the types of errors to avoid when doing so. See Loomis and Walsh (1997, pp. 159–176), Bishop and Heberlein (1990), and Johnson, Bregenzer, and Shelby (1990) for more details.

The CVM provides useful empirical information about the economic benefits of outdoor recreation, and it has also done so for proposed natural and cultural/heritage resource protection efforts through measures of existence, option, and bequest values. Those preservation values can be added to actual use/recreation participation values to

estimate total economic benefits of a specific resource. For example, Loomis and Walsh (1997, pp. 366–368) provide what they called *tentative evidence* of such total benefits of different resource protection and outdoor recreation programs derived from applications of the CVM in a representative household survey in Colorado by Aiken (1985). That study focused on the average annual willingness to pay per household for recreation use and resource protection programs in the state of Colorado. Table 19.2 shows the summary results for that study with the resource programs shown in the left column and the four economic values (benefits) considered shown in the next columns. Total WTP for the resource programs studied ranged from $47 to $102 annually, with an aggregate annual total willingness to pay of $467. Table 19.2 also shows the percentage that each type of economic value represented in terms of the total willingness to pay.

A great deal of useful information can be obtained from economic analyses like that summarized in Table 19.2. For example, it can be seen that of the total average willingness to pay (WTP) of $102 for Air Quality, 23.3% ($23.76), is willingness to pay to realize Bequest Benefits. Also notice that the sizable 40.4%, ($41.20) of the total WTP of $102 relates to the effects of Air Quality and On-Site Recreation Use. Such findings help to quantify in economic terms concerns about such things as air pollution reducing visibility. Also notice that 32.2% ($17.39) of the total average annual willingness to pay for Recreation Facilities was assigned to actual On-Site Use of those facilities, with the remaining $36.61 assigned to the three types of preservation benefits indicated. Furthermore, across all the seven resource programs indicated, On-Site Recreation Use values represented only 31.2% ($145.70) of the total aggregate annual average WTP of $467. In contrast, the three preservation benefits (bequest, existence, and option values, of 27.6%, 20.0%, and 21.2%, respectively) totaled $321.30. In summary, the largest proportion of the On-Site Recreation Use values were attributed to the resource protection programs, such as 40.4% to Air Quality, instead of to the Recreation Facilities, and the perceived economic benefits received from

Table 19.2 Percent representation of four economic values

Program	Bequest	Existence	Option	On-Site Recreation Use	Total WTP
Air quality	23.3%	14.9%	20.9%	40.4%	$102
Water quality	25.9%	16.1%	20.8%	37.2%	$93
Wild & scenic rivers	29.8%	23.0%	20.9%	26.3%	$58
Fish and Wildlife	28.0%	22.6%	19.9%	29.5%	$58
Forest quality	29.6%	21.1%	21.9%	27.4%	$47
Wilderness areas	29.8%	24.0%	21.7%	24.5%	$55
Recreation facilities	26.0%	18.5%	22.3%	32.2%	$54
Average all programs	27.6%	20.0%	21.2%	31.2%	$467

Source: Loomis and Walsh (1997, p. 367)

On-Site Recreation Use ($145.70) was less than half of the benefits perceived for the three preservation-related benefits ($321.30). These examples, and similar ones from other economic studies of the economic benefits of outdoor recreation and resource preservation programs have tremendous implications for the public financing of those programs, a topic which we return to in the section on recreation entrance and use fees. But, it should be emphasized here all three types of sizable preservation benefits were realized not only by respondents who were actually *on-site users,* but also by what are called *off-site users* (see Chapters 2 and 13). The data in Table 19.2 document such off-site users must be considered by outdoor recreation resource policy makers, planners, and managers who operate in the public and nonprofit sectors.

The CVM has been used and formally endorsed and recommended by major federal natural resource and environmental agencies. It has also stood up in court decisions related to agencies using results of its applications. CVM (i.e., stated preference) is the best way to estimate willingness to pay for certain kinds of public goods and services for which there is no way to get at revealed preferences (i.e., examining actual behavior as the travel cost model does). Nevertheless, despite many applications and refinements of the CVM methods, it still has its detractors both within and outside the fields of environmental and recreation economics. A particular concern is that the CVM involves the creation of a hypothetical market. So most, but not all, applications of the CVM do not involve the exchange of real money or impose actual and personal economic costs to the respondents of CVM surveys as real competitive markets do. Second, there are a large number of errors that can be caused by improper application of the CVM, described in the published literature. Lastly, the CVM combines principles and tested theories from both economics and psychology and interactions between them. Those interactions have yet to be examined sufficiently for the CVM, as explained in Ajzen and Driver (1992), Ajzen and Peterson (1988), Bishop and Heberlein (1990), Harris, Driver, and McLaughlin (1989), and Peterson, Driver, and Gregory (1988).

Travel Cost Method

A second approach used to estimate the consumer surplus of recreational use of public land is the *travel cost method* (TCM). According to Loomis and Walsh

> The travel cost method (TCM) has been preferred by most economists, as it is based on observed market behavior of a cross section of users in response to direct out-of-pocket and time cost of travel [to recreation/amenity resource sites]. The basic premise of the approach is that the number of trips to a

recreation site will decrease with increases in distance traveled, other things being equal. By calculating (i.e., integrating) the area under the demand curve for a site or resource, the travel cost approach provides an indirect measure of the consumer surplus benefits. (1997, p. 135)

Remember that an economic demand curve for a particular good or service shows what price customers are willing to pay for different quantities of that good or service. Given that travel costs increase with distance to a site, the out-of-pocket costs per trip of more remote users are higher than are the costs of users who live nearer the site. Therefore the nearer users can afford to make more trips. Under this logic, estimates of prices people are willing to pay to use the site are based on the costs they are actually willing to bear to travel to the site, and the quantity demanded is the total number of trips made during a specified time by the people studied. From such demand curves, estimates are made of the recreationists' net willingness to pay—that is, the consumer surplus, which is the economists' measure of the economic benefits of publicly provided recreation.

Be aware there are many variations of the TCM and most require sophisticated mathematical approaches, such as multinomial logit regression. Among other variations, the TCM has been applied to determine the economic benefits of just one site visited, of multiple sites visited during a particular trip, and of estimating not only the value of the recreation facilities of a site but also the value of particular associated amenities. Such detail about the TCM is beyond the scope of this introductory text and can be found in many publications about the TCM, such as Chapter 9 of Loomis and Walsh (1997, pp. 135–158).

Results of the TCM have been used in economic valuations of many different recreation sites by many different public agencies. Because it is based on the out-of-pocket travel costs of the recreationists and does not posit a hypothetical market as the CVM does, the TCM has received less criticism. However, it does not have the breadth of application to estimate the economic benefits of resource preservation efforts that the CVM does.

Summary Comments on the CVM and TCM

The CVM and TCM methods and their many variations (e.g., hedonic pricing as explained in McCollum & Bergstrom, 1992, pp. 164–167; and Champ, Boyle & Brown, 2003) are the methods most commonly used to estimate consumer surpluses. Sample results from many such studies that surveyed participants in many outdoor recreation activities are given in Table 19.3. The data for that table are taken from Rosenberger and Loomis (2001, p. 4). Their study reviewed results of 163 separate CVM and TCM studies conducted from 1967 to 1998, which covers a period during which much refinement in methods and therefore accuracy of estimates occurred. Those 163 separate studies estimated the average consumer surplus for the 19 different outdoor recreation activities as shown in Table 19.3 and included 760 benefit measures because a large number of separate estimates were made for particular activities. For example, 117 separate estimates were made for big game hunting. Table 19.3 shows the average and median consumer surpluses estimated for the outdoor activities indicated as well as the range of estimates for each activity. The median shows the value for which 50% of the values were greater than and 50% were lower.

It should be noted from Table 19.3 the economic benefits shown are considerable and generally greatly exceed the entrance and use fees charged by the public agencies to engage in the outdoor recreation activities shown (except for hunting and fishing, where fees for licenses have increased considerably in most states during the past decade). It is important this gap between average consumer surplus and actual fees is recognized when public officials decide how scarce government revenues should be allocated for outdoor recreation. Too often those decisions focus on the costs rather than the likely social benefits of outdoor recreation, and the benefits get depreciated. As such, policy makers often fail to consider adequately the total social benefits of recreation, either because of biases against it (their thinking has not been properly "repositioned," as described in Chapter 2), or because they are not aware of existing science-based information regarding economic and other benefits. Results of the TCM and CVM methods have helped substantially in correcting this information

deficit about the benefits of outdoor recreation. Empirical data such as that summarized in Tables 19.2 and 19.3 has proven very useful in helping to justify and in some cases increase funding for parks and recreation from legislative bodies.

Some people, including some economists, have concerns about the accuracy of CVM and TCM estimates of benefits. Those concerns include questions such as the following:

- Can people realistically estimate hypothetical prices they would be willing to pay under the CVM?
- Does the TCM adequately include consideration of the values of all dimensions of a recreation trip, such as traveling to and from the area visited?
- Do such estimates of the economic value of publicly provided amenities and resource preservation sufficiently recognize the interactions of public-sector preservation and recreation programs, such as those indicated in Table 19.2?
- Does the process of making and using the results of the CVM and TCM promote competitive market-type allocations that ignore the merit good aspects (i.e., positive spin-off benefits to society in general) of recreation, related amenities, and resource preservation efforts?
- Do attempts to price publicly provided recreation opportunities tend to distort and demean the ideal that many types of nature and heritage resource recreation opportunities should be reasonably available for all to use? In other words, do such economic

Table 19.3   Summary statistics on average consumer surplus (CS) values per person per recreation activity day

Recreation Activity	Number of Studies	Number of CS Estimates	Mean CS	Median CS	Range of CS Estimates
Camping	22	40	$30.36	$24.09	$1.69 – 187.11
Picnicking	7	12	$35.26	$24.21	$7.45 – 118.95
Swimming	9	12	$21.08	$18.19	$1.83 – 49.08
Sightseeing	9	20	$35.88	$21.13	$0.54 – 174.81
Off-Road Driving	3	4	$17.43	$15.85	$4.73 – 33.64
Motorized Boating	9	14	$34.75	$18.15	$4.40 – 169.68
Nonmotorized Boating	13	19	$61.65	$36.42	$15.04 – 263.68
Hiking	17	29	$36.63	$23.21	$1.56 – 218.37
Biking	3	5	$45.15	$54.90	$17.61 – 62.88
Downhill Skiing	5	5	$27.91	$20.90	$12.54 – 52.59
Cross-Country Skiing	7	12	$16.15	$26.73	$1.70 – 40.32
Snowmobiling	2	2	$69.97	$69.97	$36.23 – 103.70
Big Game Hunting	35	117	$43.17	$37.30	$4.75 – 209.08
Small Game Hunting	11	19	$35.70	$27.71	$3.47 – 190.17
Waterfowl Hunting	13	59	$31.61	$18.21	$2.16 – 142.82
Fishing, All Types	39	122	$35.89	$20.19	$1.73 – 210.94
Wildlife Viewing	16	157	$30.67	$28.26	$2.36 – 161.59
Horseback Riding	1	1	$15.10	$15.10	$15.10 – 15.10
Rock Climbing	2	4	$52.96	$48.14	$29.82 – 85.74

Source: Rosenberger and Loomis (2001, p. 4)

analyses treat those opportunities as commodities and nurture the image that such provision is too much like a business? This concern has been addressed more toward the charging of recreation and use fees than to attempts to estimate the economic benefits of outdoor recreation.

- Are the social benefits of recreation opportunities so great and obvious that no other justification is needed? The authors of this text disagree with this contention made by some recreation philosophers. Detractors of economic data should note that measures of consumer surplus have also helped to document the total economic and noneconomic benefits of public resource preservation programs as well. It seems that such concerns stem from a lack of understanding of why consumer surplus is measured and how.

- Can people assign economic values to things they do not know much about?

In sum, despite reservations, information about economic benefits have helped considerably to empirically document the nature of the total benefits of outdoor recreation and resource preservation programs. In addition, economic estimates of consumer surplus strongly support the contention made in Chapter 2 that when considered broadly the leisure sector of the U.S. economy (and probably of the economies of other countries) is one of the largest sectors of that economy.

Measuring the Local Economic Impacts of Tourism

In addition to estimating recreationists' consumer surplus as a measure of net economic benefits realized by society, recreation economists have also developed techniques to estimate the economic impacts of tourism on local, regional, and even national economies by use of economic impact analyses (EIAs). Measures of consumer surplus and EIAs are frequently confused because both consider economic benefits, but each defines benefits differently and each is used for very different purposes. Consumer surplus estimates the economic benefits to society from particular public investments (e.g., parks and recreation) in terms of the welfare changes to users of the public goods and services provided. In contrast, EIAs measure economic benefits to local businesses, households, and governments in terms of new monetary transactions, income, wages, and taxes generated by expenditures of tourists in a particular locality. Put slightly differently, consumer surplus focuses on obtaining data to make economically efficient public resource allocations that optimize net benefits (i.e., benefits minus costs) to society and are used in public-sector benefit-cost analyses. In contrast, EIAs evaluate the economic impacts of the tourists' expenditures on the income, employment, sales, wages, and governmental tax revenues within a particular area or region.

It is important to understand that EIAs evaluate the economic impacts of the expenditures of recreationists who visit a region or area but reside somewhere outside that region or area. They do not evaluate the economic impacts of recreationists who reside and recreate within that region or area. Because this distinction is very important when making EIAs, the word *tourist* is used technically to designate a person from outside a region who visits a different region or locality for purposes of recreation, with owners of summer/vacation homes sometimes excluded. We should mention that until rather recently, many outdoor recreation professionals working for public agencies, as well as many local residents, viewed the word *tourist* negatively, primarily because of actual and perceived negative impacts sometimes caused by tourism. Those negative perceptions are decreasing, and tourism is recognized as an important field of leisure, including outdoor recreation.

Because tourists from outside a locality or region make expenditures within the area they visit for recreational purposes, those expenditures represent real money transferred from one region to another. Therefore, although those expenditures by tourists might create only modest contributions to net national economic welfare and efficiency, they can have tremendous economic impacts on the localities in which the expenditures are made. Evaluating those economic impacts is the purpose of EIAs. This section gives an introductory overview of EIAs, about which much has been written in the literature. Selected references are cited throughout this section for readers wanting more information. This section draws heavily from Stynes (2002, 2004, in press) and Stynes and White (2003).

Visitors to outdoor recreation sites, like this whitewater river in Cherokee National Forest in Tennessee, can generate substantial local economic impacts.

General Characteristics of EIAs

EIAs are conducted for the following reasons:

- The economic impacts of tourism are important considerations in local, regional, and state planning and development decisions, especially when one locality competes with other regions to promote and enhance its economic growth and stability, as most localities do.

- Economic costs, as well as benefits, are associated with tourism. Included are the direct costs incurred by tourism businesses; costs to local governments to provide needed infrastructure; and possibly other costs associated with congestion, damage to private property from trespassing, and changed images and characteristics of a locality. These costs must be compared with the likely economic benefits, which can be better understood by information provided by EIAs.

- The results of EIAs are useful in marketing and promoting a particular area or locality or in justifying creation of improved tourism infrastruture, particularly by tourism industries.

- Public officials, especially those responsible for requesting funds to support recreational developments as well as members of governing bodies responsible for funding those requests, frequently use data from EIAs to guide and support their actions. This information is particularly important to elected officials who want to demonstrate how well they are serving their constituencies.

- EIAs provide tangible evidence of the economic linkages that exist within a local economy and enable a clearer understanding of those economic dynamics and what is needed to maintain them in desired ways.

- EIAs are used to evaluate the economic impacts of changes in the supply of recreation and tourism opportunities as well as the impacts of demands for such.

- EIAs are used to compare the economic impacts of alternative resource allocations, policies, or managerial proposals.

An EIA typically addresses the following questions (Stynes, 2004):

- How much do tourists spend in an area?

- What portion of sales by local business is due to tourism?

- How much income and new sales does tourism generate for households and businesses in the area?

- How many jobs does tourism support?

- How much tax revenue is generated from tourism?

- What is the economic structure of the economy being studied in terms of its leading and lagging economic sectors?

Stynes (2004) stated:

> A standard economic impact analysis traces flows of money from tourism spending, first to businesses and government agencies where tourists spend their money, and then to other businesses supplying goods and services to tourist businesses; households earning income by working in tourism or supporting industries; and government, through various taxes and charges on tourists, businesses, and households.

Therefore, the two most frequent uses of EIAs are to determine the economic impacts of tourism for an existing tourist market or to determine the economic impacts that would result from a change in an existing market, such as increases or decreases in tourist expenditures over those currently being made in that market. The first traces existing tourism expenditures through that locality, the second traces the impacts of the increases or decreases in expenditures. The EIA methods are the same for both applications. In either case, it is important to remember EIAs look at the economic impacts on a locality only if tourism expenditures are made within that locality.

How to Conduct an EIA

The steps of conducting EIAs will now be outlined very generally. First, visitor spending is estimated by multiplying the number of tourists visiting a clearly specified tourist area or market (e.g., a state, region, county, large municipality) during a specified period of time (usually a year) by the average spending per tourist. So, the first two steps are to determine the number of tourists and their average total spending in the study area. That total spending by tourists will include all expenditures made by tourists within the area being evaluated and exclude expenditures made by the targeted tourists before they arrived at that area (i.e., trip-related expenditures made back home or while traveling to the boundaries of the area or region being studied). These relevant direct expenditures would include costs of gas, auto repairs and servicing, lodging, food in restaurants and grocery stores, recreation equipment, film, health services, rental fees, fees for guides and outfitters, recreation entrance and use fees, souvenirs, and so on.

Next, the direct, indirect, and induced effects of the total expenditures must be estimated as that money flows through different sectors of the local economy being studied. Regional and recreation economists define these three effects as follows (cf. Stynes, 2004):

Direct effects are changes in sales and other payments associated directly with tourism expenditures—such as payments by hotels, restaurants, laundry services, and vehicle services—for increased wages and supplies needed to meet the tourists' demands. Included also would be local expenditures on construction and maintenance of needed tourism infrastructure. Some regional/recreation economists include increased property taxes that result from tourism developments as direct effects while others prefer they be omitted and considered separately in fiscal impact studies that address the question of whether additional governmental revenues from tourism will cover the costs of necessary public developments.

Indirect effects are changes in sales/payments that result from the direct effects via "backward linkages" to other economic sectors of the local economy. For example, tourist expenditures in hotels and inns will require that hotels purchase needed support services such as laundry services. Then, the local laundry will spend part of this money they receive from the hotels to pay wages of their employees and to purchase supplies from other local business. In this manner, the tourists' dollars circulate not once but several times to different economic sectors of the local economy.

Induced effects are changes in economic activity within the area studied that result from the spending of income by households that results directly or indirectly from tourism spending. For example, employees of the local supporting tourism industries (e.g., hotels, restaurants, other services) and of public park and recreation agencies spend their tourism-related income in the local area for housing, food, recreation, transportation, and the typical array of household expenditures. Indirect and induced effects are sometimes combined and called *secondary effects* to contrast them from the direct effects.

These secondary effects are estimated by applying the tourists' expenditures to a mathematical input-output (IO) model of the local economy. Those IO models use the production functions of distinct economic sectors of the local economy to estimate the number of jobs and income associated with a given level of direct expenditures. By tracing flows of money among economic sectors, IO models estimate the secondary effects (both indirect and induced) of changes in spending caused by the tourists' expenditures. These effects are estimated through use of "multipliers" that can be applied to changes in spending.

To take full advantage of the detail in IO models, tourism spending must be matched with the economic sector that receives the spending. The most important sectors for recreation and tourism impact analyses are generally the lodging, restaurants, amusements, retail trade, and transportation sectors. Business and economic accounts in the United States are organized and reported using a multidigit classification system with increasingly specific subcategories. For example, there is a one-digit code for all manufacturing, and up to five (or more) digit codes to designate very specific types of manufacturing. The United States has recently switched from reporting these accounts by use of the standard industrial classification (SIC) system reported in the *Standard Industrial Classification Manual* (U.S. Office of Management and Budget, 1987) to use of the North American Industrial Classification System (NAICS). Still problematic is the fact that no data are reported specifically for leisure, recreation, or tourism as separate economic sectors. Instead, all leisure-related commerce is included in several other NAICS codes.

According to Stynes (2004), sales multipliers are of two types: Type I and Type II. Type I sales multipliers capture direct and indirect effects, while Type II sales multipliers also include induced effects and thereby give a more complete picture of the total impact on sales in the area from tourist expenditures. Stynes (in press) states:

> The aggregate Type II sales multipliers recommended in the MGM2 [updated Money Generation Model] model range from 1.3 for rural areas to 1.6 for larger metropolitan areas. Multipliers for statewide regions generally range from 1.65 to 2.0. The tourism sales multiplier for a national model is around 2.5.

Stynes's MGM2 for estimating economic impacts is explained in detail at http://www.prr.msu.edu/mgm2/econ/.

The impacts of the increased sales in a region attributable directly to tourist expenditures can significantly affect income and employment in that region. For example Stynes (2002) found tourist spending around Great Smoky Mountains National Park in 2000 supported over 12,000 jobs in the region through direct effects and 15,000 jobs including secondary (i.e., indirect and induced) Type II effects. This represents over 10% of all jobs in that region.

Roughly 30% of sales related to tourism goes to income. So, in a region with a Type II sales multiplier of 1.5, about $0.45 of new income is created for every dollar of new sales caused by the expenditure of each dollar by tourists (i.e., a dollar of sales yields $0.30 in direct effects and another $0.15 in income from secondary sales through indirect and induced effects). But, we emphasize that sales multipliers vary from location to location, as does the relationship between sales generated and income multipliers. A common mistake is to apply multipliers for statewide regions to local areas. Multipliers for smaller regions and rural areas will be much smaller than those for an entire state or a large metropolitan region. Therefore, each region must be studied separately by qualified analysts. Generalizations from one area to another can be very misleading.

Until recently, most EIAs of tourism have been done at local or regional levels. However, they have also been done at the state and national levels to estimate the economic impacts of any sector or subsector of an economy. For example, Alward, Arnold, Niccolucci, and Winter (2002) used EIAs to estimate the contributions of 15 different programs/operations of the USDA Forest Service to the U.S. economy in 2002. Four such economic contributions were measured for each of the 15 different program areas:

1. Gross Domestic Product (GDP; a summary measure of all final goods and services produced by an economy such as a nation)

2. Total National Income (TNI)

3. Wages (W; or employee compensation)

4. Total National Jobs (TNJ)

Results of that study are shown in Table 19.4 for five of the resource management programs of the USDA Forest Service evaluated. The figures reflect the contributions of each program to GDP, TNI, W, and TNJ (representing total contributions) in 2002. In the study, those totals are broken down into four subcategories such as "by the Forest Service only" and "including backward linkages," which are not separated out here. In Table 19.4, the estimated contributions for GDP, TNI, and W are shown in millions of dollars, and TNJ is shown in total jobs created.

Notice the much greater contribution of recreation management (and related resources included in that category) to each of the four economic indicators than any of the other four resource management programs listed. Note especially, the contribution of recreation management of over $32 billion to Gross Domestic Product and creation of near 728,000 jobs in 2002. These were obviously significant contributions to the U.S economy that year.

There have been scores of EIAs made for different regions and for specific types of tourist destinations, such as national forests, national parks, Corps of Engineers projects, and so on. Those studies have documented that the economic impacts of outdoor recreation on the economic viability of local areas, regions, and the nation at large are considerable. Results of EIAs represent another very important contribution of recreation economists to documenting the economic significance of outdoor recreation. Those results further support our proposition in Chapter 2 that leisure is one of the largest economic sectors of most economies.

As mentioned earlier, tourism can cause local economic and other costs as well as beneficial impacts. Nevertheless, EIAs are very important to gaining a better understanding of the total economic benefits of recreation. They have shown that tourism generally is within the top three economic sectors of practically all states in the United States and of political subdivisions of most other countries.

Expenditures of Tourists and the Significance of Leisure-Related Industries

Sometimes just the total amount of expenditures people make on leisure, tourism, or a specific type of such are used to document the economic significance of recreation and tourism, even without making a full EIA to determine the additional indirect and induced effects of those expenditures. Another important measure of the economic significance of recreation and tourism, including outdoor recreation or nature and heritage resource based tourism, is the amount of money spent by leisure-related industries, including those that manufacture and sell the clothing, gear, equipment, supplies, and related materials (e.g., maps) used totally or partially for recreational purposes. This section briefly examines these additional measures of the economic significance of outdoor recreation.

Table 19.4   Economic contributions of four USDA Forest Service resource management programs to the U.S. economy in 2002

Resource Management Program	Contributors in 2002 (in millions of 1997 Dollars) to:			
	Gross Domestic Product (GDP)	Total National Income (TNI)	Wages (W)	Total National Jobs (TNJ)
Recreation[a]	$32,423	$29,224	$17,391	727,906
Timber	$6,029	$5,666	$2,927	97,120
Minerals & Geology	$3,838	$3,486	$1,837	50,734
Range	$431	$393	$179	13,334
Watershed & Air[b]	$217	$206	$109	3,702

[a] Includes recreation, heritage, wilderness, wildlife, fish, and rare plant resources
[b] Differs from the other four resource management categories shown, because these resources do not produce outputs or products for which prices or fees are paid on-site.

Source: Alward, Arnold, Niccolucci, and Winter (2002)

Expenditures of Tourists and Other Outdoor Recreationists

As just explained, when EIAs are being conducted, data on the expenditures of tourists within the area being studied are summarized by different categories of spending, such as for lodging, restaurants and bars, groceries, gas and oil, other transportation, admission fees, and souvenirs and fees. For example, Stynes (in press) reports the following percentage distributions of $10.6 billion spent for recreation in areas near national parks in the United States due to 280 million visits in 2001:

- lodging: 28%
- restaurants: 25%
- shopping: 16%
- gas and oil: 12%
- admissions and fees: 10%
- groceries, take-out, food, and drinks: 9%

Stynes also provided some empirical data of expenditures by similar categories from one of the many studies he and his associates have made of the local and regional impacts of tourism. These data are in an unpublished report by Stynes and White (2003) submitted to the USDA Forest Service. That two-year study randomly sampled visitors to designated recreation sites on national forests as well as general visitors to the forest, with forests sampled in each of the nine administrative regions of the Forest Service. The data in Table 19.5 represent average total spending per trip provided by 8,440 respondents, with spending limited to that made within 50 miles of the interview site. The Stynes and White report showed spending profiles by both the local visitors (living within 30 miles of the forest studied) and nonlocal visitors. Only the data for the non-local visitors are shown in Table 19.5, which shows average trip expenditures for day users (DU), visitors who spend at least one night lodging on the forest (LOF), and those who spent at least one night lodging elsewhere (LEW). Of nonlocal visits, 15% involved an overnight stay on the forest and 25% involved overnight stays off the forest.

Not shown in Table 19.5 are the average per trip expenditures of the local visitors, which were $31.57, $112.44, and $101.94, respectively for local day users, local users who spent at least one night on the forest, and local users who spent at least one night elsewhere not on the forest. As for the local users, the major categories of expenditure were for restaurants, groceries, and gas/oil/other transportation. These data show that even remote types of outdoor recreation outings, such as at national forests, can generate sizable expenditures.

The economic significance of these types of recreation-related expenditures have been documented in many other sources as well. For example, Chapter 2 pointed out the tremendous economic impacts on nations and subdivisions of expenditures by tourists. As was noted there:

> In 1995, travel and the related tourism it stimulated, was the third largest retail industry in the United States, after automotive dealers and food stores. The projections for the foreseeable future are for expenditures in that sector to continue to increase as a percent of total expenditures of the retail sale industries of the United States. (U.S. Travel Data Center, 1994)

More recently, the Travel Industry Association of America (2003) estimated travelers in the United States spent $12.1 billion in 2001, directly supporting 157,200 jobs with a total payroll of $3.4 billion. A sizable portion of these totals is, no doubt, related to outdoor recreation and natural settings that support it.

The very significant economic importance of tourism and recreation has been documented also at the national level, and for political subdivisions, of many other countries. For example, Gan (1998, p. 337) stated, "In terms of foreign exchange earnings, New Zealand tourism is a $22 (NZD) million a day business and is one of the top foreign exchange earners." He also stated:

> Just as tourism is a dominant force in New Zealand, it is also one of Australia's largest and most dynamic

Table 19.5   Average spending per trip by visitors to national forests in 2000 and 2001

Spending Per Trip	Day Users (DU)	Lodging on Forest (LOF)	Lodging Elsewhere (LEW)
Lodging (Public and Private)	$0.00	$22.34	$50.70
Restaurants	$12.41	$26.65	$47.98
Groceries	$6.72	$39.11	$29.30
Gas, Oil, Other Transportation	$16.27	$42.20	$39.96
Admissions/Fees	$4.32	$12.39	$8.45
Activities	$2.51	$6.61	$10.92
Souvenirs	$1.76	$4.60	$11.15
Other	$2.87	$10.45	$9.55
Total	*$48.88*	*$164.14*	*$207.02*

Source: Stynes and White (2003)

sectors of commerce.... It is estimated by the Australian Bureau of Tourism Research that tourism accounted for 5.5 per cent of the country's GDP [i.e, Gross Domestic Product].... It is one of Australia's largest foreign exchange earners.

Tourism is also the major generator of foreign exchange for many less economically developed countries.

Economic Significance of Leisure-Related Business Enterprises

Too frequently, published papers and texts on the economics of outdoor recreation focus only on the economics of outdoor recreation opportunities provided by public agencies. They generally ignore the economic significance of the leisure-related business activities of private and nonprofit enterprises, such as those discussed in Chapters 7 and 8. A comprehensive listing of these activities and influences of private enterprises would include the following:

- the offering of recreation opportunities, such as private campgrounds, ski areas, hunting and fishing opportunities on private land, guiding and outfitting, and operation of tourism complexes (including ecotourism operators)

- the manufacturing, advertising, distributing, and sales of recreation-related clothing, equipment, supplies, and other supporting goods and services. Included here would be a wide array of fishing, hunting, boating, skiing, camping, hiking, and birdwatching equipment, apparel, and supplies. Also included would be that proportion of the costs of purchasing and maintaining modes of transportation (e.g., cars, vans, pick-up trucks, RVs, off-highway vehicles, snowmobiles, airplanes, boats, rafts) that should be allocated to leisure to represent their use during recreational engagements

- the purchase and use of cameras, film, maps, binoculars, camcorders, privately owned homes, and cabins rented by recreationists

Outdoor recreation visitors spend money on a tremendous variety of equipment and services, including travel costs to and from recreation areas like this one in North Carolina.

Production and sales of hunting and fishing equipment is an extremely large outdoor recreation-related industry.

The production, sale, and operation of recreation-related products, like recreational vehicles, contributes greatly to economic growth.

Production and sales of outdoor recreation-related information is an industry that is larger than most people realize.

- the capital investments made and the salaries, employee benefits, and taxes paid by leisure-related private and nonprofit enterprises

As emphasized in Chapter 2, the leisure industry sector is probably one of the largest economic sectors of the United States, and many other countries, when this appropriately wide view is taken of that economic sector. Of course, not all leisure-related activity by private and nonprofit enterprises can be attributed to outdoor recreation. Nevertheless, these sectors of the outdoor recreation industry are of much greater economic significance than has been pointed out or documented in practically all published papers and texts on the economics of outdoor recreation.

Additional Measures of the Economic Value of Outdoor Recreation

In addition to consumer surplus, economic impact analyses, tourist expenditures, and activities of leisure-related business enterprises, two other measures are also used to estimate the economic value of outdoor recreation resources: *increased value of property* owned near recreation and open space lands and *opportunity pricing*. These two additional measures also help quantify the tremendous total economic benefits of recreation extolled in Chapter 2. Each will described briefly.

Increased Property Values and Tax Revenues

Crompton (1999) wrote the definitive work on the subject of this section in *The Impact of Parks and Open Space on Property Values and the Property Value Tax Base*. This section draws heavily from that source. Crompton stated:

Public parks and open spaces traditionally have not been evaluated in economic terms because there are many other appealing and rational justifications for acquiring and providing them. These may include: (1) enhancement of a community's quality of life, which embraces its livability or "feel" and aesthetic integrity, and the role of parks and open spaces in creating a sense of place or community; (2) ecological and environmental reasons relating to issues such as biological diversity, improving water quality, air cleansing, aquifer recharge and flood control; (3) and scenic vistas and places for engaging in active or passive recreation activities. (p. 7)

However, Crompton documented throughout his report that parks and open spaces do have tremendous economic importance in addition to these three traditional values used to justify them. He offered the following important points:

Park and open spaces are equally as productive contributions to a local economy as roads, utilities, and other infrastructure elements (p. 7).... The real estate market consistently demonstrates that many people are willing to pay a larger amount for a property located close to park and open space areas than for a home that does not offer this amenity. The higher values of these residences means that their owners pay higher property taxes. It [the higher taxes] means that in some instances if the incremental amount of taxes paid by each property which is attributable to the presence of a nearby park is aggregated, it will be sufficient to pay the annual debt charges required to retire the bonds

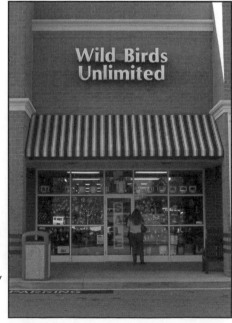

Equipment and services related to particular outdoor recreation experiences, like birding, can generate significant economic impacts.

The availability of outdoor recreation opportunities, like those provided at this county park lake, can be an important factor in corporate location decisions and can increase the values of nearby property.

used [by local governments] to acquire and develop the park. (Executive summary).

Later in his executive summary, Crompton noted the idea that increased tax revenues from the increased property values would offset the public costs of acquiring and developing the parks "...was first promulgated and empirically verified in the parks field by Frederick Law Olmsted in the context of Central Park in New York City." Crompton then shows that that principle was soon confirmed for major investments in public parks in many other cities in the United States in the late 19th century.

Crompton found increased property value effects existed for up to 200 feet away from parks and open spaces on which passive uses predominated instead of active, noisier uses.

In sum, just the presence of parks, recreation, and open space can create considerable economic value. They do so because land values near recreation developments (including large tourist attractions such as Disneyland and Disney World) are often appreciatively higher because of their proximity to recreational, open space, and tourism developments. These higher property values generate increased tax revenues to local governments.

Opportunity Pricing

Another technique for estimating the economic value of recreation and related amenity resources is opportunity pricing or opportunity costing. This technique does not try to establish the market value of a particular recreation resource, but instead estimates what its minimum economic value would be if that resource was to be used for purposes other than for providing recreation opportunities. The logic is if the resource is to be used for recreation, then its economic value should be at least equal to the maximum economic value of the highest alternative use. For example, when arguments were being made to create Redwood National Park in California, opponents argued the national economic value of such a park should be at least equal to the value of the redwood timber that could be harvested from that area over time. Note that this argument did not imply the economic value could not be higher than the value of the timber that would be foregone, but only that it should at least equal that value.

Put simply, the concept of opportunity pricing focuses on the highest valued opportunity that would be foregone. For example, it was impossible to quantify the economic value to the United States of landing a person on the moon. But the U.S. government decided in the 1960s the value was at least as great as the aggregate values that would be realized from the opportunities foregone by allocating federal revenue to that space program. In sum, opportunity pricing/costing provides only a reference point or benchmark and does attempt to quantify the actual economic benefits that would or do exist.

Recreation Entrance and Use Fees

The previous section described the methods commonly used to measure the economic benefits and values of outdoor recreation resources and opportunities. While fees charged are sometimes included in estimates of those economic benefits, they represent only a part, and usually a small part, of the expenditures of outdoor recreationists. Therefore, this section on recreation fees considers a different part of the economics of outdoor recreation. Two types of recreation fees are commonly recognized: entrance and use fees. *Entrance fees* are charged to enter a recreation area, site, or facility, and *use fees* are charged to use a particular service, such as to camp or to use a parking facility. Not included in the discussion in this section are other types of recreation fees, such as fees for guides and outfitters; permits; licenses and stamps to hunt, fish, or trap; or excise taxes on equipment needed to hunt or fish.

While many other outdoor recreation policy and managerial decisions have strong emotional components, none have been as contentious as decisions about whether to levy recreation entrance or use fees when none existed before or to increase fees that did exist. This section briefly reviews the history of establishing recreation entrance and use fees for public lands in the United States, outlines the arguments both for and against recreation fees, summarizes the authors' central positions on fees, and reviews techniques that have been used to reduce opposition to either establishing or increasing fees for publicly provided outdoor recreation opportunities. The focus here is on fees charged by public providers.

Recreation entrance and use fees, like those collected at this National Forest in Arizona, are increasingly common.

Historical Overview

This section briefly reviews the history of imposing fees for outdoor recreation opportunities provided by federal agencies of the U.S. government. Similar trends have occurred for many state park agencies and in other countries.

The U.S. Congress establishes the legal authorities for federal agencies to charge fees to use the outdoor recreation areas and sites they manage. Interestingly, until recently, Congress has shown strong bipartisan opposition to federal agencies levying fees for outdoor recreation. Driver, Bossi, and Cordell (1985) discuss the history of that opposition, as does Mackintosh (1983) for the National Park Service (NPS).

At federal areas, user fees in the form of auto entry permits (i.e., entrance fees), were first collected in 1908 at Mount Rainier National Park, followed by General Grant (1910), Crater Lake (1911), Glacier (1912), Yosemite and Sequoia (1913), Mesa Verde (1914) and Yellowstone (1915). Because the sentiment of the NPS (created in 1916) and the U.S. Congress was that excessive entrance fees should not be charged, entrance fees for these NPS units were reduced in 1917 and again in 1926, and all fees for camping were prohibited until passage of the Land and Water Conservation Fund Act (LWCFA) in 1965. (See Chapter 12 for more details about the LWCFA.)

The 1965 LWCFA was the first authorization by the U.S. Congress for several federal agencies to levy entrance fees and fees for specific services, such as to camp in areas where potable water was provided. Subsequent amendments to the LWCFA changed what fees could be charged and for what services, and how the revenues obtained

Self-service stations are a common approach to collecting entrance and use fees in outdoor recreation areas.

would be distributed—whether totally to the U.S. Treasury, or mostly to the Treasury but also partially to the agencies collecting the fees, and/or to units of state governments as grants-in-aid within guidelines that require approved State Comprehensive Outdoor Recreation Plans (SCORPs). From 1965 until the present, the fees charged by the federal agencies for outdoor recreation have increased gradually, as documented empirically in Driver, Bossi, and Cordell (1985). During that period, many state and local public park and recreation agencies also had to initiate fee programs where none existed before and/or increase existing fees to cover the increasing costs of providing recreation opportunities.

The historic strong reluctance of the U.S. Congress to provide needed fiscal allocations to the federal agencies over several decades created an undesirable situation. It reflected the fact that each of the federal agencies (especially the USDA Forest Service, the National Park Service, and the Bureau of Land Management) were facing hundreds of millions of dollars of backlogged needs (a) to refurbish facilities that had deteriorated and (b) to provide new facilities and resources to meet growing recreation demands.[2] At the urging of the federal agencies, the Congress created, on a trial basis, the Recreation Fee Demonstration (or "Fee-Demo") program in 1996. Fee-Demo greatly expanded those federal agencies' authority to levy higher fees and to charge fees for services they could not before, but only at designated Fee-Demo sites and areas. The major purpose of that legislation was to "maintain and improve recreation facilities and services." A novel part of Fee-Demo is that a high percentage of the fee revenue collected at a Fee-Demo area would be returned to the area or site at which the fees were collected. From about 2000 to the time this text was written, the Fee-Demo program has become very controversial for several reasons:

1. Many opponents did not understand why Fee-Demo was created.

2. Some managers left the impression they were being excessive in the fees they charged at Fee-Demo areas, with a few managers of particular sites/areas accused of trying to make profits or collect fee revenues greater than costs so they would have more operating funds.

3. Some people were left with perceptions that Fee-Demo revenues were being used for purposes other than proving outdoor recreation opportunities, such as to maintain wildlife species and habitat, which seemed inappropriate to the opponents of Fee-Demo.

4. Definite and felt increases in fees at Fee-Demo sites were opposed by some.

5. Some felt they already paid for access to public lands through their taxes.

6. Sentiments of people who believe public recreation opportunities should be provided free or at a low cost to everyone also led to controversy.

Many of these oppositions to the Fee-Demo program could have been avoided if managers had done a better job of explaining to users what the Fee-Demo funds were being used for and why, and if fees had never been excessive.

These trends of increasing recreation entrance and use fees have also occurred in all of the more developed countries as well as the United States. See Driver and Koch (1986) for a cross-cultural documentation of these trends.

Rationales For and Against Recreation Fees

A variety of arguments have been made, and are still being made, in support of and in opposition to recreation entrance and/or use fees (Driver & Koch, 1986, pp. 371–373; Harris & Driver, 1987).

Arguments Supporting Fees

It is the perception of the authors of this text that few proponents of fees for publicly provided outdoor recreation opportunities believe fees should be set to cover the total costs of such provision (or for public agencies to make a profit), but only that fair and reasonable fees be charged. Arguments supporting fees include the following:

Recover part of the costs. This rationale has several dimensions. Most importantly, users should bear their *equitable share* of the costs (especially the variable costs) of providing the opportunities used. Second, agencies can better justify their programs to funding authorities if higher proportions of costs are recovered than have been recovered historically.

Generate revenues to the U.S. Treasury for use by the collecting agencies. This argument goes beyond just cost-recovery; it proposes that at least part of the fee revenues be returned to the collecting agency to be used to increase the quantity and quality of recreation opportunities supplied. Too many fee-levying authorizations have proposed only that the funds are returned to the public treasury to be allocated as the responsible legislature or parliament chooses. In part, this rational for reasonable fees recognizes the historic fact that severely limited appropriations by the U.S. Congress have been made to try to meet the needs of those agencies that provide outdoor recreation opportunities.

Promote equity. This includes economic considerations but is also based on the notion of fairness. The argument is that it is unfair to tax all citizens to provide funds for recreation developments when some of the taxpayers do not use the opportunities provided. Letting the users pay more of the costs through use fees is viewed as fairer.

Reduce unfair competition with private recreation enterprises. This rationale, which also relates to fairness, states that public subsidy of recreation puts private enterprises providing similar opportunities at an economic disadvantage. Provision of public opportunities at low prices limits prices that the private firms can charge.

Promote national economic welfare. This argument is based in microeconomics and proposes that economically efficient allocations (ignoring distributional considerations) of a nation's public resources depend on the idea that those who have the ability and willingness to pay for goods and services do so in transactions where supply costs must, at least in part, be met by prices (or fees) paid. The argument has been made that recreation opportunities should go to those who are willing to pay a fee at least equal to the marginal personal benefits received. Because of the merit-good benefits to society at-large from the use of most outdoor recreation opportunities, the authors of this text reject this rationale as elaborated later.

Increase user commitment. This rationale holds that a person who pays a fee will be more committed to that opportunity than will users who pay no fee. It proposes further that the users holding these commitments would be more protective of the resources and follow the rules and regulations more closely.

Redistribute use. In addition to limiting use to the most committed users, differential fees (fees that vary by time or location) can be used to encourage or discourage use at particular times (i.e., reduce peak loads) or locations (i.e., shift use from heavily to lightly used areas or sites).

Make contact with users. This rationale has two dimensions. One proposes that even a small fee will help agency managers to identify the users and to remind them that they get a valued service. The second is that the contacts can be used to help meet management objectives (e.g., distribute fire prevention and other resource protection information, provide more accurate use statistics for planning purposes).

We pay; why shouldn't they? This final argument is not so much a rationale as a visceral response as citizens see fees increase for other public programs (e.g., postal services, housing, transportation, medical services). A citizen might reason, if I pay for my public services, so should users of public recreation services.

Arguments Opposing Fees

Although some opponents of fees advocate free recreation, especially of national parks, most of them are concerned about what they view as excessive fees. Their arguments include the following:

Restrict use. Fees will restrict use of recreation opportunities by those citizens who cannot afford them.

Provide benefits to individuals. This rationale goes beyond concern for those people who might be excluded by fees to the explicit argument that outdoor recreation participation is good and wholesome for all individuals, so everyone should have access to publicly provided opportunities, unfettered by any constraints (both psychological or economic) imposed by fees.

Provide a merit good. This argument states that recreation, like education, is a "merit good" because there are spin-off benefits (i.e., external economies) from users to nonusers, such as benefits of better heath of the users which lowers health care costs to society in general. Thus, everyone should, through general taxation, pay at least part of the costs of creating these meritorious or socially advantageous spin-offs benefits.

Benefit off-site and future users. This rationale for public subsidization of outdoor recreation opportunities is that many citizens benefit from maintenance and preservation of outdoor recreation resources by simply knowing those resources are being maintained rather than allocated to alternative uses. Those benefits relate to accepting stewardship responsibilities to protect recreation resources to preserve options for future generations. Those types of beneficiaries, who do not use the recreation areas, can pay only through general taxation.

Avoid double taxation. Another argument made in opposition to fees, or for limiting fees, for public outdoor recreation is that since the public already owns the land, there should be relatively free access—or no "double taxation." This argument focuses only on the fixed and sunk costs of land acquisition and ignores the variable operating costs associated with use.

Be cost-effective. Agency studies have shown the costs of collecting fees for some types of outdoor recreation opportunities exceed the fee revenues obtained. This is especially true for remote areas having many access points. Therefore, the argument of cost-ineffectiveness applies to those types of opportunities where fee revenues generated are less than the costs of collecting those revenues. As an aside, it is mentioned that this is the reason many outdoor recreation areas have self-registration booths with places to deposit fees in lock boxes in envelopes provided.

Limit freedom. This concern relates to the belief that imposition or expansion of fee programs will be accompanied by authoritative agency regulations, requirements, and the on-site presence of "policing" personnel to an extent that conflicts would exist with the ideal of leisure requiring perceived freedom, as discussed in Chapters 1 and 2.

Avoid adverse impacts on agencies. Several concerns about fees relate directly to possible adverse impacts on the recreation agencies. One is that return of fee revenues to the collecting agency will make it more difficult for the agency to receive supplemental appropriations and that over time total budgets will be reduced. A second is that the agency's favorable public image will be weakened and replaced with perceptions the agency has become crass, business-like, commercialized, or has adopted short time planning horizons.

Reduce recreation options. Concern has been expressed that agencies will focus on providing recreation opportunities that generate the most revenue and over time fail to provide a balanced spectrum of choice options. It is argued such motivation would affect especially the dispersed, more primitive opportunities for which fee programs usually are more difficult to implement and which generate less revenue from fees.

Maintain tradition. Several arguments against fees relate to historical precedent and reluctance to change. In some countries, for example, relatively free access to public (and even private) lands for recreation is based on time-honored rights. Included also in this rationale are instances where previously local or regional outdoor recreation areas with low fees are transferred to national administrative jurisdictions. Past perceptions of preemptive rights persist; thus, simple social inertia to change prompts some opposition to proposed alterations in fee structures.

Revenues will go to the Treasury and not to help recreation. This opposition is that, even if valid reasons can be given to support fee programs, any revenues obtained will go back to the general Treasury and will be allocated to other programs—many of which are perceived not to be as socially beneficial as recreation.

Give me mine. This final argument against expansion of fee programs is the reverse of the last one in favor of fees (*We pay; why shouldn't they?*). The position taken is that because most groups of people in a society receive some type of federal subsidy, outdoor recreation should be subsidized too, as long as those other subsidies exist.

A Reasoned Position on Recreation Fees

We believe reasonable fees for publicly provided outdoor recreation opportunities are appropriate for the following reasons:

Users should pay their fair share of the costs of publicly provided outdoor recreation opportunities. But, we believe such fees should not be set to cover all the costs of provision because of the legitimate merit-good aspects of recreation. After several decades of doing and reviewing research on the benefits of leisure, we are convinced most outdoor recreation settings are merit goods in terms of the benefits provided to all members of a society, whether participants in recreation activities or not. The only equitable way that nonusing and off-site beneficiaries can pay their fair share of the costs of their realization of these merit-good benefits is through their tax dollars, which can then be used to help subsidize provision of the meritorious opportunities.

We have no problem with charging lower or no fees for low-income people, as is done for many public services. But we do not believe that low-income people should, as a rule, be provided free outdoor recreation unless everyone is, as is done in many municipal parks and playgrounds. We have seen no evidence that reasonable fees at remote outdoor recreation areas restrain or limit their use by low-income people because the transportation costs of getting to those areas are typically a much bigger constraint.

We do not accept the argument that free access should be given to public lands because those lands have already been paid for from public funds. We believe users of those areas should pay their fair share of any increased maintenance and operating costs related to their use.

We believe the biggest problem regarding increasing fees has been that the managing agencies have not clearly communicated to the using publics why such increases are necessary.

For the reasons given in Chapter 17 on Collaborative Partnerships, we also believe managers should more widely involve relevant stakeholders collaboratively in decisions regarding any proposed increases in fees.

Reducing Public Opposition to Fees

Park and recreation practitioners and leisure scientists working with them have learned that the following actions can reduce public opposition to the implementing of recreation fees where no fees existed before or when increasing existing fees that are inappropriately low:

- Inform the using public of the needs for the fees and do so by providing clear, specific, and accurate information about existing budgets, revenues, and costs of providing specific types of recreation opportunities. It is particularly important that the costs of providing the opportunities be explained clearly. People often forget that the cost of everything tends to increase over time.

- Inform the using public what will be gained from any increases in fees, such as eliminate the need to offer fewer services, offer more and higher quality services, allow needed repairs to be made to existing facilities, and expand hours of operation. Let the people know what their fees are "buying."

- Realize people frequently oppose the percentage increase in fees more than the absolute amount of increase. For example, an increase from $1.00 to $2.00 is a 100% increase. So, it has been found to be less objectionable to raise the fee in two stages—first from $1.00 to $1.50 and then later from $1.50 to $2.00.

- Inform the customers of "referent" prices, or prices being charged by other providers of comparable services, such as a private campground, or use an example such as that the proposed increased fee costs no more than a Coke or whatever relevant numbers of Cokes or Pepsis.

Financing Public Recreation

Professionals working for public agencies that provide recreation opportunities, including outdoor recreation, are continually faced with the question of how to obtain the financial resources needed to provide those opportunities. Crompton (1999) in his excellent, comprehensive text *Financing and Acquiring Park and Recreation Resources*, pointed out the largest source of funds to finance recreation at the local municipal level is property taxes and the second largest source is sales taxes. He describes these and other potential sources of financing, including the following:

- sales and excise taxes, such as a hotel/motel tax (usually 10% to 15% added to the basic cost of lodging). An example at the federal level is the federal excise tax on fishing equipment, trolling motors, fish finders, and motorboat fuels which are added to the Dingell-Johnson Fund and earmarked for distribution to the states for sport-fishing areas, restoration of fisheries and coastal wetlands, and

Federal and state grant programs have been very important in financing the purchase of lands for outdoor recreation.

boating enhancement programs. Similarly, the Pittman-Roberston Act of the U.S. Congress provides for an excise tax on sporting arms, ammunition, archery equipment, pistols and revolvers, and related goods used in hunting, with that tax revenue going to the states for wildlife restoration and enhancement programs.

- special fees levied on snowmobiles, all-terrain vehicles, and other off-highway vehicles
- special assessments levied on developers to acquire and maintain open, green, and park lands
- general obligation and revenue bonds directed to acquiring and maintaining open spaces and other recreation resources
- recreation entrance and use fees
- transfers of development rights to assure open spaces and park lands will not be developed commercially and thereby become more costly to acquire later
- cooperation with nonprofit organizations and cost sharing with local private enterprises
- use of volunteers to keep administrative and operating costs down
- partnerships with schools and other public service agencies, such as police protection, to share resources and services
- federal grants, such as grants to states and municipalities from the Land and Water Conservation Fund (explained in Chapter 12)

- competitive grants from units of government and private charitable foundations
- donations
- revenue from lotteries earmarked for park and recreation
- special fundraising events such as fairs, festivals, and open houses

Summary

This chapter reviewed the following general characteristics of the discipline of economics: how economists define the concepts of economic value and benefit; the concepts of merit, public, and nonmarket (i.e., unpriced) goods and services; the measures used by recreation economists to estimate the economic benefits of recreation, with emphasis on measuring consumer surplus and conducting economic impact analyses; the arguments both for and against the use of recreation entrance and use fees; suggestions for reducing the adverse impacts of having to increase fees; and different means of financing park and recreation resources, programs, and services. This chapter also reinforced the contention that the leisure sector of the economy, including outdoor recreation, is likely one of the largest in the United States. From this general overview, it should be clear that the economics of recreation, especially outdoor recreation, is a very important aspect of the inquiry and concern of the outdoor recreation professional.

Literature Cited

Aiken, R. (1985). *Public benefits of environmental protection in Colorado.* Unpublished master's thesis, Colorado State University, Fort Collins, CO.

Ajzen, I. and Driver, B. (1992). Contingent value measurement: On the nature and meaning of willingness to pay. *Journal of Consumer Economics, 1*(4), 297–316.

Ajzen, I. and Peterson, G. (1988). Contingent value measurement: The price of everything and the value of nothing? In G. Peterson, B. Driver, and R. Gregory (Eds.), *Amenity resource valuation: Integrating economics with other disciplines* (pp. 65–76). State College, PA: Venture Publishing, Inc.

Alward, G., Arnold, J., Niccolucci, M., and Winter, S. (2002). *Evaluating the economic significance of the USDA Forest Service's strategic plan (2000 revision): Methods and results for programmatic evaluations* (Inventory and Monitoring Report No. 6). Fort Col-

Many counties and municipalities operate grant programs, often funded by selling bonds, to protect open space and areas for outdoor recreation.

lins, CO: USDA Forest Service, Inventory and Monitoring Institute.

Bishop, R. and Heberlein, T. (1990). The contingent valuation method. In R. J. Johnson and G. Johnson (Eds.), *Economic valuation of natural resources: Issues, theory, and applications* (pp. 81–104). Boulder, CO: Westview Press.

Brazer, H. (1970). Outdoor recreation as a public good and some problems of financing. In B. Driver and R. Tocher (Eds.), *Elements of outdoor recreation planning*. Ann Arbor, MI: University of Michigan Press.

Brown, T. (1984). The concept of value in resource allocation. *Land Economics, 60*(3), 231–246.

Callicott, J. (1985, Fall). Intrinsic value, quantum theory, and environmental ethics. *Environmental Ethics, 7*, 257–275.

Champ, P., Boyle, K., and Brown, T. (Eds.). (2003). *Primer on nonmarket valuation.* Boston, MA: Kluwer Academic Press.

Crompton J. (1999). *Financing and acquiring park and recreation resources.* Champaign, IL: Human Kinetics.

Crompton, J. (2000). *The impact of parks and open space on property values and the property value tax base.* Ashburn, VA: National Recreation and Park Association.

Decker, D. and Goff, G. (1987). *Valuing wildlife: Economic and social perspectives.* Boulder, CO: Westview Press.

Driver, B., Bossi, J., and Cordell, H. (1985). Trends in user fees at federal outdoor recreation areas. In *Proceedings, 1985 Outdoor Recreation Trends Symposium II, Volume I* (pp. 222–242). Clemson, SC: Clemson University Department of Parks, Recreation, and Tourism Management.

Driver, B. and Burch, W. (1988). A framework for more comprehensive valuations of public amenity goods and services. In G. Peterson, B. Driver, and R. Gregory (Eds.), *Amenity resource valuation: Integrating economics with other disciplines* (pp. 31–45). State College, PA: Venture Publishing, Inc.

Driver, B. and Koch, N. (1986). Crosscultural trends in user fees charged at national outdoor recreation areas. In *Proceedings, 18th International Congress of the International Union of Forest Research Organizations* (pp. 370–385). Ljubljane, Yugoslavia: IUFRO Organizing Committee.

Gan, C. (1998). Leisure and recreation: An economic perspective. In H. Perkins and G. Cushman (Eds.), *Time out?* (pp. 327–342). Aukland, New Zealand: Addison Wesley Longman New Zealand Limited.

Harris, C. and Driver, B. (1987). Recreation user fees: Pros and cons. *Journal of Forestry, 85*(5), 25–29.

Harris, C, Driver, B., and McLaughlin, W. (1989). Improving the contingent valuation method: A psychological perspective. *Journal of Environmental Economics and Management, 17*, 213–229.

Johnson, R., Bregenzer, N., and Shelby, B. (1990). Contingent valuation question formats: Dichotomous choice versus open-ended responses. In R. Johnson and G. Johnson (Eds.), *Economic valuation of natural resources: Issues, theory, and applications* (pp. 193–203). Boulder, CO: Westview Press.

Johnson, R. and Johnson, G. (1990). *Economic valuation of natural resources: Issues, theory and applications.* Boulder, CO: Westview Press.

Loomis, J. and Walsh, R. (1997). *Recreation economic decisions* (2nd ed.). State College, PA: Venture Publishing, Inc.

Mackintosh, B. (1983). *Visitor fees in the National Park Service: A legislative and administrative history.* Washington, DC: History Division, USDI National Park Service.

McCollum, D. and Bergstrom, J. (1992). Measuring net economic value and regional economic impact. In G. Peterson, C. Swanson, D. McCollum, and M. Thomas (Eds.), *Valuing wildlife resources in Alaska* (pp. 135–197). Boulder, CO: Westview Press.

McCollum, D., Peterson, G., and Swanson, C. (1992). A manager's guide to the valuation of nonmarket resources: What do you really want to know? In G. Peterson, C. Swanson, D. McCollum, and M. Thomas (Eds.), *Valuing wildlife resources in Alaska* (pp. 25–52). Boulder, CO: Westview Press.

Peterson, G., Driver, B., and Gregory, R. (Eds.). (1988). *Amenity resource valuation: Integrating economics with other disciplines.* State College, PA: Venture Publishing, Inc.

Peterson, G. and Randall, A. (1984). *Valuation of wildland resource benefits.* Boulder, CO: Westview Press.

Peterson, G., Swanson, C., McCollum, D., and Thomas, M. (Eds.). (1992). *Valuing wildlife resources in Alaska.* Boulder, CO: Westview Press.

Randall, A. (1984). Benefit-cost analysis as an information system. In G. Peterson and A. Randall (Eds.), *Valuation of wildland resource benefits* (pp. 65–75). Boulder, CO: Westview Press.

Rosenberger, R. and Loomis, J. (2001). *Benefit transfer of outdoor recreation use values: A technical document supporting the Forest Service strategic plan, 2000 revision* (General Technical Report RMRS GTR-72). Fort Collins, CO: USDA Forest Service, Rocky Mountain Research Station.

Stynes, D. (2002). *Economic impacts of Great Mountain National Park visitors on the local region.* Unpublished report. East Lansing, MI: Michigan State University, Department of Park, Recreation, and Tourism Resources.

Stynes, D. (2004). *Economic impacts of recreation and tourism.* Retrieved June 3, 2004, from http://www.prr.msu.edu/mgm2/econ

Stynes, D. (in press). *Economic significance of recreational uses of National Parks and other public lands* (National Park Service Social Science Series). Washington, DC: National Park Service.

Stynes, D. and White, E. (2003). *Spending profiles of national forest visitors.* Unpublished report to the USDA Forest Service. Joint Venture Agreement No. 01-JV-11130149-203 between USDA Forest Service's Inventory and Monitoring Unit and Michigan State University. East Lansing, MI: Michigan State University, Department of Park, Recreation, and Tourism Resources.

Travel Industry Association of America. (2003). *Economic review of travel in America.* Washington, DC: Author.

U.S. Office of Management and Budget. (1987). *The standard industrial classification manual.* Washington, DC: Author.

U.S. Travel Data Center. (1994). *Impact of travel on state economies 1994* (Periodic Report). Washington, DC: U.S. Department of Labor.

Endnotes

1. Great appreciation is expressed to John Loomis, George Peterson, and Daniel Stynes, who contributed substantially to this chapter.

2. This reluctance to provide needed funds reflects the continuing need to "reposition" the image of recreation in the minds of members of the U.S. Congress, so they will understand the real social significance of recreation, as articulated in Chapter 2.

Chapter 20
The Future of Outdoor Recreation

The simplest rule of conduct for a camper is to leave a place as he would like to find it....The duty of the camper, as one with greater opportunity in this respect than the average citizen, is to preserve the resources which nature has bestowed and to cherish the land as he would his home. (MacKaye, 1904, as cited in Anderson, 2002)

Learning Objectives

1. Recognize major changes are taking place in the outdoor recreation field and rapid change will continue.
2. Consider what the future of providing outdoor recreation opportunities might look like.
3. Describe the most important aspects of what constitutes being an outdoor recreation professional.
4. Summarize the overall conclusions regarding outdoor recreation offered at the end of the chapter.

As Appalachian Trail founder and noted conservationist Benton MacKaye said so well over a century ago, campers have a duty to leave natural areas as they would like to find them. He was also correct that campers have greater opportunities in this respect than most citizens. Outdoor recreation professionals and natural resource planners and managers in general have greater opportunities still. Consequently, outdoor recreation and natural resource professionals have the greatest duties of all to preserve and conserve the natural resources under their care and to provide for their sustained public use and enjoyment.

Outdoor recreation is a tremendously important and beneficial use of natural and cultural/historic resource areas and one growing rapidly in popularity. This text has been about outdoor recreation—what it is, providing opportunities for it, and managing it professionally. Its primary purpose has been to introduce the essentials of the professional body of knowledge necessary for outdoor recreation professionals to fulfill their challenging and important responsibilities. In this final chapter we wrap up our treatment of this broad topic by presenting visions of the future of outdoor recreation and its management, discussing emerging issues, the responsibilities of outdoor recreation professionals, and conclusions.

Visions of Our Future

Futurists use a wide variety of techniques to predict what things might look like years and decades ahead. The point of their predictions, of course, is to help people prepare for and ideally to shape what the world will look like then. Outdoor recreation resource professionals must also look toward the future to best prepare for the opportunities and challenges that lay ahead as well as to shape what the future of outdoor recreation will be. There are many possible outdoor recreation futures that we all will have some role in choosing and creating. These can be viewed as existing along a continuum from the least optimistic and desirable to the most ideal. Following are three of the possible outdoor recreation futures along this continuum.

Laissez-Faire Outdoor Recreation Future

This pessimistic possibility consists of a relatively small public outdoor recreation estate of lands and waters fragmented and under siege like isolated embattled islands. There is a recreation world of "haves and have-nots," where those able to pay can visit exclusive private "natural area resorts" but the majority are relegated to small and overused public lands that are highly regulated, provide only marginal experiences, and are managed by grossly underfunded public outdoor recreation agencies. Although some citizens are active supporters of these lands, the majority do not fully appreciate the potential benefits of outdoor recreation. Therefore, they view public lands as "locked up" and unproductive. This is the likely future if we limit ourselves to seeing the existing public land estate as complete as it now exists, and if we manage our park and forest systems in ways that attempt to please everyone.

Modestly Successful Outdoor Recreation Future

This modestly optimistic possibility sees a slightly expanded public land estate with some components being large enough to be managed as healthy ecosystems. An active minority of users and nonusers recognize the many benefits these areas provide, strongly support managing agencies, and participate in their efforts individually or through active collaborating partner organizations. Ongoing divisive battles among a vast array of stakeholders lead to some successes, but also result in many failures and huge numbers of compromises that preserve some opportunities but lose many others. This future is likely if some planners and managers are visionary and professionally prepared, but most are not.

Ideal Outdoor Recreation Future

This optimistic vision of the future consists of a large, high-quality, healthy public land system that is diverse and easily accessible to everyone. Management focuses on assuring healthy sustainable ecosystems and providing a wide range of outdoor recreation opportunities. The system is able to provide freedom for users because all users understand their responsibilities to cause as little negative impact to resources as possible and have the skills and desire to do just that. Recreation resource areas face relatively few natural and human threats because the majority of users (and voters) understand and appreciate the vast personal and societal benefits these areas generate. As a result they are willing to commit their time, private donations, and tax dollars to protecting and enhancing their public lands and outdoor recreation opportunities. This vision of a sustainable natural resource base for outdoor recreation is successful, in part, because there are high-quality outdoor recreation opportunities within 15 minutes of every American, so nearly everyone has frequent personal experience with these areas and they see firsthand the benefits that result from their existence and use. This large physically interconnected system resembles a vast web linked to large nodes of wildland spread across the nation. It begins with urban and suburban "starbursts" of greenways and other protected open space areas close to where people live and work. These concentrated starbursts are connected through a network of many different types of lands and waters available for public outdoor recreation located farther from the centers of population. These in turn, are connected to the "Crown Jewels" of the National Park System, designated Wilderness areas, and the large natural areas of the National Forest System and remote holdings of other agencies and organizations. This ideal future is only possible if outdoor recreation and natural resource professionals at all levels are well-prepared, credible, ethical, visionary, and dedicated. It also requires that all outdoor recreation and natural resource professionals work together with many like-minded partners and a supportive general public to creatively and tenaciously pursue this ideal.

Our natural resource and outdoor recreation future will fall somewhere on this continuum. What it will actually be depends on which vision we choose to embrace now and dedicate ourselves to creating, as well as mobilizing others to create. This is particularly important for the readers of this book who are now students, some of whom will eventually be in top management positions around the world.

Notice that each of the possible futures illustrated here has both natural resource dimensions and human dimensions. Outdoor recreation has always been about the intersection of these two dimensions and will continue to be in the future as well. The most successful future for outdoor recreation will be that which addresses each of these two dimensions explicitly and effectively, both of which will require excellent science and the application of the best available practices related to natural resource health and leisure behavior. It will also require that we broadly and effectively *reposition the image* of leisure in general and outdoor recreation in particular so that the vast benefits of such are more widely understood and appreciated.

Emerging Issues

To prepare for and shape the future, outdoor recreation professionals must carefully identify the obstacles to realizing their vision and develop the necessary approaches to overcome these obstacles. This requires examining the broad trends and forces affecting our field and anticipating and addressing the implications they will have. In Chapter 4 we introduced what we believe are the key trends and forces affecting recreation:

Population Changes
- growing populations
- aging populations
- increasing diversity
- continuing urbanization and suburbanization
- decreases in traditional families

Technological Innovations
- innovations changing how people communicate and live
- innovations changing how we manage recreation resources
- innovations changing how users engage in outdoor recreation

Shifts in Economic Strengths and Weaknesses

- transforming economies
- increasing debt levels

Increased Accountability of Institutions and Leaders

- shifts in political power closer to the people
- interest groups more politically aware and effective
- general mistrust of corporations and government

Changes in Transportation

- greater mobility
- concerns about travel
- fluctuating energy availability and cost
- public interest in bicycling and walking

Concern for the Environment and Its Effects on Health

- increasing concern for personal health and safety
- increase in radical groups and ecoterrorism

Greater Emphasis on Partnerships

Increasing pressure on public recreational resources

- less land available as development accelerates
- recreation use increasing on existing public lands

Changes in Recreation and Leisure in General

- people with more free time, but often used in sedentary ways
- increased rushing and stress
- increased concern about life satisfaction and quality of life

Changes in Outdoor Recreation Participation in Particular

- levels of outdoor recreation participation increasing overall
- changing participation rates in various outdoor recreation activities

To respond to these trends and forces, outdoor recreation planners and managers will need to broaden their perspectives and roles to take advantage of the tremendous opportunities the future will present. This will require new ways of thinking, new training and resources, new partners, and especially a commitment to professionalism, as described in Chapters 1 and 2. In addition to considering the broad trends and forces affecting outdoor recreation, it is helpful to look at more specific examples of changes in outdoor recreation that are taking place now. There are hundreds of new activities, user groups, and consumer preferences that present opportunities and challenges we cannot afford to ignore. Following are just a few examples of developments related to outdoor recreation occurring now.

New and Emerging Outdoor Recreation Activities

The ways creative people enjoy natural areas continues to expand. This sometimes involves entirely new activities and other times new styles of existing ones. Examples include the following:

Geocaching. Geocaching is an outdoor adventure game where users of global positioning system (GPS) technologies set up "caches" and share the cache locations on the Internet. Other GPS users then use the posted coordinates to attempt to find the caches in what amounts to an outdoor treasure hunt (geocaching.com, 2004a). Caches are typically Tupperware containers or ammo boxes that contain cheap "treasures" and a logbook. Successful geocachers take something from the cache, leave something in its place, and write an entry in the logbook. There are now over 100,000 active caches in 208 countries (geocaching.com, 2004b).

Night-vision activities. Night-vision optics, such as goggles and scopes, are allowing people to take many activities into the night that they could not before. Wildlife observation in particular can now take place around the clock, making it possible for the average user to watch nocturnal wildlife in their natural habitats.

Wheeled dogsleds and skijor. Started as a means for serious mushers to keep their dogs fit in the summer, wheeled dogsledding is becoming more popular as a warm weather activity in its own right. Skijor is a winter activity that involves one or two sled dogs towing a cross-country skier.

Off-road skateboards. All-terrain boards (e.g., Earthboards) are essentially skateboards designed for off-road use on areas such as summer ski slopes, hillsides, and trails (Earthboard, 2004). Equipped with large knobby tires and bindings to hold the rider's feet secure, these boards can negotiate surprisingly difficult downhill terrain.

Amphibious recreation vehicles. Prototype amphibious recreation vehicles (RVs) are now available for use both on the road and the water. A family could use one to, say, drive from the east coast to Lake Mead in Arizona using their RV as a camper along the way and then as a houseboat to tour the lake once they arrive. The Terra Wind model is available now for $850,000, as are other amphibious vehicles like ones designed for resorts that can carry up to 50 tourists (Smith, 2004).

Rockcrawling. Rockcrawling involves the driver of a custom-built truck/dune buggy hybrid and a spotter negotiating the vehicle through extreme courses laid out in dirt, mud, and boulders. There are now multiday United Rockcrawling and Off-Road Challenges (Juarez, 2004).

Skyrays. The Skyray is an attachable rigid wing system designed by a German firm that can be used to expand skydiving to "skyflying." The triangular shaped Skyrays are nearly ready for mass production and have enabled skyflying test pilots to maneuver like airplanes, reaching speeds of 186 miles per hour (Abrams, 2004; FreeSky, 2004).

Boom of Technology in Backcountry

The types and amounts of new technology being used are increasing in the backcountry. Although there are benefits, many outdoor recreationists, managers, and commentators are concerned about this technological "invasion" into the natural world. Even humorist Dave Barry has written about the annoyance of cell phones at the beach (Barry, 2001). Examples of new technologies now being used in or adapted for outdoor recreation areas include the following:

Geographic information systems. Global positioning system (GPS) units have become increasingly popular in the backcountry for navigation, emergency location identification, and geocaching. They have even been used in research to track the movements of elk hunters (Lyon & Burcham, 1998). These are only a few of the many actual and potential adaptations of geographic information system (GIS) technology to outdoor recreation, research, and management.

Biotechnology. Biotech companies are increasingly interested in wild places, especially hot springs and other thermal features, ocean beds, soda lakes, and even Arctic tundra as they search for potentially lucrative genetic material that may be the key to the next bioengineering breakthrough. Some compounds and organisms found in parks and other natural areas may contain the genetic instructions for producing proteins that can be adapted to a wide variety of innovative uses in industry and medicine ("Sea of Dreams," 2004).

Advertising. By some estimates, the average American is subjected to 3,000 advertising messages every day ("The Harder Hard Sell," 2004). The advertising industry has always been innovative and will certainly continue to be relentless in how it attempts to grab and hold people's attention, and affect their behavior. A team of 23 futurists predicts the advertising industry will eventually be able to use technology to recognize us as individuals and "spot sell" to each of us directly (Gentile, 2002). Certainly, there will be increasing pressure from advertisers to use new technology and approaches to influence users before, during, and after their outdoor recreation.

Communications technologies. Cell phones, satellite phones, wireless networks, and other technologies are bringing real-time worldwide communication capabilities into even the most remote parts of the backcountry. At least one urban park is even beginning to offer connections to the Internet. A park in southeast England has become the first to offer an Internet-ready park bench by discreetly wiring it with phone lines for free laptop connections (Fontaine, 2001; Microsoft, 2004).

Monitoring and identification technologies. A number of new technologies are or could be used to monitor outdoor recreation resources or even outdoor recreationists themselves. Identifying and monitoring outdoor recreation users would raise dramatic privacy concerns, of course, and just because we can monitor something does not mean we should. There may be situations where it becomes desirable or necessary however. There may also be users who are willing to give up some privacy to have access to particularly high-quality or sensitive sites where access must be carefully controlled. Some users may actually prefer some level of personal identification and/or real-time monitoring of their location rather than be subjected to more burdensome on-site management approaches. Sophisticated monitoring technologies exist now, and others will no doubt become available as technology advances. Existing technologies include the following:

- *Visitor identification.* Since the terrorist attacks of 9/11/2001 there has been a greater push to enable public officials to identify individuals. This has included biometric information such as fingerprints, retinal scans, facial recognition data, Homeland Security Department databases, and many related technologies. For example, U.S. passports will likely be fitted with electronic identification chips containing biometric data starting in 2005 (Krim, 2004). Any of these technologies could be used to monitor and control access to sensitive sites where outdoor recreation opportunities are located such as sites that contain significant national treasures (e.g., Mount Rushmore, Statue of Liberty) or reservoirs and other water supplies. Intrusive security will have to be weighed against the freedom and privacy that would be given up however.

- *Cameras and closed-circuit TV.* The use of cameras and closed-circuit TV for real-time surveillance has expanded rapidly. For example there are an estimated 1.5 million cameras monitoring public places in Britain, with the average person being recorded on closed-circuit TV about 300 times every day ("No Hiding Place," 2003). Outdoor recreation managers will always need to be sensitive to how and where they gather personal information and how they use it, of course.

- *Chemical markers.* Benign chemical markers have been placed in rare and endangered plants or the home soil they grow in to allow their original locations to be identified. These markers can be used to prove certain plants were poached from public lands and to prosecute the thieves. If widely used, such forensic technologies could make rare and endangered plants and animals as difficult to sell as a stolen Picasso.

- *GPS-enabled tags.* GPS-enabled tags surgically implanted into pets are being used to help track down lost or stolen animals. Similar tags are also being used to locate stolen vehicles. Satellite-tracked GPS tags could be used to monitor game animals, rare and endangered species, and backcountry permits.

- *Radio frequency identification.* Product identification technologies, such as bar codes, have been in use in retail settings and libraries for many years. Radio frequency identification (RFID) represents a major leap beyond existing barcodes for many identification purposes. RFID involves tiny microchips with attached antenna (called *smart tags*) that can be attached to virtually any item. When the smart tag is prompted by a reader, the tag broadcasts the unique identification information that has been programmed into it ("The Future Is Still Smart," 2004). Such technologies could be used to monitor outdoor recreation resources or even outdoor recreationists themselves where appropriate. They could, for example, be laminated into backcountry permits or recreation equipment to allow remote monitoring of users or to alert users if they enter a restricted area.

Expansion of "Citizen Science"

Good natural resource and outdoor recreation resource management decisions require detailed understanding of complicated natural processes and human dynamics. This is generally intricate and expensive research work. Unfortunately, basic and applied research related to outdoor recreation resources has never been adequately funded and probably will not be in the future. An emerging trend that may be beneficial in helping meet our research needs in this regard is something called *citizen science*. This entails scientists and trained volunteers working together on research that might otherwise not be possible because of the large scope of the projects and/or inadequate funding. Examples of existing citizen science projects related to resource and recreation management include the following:

All Taxa Biodiversity Inventory. The All Taxa Biodiversity Inventory (ATBI) is a multiyear effort to identify and understand all the species of life within the 800 square mile ecosystem of Great Smoky Mountains National Park. To accomplish this huge task the National Park Service is working with the nonprofit Discover Life In America (DLIA) to actually conduct the inventory and related educational activities. DLIA recruits, trains, and coordinates volunteers; raises funds and in-kind donations; and assists in coordinating and supporting the efforts of scientist working in the park. The project's long-term objective is to the refine methodologies developed in the ATBI in the Great Smokies and use them to conduct similar ATBIs in other national park ecosystems and natural areas around the world (Discover Life In America, 2004).

Christmas Bird Count. The National Audubon Society's annual Christmas Bird Count (CBC) enlists tens of thousands of volunteer observers to count millions of birds in locations all across the western hemisphere each winter. December 14, 2003, to January 5, 2004, was the 104th annual CBC. Observers record their counts by species and location and send the data to the Audubon Society, which compiles and analyzes the results annually. The 100-plus years of CBC data has been instrumental in identifying major changes in bird populations (National Audubon Society, 2004).

Project FeederWatch. Project FeederWatch is a volunteer bird counting survey operated by the Cornell Lab of Ornithology in partnership with the National Audubon Society, Bird Studies Canada, and Canadian Nature Federation. It enlists volunteers to count birds at backyard feeders, nature centers, community areas, and other locales in North America from November through early April. Project FeederWatch data help scientists to track movements of winter bird populations and to identify long-term trends in bird distribution and abundance (Project FeederWatch, 2004).

Adventure Racing and Other Competitive Outdoor Recreation Events

There has been very rapid growth in extreme sports competitions like Eco-Challenge, Subaru Primal Quest, and other long-distance challenge events. Since its inception in 1989, adventure racing has grown to over a thousand races worldwide with tens of thousands of participants and has become a popular genre on cable television (Subaru Primal Quest, 2004). Adventure races range from a few hours up to ten days and are nonstop, around the clock, team endurance events set in backcountry locations. They typically involve mountain biking, paddling, trekking, and rappelling. For both good and bad, these competitions draw large numbers of participants, spectators, and media into natural areas and will continue to do so in the future. Some examples of adventure racing and related activities include the following:

24-hour mountain bike races. There are now about thirty-five 24-hour mountain bike races each year across the United States. Many of them attract large crowds with camping, bonfires, and contests in a festival atmosphere for spectators and individual and team race participants (Tolme, 2004).

Ultrarunning. Ultramarathons and other long-distance running races are on the increase nationwide and around the world. Run on roads, trails, or tracks, an ultramarathon is any organized running event longer than the standard 26.2-mile marathon distance. Distances typically begin at 50 kilometers and races of 100 kilometers and 100 miles are common, as are 24-hour races (Blaikie, 2004).

Great outdoor games. These highly popular televised competitions include fishing events (e.g., fly fishing, freshwater doubles), sporting dog events (e.g., retriever, agility, disc drive, and big air), target shooting event (e.g., archery, rifle, and shotgun) for both speed and accuracy, and timber events (e.g., boom run, log rolling, team relay, endurance, speed climbing, tree topping, hot saw, and springboard; ESPN, 2004).

Possible Future Developments

The examples noted here are developments related to outdoor recreation occurring now. There are obviously many other developments on the horizon for our field. Allow us to speculate (as should all outdoor recreation professionals) about what some of these might be. Following are possibilities of what the future of some aspects of outdoor recreation and outdoor recreation management may hold:

Specification of allowable technologies. Agencies might become much more explicit about what technologies are appropriate or even allowable in particular areas under their jurisdictions. This could take many forms, from expanding the Leave No Trace principles, to discouraging cell phone use in certain backcountry areas, to developing other technology guidelines, to the creation of "technology free zones" in some wilderness and related areas. The naturalness indicator used in the Recreation Opportunity Spectrum management system could even be expanded to more explicitly address what user technologies are appropriate in each class of setting.

Major ecosystem restorations. Major ecosystem restorations might be undertaken to rejuvenate large parts of parks and other natural areas on a scale not yet attempted. These efforts could be sponsored by nonprofits or private companies, which might fund them, give their employees release time to help accomplish the initial work, and then "adopt" the site for ongoing needs.

Virtual outdoor recreation. A plethora of computer adventure games exist now. Ones based on simulated extreme sports and adventure races will likely follow. These could take some pressure off real resource areas, and perhaps introduce low-impact techniques and appropriate etiquette to those who will progress from simulated outdoor recreation to the real thing. Other virtual outdoor recreation "outings" will almost certainly become more available as well. It is not hard to imagine DVD sets for top-end exercise machines that simulate anything from a simple jog in a park to an actual thru-hike of the Appalachian Trail or climb of Mount Everest complete with sights and sounds based on actual digital video. Demand for realistic images could spawn a small industry including professional "scenery paparazzi," "adventure experienceographers," and other technicians to capture and clean up the images and integrate them into exercise equipment and facilities. Clubs of these virtual adventurers (in person and networked via computer) might issue their own awards and certificates of completion as well as develop codes of ethics and organize virtual group outings and expeditions. Some might become active in the conservation community even if they have never actually visited the sites they support. It is possible the virtual outings could benefit parks by reducing the number of visitors in heavily used areas, improving outdoor awareness and ethics, and generating income for managers through creative licensing agreements. The conservation community could certainly benefit by tapping into a new source of members and contributors.

Simulated experiences in visitor centers. Sophisticated simulated experiences will likely be increasingly offered in visitor centers. They would almost certainly be very popular and could generate income for important resource management programs. Such experiences could be designed to influence visitor attitudes and to improve support for resource protection efforts as well as for the managing agencies themselves.

New outdoor recreation activities. New outdoor recreation activities, activity styles, and experiences will almost certainly continue to be developed at a rapid rate. Most of them will probably be created by innovative participants or entrepreneurs from the private sector. Some examples might include the following:

- overflights of nonwilderness natural areas using virtually silent helicopters
- night-tracking competitions using night-vision optical equipment
- low-impact tall-tree climbing and suspended hammock or tent camping high in the forest canopy
- nonlethal hunting on both public and private lands where "hunters" use infrared marking rifles based on military infantry training technology and attached cameras to take photos of their "kills." In some private reserves tranquilizer weapons and other stunning technologies might be used that give the client

and guide time for a trophy photo before the animal revives and wanders off again.

- "retro wilderness trekking" involving individuals or outfitted groups experiencing particular areas as similarly as possible to the way it was during a particular historical period—"John Muir Treks" in the Sierras, "Lewis and Clark River Expeditions" of the Missouri and Columbia rivers, or even mountaineering adventures using equipment and approaches like those used on the first ascents of famous peaks. Growth in such *heritage re-creation experiences* could be a reaction to the increasing reliance on technology in almost every other facet of regular life. A few people even predict that real time travel may someday become the next frontier in tourism, allowing customers to take historic tours to the actual events themselves (Bleiberg, 2001). We believe retro tours like those described here will be the extent of this type of heritage experience unless the laws of physics are repealed.

Private outdoor recreation providers. There will likely be rapid growth in the development of private nature reserves and outdoor recreation in parts of the world where demand is strong and high-quality natural areas still exist in private ownership. Entrepreneurs could be especially successful at creating and tapping into high-end markets for exclusive experiences and upscale accommodations. Where these operations rely on nearby public lands for some of their trips, land managers could become much more aggressive in charging what would have once been considered very high fees for such commercial use of public land. Ideally, these fees will be based, in part, on detailed research conducted by recreation and resource economists.

Negative impacts of recreation use. Negative impacts caused by visitor use will continue to be a challenge. Technological advances in both equipment and resource protection will help, but in some cases will be more than overcome by increases in the number of users. To be widely accepted and used, quieter, less polluting, and less damaging motorized outdoor recreation equipment will need to be more economical or mandated. Important advances will need to include better and more economical four-stroke engines for ATVs, OHVs, snowmobiles and PWCs and possibly even electric and natural gas models for some applications. Better soil cements and bonding agents, natural looking and feeling but virtually bullet-proof, would be extremely valuable for trail surfaces in heavily used areas as would chameleon-like fabrics for less visual impacts in wilderness settings.

Continued expansion of fees. As the costs of managing outdoor recreation resources continues to rise, recreation fees will increase and will likely expand through most of the outdoor recreation estate. In some cases agencies may experiment with offering resort experiences in some areas and exclusive trips for higher fees in efforts to fund other operations and to provide a wider range of opportunities with the income generated. Increases in fees will not be limited to fees for recreation. For example, some agencies will have the foresight to pursue innovative licensing agreements and contracts with biotechnology firms and generate substantial income as a result. In the best cases, these contracts will require the biotech firms to pay royalties to the agency for the sale of products resulting from new organisms and other organic compounds originally "prospected" from sites under the agency's jurisdiction.

Internationalization of outdoor recreation. The mix of visitors in every nation's protected area system will continue to become more multicultural because of increased diversification of domestic user bases and influxes of international visitors. International visitation will continue to vary depending on monetary exchange rates, travel conditions, and internatioanl terrorism, but in general, outdoor recreation will become more global. The "Japanese wave" of the 1990s will be followed by others, perhaps a "Chinese wave" and a "Latin American wave." Opportunities certainly exist for expanded exchange programs for park planners and managers, perhaps funded in part by the United Nations or nongovernmental organizations (NGOs). As a beginning, 3- to 12-month exchanges of park personnel at all levels could bring staff from "visitor source" nations to "visitor recipient" nations. Each employee could be then paired at their new duty station where they would better serve their fellow nationals and teach their partners about the culture and language of their home region.

Increasing reliance on nontraditional employees. Interns, volunteers, seasonal employees, and other types of nontraditional workers will become increasingly important. Various national and international outdoor service programs do large amounts of work, much of it benefiting parks and other natural resource based areas popular for outdoor recreation. Built on the strong tradition of the Civilian Conservation Corps (CCC) from the 1930s in the United States, these programs could be greatly expanded to train and employ people of all ages. For example, the Retired Senior Volunteer Program (RSVP) successfully taps into the large and increasing number of retired people and could be particularly effective in the future.

In spite of the many dramatic changes taking place now in outdoor recreation and outdoor recreation management, and the many other changes that will certainly take place in the coming decades, the most important things will not change. Huge numbers of people will continue to seek the many benefits that outdoor recreation and natural areas offer, and a dedicated minority of these people will commit themselves to protecting and managing the outdoor recreation opportunities these benefits depend on. Outdoor recreation management will always involve natural resource dimensions and human dimensions, and will require professional training, experience, and skills related to both of these interrelated dimensions.

Outdoor Recreation Professionalism

Chapters 1 and 2 emphasized and Chapters 12 and 13 reinforced the need for professionalism in people who work in any of the many specialties of leisure. Central to that discussion was the commonly accepted notion that the most fundamental characteristic of a true profession is its reliance on an empirically supported body of knowledge. Also fundamental to professionalism is the idea that as the empirically supported body of knowledge relevant to that profession advances and grows, a professional must seek out, absorb, understand, and apply that new information. This means that all outdoor recreation professionals must stay informed about their ever-advancing body of knowledge and know how to apply it.

We proposed that one of the greatest challenges facing the leisure professions, including outdoor recreation, was achieving widespread recognition of the many tremendous benefits of recreation. This appropriate image of leisure needs to be achieved not only among leisure professions themselves but also among members of legislative bodies,

Nontraditional "employees" like these volunteers, will continue to play an increasingly important role in providing outdoor recreation opportunities on public lands.

related public agencies (and private and nonprofit organizations), and especially in the minds of the public at large. Put simply, if we are to advance as a profession, we must move well beyond viewing recreation as only fun and games. Instead, there must be widespread recognition that recreation is a service equal to any other service in terms of the benefits provided to individual, social, environmental, and economic well-being.

Now we would like to emphasize the importance of ethical behavior. We discuss that topic here, near the end of this text because it is important enough that we want all readers to be left with it at the tops of their minds. The future of outdoor recreation opportunities and the outdoor recreation field depends on ethical, well-informed, and professionally educated practitioners.

Ethics and professionalism are essential for any field. Without professional and ethical behavior, the members of a profession can have no credibility with the public they supposedly serve and no respect for one another. Without credibility and respect, no profession can be effective. Ethical and professional behavior is particularly important within the recreation profession, including outdoor recreation, because we have not yet adequately repositioned the image of our field in the eyes of most people we serve. Repositioning the image of our field is necessary to garner the public support needed to accomplish our purposes. All of this depends on clear ethical and professional standards that are adhered to by all members of our field.

As outdoor recreation professionals, we are also recreation professionals in the broader sense. As such we look, in part, to our professional association, the National Recreation and Park Association (NRPA) for guidance on ethical and professional behavior. The NRPA Code of Ethics reads, in part, as follows:

Membership in NRPA carries with it special responsibilities to the public at large, and to the specific communities and agencies in which recreation and park services are offered. As a member of the National Recreation and Park Association, I accept and agree to abide by this Code of Ethics and pledge myself to:

- adhere to the highest standards of integrity and honesty in all public and personal activities to inspire public confidence and trust

- strive for personal and professional excellence and encourage the professional development of associates and students

- strive for the highest standards of professional competence, fairness, impartiality, efficiency, effectiveness, and fiscal responsibility

- avoid any interest or activity that is in conflict with the performance of job responsibilities
- promote the public interest and avoid personal gain or profit from the performance of job duties and responsibilities
- support equal employment opportunities (NRPA, 2004)

As outdoor recreation professionals, we are—to varying degrees—natural and cultural/historic resource professionals as well as recreation professionals. This is consistent with the fact that we are always concerned with both natural resource dimensions and human dimensions. As natural resource professionals there is an overlapping but distinct set of ethical questions we must consider. The best overall guidance in this regard comes from the Society of American Foresters (SAF). The SAF Code of Ethics reads in part as follows:

Service to society is the cornerstone of any profession. The profession of forestry serves society by fostering stewardship of the world's forests. Because forests provide valuable resources and perform critical ecological functions, they are vital to the well-being of both society and the biosphere.

Members of the Society of American Foresters have a deep and enduring love for the land, and are inspired by the profession's historic traditions, such as Gifford Pinchot's utilitarianism and Aldo Leopold's ecological conscience. In their various roles as practitioners, teachers, researchers, advisers, and administrators, foresters seek to sustain and protect a variety of forest uses and attributes, such as aesthetic values, air and water quality, biodiversity, recreation, timber production, and wildlife habitat.

The purpose of this Code of Ethics is to protect and serve society by inspiring, guiding, and governing members in the conduct of their professional lives. Compliance with the code demonstrates members' respect for the land; their commitment to the long-term management of ecosystems; and ensures just and honorable professional and human relationships, mutual confidence and respect, and competent service to society.

On joining the Society of American Foresters, members assume a special responsibility to the profession and to society by promising to uphold and abide by the following:

Principles and Pledges

1. Foresters have a responsibility to manage land for both current and future generations. We pledge to practice and advocate management that will maintain the long-term capacity of the land to provide

the variety of materials, uses, and values desired by landowners and society.

2. Society must respect forest landowners' rights and correspondingly, landowners have a land stewardship responsibility to society. We pledge to practice and advocate forest management in accordance with landowner objectives and professional standards, and to advise landowners of the consequences of deviating from such standards.

3. Sound science is the foundation of the forestry profession. We pledge to strive for continuous improvement of our methods and our personal knowledge and skills; to perform only those services for which we are qualified; and in the biological, physical, and social sciences to use the most appropriate data, methods, and technology.

4. Public policy related to forests must be based on both scientific principles and societal values. We pledge to use our knowledge and skills to help formulate sound forest policies and laws; to challenge and correct untrue statements about forestry; and to foster dialogue among foresters, other professionals, landowners, and the public regarding forest policies.

5. Honest and open communication, coupled with respect for information given in confidence, is essential to good service. We pledge to always present, to the best of our ability, accurate and complete information; to indicate on whose behalf any public statements are made; to fully disclose and resolve any existing or potential conflicts of interest; and to keep proprietary information confidential unless the appropriate person authorizes its disclosure.

6. Professional and civic behavior must be based on honesty, fairness, good will, and respect for the law. We pledge to conduct ourselves in a civil and dignified manner; to respect the needs, contributions, and viewpoints of others; and to give due credit to others for their methods, ideas, or assistance. (SAF, 2004)

The SAF bylaws also specify processes for the reprimand, censure, and expulsion of members who violate the Code of Ethics.

In addition to the specific principles and pledges offered by these professional associations, outdoor recreation professions should always do a number of obvious but important things, including the following:

- Stay up-to-date on the professional literature of their field, including participating in continuing education opportunities and being certified and accredited where appropriate.

- Accept the obligation to point out mistakes and unethical behavior in a constructive and professional manner.

- Belong to, support, and be actively involved in relevant professional associations, including participating in national and state affiliate activities.

- Always act honestly and ethically, including (at a minimum) complying with all laws and profesional standards, only taking credit where appropriate, and honoring all commitments.

- Always represent the profession and field in positive and professional ways.

- Share professional information.

- Treat visitors professionally and respectfully and make all reasonable efforts to minimize burden on the recreating public while protecting natural resources.

Lastly, we mention that as an outdoor recreation professional you will at times be confronted by members of the leisure profession, by customers, and by other members of the public who disagree with positions you have taken or are about to take. From much such personal experience of the two authors of this text, our suggestion is that you always keep an open mind to be receptive to new ideas and countervailing arguments and positions. In the final analysis, if you still believe you are right and are being professionally responsible, stick by your guns. Be clear in explaining your position and why you hold it. Always remember that agreement is not usually the most important ingredient—*understanding* is! Things often change slowly. Good luck! We wish each of you much personal gratification with your personal achievements and contributions. What you are doing is of great importance.

Conclusions

Outdoor recreation and outdoor recreation management have advanced and changed dramatically during the last few decades. Faced with increased use, new recreation activities and technologies, and new pressures and challenges, outdoor recreation professionals and their many partners have responded. They have worked to protect lands and waters for public outdoor recreation use. They have developed far better understandings of participants' preferences, behavior, and experiences as well as much greater knowledge about the processes affecting the natural resources on which outdoor recreation depends. They have created and refined new science-based systems for

planning, providing, and managing high-quality outdoor recreation opportunities. They have made strides in identifying and minimizing recreation's negative impacts to natural and cultural/historic resources and developed much more effective ways to create collaborative partnerships with the many stakeholders involved in and affected by the provision of outdoor recreation opportunities. As impressive as these and many other advances are, there is, of course, much more to be done if the potential of outdoor recreation is to be fully realized. We hope this text has been a valuable step in that direction.

In this text we attempted to introduce the most important principles and practices related to the field of outdoor recreation. By necessity this has been a broad, interdisciplinary, and sometimes selective and cursory treatment. Recall that we covered an extremely large number of topics from multiple perspectives. In Part 1, Foundations and Background, we introduced

- key concepts
- benefits of leisure and its roles in society
- historical context
- social and technological forces affecting outdoor recreation

In Part 2, Outdoor Recreation Resources and Providers of Outdoor Recreation Opportunities, we discussed

- land and water resources for outdoor recreation
- public sector providers
- private sector providers
- nonprofit sector providers
- partnerships among outdoor recreation providers
- outdoor recreation opportunities from selected countries around the world

And in Part 3, Managing Outdoor Recreation Opportunities, we addressed

- policy development, management, administration, and planning
- evolution of science-based management of outdoor recreation resources
- the beneficial outcomes approach to leisure (BOAL)
- negative impacts of recreation use
- gathering data for managing outdoor recreation
- influencing and managing visitor behavior
- collaborative planning and management (CPM)
- management of special outdoor recreation resources: wilderness and trails

- economics of outdoor recreation
- the future of outdoor recreation

This has been a great deal of ground to cover. In this final section we would like to offer a few overall conclusions. They are offered as guides to people beginning or considering careers as outdoor recreation professionals—things to keep in mind while moving ahead in this field.

Outdoor recreation is tremendously beneficial and important. Outdoor recreation participation and the natural places where it occurs are tremendously important for individuals, societies, cultures, economies, and the environment. The total benefits of recreation, when considered broadly, equal or exceed the benefits of any other social service. Therefore, the outdoor recreation profession is an important and valuable one, and one worthy of the dedication and hard work of all involved. This will become more obvious as we carry out our responsibilities, and in so doing, more successfully "reposition the image" of recreation in general and outdoor recreation in particular.

Outdoor recreation depends on natural environments. Outdoor recreation involves experiences that result from activities that occur in and depend on the natural environment. As such, outdoor recreation and its management exist where people and natural resources come together. Regardless of whether a particular agency or professional calls it outdoor recreation, natural resources recreation, wildland recreation, nature-based tourism, ecotourism, or some other related term, *if there are no natural areas available with public access, there is no outdoor recreation.* Every generation inherits a finite outdoor recreation estate. As world populations continue to grow and expand into this estate, its area shrinks and the pressures on what remains intensify. Vision, determination, creativity and professionalism will be needed if we are to enhance or even preserve our outdoor recreation estate. "Conservationists have to win again and again and again," says former Sierra Club President David Brower (McPhee, 1971, p. 85). It is worth the ongoing effort.

Effective outdoor recreation management requires a focus on experiences and other benefits. Outdoor recreation planning and management should always be focused on generating benefits, including satisfying outdoor recreation experiences. Outdoor recreation professionals can and should strive to maximize recreation benefits by providing a broad spectrum of outdoor recreation opportunities as advocated in planning frameworks like the recreation opportunity spectrum (ROS) and by using science-based systems such as the beneficial outcomes approach to leisure (BOAL). This focus on generating benefits is far different from a traditional commodity focus, however. Outdoor recreation professionals carefully consider the needs for a very broad array of benefits, including difficult to quantify benefits like those that result from aesthetic appreciation, contact with nature, and spiritual development. They develop an understanding of the context of the lands and waters they manage, and they work with many other providers and publics to assure an appropriate mix of benefits. Perhaps most importantly, professionals recognize that the users themselves generate many of the benefits by taking advantage of the recreation opportunities provided by managers.

Effective outdoor recreation management requires involvement of stakeholders and other providers. The stakeholders of outdoor recreation—recreation users, customers, visitors, neighboring landowners, the general public, politicians, as well as other associated providers—will

Outdoor recreation will always depend on high-quality natural resources of many types.

To be most effective, outdoor recreation managers must focus on benefits. This includes providing opportunities for high-quality visitor experiences.

either be an outdoor recreation professional's biggest allies or biggest challenges. Which it will be depends, in many respects, on the recreation professional's perspective and approach. Public support can make the difference between success and failure for policies, programs, and the health of natural resources. The public is the political power base on which agency budgets, and ultimately, their effectiveness depends. Gaining stakeholder support, cooperation, and assistance requires involving the public constructively. This in turn depends on understanding their needs, interacting with them in many ways and places, and forming long-term constructive partnerships with them. Resource management, and therefore outdoor recreation management, is inherently political. This is not bad—just the environment in which all local, regional, national, and international resource decisions are made. Effective outdoor recreation professionals must be at least as astute and skilled at working in the human environment as they are in working in the natural resource environment.

The future of outdoor recreation depends on everyone. As outdoor recreation professionals we have a tremendous opportunity for good and the responsibility that goes hand-in-hand with that opportunity. Each outdoor recreation professional can make a profound positive difference and has the responsibility to do his or her very best to do so. The opportunity and responsibility is not limited to just outdoor recreation professionals, however. Everyone reading this text should understand that public lands and the health of the environment are the responsibility of everyone. Although not all readers will become outdoor recreation professionals, all are citizens and voters, and the vast majority will be outdoor recreationists. Each of us has a responsibility to get involved and stay involved to protect natural areas, provide high-quality outdoor recreation opportunities, and to use them responsibly. This requires professionalism, dedication, high standards, and personal integrity.

We agree with the Benton MacKaye admonition to preserve and cherish outdoor recreation resources that introduced this chapter, and believe it applies to all of us. We should leave the outdoor recreation estate in the United States and every other nation to our children and their children just as we would like to find it ourselves— healthy, sustainable, large, diverse, convenient, accessible, and offering a wide variety of high-quality opportunities. This will take foresight, creativity, courage, sacrifice, and professional commitment. It is a challenge well worth our effort and one to which all outdoor recreation professionals should dedicate themselves. Working together we can make this happen. It is our hope that this text has helped lay the necessary foundation to do so effectively. The rest is up to you.

Can we, as outdoor recreation professionals, create desirable, even *ideal* conditions where people have the opportunity to enhance their lives and, perhaps, our world? That is, after all, an essential part of what true leisure really is. We are optimistic about the future of outdoor recreation, and believe we can attain this ideal. We also believe that our field will play an increasingly important role in this regard in the decades ahead. As we stated from the outset, the field of outdoor recreation is important. We challenge you to make an important positive contribution for and through outdoor recreation and have some fun along the way. In fact, set out to save the world. If we all try that together, we just might pull it off!

Literature Cited

Abrams, M. (2004). *Wingman: Get ready to fly at 186 mph.* Retrieved July 7, 2004, from http://www.wired.com/wired/archive/11.09/wing.html

Anderson, L. (2002). *Benton MacKaye: Conservationist, planner, and creator of the Appalachian Trail* (p. 53). Baltimore, MD: Johns Hopkins University Press.

Barry, D. (2001, August 24). Sunscreen, shades, towel and cell phone? *Raleigh News and Observer*, E8.

Blaikie, D. (2004). *What is an ultramarathon?* Retrieved August 5, 2004, from http://www.ultrunr.com/what_is.html

Bleiberg, L. (2001, September 30). Time travel? Why not? *Raleigh News and Observer*, H8.

Discover Life In America. (2004). *About Discover Life In America, Inc. and the All Taxa Biodiversity Inventory.* Retrieved July 7, 2004, from http://www.dlia.org/dlia/about_dlia.html

Earthboard. (2004). *Earthboard: Ride the earth.* Retrieved August 5, 2004, from http://www.earthboards.com

ESPN. (2004). *Great outdoor games?* Retrieved August 5, 2004, from http://espn.go.com/gog04/s/event_launch_pg.html

Fontaine, C. (2001, August 27). English park bench a refuge for the tired, or the wired. *Raleigh News and Observer*, H1.

FreeSky. (2004). *Skyray.* Retrieved July 7, 2004, from http://www.freesky.de/SKYRAY.html

The Future Is Still Smart. (2004, June 26). *The Economist, 371*(8381), 63–64.

Gentile, G. (2002, July 1). Scanning the future. *Raleigh News and Observer*, C1–C3.

geocaching.com (2004a). *Frequently asked questions about geocaching.* Retrieved July 7, 2004, from http://www.geocaching.com/faq

geocaching.com (2004b). *About geocaching.* Retrieved July 7, 2004, from http://www.geocaching.com/about

The Harder Hard Sell. (2004, June 26). *The Economist, 371*(8381), 69–71.

Juarez, V. (2004, July 19). Rocking, rolling and roaring: A hot new sport pushes gravity to the limit. *Newsweek, 144*(3), 53.

Krim, J. (2004, August 6). Passports to include ID chips. *Raleigh News and Observer*, A8.

Lyon, J. and Burcham, M. (1998, February). *Tracking elk hunters with the global positioning system* (Research Paper RMRS-RP-3). Fort Collins, CO: USDA Forest Service, Rocky Mountain Research Station.

McPhee, J. (1971). *Encounters with the archdruid*. New York, NY: Farrar, Straus and Giroux.

Microsoft. (2004). *Microsoft to wire UK park bench for Web surfing*. Retrieved July 7, 2004, from http://www.wininsider.com/news/?61

National Audubon Society. (2004). *Christmas bird count homepage*. Retrieved July 7, 2004, from http://www.audubon.org/bird/cbc/index.html

National Recreation and Park Association. (2004). *NRPA professional code of ethics*. Retrieved August 3, 2004, from http://www.nrpa.org/content/default.aspx?documentId=493

No Hiding Place. (2003, January 25). A survey of the Internet society. *The Economist*, 5–11. Retrieved from http://www.economist.com

Project FeederWatch. (2004). *What is Project Feeder-Watch?* Retrieved July 7, 2004, from http://www.birds.cornell.edu/pfw/overview/whatispfw.htm

Sea of Dreams. (2004, May 1). *The Economist, 371*(8373), 81–82.

Smith, S. (2004, July 29). Terra Wind: At home on land and in water. *Raleigh News and Observer*, G1–G2.

Society of American Foresters. (2004). *SAF code of ethics*. Retrieved August 3, 2004, from http://www.safnet.org/who/codeofethics.cfm

Subaru Primal Quest. (2004). *Adventure racing 101: Learn the history of the sport*. Retrieved July 7, 2004, from http://www.subaruprimalquest.com/race2004_prerace/about/racing101.cfm

Tolme, P. (2004, July 19,). All-night shifts. *Newsweek, 144*(3), 60.

Appendix A
Domains, Scales, and Scale Items for the Recreation Experience Preference (REP) Scales

What Do the Scales Measure?

The recreation experience preference (REP) scales were developed to define and to measure the many types of recreation experiences that can be remembered by a person as satisfying or dissatisfying after that person has participated in a specific recreation activity in a particular recreation setting. As such, the REP scales focus on the salient experiences—those that can be recalled most readily—because they are foremost in one's mind several months after an on-site engagement, when the REP scales are administered. By focusing on the on-site engagement, the REP scales do not consider experiences realized from planning for the engagement, traveling to the engagement, or returning from the engagement.

The scientists who developed the scales recognize that many approaches to defining and quantifying recreation experiences exist, so they do not propose the REP scales are the only approach that should be used. However, the REP scales were refined and tested over a period of 13 years to assure they have acceptable psychometric (i.e., psychological measuring) properties, such as reasonably good validity and reliability. The scales have been applied widely in the United States and several other countries.

The scales provide the most reliable and accurate information if they are not administered on-site to first-time participants in the recreation activity being studied. This is true because first-time users have no previous experiences with the recreation activity being studied, so they cannot accurately express preferences for experiences regarding that activity. However, it is acceptable to mail such first-time users a questionnaire containing the REP scales after they return home. It is also advisable to administer the scales at least several months after participation has occurred to control for recency and latency effects.

Description of How the REP Scales Are Presented

This appendix lists the REP scales, the scale items that comprise each scale, and the domains into which the scales were grouped empirically. The organization of the scales is first explained, and then the scales are presented.

Scales

Each REP scale identifies and measures a specific desired and/or realized recreation experience (e.g., Reinforcing Self-Image, Family Togetherness). Each scale listed is represented by a number, and they are organized into domains.

Scale Items

The REP scales are comprised of two or more scale items. They are designated by small letters. The wording of each scale item attempts to capture the theme of its REP scale (e.g., "to do something the family could do together" scale item for Family Togetherness). Several scale items are needed for each scale to assure the specific recreation experience denoted by each REP scale, and not some other experience, is being captured and measured with reasonable validity and reliability. The scale items listed for each REP scale were selected for each REP scale by a research process that involved conducting many surveys of recreationists and analyzing the responses to each survey. The purpose of these many studies was to develop and refine the REP scales so that each REP scale was comprised of scale items that showed acceptable psychometric properties, such as interitem correlations of 0.4 or higher, content and other types of validity, and reliability.

Core Scale Items

Most of the REP scales are comprised of more than two scale items, which is necessary for tests that assure each scale reflects desirable psychometric properties. Inclusion of all of those scale items in a survey instrument, such as a questionnaire, would greatly increase the length of the instrument. Several studies of large numbers of recreationists showed that mean scores and standard deviations to two-core-item REP scales differed very little, to not at all, from means and standard deviations computed from the same data when the complete list of scale items for each REP scale were used. This lack of differences held even when these comparative tests were made across many "cuts" of the data by social, economic, and demographic variables, such as age, gender, different recreation activities, and amount of past participation in those activities. Therefore, to reduce the length of the survey instrument and the amount of data processing needed, a person can use the two core-item REP scales instead of all the scale items. The two core (or best) items for each REP scale are designated by asterisks.

Domains

Although each REP scale represents a separate recreation experience (or *psychological construct*), some of the REP scales are less distinct psychometrically than others. The scales related to each other psychometrically (i.e., relate to the same experimental theme or construct) and grouped together empirically (i.e., intercorrelate) are grouped together into *domains*. Domains are indicated by capital letters. The title of each domain captures the general theme of the REP scales that comprise it. For example, the seven REP scales that comprise Domain A (**ACHIEVEMENT/ STIMULATION**) all relate to recreation experiences involving achievement, and the four REP scales in Domain O (**ESCAPE PERSONAL/SOCIAL PRESSURES**) relate to that theme. It should be noticed that some domains contain only one REP Scale, and the name of the domain is the same as that for that one scale. These one-scale domains exist because the psychological construct, or recreation experiences, denoted by the name of the domain and scale did not relate psychometrically to other scales. In other words, that scale is statistically independent of the other REP scales. Because REP scales within a particular domain are intercorrelated statistically, a person can select a core scale item from each scale and make a "domain scale" if interests are in general/macro experiences instead of the more specific/micro experiences denoted by each separate REP scale.

A: ACHIEVEMENT/STIMULATION

1. Reinforcing Self-Image
* a. To gain a sense of self-confidence.
* b. To develop a sense of self-pride.
  c. To increase your feelings of self-worth.
  d. To show yourself you could do it.
  e. To help you feel like a better person.
  f. To increase your feelings of self-importance.
  g. To feel like a better person for doing it.
  h. To test the extent to which I can do it.

2. Social Recognition
* a. To have others think highly of you for doing it.
* b. To show others you can do it.
  c. To have others recognize and admire you for doing it.
  d. To have others see you do things you are good at.
  e. To do something that impresses others.
  f. To make a good impression on others.
  g. To do something impressive.
  h. To be recognized for doing it.
  i. To receive compliments on my skills and abilities.
  j. To be seen by others doing it.

3. Skill Development
* a. To become better at it.
* b. To develop your skills and abilities.
  c. To improve your skills.
  d. To be challenged.
  e. To feel like I have achieved something when through.
  f. To remind myself that I have the skills to do it.
  g. To try to achieve a high standard in it.
  h. To see if I could do it.

4. Competence Testing
* a. To test your abilities.
* b. To learn what you are capable of.

5. Excitement
* a. To have thrills.
* b. To experience excitement.
  c. To experience a lot of action.
  d. To have a stimulating and exciting experience.
  e. To experience the fast paced nature of things.
  f. To feel exhilaration.
  g. To get all charged up.
  h. To experience the exciting events that always happen here.
  i. To cause things to happen.

6. Endurance
* a. To test your endurance.
* b. To rely on your wits and skills.
  c. To gain a sense of accomplishment.

7. Telling Others (i.e., status)
* a. To tell others about the trip.
* b. To have others know that you have been there.

B: AUTONOMY/LEADERSHIP

1. Independence
* a. To feel my independence.
* b. To be on my own.

2. Autonomy
* a. To be my own boss.
* b. To be free to make your own choices.
  c. To be obligated to no one.
  d. To do things your own way.
  e. To think for myself.
  f. To be at a place where I can make my own decisions.

3. Control Power
* a. To control things.
* b. To be in control of things that happen.
  c. To have a chance to have control over things.
  d. To be more in control here.
  e. To be in charge of what's happening.
  f. To have a chance to feel in charge of what's happening.
  g. To be in command of a situation.
  h. To put yourself in a position of power of authority.
  i. To manipulate things.

C: RISK TAKING

1. Risk Taking
* a. To take risks.
* b. To chance dangerous situations.
  c. To experience the uncertainty of not knowing what will happen.
  d. To experience the risks involved.

D: EQUIPMENT

1. Equipment
* a. To use your equipment.
* b. To talk to others about (your/our) equipment.
  c. To test and use your equipment.
  d. To compare my equipment with others.

E: FAMILY TOGETHERNESS

1. Family Togetherness
* a. To do something with your family.
* b. To bring your family closer together.
  c. To do something the family could do together.
  d. To get the family together more.
  e. To realize a good experience for the family.
  f. To do what my children wanted me to.
  g. To do something the entire family would like.
  h. To get the family together for awhile.
  i. To do something so the family could spend more time together.
  j. To do something my spouse or associate wanted me to.

F: SIMILAR PEOPLE

1. Being With Friends
* a. To be with members of (your/our) group.
* b. To be with friends.
  c. To do things with your companions.
  d. To enjoy the company of people who came with me.

2. Being With Similar People
* a. To be with (others/people) who enjoy the same things you do.
* b. To be with people having similar values.
  c. To be with people who have similar interests.
  d. To be with people who are enjoying themselves.

G: NEW PEOPLE

1. Meeting New People
* a. To talk to new and varied people.
* b. To meet other people in the area.
  c. To meet new people.
  d. To meet other people.
  e. To build friendships with new people.
  f. To see new faces.

2. Observing Other People
* a. To be with and observe other people using the area.
* b. To observe other people in the area.
  c. To observe the other people.

H: LEARNING

1. General Learning
* a. To develop (your/my) knowledge of things (here/there).
* b. To learn more about things (here/there).
  c. To find out about things here.
  d. To understand things here better.

2. Exploration
* a. To experience new and different things.
* b. To discover something new.
  c. To find out about things.
  d. To explore the area.
  e. To explore things.
  f. To see new and different things.
  g. To experience the unknown.
  h. To experience the sense of discovery involved.

3. Geography of Area
* a. To get to know the lay of the land.
* b. To learn about the topography of the land.

4. Learn About Nature
* a. To study nature.
* b. To learn more about nature.
   c. To learn more about natural settings.
   d. To gain a better appreciation of nature.

I: ENJOY NATURE

1. Scenery
* a. To view the scenery.
* b. To view the scenic beauty.
   c. To enjoy the scenery.
   d. To observe the scenic beauty.
   e. To take in the scenic beauty.
   f. To look at the pretty view.
   g. To observe the scenic beauty.

2. General Nature Experience
* a. To be close to nature.
* b. To enjoy the smells and sounds of nature.
   c. To take in the natural surroundings.
   d. To be in a natural setting.
   e. To be where things are natural.
   f. To obtain a feeling of harmony with nature.

J: INTROSPECTION

1. Spiritual
* a. To develop personal, spiritual values.
* b. To grow and develop spiritually.
   c. To reflect on personal religious values.
   d. To reflect on your religious or other spiritual values.
   e. To be in closer touch with higher spiritual values.
   f. To get a greater sense of spiritual being.

2. Introspection
* a. To think about your personal values.
* b. To think about who you are.
   c. To help you understand better what your life is all about.
   d. To learn about yourself.
   e. To learn more about yourself.
   f. To rebuild the world in my mind.
   g. To think about how I would like the world to be.
   h. To think new thoughts.
   i. To paint things in my mind like an artist.

K: CREATIVITY

1. Creativity
* a. To be creative.
* b. To do something creative such as sketch, paint, take photographs.
   c. To put some thoughts or ideas together.
   d. To create something new or different.
   e. To gain a new perspective on life.

L: NOSTALGIA

1. Nostalgia
* a. To think about good times you've had in the past.
* b. To bring back pleasant memories.
   c. To reflect on past memories.
   d. To recall past satisfactions.
   e. To gain an experience I can look back on.

M: PHYSICAL FITNESS

1. Exercise/Physical Fitness
* a. To get exercise.
* b. To keep physically fit.
   c. To improve (my/your) physical health.
   d. To help keep you in shape physically.
   e. To feel good after being physically active.
   f. To tone up my muscles.

N: PHYSICAL REST

1. Physical Rest
* a. To relax physically.
* b. To rest physically.
   c. To take it easy physically.
   d. To give my body a rest.

O: ESCAPE PERSONAL/SOCIAL PRESSURES

1. Tension Release
* a. To help get rid of some clutched-up feelings.
* b. To help release or reduce some built-up tensions.
   c. To help reduce some frustrations (I/you) have been feeling.
   d. To release or reduce tension.
   e. To help get rid of some anxieties.
   f. To help get rid of some up-tight feeling.

2. Slow Down Mentally
* a. To have your mind move at a slower pace.
* b. To give your mind a rest.
   c. To recover from (my/your) usual hectic pace.
   d. To have your mind slow down for a while.
   e. To have a break from being too busy mentally.

3. Escape Role Overloads
* a. To get away from the usual demands of life.
* b. To avoid everyday responsibilities for awhile.
   c. To reduce the feeling of having too many things to do.
   d. To get away from some of the expectations people have of me back home.
   e. To rest awhile from the feeling of being overloaded at home or work.
   f. To get away from the demands of other people.
   g. To feel less tied down for awhile.

4. Escape Daily Routine
* a. To have a change from your daily routine.
* b. To have a change from everyday life.
  c. To do something different from what (I/you) do back home.
  d. To have a change of pace from everyday life.
  e. To add some variety to my daily routine.
  f. To have a change from your everyday self.

P: ESCAPE PHYSICAL PRESSURE

1. Tranquility
* a. To experience tranquility.
* b. To experience solitude.
  c. To experience the peace and calm.
  d. To experience surroundings that are soothing.
  e. To experience the calming and healing setting.
  f. To sense a feeling of balance in things around me.
  g. To enjoy the quietness and beauty.
  h. To be where it is quiet.

2. Privacy
* a. To feel isolated.
* b. To be alone.
  c. To get away from other people.
  d. To have more privacy than you have back home.

3. Escape Crowds
* a. To be away from crowds of people.
* b. To experience more elbow room.
  c. To get away from crowded situations for awhile.
  d. To experience the open space.
  e. To (seek/enjoy) distant or unobstructed views.
  f. To get away from civilization for awhile.
  g. I thought there would be less confusion here.

4. Escape Physical Stressors
* a. To get away from the clatter and racket back home.
* b. To get away from the noise back home.
  c. To get away from the ugly scenes back home.
  d. To get away from the bright lights back home for awhile.
  e. To escape the pollution back home for awhile.
  f. To get away from other people.

Q: SOCIAL SECURITY

1. Social Security
* a. To be near considerate people.
* b. To be with respectful people.
  c. To be with considerate people.
  d. To be with fairly honest people.
  e. To be where things are fairly safe.
  f. To be with people who are nice to each other.

R: ESCAPE FAMILY

1. Escaping Family
* a. To be away from the family for awhile.
* b. To escape the family temporarily.
  c. To be without the family for awhile.

S: TEACHING-LEADING OTHERS

1. Teaching/Sharing Skills (Sharing Knowledge/ Directing Others)
* a. To teach your outdoor skills to others.
* b. To share what you have learned with others.
  c. To share your skill and knowledge with others.
  d. To help others learn about things here.
  e. To teach others about things here.

2. Leading Others (Sharing Knowledge/Directing Others)
* a. To help direct the activities of others.
* b. To lead other people.
  c. To show others what to do.

T. RISK REDUCTION

1. Risk Moderation
* a. To be near others who could help if you need them.
* b. To know others are nearby.

2. Risk Avoidance
* a. To be sure of what will happen to you.
* b. To avoid the unexpected.

U. TEMPERATURE

1. Temperature
* a. To get away from the heat.
* b. To experience a nicer temperature.
  c. To have more agreeable temperature.
  d. To be where it is cooler.

Past applications of the scales have used different varieties of Likert-like response formats to measure either the importance (from none to great) of realizing the selected experience (inherent to each scale item) as a reason for engaging in the specific recreation activity in the setting studied, or how much realization of each selected experience (i.e., scale item) either added to or detracted from (with a neutral "neither added to or detracted from") the level of satisfaction the subject received when he or she engaged in the specific activity and setting studied. It is important to study experiences for the specific activities engaged in at specific settings and not for activities (e.g., camping) and settings (e.g., rivers) in general. Mean scores are then computed across the scale items for each scale. Most past applications of the scale involved collecting information on-site about the types of recreation activities selected and settings being used.

Then, with subjects' consent, follow-up questionnaires were mailed to them later. Response rates for this type of application have generally been high.

Several additional recreation experiences have been identified since the REP scales were first developed, including perceived freedom, exhilaration, and being in an environment largely unmodified by humans. So, although the REP scales were designed to comprehensively include most experience preferences related to recreational engagements, these and perhaps other more recently identified experiences might also be considered.

Appendix B
Providers of Outdoor Recreation Opportunities

This compilation provides contact information for selected outdoor recreation providers. While not possible to provide a comprehensive directory of all recreation providers, we offer the following as a convenient source of contact information for major providers and a sampling from the breadth of other providers. The providers listed are organized by sector.

Public Sector

The public sector is comprised of tax-supported government agencies at all levels. These agencies manage land for myriad purposes, but ultimately for the benefit of the citizens each particular public sector agency serves. Examples of selected public sector outdoor recreation resource providers and their contact information follow.

U.S. Federal Agencies

U.S. Army Corps of Engineers (USACE)
- 🖃 HQ, U.S. Army Corps of Engineers
  441 G Street NW
  Washington, DC 20314-1000
- ☏ 202-761-0011
- ❏ http://www.usace.army.mil

Bureau of Indian Affairs (BIA)
- 🖃 Bureau of Indian Affairs
  Office of Public Affairs
  1849 C Street NW MS-3318-MIB
  Washington, DC 20240
- ☏ 202-208-3710 (general information)
  202-208-3711 (tribal leaders directory)
- ❏ http://www.doi.gov/bureau-indian-affairs.html

Bureau of Land Management (BLM)
- 🖃 Bureau of Land Management
  Office of Public Affairs
  1849 C Street, Room 406-LS
  Washington, DC 20240
- ☏ 202-452-5125
- ✆ 202-452-5124
- ❏ http://www.blm.gov/nhp/index.htm

Bureau of Reclamation (BOR)
- 🖃 Bureau of Reclamation
  1849 C Street NW
  Washington, DC 20240-0001
- ☏ 202-513-0501
- ✆ 202-513-0315
- ❏ http://www.usbr.gov

Federal Highway Administration (FHWA)
- 🖃 Federal Highway Administration
  400 Seventh Street, SW
  Washington, DC 20590
- ☏ 202-366-0660 (Office of Public Affairs)
- ❏ execsecretariat.fhwa@fhwa.dot.gov
  http://www.fhwa.dot.gov

National Park Service (NPS)
- 🖃 National Park Service
  1849 C Street NW
  Washington, DC 20240
- ☏ 202-208-6843
- ❏ http://www.nps.gov

USDA Forest Service (USFS)
- 🖃 USDA Forest Service
  1400 Independence Avenue, SW
  Washington, DC 20250-0003
- ☏ 202-205-8333
- ❏ webmaster@fs.fed.us
  http://www.fs.fed.us

U.S. Fish and Wildlife Service (USFWS)
- 🖃 U.S. Fish and Wildlife Service
  Public Affairs Office
  1849 C Street NW Room 3359
  Washington, DC 20240
- ☏ 800-344-WILD
- ❏ http://www.fws.gov

🖃 Mailing address	☏ Phone
✆ Fax	❏ E-mail/Website address

Federal Employment Opportunities in the Public Sector

The most comprehensive source of information on employment opportunities with federal agencies in the United States is USAJOBS maintained by the U.S. Office of Personnel Management (http://www.usajobs.opm.gov).

U.S. State Agencies

All 50 states provide extensive outdoor recreation opportunities, typically through divisions of parks, forestry, wildlife, and related units. Links to each of the state park agencies can be accessed through the nonprofit National Association of State Park Directors (NASPD), which can be contacted as noted next.

National Association of State Park Directors (NASPD)

◻ NASPD@nc.rr.com
http://naspd.indstate.edu/index.html
http://naspd.indstate.edu/stateparks.html (Direct link to state park agencies)

U.S. Regional Agencies

East Bay Regional Parks District

▣ East Bay Regional Parks District
2950 Peralta Oaks Court
P.O. Box 5381
Oakland, CA 94605-0381
℩ 510-562-PARK
◻ http://www.ebparks.org

Northern Virginia Regional Park Authority

▣ Northern Virginia Regional Park Authority
5400 Ox Road
Fairfax Station, VA 22039
℩ 703-352-5900 TDD: 703-352-3165
℘ 703-273-0905
◻ Info@NVRPA.org
http://www.nvrpa.org

U.S. Municipal Agencies

Boston Department of Parks and Recreation

▣ Boston Department of Parks and Recreation
1010 Massachusetts Avenue, 3rd Floor
Boston, MA 02118
℩ 617-635-4505
℘ 617-635-3173
◻ parks@ci.boston.ma.us
http://www.cityofboston.gov/parks

Cleveland Metro Parks

▣ Cleveland Metro Parks
4101 Fulton Parkway
Cleveland, OH 44144
℩ 216-351-6300 TTY: 216-351-0808
℘ 216-635-3286
◻ http://www.clemetparks.com

Denver Parks and Recreation Department

▣ Denver Parks and Recreation Department
201 West Colfax Avenue, Department 601
Denver, Colorado 80202
℩ 720-913-0696
℘ 720-913-0791
◻ http://www.denvergov.org/Parks_Recreation/

Seattle Department of Parks and Recreation

▣ Seattle Department of Parks and Recreation
100 Dexter Avenue N
Seattle, WA 98109
℩ 206-684-4075
◻ parksinfo@seattle.gov
http://www.cityofseattle.net/parks/

Private Sector

From the purely economic perspective, the private sector is comprised of business enterprises and is sometimes referred to as the for-profit sector. Private sector organizations hold and manage land for many reasons, one of which is generating a profit for their owners and investors. Most outfitters, concessionaires, ecotourism providers, ski areas, guest ("dude") ranches, equipment rental entrepreneurs, ranching/farm vacation operations, and so forth, operate as private sector enterprises. Note that some of the following examples are actually nonprofit associations that represent groups of private sector providers.

America Outdoors

America Outdoors is a national trade association that represents professional companies that provide a wide range of outdoor recreation services and outdoor equipment.

- ✉ America Outdoors
  P.O. Box 10847
  Knoxville, TN 37939
- ☎ 865-558-3595
- 📠 865-558-3598
- 💻 infoaccount@americaoutdoors.org
  http://www.americaoutdoors.org

American Recreation Coalition (ARC)

ARC is a national coalition of prominent private sector recreation companies and recreation-related associations.

- ✉ American Recreation Coalition
  1225 New York Avenue NW
  Suite 450
  Washington, DC 20005-6405
- ☎ 202-682-9530
- 💻 arc@funoutdoors.com
  http://www.funoutdoors.com

Kampgrounds of America (KOA)

- ✉ Kampgrounds of America Corporate Offices
  P.O. Box 30558
  Billings, MT 59114-0558
- ☎ 406-248-7444
- 💻 http://www.koakampgrounds.com

Outdoor Industry Association (OIA)

OIA provides services to private sector manufacturers, distributors, suppliers, sales representatives and retailers involved in various ways in outdoor recreation.

- ✉ Outdoor Industry Association
  4909 Pearl East Circle, Suite 200
  Boulder, CO 80301
- ☎ 303-444-3353
- 📠 303-444-3284
- 💻 info@outdoorindustry.org
  http://www.outdoorindustry.org

Professional Trailbuilders Association (PTBA)

The Professional Trailbuilders Association (PTBA) is a professional association of trail specialists, professional trail contractors, designers, and consultants in North America.

- ✉ Northwest Trails, Inc.
  705 Chuckanut Drive North, P.O. Box 4323
  Bellingham, WA 98227
- ☎ 360-671-1982
- 📠 360-647-1968
- 💻 members@trailbuilders.org
  http://www.trailbuilders.org

Nonprofit Sector Organizations

The nonprofit sector is made up of nongovernmental organizations (known simply as NGOs in much of the world). The nonprofit sector is sometimes called the independent, quasi-public, or charitable sector by NGOs in the United States. Following are examples of the large number of nonprofit organizations that are involved in providing outdoor recreation opportunities.

The Access Fund

- ✉ The Access Fund
  P.O. Box 17010
  Boulder, CO 80308
- ☎ 303-545-6772
- 📠 303-545-6774
- 💻 john@accessfund.org (webmaster)
  http://www.accessfund.org/index.html

American Camping Association

- ✉ American Camping Association
  5000 State Road 67 North
  Martinsville, IN 46151
- ☎ 765-342-8456
- 💻 http://www.acacamps.org

American Hiking Society

- ✉ American Hiking Society
  1422 Fenwick Lane
  Silver Spring, MD 20910
- ☎ 301-565-6704
- 📠 301-565-6714
- 💻 http://www.americanhiking.org

Appalachian Mountain Club

- ✉ AMC Main Office
  5 Joy Street
  Boston, MA 02108
- ☎ 617-523-0636
- 📠 617-523-0722
- 💻 information@outdoors.org
  http://www.outdoors.org

Appalachian Trail Conference

▣ Appalachian Trail Conference
799 Washington Street, P.O. Box 807
Harpers Ferry, WV 25425-0807

✆ 304-535-6331

℡ 304-535-2667

▢ http://www.appalachiantrail.org

The Conservation Fund

▣ The Conservation Fund
1800 North Kent Street, Suite 1120
Arlington, VA 22209-2156

✆ 703-525-6300

℡ 703-525-4610

▢ postmaster@conservationfund.org
http://www.conservationfund.org

The Good Sam Club

▣ The Good Sam Club
P.O. Box 6888
Englewood, CO 80155-6888

✆ 1-800-234-345

▢ info@goodsamclub.com
http://www.goodsamclub.com

Land Trust Alliance

▣ Land Trust Alliance
1331 H Street NW, Suite 400
Washington, DC 20005-4734

✆ 202-638-4725

℡ 202-638-4730

▢ lta@lta.org
http://www.lta.org/index.shtml

The Nature Conservancy

▣ The Nature Conservancy
4245 North Fairfax Drive, Suite 100
Arlington, VA 22203-1606

✆ 703-841-5300

▢ comment@tnc.org
http://www.nature.org

Rails-to-Trails Conservancy

▣ Rails-to-Trails Conservancy
1100 17th Street, 10th Floor NW
Washington, DC 20036

✆ 202-331-9696

▢ railtrails@railtrails.org
http://www.railtrails.org

Student Conservation Association

▣ Student Conservation Association
689 River Road, P.O. Box 550
Charlestown, NH 03603-0550

✆ 603-543-1700

▢ http://www.sca-inc.org

Trust for Public Lands

▣ TPL National Office
116 New Montgomery Street, 4th Floor
San Francisco, CA 94105

✆ 415-495-4014

℡ 415-495-4103

▢ info@tpl.org
http://www.tpl.org

Selected International Providers and Information Sources

Conservation Volunteers (Australia)

▣ See website to obtain the mailing address for the office you would like to contact.

✆ +61 (3) 5333 1483

▢ info@conservationvolunteers.com.au
http://www.conservationvolunteers.com.au

Costa Rica Conservation Trust

▣ Costa Rica Conservation Trust
3528 17th Street
San Francisco, CA 94110

✆ 415-215-4933

℡ 415-552-5587

▢ contact@conservecostarica.org
http://www.conservecostarica.org

Department of Conservation (New Zealand)

▣ Department of Conservation
Head Office
P.O. Box 10420
Wellington, New Zealand

✆ 64 (4) 471 0726

℡ 64 (4) 471 1082 (8001)

▢ http://www.doc.govt.nz

Parks Canada

▣ Parks Canada National Office
25 Eddy Street
Gatineau, Quebec, Canada
K1A 0M5

✆ 888-773-8888

▢ information@pc.gc.ca
http://www.pc.gc.ca

World Conservation Monitoring Centre

▣ UNEP World Conservation Monitoring Centre
219 Huntingdon Road
Cambridge CB3 0DL, United Kingdom

✆ +44 (0)1223 277314

℡ +44 (0)1223 277136

▢ info@unep-wcmc.org
http://www.unep-wcmc.org

World Conservation Union (IUCN)

▪ IUCN—The World Conservation Union Headquarters
Rue Mauverney 28
Gland
1196
Switzerland
☏ +41 (22) 999-0000
✆ +41 (22) 999-0002
▢ mail@iucn.org
http://www.iucn.org

World Wildlife Fund

▪ WWF—United States
1250 24th Street NW
Washington, DC 20037-1175
United States of America
☏ 202-293-9211
✆ 202-293-4800
▢ http://www.panda.org

Glossary

This glossary defines words and concepts commonly used by outdoor recreation professionals. Some relate specifically to outdoor recreation; however, most have broader applications. This glossary is followed by a list of acronyms common to outdoor recreation.

Activity Occasion A measure of recreation use equal to a single person participating in one recreation activity for any part of one day. For example, one visitor participating in whitewater rafting, hiking, and picnicking during a one-day trip to a popular river would be counted as three activity occasions. (contrast with *recreation visit*)

Administration The organizational process concerned with those activities necessary for policy makers, managers, and planners to operate effectively, efficiently, responsibly, and legally. (see also *policy* and *management*)

Adventure Recreation Activities such as mountaineering, whitewater kayaking and rafting, spelunking, ropes courses, ski diving, SCUBA diving, etc. Adventure recreation is typically part of outdoor recreation as defined here.

Anticipation A phase of the outdoor recreation experience that includes planning and preparing for the engagement as well as looking forward to it. It may be very short and spontaneous or long and involved.

Associated Outdoor Recreation Providers The many partners that assist in providing outdoor recreation opportunities or who influence the amount, type, and quality of related goods and services. These partners manufacture, sell, or otherwise produce or provide the equipment, facilities, services, programming, expertise, information, etc., needed for outdoor recreation experiences to occur. (see also *collaborative style of planning and management*)

Backcountry A primitive, remote, or wilderness area reached primarily by hiking, boating, or horseback (based on National Park Service, 2002).

Beneficial Outcomes Approach to Leisure (BOAL) An approach to leisure that focuses on the beneficial and the negative outcomes of leisure and recreation. It is used in leisure education and to help guide leisure/recreation research, leisure resource policy development, planning, and management. One specialized application of the BOAL is benefits-based management (BBM).

Benefit of Leisure A leisure-based outcome that constitutes either (a) a change in a condition or state that is viewed as more desirable than a previously existing condition or state; (b) the maintenance of a desired condition

and thereby prevention of an unwanted condition from occurring, prevention of an undesired condition from becoming worse, or reduction of the unwanted impacts of an existing undesired condition; or (c) the realization of a satisfying recreation experience.

Benefits Based Management (BBM) A recreation and resource planning and management system used by managers and their collaborating partners (a) to assure an array of benefit opportunities are being provided and (b) to target and facilitate the realization of one or more specific types of benefits desired. BBM is one specialized application of the beneficial outcomes approach to leisure (BOAL).

Cession An area of land or rights in land that have been ceded (i.e., given up) either temporarily or permanently.

Collaborative Style of Planning and Management An approach in which resource managers work collaboratively with the customers (i.e., stakeholders) they serve as well as with associated providers to solve a set of problems none of them can solve as well individually.

Commercial Recreation Recreation opportunities or services provided by enterprises that operate in the private sector. Many outdoor recreation opportunities or services are provided by commercial providers, such as guides and outfitters, private ski area corporations, and private campground operators.

Concession Facilities, services, or business operations provided on public land by a private or nonprofit partner.

Concession Agreement A specialized contract spelling out the terms of operation for the private concession.

Concessioner (or Concessionaire) A private company or individual granted the privilege of providing facilities and services considered necessary by the public sector provider for accommodating visitors (based on National Park Service, 2002).

Conflict see *recreation conflict*

Conservation A management philosophy directed toward the wise and sustainable use of resources over the long term. Many uses may be allowed, but only in ways designed to avoid depletion and irreversible damage, and only after long-term benefits are judged to justify the costs to resources and society. Contrasts with, or is situated between, *exploitation* and *preservation*.

Consumer Surplus An economic concept denoting the net benefits received by a consumer, which are benefits above and beyond what the consumer had to pay. Sometimes referred to as net willingness to pay.

Crowding see *recreation crowding*

Cultural/Historic Resource Resources that reflect and represent the past history and/or culture of sites, areas, regions, or nations.

Customer A person who uses a particular good, service, or opportunity. In recreation resource management, they are of two types: the on-site customer (frequently called the on-site user or visitor) who visits the place where the outdoor recreation opportunity is provided, and the off-site customer (or user) who does not physically visit the site or place where the opportunity is provided, but nevertheless values it.

Direct Management Strategies Direct approaches are actions by management that directly affect what users can and cannot do. Direct strategies restrict or regulate user behavior through such means as rules, regulations, area closures, zoning, requiring mandatory permits, fees, and rationing.

Displacement When a recreation user chooses or is forced to substitute alternatives for their preferred recreation place, time, or activity, including the possibility of not participating at all. (contrast with *substitution*)

Economic Benefit An estimate of what a resource, good, or service is "worth" economically to a particular group of people. Also referred to as the total economic value to society. (contrast with *economic impact*)

Economic Impact The actual expenditures made by visitors and the effects of those expenditures on a particular economy. (contrast with *economic benefit*)

Ecosystem An ecosystem is a system formed by the interaction of all living organisms (including people) with their environment (USDA Forest Service, 1995, p. xi). As such, an ecosystem includes flora, fauna, water, air, and humans and can be very small or vast in size.

Ecosystem Management Sustainable ecosystem management is "the skillful, integrated use of ecological knowledge at various scales to produce desired resource values, products, services and conditions in ways that also sustain the diversity and productivity of ecosystems" (USDA Forest Service, 1995, p. xii). Generally, ecosystems should be managed at the size of a watershed or larger.

Ecoterrorism Illegal acts of sabotage (sometimes referred to as ecotage or monkey wrenching) directed at things the perpetrators believe are harming the environment.

Ecotourism The Ecotourism Society defines ecotourism as "responsible travel to natural areas which conserves the environment and improves the welfare of local people" (Western, 1993, p. 8). Much of ecotourism is outdoor recreation as defined in this text.

Exploitation A management philosophy directed toward extracting the maximum economic gains from resources. This approach is often associated with a short-term focus, commercial enterprises, and nonrenewable resources. (contrast with *conservation* and *preservation*)

Forecasting Making predictions about the future. In outdoor recreation planning and management, forecasting is usually directed at estimating the types and levels of recreation use that will occur in various places.

Forest Recreation A term sometimes used to refer to any outdoor recreation that "takes place in forested areas, whether or not the forest provides the primary purpose for the activity" (Douglas, 2000, p. 10). Forest recreation is part of outdoor recreation as defined here.

Greenway A linear open space established along either a natural corridor, such as a river front, stream valley, or ridge line, or over land along a railroad right-of-way converted to recreational use, a canal, a scenic road, or other route; any natural or landscaped course for pedestrian or bicycle passage; an open-space connector linking parks, nature reserves, cultural features, or historic sites with each other or with populated areas; or, locally, certain strips of linear parks designated as a parkway or greenbelt (Little, 1990, p. 1; see also *greenway trail*).

Greenway Trail A recreational trail located within a greenway. (see also *greenway*)

Guide A paid individual who accompanies an individual or group on an outdoor recreational outing to provide expertise, leadership, or assistance. (see also *outfitter*)

Impact Management System One of a number of management systems used to identify, prevent, and/or reduce adverse physical, biophysical, and social impacts of recreational use.

Indirect Management Strategies Attempts to influence user behavior indirectly rather than through regulations or restrictions. Indirect approaches tend to be subtler than direct ones and compliance is not mandatory. Examples include information and education programs and physical alterations to settings and facilities that attempt to encourage (rather than mandate) responsible behavior.

Information and Education Program A common type of indirect management approach that attempts to inform, educate, and/or influence visitors, potential visitors, or other publics.

Intermediate Area Part of an early classification of outdoor recreation areas referring to areas having characteristics somewhere between those of resource-based and user-oriented areas in terms of access, remoteness, and naturalness. Examples would include many county parks and state parks as well as regional open space systems. (see also *resource-based area* and *user-oriented area*)

Intermodal In the context of transportation planning, intermodal refers to using multiple different modes of transportation (e.g., walking on a trail to a subway station to catch a train to work, taking a bus to an airport for a flight to a vacation destination). The federal Intermodal Surface Transportation Efficiency Act (ISTEA) is used to fund many trail and greenway projects in the United States.

Land and Water Conservation Fund (LWCF) A federal funding mechanism established in the United States in 1965 to help fund outdoor recreation resource planning, and to acquire and develop outdoor recreation resources. The related federal law also established the Statewide Comprehensive Outdoor Recreation Planning (SCORP) process.

Land Trust "A nonprofit organization that, as all or part of its mission, actively works to conserve land by undertaking or assisting direct land transactions—primarily the purchase or acceptance of donations of land or conservation easements" (Land Trust Alliance, 2003).

Leisure Umbrella concept that encompasses all recreation, including outdoor recreation. Defined by various authors as free time, certain freely chosen activities, pleasant states of mind, or even a particular state of being or existence. The definition adopted for this text was that leisure is a state of being (i.e., the state of leisure) in which a person is relatively free to choose to engage in activities of their choosing (including recreational activity). Therefore, *leisure is a precondition for all recreational engagements* and is the state or condition where recreation becomes possible. This state may exist for a few minutes, hours, or much longer for some people. The leisure condition is characterized by relative freedom from obligations and other constraints.

Limits of Acceptable Change (LAC) A widely used standards-based approach to identifying and managing negative recreation impacts.

Line Position A position in an organization's "chain of command" that has authority to make policy decisions and issue instructions, orders, and directives at the level appropriate to that position.

Management The organizational process that establishes and enforces very specific guidelines about what can and cannot be done within the guidelines for action set by established policies.

Minimum Tool Rule Addressing a management challenge by applying only the minimum tools, equipment, device, force, regulation, action or practice that will bring the desired result (Hendee & Dawson, 2002, p. 201).

Multiple-Use Land Management The management of public lands for several (i.e., multiple) uses and values so that those lands are utilized in ways that will best meet present and future needs.

Natural Environment That part of our surroundings characterized by naturally occurring features, fauna, flora, and so forth, that have not been altered to any great extent from their original landscapes and environmental processes (as opposed to the built environment). Natural environments can range from large and remote landscapes and ecosystems (e.g., designated Wilderness areas) to small, highly managed sites.

Natural Resource Recreation Synonymous with *outdoor recreation* as used in this text.

Natural Resources The land, water, flora, fauna, air, geology, and minerals that comprise the natural world.

Nature-Based Tourism Sometimes referred to as nature tourism, nature-based tourism is a particular form of tourism defined as

> an aspect of adventure tourism where the focus is upon the study and/or observation of flora, fauna and/or landscape. It tends toward the small-scale, but it can become mass or incipient mass tourism in many national parks (e.g., Yosemite). It is sometimes perceived as synonymous with ecotourism since one of its aims is to protect natural areas. (France, 1997, p. 16)

Negative Recreation Impacts Any damage, intentional or otherwise, that results from outdoor recreation use. Can affect any natural or cultural/heritage recreation resource or the recreation experiences of other users. Various categorizations break these impacts into ecological (or environmental) impacts and social impacts; or physical (i.e., soil and water), biological (i.e., vegetation and wildlife), and social impacts.

Nonprofit Sector The sector comprised of nongovernmental organizations not part of the private for-profit sector. Generally known simply as NGOs in much of the world.

On-Site Experience A phase of the outdoor recreation experience that includes the actual participation in outdoor recreation activities and the experiences that result in the recreation setting.

Outdoor Adventure Pursuits "A variety of self-initiated activities utilizing an interaction with the natural environment that contain elements of real or apparent danger, in which the outcome, while uncertain, can be influenced by the participant and circumstances." (Ewert, 1989, p. 6; see also *adventure recreation*)

Outdoor Recreation Recreation experiences that result from recreation activities that occur in and depend on the natural environment.

Outdoor Recreation Engagement The actual outdoor recreation outing itself.

Outdoor Recreation Management Providing opportunities for satisfying outdoor recreation experiences while sustaining the health of the natural environments on which these opportunities depend.

Outdoor Recreation Manager The manager of outdoor recreation resources who works with collaborating stakeholders and associated providers to provide outdoor recreation opportunities. As outdoor recreation professionals, they protect, manage, maintain, and, where appropriate, improve the basic natural and cultural/heritage recreation resources necessary for outdoor recreation to occur.

Outdoor Recreation Opportunity "The availability of a real choice for a user to participate in a preferred activity within a preferred setting, in order to realize those satisfying experiences which are desired" (USDA Forest Service, 1982, p. 4).

Outdoor Recreation Professional A person who has professional responsibilities for providing outdoor recreation opportunities, teaches courses, does research on outdoor recreation, or is otherwise engaged professionally is some aspect of outdoor recreation. Being an outdoor recreation professional requires learning the body of knowledge relevant to the profession and continually staying abreast of new additions to that knowledge.

Outdoor Recreation Provider Any organization, enterprise, or individual that directly or indirectly provides outdoor recreation opportunities.

Outdoor Recreation Resources The natural and cultural/historic resources that make outdoor recreation possible and the other outdoor elements useful for recreational purposes. They include the natural resources of land, water, vegetation, wildlife, air, and minerals as well as the facilities and other developments used in outdoor recreation engagements.

Outdoor Recreation Resources Review Commission (ORRRC) A congressional commission created in 1958 to study the demand for outdoor recreation and the supply of outdoor recreation resources. It issued its 27 volumes of reports in 1962, including recommendations to Congress that led to some of the most significant outdoor recreation and environmental legislation ever enacted in the United States.

Outfitter An individual or company that provides the services, equipment, and supplies needed for an outdoor recreation trip. (see also *guide*)

Partnership Collaboration and cooperation among public agencies, nonprofit organizations, private sector companies, and/or individuals in providing outdoor recreation opportunities.

Party A recreation party is the collection of people who are engaged in recreation together. This is generally the same as the members of the travel party who came to the site together.

People at One Time (PAOT) The total number of people present in a particular area at a particular time.

Planning The organizational process undertaken to prepare various types of plans, such as policy, managerial, and administrative plans.

Policy A broad guide for the actions of the people subject to that policy. Policies are essentially the broad standing decisions that guide action. (see also *administration* and *management*)

Preservation A management philosophy directed toward protecting natural and cultural/historic resources indefinitely, with on-site use permitted to the extent that it does not deplete or cause irreversible damage to those protected resources. (contrast with *conservation* and *exploitation*)

President's Commission on Americans Outdoors A Presidential Commission, operating from 1985–1987, that had a similar charge to that of ORRRC, but with a considerably less important impact on U.S. policy.

Private Sector The sector comprised of business enterprises. Sometimes referred to as the for-profit sector.

Professional see *outdoor recreation professional*

Protected Area The term used in much of the world to describe land or water areas where some legal protection is in place to protect the natural environment and associated resources.

Public Domain One category of federal public land referring to the original acquisitions through war, purchase, treaty, cession, or other government action, that have never left federal ownership. Also includes some lands in federal ownership obtained through exchange for other public domain land or resources on public domain land (Bureau of Land Management, 1999).

Public Land Land controlled and managed by any government agency. Such lands are actually owned by all citizens. Note that public access is not permitted on all public lands.

Public Sector The sector comprised of tax-supported agencies of government at all levels.

Recollection A phase of the outdoor recreation experience that occurs after the on-site experience that includes memories, pictures, souvenirs, and so forth. It can, in some cases, be the longest and most enjoyable aspect of the total experience.

Recreation Freely chosen activities undertaken during leisure and the intrinsically rewarding experiences that result from engaging in those activities.

Recreation Conflict Interference with a visitor's recreational goals that he or she attributes to another person's behavior (based on Jacob & Schreyer, 1980).

Recreation Crowding A visitor's subjective evaluation that there are too many people in a particular area (as opposed to the objective number or even density of people actually there). Sometimes called perceived crowding.

Recreation Experience An intrinsically rewarding experience that finds its source in voluntary engagements during nonobligated time (Driver & Tocher, 1970, p. 10).

Recreation Group A collection of people engaged in recreation together (often referred to as a *party*). This is generally the same as the travel party that came to the site together.

Recreation Impacts See *negative recreation impacts*

Recreation Opportunity Spectrum (ROS) A widely used planning and management framework used for providing a diversity of outdoor recreation opportunities based on classes of settings and experiences sought.

Recreation Production Process (or System) The systematically integrated recreation resource managerial system that provides recreation opportunities targeted by managers working with collaborating partners and associated providers to optimized the realization of net benefits by the customers served. (see *customer*)

Recreation Products The recreation opportunities provided by management of the recreation production process (or system).

Recreation Resource Impacts See *negative recreation impacts*

Recreation Vehicle Any enclosed vehicle used for camping, which is more elaborate than a simple truck or car, such as a pickup truck with camper body, pop-up tent trailer, travel trailer, bus, motor coach, or mobile home (National Park Service, 2002).

Recreation Visit A measure of recreation use indicating one entry by one person for any part of a day regardless of length of stay. Recreation visits are often referred to simply as the number of visits. (contrast with *recreation visitor day* and *recreation visitor*)

Recreation Visitor A distinct individual that uses as area for recreation, regardless of their number of visits or length of stay. Sometimes referred to as a user. (contrast with *recreation visit*)

Recreation Visitor Day (RVD) An measure of recreation use that aggregates to 12 visitor hours. This accumulated 12 hours of recreation use by 1 or more persons could consist of 1 person for 12 hours, 2 people for 6 hours each, or any equivalent combination. (contrast with *recreation visit*)

Recreation Visitor Hour An accumulated 60 minutes of recreation use by 1 or more persons. This could be 1 person for an hour, or 2 people for 30 minutes each, etc. This measure can be used as a building block for RVDs depending on how the data is gathered and tabulated. (see also *recreation visitor day*)

Resource-Based Area Part of an early classification of outdoor recreation areas referring to large, remote, natural areas such as typical national parks, national forests, federal wildlife refuges, etc. (see also *intermediate area* and *user-oriented areas*)

Resource-Based Recreation Synonymous with outdoor recreation as used in this text.

Risk Recreation see *adventure recreation*

Setting Provider Any organization, enterprise, or individual that provides the natural or semi-natural settings for outdoor recreation.

Special Use Permit A formal agreement between an agency and a partner that authorizes the partner to undertake a relatively unique operation within the agency's jurisdiction.

Staff Position A position not in an organization's "chain of command." Staff positions offer advice, assistance, services, reports, and other types of support. (contrast with *line position*)

Stakeholders On-site and off-site customers who either affect or are affected by resource allocation decisions to a mangerially relevant degree, such as the provision of outdoor recreation opportunities. (see also *collaborative style of planning and management*)

State Comprehensive Outdoor Recreation Plan (SCORP) An outdoor recreation plan required by the federal Land and Water Conservation Act of 1965. A current SCORP is required for a state to be eligible for Land and Water Conservation Fund grants.

Substitution A coping strategy where a recreation visitor chooses a different activity, place, or time for their recreation when they find the original conditions unacceptable or when constraints, such as limited time, funds, or needed skills, require substituting one choice for another. (contrast with *displacement*)

Tourism The World Tourism Organization defines tourism as "the activities of persons traveling to and staying in places outside their usual environment for not more than one consecutive year for leisure, business and other purposes" (Goeldner & Richie, 2003, p. 7). Some, but by no means all, outdoor recreation is consistent with this definition of tourism.

Trail A "beaten path." According to a national trails task force, a trail is a linear corridor, on land or water, with protected status and public access for recreation or transportation (American Trails, 1990, p. 2).

Travel Back A phase of the outdoor recreation experience that involves traveling back to home or work from the outdoor recreation area.

Travel To A phase of the outdoor recreation experience that involves getting from home or work to the outdoor recreation setting.

User Impacts see *negative recreation impacts*

User-Oriented Area Part of an early classification of outdoor recreation areas referring to areas relatively close to and accessible to where users live and work. They are generally small with physical characteristics that are not too demanding. Examples would include most city parks and playgrounds. (see also *intermediate area* and *resource-based area*)

Visitor Activity Management Process (VAMP) A standards-based approach to identifying and managing negative recreation impacts as well as guiding the planning and management processes of entire parks and other areas administered by Parks Canada.

Visitor Impact Management System (VIM) A standards-based approach to identifying and managing negative recreation impacts.

Visitor Impacts see *negative recreation impacts*

Wilderness In the sociological and popular sense, wilderness is a culturally defined concept, meaning any setting people happen to think is "wild." Legally designated Wilderness in the United States, on the other hand, is an area designated as Wilderness under the Wilderness Act of 1964 or the Eastern Wilderness Act of 1975. Such Wilderness is defined in part as follows:

> A wilderness, in contrast with those areas where man and his own works dominate the landscape, is hereby recognized as an area where the earth and its community of life are untrammeled by man, where man himself is a visitor who does not remain.

Wildland Recreation Often used as a synonym for outdoor recreation. Wildland recreation is a subset of outdoor recreation that takes place in wildland areas and that is dependent on the natural resources of these areas (Hammitt & Cole, 1998, p. 3).

Literature Cited

American Trails. (1990). *Trails for all Americans: The report of the National Trails Agenda Project.* Washington, DC: U.S. Department of the Interior, National Park Service.

Bureau of Land Management. (1999). *Public land statistics 1998.* Washington, DC: U.S. Government Printing Office.

Douglas, R. W. (2000). *Forest recreation* (5th ed.). Prospect Heights, IL: Waveland Press.

Driver, B. L. and Tocher, S. (1970). Toward a behavioral interpretation of recreational engagements, with implications for planning. In B. Driver (Ed.), *Elements of outdoor recreation planning* (pp. 9–31). Ann Arbor, MI: University of Michigan Press.

Ewert, A. W. (1989). *Outdoor adventure pursuits: Foundations, models and theories.* Columbus, OH: Publishing Horizons.

France, L. (Ed.) (1997). *The Earthscan reader in sustainable tourism.* London, England: Earthscan Publications, Ltd.

Goeldner, C. R. and Richie, J. R. B. (2003). *Tourism: Principles, practices and philosophies* (9th ed.). Hoboken, NJ: John Wiley & Sons.

Hammitt, W. E. and Cole, D. N. (1998). *Wildland recreation: Ecology and management* (2nd ed.). New York, NY: Wiley.

Hendee, J. and Dawson, C. (2002). *Wilderness management: Stewardship and protection of resources and values* (3rd ed.). Golden, CO: Fulcrum.

Jacob, G. and Schreyer, R. (1980). Conflict in outdoor recreation: A theoretical perspective. *Journal of Leisure Research, 12,* 368–380.

Land Trust Alliance. (2003). *National Land Trust Census.* Retrieved June 27, 2003, from http://www.lta.org/aboutlt/census.shtml

Little, C. (1990). *Greenways for America.* Baltimore, MD: The Johns Hopkins University Press.

National Park Service. (2002). *National Park Service statistical abstract, 2002.* Denver, CO: National Park Service Public Use Statistics Office.

USDA Forest Service. (1982). *ROS users guide.* Washington, DC: USDA Forest Service.

USDA Forest Service. (1995). *Sustaining ecosystems: A conceptual framework* (Version 1.0). USDA Forest Service, Pacific Southwest Region and Station (R5-EM-TP-001).

Western, D. (1993). Defining ecotourism. In K. Lindberg and D. E. Hawkins (Eds.), *Ecotourism: A guide for planners and managers* (pp. 7–11). North Bennington, VT: The Ecotourism Society.

Commonly Used Acronyms in Outdoor Recreation

ARC	American Recreation Coalition
AT	Appalachian Trail
ATC	Appalachian Trail Conference
ATV	All-terrain vehicle
BBM	Benefits-based management
BIA	Bureau of Indian Affairs
BLM	Bureau of Land Management
BOA	Beneficial outcomes approach
BOAL	Beneficial outcomes approach to leisure
BOR	Bureau of Reclamation
COE	(U.S. Army) Corps of Engineers
CVM	Contingent valuation method (of estimating economic benefits)
EA	Environmental assessment
EIA	Economic impact analysis
EIS	Environmental impact statement
EPA	Environmental Protection Agency
FHWA	Federal Highway Administration
FLPMA	Federal Land Policy and Management Act of 1976
FWS	(U.S.) Fish and Wildlife Service
FY	Fiscal year
GIS	Geographic information system
GMP	General management plan
GPS	Global positioning system
HCRS	Heritage, Conservation and Recreation Service (sometimes called "Hookers")
I&E	Information and education
ISTEA	Intermodal Surface Transportation Efficiency Act
IUCN	The World Conservation Union (previously the International Union for Conservation of Nature and Natural Resources)
IUFRO	International Union of Forest Research Organizations
LAC	Limits of acceptable change
LWCF	Land and Water Conservation Fund
LWCFA	Land and Water Conservation Fund Act of 1965
MOU	Memoranda of understanding
MUSYA	Multiple Use and Sustained Yield Act of 1960
MWR	Morale, Welfare, and Recreation
NAI	National Association for Interpretation
NARRP	National Association of Recreation Resource Planners
NASPD	National Association of State Park Directors
NCRC	National Center for Recreation and Conservation
NEPA	National Environmental Policy Act of 1969
NFMA	National Forest Management Act of 1976
NFS	National Forest System

NGO	Nongovernmental organization
NOAA	National Oceanic and Atmospheric Administration
NPLOS	National Private Landowner Survey
NPS	National Park Service
NRA	National Recreation Area
NRPA	National Recreation and Park Association
NSPR	National Society for Park Resources
NSRE	National Survey on Recreation and the Environment
OHV	Off-highway vehicle
ORRRC	Outdoor Recreation Resources Review Commission
PCAO	President's Commission on Americans Outdoors
PWC	Personal watercraft
RCRA	Resort and Commercial Recreation Association
RO	Regional office (of the USDA Forest Service)
ROS	Recreation opportunity spectrum
RPA	Forest and Rangeland Renewable Resources Planning Act of 1974
RV	Recreation vehicle
RVD	Recreation visitor day
SCORP	State Comprehensive Outdoor Recreation Plan
SM	Scenery management
SO	Supervisor's office (in the USDA Forest Service)
TCM	Travel cost method (of estimating economic benefits)
TEA-21	Transportation Efficiency Act for the 21st Century
UPARR	Urban Park and Recreation Recovery Program
USACE	U.S. Army Corps of Engineers
USDA	U.S. Department of Agriculture
USDI	U.S. Department of the Interior
USFS	USDA Forest Service
USGS	U.S. Geological Survey
VAMP	Visitor activity management process
VERP	Visitor experience and resource protection
VIF	Volunteers in the National Forests (program of the U.S. Forest Service)
VIM	Visitor impact management
VIP	Volunteers-in-Parks (program of the National Park Service)
VRM	Visual resource management
WLRA	World Leisure and Recreation Association
WO	Washington office (headquarters of the USDA Forest Service)
WOZ	Wilderness opportunity zoning

Index

Other Books by Venture Publishing, Inc.

21st Century Leisure: Current Issues, Second Edition
by Valeria J. Freysinger and John R. Kelly

The A•B•Cs of Behavior Change: Skills for Working With Behavior Problems in Nursing Homes
by Margaret D. Cohn, Michael A. Smyer, and Ann L. Horgas

Activity Experiences and Programming within Long-Term Care
by Ted Tedrick and Elaine R. Green

The Activity Gourmet
by Peggy Powers

Advanced Concepts for Geriatric Nursing Assistants
by Carolyn A. McDonald

Adventure Programming
edited by John C. Miles and Simon Priest

Assessment: The Cornerstone of Activity Programs
by Ruth Perschbacher

Behavior Modification in Therapeutic Recreation: An Introductory Manual
by John Datillo and William D. Murphy

Benefits of Leisure
edited by B. L. Driver, Perry J. Brown, and George L. Peterson

Benefits of Recreation Research Update
by Judy M. Sefton and W. Kerry Mummery

Beyond Baskets and Beads: Activities for Older Adults With Functional Impairments
by Mary Hart, Karen Primm, and Kathy Cranisky

Beyond Bingo: Innovative Programs for the New Senior
by Sal Arrigo, Jr., Ann Lewis, and Hank Mattimore

Beyond Bingo 2: More Innovative Programs for the New Senior
by Sal Arrigo, Jr.

Both Gains and Gaps: Feminist Perspectives on Women's Leisure
by Karla Henderson, M. Deborah Bialeschki, Susan M. Shaw, and Valeria J. Freysinger

Boredom Busters: Themed Special Events to Dazzle and Delight Your Group
by Annette C. Moore

Client Assessment in Therapeutic Recreation Services
by Norma J. Stumbo

Client Outcomes in Therapeutic Recreation Services
by Norma J. Stumbo

Conceptual Foundations for Therapeutic Recreation
edited by David R. Austin, John Dattilo, and Bryan P. McCormick

Constraints to Leisure
edited by Edgar L. Jackson

Dementia Care Programming: An Identity-Focused Approach
by Rosemary Dunne

Dimensions of Choice: A Qualitative Approach to Recreation, Parks, and Leisure Research
by Karla A. Henderson

Diversity and the Recreation Profession: Organizational Perspectives
edited by Maria T. Allison and Ingrid E. Schneider

Effective Management in Therapeutic Recreation Service
by Gerald S. O'Morrow and Marcia Jean Carter

Evaluating Leisure Services: Making Enlightened Decisions, Second Edition
by Karla A. Henderson and M. Deborah Bialeschki

Everything From A to Y: The Zest Is up to You! Older Adult Activities for Every Day of the Year
by Nancy R. Cheshire and Martha L. Kenney

The Evolution of Leisure: Historical and Philosophical Perspectives
by Thomas Goodale and Geoffrey Godbey

Experience Marketing: Strategies for the New Millennium
by Ellen L. O'Sullivan and Kathy J. Spangler

Facilitation Techniques in Therapeutic Recreation
by John Dattilo

File o' Fun: A Recreation Planner for Games & Activities, Third Edition
by Jane Harris Ericson and Diane Ruth Albright

Functional Interdisciplinary-Transdisciplinary Therapy (FITT) Manual
by Deborah M. Schott, Judy D. Burdett, Beverly J. Cook, Karren S. Ford, and Kathleen M. Orban

The Game and Play Leader's Handbook: Facilitating Fun and Positive Interaction, Revised Edition
by Bill Michaelis and John M. O'Connell

The Game Finder—A Leader's Guide to Great Activities
by Annette C. Moore

Getting People Involved in Life and Activities: Effective Motivating Techniques
by Jeanne Adams

Glossary of Recreation Therapy and Occupational Therapy
by David R. Austin

Great Special Events and Activities
by Annie Morton, Angie Prosser, and Sue Spangler

Group Games & Activity Leadership
by Kenneth J. Bulik

Growing With Care: Using Greenery, Gardens, and Nature With Aging and Special Populations
by Betsy Kreidler

Hands On! Children's Activities for Fairs, Festivals, and Special Events
by Karen L. Ramey

In Search of the Starfish: Creating a Caring Environment
by Mary Hart, Karen Primm, and Kathy Cranisky

Inclusion: Including People With Disabilities in Parks and Recreation Opportunities
by Lynn Anderson and Carla Brown Kress

Inclusive Leisure Services: Responding to the Rights of People with Disabilities, Second Edition
by John Dattilo

Innovations: A Recreation Therapy Approach to Restorative Programs
by Dawn R. De Vries and Julie M. Lake

Internships in Recreation and Leisure Services: A Practical Guide for Students, Third Edition
by Edward E. Seagle, Jr. and Ralph W. Smith

Interpretation of Cultural and Natural Resources, Second Edition
by Douglas M. Knudson, Ted T. Cable, and Larry Beck

Intervention Activities for At-Risk Youth
by Norma J. Stumbo

Introduction to Recreation and Leisure Services, Eighth Edition
by Karla A. Henderson, M. Deborah Bialeschki, John L. Hemingway, Jan S. Hodges, Beth D. Kivel, and H. Douglas Sessoms

Introduction to Therapeutic Recreation: U.S. and Canadian Perspectives
by Kenneth Mobily and Lisa Ostiguy

Introduction to Writing Goals and Objectives: A Manual for Recreation Therapy Students and Entry-Level Professionals
by Suzanne Melcher

Leadership and Administration of Outdoor Pursuits, Second Edition
by Phyllis Ford and James Blanchard

Other Books by Venture Publishing, Inc.

Venture Publishing, Inc.
1999 Cato Avenue
State College, PA 16801
Phone:(814) 234-4561
Fax: (814) 234-1651